T0394946

The Palgrave Handbook of Servitization

Marko Kohtamäki · Tim Baines ·
Rodrigo Rabetino · Ali Ziaee Bigdeli ·
Christian Kowalkowski · Rogelio Oliva ·
Vinit Parida
Editors

The Palgrave Handbook of Servitization

palgrave
macmillan

Editors
Marko Kohtamäki
School of Management
University of Vaasa
Vaasa, Finland

Rodrigo Rabetino
School of Management
University of Vaasa
Vaasa, Finland

Christian Kowalkowski
Department of Management
and Engineering
Linkoping University
Linköping, Sweden

Vinit Parida
Department of Business Administration
Luleå University of Technology
Luleå, Sweden

Tim Baines
Aston Business School
Aston University
Birmingham, UK

Ali Ziaee Bigdeli
Aston Business School, Aston Triangle
Aston University
Birmingham, UK

Rogelio Oliva
Mays Business School
Texas A&M University
College Station, TX, USA

ISBN 978-3-030-75770-0   ISBN 978-3-030-75771-7   (eBook)
https://doi.org/10.1007/978-3-030-75771-7

Cover credit: Pitinan Piyavatin/Alamy Stock Photo

This Palgrave Macmillan imprint is published by the registered company Springer Nature Switzerland AG
The registered company address is: Gewerbestrasse 11, 6330 Cham, Switzerland

Contents

Notes on Contributors

Tor Helge Aas serves as a Professor at University of Agder and as a Research Professor at NORCE Norwegian Research Centre AS. He holds a Ph.D. in Strategy and Management from Norwegian School of Economics (NHH) and a M.Sc. in Information and Communication Technology Management from University of Agder. Tor Helge Aas is researching innovation management, and his research concentrates on topics such as the organizational effects of innovation, innovation processes and capabilities, collaboration for innovation, and management control of innovation. The research conducted by Tor Helge Aas has been published in international journals such as *Technovation, Technological Forecasting and Social Change, International Journal of Innovation Management, Service Industries Journal* and *Journal of Service Theory and Practice* among others.

Federico Adrodegari is a postdoc researcher at the Department of Industrial and Mechanical Engineering at University of Brescia, where he teaches in the operations management area. Since 2011 he is a member of the RISE Laboratory (www.rise.it). His research activity concerns the areas of supply chain management and service management, in particular the servitization and digital servitization fields. He is the author of numerous scientific publications on national and international conferences and journals. He is a member of the the IFIP WG5.7 "Advances in Production Management Systems" and currently the national coordinator of the ASAP Service Management

Forum, an industry-academia community about servitization and product-service systems, performing research transfer projects with companies and dissemination activities in these fields (www.asapsmf.org).

Maria Åkesson holds a Ph.D. in Business Administration at the Service Research Center (CTF) at Karlstad University in Sweden. Her main research interest is in the areas of service innovation and value co-creation through service, especially with a focus on servitization. Her work has been published in journals such as *Journal of Business Research, Journal of Business and Industrial Marketing, Journal of Service Management*, and *Journal of Service Theory and Practice*.

Tim Baines, Ph.D. is a Professor of Operations Strategy and Executive Director of the Advanced Services Group at Aston University. He is a leading international authority on servitization and spends much of his time working hands-on with both global and local manufacturing companies to understand servitization in practice and help to transform businesses. His book Made to Serve described as, "Essential reading for any companies or executives looking to explore this option for their business" provides a practical guide to servitization, based on in-depth research with leading corporations such as Xerox, Caterpillar, Alstom and MAN Truck & Bus UK.

Ali Ziaee Bigdeli, Ph.D. is an Associate Professor of Industrial Service Innovation at The Advanced Services Group at Aston Business School, Aston University. His interests lie in the organizational change and business model innovation brought about when organizations move toward providing capabilities rather than just selling products on a transactional basis. He is extensively engaged with both multinational and SME manufacturers to understand servitization in practice, and help the acceleration of the adoption of advanced services. His research has been published in the leading management journals including *International Journal of Operations & Production Management, Journal of Business Research, Production Planning & Control*, and *International Journal of Production Research*.

Karl Joachim Breunig is Head of the Department of Strategy, Innovation, and Marketing and Full Professor of Strategic Management at Oslo Business School—OsloMet–Oslo Metropolitan University. At OsloMet he currently serves as a deputy member of the University Board and is responsible for the Ph.D. program at the Oslo Business School. He initiated and also heads the interdisciplinary research group DISCO: Digital Innovation and Strategic Competence in Organizations. He received his Ph.D. from BI Norwegian Business School and M.Sc. from London School of Economics.

Prof. Breunig's research concentrates on the interception of strategy—and innovation theory, and currently focus on digitalization in a number of different industries and organizations.

Dr. Jamie Burton is a Professor of Marketing and Head of the Management Sciences and Marketing Division at Alliance Manchester Business School. His research interests include services marketing including customer feedback, customer experience and engagement, customer management, and servitization. Jamie has held a wide variety of service roles and delivered a number of executive training presentations and invited presentations for Shell, Vertex, the British Quality Foundation, the social housing sector, Lancaster University Management School and the University of Maastricht,. Jamie co-hosted the 2016 Spring Servitization Conference in Manchester and co-chaired, organized and ran the 1st and 2nd CMLG academic-practitioner research with impact workshops in January 2016 and June 2018 in Manchester, leading to edited special sections in the *Journal of Services Marketing* in 2017 and the *Journal of Business Research* in 2020. Jamie has won several awards for his research and has over 180 publications including in the *Journal of Service Research*, the *International Journal of Operations and Production Management*, *Industrial Marketing Management*, *International Journal of Production Economics*, *Journal of Service Management*, *Journal of Services Marketing*, and the *Journal of Marketing Management*. Jamie is co-author of the book *Converting Customer Value* and a chapter in the book: *Practices and Tools for Servitization*.

Koteshwar Chirumalla is an Associate Professor and subject representative in Product and Process Development at Mälardalen University, Sweden. His research interests include servitization, product and production development, business models, digital transformation, and knowledge management. He is currently leading research projects on topics: digital twin ecosystems, second life of electric vehicle batteries, and digitalization of manufacturing. He has published around 50 articles in leading international journals, conferences, book chapters and industry handbooks.

Wim Coreynen is a Postdoctoral Researcher at the Vrije Universiteit (VU) Amsterdam and Utrecht University (UU) in The Netherlands. He obtained his Ph.D. at the Faculty of Business and Economics at the University of Antwerp (UA) in Belgium. He previously also worked for Antwerp Management School (AMS), the Jheronimus Academy of Data Science (JADS), and Zhejiang University School of Management (ZJUSOM). His research revolves around the transformation of companies through servitization and digitalization, entrepreneurship, intellectual property management, and recently also data science. His work has been published in journals such as *Industrial Marketing Management* (IMM), the *International Journal of Production Research* (IJPR), and *Journal for Business Research* (JBR) as well as books such as *Practices and Tools for Servitization: Managing Service Transition.*

Philip Davies is a Lecturer in Operations Management at Henley Business School, University of Reading after completing his Ph.D. in Operations Management at the University of Warwick in 2018. He previously worked as a design engineer for various companies and worked in a range of industries including automotive, aerospace, fashion, medical, television, and film. His research focus includes service operations management, service design, service modularity, servitization and digitalization of manufacturing and service organizations with emphasis placed on additive manufacturing and the Internet of Things.

Ibon Gil de San Vicente holds a Degree in Economics from the University of the Basque Country. Following this he continued his studies with a master's degree in Business Administration from the University of Kent (UK) and a master's degree in Business Innovation from the University of Deusto. Since 2006 he has worked at Orkestra-Basque Institute of Competitiveness where he has had a number of responsibilities, primarily in the area of general and project management, communication, and institutional relations. Before joining Orkestra he developed his career in different financial entities, where he assumed responsibilities linked to commercial banking and risk management.

Suvi Einola (Ph.D.) works as an Assistant Professor at the University of Vaasa. Before joining the academia, Suvi worked in the public sector for fifteen years in managerial, management, training, and development positions. She has facilitated strategy workshops in different types of organizations over ten years and has been in charge of managerial training for a medium-sized city organization for five years. In her research, Einola has focused on strategic practices and the challenges of servitization in both public and private sectors. Her research has been published in scientific journals and books in both the public sector and industrial marketing.

Dr. Thomas Frandsen is an Associate Professor at the Department of Operations Management, Copenhagen Business School, Denmark. He is co-principal investigator on the collaborative research project *Driving competitiveness through servitization* which focuses on service strategies in Danish industrial firms. His current research interests are in the area of service operations management, service architecture and modularity, servitization,

3D printing, pricing, and managerial decision making. He has published research in journals such as *International Journal of Operations & Production Management*, *International Journal of Production Economics*, *Journal of Business Research*, and *Technological Forecasting & Social Change*.

Paolo Gaiardelli is an Associate Professor at the Department of Management, Information, and Production Engineering of the University of Bergamo. His teaching and research mainly focus on Production and Service Management, with a specific interest in Lean Management. Recently, his research interests have extended to exploring lean management's role within operation and service management. He is mainly involved in understanding how the adoption of lean paradigms increases Product-Service System design and development, as well as its impact on management's efficiency and effectiveness. He is European Chair of IFIP Working Group 5.7 (Advances in Production Management Systems) and coordinator of its Special Interest Group in Service Systems Design, Engineering, and Management. Paolo is also a member of ASAP Service Management Forum, an Italian industry-academic initiative that aims to promote service management's culture and excellence through research projects, practice, education, and technological transfer.

Magnus Hellström works as an Associate Professor within The Sea at the Faculty of Science and Engineering at Åbo Akademi University. He also holds a position in project and supply chain management at the School of Business and Law at University of Agder in Norway. Dr. Hellström's research interests revolve around new B2B business models especially in the marine industry, such as ones based on modularization, servitization, collaborative business practices, and sustainability. His work has appeared in journals such as *Industrial Marketing Management*, *Journal of Cleaner Production*, and *International Journal of Project Management*. In addition to his academic work, Hellström has been consulting large and medium-sized technology companies.

Prof. Dr. Michael Henke holds the Chair of Enterprise Logistics at the faculty of Mechanical Engineering at TU Dortmund University and also completes the board of directors of Fraunhofer IML as director of the section Enterprise Logistics. His research focuses among others on purchasing, logistics, and supply chain as well as the management of Industry 4.0.

Ellen Hughes is a Research Fellow at the Surrey Business School. She completed her Ph.D. in Economic Geography at the University of the West of England in 2020. She previously worked as an oral historian, conducting life-story interviews, and as a researcher mapping design enterprises in the

Bristol and Bath region. Her work now focusses on value creation and service ecosystems.

Tuomas Huikkola is an Assistant Professor at the School of Management at the University of Vaasa. His special interest is in digital servitization and incumbent firm's strategic change. He has published in a number of journals, including *Industrial Marketing Management*, *Research-Technology Management*, and *Journal of Business and Industrial Marketing*.

Katja Maria Hydle works as an Associate Professor at the University of Oslo, Department of Informatics and serves as a Research Professor at NORCE Norwegian Research Centre AS. She holds a Ph.D. in Strategic Management from BI Norwegian Business School and an M.A. in European Politics and Administration from College of Europe. Hydle's research interests include digital transformation, ecosystems, and platformization with a focus on servitization, collaborative business practices, and strategizing. Her work has appeared in journals such as *Organization Studies, Human Relations, Journal of World Business, and Management Learning*.

Anmar Kamalaldin is a Ph.D. candidate in entrepreneurship and innovation at Luleå University of Technology (Sweden). His research focuses on business-to-business relationships and innovation ecosystems in digital servitization context.

Bart Kamp is a Principal Investigator in the focus area of Business Internationalization and Servitization at Orkestra-Institute of Basque Competitiveness. His research focuses on competitive strategies that enable firms to be leaders in their niches on the international market and on servitization processes among manufacturing firms. With over 25 years of professional experience, Bart has held positions as a researcher and advisor in fields like: innovation policies, industrial competitiveness, foreign investment attraction, and business development. Bart has authored many articles and edited several books on these subjects. His work has been published in Dutch, English, Spanish, Basque, Portuguese, and Japanese. He has rendered services to multilateral institutions, governmental organizations, SMEs, and multinationals from Belgium, The Netherlands, Luxembourg, Germany, France, Portugal, Spain, Romania, Lithuania, Argentina, Chile, and Colombia. Apart from his work at Orkestra, he teaches at Deusto Business School (Spain) and the Louvain School of Management (Belgium).

Marko Kohtamäki is a Professor of Strategy, and a director of the "Strategic Business Development" (SBD) research group at the University of Vaasa, a Visiting Professor at Luleå University of Technology and University of South-Eastern Norway, and as a Docent at University of Oulu. Prof. Kohtamäki takes special interest in digital servitization, product-service-software innovation, organizational change, strategic practices, business intelligence, and strategic alliances. Prof. Kohtamäki has published in *Strategic Management Journal*, *International Journal of Operations and Production Management*, *Strategic Entrepreneurship Journal*, *International Journal of Management Reviews*, *International Journal of Production Economics*, *Long Range Planning*, Technovation, *Industrial Marketing Management*, *Journal of Business Research*, among others.

Mr. Lauri Korkeamäki is a Ph.D. Candidate (Econ.) and a Project Researcher at the University of Vaasa, School of Management, majoring in Management and Organizations. His dissertation concerns outcome-based business models (OBMs) of manufacturing firms. Korkeamäki's research focuses on servitization of manufacturers and his research interests include but are not limited to service business models, strategic management, sociology in organizations, and paradox theory. Korkeamäki has presented his research in international forums, such as the annual meeting of Academy of Management and the CIRP conference on industrial product service systems and his work has been published in Industrial Marketing Management.

Christian Kowalkowski is a Professor of Industrial Marketing at Linköping University and is affiliated with the Centre for Relationship Marketing and Service Management at Hanken School of Economics in Helsinki. Dr. Kowalkowski's research interests include service growth strategies, service innovation, and B2B subscription business models. His work has been published in journals such as *Industrial Marketing Management*, *Journal of Business Research*, and *Journal of Service Research*. He is the servitization editor for the *Journal of Service Management*, associate editor of the *Journal of Services Marketing*, and advisory board member of *Industrial Marketing Management*. He is the co-author of *Service Strategy in Action: A Practical Guide for Growing Your B2B Service and Solution Business* (www.Servic eStrategyInAction.com; Service Strategy Press, 2017), the leading book for industry executives on how to navigate the transition from a goods-centric to a service-savvy business model.

Dr. Melanie E. Kreye is an Associate Professor in Operations Management at the Department of Technology, Management and Economics, Technical University of Denmark (DTU Management). Her research focuses on uncertainty in different industrial and academic areas including engineering service operations (servitization), product development and solution development. Her research has been published in peer-reviewed journals such as *Omega— The International Journal of Management Science*, *The International Journal of*

Operations & Production Management, and *Production Planning and Control*. She is an Associate Editor for the *International Journal of Operations & Production Management*.

Alexander Kreyenborg is a research associate at the Chair of Enterprise Logistics at the faculty of Mechanical Engineering at TU Dortmund University and coordinator of the field of maintenance and service management. His research focuses on service management, servitization, and the development of industrial product-service systems in SMEs.

Luna Leoni is an Assistant Professor in Management at the University of Rome Tor Vergata. In the same University, she is Professor of "Creative Enterprise" and "Knowledge Management" as well as Program Manager of the "Master in Economics and Management of Cultural and Tourist Activities". Her main research interest areas are: servitization, knowledge management, tourism, and creativity. Moreover, she is a Council Member of the European Association for Research on Services (RESER). Luna's research findings have appeared in top-tier business, management, and tourism journals.

Leandro Lepratte is an Associate Professor and Director of the Research Group on Development, Innovation, and Competitiveness at the National Technological University (UTN) in Argentina. Member of the Scientific Committee on Technology of Organizations at the UTN. His research interests are innovation capabilities, socio-technical analysis, and technological change.

Lina Linde is a Ph.D. candidate in entrepreneurship and innovation at Luleå University of Technology (Sweden). Her research focuses on business model innovation and innovation ecosystems in digital servitization context.

Nina Löfberg is a researcher at the Service Research Center (CTF) at Karlstad University, Sweden. She holds a Ph.D. in Business Administration from Karlstad University and her research interest is in servitization, service logic, value creation and service innovation. Nina has published research in scholarly journals such as *Journal of Business Research*, *Production Planning and Control*, *Managing Service Quality*, and *Journal of Business and Industrial Marketing*.

Anet Mathews graduated in Master of Science in Engineering in February 2020. During her Master Degree her focus was on product and service innovation. She did her first research project in challenges of servitization and has been invested in this research topic since. She was also active in the airline industry, where she completed two more projects in the topic project management and digitalization as a part of her master's degree. Anet is currently working as a Junior Project Consultant where she is responsible for carrying out operative project management for an R&D Project. When she is not working, she can be found traveling around the world, trying new cuisines. Unless, we are mid-pandemic—then you can find her trying new cuisines in her own kitchen.

Prof. Dr. Paul Matthyssens is a Professor of Global Business and Global Marketing at the University of Milano-Bicocca Department of Economics, Quantitative Methods, and Business Strategy. He teaches Strategic Management at the University of Antwerp (Department of Management) and Antwerp Management School (AMS). He has published in academic journals such as *Industrial Marketing Management*, *Journal of Management Studies*, *Strategic Organization*, *Long Range Planning*, *Technovation*, *Journal of Business & Industrial Marketing*, *Psychology & Marketing*, *International Marketing Review*, *Journal of Engineering & Technology Management*, *International Journal of Production Research* and *Journal of Purchasing & Supply Management*. His research interests include business and industrial marketing, value innovation, servitization, global strategy, industry transformation, business modeling, ecosystems, and purchasing strategy. Matthyssens is a member of the Strategy Council to the Board of the European top research institute VITO (2017-now).

Frederik Möller is a Chief Engineer at the Chair for Industrial Information Management at TU Dortmund University. He holds a Masters's degree in Industrial Engineering, and his research focuses on design theory, business models, and Logistics.

Khadijeh Momeni received a Ph.D. degree in business and technology management from Tampere University. She currently works as a postdoctoral research fellow at the Department of Industrial Engineering and Management, Tampere University. Her current research interests include managing industrial service business and digital servitization of manufacturing firms.

Max Niemann studies industrial engineering at TU Dortmund University and works as a student assistant in the field of maintenance and service management at the Chair of Enterprise Logistics at the faculty of Mechanical Engineering of TU Dortmund University.

Rogelio Oliva is the Bob and Kelly Jordan Professor of Business in the Department of Information and Operations Management at Mays Business School, Adjunct Professor at the Zaragoza Logistics Center, and Research

Affiliate at MIT Center for Transportation & Logistics. His research explores how behavioral and social aspects of an organization interact with its technical components to determine the firm's operational performance. His current research interests include behavioral operations management, retail and service operations, and the transition that product manufacturers are making to become service providers. His research work has been published in several academic journals, among them: *Management Science, Organization Science, Journal of Operations Management, Production and Operations Management*, and *California Management Review*. He is the recipient of the 2019 Jay W. Forrester Award for the best written contribution to the System Dynamics field in the preceding five years.

Mădălina Pană is a Ph.D. student at the Department of Technology, Management and Economics, Technical University of Denmark (DTU Management). Her research focuses on the organizational transition to servitization with a specific focus on employee management.

Vinit Parida is a Chaired Professor of Entrepreneurship and Innovation at Luleå University of Technology. His researches subjects are about how companies can evolve their business to higher profitability with digitalization through servitization and business model innovation in collaboration with leading companies in different industrial sectors. The research work involves cooperation with large companies like ABB, Billerudkorsnäs, Boliden, Epiroc, Ericsson, Gestamp HardTech, IBM, Komatsu Forest, Lindbäcks, Metso, Sandvik Coromant, SCA, Scania, Volvo Cars, and Volvo Construction Equipment. His research results has been published in 200+ leading international peer-reviewed journals, conferences, book chapters, and industry/popular publications. Such as *Strategic Management Journal, Journal of Management Studies, Entrepreneurship Theory and Practice, Journal of Product Innovation Management, California Management Review, Long Range Planning, Industrial Marketing Management, Journal of Business Research, International Journal of Production Economics, Production and Operation Management, International Journal of Operations & Production Management, Strategic Entrepreneurship Journal, Entrepreneurship and Regional Development, Journal of Small Business Management, and Journal of Cleaner Production*. He is active within different academic communities and has presented research results in well-known international conferences, such as *Babson College Enterprise Research Conference, Research in Entrepreneurship and Small Business (RENT), The Annual ICSB World Conference, International Conference on Management of Technology (IAMOT), International Product Development Management Conference, and CRIP IPSS Conference*. Associate Editor of Journal of Business

Research (2018-). Editorial Review Board Member of *Industrial Marketing Management*, *Journal of Small Business Management*, and *Journal of Business Research*. He has been special issue guest editor for *Industrial Marketing Management* (2020), *Journal of Business Research* (2019), *Sustainability an Open Access Journal from MDPI* (2018), and *International Entrepreneurship and Management Journal* (2018). He has also been working in several policy and consultancy-oriented projects for Swedish IT Ministry, EU Commission, VINNOVA, Growth Analysis, and directly toward companies.

Prof. Glenn Parry is the Chair in Digital Transformation in Surrey Business School, University of Surrey. He completed his Ph.D. at Cambridge and then worked as at LEK as a management consultant. He then returned to academia, working closely with business on major transformational projects. His work focusses on the meaning of value and how business co-create value within their supply chains. He has worked in and led international projects in Aerospace, Automotive, Construction, Media, and HealthCare, helping business understand the challenges of data collection and use. He is currently CoDirector of £10m DECaDE: Centre for the Decentralised Digital Economy, a UK research center exploring the potential for decentralized platforms to disrupt the Digital Economy.

Dr. Sophie Peillon is an Associate Professor in Management at the Henri Fayol Institute of the Ecole des mines de Saint-Etienne, France. Her research focuses on business model innovation, especially through servitization and product-service systems, with a particular attention to SMEs. She has published various articles on these phenomena in academic journals.

Isabelle Prim-Allaz is a Professor of Marketing and Director of the Coactis Research Centre at Lumière Lyon 2 University. Her work focuses on customer relationship management as well as sustainable marketing. She has published work on servitization in journals including *Industrial Marketing Management* and the *Journal of Service Management*. Her co-authored book, *Augmented Customer Strategy*, questions how digital transformation is shaping a new landscape for businesses and their customers.

Dr. Rodrigo Rabetino is an Associate Professor of Strategic Management in the School of Management and the Vaasa Energy Business Innovation Centre (VEBIC) at the University of Vaasa. His current research activities concern servitization and product-service systems, industrial service business, business intelligence, business models, strategy as practice, and small business management. He has published articles in international journals such as

Regional Studies, International Journal of Operations and Production Management, Industrial Marketing Management, International Journal of Production Economics, Journal of Business Research, Journal of Small Business Management, and *Journal of Small Business* and *Enterprise Development.*

Chris Raddats is a Senior Lecturer in Marketing and the Director of Research for the University of Liverpool Management School's Marketing group. Chris completed a Ph.D. at Alliance Manchester Business School in 2009 and previously had a 20-year career in the telecommunications industry, where he worked as a marketing manager for both telco operators and an equipment manufacturer. Chris' primary research addresses how traditionally product-centric business-to-business (B2B) firms can build a chargeable services capability to enhance market differentiation and sales (servitization). He publishes his work in leading marketing (e.g., *Industrial Marketing Management*), operations (e.g., *International Journal of Operational & Production Management*), and general management (e.g., *Journal of Business Research*) journals.

Dr. Jawwad Z. Raja is an Associate Professor at the Department of Operations Management, Copenhagen Business School, Denmark. His current research interests are in the areas of service operations, servitization, network configurations, customer value and human resource management. He has published research in journals such as *Human Resource Management Journal*, *Journal of Product Innovation Management*, *International Journal of Operations & Production Management*, *International Journal of Production Economics*, *Journal of Business Research* and *Construction Management and Economics.*

Mario Rapaccini is an Associate Professor at the Department of Industrial Engineering, University of Florence, where he teaches Economics and Business Organisation, Business Strategy, and Innovation Management. He is also on the faculty staff of Scuola Sant'Anna in Pisa. His primary fields of research are digital transformation (Industry 4.0) and servitization of industrial enterprises, in this latter he has done research for +15 years. He serves on the board of ASAP Service Management Forum (www.asapsmf.org) and he is currently a member of the IFIP WG5.7 "Advances in Production Management Systems" and of the joint doctoral course of Universities of Pisa, Firenze, and Siena on the topic of "Smart Industry." He has collaborated in technology transfer, vocational training, and consultancy initiatives for global companies.

Wiebke Reim is an Associate Senior lecturer in Entrepreneurship and Innovation at Luleå University of Technology. Her research interests include business model innovation, the circular economy, and servitization. She studies the implementation of new business models and how that affects the whole business ecosystems as well as how to secure that economic, environmental, and social value is generated. The circular economy research is well aligned with the industrial symbiosis concept and is of great value when combines with business model thinking. The results of her work have been published in over 20 leading international peer-reviewed journals, conferences, book chapters, and industry/popular publications., such as *Journal of Cleaner Production, International Journal of Production and Operations Management, and Industrial Marketing Management.*

Eugen Rodel holds a Doctor of Business Administration (DBA) degree from Charles Sturt University in Australia. With respect to this, he studied Business Models and the transition of capital goods companies from manufacturers to service providers. After graduation as a Master of Engineering (Old Dominion University, USA), he worked as a Research Engineer for a start-up in the telecommunication industry. Subsequently, he received an Executive M.B.A. degree (Bern University of Applied Science, Switzerland) and held the position of product manager in the industrial goods sector. Today he works as an independent consultant and researcher. His areas of interest include Digital Transformation, Innovation, and Visual Thinking. Moreover, he is very tech-savvy and thus enthusiastic for information and communication technology, especially the topics Computer Programming and Artificial Intelligence.

María Alejandra Rodríguez is a master candidate in Economics and Industrial Development at Universidad Nacional General Sarmiento in Argentina. She is an assistant professor of Strategic Management and junior researcher of the Research Group on Development, Innovation, and Competitiveness at the National Technological University in Argentina. Her research interests are in digital servitization, strategic management, and intellectual property.

Nicola Saccani is an Associate Professor at the Department of Industrial and Mechanical Engineering at the University of Brescia (Italy), where he is part of the RISE laboratory (Research and Innovation for Smart Enterprise, www.rise.it). He is a member and past coordinator of the ASAP Service Management Forum. His research activities concern service and supply chain management, with particular reference to the impact of phenomena such as the digital transformation, servitization, and circular economy on business models, supply chain configuration and operations management. He is the author of several scientific publications in such fields. He has also taken part to several company transfer projects on such topics.

Anna Salonen (D.Sc. Econ.) is a University Lecturer in Marketing at the Turku School of Economics, University of Turku, Finland and an Adjunct Professor in B2B marketing at the University of Jyväskylä, Finland. Anna's research focuses on B2B marketing and sales related topics with an emphasis on understanding solution business transformations. Her research has been published in the *Journal of the Academy of Marketing Science, Industrial Marketing Management, International Journal of Operations Management, Journal of Business-to-Business Marketing*, and the *Journal of Service Management*.

David Sjödin is an Associate Professor of Entrepreneurship and Innovation at Luleå University of Technology. He researches questions about how companies can change their business to profit from digitalization through servitization and business model innovation in collaboration with leading Swedish companies and regularly consult the industry. The research work involves close collaboration with large firms, such as Volvo Construction Equipment, LKAB, Scania, Ericsson, Boliden, ABB, Metso, and Epiroc as well as many SMEs. The results of his work have been published in over 90 leading international peer-reviewed journals, conferences, book chapters, and industry/popular publications, such as the *California Management Review, Industrial Marketing Management, Journal of Business Research, Long Range Planning, International Journal of Production Economics, Journal of Engineering Technology Management* and *Journal of Product Innovation Management*.

David Sörhammar is an Associate Professor of Marketing at Stockholm Business School, Stockholm University, Sweden. His research interests include service innovation, co-creation, and user innovations. His current research focuses on the interplay between digitization and servitization, and as well as investigating how internationalization occur on the internet. His research has been published in journals such as *Industrial Marketing Management, Journal of Business Research*, and *Marketing Theory*.

Oliver Stoll gained a Master of Science in Engineering and works as a research assistant at the Institute of Innovation and Technology Management (IIT) and a member of Research Group Digital Business Engineering. Simultaneously, he is doing his Ph.D. at Glasgow Caledonian University. In his Ph.D. work, he is investigating the characterization of digital-enabled product-service systems to better understand how such systems can be managed over the life cycle. His past professional career includes boatbuilding of wooden luxury boats. Today's professional work is related to the design, development and commercialization of smart services in the facility management sector. His current and past professional and academic experience have allowed him to gain and build expertise in various fields. When he is not researching and working, he can be found up to 70 meters underwater in the cold lakes of Switzerland.

Prof. Vicky M. Story is a Professor of Marketing at the School of Business and Economics, Loughborough University, United Kingdom. Her primary research interests lie in the fields of fields of marketing strategy, innovation and services, including entrepreneurial orientation and firm performance, radical innovation, servitization, including capabilities and network implications. She has published on these issues in such journals as: *Journal of Product Innovation Management*; *Journal of Business Venturing*; *Industrial Marketing Management*; and *International Journal of Operations and Production Management*. She received her Ph.D. in marketing from Loughborough University in 1998.

Bieke Struyf is a Ph.D. Candidate at the University of Antwerp and researcher at the Antwerp Management School. She obtained her master's degree in Applied Economics at the KU Leuven and is currently part of the multidisciplinary team surrounding FWO-project Paradigms 4.0 which investigates how manufacturing companies can implement Industry 4.0 technology in a sustainable manner. As a Ph.D. Candidate, she focuses on the identification of value-creating strategies, barriers, and critical success factors which contribute to effective digital transformation. She does so under the supervision of Prof. Dr. Paul Matthyssens. Mainly qualitative research methods are used in her multilevel and multidisciplinary research of transformation processes which investigate the impact on and mobilization of individual employees, the organization, and its surrounding ecosystem.

Viktor Sundholm main interest is in industrial business development, and has been involved in several research projects and consulting assignments in this area. The Ph.D. research (in final phase) has been based on solution business strategy and value-based selling. Currently, Mr. Sundholm is mainly involved in teaching through the FITech Network University and in Finland's leading ecosystem on digitalizing the manufacturing industry, REBOOT IoT Factory.

Tinhinane Tazaïrt is a Ph.D. candidate in Management Sciences and a Member of the Coactis research center at Lumière Lyon 2 University, where she also teaches strategic marketing. Her Ph.D. research is funded by the Auvergne-Rhône-Alpes (AURA) district. Her research interests are in the areas of servitization and digitalization, with a focus on performance issues in servitized industrial SMEs that attempt to digitalize their servitization.

Harri Terho is an Adjunct Professor and Senior Research Fellow in Marketing at the Turku School of Economics, University of Turku, Finland. His research interests focus on B2B marketing, customer value, selling, digital marketing and management of customer relationships. His research has been published in the leading general marketing and business marketing outlets, such as the *Journal of the Academy of Marketing Science, Industrial Marketing Management, Journal of Business Research, Journal of Business-to-Business Marketing* and *Journal of Personal Selling & Sales Management*, among others.

Bård Tronvoll is a Professor of Marketing at Inland Norway University of Applied Sciences, Norway and at CTF-Service Research Center at Karlstad University, Sweden. Tronvoll is a member of the editorial advisory board at *Journal of Service Management*, and his work has been published in journals such as *Journal of the Academy of Marketing Science, Journal of Service Research, Journal of Business Research, Industrial Marketing Management, European Journal of Marketing, Journal of Service Management and Marketing Theory*. His research interests include marketing theory, service innovation, customer complaining behavior/service recovery, and digitalization.

Wouter Van Bockhaven is a Professor of Innovation Ecosystems at the Antwerp Management School knowledge cluster on Smart Networks and Ecosystems. He is a project and work package leader on several nationally and EU-funded projects on topics of smart port ecosystems, Industry 4.0, and entrepreneurship. His research focuses on the nexus between institutional innovation value systems (IMP) and multi-stakeholder field development. It tackles questions of how collaborative value-creating systems of stakeholders are designed, mobilized and governed, and bridges multidisciplinary theories with links to action. As such, his work has resulted in peer-reviewed publications, as well as in actual ecosystem innovations and adopted policies at different levels.

Shaun West gained a Ph.D. from Imperial College in London, Shaun worked for over 25 years in several businesses related to industrial services. He started his industrial career with AEA Technology before moving to National Power, where he developed and sold services to external businesses. After studying at HEC (Paris) for an M.B.A., he moved to GE Energy Services, modeling and negotiating long-term service agreements. At Sulzer, he drafted the strategy that led to the service division tripling in size over ten years and executed part of the strategy by acquiring a 220M CHF service business. Now at the Lucerne University of Applied Sciences and Arts, he is the Professor of Product-Service System Innovation. He focuses his research on supporting industrial firms to develop and deliver new services and service-friendly business models. He is a member of the advisory board for ASAP Service Management Forum and a member of the Swiss Alliance of Data-Intensives Services. He lives close to Zurich with his wife and two children. He climbs, skis and runs.

Lars Witell is a Professor of Marketing at Linköping University, Sweden and holds a position as Professor of Service Research at the CTF-Service Research Center at Karlstad University in Sweden. His research interests concern service innovation, service infusion, and customer experience. We do research with major Swedish firms such as Volvo and IKEA. He has published about 75 papers in scholarly journals such as *Journal of Service Research, International Journal of Operations and Production Management, Journal of Service Management*, and *Industrial Marketing Management*. He is also an Associate Editor for *Journal of Business Research* and *Journal of Services Marketing*.

Dr. Judy Zolkiewski is a Professor in Marketing at Alliance Manchester Business School. Before becoming an academic she worked for 15 years in the industrial controls industry. She received her Ph.D. in 1999 from UMIST and has worked at Manchester since then, initially at Manchester School of Management (UMIST) and, following the merger of UMIST and University of Manchester, at AMBS. Her research interests are focused on understanding business markets, relationships and networks both in the traditional manufacturing and engineering industries and in the evolving business-to-business services sector with specific focus on relationship and network dynamics, servitization, strategy, and technology. Her current research projects focus on the processes underpinning relationships and networks and the transformations that are needed for manufacturers to successfully deliver services. She has been heavily involved in knowledge transfer projects and has published in *Journal of Business Research, European Journal of Marketing, Industrial Marketing Management, International Journal of Operations & Production Management, International Journal of Production Economics, Journal of Services Marketing*, the *Journal of Marketing Management*, and *Journal of Business & Industrial Marketing*.

Wenting Zou is a Ph.D. student at the Department of Industrial Engineering and Management (DIEM) at Aalto University in Finland. From June 2016 to the 2021, she has been dedicated to doctoral research on managing service contracting in buyer-supplier collaboration. She has been published her doctoral work in *International Journal of Operations and Production Management* as the first author. She was awarded the scholarship for the first refereed article at the doctoral program in Science at Aalto University in 2018. She has reviewed papers for *International Journal of Operations & Production Management*, and *Journal of Purchasing and Supply Management*. She is due to graduate in Spring 2021. Now she lives in Canton of Zurich with her husband and son. She likes traveling, swimming, running, and playing cards (e.g., Swiss Jass).

List of Figures

A Conceptual Guideline to Support Servitization Strategy Through Individual Actions

Employee Reactions to Servitization as an Organizational Transformation

Digital Servitization: Strategies for Handling Customization and Customer Interaction

Service-Dominant Logic: A Missing Link in Servitization Research?

Value Co-creation in Digitally-Enabled Product-Service Systems

Manufacturers' Service Innovation Efforts: From Customer Projects to Business Models and Beyond

Configurational Servitization Approach: A Necessary Alignment of Service Strategies, Digital Capabilities and Customer Resources

Service Integration: Supply Chain Integration in Servitization

Coordinating and Aligning a Service Partner Network for Servitization: A Motivation-Opportunity-Ability (MOA) Perspective

List of Tables

Theoretical Landscape in Servitization

Marko Kohtamäki, Tim Baines, Rodrigo Rabetino,
Ali Z. Bigdeli, Christian Kowalkowski, Rogelio Oliva,
and Vinit Parida

1 Introduction

Manufacturers have shifted their focus from products to smart solutions in the search for higher returns and additional growth opportunities (Lightfoot et al., 2013; Matthyssens & Vandenbempt, 2008; Rabetino et al., 2015). This shift, described as servitization (Vandermerwe & Rada, 1988) or later as digital servitization (Coreynen et al., 2017; Kohtamäki, Parida et al., 2019), is

M. Kohtamäki (✉) · R. Rabetino
School of Management, University of Vaasa, Vaasa, Finland
e-mail: mtko@uwasa.fi

R. Rabetino
e-mail: rodrigo.rabetino@uwasa.fi

T. Baines
Aston Business School, Aston University, Birmingham, UK
e-mail: t.baines@aston.ac.uk

A. Z. Bigdeli
Aston Business School, Aston Triangle, Aston University, Birmingham, UK
e-mail: a.bigdeli@aston.ac.uk

C. Kowalkowski
Department of Management and Engineering, Linkoping University, Linköping, Sweden
e-mail: christian.kowalkowski@liu.se

M. Kohtamäki et al. (eds.), *The Palgrave Handbook of Servitization*,
https://doi.org/10.1007/978-3-030-75771-7_1

a lengthy and complex process for which positive outcomes cannot be guaranteed (Gebauer et al., 2005; Oliva & Kallenberg, 2003). The present chapter consolidates contemporary research on servitization and sheds light on the structure and relevant concepts in this multidisciplinary field (Rabetino et al., 2018).

Servitization—the shift from a product-centric to a service-centric business model and logic (Kowalkowski, Gebauer, Kamp, & Parry, 2017)—represents a powerful growth engine for firms seeking to expand beyond their traditional product core. Examples include both traditional machine manufacturers and software companies that have shifted to cloud-based subscription models. Today, servitization has become a flourishing and active research domain, attracting interest from a wide range of disciplines, including marketing, operations, engineering management, service management, and environmental research (Rabetino et al., 2018; Raddats et al., 2019).

Whereas managers generally agree that they must move into services, empirical research suggests mixed outcomes from such transformations. The link between servitization and performance has been demonstrated to be potentially nonlinear and complex (Fang et al., 2008; Kohtamäki, Parida et al., 2020; Kohtamäki et al., 2013). Frequently, failures have been argued to emerge from poor implementation, lack of required capabilities, poorly executed processes, organizational tensions, and other factors (Lenka et al., 2018; Martinez et al., 2017; Parida et al., 2014; Visnjic Kastalli et al., 2013). Recent studies highlight the important role of digitalization in ensuring profitable servitization (Cenamor et al., 2017; Lenka et al., 2017). This interplay between digitalization and servitization has been captured under the term "digital servitization," which emphasizes value creation through the interplay between products, services, and software (Kohtamäki, Parida et al., 2019; Porter & Heppelmann, 2014) and represents an important future research stream in the servitization literature.

This chapter provides an overview of the changing landscape of servitization research, including the transformation process, business model content, and context with various contingencies (Kohtamäki, Henneberg et al., 2019).

R. Oliva
Mays Business School, Texas A&M University, College Station, TX, USA
e-mail: roliva@tamu.edu

V. Parida
Department of Business Administration, Luleå University of Technology, Luleå, Sweden
e-mail: vinit.parida@ltu.se

Although our core focus is on servitization, we intend to broaden the rich conceptual landscape evolved around this literature, including related concepts such as digital servitization and product-service systems (PSS). We provide some theoretical background and methodological angles to demonstrate future directions for expanding servitization research further.

The remainder of the chapter is structured as follows. We first present the definition and content of servitization and related concepts, highlighting the role of software as part of product-service-software systems. We then review the current structure of the servitization field and then the conceptual landscape of the servitization literature, followed by a discussion of the servitization concept from the perspectives of content, process, and context. We offer some notes on the methodological landscape in servitization before we end the article discussing the future avenues of servitization research.

2   Evolution of the Field of Servitization

Defining Servitization

Since Vandermerwe and Rada first introduced the concept of servitization in (1988), we have witnessed its conceptual emergence and development. The early developments were slow, and the literature did not significantly take off before the early 2000s, when some of the seminal papers were published. Since then, servitization has gained enormous attention by researchers, and 726 scholarly papers have been published on and around the topic. In addition, dedicated academic conferences and conference tracks have been established during the last decade (Kowalkowski, Gebauer, Kamp, & Parry, 2017), and managerial books have been written (e.g., Baines & Lightfoot, 2014; Kowalkowski & Ulaga, 2017). Studies from Oliva and Kallenberg (2003), Mathieu (2001), Davies (2004), Gebauer et al. (2005), Tukker (2004), Brax (2005) and Baines et al. (2007) initiated the stream of servitization literature, and we see a growing trend in publishing on this topic today (Rabetino et al., 2018).

Table 1 synthesizes the definitions of servitization-related concepts within these traditions. At the core, *servitization is about the transition from product to service logic, often involving a complex integration of product-service-software systems, where the ideal–typical form of service logic can be understood as a customer paying for the realized value in use.* Researchers have also noted the lack of software or digital emphasis in the prior servitization literature, perhaps resulting from the lack of advanced digital technologies, which we

Table 1 Definitions of key servitization-related concepts

Study	Concept	Definition
Offerings		
Baines et al. (2007: 3)	Product-Service system	PSS is *"an integrated product and service offering that delivers value in use. A PSS offers the opportunity to decouple economic success from material consumption and hence reduce the environmental impact of economic activity"*
Sawhney (2006: 369)	Customer solution	*"an integrated combination of products and services customized for a set of customers that allows customers to achieve better outcomes than the sum of the individual components"*
Brady et al. (2005: 572)	Integrated solutions	*"bringing together of products and services in order to address a customer's particular business or operational requirements"*
Servitization process		
Kowalkowski, Gebauer, Kamp, and Parry (2017: 5)	Servitization	A transformation from a product-centric to a service-centric business model and logic
Kowalkowski, Gebauer, Kamp, and Parry (2017: 5)	Service infusion	*"The process whereby the relative importance of service offerings to a company or business unit increases, amplifying its service portfolio and augmenting its service business orientation"*

(continued)

Table 1 (continued)

Study	Concept	Definition
Kohtamäki, Parida et al. (2019)	Digital servitization	The transition toward smart solutions (product-service-software systems) that enable value creation and capture through monitoring, control, optimization, and autonomous function. Digital servitization emphasizes value creation through the interplay between products, services, and software

see emerging currently. Studies have called for the concept of digital servitization to emphasize the role of software as the core of novel product-service systems, so-called product-service-software systems (Coreynen et al., 2017; Kohtamäki, Parida et al., 2019). These offerings and the interplay between products, services, and, more recently, software modules are central to the servitization literature (Cenamor et al., 2017). Manufacturers engage in a both-and game, where they must accept various paradoxical tensions that emerge due to the simultaneous engagements in product, service, and software development, lifecycle, and upgrading cycles (Kohtamäki, Einola, & Rabetino, 2020; Lenka et al., 2018). Such product, service, and software offerings have played an important role in servitization research, where offerings are often used as an obvious indicator of strategy and value proposition (Kohtamäki et al., 2013; Rabetino et al., 2015).

Servitization studies have incorporated the concepts of product-service systems (Reim et al., 2015), customer solutions, integrated solutions, services supporting the product (SSP), and services supporting the customer (SSC) (Mathieu, 2001), to name a few. It is important to remember that, from the infancy of servitization, the data-related software element has been part of the servitization literature (Vandermerwe & Rada, 1988). Vandermerwe and Rada (1988), in their seminal piece, emphasized the interplay between goods, services, and information (cf. Page and Siemplenski's [1983] concept of product systems marketing). The connection, integration, or bundling between products, services, and software can be seen as one of the central elements in the servitization literature—yet, the dynamics related to operational integration have not been discussed in great detail. For instance,

Rabetino et al. (2015) argue in their empirical study that it is the product lifecycle that enables intuitive integration of products and services. Similarly, Cenamor et al. (2017) discuss how advanced service offerings by manufacturing firms would require viewing software or information modules as a core around which different product and service modules are integrated to efficiently create a customized solution for customers. Practical examples of such offerings can include fleet solutions, site optimizations, or even autonomous solutions, as offered by manufacturing firms. Thus, further attention to software elements is central to adapting servitization in the current digital age.

Structure of the Servitization Field

Figure 1 shows the yearly number of scientific journal articles and citations from 1988 to 2020 in the field of servitization, totaling 726 servitization studies across all disciplines and journals included in Scopus. Based on the figures, we can see a sharp increase in the number of published articles, which increased from 13 papers per year before 2010 to 152 articles per year by

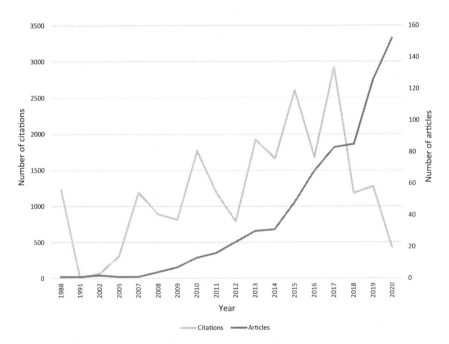

Fig. 1 Increase in the number of articles and citations per year from 1988 to 2020

2020. Indeed, the publication rate has doubled every three years, and 93% of the articles have been published since 2010 (93%).

Similarly, the yellow curve demonstrates the increase in citations per paper published in servitization per year. The papers published in 2017 received 2,921 citations until the end of 2020 (yellow line). As it takes time for papers to gather citations, the citation count of 2017 provides a better picture of the progress than 2018 or later, after which the papers have had much less time to collect citations. Overall, Fig. 1 demonstrates the drastic increase in published papers and paper citations, depicting the increase in servitization during the past years.

Next, Fig. 2 describes the current structure of the servitization field based on a cocitation analysis and VOSviewer software, with the data of 726 studies. Author cocitation analysis considers the number of times each pair of authors has been cocited in the studied data (Zupic & Čater, 2015), as cocited authors often share similar ideas. In the figure, color indicates the cluster, the size of

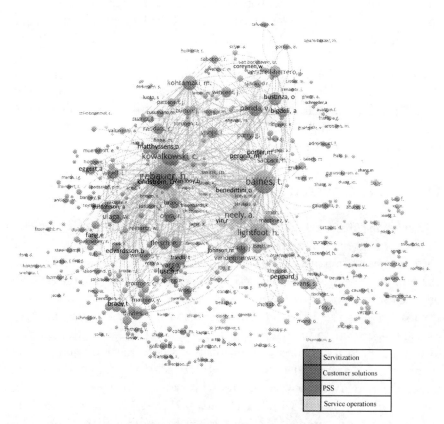

Fig. 2 Structure of the servitization field 1988–2020 (based on cocitation analysis of 726 articles)

the circle signals the number of citations (larger circle means a higher number of citations), closer location between authors means that the authors are often cocited, and the 500 most frequently cocited pairs of authors are indicated by lines.

Based on the analysis, we found four clusters: (1) customer solutions, (2) servitization, (3) product-service systems (PSS), and (4) service operations. The red cluster involves customer solutions, integrated solutions, service logic and services-dominant logic, value cocreation, and related literature. Most of these studies are within marketing, although scholars such as Brady and Davies are within innovation management. The blue cluster includes management-oriented servitization studies, strategy, structure, innovation, and digital servitization papers. The green cluster is a PSS-oriented stream with strong engineering emphasis and involves sustainability-oriented writings in servitization. Finally, the yellow group is oriented toward service operations and service technologies, including the service science approach. Understandably, the borders between clusters are blurry and there are boundary spanners, which are located at the intersections of different communities, such as Kowalkowski, Gebauer, Baines, or Lightfoot. Reasons include cross-disciplinary publishing and the use of different terminology. The customer solutions, servitization, PSS, and service operations clusters in Fig. 2 seem consistent when compared with other reviews (Rabetino et al., 2018). These streams also consist of smaller substreams, which can be recognized by looking at the most cited authors in any location of the picture and their publications over the years.

Conceptual Landscape in Servitization

The anatomy of the servitization literature can be understood by depicting and analyzing the concepts embedded in servitization studies. For this purpose, we used textual analysis of the servitization articles and a linguistic text mining process. We utilized Leximancer software, following the examples provided by previous strategy and innovation studies (Wilden et al., 2016). Leximancer uses thematic and semantic analyses and a Bayesian machine-learning algorithm to analyze the text in the sampled journal articles and to reveal concepts and themes based on the cooccurrence of words, as the context defines any word (Wilden et al., 2016: 1010). Thus, the analysis reveals the primary conceptual themes (clusters) in the literature and represents the main concepts within each cluster. In addition to linguistic text mining, we use traditional narrative review to understand the conceptual landscape in the servitization literature. Figure 3 synthesizes five main clus-

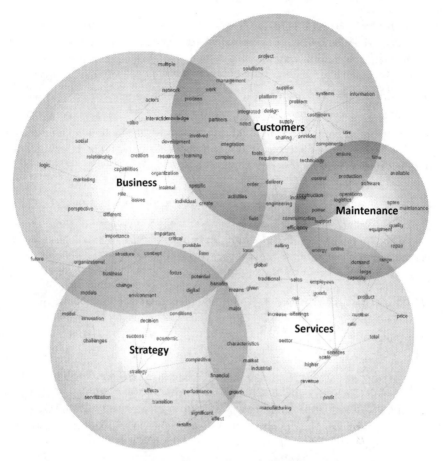

Fig. 3 The conceptual landscape of servitization resulting from concept mapping

ters of concepts stemming from the servitization literature. The dimensions and the most typical concepts emerging from the studies were (1) services, (2) customers, (3) business, (4) strategy, and (5) maintenance. Servitization centers around offerings, customers, value, and maintenance operations, which are part of the business model. This objective depiction from the literature involves the most typical concepts in the servitization literature, providing a valuable lens to view the literature.

The first cluster is about *services*, including offerings, and related concepts (product, goods) and the effects of services (revenue, growth, profit). The cluster also contains concepts related to risk, sales, selling, and contextual factors (e.g., manufacturing). The second cluster centers on *customers* covers concepts such as solutions, processes, activities, platforms, tools, problems, and sharing. Indeed, the role of customers has been emphasized in the servitization literature, for instance, by the service infusion concept, the transition toward service logic. The third cluster, *business*, captures the concepts around value, capabilities, organization, structure, logic, learning, and interactions. Many of these concepts interact with customers and strategy and link to other concepts around different forms of value creation, which are undoubtedly relevant to the servitization literature. Fourth, the concept *strategy* involves servitization, business models, transition, change, digital, effects, and success—all typical concepts from strategy-related servitization studies. Finally, the fifth cluster involves *maintenance*-related concepts linked to operations, equipment, production, control, efficiency, available, spare, capacity, software, repair, and online. These concepts focus on operations and service technologies. The five clusters of concepts reveal the typical themes and concepts covered in servitization research. The picture is not complete because it includes only the most typical concepts.

Servitization as Content, Process, and Context

If we look at the servitization literature through the lens of strategy, we can divide the analysis into (1) content, (2) process, and (3) context (Ketchen et al., 1996). Such categorization helps to analyze the research from an inside-out perspective (business model of value creation content), as a process view (how the servitization strategy content is created, or how servitization progresses as planned and emergent), and from an outside-in perspective (contingency).

The largest proportion of studies focuses on pure strategy or business model content, and the lowest number ($\sim$20) focuses on the servitization process. Contingency-theoretic or configurational research is somewhere in between the content and process. The proportion of papers focusing on the servitization process is surprisingly low, particularly those using the processual approach. There are several papers using the terms process or change, but most of these studies do not explore the servitization process, instead focusing on value creation, innovation process, behavioral processes, and so forth. Most of the servitization work to date has analyzed the strategy, business model content, capabilities, service offerings, PSS, value creation, service innovation, technologies, performance, or related constructs. Servitization studies are predominantly content oriented, or they analyze more microlevel relevant processes but rarely servitization processes. Finally, a significant research effort has identified contingency factors, such as the nature of the business environment, or internal contingency factors, such as the nature of the business models, offerings, or technologies, depending on the research settings. In what follows, we describe in more detail the focus of the research found under the themes.

Servitization as a Content: Servitization Business Models

We first focus on servitization from a content perspective given the large proportion of the published papers that have dealt with strategy or business model content, different kinds of servitization strategies, product-service offerings, product and service operations that servitized companies have been running, capabilities, value creation, value capture, and pricing, remote technologies. Another topic that has received attention is the effects or outcomes of servitization, for instance, the performance effects of servitization, such as the impact on revenues, profits, and company valuation.

Servitization strategy and business models have received much attention in the literature. Multiple concepts have been used, such as the servitization business model, solution business model, PSS business model, or service business model. In their study, Kowalkowski et al. (2015) identified three different business models and trajectories: availability provider, performance provider, and industrializer (see also Matthyssens & Vandenbempt, 2008; Penttinen & Palmer, 2007). While firms generally move from basic, product-oriented services toward offerings that include more complex, process-oriented services and solutions, the researchers also identified cases where firms shift the emphasis from more advanced to more standardized service offerings. In addition, Kohtamäki, Parida et al., (2019) developed a typology of five alternative servitization business models, including a product-oriented service provider, industrializer, integrated solutions provider, outcome provider, and platform provider, which they discussed by using four theories of the firm. Recent studies have also looked more into a specific type of servitization business model, such as Sjödin, Parida, Jovanovic, and Visnjic (2020), investigating how to design, develop, and implement outcome-based business models.

Customers have been an important starting point for the servitization literature. The research highlights the role of value cocreation, value coproduction, and value capture (Sjödin et al., 2016). Thus, service-dominant logic and service logic are theoretical lenses often used in the servitization literature. As such, one of the core emphases has related to customer importance, or customer orientation, which is an inherent part of the service logic (Kowalkowski & Ulaga, 2017). Kohtamäki and Partanen (2016) study the role of customer cocreation in advanced services, finding the positive moderating impact of customer cocreation on the relationship between a manufacturer's R&D services and relationship profitability to the manufacturer. Recent studies also recognize the need to develop an agile approach toward advanced service delivery, as both often call for both providers and customers to significantly transform their relationships and the associated value creation process (Sjödin, Parida, Kohtamäki, & Wincent, 2020).

The servitization literature emphasizes the role of service offerings as an important indicator of servitization. Studies have conceptualized offerings using many different concepts, such as product-service systems (PSS), service offerings, customized solutions, customer solutions, integrated solutions, hybrid offerings, and others. Rabetino et al. (2015) studied product-service bundling in manufacturers and used the product lifecycle to understand how manufacturers integrate services into the product lifecycle. In one of the most influential studies, Tuli et al. (2007) conceptualize solutions as a set of customer–supplier relational processes and highlight that the effectiveness of a customer solution depends not only on supplier variables but also on several customer variables.

The transition from products to product-service-software systems requires a major evolution in strategic capabilities, such as the unique set of resources and capabilities the firm possesses (or can harness from its network). The resource-based view is one of the primary strategy theories involving a large body of academic research. From the 726 papers, we identified 152 papers related to capabilities (strategic or dynamic capabilities). This relevance is also seen in servitization; the capability approach is one of the most significant research streams, not least due to the managerial value the RBV provides. The literature involves a large body of contributive papers. For example, Ulaga and Reinartz (2011) identified a set of overarching resources and capabilities required for successful servitization. Acknowledging that resources do not confer competitive advantage per se, as they need to be leveraged for capability building, they support five critical capabilities: 1) service data processing and interpretation, 2) implementation risk assessment and mitigation, 3) design-to-service, 4) solution sales, and 5) offering deployment. Storbacka (2011) conceptualized a solution process with four phases (develop solutions, create demand, sell solutions, and deliver solutions) and three groups of cross-functionality issues (commercialization, industrialization, and solution platform), with 12 capability categories and 64 capabilities and management practices pertinent to the effective management of solution business. Baines and Lightfoot (2014) created an integrative framework combining various critical resources (e.g., factories and location, supplier relationships, information and communication technologies, performance measurement, value demonstration, people management, processes, and customer relationships). Hasselblatt et al. (2018) recognized five strategic capabilities that develop, sell and deliver IoT-related capabilities: (1) building a scalable solution platform, (2) value selling, (3) value delivery, (4) digital business model development, and (5) business intelligence. Kindström et al. (2013) identified 11 microfoundations associated with the sensing, seizing, and reconfiguring capabilities geared to the facilitation of servitization. Finally, recent studies recognize the importance of digitalization capability to successfully develop and deliver advanced services to customers (Annarelli, Battistella, Nonino, Parida, & Pessot, 2021; Lenka et al., 2017).

Servitization as a Process (From—To)

Multiple concepts have been used when referring to servitization. Concepts such as service transition (Fang et al., 2008; Oliva & Kallenberg, 2003), service transformation, and service infusion (Brax, 2005; Forkmann et al., 2017; Kowalkowski et al., 2012) have been used to refer to the transformation from products to product-service-software systems. At its core, servitization as a process refers to the transition from a product business to product-service systems. This characterization means that in an ideal–typical situation, the other end of a continuum reflects a product logic, in practice, a standard product business with add-on services; at the other end of the continuum is the service logic, or in practice, the pure service business model (e.g., an outcome-based service business) (Kowalkowski, Gebauer, & Oliva, 2017; Oliva & Kallenberg, 2003). There may be a mixture of business models in between that configure the components of products, services, and software (Parida et al., 2014). In practice, different business models may coexist within the same organization (Kowalkowski et al., 2015). Hence, a firm may have a product-centric business model, aiming to maximize equipment sales, and a service-centric model, aiming to improve its customers' processes in parallel, even if the latter implies selling fewer products. One of the most challenging elements of the processes is shifting to a service-centric business logic, which includes changing norms, values, practices, and mental models (Kindström et al., 2013).

Transition, strategic, and organizational change is at the core of the concept of servitization. However, when we look at servitization studies, few can be found on the actual transition process, and only a handful of processual studies about servitization process exist. For instance, Lenka et al. (2018) show that the servitization process requires changes to a different organization level, such as strategic, tactical, and operational levels, which creates ambivalence toward organizational change. Baines et al. (2020) found in their study of 14 manufacturers that the servitization process can be conceptualized through four phases: exploration, engagement, expansion, and exploitation. Moreover, they identify a few contextual factors shaping the process. Martinez et al. (2017) investigated the servitization journey. Their study finds servitization as a process of continuous change, emphasizes some contingency factors, and specifies the pace of servitization advancing through different stages from basic through intermediate to complex services. Tronvoll et al. (2020) emphasize the role of organizational identity, dematerialization, and collaboration, specifically in the process of digital servitization. Kohtamäki, Einola, & Rabetino, (2020) highlight the paradoxical tensions in servitization emerging between effectiveness in customizing solutions and efficiency in product manufacturing; this constant struggle between effectiveness and efficiency, which cannot be solved, and is therefore paradoxical. Tronvoll et al. (2020) studied the digital servitization process and identified the key roles of identity change, dematerialization, and collaboration in the change process.

Servitization as Context

The third approach sees servitization as a context for various factors around the business environment. At its core, contingency theory sees strategy and structure as contingent on the factors shaping the business environment. Strategy and structure should fit with changes in the business environment. The configurational approach considers a variety of configurations as contingent on the environment. The configurations can be used by different dimensions, such as strategy and structure, or different business model dimensions. The configurational approach carries the idea of equifinality, which suggests that multiple routes can lead to successful outcomes as long as the configuration provides fit (Doty et al., 1993).

In any case, servitization as a transition relates to strategy and structures inside and outside the firm. The former refers to microlevels, whereas the latter refers to the meso- (ecosystem or value system) or macrolevel (industry and society at large). Typically, configurational studies consider this combination a configuration that should fit the environment-strategy-structure (Kohtamäki, Henneberg et al., 2019). Thus, we can separate the three organizational levels where servitization occurs: (1) the business environment, (2) the ecosystem, and (3) the firm and its divisions, units, and individual actors. The firm is obviously at the center of any strategic transition, so it also is in servitization. The competitive macroenvironment has implications, for example, a transition toward a carbonless society or digitalization.

Ecosystems set many boundaries for development—what ecosystem partners are willing to accept, what can be achieved, and to what extent the existing ecosystems and markets can be shaped. Eventually, the firm is the strategic entity that makes the strategic decision to move toward digital servitization. In this process, individual actors, service workers, middle managers, and top management are needed. To be successful, Kowalkowski and Ulaga (2017) argue that key stakeholders on all three levels—top management, middle management, and frontline employees—need to be engaged. Notably, servitization is often studied only at the level of companies, typically the supplier firm, but sometimes it is studied from the customer's perspective (e.g., Macdonald et al., 2016). Recently, a growing number of studies have adopted a service ecosystem perspective to go beyond the customer–supplier dyad to better understand the complex relationships and interdependencies between intrafirm and interfirm entities. Based on service-dominant logic and industrial network theory, a service ecosystem perspective examines servitization through a holistic, multiactor lens and emphasizes that the systemic, dynamic, and contextual aspects of the phenomenon are influenced by the interactions between actors (Sklyar et al., 2019).

Methodological Insights on the Field of Servitization

Servitization research involves a variety of methodologies and methods. Most servitization studies predominantly build on a realist philosophical approach, using positivist, interpretative, or socioconstructionist orientations. For instance, the servitization literature has strong emphases on qualitative field studies (e.g., multiple case studies), quantitative studies, and literature reviews. There are fewer studies using nominalist or subjectivist orientations, or, for instance, discursive and narrative methods (Luoto et al., 2017), which could be highly relevant in managing complex and lengthy organizational change processes, such as digital servitization. In addition, most studies—explicitly or implicitly—build upon or extend the established body of literature within a certain servitization subcommunity; only a few studies set out to challenge underlying assumptions that exist within the field (Kowalkowski et al., 2015; Luoto et al., 2017; Rabetino et al., 2018; Raddats et al., 2019).

Many previous reviews (Baines et al., 2009; Rabetino et al., 2018; Raddats et al., 2019; Velamuri et al., 2011; West et al., 2018) have pointed out that the vast majority of research in servitization has been qualitative and often case-based. This emphasis on exploratory grounded work is understandable considering the nascent nature of servitization research, where the focus has been to define precisely what is meant by servitization and create the right typologies to observe the phenomena (Kowalkowski, Gebauer, & Oliva, 2017). The majority of empirical studies are based on qualitative data, although the number of quantitative papers is increasing (Raddats et al., 2019). There is also increasing methodological diversity in quantitative papers, including those focused on fuzzy-set qualitative comparative analysis (Forkmann et al., 2017; Sjödin et al., 2019) or those focusing on analysis of large sets of secondary data (Fang et al., 2008; Patel, Ii, & Guedes, 2019; Visnjic Kastalli & Van Looy, 2013). Overall, however, the field has struggled to shift its methodological focus toward the generation of testable propositions or the careful description of complex relationships between the strategic concepts, the transformation process, and the contingency factors that affect this transformation (Oliva, 2016). Without generating these testable propositions and provisional models, it will not be possible for the field to move into a mature stage of theoretical development where hypotheses are being tested and specific quantitative measures of constructs are developed (Edmondson & McManus, 2007). It is not until we gain some confidence in these theoretical developments that we can aspire to develop actionable and prescriptive theories to guide interventions and improve practice (Oliva, 2019).

3   Discussion—Where to Go from Here?

Servitization research has been growing rapidly during the past 20 years, with an increasing number of yearly publications. Over these years, we have witnessed the emergence of four subcommunities in servitization research: (1) servitization, (2) customer solutions, (3) product-service systems, and (4) operations management, as demonstrated by the cocitation analysis. The thematic and semantic analyses of the most typical concepts used in the servitization literature revealed five main clusters of concepts, including (1) services, (2) customers, (3) business, (4) strategy, and (5) maintenance-related concepts. The conceptual landscape in servitization research will keep evolving, while we move forwards, with the effort of the striving servitization community and subcommunities. Hence, it is perhaps safe to conclude that servitization literature is not singular but has many areas, and there is plenty of richness in the literature to move forward. While acknowledging the substantial accumulation of knowledge, particularly in the past decade, recent research agendas point to a wide array of research priorities (Rabetino et al., 2018; Raddats et al., 2019). In particular, digitalization will continue to fundamentally affect industries and accelerate servitization, thereby providing further research opportunities.

Regarding the methods in servitization, we concluded that content-focused variance research is dominant in the servitization literature. However, we can also conclude that many opportunities exist to continue to advance the variance-theoretical research on the servitization business model, antecedents, processes, and outcomes. Advancing servitization theory would certainly be beneficial, as we currently lack precise definitions and measurements for even the most basic constructs surrounding servitization. There is, however, a complementary perspective for theoretical development that has promising potential given the nature of the phenomena that servitization research is attempting to explain, namely, a process.

Another perspective is process theories, which, in contrast to variance theories, focus on processual explanations, of how and why things happen and identify how entities participate in and are affected by the sequence of events; i.e., timing is critical to the outcomes in process theories (Mohr, 1982). Clearly, the relevant constructs (e.g., agents, events) and framing of hypotheses are very different for process theories when compared to the traditional statistical hypothesis testing done for variance theories. As we concluded in our analysis, servitization research lacks process research about the very core of servitization, the transition process. One possible explanation is that, typically, we are not trained in developing and testing process theories (Oliva, 2019). Another is that some journals and reviewers may not be ready to accept process research. Recent methodological developments and calls for more process theories across disciplines (e.g., Langley et al., 2013; Monge, 1990; Poole et al., 2000; Sterman et al., 2015) seem to be removing these traditional obstacles. We should leverage the nature of the servitization phenomenon and use process research to develop improved theorizing on service transition (Kohtamäki, Parida et al., 2019; Oliva, 2020).

Finally, we have all witnessed the massive disruption caused by the recent COVID-19 pandemic (Rapaccini et al., 2020), which has challenged some of the presumed advantages of servitization (e.g., outcome-based contracts) and revealed downsides of these complex offerings (Bond et al., 2020). Hence, research regarding the servitization context, contingency-theoretic, and configurational research on the environment-strategy-structure in servitization requires more attention. As we concluded in our analysis, the servitization literature involves research using contingency-theoretical settings and configurational settings (for configurational research, see the review from Kohtamäki, Henneberg et al., 2019). While servitization scholars may have given some attention to these issues, they offer additional opportunities for further research.

This article provided a short introduction to The Handbook of Servitization, a handbook with articles providing perspectives on servitization strategy and business model, servitization process, customers and value cocreation, innovation and managing operations.

References

Annarelli, A., Battistella, C., Nonino, F., Parida, V., & Pessot, E. (2021). Literature review on digitalization capabilities: Co-citation analysis of antecedents, conceptualization and consequences. *Technological Forecasting and Social Change, 166*.

Baines, T., Bigdeli, A. Z., Sousa, R., & Schroeder, A. (2020, March). Framing the servitization transformation process: A model to understand and facilitate the servitization journey. *International Journal of Production Economics, 221*.

Baines, T., & Lightfoot, H. (2014). Servitization of the manufacturing firm: Exploring the operations practices and technologies that deliver advanced services. *International Journal of Operations & Production Management, 34*(1), 2–35.

Baines, T., Lightfoot, H., Evans, S., Neely, A., Greenough, R., Peppard, J., Roy, R., Shehab, E., Braganza, A., Tiwari, A., Alcock, J. R., Angus, J. P., Bastl, M., Cousens, A., Irving, P., Johnson, M., Kingston, J., Lockett, H., Martinez, V., ... Wilson, H. (2007). State-of-the-art in product-service systems. *Proceedings of the Institution of Mechanical Engineers, Part B: Journal of Engineering Manufacture, 221*(10), 1543–1552.

Baines, T., Lightfoot, H., Peppard, J., Johnson, M., Tiwari, A., Shehab, E., & Swink, M. (2009). Towards an operations strategy for product-centric servitization. *International Journal of Operations & Production Management, 29*(5), 494–519.

Bond, E. U., de Jong, A., Eggert, A., Houston, M. B., Kleinaltenkamp, M., Kohli, A. K., Ritter, T., & Ulaga, W. (2020). The future of B2B customer solutions in a post-COVID-19 economy: Managerial issues and an agenda for academic inquiry. *Journal of Service Research, 23*(4), 401–408.

Brady, T., Davies, A., & Gann, D. M. (2005). Creating value by delivering integrated solutions. *International Journal of Project Management, 23*(5), 360–365.

Brax, S. (2005). A manufacturer becoming service provider–challenges and a paradox. *Managing Service Quality, 15*(2), 142–155.

Cenamor, J., Sjödin, D., & Parida, V. (2017). Adopting a platform approach in servitization: Leveraging the value of digitalization. *International Journal of Production Economics, 192*(October), 54–65.

Coreynen, W., Matthyssens, P., & Van Bockhaven, W. (2017). Boosting servitization through digitization: Pathways and dynamic resource configurations for manufacturers. *Industrial Marketing Management, 60*(42–53), 42–53.

Davies, A. (2004). Moving base into high-value integrated solutions: A value stream approach. *Industrial and Corporate Change, 13*(5), 727–756.

Doty, H. D., Glick, W. H., & Huber, G. P. (1993). Fit, equifinality, and organizational effectiveness: A test of two configurational theories. *Academy of Management Journal, 36*(6), 1196–1250.

Edmondson, A. C., & McManus, S. E. (2007). Methodological fit in management field research. *Academy of Management Review, 32*(4), 1155–1179.

Fang, E., Palmatier, R., & Steenkamp, J.-B. (2008). Effect of service transition strategies on firm value. *Journal of Marketing, 72*(5), 1–14.

Forkmann, S., Henneberg, S. C., Witell, L., & Kindström, D. (2017). Driver configurations for successful service infusion. *Journal of Service Research, 20*(3), 275–291.

Gebauer, H., Fleisch, E., & Friedli, T. (2005). Overcoming the service paradox in manufacturing companies. *European Management Journal, 23*(1), 14–26.

Hasselblatt, M., Huikkola, T., Kohtamäki, M., & Nickell, D. (2018). Modeling manufacturer's capabilities for the Internet of Things. *Journal of Business & Industrial Marketing, 33*(6), 822–836.

Ketchen, D. J., Thomas, J. B., & McDaniel, R. R., Jr. (1996). Process, content and context: Synergistic effects on organizational performance. *Journal of Management, 22*(2), 231–257.

Kindström, D., Kowalkowski, C., & Sandberg, E. (2013). Enabling service innovation: A dynamic capabilities approach. *Journal of Business Research, 66*(8), 1063–1073.

Kohtamäki, M., Einola, S., & Rabetino, R. (2020). Exploring servitization through the paradox lens: Coping practices in servitization. *International Journal of Production Economics, 226*, 1–15.

Kohtamäki, M., Henneberg, S. C., Martinez, V., Kimita, K., & Gebauer, H. (2019). A configurational approach to servitization: Review and research directions. *Service Science, 11*(3), 213–240.

Kohtamäki, M., Parida, V., Oghazi, P., Gebauer, H., & Baines, T. (2019). Digital servitization business models in ecosystems: A theory of the firm. *Journal of Business Research, 104*, 380–392.

Kohtamäki, M., Parida, V., Patel, P., & Gebauer, H. (2020). The relationship between digitalization and servitization: The role of servitization in capturing the financial potential of digitalization. *Technological Forecasting and Social Change, 151*, 1–9.

Kohtamäki, M., & Partanen, J. (2016). Co-creating value from knowledge-intensive business services in manufacturing firms: The moderating role of relationship learning in supplier-customer interactions. *Journal of Business Research, 69*(7), 2498–2506.

Kohtamäki, M., Partanen, J., Parida, V., & Wincent, J. (2013). Non-linear relationship between industrial service offering and sales growth: The moderating role of network capabilities. *Industrial Marketing Management, 42*(8), 1374–1385.

Kowalkowski, C., Gebauer, H., Kamp, B., & Parry, G. (2017). Servitization and deservitization: Overview, concepts, and definitions. *Industrial Marketing Management, 60*(1), 4–10.

Kowalkowski, C., Gebauer, H., & Oliva, R. (2017). Service growth in product firms: Past, present, and future. *Industrial Marketing Management, 60*(1), 82–88.

Kowalkowski, C., Kindström, D., Alejandro, T. B., Brege, S., & Biggemann, S. (2012). Service infusion as agile incrementalism in action. *Journal of Business Research, 65*(6), 765–772.

Kowalkowski, C., & Ulaga, W. (2017). *Service strategy in action: A practical guide for growing your B2B service and solution business.* Service Strategy Press.

Kowalkowski, C., Windahl, C., Kindström, D., & Gebauer, H. (2015). What service transition? Rethinking established assumptions about manufacturers' service-led growth strategies. *Industrial Marketing Management, 45*(1), 59–69.

Langley, A., Smallman, C., Tsoukas, H., & Van de Ven, A. H. (2013). Process studies of change in organization and management: unveiling temporality, activity, and flow. *Academy of Management Journal, 56*(1), 1–13.

Lenka, S., Parida, V., Sjödin, D. R., & Wincent, J. (2018). Towards a multi-level servitization framework: Conceptualizing ambivalence in manufacturing firms. *International Journal of Operations and Production Management, 38*(3), 810–827.

Lenka, S., Parida, V., & Wincent, J. (2017). Digital capabilities as enablers of value co-creation in servitizing firms. *Psychology & Marketing, 34*(1), 92–100.

Lightfoot, H., Baines, T., & Smart, P. (2013). The servitization of manufacturing: A systematic literature review of interdependent trends. *International Journal of Operations & Production Management, 33*(11), 1408–1434.

Luoto, S., Brax, S., & Kohtamäki, M. (2017). Critical meta-analysis of servitization research: Constructing a model-narrative to reveal paradigmatic assumptions. *Industrial Marketing Management, 60*(1), 89–100.

Macdonald, E. K., Kleinaltenkamp, M., & Wilson, H. N. (2016). How business customers judge solutions: Solution quality and value in use. *Journal of Marketing, 80*(3), 96–120.

Martinez, V., Neely, A., Velu, C., Leinster-Evans, S., & Bisessar, D. (2017, October). Exploring the journey to services. *International Journal of Production Economics, 192*, 66–80.

Mathieu, V. (2001). Product services: From a service supporting the product to a service supporting the client. *Journal of Business and Industrial Marketing, 16*(1), 39–53.

Matthyssens, P., & Vandenbempt, K. (2008). Moving from basic offerings to value-added solutions: Strategies, barriers and alignment. *Industrial Marketing Management, 37*(3), 316–328.

Mohr, L. (1982). *Explaining organizational behavior.* San Francisco: Jossey-Bass.

Monge, P. P. (1990). Theoretical and analytical issues in studying organizational processes. *Organization Science, 1*(4), 406–430.

Page, A. L., & Siemplenski, M. (1983). Product systems marketing. *Industrial Marketing Management, 12*(2), 89–99.

Oliva, R. (2016). Servitization theory stunted growth: Diagnosis and proposed treatment. In *Spring Servitization Conference (SSC2016)*. Manchester.

Oliva, R. (2019). Intervention as a research strategy. *Journal of Operations Management, 65*(7), 710–724.

Oliva, R. (2020). On structural dominance analysis. *System Dynamics Review, 36*(1), 8–28.

Oliva, R., & Kallenberg, R. (2003). Managing the transition from products to services. *International Journal of Service Industry Management, 14*(2), 160–172.

Parida, V., Sjödin, D., Wincent, J., & Kohtamäki, M. (2014). Mastering the transition to product-service provision: Insights into business models, learning activities, and capabilities. *Research Technology Management, 57*(3), 44–52.

Patel, P. C., Ii, J. A. P., & Guedes, M. J. (2019). The survival benefits of service intensity for new manufacturing ventures: A resource-advantage theory perspective. *Journal of Service Research.*

Penttinen, E., & Palmer, J. (2007). Improving firm positioning through enhanced offerings and buyer–seller relationships. *Industrial Marketing Management, 36*(5), 552–564.

Poole, M. S., van de Ven, A. H., Dooley, K., & Holmes, M. E. (2000). *Organizational change and innovation processes: Theory and methods for research.* Oxford University Press.

Porter, M., & Heppelmann, J. (2014). How smart, connected products are transforming competition. *Harvard Business Review, 92*(11), 66–68.

Rabetino, R., Harmsen, W., Kohtamäki, M., & Sihvonen, J. (2018). Structuring servitization-related research. *International Journal of Operations and Production Management, 38*(2), 350–371.

Rabetino, R., Kohtamäki, M., Lehtonen, H., & Kostama, H. (2015). Developing the concept of life-cycle service offering. *Industrial Marketing Management, 49*(August), 53–66.

Raddats, C., Kowalkowski, C., Benedittini, O., Burton, J., & Gebauer, H. (2019). Servitization: A contemporary thematic review of four major research streams. *Industrial Marketing Management* (October 2018), 1–70.

Rapaccini, M., Saccani, N., Kowalkowski, C., Paiola, M., & Adrodegari, F. (2020). Navigating disruptive crises through service-led growth: The impact of COVID-19 on Italian manufacturing firms. *Industrial Marketing Management, 88*, 225–237.

Reim, W., Parida, V., & Örtqvist, D. (2015). Product-Service Systems (PSS) business models and tactics—A systematic literature review. *Journal of Cleaner Production, 97*, 61–75.

Sawhney, M. (2006). Going beyond the product: Defining, designing and delivering customer solutions. In R. F. Lusch & S. L. Vargo (Eds.), *The service dominant logic of marketing dialogue debate and directions* (pp. 356–380). M.E. Sharpe.

Sjödin, D., Parida, V., Jovanovic, M., & Visnjic, I. (2020). Value creation and value capture alignment in business model innovation: A process view on outcome-based business models. *Journal of Product Innovation Management, 37*(2), 158–183.

Sjödin, D., Parida, V., & Kohtamäki, M. (2019). Relational governance strategies for advanced service provision: Multiple paths to superior financial performance in servitization. *Journal of Business Research, 101*(August), 906–915.

Sjödin, D., Parida, V., Kohtamäki, M., & Wincent, J. (2020). An agile co-creation process for digital servitization: A micro-service innovation approach. *Journal of Business Research, 112*(June 2019), 478–491.

Sjödin, D., Parida, V., & Wincent, J. (2016). Value co-creation process of integrated product-services: Effect of role ambiguities and relational coping strategies. *Industrial Marketing Management, 56*, 108–119.

Sklyar, A., Kowalkowski, C., Tronvoll, B., & Sörhammar, D. (2019). Organizing for digital servitization: A service ecosystem perspective. *Journal of Business Research, 104*(October 2017), 450–460.

Sterman, J. D., Oliva, R., Linderman, K., & Bendoly, E. (2015). System dynamics perspectives and modeling opportunities for research in operations management. *Journal of Perations Management, 39–40*, 1–5.

Storbacka, K. (2011). A solution business model: Capabilities and management practices for integrated solutions. *Industrial Marketing Management, 40*(5), 699–711.

Tronvoll, B., Sklyar, A., Sörhammar, D., & Kowalkowski, C. (2020). Transformational shifts through digital servitization. *Industrial Marketing Management, 89*, 293–305.

Tukker, A. (2004). Eight types of product–service system: Eight ways to sustainability? Experiences from SusProNet. *Business Strategy and the Environment, 13*(4), 246–260.

Tuli, K. R., Kohli, A. K., & Bharadwaj, S. G. (2007). Rethinking customer solutions: From product bundles to relational processes. *Journal of Marketing, 71*(3), 1–17.

Ulaga, W., & Reinartz, W. J. (2011, November). Hybrid offerings: How manufacturing firms combine goods and services successfully. *Journal of Marketing, 75*, 5–23.

Vandermerwe, S., & Rada, J. (1988). Servitization of business: Adding value by adding services. *European Management Journal, 6*(4), 314–324.

Velamuri, V. K., Neyer, A. K., & Möslein, K. M. (2011). Hybrid value creation: A systematic review of an evolving research area. *Journal Fur Betriebswirtschaft, 61*(1), 3–35.

Visnjic Kastalli, I., & Van Looy, B. (2013). Servitization: Disentangling the impact of service business model innovation on manufacturing firm performance. *Journal of Operations Management, 31*(4), 169–180.

Visnjic Kastalli, I., Van Looy, B., & Neely, A. (2013). Steering manufacturing firms towards service business model innovation. *California Management Review, 56*(1), 100–123.

West, S., Rohner, D., Kujawski, D., & Rapaccini, M. (2018). Value-scope-price: Design and pricing of advanced service offerings based on customer value. In M. Kohtamäki, T. Baines, R. Rabetino, & A. Bigdeli (Eds.), *Practices and tools for servitization: Managing service transition* (pp. 141–167). Springer International.

Wilden, R., Devinney, T. M., & Dowling, G. R. (2016). The architecture of dynamic capability research. *The Academy of Management Annals, 10*(1), 997–1076.

Zupic, I., & Čater, T. (2015). Bibliometric methods in management and organization. *Organizational Research Methods, 18*(3), 429–472.

Strategic Approaches in Servitization

Digital Servitization: How Manufacturing Firms Can Enhance Resource Integration and Drive Ecosystem Transformation

Christian Kowalkowski, David Sörhammar, and Bård Tronvoll

1   Introduction

The integration of data-enabled services into an ever-increasing number of business practice aspects exemplifies how digitalization and servitization are two closely intertwined transformations. For manufacturing firms, such *digital servitization* gives rise to new opportunities for long-term competitive advantage. However, it also poses new challenges as it blurs industry boundaries and alters the established positions of firms. In addition, digital

C. Kowalkowski (✉)
Department of Management and Engineering, Linköping University, Linköping, Sweden
e-mail: christian.kowalkowski@liu.se

D. Sörhammar
Stockholm University, Stockholm, Sweden
e-mail: david.sorhammar@sbs.su.se

B. Tronvoll
Inland Norway University of Applied Sciences, Hamar, Norway

Karlstad University, Karlstad, Sweden

B. Tronvoll
e-mail: bard.tronvoll@inn.no

M. Kohtamäki et al. (eds.), *The Palgrave Handbook of Servitization*,
https://doi.org/10.1007/978-3-030-75771-7_2

servitization changes not only involve intra-firm processes and customer relationships but the overall ecosystem dynamics as well (Kohtamäki et al., 2019; Sklyar et al., 2019a).

Services have traditionally helped manufacturers stabilize their business during turbulent times, such as the Great Depression in the 1930s (McNeill, 1944) and the global financial crisis in 2008–2009 (Kowalkowski & Ulaga, 2017). The crisis caused by the COVID-19 pandemic has partially or totally interrupted production and economic activities across the globe and has wrought major negative effects in many industry sectors. However, it has dramatically accelerated digitalization across sectors; as Microsoft CEO Satya Nadella put it, "We've seen two years' worth of digital transformation in two months" (Spataro, 2020). In addition, servitization business models have proven more resilient compared with traditional product-centric models. A study of 177 manufacturing firms in Northern Italy, the European region that was first and most extensively affected by the first wave of the pandemic, shows a striking difference between product and service sales (see Fig. 1). Whereas executives anticipated a substantial impact on product sales, the impact on advanced services, such as the sales of connectivity-based services, was much more limited (Rapaccini et al., 2020). Therefore, companies that can successfully seize the opportunities that digital servitization brings are likely to bounce back faster compared with their competitors.

While manufacturers are investing strategically in data collection, analytics capabilities, and in cloud-based platforms, many firms remain concerned

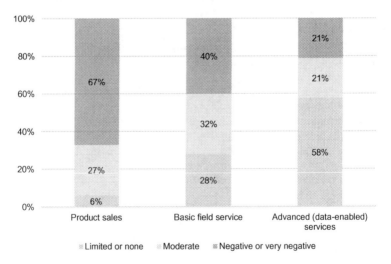

Fig. 1 COVID-19: Expected impact on product and service sales (based on Rapaccini et al., 2020: 229)

about how to best address digital disruption and enable digitalization. The COVID-19 pandemic has accelerated the change and placed additional pressure on firms. Unless a firm is able to transform accordingly, it risks being outpaced by its competitors. Despite being a topic that is front and center for most firms, there is a dearth of theories that guide firm actions in structuring operations for digitalization (Zeithaml et al., 2020). As Raddats et al. (2019) point out, increasing our knowledge about how manufacturing firms can manage digital servitization successfully is a key research priority. Against this backdrop, this chapter sheds light on how manufacturers can transition into a digitalized stage by examining the resource integration patterns that connect ecosystem actors and the organizational shifts needed. Our chapter reveals the dual role of technology in increasing pattern complexity and facilitating the coordination of that complexity. Furthermore, it discusses how firms need to foster service-centricity and execute strategic change initiatives geared toward the internal organization, as well as the wider ecosystem, to take full advantage of digitalization beyond purely technological benefits.

2 Theoretical Background

Digital Servitization

Servitization refers to a firm's transition from a product-centric business model and logic focusing on selling products to a more service-oriented business model and logic that focuses on facilitating customer value creation through the provision of advanced services and solutions that better fulfill customer-specific needs (Baines & Lightfoot, 2014; Kowalkowski et al., 2017). By its very nature, service requires more intense and closer customer interactions that facilitate connections at different organizational levels and help a firm acquire a better understanding of its customers' businesses and needs, and those of its customers' customers (Kowalkowski & Ulaga, 2017). Merging the physical and digital worlds has become an emerging area within the servitization domain under the scope of the term "digital servitization," which we define as the utilization of digital technologies for transformational processes from a product-centric to a service-centric business model and logic (Coreynen et al., 2017; Sklyar et al., 2019a). Digital servitization enables value co-creation through monitoring, control, optimization, and autonomous function (Kohtamäki et al., 2019).

Here, the difference between digitization, which means turning analog data into digital data, and digitalization, which refers to the use of digital technology to provide new value-creating and revenue-generating opportunities (i.e., to change a business model) becomes relevant. Digitization in itself is seldom sufficient for (long-term) competitive advantage as it is rapidly becoming commoditized (Carr, 2003). Rather, differentiation depends on the new practices enabled by it (Brown & Hagel, 2003). Therefore, to be successful, a firm needs to manage digitalization, which includes the socio-technical processes that accompany digitization (Lusch & Nambisan, 2015). Drawing on the concept of the resource-based view (e.g., Barney, 1991), this implies that a firm can achieve competitive advantage by developing and deploying digital resources and capabilities. However, as Ulaga and Reinartz (2011: 6) point out, "Resources per se do not confer competitive advantage but must be transformed into capabilities to do so." For example, the acquisition of installed base product usage and process data is a necessary, but not a sufficient, condition for service-related data processing and interpretation capability. Concomitantly, the acquisition of strategic customer data is a necessary, but not a sufficient, condition for servitization (Ulaga & Reinartz, 2011).

A technology-oriented firm with a product-centric mindset may have little difficulty in implementing digitization, as when record companies moved from selling LPs to CDs. However, rather than embracing the new digital opportunities enabled by digitalization (e.g., "softwareization"), which changed the way people interact with music, record companies generally clung to a product-centric business logic of selling CDs. Rather than developing business models based on Internet distribution, they strived to protect their business model by using items like copy-protected CDs. Ironically, this defensive stance pushed many people to engage in illegal downloading to conveniently access software-based music (e.g., mp3), thereby undermining their product-centric model even further. There are many successful examples of firms providing digitally enabled services for years or even decades. For example, Rolls-Royce's archetypal solution TotalCare began in 1997 (Macdonald et al., 2016) and BT Industries (since 2000 part of Toyota Material Handling) created its logistics-planning software system BT Compass in 1993, to help customers improve their performance (Anderson & Narus, 1998). Similarly, leading bearings manufacturer SKF started early on to remotely monitor bearings usage data flowing from its customers' equipment installed around the globe (Kowalkowski & Ulaga, 2017). As the number of digital business opportunities are rapidly growing, the challenge is seldom to develop or acquire the required resources but rather to have control of and be able to deploy the digital capabilities needed.

Furthermore, digital technology can be a double-edged sword when it comes to servitization. A case study by Perks et al. (2017) illustrates how many manufacturers have been carried away by technical possibilities (e.g., remote connectivity) without having a clear service business model in mind. Rather than truly understanding the customer's business needs and how to conduct value-based selling based on enhanced customer performance, it is tempting to either mimic what competitors are doing or give the service away for free with the hope that customers would eventually discover (some of) its value and be willing to pay for it. However, as the connected installed base grows and the costs of collecting and managing data increase year over year, it becomes more and more difficult to defend such a technology-centric approach unless service sales start to materialize. By giving services away for free, the perceived value of the service offering diminishes in the eyes of the customer (Kowalkowski & Ulaga, 2017).

Resource Integration

To create competitive advantage through digital servitization, both digital resources (i.e., digitization) and capabilities to implement and transform (i.e., digitalization) are necessary. Moreover, resource integration, or the means by which actors co-create context-specific, uniquely determined value for themselves and for other actors in the ecosystem (Kleinaltenkamp et al., 2012), is a key capability in terms of the digital context. For example, a manufacturer may use its knowledge and skills to identify, select, and coordinate suppliers across different supply chains, integrating the hardware, software, and service components into a customer-specific solution. Once deployed, the manufacturer and customer interact through various service activities, including the deployment of new components in response to evolving customer requirements (e.g., the supplier helping install and manage a private 5G network for connected equipment).

Resource integration within an ecosystem—a system of actors, technologies, and institutions (Aarikka-Stenroos & Ritala, 2017)—occurs between strongly and weakly tied actors. Strongly tied actors have close relationships and interact frequently, such as members of the same organizational team, whereas weakly tied actors have distant relationships and interact infrequently, such as members of different firms or business networks that only interact on an irregular basis. Within a network of strong ties, actors with weak ties outside the network can act as bridges to other networks within the ecosystem (Granovetter, 1983).

Increasingly, digital technology acts as a critical facilitator of value creation as it modifies resource integration patterns that connect ecosystem actors between and within organizations (Sklyar et al., 2019b). Whereas the resource-based view of the firm (e.g., Barney, 1991) tends to focus on resources that are controlled within the four walls of the firm, such an ecosystem perspective acknowledges that a single actor is dependent at varying degrees on resources controlled by other actors for its own competitive advantage, as well as for the viability of the ecosystem as a whole. The rapid and potentially disruptive nature of technological change makes it critical for manufacturing firms to be able to make changes to their resource integration patterns when pursuing digital servitization (Sklyar et al., 2019b).

Inter-firm and intra-firm actors within ecosystems generally become strongly tied over time as they learn to draw on each other's heterogeneous resources in a more efficient and effective manner. The more the actors mutually adapt their process and routines, the stronger the ties between them become (Granovetter, 1983). Such adaptation and close relationship are generally seen as a prerequisite for the provision of complex services and customer solutions (Tuli et al., 2007). However, in pursuing digital servitization, manufacturers may encounter a paradox. The mutual adaptation and resources that brought success in the traditional product domain may become what Leonard-Barton (1992) refers to as "core rigidities" that emerge within the preexisting network of strong and weak ties and constrain the transformation effort. In particular, strongly tied patterns of resource integration make it more difficult to adapt to technology-driven environmental changes (Lieberman & Montgomery, 1988; Sklyar et al., 2019b).

While strongly tied actors integrate more resources with each other than with weakly tied actors, the rigidities formed by such institutionalization may inhibit more extensive change and even create resistance ("incumbent inertia;" Lieberman & Montgomery, 1988). In such circumstances, in order to acquire novel resources beyond those already available, such as data science skills, an actor may have to interact with weakly tied actors (Granovetter, 1983). Here, weak ties play an important role in ecosystem transformation and change, such as digital servitization (Sklyar et al., 2019b).

3   Theory Development and Discussion

As firms pursue digital servitization, they move from a pre-digitalized to a digitalized state, which affects both the internal organization and the ecosystem. Drawing on an extensive study of a market-leading systems integrator in the marine industry (Sklyar et al., 2019b; Tronvoll et al., 2020), we identify major differences between the two states. The study draws on 41 in-depth interviews with 33 key informants at the business unit and within the wider multinational corporation conducted from 2016 to 2020. The systems integrator is part of a business ecosystem providing maritime solutions, including a wide range of equipment and onshore and offshore services. The customers are typically operators and vessel owners who are responsible for large international fleets. Figure 2 summarizes the characteristics of the transformational shifts required to achieve digital servitization and move from a pre-digitalized to a digitalized ecosystem based on changes in technology, strong and weak ties, resource integration patterns, as well as shifting from planning to discovery, from scarcity to abundance, and from hierarchy to partnership.

In addition, the findings demonstrate the dual role of technology in (1) increasing the complexity of resource integration patterns and (2) enabling actors to successfully coordinate and manage that complexity. Moreover, they reveal three interconnected shifts that are crucial in achieving digital servitization. As digital, software-based services become central to resource integration, the integration becomes increasingly effective through (1) technological support for connectivity and continuous interaction and (2) the related need for more extensive coordination. By referring to ecosystems rather than inter-organizational networks, we acknowledge that new ecosystems are likely to emerge as firms when firms pursue digital servitization. These ecosystems are not necessarily organized as traditional inter-organizational networks but can instead be organized as markets (Kohtamäki et al., 2019).

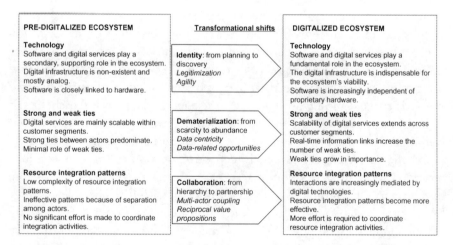

Fig. 2 Ecosystem transformations for digital servitization (based on Sklyar et al., 2019b: 983; Tronvoll et al., 2020: 300)

From Pre-digitalized to Digitalized Ecosystem

In the pre-digitalized ecosystem, the focus of the firm's servitization initiatives was on hardware rather than software, resulting in limited scalability across customer segments and restriction on the extent by which third-party actors could connect and integrate. Due to a lack of digital infrastructure that would enable real-time connectivity, the actors typically interacted by means of analog or one-way digital communication, such as email. During the 2010s, the firm's ecosystem changed into what we refer to as a digitalized state. The firm acted as a network orchestrator—assembling and managing an inter-organizational network to achieve a collective goal (Paquin & Howard-Grenville, 2013)—and drove the change. Rapid technological development enabled the key actors in the ecosystem to build the digital infrastructure needed for continuous real-time connectivity, which resulted in digital technology mediating all interactions among the actors. Examples include onshore operations centers and customized user portals and interfaces supported by third-party cloud services. Notably, the interaction between onshore and offshore units, which had traditionally been (relatively) isolated, was enhanced and simultaneous remote access for both the captain and the chief engineer enhanced the decision-making processes. From having a secondary and supporting role in the pre-digitalized ecosystem, digital technology became critical to interactions in the digitalized stage and functioned as the digital service key selection criterion when fleet owners and operators selected equipment suppliers. The new digital infrastructure further enabled scalability and third-party compatibility, which would have been impossible to achieve in earlier stages (Sklyar et al., 2019b).

In terms of resource integration, our findings shed light on major differences between the pre-digitalized and digitalized ecosystems in terms of (1) interplay between technology, (2) strong and weak ties, and (3) resource integration patterns. In the pre-digitalized state, digital infrastructure was non-existent and mostly analog in its efficiency. Software was closely linked to hardware, usually within (but not across) firms, and to digital services that were mainly scalable within (but not across) customer segments. Furthermore, the ecosystem actors largely depended on non-continuous communication, and strong ties dominated the resource integration patterns due to a scarcity of continuous real-time information links. The role of weak ties was minimal because software and hardware integration occurred mainly within suppliers. However, the dependence on strong ties could create core rigidities (Leonard-Barton, 1992), resulting in less effective resource integration patterns. The secondary supporting role in the ecosystem reflected technology's role as an operand resource, that is, a resource upon which an act is performed (Lusch & Nambisan, 2015). Interactions between actors were not continuously mediated by digital technology, as software and digital services were less prominent. In addition, the resource integration patterns were relatively ineffective because of isolation among the ecosystem's main actors. The low complexity of resource integration patterns meant that no significant effort was exerted to coordinate the actors' integration activities.

The digitalized state, on the other hand, allowed weaker ties to play a central role in the mediation of interactions among actors due to the widespread integration of software interfaces and continuous real-time information links between actors. On the whole, the scalability of digital services extended across customer segments. The created digital infrastructure became indispensable for the ecosystem's viability and software that was increasingly independent of any single supplier's hardware and was extended to third-party offerings. For example, onboard operations of vessels could now be connected to onshore operations, thereby coupling actors who had previously been disconnected (i.e., weak ties). As digital technologies facilitated such weakly tied interactions, new resource integration patterns emerged, which involved more spatially dispersed actors and engendered more effective resource integration patterns (Sklyar et al., 2019b). This change also reflected technology's role as an operant resource, that is, a resource that produces effect. Nonetheless, as the complexity of patterns significantly increased, more effort was required to coordinate the actors' resource integration activities.

Transformational Shifts for Digital Servitization

In order to transform from a pre-digitalized to a digitalized ecosystem state, a firm needs to carry out three interrelated transformational shifts: (1) from planning to discovery, (2) from scarcity to abundance, and (3) from hierarchy to partnership (Tronvoll et al., 2020). The first shift relates to a firm's identity and self-perception of its business model. The case firm transformed from a traditional planning-oriented identity to a more discovery-oriented one and defined itself as a digital technology company. Legitimization and agility facilitated this shift. Here, legitimization mechanisms facilitated the digital servitization of both internal and external actors. For example, the firm provided a vision for transformation, envisioned how it and its customers would operate in the future, and invited customers to its new digital operations centers to be able to experience the new software-centric services firsthand. This emphasis and focus on visionary leadership is vital also for "conventional" servitization (Kowalkowski & Ulaga, 2017), although the specific focus here was on the digital facets of the change. Another key component was to meet the demands of agility linked to digital servitization, which required changing some practices and elements of organizational culture in order to cope with faster software development lifecycles. This included standardizing and formalizing customer-specific solutions and striving for greater scalability (i.e., industrializing and productizing). The entrepreneurial mindset and culture within the firm helped drive the change (see also Fischer et al., 2010).

The second shift concerns dematerialization—the separation between data and physical manifestations—when moving from scarcity to abundance. In the pre-digitalized stage, high-quality performance data were generally scarce. However, in the digitalized stage, the ongoing dematerialization created abundance of data. The shift was facilitated by data centricity and the seizing of data-related opportunities. First, the firm developed new digital capabilities and was able to create competitive advantage by recombining sets of data. Thus, it was able to provide new services. Concurrently, a new set of employees had to be recruited, which led to a more diverse set of human resources. Growing concerns among customers about cybersecurity accelerated the firm's decision to hire employees with data science skills. Second, the firm was able to recognize favorable growth opportunities by leveraging longitudinal customer data, which could be used to enhance existing services and develop new ones (Tronvoll et al., 2020).

Fostering collaboration was the third shift, which was required to break the silo mentality and move from hierarchy to partnership. Multi-actor coupling, which refers to the joint activities of ecosystem actors, and reciprocal value propositions with clear benefits to both parties facilitated the change. Digital services, such as voyage advisory, conditioning monitoring, and cybersecurity services, considerably reduced the amount of time that the firm's service employees had to spend onboard customer vessels as more activities could be conducted remotely. However, in order to take advantage of this benefit, collaborative learning was required to improve the knowledge and skills of the customer service staff. The abundance of data drew the firm closer to many of its customers operationally and strategically. Furthermore, the firm had to foster collaboration among its different units, including its traditional front-end and back-end units, as well as its new digital entity (Sklyar et al., 2019a). While there was concern among some executives that digital services would cannibalize the firm's established service business, the resistance decreased as the firm placed specific emphasis on gaining a profound knowledge of customers' businesses in order to craft value propositions with clear benefits to both parties. In order to develop more competitive value propositions, it became vital to assess the digital maturity of each customer (Tronvoll et al., 2020).

Managerial Implications

At a practical level, our findings indicate that digital services alone are not sufficient to achieve effective resource integration due to the low levels of digital maturity and strong ties among actors in the pre-digitalized ecosystem. A comprehensive digital infrastructure has to be implemented in order to establish a large number of weak ties, thereby enabling more effective resource integration patterns. In this case, as in many other industries and ecosystems, intra-firm and inter-firm core rigidities inhibited the changes needed to drive digital servitization. Here, better connectivity and information exchange can improve decision-making and increase the transparency of operations within and among ecosystem actors. Having a digital infrastructure also helps in responding to environmental changes and taking advantage of further technological advancements, leading to the creation of competitive advantage for both the individual firm and the ecosystem as a whole.

In order to drive transformation, management needs to develop a credible and captivating vision for the firm and its key customers and partners. Furthermore, to transform vision and strategy into realization, a firm needs new types of employees, such as data scientists, which means increasingly competing with the IT industry (and other manufacturers) for talent. While servitization is perceived traditionally as a largely incremental and emergent process, the digital side of the change requires more purposeful and coordinated effort (Sklyar et al., 2019a). Finally, managers need to acknowledge that competition in the digital domain may be fundamentally different than that for "conventional" servitization, such as spare part provision and field service. As we have observed, customers are increasingly looking for providers who are able to integrate systems and provide a uniform platform beyond traditional product and industry categories. Therefore, competition may come from various software and hardware companies, as well as established incumbent manufacturers. Regardless of industry and service maturity, manufacturing firms need to be able to undertake the requisite transformations for digital servitization in order to build and sustain competitive advantage.

References

Aarikka-Stenroos, L., & Ritala, P. (2017). Network management in the era of ecosystems: Systematic review and management framework. *Industrial Marketing Management, 67*, 23–36.

Anderson, J. C., & Narus, J. A. (1998). Business marketing: Understand what customers value. *Harvard Business Review, 76*(6), 53–67.

Baines, T., & Lightfoot, H. W. (2014). Servitization of the manufacturing firm. *International Journal of Operations & Production Management, 34*(1), 2–35.

Barney, J. B. (1991). Firm resources and sustained competitive advantage. *Journal of Management, 17*(1), 99–120.

Brown, J. S., & Hagel, J. (2003). Does IT matter? *Harvard Business Review, 81*(7), 109–112.

Carr, N. G. (2003). IT doesn't matter. *Harvard Business Review, 81*(5), 41–49.

Coreynen, W., Matthyssens, P., & Van Bockhaven, W. (2017). Boosting servitization through digitization: Pathways and dynamic resource configurations for manufacturers. *Industrial Marketing Management, 60*, 42–53.

Fischer, T., Gebauer, H., Gregory, M., Ren, G., & Fleisch, E. (2010). Exploitation or exploration in service business development? Insights from a dynamic capabilities perspective. *Journal of Service Management, 21*(5), 591–624.

Granovetter, M. (1983). The strength of weak ties: A network theory revisited. *Sociological Theory*, 201–233.

Kleinaltenkamp, M., Brodie, R. J., Frow, P., Hughes, T., Peters, L. D., & Woratschek, H. (2012). Resource integration. *Marketing Theory, 12*(2), 201–205.

Kohtamäki, M., Parida, V., Oghazi, P., Gebauer, H., & Baines, T. (2019). Digital servitization business models in ecosystems: A theory of the firm. *Journal of Business Research, 104*, 380–392.

Kowalkowski, C., Gebauer, H., Kamp, B., & Parry, G. (2017). Servitization and deservitization: Overview, concepts, and definitions. *Industrial Marketing Management, 60*, 4–10.

Kowalkowski, C., & Ulaga, W. (2017). *Service strategy in action: A practical guide for growing your B2B service and solution business*. Service Strategy Press.

Leonard-Barton, D. (1992, Summer). Core capabilities and core rigidities: A paradox in managing new product development. *Strategic Management Journal, 13*, 111–125.

Lieberman, M. B., & Montgomery, D. B. (1988, Summer). First-mover advantages. *Strategic Management Journal, 9*, 41–58.

Lusch, R. F., & Nambisan, S. (2015). Service innovation: A service-dominant logic perspective. *MIS Quarterly, 39*(1).

Macdonald, E. K., Kleinaltenkamp, M., & Wilson, H. N. (2016). How business customers judge solutions: Solution quality and value in use. *Journal of Marketing, 80*(3), 96–120.

McNeill, R. B. (1944). The lease as a marketing tool. *Harvard Business Review, 22*(4), 415–430.

Paquin, R. L., & Howard-Grenville, J. (2013). Blind dates and arranged marriages: Longitudinal processes of network orchestration. *Organization Studies, 34*(11), 1623–1653.

Perks, H., Kowalkowski, C., Witell, L., & Gustafsson, A. (2017). Network orchestration for value platform development. *Industrial Marketing Management, 67*, 106–121.

Raddats, C., Kowalkowski, C., Benedettini, O., Burton, J., & Gebauer, H. (2019). Servitization: A contemporary thematic review of four major research streams. *Industrial Marketing Management, 83*, 207–223.

Rapaccini, M., Saccani, N., Kowalkowski, C., Paiola, M., & Adrodegari, F. (2020). Navigating disruptive crises through service-led growth: The impact of COVID-19 on Italian manufacturing firms. *Industrial Marketing Management, 88*, 225–237.

Sklyar, A., Kowalkowski, C., Sörhammar, D., & Tronvoll, B. (2019a). Resource integration through digitalisation: A service ecosystem perspective. *Journal of Marketing Management, 35*(11–12), 974–991.

Sklyar, A., Kowalkowski, C., Tronvoll, B., & Sörhammar, D. (2019b). Organizing for digital servitization: A service ecosystem perspective. *Journal of Business Research, 104*, 450–460.

Spataro, J. (2020). 2 years of digital transformation in 2 months [Microsoft Press release].

Tronvoll, B., Sklyar, A., Sörhammar, D., & Kowalkowski, C. (2020). Transformational shifts through digital servitization. *Industrial Marketing Management, 89*, 293–305.

Tuli, K. R., Kohli, A. K., & Bharadwaj, S. G. (2007). Rethinking customer solutions: From product bundles to relational processes. *Journal of Marketing, 71*(July), 1–17.

Ulaga, W., & Reinartz, W. J. (2011). Hybrid offerings: How manufacturing firms combine goods and services successfully. *Journal of Marketing, 75*(6), 5–23.

Zeithaml, V. A., Jaworski, B. J., Kohli, A. K., Tuli, K. R., Ulaga, W., & Zaltman, G. (2020). A theories-in-use approach to building marketing theory. *Journal of Marketing, 84*(1), 32–51.

Typologies of Manufacturer Identities in the Age of Smart Solutions

Tuomas Huikkola, Suvi Einola, and Marko Kohtamäki

1   Introduction

Recently, manufacturing companies have been digitizing their offerings to sustain a competitive advantage in the markets and differentiate themselves from their rivals (Kohtamäki et al., 2019; Porter & Heppelmann, 2015; Sklyar et al., 2019). To differentiate themselves, generate financial benefits and obtain deeper customer understanding, manufacturers have invested in building connectivity elements into their equipment to better monitor, control, and analyze the usage of their products (Hasselblatt et al., 2017). This digital development has required manufacturers to acquire new skills, namely, software development and acquisition skills (Allmendinger & Lombreglia, 2005; Iansiti & Lakhani, 2014) and sales competencies (Töytäri et al., 2018; Ulaga & Reinartz, 2011). Some people have argued that manufacturers will be reminiscent of software companies in the future. GE's former CEO Jeff Immelt famously said that *"every industrial company must become a*

T. Huikkola (✉) · S. Einola · M. Kohtamäki
School of Management, University of Vaasa, Vaasa, Finland
e-mail: thui@uwasa.fi

S. Einola
e-mail: suvi.einola@uwasa.fi

M. Kohtamäki
e-mail: mtko@uwasa.fi

© The Author(s), under exclusive license to Springer Nature
Switzerland AG 2021
M. Kohtamäki et al. (eds.), *The Palgrave Handbook of Servitization*,
https://doi.org/10.1007/978-3-030-75771-7_3

41

software company" (Porter & Heppelmann, 2015: 108). Many other executives of traditional manufacturing companies have taken a similar approach and made similar statements, such as "…*we are becoming a software company*" or "…*we are a software company*," to foster change and communicate their digital strategies to different stakeholders.

On the other hand, personnel and customers may be confused about these types of statements because they still see firms as "*traditional engine suppliers.*" They may also view these types of announcements as similar to marketing speeches disconnected from reality and as inaccurate signals of the manufacturers' positions and initial strengths. For instance, one manager told us in an interview that "…*there is no point for us being a software company, it's better for us to be a manufacturer that adds some digital elements into our cutting-edge products.*" Therefore, changing a firm's identity is far from easy, as it is unclear whether the entire identity must be changed or if the old identity can be a basis upon which to add digital elements. Moreover, changing an identity does not happen overnight; it requires profound changes in a firm's capabilities, structures, routines, processes, boundaries, and offerings as well as in collective sense making and sensegiving (Gioia & Chittipeddi, 1991; Weick, 1995) and in managers' cognitions and mental models (Danneels, 2011; Helfat & Peteraf, 2015).

This conceptual chapter contributes to the intersection of the digital servitization and organizational identity literature by demonstrating how digital servitization affects manufacturer identity in the era of smart solutions. Answering the question "Who are we as an organization?" and identifying the types of challenges manufacturers might face when trying to change their identities allows manufacturers to address the question "Who will we become as an organization?" We propose different archetypes to (re)define manufacturers' identities in the age of smart solutions and discuss how firm identity can be altered.

2   Theory Development

Defining Digital Servitization

Manufacturing companies have been embracing the opportunity to create value by digitizing downstream activities (Brax & Jonsson, 2009; Porter & Heppelmann, 2014). Studies use various terms, such as "digital servitization" (Kohtamäki et al., 2019) or "digital transformation" (Warner & Wäger, 2019), to denote the concept of a transition toward value creation and capture through product-service-software systems (PSSSs). Digital servitization can be described as a continuum ranging from sales of pure products to sales of purely digitally enabled services. Through digital servitization, manufacturers attempt to seek both economic and strategic advantages by moving away from the eroding product business and trying to provide more added value to clients, whether through decreased costs or increased revenues (Töytäri et al., 2018). Manufacturers thus try to avoid falling into a "commoditization trap" (Huikkola et al., 2016) by digitizing their offerings and processes. Through digitization, a manufacturing company can provide valuable fleet information to both its clients and focal company (e.g., productivity measures, cost information, and predictions). These collected data can enable manufacturers to develop better and more cost-efficient solutions. These digitally enabled solutions can include connectivity elements, thus leading to system-of-system effects (Porter & Heppelmann, 2014) and contributing to their customers' broader business development. Industrial equipment is thus no longer a stand-alone product but is connected to larger systems. For instance, elevators can be connected to other systems in a building and communicate with other products and systems at a customer's site, potentially leading to improved energy efficiency, process flow, and user experience.

Organizational Identity

In 1985, Albert and Whetten (1985a) suggested that organizations have identities. In their seminal work, they defined organizational identity as *central*, *enduring*, and *distinctive*. Organizational identity refers to firm personnel's self-reflective questions related to the core of the firm's existence, such as "Who are we as an organization?" or "Who do we want to be as an organization?" (Albert & Whetten, 1985b; Corley & Gioia, 2004). Therefore, organizational identity aligns with organization members' collective and shared answers to the questions "What kind of organization is this?" and "How is our organization distinctive from others?" The defining aspects of an organization's identity are based on the organization's founding and history and are typically seen as relatively stable. Although previous studies have considered organizational identity to be a relatively stable cognitive structure (Narayanan et al., 2011), an increasing number of studies discuss organizational identity as a dynamic process (Gioia & Patvardhan, 2012). Identity has also been said to address a firm's boundaries, i.e., how different stakeholders such as customers and suppliers view an organization. One way to define, strengthen, and clarify organizational identity is to describe it by addressing questions such as "What kind of organization are we not?" and "What kind of organization do we not want to be?" For instance, Apple did not want to define itself as a traditional engineering/software company ("those are nerds") but rather as a design company that develops technology ("we are cool") (Isaacson, 2011).

Identity has been approached in the literature through different theoretical frameworks. First, researchers have approached identity through an institutional theory-driven lens in which identity is seen to be more or less resistant to change, as labels never change easily. In this view, organizational leaders have an important sensegiving role in which managers provide a consistent *"narrative to construct a collective sense of self"* (Ravasi & Schultz, 2006: 434). Another stream of identity research has its roots in social constructivism, where organizational identity is seen as a shared understanding of and set of beliefs about the central attributes of an organization (Gioia et al., 2000; Vaara & Tienari, 2011). Identity is a relational construct formed through ongoing interactions with others, and sensemaking processes are carried out by all organizational members (Gioia et al., 2013). Through ongoing discussions, members build a shared understanding about the distinctive elements of their organization (Ravasi & Schultz, 2006). In this article, both institutional and socioconstructivist views are acknowledged, and both sensegiving and sensemaking are seen as important processes when manufacturing companies aim to change their identities toward smart solutions.

Creating a New Identity

Constructing a new identity for a firm takes time and occurs relatively slowly because the defining aspects of a firm's identity typically have a relatively stable foundation in the organization's roots, cultural aspects, and history (Corley & Gioia, 2004). Constructing a new identity requires not only the attention of top management (Vaara & Tienari, 2011), a clear vision of the organization's future position, and active and continuous communication to different stakeholders but also a deeper understanding of the characteristics of organizational identity. Identity changes have been studied in the merger and acquisition process (Vaara & Tienari, 2011), spinoffs (Corley & Gioia, 2004), the process of diversification (Barney, 1998), new ventures (Fisher et al., 2016), or the process of creating new divisions within firms (Brown & Gioia, 2002). Therefore, clear triggers have been identified in previous studies from which to start to investigate how firms (re)create their identities. Previous studies (see Albert, 1992) have suggested that additive changes are easier to manage than subtractive changes (Corley & Gioia, 2004). In the servitization literature, "service infusion" is reminiscent of an additive change, whereas strategic, complete renewal, and "morphing" are more indicative of subtractive changes.

Identity consists of both *language* and *meanings* (Gioia et al., 2000). First, language refers to how an organization's members respond to the question "Who are we as an organization?" For instance, responses such as "We are an innovative start-up" align with self-reflective labels such as "innovative" and "start-up." However, these labels have different meanings for internal and external stakeholders, as innovative and start-up can mean different things to different organization members. For some, innovative may refer to the "ability to develop cutting-edge technologies," whereas for others, it may mean the "ability to enter markets first." The term start-up may indicate being entrepreneurial and agile to some, whereas for others, it may mean that a company is still seeking a well-tested and functional earning logic.

Identity Ambiguity

Identity ambiguity refers to there being multiple different interpretations of an organization's core features, thereby leading to uncertainty and confusion among personnel and stakeholders regarding the organization's future image (Corley & Gioia, 2004). This confusion may lead to tensions between units and organization members regarding their collective understanding of "What kind of organization is this?" Ambiguity typically stems from corporate spinoffs, acquisitions, divestments, unclear goals, and weak management communication. Even though identity ambiguity has a negative connotation, organizational resistance and inertia may be beneficial for identity renewal, as they indicate that an organization's members are interested in the firm's direction and in how its executives will try to redirect the company.

Typology of Identities in Digital Servitization

Figure 1 presents eight ideal pure forms of manufacturer identity that are possible in the age of smart services. These "We form" archetypes are categorized as reflections of potential ways to describe a company: (1) "We are a software company," (2) "We are a manufacturer," (3) "We are a smart manufacturer," (4) "We are a service company," (5) "We are a smart service company," (6) "We are a manufacturer that provides services," (7) "We are a smart manufacturer that provides services," and (8) "It is unclear who we are." These identities are typologized based on how weak or strong a firm's manufacturing, service, and software identities are interpreted to be.

A typology of manufacturers' identities in the age of smart solutions

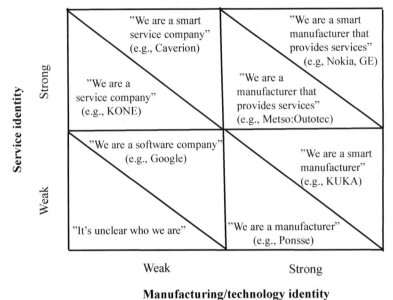

Weak software identity in lower left triangle,
strong software identity in upper right triangle

Fig. 1 Typology of different identities of manufacturing companies

The "*We are a software company*" statement highlights the role of software for a manufacturer and diminishes the role of manufacturing and services. This is a powerful utterance from executives and is typically used in manufacturing firms that have taken strategic initiatives toward smart solutions. The statement clearly describes the manufacturers' strategic intent but has several drawbacks and causes doubts related to the manufacturers' existing capabilities, culture, and position in the markets. First, before expressing this type of goal for a firm's future identity, executives should have a proper understanding of the firm's extant capabilities (Danneels, 2011) and of how the firm can develop digital/software capabilities (e.g., through acquisitions or hiring software developers; see Huikkola et al., 2020). Second, executives should understand a firm's organizational culture, namely, how agile and enduring it is. In software companies, organizational culture traditionally emphasizes flexibility, informality, and agility, whereas traditional manufacturers can be described as relatively inflexible, formal, and rigid (Immelt, 2017). Hence, there is potential for tensions to accrue within companies, and executives should give special attention to identifying routines to "get things done" within their organizations. Third, regarding market position, being a software company provides the possibilities of leveraging software to enter other markets and being free from products and developing stand-alone digital offerings.

"*We are a manufacturer*" and "*We are a technology company*" are relatively natural descriptions for manufacturers and technology companies. However, many times, they are reflections of a company's current situation and do not provide guidelines regarding what kind of company it will be in the future. These clear identities emphasize that products and manufacturing assets are the core of the company. They do not indicate that manufacturers would not develop software internally or provide services to their clients. For instance, the Finnish forest machine manufacturer Ponsse has clearly stated that its mission is to "produce the best forest machines in the world." These machines contain many smart elements, as PCs have been embedded in them since the 1990s, and they need to be serviced regularly. It must be remembered that key stakeholders such as customers view these companies through their products, as customers use the products daily at their sites. This does not mean that services and software elements are not important, but the core of such firms is built around their equipment.

"*We are a smart manufacturer*" minimizes the role of services and emphasizes the role of technology and software as distinctive elements of the manufacturer. This identity description is typically used in robotics, additive manufacturing (3D printing), and smart factory contexts, where manufacturers possess deep knowhow of certain technological solutions. Typically, this identity requires capability development in areas such as big data, modeling and simulation, and intelligent automation. For instance, robotics companies KUKA Robotics and ABB are examples of manufacturing companies whose identities could be described in such a way.

The "*We are a service company*" reflection stresses the importance of services to a manufacturer. This statement has been used particularly among manufacturers who have started to provide traditional after-sales services (Cohen et al., 2006), such as maintenance and repair services, to their clients to obtain more stable income and higher margins (Neu & Brown, 2005). The idea behind this utterance is to highlight customer intimacy. One of the key ways to sell new equipment is through existing customer relationships; relevance at customer sites also facilitates sales of new products. In this identity archetype, business logic originates from service sales, e.g., how new equipment and smart elements can boost service sales. For instance, the Finnish elevator manufacturer KONE started to describe itself merely as "a service company," highlighting that services and service contracts are seen as key differentiators and sources of income for the company.

"*We are a smart service company*" describes a company that stresses the role of software and services in its core business. Software and services are intertwined in this typology, thereby diminishing the role of traditional manufacturing and equipment. A key distinction emerges from a manufacturer's ability to deliver software-as-a-service types of solutions to its clients. In this archetype, products are seen merely as "add-ons" for companies, and manufacturers are reminiscent of consultancies or project companies. Schneider Electric and Caverion are potential examples of companies pursuing a smart service company identity.

The "*We are a manufacturer that provides services*" identity combines the traditional product business with a service business. Another form of this identity could be "*We are a service company that provides equipment.*" Before the Internet of Things (IoT) era, this approach became popular among technology companies, as manufacturers possessed two subidentities: (1) a manufacturing/technology identity and (2) a service identity. Those subidentities were typically even separately organized within the manufacturing companies. Many times, they were well balanced in each company in terms of proportion and strategic importance.

"*We are a smart manufacturer that provides services*" indicates that the manufacturer is attempting to excel in three different arenas (manufacturing, services, and software). This is perhaps the most challenging initiative to accomplish in practice, as there exists a danger of identity ambiguity. Moreover, developing capabilities and culture to facilitate positioning has become increasingly difficult. Integrated solution providers (see Davies et al., 2006; Wise & Baumgartner, 1999), such as Alstom (mobility provider) and Nokia (network provider), are examples of companies that could credibly pursue such an identity.

The "*It is unclear who we are*" category refers to manufacturers who do not stress or communicate enough about any of the three distinctive features, as all of the distinct identity elements are minimal or ambiguous. In these situations, organizations typically have unclear goals and measures, which causes different organizational levels and units to compete against each other and aim toward different goals, resulting in ambiguity. This archetype is sometimes observed in manufacturers that are struggling toward smart services while also aiming to increase their profits from traditional manufacturing activities.

The eight identity archetypes presented above are illustrations of possible identities for manufacturing companies in an era when services, solutions, and software are complexly intertwined. We acknowledge that these pure forms rarely exist in real life, but they are important for managers to consider when evaluating what type of company their organization is or what direction their company will potentially take in the future.

Creating a New Identity

To create a new firm identity, executives should have a proper understanding of the firm's current identity, its strengths, and its weaknesses. Furthermore, they need to draw a picture of the firm's desired future position in the industrial ecosystem. This position may be far from the firm's current position, and firms rarely have the capabilities necessary to obtain that position. In the beginning, managers need to understand the current organizational culture and its three levels, namely, (1) artifacts, (2) beliefs and values, and (3) basic assumptions (Schein, 2010), which are interrelated with organizational identity. Organizational culture is perceived to have a dynamic relationship with identity and image (Ravasi & Schultz, 2006) in which identity expresses cultural understandings (Hatch & Schultz, 2002) and is socially constructed (Gioia et al., 2000). These organizational beliefs, structures and basic assumptions potentially hinder organizational identity change. Some level of resistance may even be beneficial for an organization because it indicates that the organization's members are interested in the firm's position and strategy. For executives, it becomes relevant to identify key internal rigidities that potentially hinder that change. Moreover, they must identify possibilities and weaknesses related to the desired position and identity in the market. For instance, if a manufacturer wants to become "a software company," it must decide what role equipment and services will play related to that position—will the manufacturer develop software for other equipment, including its rivals' products, and will it sell software as projects or services (SaaS)? A manufacturer must also decide on an organizational structure for the software business—will software be a profit-and-loss responsible unit within the organization or will it be integrated with the product and service units? In addition, companies need to have a clear roadmap related to personnel and routine development—i.e., how to hire, retain and train software engineers and developers who could be employed by world-class software companies such as Google, Apple, Amazon, and Microsoft.

In the moving, transitioning, or changing phase (Lewin, 1951), change becomes reality and may be viewed with fear and uncertainty by organization members. In this mode, employees need to learn new routines, processes, and modus operandi. In this phase, communication from executives and managers is vital—what does the firm want to achieve with this new identity, and why is this change required? Both sensegiving and sensemaking are needed. This change does not happen overnight, and managers must continuously communicate about the new identity to the key stakeholders—this communication can take place through e-mails, management letters, shareholder speeches, annual reports, personnel info, development discussions, letters from the CEO, media interviews, investor meetings, etc. All of these actions are part of the sensegiving process, which needs to be ongoing, active, and repetitive to be effective. In the sensegiving process, managers should present the changes in ways that relate the changes to the previous experiences of the organization's members to facilitate a collective sensemaking process (Gioia, 1986). Other ways to facilitate organizational sensemaking processes are to ensure that members have time to discuss, debate, ask, and build shared understandings about the identity change. Production meetings, team meetings, weekly meetings, and even coffee breaks are important arenas for the sensemaking process. Furthermore, firms typically take many actions to pursue a new identity. For instance, firms may hire software engineers, build new digital organizations, appoint Chief Digital Officers (CDOs), or craft new vision/mission statements regarding the desired new identity.

After these continuous actions, communication initiatives, and sensegiving and sensemaking processes, the changes must be reinforced and stabilized. In this phase, the new identity will be cemented, and executives must ensure that organizational processes and members' ways of doing things (routines) are systematically employed. In practice, goals, measures, and rewards must be established, and executives need to verify that the changes have taken place through mutually accepted measures. For instance, if a manufacturer's goal is to become "a service company," it most likely will begin to measure its (1) sales of services, (2) services' profitability (e.g., service margins and customer-based profitability), (3) customer lock-in (e.g., customer retention rate), and (4) number of installed base/service contracts. To establish this service identity, executives must verify through such measures that the organization's actions support and convey the new identity. Figure 2 outlines organizational identity as a socially constructed process (Gioia & Chittipeddi, 1991; Schein, 2010).

Based on the actions described above, a new identity is created or a firm starts to re-evaluate its identity (do we continue or attempt to change our identity?). The reflections of the new identity formation include artifacts (How can the new identity be depicted in practice through visualizations?), shared language among organization members, and acceptance of the new identity among internal and external stakeholders. In particular, customers

Smart solution provider identity as a socially constructed process

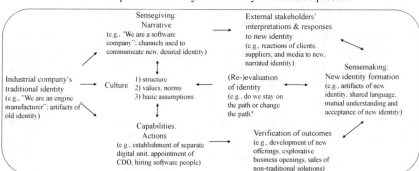

Fig. 2   Smart solution provider's identity as a socially constructed process

and users are important when evaluating how a new identity is established. For instance, in 2008, Nokia's then CEO, Olli-Pekka Kallasvuo, publicly stated, "Nokia is a service company." However, large audiences, consumers, and operators probably did not understand or believe that statement because they only viewed Nokia through its products and powerful "connecting people" mission statements. In contrast, the public and operators were more easily convinced that Apple, Microsoft, and Google are real software companies. However, these companies would encounter difficulties in being viewed as manufacturers even though all of them also produce devices.

3   Discussion

As the world and industrial equipment are becoming increasingly connected and Industry 4.0 and IoT are becoming more relevant to both manufacturers and their customers, new technologies and digitization provide opportunities to increase sales and decrease costs. To thrive in this era of smart services, manufacturers need not only new capabilities, structures, offerings, and processes but also redefined corporate identities. This redefinition is far from easy, as a manufacturer's new identity should not be too similar to its existing identity, it needs to motivate internal and external stakeholders, and it needs to be inspiring yet realistic to achieve. Establishing a new identity may also lead to mixed identities and identity ambiguity among organization members (Corley & Gioia, 2004).

Theoretical Contributions

This book chapter makes two theoretical contributions. It (1) typologizes eight distinct archetypes of manufacturer identities using three perspectives—(a) manufacturing/technology, (b) service, and (c) software)—and their dichotomies and (2) describes organizational identity change as a socially constructed process.

For its first theoretical contribution, this article conceptualizes and categorizes eight possible identities for manufacturers in the age of smart services. Specifically, this article contributes to the literature on digital servitization (Kohtamäki et al., 2019; Sklyar et al., 2019) by describing how new smart identities are socially constructed (Corley & Gioia, 2004; Gioia et al., 2013). Based on three distinct identity elements (technology provider/manufacturer, service, and software) and configurations of how strong or weak the elements are considered, we typologize eight distinct organizational identities that are possible for manufacturing companies to adopt. Although these pure forms are far from the forms taken by manufacturers in reality, these archetypes enable manufacturers to identify both their existing identities and their desired future identities, hence giving them direction. Pure forms help executives identify possible alternatives and redirect companies when altering their identities, even though the pure identities are far from real.

For its second theoretical contribution, this article describes the identity change process as a socially constructed process, thus contributing to the literature on identities and digital servitization (Huikkola et al., 2020; Keränen et al., 2020; Kohtamäki et al., 2019; Salonen & Jaakkola, 2015). Building a new corporate identity requires changing the executives' narratives about the company ("Who are we as an organization?), organizational culture (structures, norms, values, and basic assumptions), and corporate resources and capabilities (reallocating resources, building new capabilities, and unlearning). We propose that when an organization changes its identity, its executives and managers need to identify the existing and desired future identities in the beginning, communicate the new identity when taking actions, and verify the new identity. Each process has its own challenges. When identifying the old identity and establishing a picture of the desired new identity, the most difficult challenge is to understand the sources of resistance among organization members and create a credible identity that is both ambitious but realistic. When changing the identity in practice, the most difficult challenge is to communicate the message and change the personnel's way of doing things because changing routines is perhaps one of the most challenging tasks for managers to execute (Gilbert, 2005). When stabilizing the identity, the managers should pay attention to artifacts, shared language, and perceptions of the new identity among the key internal and external stakeholders.

In sum, particularly in larger companies, many identities may coexist. Executives should be aware of possible subidentities and define their companies' "master identity." The challenge is to define the identity and what kind of organization the company wants to become. In changing that identity, there is danger of identity ambiguity and confusion among personnel and stakeholders. To avoid this identity ambiguity, we suggest that executives and managers could benefit from implementing identity identification, communication, and verification phases. Moreover, identity is socially constructed and requires active dialogue and communication between managers, personnel, and other key stakeholders (Gioia et al., 2013; Vaara & Tienari, 2011).

Managerial Implications

For managers, the present article shows the elements involved in the process of identity change that should be considered when aiming to alter organizational identity. This article does not give special attention to any specific change process triggers, such as mergers and acquisitions, alliances, spinoffs, or divestments, but reviews the strategic change process in general. In particular, to facilitate new identity formation, executives and managers should give attention to identifying the new organizational identity, communicating the identity, and verifying the organizational actions' outcomes. Thus, we suggest that executives should be aware of the typical bottlenecks during the different phases of the identity change process.

Future Research Directions

Future studies could delve deeper into the processes and practices related to specific digital servitization triggers and actions, such as software firm acquisitions and the establishment of separate digital units. Future studies could investigate in-depth how those special triggers and actions affect firms' (software) identities. Studies could also investigate how a manufacturer's identity facilitates digital servitization. Moreover, more studies are needed about how "storytelling" and "antenarratives" are applied when facilitating organizational identity change toward smart services (Vaara & Tienari, 2011). We suggest that future studies investigate artifacts as reflections of corporate identity formation and how identity change can be depicted through visualizations.

References

Albert, S., & Whetten, D. (1985a). Organizational identity. *Research in Organizational Behavior, 7*, 263–295.

Albert, S., & Whetten, D. A. (1985b). Organizational identity. In L. L. Cummings & B. M. Staw (Eds.), *Research in organizational behavior* (Vol. 7, pp. 263–295). JAI Press.

Albert, S. (1992). The algebra of change. In L. L. Cummings & B. M. Staw (Eds.), *Research in organizational behavior* (Vol. 14, pp. 179–229). JAI Press.

Allmendinger, G., & Lombreglia, R. (2005). Four strategies for the age of smart services. *Harvard Business Review, 83*(10), 131–145.

Barney, J. (1998). Koch industries: Organizational identity as moral philosophy. In D. Whetten & P. Godfrey (Eds.), *Identity in organizations developing theory through conversations* (pp. 106–109). Sage.

Brax, S. A., & Jonsson, K. (2009). Developing integrated solution offerings for remote diagnostics: A comparative case study of two manufacturers. *International Journal of Operations & Production Management, 29*(5), 539–560.

Brown, M. E., & Gioia, D. A. (2002). Making things click, distributive leadership in an online division of an offline organization. *The Leadership Quarterly, 13*, 397–419.

Cohen, M. A., Agrawal, N., & Agrawal, V. (2006). Winning in the aftermarket. *Harvard Business Review, 84*(5), 129–138.

Corley, K. G., & Gioia, D. A. (2004). Identity ambiguity and change in the wake of a corporate spin-off. *Administrative Science Quarterly, 49*(2), 173–208.

Danneels, E. (2011). Trying to become a different type of company: Dynamic capability at Smith Corona. *Strategic Management Journal, 32*(1), 1–31.

Davies, A., Brady, T., & Hobday, M. (2006). Charting a path toward integrated solutions. *MIT Sloan Management Review, 47*(3), 39–48.

Fisher, G., Kotha, S., & Lahiri, A. (2016). Changing with the times: An integrated view of identity, legitimacy, and new venture life cycles. *The Academy of Management Review, 41*(3), 383–409.

Gilbert, C. (2005). Unbundling the structure of inertia: Resource versus routine rigidity. *Academy of Management Journal, 48*, 741–763.

Gioia, D. (1986). Symbols, scripts, and sensemaking: Creating meaning in the organizational experience. In *The thinking organization* (pp. 49–74). Jossey-Bass.

Gioia, D., & Chittipeddi, K. (1991). Sensemaking and sensegiving in strategic change initiation. *Strategic Management Journal, 12*(6), 433–448.

Gioia, D. A., Schultz, M., & Corley, K. G. (2000). Organizational identity, image, and adaptive instability. *The Academy of Management Review, 25*(1), 63–81.

Gioia, D., & Patvardhan, S. (2012). Identity as process and flow. In M. Schultz, S. Maguire, A. Langley, & H. Tsoukas (Eds.), *Constructing identity in and around organizations* (pp. 50–62). Oxford University Press.

Gioia, D., Patvardhan, S., Hamilton, A., & Corley, K. G. (2013). Organizational identity formation and change. *The Academy of Management Annals, 7*(1), 123–193.

Hasselblatt, M., Huikkola, T., Kohtamäki, M., & Nickell, D. (2017). Modeling manufacturer's capabilities for the Internet of Things. *Journal of Business & Industrial Marketing, 33*(6), 822–836.

Hatch, M. J., & Schultz, M. (2002). The dynamics of organizational identity. *Human Relations, 55*(8), 989–1018.

Helfat, C. E., & Peteraf, M. A. (2015). Managerial cognitive capabilities and the microfoundations of dynamic capabilities. *Strategic Management Journal, 36*(6), 831–850.

Huikkola, T., Kohtamäki, M., & Rabetino, R. (2016). Resource realignment in servitization. *Research-Technology Management, 59*(4), 30–39.

Huikkola, T., Rabetino, R., Kohtamäki, M., & Gebauer, H. (2020). Firm boundaries in servitization: Interplay and repositioning practices. *Industrial Marketing Management, 90*, 90–105.

Iansiti, M., & Lakhani, M. R. (2014). Digital ubiquity: How connections, sensors, and data are revolutionizing business. *Harvard Business Review, 92*(11), 90–99.

Immelt, J. R. (2017). How I remade GE: And what I learned along the way. *Harvard Business Review, 95*(5), 42–51.

Isaacson, W. (2011). *Steve Jobs: The exclusive biography*. Simon & Schuster.

Keränen, J., Salonen, A., & Terho, H. (2020). Opportunities for value-based selling in an economic crisis: Managerial insights from a firm boundary theory. *Industrial Marketing Management, 88*, 389–395.

Kohtamäki, M., Parida, V., Oghazi, P., Gebauer, H., & Baines, T. (2019). Digital servitization business models in ecosystems: A theory of the firm. *Journal of Business Research, 104*, 380–392.

Lewin, K. (1951). *Field theory in social science*. Harper.

Narayanan, V., Zane, L., & Kemmerer, B. (2011). The cognitive perspective in strategy: An integrative review. *Journal of Management, 37*(1), 305–351.

Neu, W., & Brown, S. (2005). Forming successful business-to-business services in goods-dominant firms. *Journal of Service Research, 8*(3), 3–17.

Porter, M. E., & Heppelmann, J. E. (2014). How smart, connected products are transforming competition. *Harvard Business Review, 92*(11), 64–88.

Porter, M. E., & Heppelmann, J. E. (2015). How smart, connected products are transforming companies. *Harvard Business Review, 93*(10), 96–114.

Ravasi, D., & Schultz, M. (2006). Responding to organizational identity threats: Exploring the role of organizational culture. *Academy of Management Journal, 49*(3), 433–458.

Salonen, A., & Jaakkola, E. (2015, November). Firm boundary decisions in solution business: Examining internal vs. external resource integration. *Industrial Marketing Management, 51*, 171–183.

Schein, E. H. (2010). *Organizational culture and leadership*. Jossey-Bass.

Sklyar, A., Kowalkowski, C., Tronvåll, B., & Sörhammar, D. (2019). Organizing for digital servitization: A service ecosystem perspective. *Journal of Business Research, 104*, 450–460.

Töytäri, P., Turunen, T., Klein, M., Eloranta, V., Biehl, S., & Rajala, R. (2018). Aligning the mindset and capabilities within a business network for successful adoption of smart services. *Journal of Product Innovation Management, 35*(5), 763–779.

Ulaga, W., & Reinartz, W. J. (2011, November). Hybrid offerings: How manufacturing firms combine goods and services successfully. *Journal of Marketing, 75*, 5–23.

Vaara, E., & Tienari, J. (2011). On the narrative construction of multinational corporations: An antenarrative analysis of legitimation and resistance in a cross-border merger. *Organization Science, 22*(2), 370–390.

Warner, S. R., & Wäger, M. (2019). Building dynamic capabilities for digital transformation: An ongoing process of strategic renewal. *Long Range Planning, 52*(3), 326–349.

Weick, K. E. (1995). *Sensemaking in organizations*. Sage.

Wise, R., & Baumgartner, P. (1999). Go downstream: The new profit imperative in manufacturing. *Harvard Business Review, 77*(5), 133–142.

PSS Business Models: A Structured Typology

Federico Adrodegari, Nicola Saccani, and Mario Rapaccini

1   Introduction

Previous literature shows that the shift from product—to PSS-based competition (servitization) is a way to increase revenues and create competitive advantage in manufacturing firms (Baines et al., 2009). However, this transformation is challenging (Adrodegari & Saccani, 2020; Reim et al., 2015), as it requires to rethink—and change—numerous aspects of the firm's business model (Raddats et al., 2019). Although a configurational analysis could facilitate the understanding of the impacts induced by embracing servitization strategies, these modifications are yet not fully understood (Adrodegari & Saccani, 2017; Storbacka et al., 2013). A BM perspective is useful to understand and shape the characteristics of a PSS offering (Adrodegari & Saccani, 2020; Dimache & Roche, 2013). However, very little research has

F. Adrodegari (✉) · N. Saccani
Department of Industrial and Mechanical Engineering, University of Brescia, Brescia, Italy
e-mail: federico.adrodegari@unibs.it

N. Saccani
e-mail: nicola.saccani@unibs.it

M. Rapaccini
Department of Industrial Engineering, University of Florence, Florence, Italy
e-mail: mario.rapaccini@unifi.it

© The Author(s), under exclusive license to Springer Nature Switzerland AG 2021
M. Kohtamäki et al. (eds.), *The Palgrave Handbook of Servitization*,
https://doi.org/10.1007/978-3-030-75771-7_4

analysed the different types of PSS through the lens of BM. This chapter defines a structured typology that gives a deeper understanding of the impact of the different PSS offerings on the manufacturer's BM. Showing how the configuration of each BM element changes, the typology can support the shaping of future research on this subject as well as practical implementation of servitization strategies.

2   Theory Development

PSS Options: Background

Since a spectrum of different options exists in the continuum between pure product sales and pure service provision (Oliva & Kallenberg, 2003), the servitization literature has suggested different kinds of PSSs. Wise and Baumgartner (1999) identified four BMs (namely, embedded services, comprehensive services, integrated solutions and distribution control). Tukker identified three PSS categories based on the value proposition and the revenue model components, namely: product-oriented, service-oriented and result-oriented. Although this typology remains widely accepted, it is affected by some limitations (Van Ostaeyen et al., 2013). For example, it appears not sufficiently refined to discriminate between different kinds of either result- or use-oriented PSSs. Another limitation refers to the fact that the typology focuses on the features of each offering and tells little on how the organization should configure its activities. Over the years, numerous authors have proposed their own classifications. Adrodegari and Saccani (2017) have reviewed this literature as presented in Table 1.

Most of these classifications are good at discriminating the BM core components, such as the value proposition and the revenue model, for instance, distinguishing between pay-per-equipment and pay-per-use PSS. But the discussion over other components such as key resources, activities, customers, partners, etc.—is rather neglected. Exceptions are the studies by Kujala et al. (2011), Lay et al. (2010) and Meier et al. (2011) considering a wider combination of BM components.

In sum, the extant literature shows a clear gap, that this paper aims at filling through the definition of a novel PSS typology, that includes a comprehensive analysis of the impact brought by servitization on each component of a BM.

Table 1 Relevant PSS typologies adopting BM perspective in the literature

Paper	No. of PSS types	Typology description	Criteria used to define the types
Tukker (2004)	8	Unstructured PSS typology identifying 3 main types and 8 subtypes: (1a) Product-related service; (1b) Advice and consultancy; (2a) Product lease; (2b) Product renting or sharing; (2c) Product pooling; (3a) Activity management/outsourcing; (3b) Pay per service unit; (3c) Functional result	Not explicitly defined by the author. According to other authors that adopt Tukker's classification in their work, the criteria used are referable to the allocation of property rights of a product (*value proposition*) and revenue model (*revenue*)
Lay et al. (2010)	5	Structured typology for service-based BMs: (1) Focused on payment and ownership; (2) Operational focus; (3) Finance/operational focus at customer site; (4) Finance/ operational focus at supplier site; (5) Involving a joint venture	Authors used the components of the proposed BM framework (i.e. Ownership; Employer of manufacturing personnel; Employer of maintenance personnel; Location of operation; Single/multiple customer operation; Payment model)
Kapletia and Probert (2010)	4	Unstructured typology to classify the more advanced forms of customer system: (1) product system support; (2) life cycle product system support; (3) functional system support; (4) enterprise system support	(1) Relational: interdependence *vs* integration (*customers*); (2) Orientation: product or customer (*value proposition*)
Kujala et al. (2010)	4	Structured typology of solution-specific BMs: (1) Basic installed base services; (2) Customer support services; (3) Operations and maintenance outsourcing; (4) Life-cycle solutions	(1) The value proposition for the customer (*value proposition*); (2) The revenue generation logic for the supplier. (*revenue*)

(continued)

Table 1 (continued)

Paper	No. of PSS types	Typology description	Criteria used to define the types
Meier et al. (2011)	3	Structured typology of industrial PSS BMs: (1) function-oriented use model; (2) availability-oriented use model; (3) result-oriented business model	Authors used the components of the proposed BM (i.e. Production responsibility; Supply of operating personnel; Service initiative; Ownership; Supply of maintenance personnel, Service turnover model)
Richter et al. (2010)	2	2 subcategories of Use-oriented BM: Cost-plus contracts, Fixed-price models	(1) The *revenue model*, which determines the suppliers' pricing scheme; (2) The distribution of decision rights and ownership rights (*value proposition*); (3) The allocation of risk (*finances*)
Windahl and Lakemond (2010)	4	Unstructured typology for integrated solutions: (1) Rental; (2) Maintenance; (3) Operational: (4) Performance offering	(1) Ownership: customer or supplier; (2) Type of offering: product or process (*value proposition*)
Gao et al. (2011)	3	Unstructured PSS typology: (1) Product-oriented; (2) Application-oriented; (3) Utility-oriented	(1) Competitive advantage of a PSS: it can be based on the product or on service (*value proposition*); (2) The ownership of a PSS: may or may not be transferred from provider to customers during transactions
Kujala et al. (2011)	3	Structured typology for defining variations in solution BMs: (1) Transactional project delivery; (2) Project led solution; (3) Life-cycle solution	Authors used the components of the BM framework proposed in Kujala et al., 2010
Meier et al. (2011)	3	Structured typology for industrial product-service systems (see Meier et al., 2011)	Authors used the components of the BM framework proposed in Meier et al. (2011)

Paper	No. of PSS types	Typology description	Criteria used to define the types
Barquet et al. (2013)	4	The different BM options are based on Tukker's typology: (1) Product-oriented PSS for an existent product; (2) Use-oriented PSS for an existent product; (3) Result-oriented PSS for an existent product; (4) Use-oriented PSS for a new business	(1) Relationship between the provider and customer (*customer*); (2) Service offering (*value proposition*); (3) Revenue model (*revenue*)
Dimache and Roche (2013)	5	Unstructured typology used as a reference for the PSS transition: (1) Mass production; (2) Product-oriented services; (3) Use-oriented services; (4) Result-oriented services; (5) Mass services	The different BM types are based on Tukker's classification; the authors do not indicate the criteria used to define the different types
Van Ostaeyen et al. (2013)	18	Unstructured PSS typology using a Functional Hierarchy Modeling (FHM) method. Distinguish a comprehensive spectrum of 18 PSS options for the manufacturer	The BM types are characterized by a different combination of: (1) The performance orientation of the dominant revenue mechanism of the PSS: input-based, availability based, usage-based, performance, based (*revenue*); (2) The level of integration of the PSS elements: segregated, semi-integrated, fully integrated (*value proposition*)
Smith et al. (2014)	4	Unstructured PSS typology: (1) Asset value proposition; (2) Recovery value proposition; (3) Availability value proposition; (4) Outcome value proposition	Defines 4 types of value proposition based on customer value creation
Visnjic et al. (2016)	3	Unstructured typology (1) Product-only business model; (2) Product-oriented business model; (3) Customer-oriented business model	The typology is based on the service portfolio offered (*value proposition*)
Reim et al. (2015)	3	Structured typology for PSS BM: (1) Product-oriented; (2) Use-oriented; (3) Result-oriented	Authors adopt Tukker's typology and do not specific the criteria that differentiate the types

Source Modified byAdrodegari and Saccani (2017)

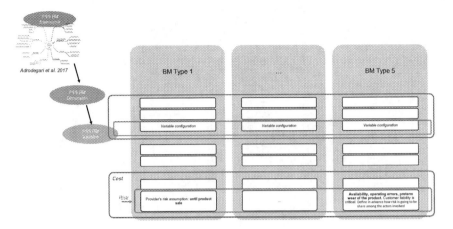

Fig. 1 Approach used for the proposed PSS BM typology

Theoretical Process and Outcomes

Following the discussion in section "PSS Options: Background", we adopt the configurational approach proposed by Kohtamäki et al. (2019) to develop the mentioned typology. In particular, we first adopt the framework proposed by Adrodegari et al. (2017) that defines "*the most relevant aspects that need be characterised in order to describe each BM component in the case of PSS*" (p. 1523). Second, for the suggested dimensions and variables, we elaborate a specific configuration based on previous literature on this topic. This process is exemplified in Fig. 1.

Last, based on the revenue mechanism, the product ownership and value propositions, we identify five archetypes of PSS BMs, that are successively grouped into two categories, namely (i) *product-* and (ii) *service-oriented BMs*. The first group includes the archetypes in which the product sale remains the most significant revenue generation driver, since its ownership is transferred to the customer, and aftermarket services are then sold—as product add-ons—in different ways (e.g. through specific deals, through multi-year contracts). The second group includes those archetypes that generate more revenues the more the product is used. In this case, the product ownership is always retained in the supplier's hands and the customer is granted with its access/use (Fig. 2).

In the following sections, we illustrate each BM archetype by briefly describing the configuration of the corresponding variables.[1]

---

[1] The table with detailed configuration of each variables along with different PSS BM types can be provided by authors upon request.

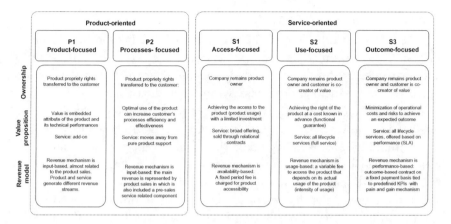

Fig. 2 The PSS BM typology

P1—Product-focused BM

Central to this archetype is the value potential that are embedded in the product, either in the form of (proprietary) know-how, brand, product design, performance, etc. This proposition sounds familiar to customers and suppliers, since it is based on value-in-exchange and market price. Thus, products are sold to the customer in exchange for money. Aftermarket services are then sold as product add-ons or provided for free (e.g. under warranty obligations) with the typical aim of recovering the product from malfunctioning and faults. In this BM, the provision of services is frequently seen as a "necessary evil", as there is little interest in exploring the customer's problems, needs and expectations in search of new business opportunities. This also explains why OEMs adopting this BM frequently recur to independent service providers to deliver aftermarket services and spare parts on their behalf (Gebauer et al., 2013; Kujala et al., 2010). The few information collected from the field are usually limited to product usage and reliability aspects (Saccani et al., 2014). Additional data pertaining to the need of the customer as well as any opportunity for improving the performance of the process in which the product is involved is rarely disclosed (Neff et al., 2014). Despite the fact that customers could need remarkable amounts of services along the product life cycle, we rarely found in these BMs the development of lifelong customer support contracts. Aftermarket services are purchased on the basis of deals, that often remain uncorrelated from each other (Barquet et al., 2013). It follows that OEMs that are stuck with this BM, invest significantly less in service innovation than they do in product innovation. Their key capabilities, actually, reside in new product development, engineering and manufacturing.

P2—Processes focused BM

This BM is an extension of the previous one: the main difference here is that the company, in addition to the services described in P1, offers also pre and after-sale services that aim to improve the performance of the customer process as well as the user experience with the product (Rapaccini & Visintin, 2015). Typical of this BM is the great emphasis put on process-related services, such as co-design, consultancy, process engineering and simulation, or user training services (Tukker, 2004). Therefore, the product manufacturer has developed knowledge about the optimal configuration of the customer processes, and can thus capture value by selling this knowledge. In some situations, these knowledge-intensive services are also provided independently from the product sale (Kindström & Kowalkowski, 2014). This is usually the case, for instance, of complex equipment that are remarkably critical to the customer's business (Rapaccini & Visintin, 2015). A service department has thus the responsibility of a separate business unit. It follows that the competences of the frontline people in the service department are of paramount importance, as they are actually expected to give advices that are customer- and industry-specific. Although the intensity of the interactions can vary to a large extent, it is not infrequent that the service expert teams can establish rich relationships with their customers (Gaiardelli et al., 2014). Analogously, the information exchanged between the parties are more intense, and focused on the sharing of business knowledge (Saccani et al., 2014). Any information systems that can facilitate the mentioned interactions are therefore of great value (Neff et al., 2014).

In the following group of BMs (*service-oriented*), we assume that the customer does not buy the product, but just pays to either get access or use the product, or for the results generated through the product use.

S1—Access-focused BM

In this case, most value is captured by enabling product access, since customers pay regular fees just to have an unconditioned possibility of accessing the product. In certain cases, the supplier receives additional money that cover the product operational costs, or its wear (Reim et al., 2015). Thus, the main advantage for the customer lays in the fact that she/he no longer needs to bear any capital cost (CAPEX) for having the product installed and ready/available to use. Thus, this BM can be particularly effective to reach—for instance—small companies, seasonal operators and start-ups, that are not willing to make significant investments in capital equipment, and prefer some sort of long-term rental to run their business. Despite the fact that this BM can be implemented as an extension of the product-dominated one (P1), it requires a shift of the company mindset, a higher service culture/orientation, greater commitment towards the customer pain points and more cross-functional communication between the product and service divisions of the firm. Since the ownership of the product is retained on the OEM's hands, OEM takes responsibility for keeping it at its best conditions for the longest possible time, providing repair and maintenance services, as well as for substitingend-of-life products. These latter are usually reconditioned and sold as "second-hand but original quality products" in secondary markets. In this BM, the service department is responsible to develop the key resources (i.e. people competences, knowledge, tools, systems, partner network) that are requested to deliver remote and field services in the most efficient and effective way. At the same time, it becomes crucial for the capacity of detecting proactively any business opportunity (Kindström & Kowalkowski, 2014). As a consequence, longer agreements and closer relationships with the customers are established (Barquet et al., 2013). It is obvious that this rental-like model cannot be implemented without having accurate and timely information from the installed base. For this purpose, OEMs are introducing IoT technologies (Ardolino et al., 2018) and web-based applications, to collect more and more field data from their connected fleet of goods (Neff et al., 2014). Fleet management systems are used to elaborate these data, plan and deliver maintenance interventions in order to prolong the product life. This BM is predominantly based on the capacity of the OEM to make customers evaluate and appreciate the benefits of this (access-based) offering. This is done by training frontline employees and sales reps and using specific commercial tools. It is also said that incentives should be rethought to be aligned with service delivery performances. In this model the payments are primarily based on recurrent fixed fees, which cover both the costs of the product and services are made available throughout the contract lifetime (Rapaccini, 2015). As the OEM sustains most costs of the offered solution, this implies higher financial and operational risks by its side, so far that a premium fee is issued to mitigate these risks. More specifically, service-oriented BMs implicate innovative revenue models and pricing strategies that are primarily value—rather than competition—or cost-based (Rapaccini, 2015). Anyway, this does not mean that the company should pay less attention to cost issues: conversely, the customer lifetime costs (sustained) and revenues (captured) have to be evaluated more precisely than in traditional models, to avoid financial troubles.

S2—Use-focused BM

Differently from the previous BM, in this case, the customer pays a (mostly) variable fee that depends on the "actual" usage of the product, not on the (potential) availability and/or easiness of access. The value, therefore, lays in the fact that the customer can use the product and produce its outputs at a predetermined cost. Setting up this commercial model requires that customer and provider agree on the metrics through which the intensity of product usage, and correspondingly the amount of money that must be paid to the product owner, can be computed easily and transparently. In this situation, the value is always co-created by the interplay between the customer and the product/service provider and value creation depends on capabilities and mutual resources from both parties (Storbacka, 2011). The fact that the OEM is responsible for all the costs along the product lifecycle is a powerful incentive towards the design of more reliable products that can be "serviced by design" (Kujala et al., 2010). Advanced services, such as remote monitoring, remote control and process optimization, predictive maintenance, are core to this BM. For the same reason, enterprise asset management (EAM) and customer relationship management systems (CRM) are milestones of the company's application portfolio (Neff et al., 2014). In this BM, the customer plays a key role in the marketing process, as she/he greatly influences the definition of the solution requirements. Therefore, the OEM must develop closer ties with key stakeholders of the customer's organization. It is in fact crucial to get aware of preferences, needs, problems, worries, interests, usage patterns, etc. (Kindström & Kowalkowski, 2014). In this regard, some studies claim that open collaboration platforms can be beneficial to the development of these BMs (Reim et al., 2015). In addition to the capabilities for selling and delivering services, that are key for the success of this BM, OEMs should integrate product and service innovation effectively (Kindström & Kowalkowski, 2014). For this reason, new organizational structures and roles need to be developed (Storbacka, 2011), as well as new rewards systems that can effectively promote the service sales (Kindström, 2010) and avoid conflict with people from the product business (Kindström & Kowalkowski, 2014). As in the previous model (S1), a change is required also in people's mindset and company's culture that has to become more service- and customer-centric. Value-driven communication becomes crucial to promote this kind of service (Reim et al., 2015), as a result, companies should develop cost assessment and configuration tools that can facilitate the sales force (Storbacka, 2011).

As in the previous case, this model shows payback times that are usually longer than the ones corresponding to the sale of physical products (Tukker, 2004). Therefore, companies must be endowed with adequate financial resources or receive support from financial partners to bridge this lag. Financial and accounting practices need therefore adaptation since the timescale of the financial flows changes considerably. The company's responsibility is greater here and the complexity increases (Reim et al., 2015). In other words, the more the firm provides customized solutions, the greater the value potential, complexity and risk. Thus, managing costs and risks all over the lifetime of the service agreement is a key capability. Consequently, the pricing strategies change accordingly, and the fees are commensurate to the costs, the customer value and the uncertainty/risk that is present in each specific agreement. Empowering at the maximum level these capabilities is a prerequisite of the BM described in the next section.

S3—Outcome-focused BM

In this case, the value lays in the fact that the OEM guarantees that the customer is going to pay a price that is proportional to some agreed performances, that the product will enable. The target performances are in fact contractually determined in terms of Service Level Agreements (SLAs), that the provider is requested to meet. Then, in this model, the focus is not on the lifecycle services per se (Kujala et al., 2010), but on the fact that these services must enable (or reach) certain level of performances of the customer process (Kindström & Kowalkowski, 2014). The value for the customer is generated not only by the reduction of the initial investment and of the operational costs, but also by the minimization of the residual risks of not achieving the expected outcome (Tukker, 2004). The provider has then the full responsibility of designing and delivering the combination of products and services that can meet the expected results. Therefore, value-in-use becomes value-in-results, as value is defined by the results achieved by the complex network of actors (included the customer) that provide and integrate resources and competencies (Saccani et al., 2014). Partnering with other actors is therefore of paramount importance, as well as the capacity of orchestrating the value creation processes throughout the product lifecycle (Barquet et al., 2013; Paiola et al., 2013). Digital technologies play of course a key role in enabling this kind of BM (Ardolino et al., 2018), for instance, adaptable back-office infrastructure with clever ICT systems can enable cost-efficient operations and higher service quality, better resource allocation and more accurate information sharing among field technicians (Kindström & Kowalkowski, 2014). In fact, the company has to collect and manage manifold types of data (product, process, customer, etc.). In sum, this BM requires a "case-by-case design", which defines the "right" outcome by the "right" product-service solution. For this reason, price and cost management is challenging in these kinds of offerings. In fact, the risk increases even further with this BM, because the OEM has complete responsibility for delivering the agreed-upon result (Reim et al., 2015). With increasing levels of responsibility, the terms of the agreement become extremely important and should focus on developing the terms carefully and accurately. This implies that contracts are complex as they may outline roles, procedures and penalties for non-compliance and determine outcomes to be delivered (Ng et al., 2013). Thus, the key issue is to design performance-based contracting, that is a form of contracting that explicitly includes a clear definition of objectives by which to measure the contractor's performance, the way data are collected and KPIs monitored, as well as the consequences (penalties, bonus-malus) for the contractor that is not able to meet those performances. It follows that payments are adjusted on the basis of the achieved result, making clear the core concept behind this model: the customer buys the performance, not the product and the related services (Reim et al., 2015). For example, a contract could be contracted on a fixed payment basis tied to predefined KPIs of the identifiable outcome, with risk/rewards sharing in place (Ng et al., 2013) or on an output-based process relating to performance levels. As in the previous BMs, financial issues should not be underestimated. Moreover here, the company's risk assumption now implies to obtain the result, and includes, as an example, availability, operating errors, preterm wear, not conformity production, etc. Thus, only manufacturers that are willing to sustain higher risks and gain the corresponding premium, offer this kind of solution (Reim et al., 2015). Therefore, risk assessment/sharing and mitigation capability are required (Kindström & Kowalkowski, 2014).

3   Discussion

Although seminal studies show that companies have alternatives when undertaking the servitization journey, the literature struggles in characterizing such pathways from a BM perspective. The definition of a structured PSS BM typology can be very useful to describe the transition from product-dominated to the numerous nuances of service-based business. Therefore, this paper develops a structured typology for PSSs that relies on the PSS BM framework presented by Adrodegari et al. (2017) and is grounded on a review of the literature on this topic. This approach also helps making the different PSS concepts more comparable and transparent and contributes also to the managerial debate. In fact, practitioners could benefit from this study to develop a deeper understanding of PSS BM characteristics through the configuration of these five archetypes. Moreover, the new PSS BM typology can be also seen as a practical guideline to help companies in the journey towards servitization.

Although this paper contributes to the development of a typological classification of BM as advocated by the general BM literature, the study focused on product-centric businesses and this could limit its generalizability. Moreover, although empirical applications to case studies exist, research has not addressed yet the issue of validating empirically the existence of different types. Finally, since companies often adopt different value propositions and BM simultaneously, for different products, markets or customers, such research direction can also lead to the mapping of the analysis of the alignment or synergy of simultaneous multiple positions of companies in a PSS BM typology (i.e. existing "service oriented" resources can leverage one another or, vice versa, questions can arise about how to prioritize resources and product- and service-related activities).

References

Adrodegari, F., & Saccani, N. (2017). Business models for the service transformation of industrial firms. *The Service Industries Journal, 37*(1), 57–83.

Adrodegari, F., Saccani, N., Kowalkowski, C., & Vilo, J. (2017). PSS business model conceptualization and application. *Production Planning and Control, 28*(15), 1251–1263.

Adrodegari, F., & Saccani, N. (2020). A maturity model for the servitization of product-centric companies. *Journal of Manufacturing Technology Management, 31*(4), 775–797.

Ardolino, M., Rapaccini, M., Saccani, N., Gaiardelli, P., Crespi, G., & Ruggeri, C. (2018). The role of digital technologies for the service transformation of industrial companies. *International Journal of Production Research, 56*(6), 2116–2132.

Baines, T. S., Lightfoot, H. W., Benedettini, O., & Kay, J. M. (2009). The servitization of manufacturing: A review of literature and reflection on future challenges. *Journal of Manufacturing Technology Management, 20*(5), 547–567.

Barquet, A. P. B., de Oliveira, M. G., Amigo, C. R., Cunha, V. P., & Rozenfeld, H. (2013). Employing the business model concept to support the adoption of product-service systems (PSS). *Industrial Marketing Management, 42*(5), 693–704.

Dimache, A., & Roche, T. (2013). A decision methodology to support servitisation of manufacturing. *International Journal of Operations and Production Management, 33*(11), 1435–1457.

Gaiardelli, P., Resta, B., Martinez, V., Pinto, R., & Albores, P. (2014). A classification model for product-service offerings. *Journal of Cleaner Production, 66*, 507–519.

Gao, J., Yao, Y., Zhu, V. C. Y., Sun, L., & Lin, L. (2011). Service oriented manufacturing: A new product pattern and manufacturing paradigm. *Journal of Intelligent Manufacturing, 22*(3), 435–446.

Gebauer, H., Paiola, M., & Saccani, N. (2013). Characterizing service networks for moving from products to solutions. *Industrial Marketing Management, 42*(1), 31–46.

Kapletia, D., & Probert, D. (2010). Migrating from products to solutions: An exploration of system support in the UK defense industry. *Industrial Marketing Management, 39*(4), 582–592.

Kohtamäki, M., Henneberg, S. C., Martinez, V., Kimita, K., & Gebauer, H. (2019). A configurational approach to servitization: Review and research directions. *Service Science, 11*(3), 213–240.

Kindström, D. (2010). Towards a service-based business model—Key aspects for future competitive advantage. *European Management Journal, 28*(6), 479–490.

Kindström, D., & Kowalkowski, C. (2014). Service innovation in product-centric firms: A multidimensional business model perspective. *Journal of Business and Industrial Marketing, 29*(2), 96–111.

Kujala, S., Artto, K., Aaltonen, P., & Turkulainen, V. (2010). Business models in project-based firms—Towards a typology of solution-specific business models. *International Journal of Project Management, 28*(2), 96–106.

Kujala, S., Kujala, J., Turkulainen, V., Artto, K., Aaltonen, P., & Wikstrom, K. (2011). Factors influencing the choice of solution-specific business models. *International Journal of Project Management, 29*(8), 960–970.

Lay, G., Biege, S., Copani, G., & Jager, A. (2010). Relevance of services in European manufacturing industry. *Journal of Service Management, 21*(5), 715–726.

Meier, H., Volker, O., & Funke, B. (2011). Industrial product-service systems (IPS2): Paradigm shift by mutually determined products and services. *International Journal of Advanced Manufacturing Technology, 52*(41982), 1175–1191.

Neff, A. A., Hamel, F., Herz, T. P., Uebernickel, F., Brenner, W., & vom Brocke, J. (2014). Developing a maturity model for service systems in heavy equipment manufacturing enterprises. *Information and Management, 51*(7), 895–911.

Ng, I. C. L., Ding, D. X., & Yip, N. (2013). Outcome-based contracts as new business model: The role of partnership and value-driven relational assets. *Industrial Marketing Management, 42*(5), 730–774.

Oliva, R., & Kallenberg, R. (2003). Managing the transition from products to services. *International Journal of Service Industry Management, 14*(2), 160–172.

Paiola, M., Saccani, N., Perona, M., & Gebauer, H. (2013). Moving from products to solutions: Strategic approaches for developing capabilities. *European Management Journal, 31*(4), 390–409.

Raddats, C., Kowalkowski, C., Benedettini, O., Burton, J., & Gebauer, H. (2019). Servitization: A contemporary thematic review of four major research streams. *Industrial Marketing Management, 83*, 207–223.

Rapaccini, M. (2015). Pricing strategies of service offerings in manufacturing companies: A literature review and empirical investigation. *Production Planning & Control, 26* (14–15), 1247–1263.

Rapaccini, M., & Visintin, F. (2015). Devising hybrid solutions: An exploratory framework. *Production Planning & Control, 26* (8), 654–672.

Reim, W., Parida, V., & Örtqvist, D. (2015). Product–Service Systems business models and tactics—A systematic literature review. *Journal of Cleaner Production, 97*, 61–75.

Richter, A., Sadek, T., & Steven, M. (2010). Flexibility in industrial product-service systems and use-oriented business models. *CIRP Journal of Manufacturing Science and Technology, 3* (2), 128–134.

Saccani, N., Visintin, F., & Rapaccini, M. (2014). Investigating the linkages between service types and supplier relationships in servitized environments. *International Journal of Production Economics, 149*, 226–238.

Smith, L., Maull, R., & Ng, I. C. L. (2014). Servitization and operations management: A service dominant-logic approach. *International Journal of Operations & Production Management, 34* (2), 242–269.

Storbacka, K. (2011). A solution business model: Capabilities and management practices for integrated solutions. *Industrial Marketing Management, 40* (5), 699–711.

Storbacka, K., Windahl, C., Nenonen, S., & Salonen, A. (2013). Solution business models: Transformation along four continua. *Industrial Marketing Management, 42* (5), 705–716.

Tukker, A. (2004). Eight types of product–service system: Eight ways to sustainability? Experiences from SusProNet. *Business Strategy and the Environment, 13* (4), 246–260.

Van Ostaeyen, J., Van Horenbeek, A., Pintelon, L., & Duflou, J. R. (2013). A refined typology of product–service systems based on functional hierarchy modeling. *Journal of Cleaner Production, 51*, 261–276.

Visnjic, I., Wiengarten, F., & Neely, A. (2016). Only the brave: Product innovation, service business model innovation, and their impact on performance. *Journal of Product Innovation Management, 33* (1), 36–52.

Windahl, C., & Lakemond, N. (2010). Integrated solutions from a service-centered perspective: Applicability and limitations in the capital goods industry. *Industrial Marketing Management, 39* (8), 1278–1290.

Wise, R., & Baumgartner, P. (1999). Go downstream: The new profit imperative in manufacturing. *Harvard Business Review, 77* (5), 133–141.

Product-Service Systems in the Digital Era: Deconstructing Servitisation Business Model Typologies

Tor Helge Aas, Karl Joachim Breunig, Magnus Hellström, and Katja Maria Hydle

1 Introduction

A business model [BM] is understood as the logic by which a company creates value for its customers, delivers that value to customers and captures a part of that value for itself (Osterwalder & Pigneur, 2010; Teece, 2010; Zott et al., 2011). The application of a servitisation strategy potentially invokes many

T. H. Aas (✉) · M. Hellström
School of Business and Law, University of Agder, Kristiansand, Norway
e-mail: tor.h.aas@uia.no

M. Hellström
e-mail: mhellstr@abo.fi

K. J. Breunig
Oslo Business School, Oslo Met - Oslo Metropolitan University, Oslo, Norway
e-mail: karjoa@oslomet.no

M. Hellström
Åbo Akademi University, Turku, Finland

K. M. Hydle
NORCE - Norwegian Research Centre, Oslo, Norway

University of Oslo, Oslo, Norway

K. M. Hydle
e-mail: katjahy@ifi.uio.no; katjahy@uio.no

M. Kohtamäki et al. (eds.), *The Palgrave Handbook of Servitization*,
https://doi.org/10.1007/978-3-030-75771-7_5

changes in, and decisions about, a company's BM(s). Service-oriented BMs provide various ways in which to operationalise servitisation strategies.

The most obvious change associated with servitising is that the core of a company's offerings shifts from products to services. Other potential changes involve the ways in which focal supplier companies interact through value co-creation with their customers (Vargo & Lusch, 2008), focal firms interact with other parties in surrounding ecosystems (e.g. Kohtamäki, Parida et al., 2019) and value is appropriated through performance-based contracts (Parida et al., 2019).

Not surprisingly, researchers have made several attempts to categorise service BM archetypes (e.g., Brax & Visintin, 2017; Kowalkowski et al., 2015). In an early work on servitisation, Wise and Baumgartner (1999) described four 'downstream' BMs that focused on the service content of offerings (embedded services, comprehensive services and integrated solutions) and value chain migration (distribution control). Subsequently, Michelini and Razzoli (2004) introduced a distinction based on product ownership.

Another literature stream has focused on product-service systems (PSSs), defined as '*tangible products and intangible services designed and combined so that they jointly are capable of fulfilling specific consumer needs*' (Tukker, 2004, p. 246). The PSS concept emerged as an approach for resource efficiency, theoretically achieved by shifting from the need for a product to the need for the function that the product enables (Mont, 2002). It has, however, come to encompass the general transition towards the use of new, service-oriented BMs (Tukker, 2015; Tukker & Tischner, 2006) and can be understood as '*an integrated combination of products and services*' (Baines et al., 2007).

Tukker (2004) proposed three main categories of PSS on a spectrum ranging from product-oriented to results-oriented services, with decreasing tangible product content and increasing intangible service content, and argued that BMs vary according to this spectrum. Tukker's (2004) typology has been cited widely, but it arguably conflates two key dimensions of BMs: results-orientedness and ownership (Michelini & Razzoli, 2004). Moreover, the current widespread digitalisation trend was not as strong when Tukker introduced this typology; today, digitalisation is central to much BM innovation (Kohtamäki, Parida et al., 2019). Manufacturing businesses are now '*entering the fourth industrial revolution (Industry 4.0) through capitalizing digitalization*' (Parida et al., 2019, p. 2). In this regard, Aas et al. (2020) empirically found that PSS BMs vary along three dimensions: results-orientedness, ownership and smartness of the provided services.

The aim of this chapter is to continue the discussion on service BM categorisation, especially in the PSS context. In this conceptual essay, we use

Tukker's (2004) typology as a starting point and elaborate on extant theory. During the discussion, we use findings from empirical research such as Aas et al. (2020) to illustrate our main arguments (Siggelkow, 2007).

The chapter is organised as follows. We first discuss the theory underlying typologies. In the ensuing section, we discuss and deconstruct Tukker's (2004) 15-year-old typology, first with respect to the results-orientedness and owner-ship dimensions, and then in light of digitalisation. From this discussion, a new typology that corresponds to the taxonomy proposed by Aas et al. (2020) emerges. We then expand this typology, discuss and illustrate the resulting eight BM types and compare them with other typologies.

2   Theory Development

Typologies

The identification of PSS BM typologies, such as the typology of Tukker (2004), is part of a long research tradition in organisational studies often referred to as the configurational approach (Kohtamäki, Henneberg et al., 2019). Configuration theory acknowledges that the suitableness of a partic-ular organisational configuration (where a configuration includes organi-sational dimensions such as processes, structures, practices, cultures and strategies) depends on its fit with the context (Venkatraman, 1989). Thus, discovering organisational configurations, in the form of typologies, is recog-nised as a fundamental approach in organisational theorising (Meyer et al., 1993). Typologies have the potential to provide parsimonious frameworks for complex organisational phenomena (Doty & Glick, 1994), and can contribute to a range of tasks, such as concept formation and refinement, the elucidation of underlying dimensions and the creation of categories for classification and measurement (Collier et al., 2012).

Below we discuss two pressing issues related to Tukker's (2004) typology. First, how more recent literature has addressed the conflation of the owner-ship and results-orientedness dimensions in this typology, and second, how recent research explains the relationship between the contemporary digitali-sation and PSS BMs.

PSS BM Typologies, and the Dimensions of Ownership and Results-Orientedness

Tukker's (2004) typology was originally published in *Business Strategy and the Environment*. The first of the three main categories, product-oriented

BMs, centres on product sales, with services sold as product add-ons and a low degree of results-orientedness. In the second main category, use-oriented BMs, manufacturers retain ownership of the products, which are made available to customers through various leasing, renting or sharing arrangements. The third main category, results-oriented BMs, centres on contracts between providers and buyers for the provision of functional results, rather than on the delivery of specific products.

Although Tukker (2004) implicitly recognises the issue of ownership, 'use-oriented' may not be the best label for that particular BM dimension, as users' needs can be taken into account when implementing product- and results-oriented BMs (e.g. Resta et al., 2015). Thus, this category may be more accurately conceptualised according to the 'degree of ownership retention', which is more suitable from the viewpoint of environmental sustainability and material resource efficiency. By pooling products among different buyers and being incentivised to maintain and extend products' lifespans, a provider can maximise capacity utilisation and requires fewer products. Thus, less raw material and energy are needed for the production of new products.

Whether the 'retention of ownership' belongs on the same continuum as results orientation may also be questioned. In some reported cases (e.g. Kowalkowski et al., 2017), manufacturers retain ownership of products while simultaneously establishing results-oriented contracts with customers. For example, Michelin offers a range of efficiency services to commercial transportation firms in addition to tires (Kowalkowski et al., 2017). This example is contrary to findings from capital-intensive industries, where the retention of ownership and results orientation do not always go together (Aas et al., 2020). For customers in these industries, an 'asset-light' strategy involving the leasing of products may be attractive for purely financial reasons, rather than environmental sustainability. Thus, an ownership-based BM requires that the supplier has a solid financial position and assets (i.e. a 'strong balance sheet'), often generated in cooperation with a financial institution. Such a BM requires that the supplier can provide services to, and take custody of, a product regardless of its location, which may not be easy or desirable in the case of mobile products (e.g. those installed onboard ships).

Results-orientation, in turn, is a strong trend in contemporary service sales. For example, outcome- and performance-based contracting (Liinamaa et al., 2016; Ng et al., 2013) has been advocated as a fundamental element of new BMs (if not a BM in its own right). This trend is exemplified by the increased interest in value-based pricing (e.g. Reen et al., 2017; Töytäri et al., 2015) and value-based selling of services (e.g. Luotola et al., 2017; Töytäri & Rajala, 2015). However, the implementation of a results-oriented BM is not easy or risk-free. For this reason, many services are still sold through product-oriented contracts, with fewer rewards for the actual results.

Thus, we propose that 'results-orientedness' and the 'degree of ownership retention' are two BM dimensions of servitised firms that do not belong on a one-dimensional continuum, as proposed by Tukker (2004). From a BM perspective (Osterwalder & Pigneur, 2010; Teece, 2010; Zott et al., 2011), we suggest that these dimensions belong on separate continuums related to how value is captured and how value for customers is created, respectively.

PSS BM Typologies and the Digital Dimension

Existing service BM typologies have previously been very useful (e.g. Williams, 2007), but their relevance may be questioned in the contemporary context, as we enter the fourth industrial revolution and companies rely increasingly on digital technologies to maintain competitiveness.

Companies' strategies and BMs are likely to change with the increased offering of smart products and services (Allmendinger & Lombreglia, 2005; Porter & Heppelmann, 2015). This shift, here referred to as 'digital servitization' (Kohtamäki, Parida et al., 2019), involves revisiting existing PSS BM typologies. For example, Baines and Lightfoot (2013, 2014) used different customer profiles as the basis for the categorisation of PSSs offerings by manufacturers as 'base', 'intermediate' and 'advanced' services. Specifically, to deliver advanced services, they observed that manufacturers typically deploy information and communication technologies that enable the provision of remote monitoring services related to product location, condition and use. Kohtamäki, Parida et al., (2019) furthered the theoretical development in this field by presenting a framework for the construction of offerings in digital servitisation along three dimensions: solution customisation, solution pricing and solution digitalisation. The latter dimension is related to the capabilities that smart products and services offer in terms of monitoring, control, optimisation and autonomy (Porter & Heppelmann, 2015).

Aas et al. (2020) extended Kohtamäki, Parida et al.'s (2019) framework by proposing a taxonomy covering the three generic BM dimensions of value creation, value delivery and value capture (Fig. 1). In this empirically derived taxonomy, the smart digital element is a means of delivering the service, and not the core of the offering. This approach is in line with Amit and Zott's (2001; Zott & Amit, 2010) activity systems perspective. Inspired by examples from early e-commerce, they argued that BM innovation can occur by altering the content, sequence or governance of underlying activities (Amit & Zott, 2001; Zott & Amit, 2010). A case in point is the way in which

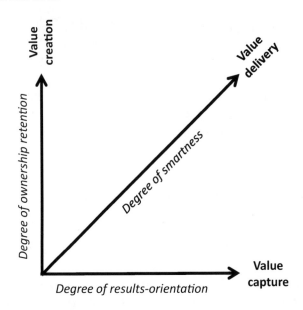

Fig. 1 PSS BM dimensions

e-marketplaces bypass incumbent distribution channels. Hence, in the value delivery dimension of our framework, we distinguish BMs with high and low degrees of 'smartness'. Similarly, Allmendinger and Lombreglia (2005) distinguished traditional and smart (digital) services. We claim that this extension is important, specifically since empirical research has found that traditional and digital services co-exist (Aas et al., 2020).

Thus, the extant literature identifies three main dimensions of PSS BMs, related to the three main BM components (value creation, value delivery and value capture). These dimensions are illustrated in Fig. 1 as the degrees of ownership retention, smartness and results orientation.

3   The Eight Types of Service-Oriented BM

The dimensions illustrated in Fig. 1 are not dichotomous (e.g. whether or not to implement a results-oriented contract), but rather fall along continuums, as captured by the use of the term 'degree'. In an empirical study, Aas et al. (2020) found several examples in which some parts of PSSs were accompanied by results-oriented contracts and others were accompanied by more traditional product-oriented contracts. The same principle applies to the other dimensions. Smart digital technology may be heavily used in some parts of a PSS and to a lesser extent in others, and some parts of the system

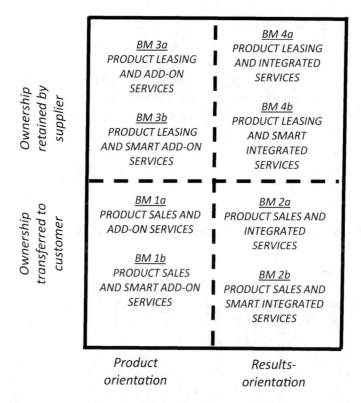

Fig. 2 New typology with eight PSS BM categories

can be made available through leasing arrangements while other parts are sold to customers. As companies can choose different degrees of results orientation, ownership retention and smartness, and combine these dimensions in different ways, an infinite number of PSS BMs is possible, rendering BM decision-making in this context very challenging.

Nevertheless, with the aim of increasing the manageability of this complexity, we focus on the outliers in each dimension, resulting in the creation of a new typology with eight PSS BM categories (Fig. 2). In this section, we briefly describe and discuss these PSS BM types.

BM 1a: Product Sales and Add-On Services

This BM type is arguably the most traditional PSS BM (Tukker, 2004). A manufacturing firm sells a product to customers, with add-on services related to the product sold on a case-by-case basis. The price of the services can be based on supplier costs (e.g. the customer pays a fixed fee or according to a cost-plus contract) or customer use intensity (e.g. the customer pays an hourly rate) (e.g. Bonnemeier et al., 2010). A wide range of add-on services is relevant when implementing BM 1a, and Partanen et al. (2017) provide a useful overview with the distinction of pre-sales, R&D, operational, product support and product lifecycle services. In their empirical study, Aas et al. (2020) observed that companies providing complex products, such as advanced offshore load handling equipment, often provided add-on services in most of these categories, whereas companies providing less-complex products, such as flat hoses, provided add-on services in fewer categories.

BM 1b: Product Sales and Smart Add-On Services

This BM is similar to the traditional BM 1a, since product ownership is transferred to the customer and product-related add-on services are provided on a case-by-case basis, and priced using a supplier cost or service use intensity regime. However, when implementing BM 1b and delivering a smart add-on service, a supplier utilises digital technology and data to a large extent. As also argued by other authors, increasingly physical products are digitally networked and integrated with information systems, which '*enable*[s] *the co-creation of "smart service" that is based on monitoring, optimization, remote control, and autonomous adaptation of products*' (Beverungen et al., 2019, p. 7; see also e.g. Zheng et al., 2018). Empirical findings from Aas et al. (2020) suggest that BM 1b is used quite commonly; one example is a supplier of advanced offshore drilling equipment that had integrated numerous sensors in its equipment. Data from these sensors was not only useful when providing product lifecycle services, such as maintenance, but also enabled the firm to provide advanced operational services by which they helped customers to use the equipment optimally.

BM 2a: Product Sales and Integrated Services

When implementing BM 2a, a manufacturer transfers ownership of a product to a customer in the same manner as in BMs 1a and 1b. However, rather than selling add-on services on a case-by-case basis, the manufacturer establishes a results-oriented service contract (often long-term) with the customer. According to Selviaridis and Wynstra (2015, p. 3505) a results-oriented contract '*can be briefly defined as the contractual approach of tying at least a portion of supplier payment to performance*'. Key performance indicators (KPIs) are fundamental elements of such contracts, as they provide the basis for supplier payments (Selviaridis & Wynstra, 2015) and a value-based pricing strategy (rather than supplier cost or service use intensity) is typically used to determine the prices of services included in the contracts (e.g. Lindström, 2013). A challenge associated with the implementation of results-oriented contracts is that '*service performance is often not only dependent on supplier effort but also on the behavior of the buying firm*' (Akkermans et al., 2019, p. 22), implying that suppliers and customers often need to co-create such contracts (Luotola et al., 2017). Aas et al. (2020) identified a few cases in which results-oriented contracting was used without digital technology; for example, one supplier provided equipment that was supposed to reduce the need for manual labour and was paid accordingly.

BM 2b: Product Sales and Smart Integrated Services

This BM is similar to the more traditional BM 2a in that product ownership is transferred to a customer while services are sold through results-oriented contracts. The difference between BMs 2a and 2b is the utilisation of digital technologies to provide smart services in the latter. Several firms in the empirical study of Aas et al. (2020) employed BMs of this type. For example, a supplier of advanced offshore drilling equipment had established a long-term results-oriented maintenance contract with a customer in which the main KPIs were related to the equipment uptime. To optimise maintenance, the supplier analysed large amounts of data from sensors installed in its equipment. Similar cases in sectors such as defence, transportation and construction have been reported (Kowalkowski et al., 2017).

BM 3a: Product Leasing and Add-On Services

This BM is similar to BM 1a, although a supplier retains ownership of its product, which is made available to a customer through a leasing arrangement. The customer purchases add-on services related to the product in the same manner as in BM 1a. This option is viable for expensive equipment (Aas et al., 2020). Leasing, rather than buying, equipment could be financially beneficial for the customer. The use of BM 3a, sometimes referred to as 'dry leasing', has also been reported in the airline industry (Hsu et al., 2013).

BM 3b: Product Leasing and Smart Add-On Services

Another option is to use digital technology to sell smart add-on services in combination with the leasing of a product to a customer. This BM is similar to the more traditional BM 1b, with the difference being the use of digital technology to provide smart services. BM 3b is also used in other industries, such as the automobile industry, in which vehicles packed with digital technologies are leased to consumers and business customers (e.g. Williams, 2007).

BM 4a: Product Leasing and Integrated Services

In BM 4a, a product is made available to a customer with no transfer of ownership, and services are sold through a combined leasing and results-oriented contract. This BM is similar to BM 2a, with the exception of the ownership dimension. It is also used, for example, in the airline industry, and is sometimes referred to as 'wet leasing' (Hsu et al., 2013). BM4a may be suitable, for example, for risk-averse customers with limited equity who need capital-intensive equipment to carry out their operations.

BM 4b: Product Leasing and Smart Integrated Services

In BM 4b, a manufacturing firm makes a product available to a customer without transferring ownership while selling smart services through a combined leasing and results-oriented contract. Many examples of the use of this BM in the market (e.g. Xerox's offering of pay-per-use services) have been described (Kowalkowski et al., 2017). BM 4b is probably more common than BM 4a, as it incentivises suppliers to use digital technologies to optimise maintenance and operations when these services are not purchased traditionally as add-ons (Selviaridis & Wynstra, 2015). BMs 4a and 4b are arguably the most service-oriented BMs available to manufacturers, as they do not involve the offering of any tangible product.

4   Concluding Remarks

In this chapter, we provide a framework bridging extant PSS typologies, emphasising the role of digital technologies in servitisation BMs. The proposed three PSS BM continuums and the new typology, which distinguishes eight types of BMs available to servitized manufacturers, are built on

Tukker (2004), Kohtamäki, Parida et al., (2019) and Aas et al. (2020). The proposed typology serves to bridge the contributions of Tukker (2004) and Kohtamäki, Parida et al., (2019) to achieve relevance in the digital era.

Extant research on PSS BMs has a wide variety of theoretical bases. The ownership dimension of PSSs is examined using frameworks derived from sustainability science, whereas the results orientation is considered based on various forms of governance theory (e.g., transaction cost economies and contract theory). In developing their framework, Kohtamäki, Parida et al., (2019) drew on a wide range of foundational theories of the firm, in line with Santos and Eisenhardt's (2005) solid conceptions. Aas et al. (2020), in turn, based their taxonomy on empirical observations, as in much servitisation research (Rabetino et al., 2018). Thus, the proposed framework represents an amalgamation of multiple academic traditions for PSSs underpinned by digitally enabled intangible deliverables.

It has been argued that BMs may be used to operationalise servitisation strategies (Gebauer et al., 2010). Thus, from a configuration theory viewpoint, the typology presented in this chapter may be perceived as different configurations of servitisation strategies. The suggested typology may therefore be useful for future configuration research aiming to identify the antecedents, processes and effects of servitisation in different contexts (Kohtamäk, Henneberg et al., 2019).

The proposed typology is also useful for practitioners in two ways: First, the framework can be used as a sensitising concept (Blumer, 1954) that enables practitioners to assess BM options along the three identified continuums. According to Blumer (1954, p. 7), sensitising concepts lack a clear definition in terms of attributes or fixed benchmarks, but give the user a general sense of reference and guidance in approaching empirical cases.

Second, the three PSS BM continuums and eight types of PSS BM can be conceived as a navigational tool for manufacturing firm managers who aim to develop innovative BMs in the digital era. The framework provides users with a common language that simplifies communication and makes the evaluation of different opportunities more robust. BMs are often used for constant testing and fine-tuning. In this regard, we recommend that the typology be used as a learning tool for organisations experimenting with service-oriented BMs.

References

Aas, T. H., Breunig, K. J., Hellström, M. M., & Hydle, K. M. (2020). Service-oriented business models in manufacturing in the digital era: Toward a new taxonomy. *International Journal of Innovation Management, 24*(8), 2040002.

Akkermans, H., Oppen, W. V., Wynstra, F., & Voss, C. (2019). Contracting outsourced services with collaborative key performance indicators. *Journal of Operations Management, 65*(1), 22–47. https://doi.org/10.1002/joom.1002.

Allmendinger, G., & Lombreglia, R. (2005). Four strategies for the age of smart services. *Harvard Business Review* (October 2005). https://hbr.org/2005/10/four-strategies-for-the-age-of-smart-services.

Amit, R., & Zott, C. (2001). Value creation in e-business. *Strategic Management Journal, 22*(6–7), 493–520.

Baines, T., & Lightfoot, H. (2013). *Made to serve: How manufacturers can compete through servitization and product service systems.* Wiley. https://www.wiley.com/en-us/Made+to+Serve%3A+How+Manufacturers+can+Compete+Through+Servitization+and+Product+Service+Systems-p-9781118585313.

Baines, T. S., Lightfoot, H. W., Evans, S., Neely, A., Greenough, R., Peppard, J., Roy, R., Shehab, E., Braganza, A., Tiwari, A., Alcock, J. R., Angus, J. P., Bastl, M., Cousens, A., Irving, P., Johnson, M., Kingston, J., Lockett, H., Martinez, V., ... Wilson, H. (2007). State-of-the-art in product-service systems. *Proceedings of the Institution of Mechanical Engineers, Part B: Journal of Engineering Manufacture, 221*(10), 1543–1552. https://doi.org/10.1243/09544054JEM858.

Baines, T., & Lightfoot, H. (2014). Servitization of the manufacturing firm: Exploring the operations practices and technologies that deliver advanced services. *International Journal of Operations & Production Management, 34*(1), 2–35. https://doi.org/10.1108/IJOPM-02-2012-0086.

Beverungen, D., Müller, O., Matzner, M., Mendling, J., & vom Brocke, J. (2019). Conceptualizing smart service systems. *Electronic Markets, 29*(1), 7–18. https://doi.org/10.1007/s12525-017-0270-5.

Blumer, H. (1954). What is wrong with social theory? *American Sociological Review, 19*(1), 3–10. https://doi.org/10.2307/2088165.

Bonnemeier, S., Burianek, F., & Reichwald, R. (2010). Revenue models for integrated customer solutions: Concept and organizational implementation. *Journal of Revenue and Pricing Management, 9*(3), 228–238. https://doi.org/10.1057/rpm.2010.7.

Brax, S. A., & Visintin, F. (2017). Meta-model of servitization: The integrative profiling approach. *Industrial Marketing Management, 60*, 17–32.

Collier, D., LaPorte, J., & Seawright, J. (2012). Putting typologies to work: Concept formation, measurement, and analytic rigor. *Political Research Quarterly, 65*(1), 217–232. https://doi.org/10.1177/1065912912437162.

Doty, D. H., & Glick, W. H. (1994). Typologies as a unique form of theory building: Toward improved understanding and modeling. *The Academy of Management Review, 19*(2), 230–251. https://doi.org/10.2307/258704.

Gebauer, H., Edvardsson, B., Gustafsson, A., & Witell, L. (2010). Match or mismatch: Strategy-structure configurations in the service business of manufacturing companies. *Journal of Service Research, 13*(2), 198–215.

Hsu, C., Chao, C., & Huang, P. (2013). Fleet dry/wet lease planning of airlines on strategic alliance. *Transportmetrica a: Transport Science, 9*(7), 603–628. https://doi.org/10.1080/18128602.2011.643508.

Kohtamäki, M., Henneberg, S. C., Martinez, V., Kimita, K., & Gebauer, H. (2019). A configurational approach to servitization: Review and research directions. *Service Science, 11*(3), 213–240.

Kohtamäki, M., Parida, V., Oghazie, P., Gebauerf, H., & Baines, T. (2019). Digital servitization business models in ecosystems: A theory of the firm. *Journal of Business Research, 104*, 380–392. https://doi.org/10.1016/j.jbusres.2019.02.012..

Kowalkowski, C., Gebauer, H., Kamp, B., & Parry, G. (2017). Servitization and deservitization: Overview, concepts, and definitions. *Industrial Marketing Management, 67*, 4–10. https://doi.org/10.1016/j.indmarman.2017.09.009.

Kowalkowski, C., Windahl, C., Kindström, D., & Gebauer, H. (2015). What service transition? Rethinking established assumptions about manufacturers' service-led growth strategies. *Industrial Marketing Management, 45*, 59–69.

Liinamaa, J., Viljanen, M., Hurmerinta, A., Ivanova-Gongne, M., Luotola, H., & Gustafsson, M. (2016). Performance-based and functional contracting in value-based solution selling. *Industrial Marketing Management, 59*, 37–49. https://doi.org/10.1016/j.indmarman.2016.05.032.

Lindström, J. (2013). A model for value-based selling: Enabling corporations to transition from products and services towards further complex business models. *Journal of Multi Business Model Innovation and Technology, 2*(1), 67–98. https://doi.org/10.13052/jmbmit2245-456X.213.

Luotola, H., Hellström, M., Gustafsson, M., & Perminova-Harikoski, O. (2017). Embracing uncertainty in value-based selling by means of design thinking. *Industrial Marketing Management, 65*, 59–75. https://doi.org/10.1016/j.indmarman.2017.05.004..

Meyer, A. D., Tsui, A. S., & Hinings, C. R. (1993). Configurational approaches to organizational analysis. *Academy of Management Journal, 36*(6), 1175–1195.

Michelini, R. C., & Razzoli, R. P. (2004). Product-service eco-design: Knowledge-based infrastructures. *Journal of Cleaner Production, 12*(4), 415–428. https://doi.org/10.1016/S0959-6526(03)00036-2.

Mont, O. K. (2002). Clarifying the concept of product–service system. *Journal of Cleaner Production, 10*(3), 237–245. https://doi.org/10.1016/S0959-6526(01)00039-7.

Ng, I. C. L., Ding, D. X., & Yip, N. (2013). Outcome-based contracts as new business model: The role of partnership and value-driven relational assets. *Industrial*

Marketing Management, 42(5), 730–743. https://doi.org/10.1016/j.indmarman.2013.05.009.

Osterwalder, A., & Pigneur, Y. (2010). *Business model generation*. Wiley.

Parida, V., Sjödin, D., & Reim, W. (2019). Reviewing literature on digitalization, business model innovation, and sustainable industry: Past achievements and future promises. *Sustainability, 11*(2), 391. https://doi.org/10.3390/su11020391.

Partanen, J., Marko, K., Vinit, P., & Joakim, W. (2017). Developing and validating a multi-dimensional scale for operationalizing industrial service offering. *Journal of Business & Industrial Marketing, 32*(2), 295–309. https://doi.org/10.1108/JBIM-08-2016-0178.

Porter, M. E., & Heppelmann, J. E. (2015, -10–01T04:00:00Z). How smart, connected products are transforming companies. *Harvard Business Review.* https://hbr.org/2015/10/how-smart-connected-products-are-transforming-companies.

Rabetino, R., Harmsen, W., Kohtamäki, M., & Sihvonen, J. (2018). Structuring servitization-related research. *International Journal of Operations & Production Management, 38*(2), 350–371. https://doi.org/10.1108/IJOPM-03-2017-0175.

Reen, N., Hellström, M., Wikström, K., & Perminova-Harikoski, O. (2017). Towards value-driven strategies in pricing IT solutions. *Journal of Revenue and Pricing Management, 16*(1), 91–105. https://doi.org/10.1057/s41272-017-0079-z..

Resta, B., Powell, D., Gaiardelli, P., & Dotti, S. (2015). Towards a framework for lean operations in product-oriented product service systems. *CIRP Journal of Manufacturing Science and Technology, 9*, 12–22. https://doi.org/10.1016/j.cirpj.2015.01.008.

Santos, F. M., & Eisenhardt, K. M. (2005). Organizational boundaries and theories of organization. *Organization Science, 16*(5), 491–508. https://doi.org/10.1287/orsc.1050.0152.

Selviaridis, K., & Wynstra, F. (2015). Performance-based contracting: A literature review and future research directions. *International Journal of Production Research, 53*(12), 3505–3540. https://doi.org/10.1080/00207543.2014.978031.

Siggelkow, N. (2007). Persuasion with case studies. *Academy of Management Journal, 50*(1), 20–24. https://doi.org/10.5465/AMJ.2007.24160882.

Teece, D. J. (2010). Business models, business strategy and innovation. *Long Range Planning, 43*(2), 172–194. https://doi.org/10.1016/j.lrp.2009.07.003.

Töytäri, P., & Rajala, R. (2015). Value-based selling: An organizational capability perspective. *Industrial Marketing Management, 45*, 101–112. https://doi.org/10.1016/j.indmarman.2015.02.009.

Töytäri, P., Rajala, R., & Alejandro, T. B. (2015). Organizational and institutional barriers to value-based pricing in industrial relationships. *Industrial Marketing Management, 47*, 53–64. https://doi.org/10.1016/j.indmarman.2015.02.005.

Tukker, A. (2004). Eight types of product–service system: Eight ways to sustainability? Experiences from SusProNet. *Business Strategy and the Environment, 13*(4), 246–260. https://doi.org/10.1002/bse.414.

Tukker, A. (2015). Product services for a resource-efficient and circular economy—A review. *Journal of Cleaner Production, 97*, 76–91. https://doi.org/10.1016/j.jcl epro.2013.11.049.

Tukker, A., & Tischner, U. (2006). Product-services as a research field: Past, present and future. Reflections from a decade of research. *Product Service Systems: Reviewing Achievements and Refining the Research Agenda, 14*(17), 1552–1556. https://doi.org/10.1016/j.jclepro.2006.01.022.

Vargo, S. L., & Lusch, R. F. (2008). Service-dominant logic: Continuing the evolution. *Journal of the Academy of Marketing Science, 36*(1), 1–10.

Venkatraman, N. (1989). The concept of fit in strategy research: Toward verbal and statistical correspondence. *Academy of Management Review, 14*(3), 423–444.

Williams, A. (2007). Product service systems in the automobile industry: Contribution to system innovation? *Journal of Cleaner Production, 15*(11), 1093–1103. https://doi.org/10.1016/j.jclepro.2006.05.034.

Wise, R., & Baumgartner, P. (1999). Go downstream: The new profit imperative in manufacturing. *Harvard Business Review, 77*(5), 133–141.

Zheng, P., Lin, T., Chen, C., & Xu, X. (2018). A systematic design approach for service innovation of smart product-service systems. *Journal of Cleaner Production, 201*, 657–667. https://doi.org/10.1016/j.jclepro.2018.08.101.

Zott, C., Amit, R., & Massa, L. (2011). The business model: Recent developments and future research. *Journal of Management, 37*(4), 1019–1042. https://doi.org/10.1177/0149206311406265.

Zott, C., & Amit, R. (2010). Business model design: An activity system perspective. *Long Range Planning, 43*(2), 216–226. https://doi.org/10.1016/j.lrp.2009.07.004.

Digital Business Model Innovation for Product-Service Systems

Wiebke Reim, Vinit Parida, and David Sjödin

1 Introduction

The integration of products and services by manufacturing companies is a growing trend in today's globally competitive business environment (Boehm & Thomas, 2013; Mont, 2002). This trend is fueled by the expectation to utilize the opportunities that come with digitalization and Industry 4.0. (Parida et al., 2019). In this regard, offering product-service systems (PSS) is proposed as an attractive solution for manufacturing companies to achieve economic, environmental, and social benefits (Vezzoli et al., 2015).

Moving toward offering digital-enabled PSS implicates that the companies' business model undergoes significant modifications (Meier et al., 2010). The business model has become a common unit of analysis in PSS literature as the crucial factor that may differentiate successful and unsuccessful PSS companies (Barquet et al., 2013; Ng et al., 2013). Furthermore, the business model perspective is not only suitable for classifying businesses with similar

W. Reim (✉) · V. Parida · D. Sjödin
Luleå University of Technology, Luleå, Sweden
e-mail: wiebke.reim@ltu.se

V. Parida
e-mail: vinit.parida@ltu.se

D. Sjödin
e-mail: david.sjodin@ltu.se

© The Author(s), under exclusive license to Springer Nature
Switzerland AG 2021
M. Kohtamäki et al. (eds.), *The Palgrave Handbook of Servitization*,
https://doi.org/10.1007/978-3-030-75771-7_6

89

characteristics but also to provide a lens for redesign activities to innovate the business model (Visnjic Kastalli et al., 2013). However, implementing a PSS business model successfully is a complex and challenging task, as demonstrated by the high failure rates in which companies do not generate the expected higher returns (Gebauer et al., 2005).

PSS offerings without careful consideration of business models run the risk that the economic and environmental potential will be offset by rebound effects and adverse behavior (Tukker, 2004). Thus, PSS business model implementation is a complex process that needs to take many aspects and strategic decisions into account. However, aggregated insights into how digital business model innovation for PSS can be successfully managed has been lacking in the literature (Baines et al., 2017; Kindström & Ottosson, 2016; Reim, 2018).

The arguments put forward highlight that the innovation of digital-enabled PSS business models is a challenging process, which is a major reason why companies struggle to increase the digitalization and service degree of their offerings. Therefore, the purpose of this chapter is *to advance understanding of the process of digital business model innovation for PSS in manufacturing companies.* This chapter is written based on findings from existing literature and extensive empirical studies in the Swedish manufacturing industry. In the following, the chapter presents relevant theoretical aspects of digital business model innovation in PSS that result in the development of a four-phase framework. The chapter concludes with theoretical and managerial implications.

2   Theory Development

Product-Service Systems

Initial studies on PSS defined the concept of PSS as a marketable set of products and services capable of jointly fulfilling customers' needs in an economical and sustainable manner (Mont, 2002). While PSS has significant potential to be beneficial for providers, customers, and the environment, there are several barriers that hinder its implementation, e.g., customers may hesitate to use PSS because they dislike ownerless consumption, or the provider organization may be unwilling to provide resources to shift the company toward PSS provision (Baines et al., 2007).

In order to define and understand PSS, it is helpful to look at the categorization into product-, use-, and result-oriented PSS (Tukker, 2004).

These categories differ in the degree of product emphasis, responsibilities, and ownership. This also shows that PSS is broadly defined, as it includes everything that has some product and service dimension reaching from maintenance over leasing to even outsourcing. In the PSS literature, most of the studies focus on case studies and examples to show the value of PSS and further to identify characteristics of PSS offers (Baines et al., 2007). Implementing and adopting PSS, however, has not been as widespread as expected, and especially higher PSS level implies even more challenges and risks that make providing PSS more difficult. The challenges that hinder successfully operating PSS usually concern the transformation process required when implementing PSS as well as strategic alignment within the company and with customers (Martinez et al., 2010). Additionally, many researchers have pointed out that the challenges companies face when implementing PSS often negatively affect company performance (Gebauer et al., 2005; Parida et al., 2014). To address these challenges, researchers have proposed that designing a well-structured business model could contribute to a comprehensive approach in PSS provision (Kindström & Kowalkowski, 2014). Such an approach has the potential to contribute to improved performance, especially in companies that implement advanced, digital-enabled PSS (Parida et al., 2014).

Digital Business Model Innovation

The business model as a concept has been part of the business jargon for a long time and is even considered as a widely used buzzword. Recently, critical and developmental management research about business models has begun to emerge (Luz Martín-Peña et al., 2018). A common argument in the literature states that the business model refers to the logic of the company, including how it operates and how it creates value for stakeholders (Magretta, 2002). However, over the last few years, more and more agreement has arisen for a common definition, as used by Teece (2010), which basically states that business models describe the design or architecture of the value creation, value delivery, and value capturing mechanisms that a company employs.

The implementation of digitalization is a challenging undertaking and requires a continuous commitment to making the organization fully capable and mature. However, this commitment to digitalization initiatives coupled with judicious implementation of business model innovation can certainly yield important benefits to the triple bottom line (Parida et al., 2019). Many companies are working with this holistic perspective in mind, and digitalization is the essential enabler to make this development a reality. It is important to highlight that the benefits can be achieved either through direct or indirect effects that are created simultaneously; it is important to visualize these and to facilitate them.

Increased process efficiency is achieved through continuous analysis of operational data, facilitating the identification of process-performance bottle-necks to be eliminated (Cenamor et al., 2017). Autonomously self-correcting systems can increase process efficiency, translate into less equipment down-time, optimized capacity, and reduced repair-time averages, to name only some of the potential benefits (Sjödin et al., 2018). Second, lower opera-tional costs are achieved through process optimization and monitoring in the interests of cost-efficient resource utilization. Enhanced predictive approaches allow quality defects and operational problems to be spotted sooner rather than later. In addition, analytics can facilitate identification of the root causes of defects—whether they are human, machine, or environmental—leading to the gains of lower scrap rates and lead times (Porter & Heppelmann, 2015). The logic of PSS business models is very well adapted to enable a successful commercialization of digital technologies in service-based offers.

PSS Business Models

Following the studies of Casadesus-Masanell and Ricart (2010), it has been argued that selecting a business model is one key choice that drives the fulfil-ment of a company's differentiation strategy. Indeed, recent PSS studies have highlighted the fact that business models are central to implementing PSS successfully and need to be carefully evaluated from start (Adrodegari & Saccani, 2017; Rabetino et al., 2017).

Value in PSS is created by taking over work tasks from customers and accomplishing them more efficiently, which also improves the relationship with the customer and enhances his or her loyalty (Meier et al., 2010). Value delivery is characterized by the high skill, competence, and experience levels required to control the entire process of providing PSS with support of digital technology (Meier et al., 2010). In addition, new organizational structures and new partners need to be integrated into PSS provision. To capture value, it is important to design PSS such that customers are willing to pay for the added value (Mont, 2002). At the same time, costs need to be handled effi-ciently. In addition, the profitability of PSS is often difficult to show because cash flows are uncertain, and quantifying savings may be difficult (Erkoyuncu et al., 2013; Gebauer et al., 2005).

Previous studies have acknowledged the importance of PSS business model implementation (Reim et al., 2015), but only a few studies have explained the mechanism by which such intent can lead to competitiveness. When companies pursue PSS implementation strategies, they add service or digital elements to their operations in different ways and under varying conditions. This explains why certain companies are more successful with PSS, whereas others fail despite adopting a similar PSS strategy. Several methodologies can be found in the literature that, for example, focus on life-cycle assessment or digital capabilities relevant for PSS business model implementation (Pagoropoulos et al., 2017). However, most frameworks only describe or analyze PSS business models without providing insight into how a company should implement the developed business models.

The framework developed by Casadesus-Masanell and Ricart (2010), which looks at the relation among strategy, business models, and tactics, is helpful in understanding the relationship between PSS and business models. The authors suggest that a company's strategy decides which potential business models it can adopt. Furthermore, tactics are defined as the residual choices at operational level that are left after deciding which business model to go for. After choosing a particular PSS business model, which decides how value is created, delivered, and captured, the tactical sets will decide how much value in the end is created and captured.

More specifically, research findings can be accumulated from the field to present a framework supporting the implementation of well-established categories of PSS business models, that is, product-oriented, use-oriented, and result-oriented business models. Each business model category can be linked to six operational-level tactics (contracts; marketing; networks; product and service design; sustainability; and digital technology) that ensure that the model can be implemented successfully and subsequently generate value (Reim et al., 2015).

PSS Risk Management

Prior studies have highlighted that reducing risks for customers tends to be the most common reason for adopting PSS (Meier et al., 2010). The assumption that customers want more reliability (Roy & Cheruvu, 2009) and are willing to pay extra (i.e., a risk premium) for the reduced risk has driven providers to engage in PSS. This implies that the risks for providers in most cases increase significantly (Ng et al., 2013) and that risk management is an important step of the innovation process of PSS business models.

PSS operational risks can be classified into three categories: competence risks, technical risks, and behavioral risks (Reim et al., 2016). Authors often focus on unexpected breakdowns of the product (Steven, 2012), which leads to increased repair and maintenance costs (Meier et al., 2010) and other penalties. These technical issues may also relate to risks that are more readily associated with the state of the technology such as obsolescence (Richter et al., 2010).

In addition, the likelihood of adverse customer behavior increases significantly because the provider takes over responsibility for product performance from the customer (Erkoyuncu et al., 2013; Ng & Yip, 2009). PSS literature has merely acknowledged such adverse behavior, but this behavior is poorly understood (Roy & Cheruvu, 2009). A specific example is when a customer only buys PSS agreements for machinery that the customer knows is prone to breaking down (Hypko et al., 2010). Operational risk can also be related to the company's competence and capability to provide the agreed-upon product-service to customers (Mont, 2002). This is important for PSS because the company must acquire numerous new capabilities and resources to be able to offer digital-enabled PSS (Parida et al., 2019). Conditions under which each risk can be mitigated can be explained using different risk management strategies (avoidance, reduction, sharing/transfer, and retention) and can be integrated into a decision framework for PSS risk management (Reim et al., 2016).

PSS Service Networks

The PSS literature typically focuses on the manufacturers' internal implementation processes or the relationship between provider and customer (Barquet et al., 2013; Stoughton & Votta, 2003; Tukker, 2004). In contrast, the role of the service network in manufacturers' PSS business model implementation efforts has largely been overlooked, but is an important step in the innovation process.

In PSS, service network actors such as distributors can be regarded as the intermediaries in an extended value creation network, providing the forward link to customers and the backward link to the manufacturer (Story et al., 2017), thus ensuring delivery of PSS business models. Thus, investigating the role of service network actors in PSS provision is vital to understand not only their role in mediating partnerships between providers and customers (Evans et al., 2007) but also the underlying dynamics that explain the service network actors' commitment, digital competence, and distributed work practices in PSS provision.

Service networks face major internal and market-related challenges that hinder their servitization and four unique strategies (service extension, service benchmarking, digitalization, customer co-creation) can be identified that distributors implement to meet these challenges (Reim et al., 2018). Zarpelon-Neto et al. (2015) highlight local regulations, resource allocation, internal culture, commercial feasibility, and lack of knowledge as major problems that prevent service network actors from offering PSS. Thus, understanding the challenges and complexity associated with PSS business model implementation in service networks is an important area of inquiry (Raja & Frandsen, 2017).

PSS Business Model Alignment

During the innovation process of a PSS business model, many aspects and functions are developed in isolation and it is important to assure alignment of the business model during its implementation. Based on its definition, the business model describes the architecture that aligns various elements to capture the essence of the cause–effect relationships among customers, the organization, and money (Teece, 2010). Accordingly, alignment in the literature has been defined as the adjustment of an object in relation to other objects so that the arrangement can lead to the optimization of results (Venkatraman, 1989). Adjustment of the constituents of the business model is therefore necessary in order to align them with the overall business logic of a company when it moves toward providing PSS. This is because the way value is created, delivered, and captured differs substantially from the way it is configured in the product-based business model. Consequently, the company's activities must also evolve to enable the implementation of the new PSS business model (Kindström & Ottosson, 2016).

There is a need for horizontal alignment (i.e., aligning activities within business model components), as well as vertical alignment (i.e., aligning activities across business model components), which is necessary to ensure both internal as well as external fit of how it creates, delivers, and captures value through PSS (Reim et al., 2017).

Digital Business Model Innovation Framework

Based on the theoretical insides from the previous sections and extensive empirical studies in the Swedish manufacturing industry, a digital business model innovation framework for PSS (Fig. 1) has been developed. The framework provides a stepwise approach for companies that make a strategic decision to increase the service extent of their digitalized operations. The framework is a result of a highly iterative process and inductive reasoning

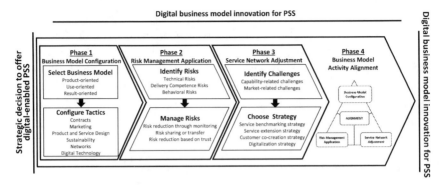

Fig. 1 Digital business model innovation for PSS

based on the findings from the literature and the empirical studies. The framework does not claim that all possible aspects are included, but it makes a synthesis of the key aspects.

The framework shows that the first phase of digital business model innovation is the business model configuration. This phase includes the PSS business model selection, which defines how value will be generated with the PSS offer as well as the configuration of PSS business model tactics, which affects how much value is generated. Implementing a PSS business model is usually accompanied by an increased risk level at the provider company because the company takes on additional tasks and a higher responsibility for the performance of its products. Dependent on the chosen PSS business model and the applied tactics, the provider is exposed to different risks that, in the second phase of the framework, need to be identified and then managed. The third phase takes into consideration that most manufacturers have to rely on service network actors to provide PSS to their customers. PSS provision implies an intensified relation to the customers compared with a pure product sale, which therefore requires adjusting the delivery practice of the service network to the PSS offer. These service network actors are exposed to various challenges, and different strategies can be applied to overcome these challenges in order to successfully offer PSS. The three first phases show many different ongoing activities related to PSS business model innovation in terms of value creation (e.g., which business model and tactics to choose), value delivery (e.g., how to integrate the distributor network), and value capture (e.g., how to manage PSS risks). These activities are all critical, and their outcomes need to be optimized. However, to secure an overall positive result of the PSS, it is crucial that all activities are aligned with each other toward the common goal of successful PSS business model implementation.

In conclusion, after going through the phases of the digital business model innovation framework for PSS, the company should be well-prepared to provide the developed digital-enabled PSS business model. The alignment of all activities is crucial to achieve the benefits of a PSS offer. Positive outcomes resulting from the framework application could be increased revenue share coming from service because the PSS business model has been designed with focus on the customer value. Furthermore, the PSS business model could be offered to a larger share of customers because the PSS-related risks are well understood and managed for the specific customer segment. Similarly, through the adjustment of the service network, PSS business models can be offered in more markets. Thus, aligning all activities related to PSS business model innovation creates an effective PSS offer in which the combination of products, services, and digital technology provides a much higher value than standalone products or services.

3   Discussion

Theoretical Contribution

The purpose of this chapter is to advance the understanding of digital business model innovation for PSS. Understanding the phases of the PSS business model innovation process is crucial, as challenges during implementation are a main hindrance to realize the high potential of PSS offers (Barquet et al., 2013). This chapter provides new theoretical insights to further develop multiple aspects of digital-enabled PSS and to facilitate successful PSS provision based on digitalization. More importantly, the major contribution lies in advancing our understanding of PSS operational tactics, which related articles frequently recognize and discuss as being central for business models and PSS literature (Casadesus-Masanell & Ricart, 2010; Evans et al., 2007). By unravelling the role of identified tactics in relation to PSS business models, a novel relationship is established between PSS business models and tactics.

Both in theory and practice, risk is frequently mentioned and is a major reason why companies shy away from high-level PSS business model innovation (Meier et al., 2010). Identifying the possible risks and finding the right risk response are crucial for the implementation of PSS business models, as it increases confidence and control in regard to the new PSS offer. This chapter contributes to the categorization of risks into technical, behavioral, and delivery competence risks that structures the fragmented discussion of risks in the literature (Steven, 2012). An important contribution is to identify and explain the key decision criteria that provide guidance to selecting an appropriate risk response.

Another contribution is the identification of four servitization strategies (digitalization, service benchmarking, service extension, and customer co-creation strategy) that can cope with specific or combinations of challenges. Previous literature acknowledges that, due to market heterogeneity, the need for developing customized strategic responses is critical (Zarpelon Neto et al., 2015). Still, we know little about which approaches are relevant and under which conditions. Identifying and decoding these distributor strategies provide evidence of how practically service network actors manage heterogeneity to achieve PSS business model implementation.

Managerial Implications

This chapter has several implications for managers in manufacturing companies that are responsible for PSS implementation and strategy development. First, the implementation of PSS is crucial for the overall generated value economically, socially, and environmentally. Implementing PSS is challenging and complex, and it requires activities in many areas to make use of the full potential of PSS. This study helps managers to make better decisions and takes them stepwise through the implementation of PSS. Second, for managers responsible for developing and operating PSS offerings, it is especially important to realize that risk management is a vital activity that extends beyond technical risks that lead to breakdowns of the product to also include risks related to customer behavior and insufficient competence at the providers' end (e.g., service network). Third, this study has managerial implications not only for senior management within manufacturing companies but also for the service network. Any manager who is responsible for developing advanced service offers within a distributor must identify the unique challenges that the distributor faces. Finally, practicing managers can take inspiration from this chapter regarding how the business model concept can be used as an organizing device to effectively provide PSS in their companies. The activity-based business model framework could also be used as a guiding and evaluation tool for the ongoing PSS implementation process within the company.

References

Adrodegari, F., & Saccani, N. (2017). Business models for the service transformation of industrial firms. *The Service Industries Journal, 37*(1), 57–83.

Baines, T. S., Lightfoot, H. W., Evans, S., Neely, A., Greenough, R., Peppard, J., Roy, R., Shehab, E., Braganza, A., Tiwari, A., Alcock, J. R., Angus, J. P., Basti, M., Cousens, A., Irving, P., Johnson, M., Kingston, J., Lockett, H., Martinez, V., … Wilson, H. (2007). State-of-the-art in product-service systems. *Proceedings of the Institution of Mechanical Engineers, Part B: Journal of Engineering Manufacture, 221*(10), 1543–1552.

Baines, T., Ziaee Bigdeli, A., Bustinza, O. F., Guang Shi, V., Baldwin, J., & Ridgway, K. (2017). Servitization: Revisiting the state-of-the-art and research priorities. *International Journal of Operations & Production Management, 37*(2), 256–278.

Barquet, A. P. B., de Oliveira, M. G., Amigo, C. R., Cunha, V. P., & Rozenfeld, H. (2013). Employing the business model concept to support the adoption of product–service systems (PSS). *Industrial Marketing Management, 42*(5), 693–704.

Boehm, M., & Thomas, O. (2013). Looking beyond the rim of one's teacup: A multidisciplinary literature review of product-service systems in information systems, business management, and engineering & design. *Journal of Cleaner Production, 51*, 245–260.

Casadesus-Masanell, R., & Ricart, J. E. (2010). From strategy to business models and onto tactics. *Long Range Planning, 43*(2), 195–215.

Cenamor, J., Sjödin, D. R., & Parida, V. (2017). Adopting a platform approach in servitization: Leveraging the value of digitalization. *International Journal of Production Economics, 192*, 54–65.

Erkoyuncu, J. A., Durugbo, C., & Roy, R. (2013). Identifying uncertainties for industrial service delivery: A systems approach. *International Journal of Production Research, 51*(21), 6295–6315.

Evans, S., Partidário, P. J., & Lambert, J. (2007). Industrialization as a key element of sustainable product-service solutions. *International Journal of Production Research, 45*(18–19), 4225–4246.

Gebauer, H., Fleisch, E., & Friedli, T. (2005). Overcoming the service paradox in manufacturing companies. *European Management Journal, 23*(1), 14–26.

Hypko, P., Tilebein, M., & Gleich, R. (2010). Benefits and uncertainties of performance-based contracting in manufacturing industries: An agency theory perspective. *Journal of Service Management, 21*(4), 460–489.

Kindström, D., & Kowalkowski, C. (2014). Service innovation in product-centric firms: A multidimensional business model perspective. *Journal of Business & Industrial Marketing, 29*(2), 96–111.

Kindström, D., & Ottosson, M. (2016). Local and regional energy companies offering energy services: Key activities and implications for the business model. *Applied Energy, 171*, 491–500.

Luz Martín-Peña, M., Díaz-Garrido, E., & Sánchez-López, J. M. (2018). The digitalization and servitization of manufacturing: A review on digital business models. *Strategic Change, 27*(2), 91–99.

Magretta, J. (2002). Why business models matter. *Harvard Business Review, 80*(5), 86–92.

Martinez, V., Bastl, M., Kingston, J., & Evans, S. (2010). Challenges in transforming manufacturing organisations into product-service providers. *Journal of Manufacturing Technology Management, 21*(4), 449–469.

Meier, H., Roy, R., & Seliger, G. (2010). Industrial Product-Service Systems—IPS2. *CIRP Annals, 59*(2), 607–627.

Mont, O. K. (2002). Clarifying the concept of product–service system. *Journal of Cleaner Production, 10*(3), 237–245.

Ng, I. C., & Yip, N. (2009). Identifying risk and its impact on contracting through a benefit based-model framework in business to business contracting: Case of the defence industry.

Ng, I. C., Ding, D. X., & Yip, N. (2013). Outcome-based contracts as new business model: The role of partnership and value-driven relational assets. *Industrial Marketing Management, 42*(5), 730–743.

Pagoropoulos, A., Maier, A., & McAloone, T. C. (2017). Assessing transformational change from institutionalising digital capabilities on implementation and development of product-service systems: Learnings from the maritime industry. *Journal of Cleaner Production, 166*, 369–380.

Parida, V., Sjödin, D., & Reim, W. (2019). Reviewing literature on digitalization, business model innovation, and sustainable industry: Past achievements and future promises. *Sustainability, 11*(2), 391.

Parida, V., Sjödin, D. R., Wincent, J., & Kohtamäki, M. (2014). Mastering the transition to product-service provision: Insights into business models, learning activities, and capabilities. *Research-Technology Management, 57*(3), 44–52.

Porter, M. E., & Heppelmann, J. E. (2015). How smart, connected products are transforming companies. *Harvard Business Review, 93*(10), 96–114.

Rabetino, R., Kohtamäki, M., & Gebauer, H. (2017). Strategy map of servitization. *International Journal of Production Economics, 192*, 144–156.

Raja, J. Z., & Frandsen, T. (2017). Exploring servitization in China: Challenges of aligning motivation, opportunity and ability in coordinating an external service partner network. *International Journal of Operations & Production Management, 37*(11), 1654–1682.

Reim, W. (2018). *Towards a framework for product-service system business model implementation* (Doctoral dissertation, Luleå tekniska universitet).

Reim, W., Lenka, S., Frishammar, J., & Parida, V. (2017). Implementing sustainable product–service systems utilizing business model activities. *Procedia CIRP, 64*, 61–66.

Reim, W., Parida, V., & Örtqvist, D. (2015). Product-service systems (PSS) business models and tactics–A systematic literature review. *Journal of Cleaner Production, 97*, 61–75.

Reim, W., Parida, V., & Sjödin, D. R. (2016). Risk management for product-service system operation. *International Journal of Operations & Production Management, 36*(6), 665–686.

Reim, W., Sjödin, D., & Parida, V. (2018). Mitigating adverse customer behaviour for product-service system provision: An agency theory perspective. *Industrial Marketing Management, 74*, 150–161.

Richter, A., Sadek, T., & Steven, M. (2010). Flexibility in industrial product-service systems and use-oriented business models. *CIRP Journal of Manufacturing Science and Technology, 3*(2), 128–134.

Roy, R., & Cheruvu, K. S. (2009). A competitive framework for industrial product-service systems. *International Journal of Internet Manufacturing and Services, 2*(1), 4–29.

Sjödin, D. R., Parida, V., Leksell, M., & Petrovic, A. (2018). Smart factory implementation and process innovation: A preliminary maturity model for leveraging digitalization in manufacturing moving to smart factories presents specific challenges that can be addressed through a structured approach focused on people, processes, and technologies. *Research-Technology Management, 61*(5), 22–31.

Steven, M. (2012). Risk management of industrial product-service systems (IPS2)– How to consider risk and uncertainty over the IPS2 lifecycle? *Leveraging Technology for a Sustainable World* (pp. 37–42). Springer.

Story, V. M., Raddats, C., Burton, J., Zolkiewski, J., & Baines, T. (2017). Capabilities for advanced services: A multi-actor perspective. *Industrial Marketing Management, 60*, 54–68.

Stoughton, M., & Votta, T. (2003). Implementing service-based chemical procurement: Lessons and results. *Journal of Cleaner Production, 11*(8), 839–849.

Teece, D. J. (2010). Business models, business strategy and innovation. *Long Range Planning, 43*(2), 172–194.

Tukker, A. (2004). Eight types of product–service system: Eight ways to sustainability? Experiences from SusProNet. *Business Strategy and the Environment, 13*(4), 246–260.

Venkatraman, N. (1989). The concept of fit in strategy research: Toward verbal and statistical correspondence. *Academy of Management Review, 14*(3), 423–444.

Vezzoli, C., Ceschin, F., Diehl, J. C., & Kohtala, C. (2015). New design challenges to widely implement 'sustainable product-service systems.' *Journal of Cleaner Production, 97*, 1–12.

Visnjic Kastalli, I., Van Looy, B., & Neely, A. (2013). Steering manufacturing firms towards service business model innovation. *California Management Review, 56*(1), 100–123.

Zarpelon Neto, G., Pereira, G. M., & Borchardt, M. (2015). What problems manufacturing companies can face when providing services around the world? *Journal of Business & Industrial Marketing, 30*(5), 461–471.

Business Models for Digital Service Infusion Using AI and Big Data

Lars Witell

1 Introduction

Manufacturing firms routinely add services and, more recently, digital services to their value proposition (Baines et al., 2017). When this leads to organizational transformation, it is known as *servitization*; when the change relates only to the firm's offering, it is called *service infusion* (Kowalkowski et al., 2017). Service infusion involves a change in the business model to improve competitiveness (Forkmann et al., 2017). In manufacturing firms, digitalization aids service infusion, creating new opportunities for services, platforms, intelligent products and novel business models (Kohtamäki et al., 2019), and increasing sales of digital services can lead to organizational transformation through *digital servitization*. The present chapter explores how digitalization supports service infusion, which may lead in the longer term to digital servitization.

Firms such as Volvo, SKF and Ericsson are investing heavily into developing and growing their range of digital services. However, this far the digital services are only a small part of the turnover from these services. Gebauer, Fleisch et al. (2020) even suggest that there is a digital paradox, i.e. that

L. Witell (✉)
Linköping University, Linköping, Sweden
e-mail: lars.witell@kau.se; lars.witell@liu.se

Karlstad University, Karlstad, Sweden

© The Author(s), under exclusive license to Springer Nature Switzerland AG 2021
M. Kohtamäki et al. (eds.), *The Palgrave Handbook of Servitization*,
https://doi.org/10.1007/978-3-030-75771-7_7

investments to procure and develop digital technologies rarely pay off. It might seem counterintuitive since the digital potential of manufacturers is often emphasized, but can Internet of Things (IoT), Artificial Intelligence (AI) and Big Data unlock the digital paradox? The present chapter reflects on the role of these technologies in different business models and how they influence service provision, highlighting theoretical and managerial implications for digital service infusion.

2   Theoretical Framework

Digital Service Infusion

Kowalkowski et al., (2017, p. 7) characterized servitization as '*the transformational process of shifting from a product-centric business model and logic to a service-centric approach*'. This description implies a reconfiguration of the manufacturer's resources, capabilities and structures—that is, an organizational transformation. However, the so-called *digital paradox* means that few manufacturers have achieved this organizational transformation when digitalizing because it is unfeasible to reorganize a firm for digital services when these account for only 1–4% of turnover (Gebauer, Arzt et al., 2020). As a service-induced change in the offering (Nilsson et al., 2001) or business model, service infusion is a more limited change than servitization (Kowalkowski et al., 2017). Digital service infusion exploits digital technologies, data and information to provide new services. The key assumption is that digital service infusion will provide opportunities for value co-creation with customers and value capture for the service provider. According to Eloranta and Turunen (2015), co-operation between different actors in the service ecosystem may be a prerequisite for value co-creation through digital service infusion.

The service encounter has traditionally been understood as any interaction between an employee and a customer (Solomon et al., 1985), either in person or over the phone. Over time, the boundaries of the service encounter have expanded to include all interactions mediated by technology, including online and IoT interactions. Larivière et al. (2017, p. 239) defined the service encounter as '*any customer-company interaction that results from a service system that is comprised of interrelated technologies (either company- or customer-owned), human actors (employees and customers), physical/digital environments and company/customer processes*'. One implication of digital service infusion is that service encounters will increasingly involve digital interactions between employees and customers, and in some cases, automated digital service encounters. Infusing digital technologies can change the service encounter in three ways. First, digital technology can augment the capabilities of employees during the service encounter (Marinova et al., 2017). Second, automated service encounters can reduce costs and standardize service encounters by replacing service employees with digital technologies (Marinova et al., 2017). Finally, digital technologies can facilitate network connections and relationships through digital platforms and IoT. From a business model perspective, such service encounters must ensure value co-creation, even in the absence of service employees.

IoT, AI and Big Data

IoT, AI and Big Data are important digital technologies in a service infusion strategy of a firm. By investing in IoT and AI, service providers can offer digital services based on monitoring and analysing equipment performance (Sjödin et al., 2020). The term *internet of things* (IoT) was coined by Kevin Ashton in 1999 to describe the interconnection of physical objects through sensors that aid identification, sensing, communication and data collection, making equipment 'smart' (Ashton, 2009). By capturing in-depth information about how customers are using the equipment, service providers can develop innovative solutions and data- and information-driven digital services (Suppatvech et al., 2019).

In the two major research streams in social sciences on the progress of AI, the service and technology literatures tend to focus on the positive aspects of AI as technology, while the economics literature typically explores the effects of AI on employees and employment (Huang & Rust, 2021). Discussing these alternative views of AI in more detail, Davenport et al. (2020) distinguished between (1) the use of AI to interpret external data and to learn and adapt in a flexible way; and (2) its use to automate business processes, gain insights from data and engage employees or customers.

Huang and Rust (2021) argue that AI involves digital technologies that can learn, connect and adapt. In certain cases, learning is the key capability, but not all AI is designed to learn. The authors further argue that AI has two key characteristics, self-learning and connectivity. These characteristics result in AI being able to adapt to changing customer needs. AI can self-improve automatically by learning from various inputs (e.g. Big Data and machine learning). AI's connectivity is most apparent in Internet of Things (IoT) applications, which link machines, objects and data flow to facilitate learning.

AI is commonly associated with Big Data, which Manyika (2012) characterized as datasets whose size makes them impossible to capture, store, manage or analyse using traditional software tools. Examples include enterprise data, sensor data and social data (Opresnik & Taisch, 2015), where the key concerns are volume, velocity, variety, verification and value. By incorporating IoT in their equipment, servitizing manufacturers can already control the volume, velocity and variety of data, and work is progressing on verification and value. In particular, the challenge for many manufacturers is to identify how access to Big Data can be used to co-create and capture value.

Business Models

Changing the offering through digital technologies enables a new service business model for manufacturing firms which represents how a firm intends to compete in a specific market (Forkmann et al., 2017). Teece (2010) characterized the business model as '*the design or architecture of the value creation, delivery, and capture mechanisms*' (p. 191). For present purposes, we have adopted Johnson et al. (2008) conceptualization of how business models can be effectively developed and changed. On this view, a business model comprises four interconnected elements that drive value co-creation and value capture: value proposition, profit formula, key resources and key processes. In the context of digital service infusion, a *value proposition* can be understood in terms of the characteristics of different service offerings (Eggert et al., 2014); the *profit formula* reflects how a firm captures value; and as prerequisites for the value proposition, *key resources* and *key processes* encompass digital technology and service capabilities (Valtakoski & Witell, 2018). According to Forkmann et al. (2017), key resources and processes can reside within the firm, partners and customers. For digital service infusion, the focus is on changes in the value proposition and profit formula, but when these lead to major changes in key resources and key processes, it starts digital servitization.

Business Models for IoT, AI and Big Data

In much the same way as they began to test different business models when moving services from free to fee (Witell & Löfgren, 2013), manufacturers now test business models for digital services. During the trial-and-error phase of business models to grow their digital service business, manufacturers commonly preinstall IoT in their equipment and encourage customers to try it free of charge, which provides access to valuable operational data.

Vendrell-Herrero et al. (2018) contended that digital service infusion can change business models in three ways: by implementing IoT to enhance business models based on traditional equipment and services; through innovative use of digital technologies to enhance value creation, delivery and capture for an existing digital service; and in the case of new entrants, by using digital technologies and services to compete with traditional manufacturers.

Among empirical studies of business models for digital services, Paiola and Gebauer (2020) identified three business models employing IoT for product-, process- and outcome-oriented digital servitization, oriented, respectively, to the firm's product, the customer's process and the customer's business. The success of these business models depends on gaining access to data from customer operations, enabling the manufacturer to fully understand customer needs and exploiting IoT to incorporate digital services in their new service strategy. Rymaszewska et al. (2017) identified four business models based on IoT: (1) option in a product (no fee), (2) IoT sold as an investment, (3) part of a larger service contract and (4) monthly fee. However, not all manufacturers provide equipment that makes it financially viable for the customer to invest in IoT or to use such digital services. In their review of existing research on digital services, Suppatvech et al. (2019) identified four types of IoT-enabled business models: add-on, sharing, usage-based and solutions-oriented (see Table 1). In the trial-and-error phase of developing an offering based on digital technologies, most larger manufacturers offer digital services following these four business models. Depending on their position in the market, the competitive situation and the type of customer, which business model that grow the fastest might vary. In the following, we will discuss digital service infusion based on these IoT-enabled business models.

3   Discussion

This theoretical framework allows us to identify a number of critical issues for digital service infusion in terms of the different demands of the three main actors (manufacturer, customer, new entrant). The *manufacturer* wants to increase value co-creation and productivity by providing advanced digital services that will reduce costs and, ideally, capture a larger proportion of co-created value. The *customer* would like to increase productivity while paying less for digital services, as they can see that the manufacturer has lowered costs by reducing the involvement of employees in service encounters. Finally, the new entrants would like to access or install IoT in existing equipment to aid customers in more efficient value creation and capture some of this value.

Table 1 An overview of business models for digital services

	Add-On	Sharing	Usage-based	Solutions-oriented
Description	Using IoT to enable digital services to existing equipment and purchased services	Customers pay to use or access equipment for a limited period, allowing different users to access the equipment	Using IoT to measure equipment usage; customers pay for or subscribe to a plan based on their needs	Using IoT to enable provision of solutions to customers. Firms make agreements with customers to deliver a specified outcome
Value proposition	IoT connects and attaches digital services to equipment	IoT enables customers to identify and access free equipment when they need it	IoT enables customers to pay for the degree to which they use a specific equipment	IoT enables the firm to improve customer production processes to ensure a specific outcome
Profit formula	Transactional or paid for through equipment charges	Pay-per-use	Pay-per-use, subscription, performance-based contract	Long-term contracts
Key resources	IoT	IoT	IoT, AI	IoT, AI, Big Data
Key processes	Value co-creation and value capture	Asset utilization	Transparency and full control of costs	Improvement and optimization
Example	Valmet, Volvo	Car2Go	Xerox	Valmet, Volvo

In other words, business models for digital service infusion must meet the differing needs of manufacturers and customers, otherwise, the manufacturer will meet the competition of new entrants.

The Customer Perspective

For present purposes, customer equipment can be assigned to three categories (see Fig. 1). In the case of *critical equipment*, it is often financially preferable to use built-in IoT, which often includes expensive sensors and related technology that provides detailed information about equipment status, aided by AI that analyses the data using Big Data algorithms. This gives the manufacturer a competitive advantage, as they are familiar with their equipment and understand what is measured, and how. However, in competitive markets where customers use equipment from several manufacturers, it may be inconvenient to use multiple digital platforms to access the various machines and data, digital platforms that support different equipment brands may prove attractive.

A second category is an *important equipment* for which the manufacturer's original IoT may prove too expensive; in such cases, less sophisticated IoT sensors may offer an adequate alternative at a fraction of the cost. New entrants can provide these sensors for different brands of equipment using a single digital platform. This poses a threat to equipment manufacturers, who resort to mergers and acquisitions or partnering to provide less expensive alternatives. Finally, there is equipment that offers *little or no payoff* for investing in digital services. In such cases, it may be preferable to invest in

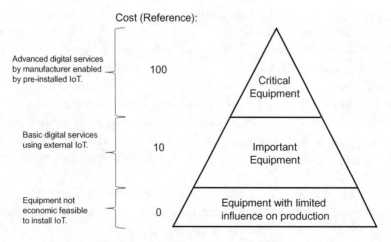

Fig. 1 An overview of digital services from the customer perspective

improving the equipment. Even in the case of equipment that is not critical for productivity, there may be legislative or safety issues that IoT can help to address. For example, in the case of equipment positioned in a physically challenging location where inspection and maintenance are difficult, IoT can offer a cheap solution that also ensures a safer work environment for maintenance staff.

The Manufacturer Perspective: From Digital Service Infusion to Digital Servitization

Manufacturers of critical equipment are uniquely placed to provide digital services to their customers. IoT business models of every type can be provided by the same manufacturer—in some cases to the same customer. Digital services based solely on IoT can be incorporated in all of the four suggested digital business models (Suppatvech et al., 2019). However, solutions-oriented business models may make value creation and capture difficult, as the investment may not be worthwhile for all customers. It all depends on how they can use the improved production process to capture more value from their customers, through increased volumes or improved quality.

One key issue for manufacturers is when to allow changes in the offering and revenue model to drive organizational transformation. In light of the digital paradox, most manufacturers remain focused on the 'bread and butter' of product sales and service provision while developing and testing new digital business models. Gebauer, Arzt et al. (2020) found that manufacturers who focus on adding digital services to product sales find it difficult to reach challenging targets for digital service infusion. As compared to traditional service infusion, there is a need for better customer knowledge at a more granular level (see Johansson et al., 2019) to ensure a better fit between service portfolio and customer segments. In particular, it is key to understand which customers have a business situation where they could take advantage of the benefits with the Usage-based and Solutions-oriented digital business models. To enable scaling these business models, increasing the knowledge about customers enable better segmentation of customers and an opportunity to scale these business models to the customers that have the largest benefit of them.

According to Gebauer, Arzt et al. (2020), manufacturers face three particular difficulties when moving into digital services: (1) failure to make progress towards changing the main business logic; (2) failure to overcome the management barrier; and (3) failure to fully develop and modify the value proposition and profit formula. A further key obstacle that is rarely discussed is the need to identify the right customer segments for digital services. In some industries where this customer segment may not be large enough to support rapid digital service infusion, the key question is what pace of investment in digital technologies will suffice, without limiting the manufacturer's further development.

How Digital Services and Business Models Influence the Service Encounter

As noted above, manufacturers of critical equipment are uniquely placed to provide digital services to their customers. Here, we discuss how different digital technologies influence the service encounter (see Larivière et al., 2017). Digital services based on IoT, AI and Big Data have significant potential to change the service encounter when used in solutions-oriented business models. As well as augmenting employees' ability to ensure better service encounters, these technologies can also replace service employees both at the service provider and the customer (Forkmann et al., 2017). By combining data from different sites or customers, AI can support network facilitation and knowledge co-creation with different customers.

Digital services based on IoT, AI and Big Data have the potential to change the service encounter in novel ways by creating new service encounters and by influencing service encounters further down the value network (i.e. the customers' customer). Big Data has the potential to disrupt the service encounter and to link such encounters in new ways. These services may prove crucial for many manufacturers in enhancing value co-creation and capture.

For new entrants seeking to disrupt an existing business relationship using new digital services (Vendrell-Herrero et al., 2018), three strategies in particular have significant potential: (1) To focus on the important equipment; Digital services using AI can aid customers in both improving working conditions, improving maintenance and through cost savings; (2) To provide a digital platform for all types of equipment; This enables the customer to access all data through one platform independent of brand or type of equipment; (3) To focus on digital services where Big Data can be used for the customers' customer.

Theoretical Contributions

This book chapter has three main theoretical implications for the use of digital services based on IoT, AI and Big Data. First, it discusses digital service infusion in relation to the digital paradox (Gebauer, Fleisch et al., 2020) and takes a critical perspective and suggests that digital service infusion might not necessarily be a quick route to infusing the business model with digital technologies. It further suggests that that the add-on business model, in the short term, has limited business potential, while more advanced digital business models have higher business potential, but that these might not be viable for most customer segments. Increased customer knowledge is the key, to better match the service portfolio and customer segment.

Second, it connects new digital technologies, business models and how they influence the service encounter. In relation to the three ways digital technology can change the service encounter (Larivière et al., 2017), this research identifies additional ways that a service provider can disrupt the service encounter. In particular, AI and Big Data have the potential to not only change the existing service encounter but connect it to subsequent service encounters. This is a key insight, since more knowledge is needed on the implications of digital technologies to understand both value creation and value capture.

Third, the research on servitization and service infusion has emphasized the key role of the installed base (Oliva & Kallenberg, 2003) and most research has taken the perspective of the manufacturer (Forkmann et al., 2017). In addition to the key role of the manufacturer, this research discusses the opportunities for new entrants to pursue digital service infusion (Vendrell-Herrero et al., 2018). The three strategies for new entrants complement existing strategies for manufacturers and can in further research be used to understand how the competitive situation changes when pursuing different digital service strategies. By taking a customer perspective, the book chapter discusses for what equipment that new entrants might have a better value proposition than the digital services offered by the manufacturer.

Managerial Contributions

A key managerial insight is to understand for whom and when to offer services based on the advanced digital business models and when to resolve to offer services based on the less advanced digital business models. The ability to identify customers and equipment that can benefit from IoT, Big Data and AI can enhance value capture through cost savings and additional sales. The fierce competition generated by IoT, AI and Big Data means there is a pressing need to decide how to address the digital paradox. Should your firm invest in developing in-house solutions? Should your firm begin by providing these to customers free of charge? How should you approach digital service infusion? These are key questions and many of them can only be answered by creating a strategic roadmap for digital service infusion and digital servitization. If the pandemic has taught us anything, it is that digital service infusion can be extremely rapid if the motivation is right.

A final key managerial insight is that the service ecosystem can be developed by incorporating cheaper IoT, depending on the needs of customers and service providers. The ability to offer cheaper solutions, at least for support equipment, is important for many customers. For service providers, offering such solutions can drive business growth and help to develop a platform that includes competitor brands.

References

Ashton, K. (2009). That 'Internet of Things' thing. *RFID Journal, 22*(7), 97–114.

Baines, T., Bigdeli, A. Z., Bustinza, O. F., Shi, V. G., Baldwin, J., & Ridgway, K. (2017). Servitization: Revisiting the state-of-the-art and research priorities. *International Journal of Operations & Production Management, 37*(2), 256–278.

Davenport, T., Guha, A., Grewal, D., & Bressgott, T. (2020). How artificial intelligence will change the future of marketing. *Journal of the Academy of Marketing Science, 48*(1), 24–42.

Eggert, A., Hogreve, J., Ulaga, W., & Muenkhoff, E. (2014). Revenue and profit implications of industrial service strategies. *Journal of Service Research, 17*(1), 23–39.

Eloranta, V., & Turunen, T. (2015). Seeking competitive advantage with service infusion: A systematic literature review. *Journal of Service Management, 26*(3), 394–425.

Forkmann, S., Henneberg, S. C., Witell, L., & Kindström, D. (2017). Driver configurations for successful service infusion. *Journal of Service Research, 20*(3), 275–291.

Gebauer, H., Arzt, A., Kohtamäki, M., Lamprecht, C., Parida, V., Witell, L., & Wortmann, F. (2020). How to convert digital offerings into revenue enhancement—Conceptualizing business model dynamics through explorative case studies. *Industrial Marketing Management, 91,* 429–441.

Gebauer, H., Fleisch, E., Lamprecht, C., & Wortmann, F. (2020). Growth paths for overcoming the digitalization paradox. *Business Horizons, 63*(3), 313–323.

Huang, M. H., & Rust, R. T. (2021). Engaged to a robot? The role of AI in service. *Journal of Service Research, 24*(1), 30–41.

Johansson, A. E., Raddats, C., & Witell, L. (2019). The role of customer knowledge development for incremental and radical service innovation in servitized manufacturers. *Journal of Business Research, 98,* 328–338.

Johnson, M. W., Christensen, C. M., & Kagermann, H. (2008). Reinventing your business model. *Harvard Business Review, 86* (12), 57–68.

Kohtamäki, M., Parida, V., Oghazi, P., Gebauer, H., & Baines, T. (2019). Digital servitization business models in ecosystems: A theory of the firm. *Journal of Business Research, 104*, 380–392.

Kowalkowski, C., Gebauer, H., Kamp, B., & Parry, G. (2017). Servitization and deservitization: Overview, concepts, and definitions. *Industrial Marketing Management, 60*, 4–10.

Larivière, B., Bowen, D., Andreassen, T. W., Kunz, W., Sirianni, N. J., Voss, C., Wünderlich, N. W., & De Keyser, A. (2017). "Service Encounter 2.0": An investigation into the roles of technology, employees and customers. *Journal of Business Research, 79*, 238–246.

Manyika, J. (2012). *Manufacturing the future: The next era of global growth and innovation.* McKinsey Global Institute, NY.

Marinova, D., de Ruyter, K., Huang, M. H., Meuter, M. L., & Challagalla, G. (2017). Getting smart: Learning from technology-empowered frontline interactions. *Journal of Service Research, 20* (1), 29–42.

Nilsson, L., Johnson, M. D., & Gustafsson, A. (2001). The impact of quality practices on customer satisfaction and business results: Product versus service organizations. *Journal of Quality Management, 6* (1), 5–27.

Oliva, R., & Kallenberg, R. (2003). Managing the transition from products to services. *International Journal of Service Industry Management, 14* (2), 160–172.

Opresnik, D., & Taisch, M. (2015). The value of big data in servitization. *International Journal of Production Economics, 165*, 174–184.

Paiola, M., & Gebauer, H. (2020). Internet of things technologies, digital servitization and business model innovation in BtoB manufacturing firms. *Industrial Marketing Management, 89*, 245–264.

Rymaszewska, A., Helo, P., & Gunasekaran, A. (2017). IoT powered servitization of manufacturing–an exploratory case study. *International Journal of Production Economics, 192*, 92–105.

Sjödin, D., Parida, V., Kohtamäki, M., & Wincent, J. (2020). An agile co-creation process for digital servitization: A micro-service innovation approach. *Journal of Business Research, 112*, 478–491.

Solomon, M. R., Surprenant, C., Czepiel, J. A., & Gutman, E. G. (1985). A role theory perspective on dyadic interactions: The service encounter. *Journal of Marketing, 49* (1), 99–111.

Suppatvech, C., Godsell, J., & Day, S. (2019). The roles of internet of things technology in enabling servitized business models: A systematic literature review. *Industrial Marketing Management, 82*, 70–86.

Teece, D. J. (2010). Business models, business strategy and innovation. *Long Range Planning, 43* (2–3), 172–194.

Valtakoski, A., & Witell, L. (2018). Service capabilities and servitized SME performance: Contingency on firm age. *International Journal of Operations & Production Management, 38* (4), 1144–1164.

Vendrell-Herrero, F., Parry, G., Bustinza, O. F., & Gomes, E. (2018). Digital business models: Taxonomy and future research avenues. *Strategic Change, 27*(2), 87–90.

Witell, L., & Löfgren, M. (2013). From service for free to service for fee: Business model innovation in manufacturing firms. *Journal of Service Management, 24*(5), 520–533.

Towards Servitization: A Taxonomy of Industrial Product-Service Systems for Small- and Medium-Sized Manufacturers

Alexander Kreyenborg, Frederik Möller, Michael Henke, and Max Niemann

1 Introduction

In light of globalized markets, manufacturers face the transition from conventional product-dominant business models to solution provider business models (Kohtamäki et al., 2019, p. 213), because the resulting industrial product-service systems (IPSS) can be significant differentiators. Nevertheless, many companies struggle to evaluate their IPSS portfolio and identify the amendments required to implement advanced IPSS, especially in light of digitalization. That is particularly critical for small and medium-sized

A. Kreyenborg (✉) · F. Möller · M. Henke · M. Niemann
Chair of Enterprise Logistics, TU Dortmund University, Dortmund, Germany
e-mail: alexander.kreyenborg@tu-dortmund.de

F. Möller
e-mail: frederik.moeller@tu-dortmund.de

M. Henke
e-mail: michael.henke@tu-dortmund.de

M. Niemann
e-mail: max.niemann@tu-dortmund.de

F. Möller
Chair for Industrial Information Management, TU Dortmund University, Dortmund, Germany

© The Author(s), under exclusive license to Springer Nature Switzerland AG 2021
M. Kohtamäki et al. (eds.), *The Palgrave Handbook of Servitization*,
https://doi.org/10.1007/978-3-030-75771-7_8

manufacturers (SMMs) as they have limited resources and usually lack a comprehensive servitization strategy (Michalik et al., 2019, p. 2328). Following Rondini et al. (2018), SMMs still receive insufficient attention in IPSS research. In particular, that is important when considering that 85% of all German companies are SMMs (VDMA, 2015, p. 22). Additionally, the manufacturing sector is Germany's largest industrial employer (VDMA, 2015, p. 8). A suitable approach is to generate a taxonomy (Glass & Vessey, 1995), which is useful to make complex domains accessible by classifying objects and deconstructing them (Nickerson et al., 2013, p. 336). That enables manufacturers and researchers to classify their current and intended product-service-portfolios within an IPSS continuum (Lay, 2014, p. 59). Because there is a lack of taxonomies explicitly addressing SMMs, the authors propose a socio-technical based approach. Although the motivation primarily addresses SMMs, the proposed taxonomy development considers both SMMs and large manufacturers providing the broadest possible coverage. We follow a configurational approach to identify central dimensions and characteristics and, subsequently, offer insight into which IPSS configurations SMMs and large manufacturers exhibit. Thus, we correlate the findings with financial data and address the following research question (**RQ**):

Are there typical IPSS configurations, and do they affect financial success?

2   Theoretical Background

Configuration Approach

Configurations enable their user to identify, conceptualize and, ultimately, reuse fundamental mechanisms and determinants of the object under consideration (Kohtamäki et al., 2019). In Service Science, there is vast potential in identifying determinants (i.e. design dimensions) to design and conceptualize new business models (Kohtamäki et al., 2019). A suitable tool to assist the configuration approach is the morphology, which explicitly analyses an object's constituent characteristics, i.e. the *Gestalt* (Ritchey, 2014). Recently, a strain of research has emerged that develops morphologies taxonomically, i.e. through collecting empirical and literature-based data to conceptualize design dimensions and characteristics of, for example, business models or services in manufacturing industries (e.g. Azkan et al., 2020). According to Nickerson et al. (2013, p. 340), a taxonomy consists of dimensions, each with "*mutually exclusive and collectively exhaustive characteristics*", enabling an intuitive way to characterize even complex IPSS. The characterization of IPSS constellations and business models is a focal point for researchers. Reim et al. (2015, p. 66f) identify five tactics, namely "*contracts, marketing, network, product and service design and sustainability*". Lay et al. (2009, p. 447) propose a morphological framework, which emphasizes organizational elements such as "payment model", to support managerial decisions. Weking et al. (2018) published a taxonomy of industry 4.0 business models, focusing on value creation elements, target customers and business model architecture. Frank et al. (2019) elaborate on adopting and using industry 4.0 technologies in increasingly complex systems. They identify three stages of implementation and allocate appropriate technologies. Gebauer et al. (2013, p. 44) identify four types of service networks and provide a catalogue of capabilities required for providing services. Boßlau and Meier (2012) develop an IPSS business model morphology, which includes the partial models "value", "organization", "risk distribution", "revenue streams" and "property rights". Azkan et al. (2020) propose a taxonomy of data-driven services in manufacturing industries, focusing heavily on leveraging data as the central resource to generate novel services. In summary, some approaches for IPSS characterization have been identified, but none focuses explicitly on the socio-technical aspects of SMMs in the servitization process.

Servitization and Industrial Product-Service Systems

The term servitization was introduced by Vandermerwe and Rada (1988) and describes—in context of manufacturing—the shift from product-oriented to service-oriented value creation alongside an IPSS continuum. According to Rabetino et al. (2018), servitization-related research can be divided into three communities: PSS group, Solution Business, and Service Science. They encourage further linking of these communities and point out that the human dimension of servitization needs to be considered. The need for new approaches is emphasized, "*addressing the servitization process, especially the particularities of organisational change processes during servitization*" (Rabetino et al., 2018, p. 363). Any servitization effort requires a holistic management perspective (Clegg et al., 2017, p. 82), which includes recognizing IPSS as a socio-technical challenge (Meier et al., 2010, p. 608). IPSS are hybrid solutions consisting of tangible goods and an immaterial service offering, consequently blurring the boundaries between both (Goedkopp et al., 1999, p. 19). The categorization of IPSS configurations as product-oriented, use-oriented or result-oriented by Tukker (2004) very common and adopted in this paper. Scholars have also proposed different approaches to characterizing IPSS according to the value created or business model morphology perspectives (Boßlau et al., 2017; Brax & Visintin, 2018; Weking et al., 2018). Several factors have accelerated the process of servitization. These include saturated markets, low margins in sales of equipment, rising demand for digital or customized solutions and high volatility. The understanding that the offering of services can mitigate the adverse influences mentioned above is widespread (Annarelli et al., 2019, p. 21ff). However, the relationship between services provided and positive (financial) effects may not be linear. The provision of advanced services often leads to higher costs than increasing margins (Sousa & da Silveira, 2017). Some authors such as Sklyar et al. (2019) explore the interplay between servitization and digitalization, analysing the incorporation of digital tools and capabilities into the transformation process. Kohtamäki et al. (2020) propose a non-linear interaction between digitalization and servitization on one side and financial performance on the other side. Mirroring the "service paradox" (Gebauer et al., 2005), a "digitalization paradox" is formulated, which emphasizes the importance of effective servitization management (Kohtamäki et al., 2020, p. 25f). IPSS development is also hampered by factors such as the financial resources available, which can differ considerably, particularly when comparing SMMs and large manufacturers (Jesus Pacheco et al., 2019, p. 905ff). Baines et al. (2017) identify the possible influence of disruptive innovations, technological shifts and social aspects of servitization as an essential avenue for future research. Financial frameworks able to support successful IPSS have also been determined to be of interest.

Understanding IPSS as a socio-technical continuum aims to shed ample light on the servitization process, including the human dimension, which has often been ignored. Thus, the paper at hand aims to add to this matter in the form of a taxonomy, which is deeply rooted in a socio-technical approach, supported by the Dortmunder Management Modell (DMM) (Henke et al., 2019). We chose the DMM as it is a suitable conceptual framework that includes all elements that we have identified as highly important above, i.e. technology, human, organization and digital information (Michalik et al., 2019). The fourth dimension reflects digitalization as a significant component for servitization (Kohtamäki et al., 2020, p. 24).

Research Design for Taxonomy Development

For systematic taxonomy development and evaluation, the authors follow the guidelines by Nickerson et al. (2013), a widely used and accepted method. To

Table 1 Abbreviated objective and subjective ending conditions as proposed by Nickerson et al. (2013, p. 344)

Objective ending conditions	Subjective ending conditions
• All objects or a representative sub-sample have been classified and no changes were made in the last iteration	• The taxonomy gives purposeful information on an object, i.e., it is meaningful and explanatory without being overwhelming
• No characteristic or dimension is empty or was added/merged in the last iteration	• The taxonomy can be used to classify objects and new dimensions and characteristics can easily be added
• Every characteristic and dimension is unique and free of redundancy	

ensure a robust conceptual foundation, the authors constructed the taxonomy by synthesizing literature. The taxonomy was then validated by building a database of 60 randomly selected firms, using the DAFNE database, which contains information on more than 1.000.000 German companies (dafne, 2019), and analysing their IPSS portfolios. For each iteration, five to ten firms were analysed. Upon reaching the ending conditions presented in Table 1, the iterative process was terminated.

The selected manufacturers were analysed based on their web presence, which is considered to be target-oriented, as companies tend to present their offerings transparently (Hartmann et al., 2016, p. 1389; Teece, 2010). Analysing both SMMs and large manufacturers enables a broader coverage of the IPSS continuum and an analysis of the actual differences in IPSS portfolios. By linking manufacturers' IPSS portfolios and financial indicators, we can derive new insights into the influence of IPSS configurations on financial indicators. As this research focuses on manufacturers of industrial machinery and equipment, the query was limited to manufacturers belonging to the NACE sector (Nomenclature statistique des activités économiques dans la Communauté Européenne) classified with code 28 (European Union, 2006). Following the German Institut für Mittelstandsforschung (2016), manufacturers with up to 499 employees and a turnover of 50 million € are classified as SMMs. Altogether, there are 1.551 SMMs and 203 large manufacturers that fit their respective definitions. For further research, only solvent companies with financial data from 2006–2018 were included. The sample used for this analysis includes 30 SMMs and 30 large manufacturers.

3   IPSS Taxonomy as Analysis Framework

At its core, the taxonomy shown in Table 2 is built upon the four dimensions (D) of the DMM, ensuring a robust socio-technical foundation (see Sect. 2 in chapter "Digital Servitization: How Manufacturing Firms Can Enhance Resource Integration and Drive Ecosystem Transformation"). In total, the design required four iterations until no further adjustments were necessary. The paper focuses on describing the dimensions rather than illustrating the iteration steps to ensure comprehensibility. Sub-dimensions (SD) are formulated (italicized in the text) based on the overarching dimensions, synthesizing previous literature on IPSS taxonomies (see Sect. 3 in chapter "Digital Servitization: How Manufacturing Firms Can Enhance Resource Integration and Drive Ecosystem Transformation") and resulting in conceptual characteristics. They are further developed and validated by applying the taxonomy to classify IPSS of randomly selected manufacturers (see Sect. 1 in chapter "Product-Service Systems in the Digital Era: Deconstructing Servitization Business Model Typologies").

Human Resources

The *nature of labour* SD is heavily influenced by the classification model for intellectual work by Hacker and Richter (2003). Our research has shown that the classification of tasks fulfilled by employees in the manufacturing sector as solely manual labour is not fitting. That is corroborated by the respective literature (Modrow-Thiel et al., 2010, p. 134ff).

The employees require specific competencies or capabilities (Dotti et al., 2013, p. 2067). For instance, operating a machine tool correctly and efficiently requires "process know-how" (Ani & Baghdadi, 2015, p. 5). By including characteristics that describe both the general type of work and the required skills, the taxonomy offers additional value compared to other approaches to classifying the human role regarding IPSS.

Technical Dimension

The "Industry 4.0 Maturity Index" published by Schuh et al. (2017) offers unique guidance in classifying businesses according to their prowess in terms of digital processes. Moreover, enterprises can be located along a transformation axis, ideal for a taxonomy. Data used to provide or support services must travel through predetermined data channels that need to conform to

Table 2 Taxonomy used to compare two offerings, Blue pattern = repair service, Orange pattern = total solution

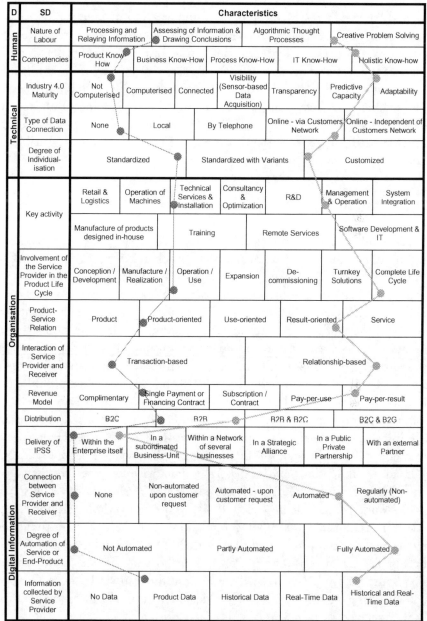

D	SD	Characteristics							
Human	Nature of Labour	Processing and Relaying Information	Assessing of Information & Drawing Conclusions		Algorithmic Thought Processes		Creative Problem Solving		
	Competencies	Product Know-How	Business Know-How		Process Know-How		IT Know-How		Holistic Know-how
Technical	Industry 4.0 Maturity	Not Computerised	Computerised	Connected	Visibility (Sensor-based Data Acquisition)	Transparency		Predictive Capacity	Adaptability
	Type of Data Connection	None	Local		By Telephone	Online - via Customers Network		Online - Independent of Customers Network	
	Degree of Individualisation	Standardized			Standardized with Variants			Customized	
Organisation	Key activity	Retail & Logistics	Operation of Machines	Technical Services & Installation	Consultancy & Optimization	R&D		Management & Operation	System Integration
		Manufacture of products designed in-house		Training		Remote Services		Software Development & IT	
	Involvement of the Service Provider in the Product Life Cycle	Conception / Development	Manufacture / Realization	Operation / Use	Expansion		De-commissioning	Turnkey Solutions	Complete Life Cycle
	Product-Service Relation	Product	Product-oriented		Use-oriented		Result-oriented		Service
	Interaction of Service Provider and Receiver	Transaction-based				Relationship-based			
	Revenue Model	Complimentary	Single Payment or Financing Contract		Subscription / Contract		Pay-per-use		Pay-per-result
	Distribution	B2C		B2B		B2B & B2C		B2C & B2G	
	Delivery of IPSS	Within the Enterprise itself	In a subordinated Business-Unit		Within a Network of several businesses	In a Strategic Alliance		In a Public Private Partnership	With an external Partner
Digital Information	Connection between Service Provider and Receiver	None	Non-automated upon customer request		Automated - upon customer request		Automated		Regularly (Non-automated)
	Degree of Automation of Service or End-Product	Not Automated			Partly Automated			Fully Automated	
	Information collected by Service Provider	No Data	Product Data		Historical Data		Real-Time Data		Historical and Real-Time Data

the offering at hand. Weking et al. (2018) identify offline, online, and intermediary channels of data between the service provider and service receivers. Ani and Baghdadi (2015) also propose using legacy and cloud solutions.

An additional SD has been derived from literature to characterize the complexity and the degree of individualization of the solutions offered. Individualization is a key element of IPSS, as it integrates the customer into the provisioning process (Meier et al., 2010, p. 607). Differentiating between mass or niche markets is also a helpful means of classifying products and services (Boßlau et al., 2017, p. 307). Thus, the taxonomy includes characteristics that differentiate standard, customized, and products available in variants.

Organization

Processes, next to resources and capabilities, are at the core of every IPSS and influence other organizational aspects (Boßlau et al., 2017, p. 307). The *key activity* SD has been designed to allow for meaningful differences to be detected between the products and services offered. Other scholars such as Mastrogiacomo et al. (2019) or Gaiardelli et al. (2014) have identified archetypes of product-oriented services. Building upon these publications, the authors have refined the concept regarding SMMs and the use in the taxonomy. The possibility to engage with customers more intensively is a key benefit of IPSS (Annarelli et al., 2019, p. 22f). To illustrate this, the product life cycle aspect has been included to allow insights into which life cycle phases the manufacturer is involved in (DIN, 2014). Furthermore, characteristics identifying turnkey solutions and complete life cycle offerings have been added (Brax & Visintin, 2018, p. 92f). Following Tukker (2004) we adopted the dimension *Product-Service Relation* with its respective characteristics. The SD *interaction of service provider and receiver* has been inspired by the work of Gaiardelli et al. (2014), who classify IPSS as transaction-based or relationship-based. In conjunction with the SD concerning the involvement in the product life cycle, this SD offers unique insights into the supplier–client relationship. Previous analyses of revenue models in the IPSS context have been screened concerning their applicability to German manufacturing enterprises (Boßlau & Meier, 2012, p. 8; Weking et al., 2018, p. 5). The *revenue model* SD in this taxonomy results from this literature review. Similarly, the *distribution* SD was inspired by previous entries in the IPSS literature by scholars such as J. H. Lee, D. I. Shin, Y. S. Hong and Y. S. Kim (2011). The fact that IPSS may be provided to customers by a network of businesses has been explored by several authors (Lim et al., 2012; Reim et al., 2015). For this taxonomy, the authors have reviewed the literature on business cooperation and implemented appropriate characteristics into the taxonomy (Jansen, 2016). Furthermore, the sub-dimensions *revenue model*, *distribution* and *delivery of IPSS* can be traced back to the Business Model Canvas by Osterwalder and Pigneur (2010).

Digital Information

The final dimension *digital information* regards the character and type of information exchanged between the service provider and service receiver. Coreynen et al. (2017) postulate "back-end" and "front-end" paths for digitalization in servitization contexts. Whereas the technical dimension entries may be interpreted as back-end components, the *information* dimension details front-end components. Data can be collected in a multitude of ways, the most advanced being real-time data acquisition programmes (Dotti et al., 2013, p. 2065). Other data-based services may rely on historical data (Herterich et al., 2016, p. 1240). Data may also be used to automate certain parts of a service or even entire offerings. The authors adopt the categorization used by Feng et al. (2011) and differentiate between *not, partly* and *fully automated* processes.

Analysis of Two Manufacturers by Exemplary Taxonomy Application

Table 2 shows two excerpts from specific offerings within separate IPSS-portfolios visualized as patterns. In the interest of brevity, the authors have decided to show the taxonomy's applicability by contrasting two examples—an SMM and a large manufacturer—that have stemmed from the analysis of the manufacturers.

The **blue pattern** shows a typical product-oriented repair service. The *taxonomy's human dimension* illustrates that for a service like this, employees require know-how regarding the product to be maintained and need to conclude from the information presented. The digital maturity of this service is low. Technicians can only assess the damage on-site, and no supporting information is passed through any data channels. The service is applicable only in the life cycle phase of actual use. Since these services are mostly requested on-demand, with contract-based services being the exception, the provider-receiver relationship is classified as transaction-based. These characteristics align with our observations in the technical dimension regarding the digital information dimension. As the service is not data-driven, only basic data is collected, and the service is carried out manually.

The comprehensive solution offering depicted by the **orange pattern** in Table 2 shows a high maturity in almost all respects. The solution is tailored to every customer's needs and spans the entire life cycle. Employees must adapt to new circumstances and demands constantly. They need to know how to deploy the product effectively and integrate all the solution components into customer's processes. The solution displays a high degree of industry 4.0 maturity. It can adapt autonomously to conditions made possible by the automated analysis of real-time and historical data. They are establishing a relationship-based affiliation between the service provider and service receiver. The revenue model binds customers in long-term contracts, which are of the "pay-per-result" fashion, further underlining this offering's result-oriented nature.

In summary, the taxonomy allows the characterization of both simple services and complex solutions. That provides coverage of the IPSS portfolio in the manufacturing industry and offers the conceptual basis for further research, addressing the **RQ** regarding typical IPSS configurations with its dimensions and characteristics of the taxonomy. Furthermore, it can be confirmed that there are typical IPSS configurations assigned to established IPSS classification approaches, e.g. according to Tukker (2004). It is noteworthy that no manufacturer classifies as a pure service provider or pure product manufacturer. Most manufacturers' IPSS portfolios are product-oriented. Figure 1 illustrates the IPSS classifications compared to the total profit margin, using the DAFNE database (see chapter "Typologies of Manufacturer Identities in the Age of Smart Solutions").

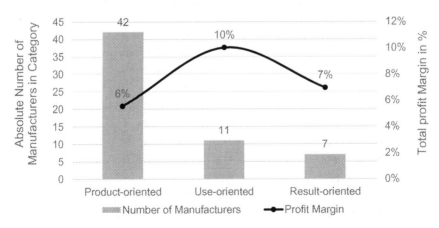

Fig. 1 Analysed manufacturers in classification scheme based on Tukker (2004)

Based on an analysis of all 678 products and services offered by the 60 manufacturers, on average, those offering use- or result-oriented IPSS display a higher profit margin than those who do not. Therefore, advanced IPSS configurations might be accompanied by financial success regarding the **RQ**. Admittedly, this is preliminary because the apparent link between IPSS configurations and financial indicators has not been statistically investigated, and therefore, no significant correlation can be confirmed within this contribution. Furthermore, the taxonomy may be used for more than pure classification since it might offer much more in-depth insights based on further analysis, such as a cluster analysis of the identified dimensions, to derive socio-technical IPSS configuration-patterns. That could provide important insights into which socio-technical aspects require special attention both in future research and practice.

4   Discussion

Current literature identifies numerous research opportunities, including new approaches to service strategies and decision support systems (Baines et al., 2017) and a lack of research on the "*interplay within and among the domains of strategy, structure, and business environment*" (Kohtamäki et al., 2019, p. 233). This contribution addresses the research gap in the domain of SMMs (Rondini et al., 2018). The authors propose a conceptually derived and empirically validated taxonomy covering the IPSS continuum of manufacturers in Germany. The taxonomy and the link to financial indicators will form the basis for further research work and new management approaches for sustainable servitization strategies.

Conceptual Contributions

Our taxonomy provides numerous contributions. First, as taxonomies are a type of analytic theory, they enable conceptualizing empirical knowledge and elevating it from a single instance (Gregor, 2006). Subsequently, it is a vehicle for generalization, a primary mechanism to contribute to the knowledge base on PSS configurations (Lee & Baskerville, 2003). Additionally, the taxonomy is a starting point for researchers to identify new types (e.g. with other *foci* than financial success), enabling structuring the field and finding innovative configurations. These types also help differentiation between generally and abstracted-from-detail idealized types (Weber, 1949).

Practical Implications

Using resources as efficiently as possible to compete in the global market is crucial for every company. However, this is a particular challenge for SMMs, operating successfully in the capital goods business for decades, which are now confronted with a holistic service transformation. Managers must understand moving in short steps along an IPSS continuum. It depends on the individual degree of servitization which dimensions of the taxonomy have to be considered less or more strongly. Therefore, managers can use the taxonomy as a starting point for understanding the socio-technical dimensions of servitization and deriving an idea of necessary fields of action at an early stage.

Limitations

There are also some limitations: Firstly, the applicability was examined with 60 companies and illustrated with two offers as examples. However, the taxonomy may evolve as more companies are considered. Secondly, the taxonomy application has not yet been tested in practice. Thirdly, the financial context is based on data that does not decompose the actual service revenue. However, in the academic community, this is an important indicator of the impact of servitization. Therefore, the link between IPSS configurations and total turnover can only be indirect evidence at most.

Acknowledgements This research was supported by the *Innovationlab Hybrid Services in Logistics* funded by the Germany Federal Ministry of Education.

References

Ani, B. A., & Baghdadi, Y. (2015). A taxonomy-centred process for service engineering. *International Journal of Computer Applications in Technology, 52*(1). https://doi.org/10.1504/IJCAT.2015.071415.

Annarelli, A., Battistella, C., & Nonino, F. (2019). *The road to servitization: How product service systems can disrupt companies' business models.* Springer.

Azkan, C., Iggena, L., Gür, I., Möller, F., & Otto, B. (2020). A taxonomy for data-driven services in manufacturing industries. In *Proceedings of the 24th Pacific Asia Conference on Information Systems,* Dubai, UAE.

Baines, T., Ziaee Bigdeli, A., Bustinza, O. F., Shi, V. G., Baldwin, J., & Ridgway, K. (2017). Servitization: Revisiting the state-of-the-art and research priorities.

International Journal of Operations & Production Management, 37(2), 256–278. https://doi.org/10.1108/IJOPM-06-2015-0312.

Boßlau, M., Gesing, J., Meier, H., & Wieseke, J. (2017). Geschäftsmodelle für Industrielle Produkt-Service Systeme. In H. Meier & E. Uhlmann (Eds.), *Industrielle Produkt-Service Systeme* (pp. 299–324). Springer Berlin Heidelberg. https://doi.org/10.1007/978-3-662-48018-2_13.

Boßlau, M., & Meier, H. (2012). *Dynamic business models for industrial product-service systems.* https://doi.org/10.13140/RG.2.1.5018.8960.

Brax, S. A., & Visintin, F. (2018). Value constellations in servitization. In M. Kohtamäki, T. Baines, R. Rabetino, & A. Z. Bigdeli (Eds.), *Practices and tools for servitization: Managing service transition* (pp. 83–95). Springer International Publishing. https://doi.org/10.1007/978-3-319-76517-4_5.

Clegg, B., Little, P., Govette, S., & Logue, J. (2017). Transformation of a small-to-medium-sized enterprise to a multi-organisation product-service solution provider. *International Journal of Production Economics, 192,* 81–91. https://doi.org/10.1016/j.ijpe.2017.01.012.

Coreynen, W., Matthyssens, P., & van Bockhaven, W. (2017). Boosting servitization through digitization: Pathways and dynamic resource configurations for manufacturers. *Industrial Marketing Management, 60,* 42–53. https://doi.org/10.1016/j.indmarman.2016.04.012.

Dafne. (2019). Retrieved from https://dafne.bvdinfo.com/.

de Jesus Pacheco, D. A., ten Caten, C. S., Jung, C. F., Sassanelli, C., & Terzi, S. (2019). Overcoming barriers towards Sustainable Product-Service Systems in small and medium-sized enterprises: State of the art and a novel Decision Matrix. *Journal of Cleaner Production, 222,* 903–921. https://doi.org/10.1016/j.jclepro.2019.01.152.

DIN. (2014). *DIN EN 60300-3-3:2014-09, Zuverlässigkeitsmanagement_Teil_3-3: Anwendungsleitfaden_ Lebenszykluskosten (IEC_56/1549/CD:2014).* Beuth Verlag GmbH. https://doi.org/10.31030/2232714.

Dotti, S., Gaiardelli, P., Pinto, R., & Resta, B. (2013). ICT functionalities in the servitization of manufacturing. *IFAC Proceedings Volumes, 46*(9), 2063–2068. https://doi.org/10.3182/20130619-3-RU-3018.00504.

European Union. (2006). *REGULATION (EC) No 1893/2006 OF THE EUROPEAN PARLIAMENT AND OF THE COUNCIL: L 393/1.*

Feng, Z., He, K., Peng, R., & Ma, Y. (2011). Taxonomy for evolution of service-based system. *IEEE World Congress on Services, 2011,* 331–338. https://doi.org/10.1109/SERVICES.2011.28.

Frank, A. G., Dalenogare, L. S., & Ayala, N. F. (2019). Industry 4.0 technologies: Implementation patterns in manufacturing companies. *International Journal of Production Economics, 210,* 15–26. https://doi.org/10.1016/j.ijpe.2019.01.004.

Gaiardelli, P., Resta, B., Martinez, V., Pinto, R., & Albores, P. (2014). A classification model for product-service offerings. *Journal of Cleaner Production, 66,* 507–519. https://doi.org/10.1016/j.jclepro.2013.11.032.

Gebauer, H., Fleisch, E., & Friedli, T. (2005). Overcoming the service paradox in manufacturing companies. *European Management Journal, 23*(1), 14–26. https://doi.org/10.1016/j.emj.2004.12.006.

Gebauer, H., Paiola, M., & Saccani, N. (2013). Characterizing service networks for moving from products to solutions. *Industrial Marketing Management, 42*(1), 31–46. https://doi.org/10.1016/j.indmarman.2012.11.002.

Glass, R. L., & Vessey, I. (1995). Contemporary application-domain taxonomies. *IEEE Software, 12*(4), 63–76. https://doi.org/10.1109/52.391837.

Goedkopp, M. J., van Halen, C. J. G., te Riele, H. R. M., & Rommens, P. J. M. (1999). Product service systems: Ecological and economic basics. *Product Innovation Technology Management, 36*(1), 1–22.

Gregor, S. (2006). The nature of theory in information systems. *MIS Quarterly, 30*(3), 611. https://doi.org/10.2307/25148742.

Hacker, W., & Richter, G. (2003). *Tätigkeitsbewertungssystem - Geistige Arbeit: Für Arbeitsplatzinhaber. Mensch - Technik - Organisation: v. 35.* Vdf Hochschulverlag AG an der ETH Zürich.

Hartmann, P. M., Zaki, M., Feldmann, N., & Neely, A. (2016). Capturing value from big data—A taxonomy of data-driven business models used by start-up firms. *International Journal of Operations & Production Management, 36*(10), 1382–1406. https://doi.org/10.1108/IJOPM-02-2014-0098.

Henke, M., Besenfelder, C., & Kaczmarek, S. (2019). Dortmunder management-modell. In M. ten Hompel, B. Vogel-Heuser, & T. Bauernhansl (Eds.), *Springer Reference Technik. Handbuch Industrie 4.0* (pp. 1–17). Springer Berlin Heidelberg. https://doi.org/10.1007/978-3-662-45537-1_115-1.

Herterich, M. M., Buehnen, T., Uebernickel, F., & Brenner, W. (2016). A taxonomy of industrial service systems enabled by digital product innovation. In *2016 49th Hawaii International Conference* (pp. 1236–1245). https://doi.org/10.1109/HICSS.2016.157.

Institut für Mittelstandsforschung. (2016). *KMU Definition des IfM Bonn.* https://www.ifm-bonn.org/definitionen/kmu-definition-des-ifm-bonn/.

Lee, J. H., Shin, D. I., Hong, Y. S., & Kim, Y. S. (2011). Business model design methodology for innovative product-service systems: A strategic and structured approach. In *2011 Annual SRII Global Conference*.

Jansen, S. A. (2016). *Mergers & Acquisitions.* Springer Fachmedien Wiesbaden. https://doi.org/10.1007/978-3-8349-4772-7.

Kohtamäki, M., Henneberg, S. C., Martinez, V., Kimita, K., & Gebauer, H. (2019). A configurational approach to servitization: Review and research directions. *Service Science, 11*(3), 213–240. https://doi.org/10.1287/serv.2019.0245.

Kohtamäki, M., Parida, V., Patel, P. C., & Gebauer, H. (2020). The relationship between digitalization and servitization: The role of servitization in capturing the financial potential of digitalization. *Technological Forecasting and Social Change, 151.* https://doi.org/10.1016/j.techfore.2019.119804.

Lay, G. (2014). *Servitization in industry.* Springer International Publishing. https://doi.org/10.1007/978-3-319-06935-7.

Lay, G., Schroeter, M., & Biege, S. (2009). Service-based business concepts: A typology for business-to-business markets. *European Management Journal, 27*(6), 442–455. https://doi.org/10.1016/j.emj.2009.04.002.

Lee, A. S., & Baskerville, R. L. (2003). Generalizing generalizability in information systems research. *Information Systems Research, 14*(3), 221–243. https://doi.org/10.1287/isre.14.3.221.16560.

Lim, C.-H., Kim, K.-J., Hong, Y.-S., & Park, K. (2012). PSS Board: A structured tool for product–service system process visualization. *Journal of Cleaner Production, 37*, 42–53. https://doi.org/10.1016/j.jclepro.2012.06.006.

Mastrogiacomo, L., Barravecchia, F., & Franceschini, F. (2019). A worldwide survey on manufacturing servitization. *The International Journal of Advanced Manufacturing Technology, 103*(9–12), 3927–3942. https://doi.org/10.1007/s00170-019-03740-z.

Meier, H., Roy, R., & Seliger, G. (2010). Industrial Product-Service Systems—IPS 2. *CIRP Annals, 59*(2), 607–627. https://doi.org/10.1016/j.cirp.2010.05.004.

Michalik, A., Besenfelder, C., & Henke, M. (2019). Servitization of Small- and Medium-Sized Manufacturing Enterprises: Facing barriers through the Dortmund management model. *IFAC-PapersOnLine, 52*(13), 2326–2331. https://doi.org/10.1016/j.ifacol.2019.11.553.

Modrow-Thiel, B., Meyer, R., Müller, J. K., & Pier, M. (2010). Arbeitsintegrierter Kompetenzaufbau. In J. C. Aurich & M. H. Clement (Eds.), *Produkt-Service Systeme* (pp. 117–162). Springer Berlin Heidelberg. https://doi.org/10.1007/978-3-642-01407-9_7.

Nickerson, R. C., Varshney, U., & Muntermann, J. (2013). A method for taxonomy development and its application in information systems. *European Journal of Information Systems, 22*(3), 336–359. https://doi.org/10.1057/ejis.2012.26.

Osterwalder, A., & Pigneur, Y. (2010). *Business model generation: A handbook for visionaries, game changers, and challengers.* Flash Reproductions.

Rabetino, R., Harmsen, W., Kohtamäki, M., & Sihvonen, J. (2018). Structuring servitization-related research. *International Journal of Operations & Production Management, 38*(2), 350–371. https://doi.org/10.1108/IJOPM-03-2017-0175.

Reim, W., Parida, V., & Örtqvist, D. (2015). Product-Service Systems (PSS) business models and tactics—A systematic literature review. *Journal of Cleaner Production, 97*, 61–75. https://doi.org/10.1016/j.jclepro.2014.07.003.

Ritchey, T. (2014). On a morphology of theories of emergence. *Acta Morphologica Generalis, 3*(3), 1–17.

Rondini, A., Matschewsky, J., Pezzotta, G., & Bertoni, M. (2018). A simplified approach towards customer and provider value in PSS for small and medium-sized enterprises. *Procedia CIRP, 73*, 61–66. https://doi.org/10.1016/j.procir.2018.03.330.

Schuh, G., Anderl, R., Gausemeier, J., ten Hompel, M., & Wahlster, W. (Eds.). (2017). *acatech STUDIE. Industrie 4.0 Maturity Index: Die digitale Transformation von Unternehmen gestalten.* Herbert Utz Verlag.

Sklyar, A., Kowalkowski, C., Tronvoll, B., & Sörhammar, D. (2019). Organizing for digital servitization: A service ecosystem perspective. *Journal of Business Research, 104,* 450–460. https://doi.org/10.1016/j.jbusres.2019.02.012.

Sousa, R., & da Silveira, G. J. C. (2017). Capability antecedents and performance outcomes of servitization. *International Journal of Operations & Production Management, 37*(4), 444–467. https://doi.org/10.1108/IJOPM-11-2015-0696.

Teece, D. J. (2010). Business models, business strategy and innovation. *Long Range Planning, 43*(2–3), 172–194. https://doi.org/10.1016/j.lrp.2009.07.003.

Tukker, A. (2004). Eight types of product–Service system: Eight ways to sustainability? Experiences from SusProNet. *Business Strategy and the Environment, 13*(4), 246–260. https://doi.org/10.1002/bse.414.

Vandermerwe, S., & Rada, J. (1988). Servitization of business: Adding value by adding services. *European Management Journal, 6*(4), 314–324. https://doi.org/10.1016/0263-2373(88)90033-3.

VDMA. (2015). *Investieren in die Zukunft: Gemeinsame wirtschaftspolitische Positionen des deutschen Maschinen- und Anlagenbaus 2105.*

Weber, M. (1949). *Methodology of the social sciences.* Free Press.

Weking, J., Böhm, M., Kowalkiewicz, M., & Krcmar, H. (2018). Archetypes for Industry 4.0 Business Model Innovations. In *Twenty-fourth Americas Conference on Information 2018.*

Further Semiotic Perspectives on the Outcome-Based vs Performance-Based Semantic Dispute

Lauri Korkeamäki

1   Introduction

To ensure the added value of their services, providers use performance- and outcome-based contracts (PBCs & OBCs) instead of billing based on the time and materials dedicated to the service activity. The interchangeable use of the terms "outcome" and "performance," however, has often caused confusion (Datta & Roy, 2011; Grubic & Jennions, 2018; Hou & Neely, 2018; Hypko et al., 2010a, b) Recently, however, arguments have been made in favor of "outcome" as the preferred prefix (Schaefers et al., 2021) to be used when discussing what the associated contracts are based on. The reasoning behind the given arguments has leaned much on semantics, that is, the meaning(s) attached to these terms. For example, "performance" can refer to an artist's presentation of artwork, the manner in which a mechanism operates, or the action of performing a task. Given this semantic ambiguity (Rodd et al., 2004), the term "performance-based contract" has been accompanied by an alternative term, "outcome-based contract," in academic discourse. However, because semantics constitutes only a part of the entire semiotics of

L. Korkeamäki (✉)
School of Management, University of Vaasa, Vaasa, Finland
e-mail: lauri.korkeamaki@uwasa.fi

the topic, this chapter contributes by systematically reviewing over 80 top-tier journal articles from the perspectives of pragmatics and syntax as well.

With regard to the chicken-or-the-egg dilemma, it seems clear that "performance" was the first to emerge in the late 1980s and early 1990s (Selviaridis & Wynstra, 2015). From the syntax perspective, however, simultaneously with the surfacing of the terms "business model" and "innovation," the term "outcome" has started to capture shares in the academic discourse. Furthermore, in terms of pragmatics, the more innovation- and marketing-oriented research outlets tend to emphasize the term "outcome." To summarize the contributions of the current paper, it provides further understanding of the antecedents of the "outcome-based vs. performance-based" debate in the related leading level literature, resulting in a fuller description of the semiotics at play in the recent pro-outcome arguments. Thus, the current chapter contributes to the concept stream of the literature concerning outcome-based contracts (Schaefers et al., 2021).

2   Theory Development

The literature to be reviewed was collected following the guidelines for systematic literature review (Kohtamäki et al., 2018; Tranfield et al., 2003). I began by *defining the keywords* to collect the studies of interest. The choice of keywords was guided by prior literature reviews (Grubic & Jennions, 2018; Hypko et al., 2010b; Selviaridis & Wynstra, 2015) concerning outcome-based business arrangements. Studies were collected from the *Scopus* database using the advanced search function. The search string used was as follows: TITLE-ABS-KEY ("outcome-based contract*" OR "performance-based contract*" OR "outcome business model*" OR "performance-based logistic*" OR "performance contract*") AND (LIMIT-TO (DOCTYPE, "ar")). The query produced 853 hits (in January 2020). To address the requirement of *deciding target journals*, the search results were further refined by limiting them to journals with *Academic Journal Guide 2018 ranking 3, 4 or 4** to guarantee the high quality of the publications. The given ranks indicate highly regarded, top tier and distinguished research quality, respectively (Academic Journal Guide, 2018).

After the application of the second-stage criteria, 81 articles were left. Next, to assess the suitability of the studies, I scrutinized the abstracts of the papers. I excluded studies that focused on employee/manager performance-rewarding contracts (7 in total, e.g., Fehrenbacher et al., 2017). As a result, 74 studies remained to be reviewed, to which I added 9 articles published/indexed after the initial search (e.g., Huang et al., 2020; Korkeamäki & Kohtamäki, 2020; Sjödin et al., 2020) and which I deemed relevant based on the references of the reviewed papers (e.g., Datta & Roy, 2011; Jain et al., 2013; Selviaridis & Van der Valk, 2019; Visnjic et al., 2018). The outlets and the number of publications are compiled in Table 1. In addition to the collected literature, I scanned the lists of references of the collected articles for further insights for secondary data consisting of conference proceedings, academic book articles, and anecdotal evidence (such as industry and working group reports). These insights and data were not included in the following analyses but rather worked as a data triangulation practice grounding the analytical work.

Table 1 OBS publications by journal

Journal	AJG2018	No. Papers
Management Science	4*	6
Operations Research	4*	2
Strategic Management Journal	4*	2
European Journal of Operational Research	4	8
International Journal of Operations and Production Management	4	7
Journal of Product Innovation Management	4	1
Production and Operations Management	4	5
American Journal of Agricultural Economics	3	2
American Review of Public Administration	3	2
Energy Economics	3	2
European Economic Review	3	1
Health Services Research	3	2
Industrial Marketing Management	3	10
International Journal of Production Economics	3	8
International Journal of Production Research	3	7
International Review of Administrative Sciences	3	3
Journal of the Operational Research Society	3	4
Management Accounting Research	3	2
Milbank Quarterly	3	2
Public Management Review	3	4
Technovation	3	1
Journal of Business Research	3	1
Production Planning and Control	3	1
Grand total		83

Pragmatics

Pragmatics is concerned with how context and practices influence meanings (Levinson, 1983). Thus, just as in the literature review by Selviaridis and Wynstra (2015), the articles reviewed were first categorized by the AJG 2018 fields. The fields included in the sample were Innovation (INNOV), Marketing (MKT), General Management, Ethics, Gender and Social Responsibility (ETHICS-CSR-MAN), Public Sector and Health Care (PUB-SEC), Operations and Technology Management (OPS-TECH), Accounting (ACCOUNT), Operations Research and Management Science (OR-MANSCI), Economics, Econometrics and Statistics (ECON) and Strategy (STRAT). The number of papers by field was INN = 2, MKT = 10, ETHICS-CSR-MAN = 1, PUB-SEC = 13, OPS-TECH = 29, ACCOUNT = 1, OR-MANSCI = 20, ECON = 5 and STRAT = 2. In particular, related research in the OPS-TECH and MKT fields has been published at a growing pace, especially in the latter decade of the century.

To investigate how the academic field influences the frequency of use of the terms "outcome" and "performance," the publications were searched using the find function provided by either the publisher or the browser. The papers were scrutinized one by one, and the search hits in the affiliations, repeated titles, lists of references, acknowledgments, and direct quotations were excluded from the count. In other words, "outcome" and "performance" hits were counted only if they belonged to the original body text. The average frequencies of the terms "outcome" and "performance" per paper were used to compare the fields. The resulting chart (Fig. 1) shows that "outcome" as a term is endorsed more in the innovation and marketing-oriented fields, while the term "performance" is emphasized in the more technical fields. In alignment with prior literature reviews (see, e.g., Grubic & Jennions, 2018; Selviaridis & Wynstra, 2015), the terms often seem to go hand in hand. Earlier research has also pinpointed that the terms are often used interchangeably (Grubic & Jennions, 2018). What is worth noting is that I conducted the search using the words "outcome" and "performance" per se, not variants including them (e.g., performance-based logistics, outcome business models). This is to create a general overview.

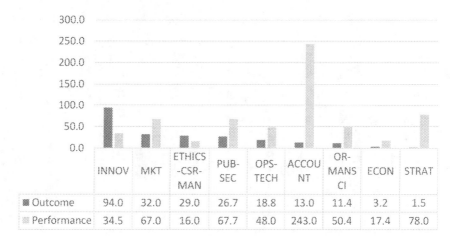

	INNOV	MKT	ETHICS -CSR- MAN	PUB- SEC	OPS- TECH	ACCOU NT	OR- MANS CI	ECON	STRAT
▓ Outcome	94.0	32.0	29.0	26.7	18.8	13.0	11.4	3.2	1.5
▓ Performance	34.5	67.0	16.0	67.7	48.0	243.0	50.4	17.4	78.0

Fig. 1 Average frequency (per paper) of "outcome" and "performance" terms by field

Syntax

Syntax is a study of relations between expressions in language (Carnie, 2006). To illustrate the balance between the terms "outcome" and "performance," the annual sums of the frequencies were rendered into stacked yearly percentage columns and overlaid with the respective number of publications per year. Figure 2 illustrates two trends in the given literature during the first decades of the twenty-first century (excluding 2004 with no publication data). First, the number of publications per year concerning the topic has rapidly increased in top-tier journals, especially in the latter decade. Second, although the term "performance" has historically been the dominant of the two, there seems to be a trend toward "outcome" capturing shares as an alternative term, especially in the latter decade of the current century.

To retrace antecedents of this shift, I first turned to Google Trends. For instance, Google Trends' index (0–100) on topic popularity shows that from February 2004 to October 2020 (the longest available timeframe), the popularity of the topic "performance-based logistics" peaked at the beginning of the century. On the other hand, the popularity index for the keyword "outcome business model" began generating continuing monthly interest only around the year 2010. Furthermore, referring to the discussions I

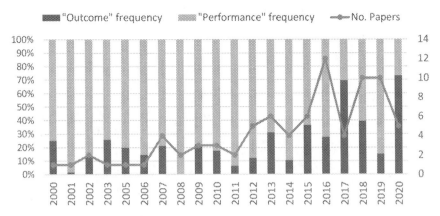

Fig. 2 The annual balance between the use of the terms "Outcome" and "Performance"

have shared with fellow scholars, it appears that the term "performance" is preferred in more operational and purchasing-related journals, while innovation- and marketing-related facets endorse "outcomes." Indeed, innovation and marketing scholars use the expression "outcome business model" (Ng et al., 2013; Sjödin et al., 2020; Visnjic et al., 2017), but rarely is the business model referred to as a "performance business model." To explore these premises, complementary data on the frequency of the terms related to innovation ("innovat" was used to capture alternative endings, such as "innovative"), and "business model" was collected using the search functions once again. The frequency of each term was divided by the number of papers in each of the fields to derive the average frequencies. The results are presented in Fig. 3, which is essentially a further refined version of Fig. 1. Veritably, not only did the use of innovation- and business model-related terms increase over time, but there was also a reason to suspect that syntax-wise, the use of the given terms were related to higher "outcome" term frequency.

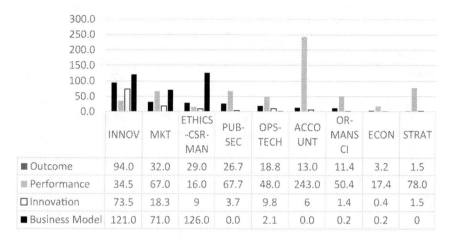

	INNOV	MKT	ETHICS -CSR- MAN	PUB- SEC	OPS- TECH	ACCO UNT	OR- MANS CI	ECON	STRAT
■ Outcome	94.0	32.0	29.0	26.7	18.8	13.0	11.4	3.2	1.5
▨ Performance	34.5	67.0	16.0	67.7	48.0	243.0	50.4	17.4	78.0
□ Innovation	73.5	18.3	9	3.7	9.8	6	1.4	0.4	1.5
■ Business Model	121.0	71.0	126.0	0.0	2.1	0.0	0.2	0.2	0

Fig. 3 Average frequency (per paper) of the terms used by the field

To test this hypothesis, a multiple regression analysis was conducted. The analysis started by fitting a simple linear regression with the sum of innovation-related terms (per year) as a predictor of the annual use of the outcome term. The model was significant (prob > F = 0.0013) and produced a positive coefficient for the predictor (p-value = 0.001) and an R^2 of 0.4455 (adjusted R^2 = 0.4146). Next, the annual sum of the term "business model" was added as a predictor. Again, the model was significant (prob > F = 0.0003) and produced positive and significant coefficients for both regressors. Furthermore, the adjusted R^2 increased to 0.5773. Last, the annual sum of the term "performance" was modeled, and the adjusted R^2 increased to 0.6486 in effect. The normality of the residuals was tested using the skewness/kurtosis test for normality (prob > chi^2 = 0.3304) and the Shapiro-Wilk test (Shapiro & Wilk, 1965) for normality (prob > z = 0.07997). To test whether the model met the assumption of constant variance, a Breusch-Pagan/Cook-Weisberg test (Breusch & Pagan, 1979) for heteroscedasticity (prob > chi^2 = 0.1057) was performed. To inspect influential data points, both DFFITS (Belsley et al., 1980) and Cook's distance (Cook, 1977, 1979) diagnostics were used and plotted. The results showed that 2019 was an outlier in terms of influence. To test the effect of this observation, the model

Table 2 Regression results

"Outcome"	Coef.	Robust std. error	t	P >| t|	[95% Conf. Interval]	
"Business model"	.8273419	.351236	2.36	0.032	.0827548	1.571929
"Innovation"	.39374	.1660052	2.37	0.031	.0418248	.7456552
"Performance"	.1799559	.0825943	2.18	0.045	.0048639	.3550479
Constant	5.957126	15.38481	0.39	0.704	−26.6572	38.57146

was fitted again without it, and another Breusch-Pagan/Cook-Weisberg test for heteroscedasticity was performed subsequently.

The results yielded improvements in the goodness of fit ($R^2 = 0.8388$ c.f. 0.7041, adj. $R^2 = 0.8066$ c.f. 0.6486) and indicated that the 2019 observation was a major factor for heteroscedasticity (Breusch-Pagan: prob > $\chi^2 = 0.8575$ c.f. 0.1057). However, as demonstrated in Fig. 2, 2019 was among the top three years in terms of published papers. Hence, I chose not to omit it from the analysis and used the model including it with robust standard errors instead. Thus, the final significant (prob > $F = 0.0000$) model produced an adjusted R^2 of 0.6486 and positive coefficients for all the predictors (p-values $= < 0.05$). The results of the analysis are reported in Table 2. For the sake of comparison, using the term "performance" as the dependent variable, the regression results for none of the other terms as predictors were significant (p-value $= > 0.05$). Although rudimentary, the results of the analysis support the hypothesis that there is a direct positive relationship between the use of business model- and innovation-related terminology and the frequency of the term outcome. However, a more detailed analysis should be conducted using dynamic topic modeling (Blei & Lafferty, 2006) or Poisson regression, for instance.

Semantics

Finally, semantics is interested in the meaningful relations between expressions in language (Jackendoff, 1990). Thus, as semantics centers on the meanings attached to terms, it is a vital part of understanding language, which is defined as a tool of expression that reflects and constructs its surroundings (Samra-Fredericks, 2005). First, the dictionary definitions of the words "performance" and "outcome" were looked up. The Merriam-Webster definition for "performance" is twofold: "*the fulfillment of a claim, promise, or request*" or "*the manner in which a mechanism performs*," the latter of which is often an appropriate meaning in manufacturing contexts. An outcome, on the other hand, is defined more univocally as "*something that follows as a result or consequence*" (Merriam-Webster.com). Thus, the word "performance" as a term[1] is considerably more polysemic (Cruse, 2000, pp. 103–124). Moreover, and importantly, the term "performance" can refer to multiple other things, such as the performance of an actor in a play. This makes "performance" also homonymic (Rice et al., 2019), meaning that despite the identical spelling (or pronunciation), the word carries multiple unrelated meanings. For example, the word "mean" can *mean* unkind or average.

Due to the polysemic nature of the term "performance," I argue that it is necessary to define the scope of its usage in academic discourse. Both arguments presented next are also strongly related to pragmatism. First, the given result-oriented service offerings have been found to be particularly important for capital-intensive (Grubic & Jennions, 2018; Hypko et al., 2010a, 2010b) and complex systems (Essig et al., 2016; Ng & Nudurupati, 2010) that are driven by life cycle logic (Grubic & Jennions, 2018; Kleemann & Essig, 2013). Thus, the term "performance" as a central signal attached to industrial objects (thus also reflecting pragmatics), such as machines or systems (i.e., extralinguistic objects), should be used to describe *the manner in which a mechanism operates*. For example, Li et al. (2014) investigated 140 energy performance contracts in China, where the providers intended to improve *energy performance* together with their clients. Adapted from Nowicki et al. (2008), a step function (Eq. 1) representing such revenue functions was formulated accordingly:

$$R(P_i) \begin{cases} R^f & \text{if } P_i \leq P_{min} \\ R^f + R^v \times (P_i - P_{min}) & \text{if } P_i > P_{min} \end{cases} \tag{1}$$

where R^f is the fixed part of the revenue function and R^v is the variable part of the revenue that is conditionally tied to the improved performance (P_i) over the agreed minimum performance (P_{min}). In addition to the design in Eq. (1), the variable revenue logic can be designed as an exponential, a polynomial or a step function (Brown & Burke, 2000; Nowicki et al., 2008). The second important argument in favor of separate definitions is legal technical. In advanced technical systems, such as power plants, manufacturing systems and e-commerce computer systems, the liquidated damages due to downtime are often measured in millions per hour, which is why investments in extensive maintenance efforts usually account for a major share of the total cost

---

[1] The distinction between "word" and "term" is that while a word is only component of language, a term is a word that has meaning(s) attached to it.

of ownership of the system (Öner et al., 2015). Following the work of Patra et al. (2019), the operational availability (A_o) of a machine can be defined as presented in Eq. (2):

$$A_o = \frac{H^{Max} - H^{Sched} - H^{DT}}{H^{Max} - H^{Sched}} \tag{2}$$

where H^{Max} is the maximum operating hours of the machine during a specified timeframe, H^{Sched} is the scheduled maintenance time and H^{DT} is the downtime of the machine during the timeframe (Patra et al., 2019). Alternatively, availability can be based on the sample average of downtimes (Grubic & Jennions, 2018; Kim et al., 2010). These types of contracts have been typified as availability outcome-based contracts (Böhm et al., 2016). However, customers are not only concerned with availability: "*The movement towards a service-based economy has led many manufacturing firms to recognize the strategic importance of after-sales product support services that enable the availability of* **properly functioning products**" (Guajardo et al., 2012, p. 961). Especially concerning machinery-focused OEMs, calculations based on mere equipment availability (measured in, e.g., operating hours) may disregard important performance specifications, according to anecdotal evidence (Klise & Balfour, 2015, p. 25). In a legal sense, the machine/system could be operational and thus considered available, although it would operate in a degraded state (e.g., produce less energy). The conclusion follows that it is in the interest of both the provider and the customer to have separate definitions for performance and availability. Thus, in these types of contracts, the aforementioned mechanical performance is an integrated part of the offering. The underlying subordination argument is as follows: availability is more important than performance because the level of performance has no significance if it is not available. The two, however, have a reciprocal influence. Correspondingly, the level of availability has lower importance if performance decreases.

3   Discussion

Theoretical Contributions

In the current chapter, I briefly synthesized the semiotics of top-tier literature concerning outcome- and performance-based contracts. Thus, this chapter contributes to the debate (Grubic & Jennions, 2018; Hypko et al., 2010b; Schaefers et al., 2021) regarding which term is the more appropriate prefix for describing the given advanced services. By doing so, the current chapter contributes to the concept stream of literature concerning the topic (Schaefers et al., 2021). The pragmatics analysis showed that although the terms "performance" and "outcome" seem to go hand in hand and are even used interchangeably (as noted by Grubic & Jennions, 2018; see, e.g., Selviaridis & Wynstra, 2015), the term "outcome" is used more frequently in journals in the fields of innovation, marketing, general management, ethics, gender, and social responsibility, and the public sector and health care. Diving deeper into the syntax between the words, it was found that over time, the use of the term "outcome" has increased. Moreover, further analysis confirmed that both "business model" and "innovation" terms are directly related to the frequency of the term "outcome." Last, in support of recent research on the topic (Schaefers et al., 2021), semantic analysis supported the argument that the term/prefix "outcome" should be preferred over "performance" in academic literature discussing the associated contracts because the latter term is more polysemic and homonymic. Linking the argument back to pragmatics, it was found that due to the ambiguity of the term "performance," its use may cause legal technical issues if it is not sufficiently distinguished from outcome-related metrics, such as availability. In conclusion, I argue that "outcome-based" is the more appropriate phrase due to its univocal nature. Thus, the current chapter provides further insights into pragmatics- and syntax-wise antecedents of terminological practices in high-quality research concerning outcome-based services.

Managerial Contributions

The current chapter offers managers multiple contributions. First, it offers managers some contextualized explanations and causes of the terminological differences present in the top-tier journal papers concerning the topic. This is important, because the variance of the terms used may not only confuse the readers, but also cause the readers to give preference to the studies endorsing one term and disregard the theoretical insights in studies using the other. Second, it summarizes current research trends and provides a catalog of the research outlets publishing papers on the topic. Furthermore, managers can rest assured of the high quality of the given facets because they represent the top level of business research regardless of the discipline. Third, although the current chapter is focused on academic discourse, it highlights some important managerial considerations, such as aspects of contract language and basic formulas for revenue functions or outcome metrics.

Limitations and Suggestions for Future Research

Like all research, the current study also has limitations. First, as the goal of the study was to look into and contribute to the debate on "outcome/performance" terminology specifically, the choice was made to focus on research endorsing the given terms. Alternative and closely related concepts include but are not limited to result-oriented product service systems (Van Ostaeyen et al., 2013), advanced services (Baines & Lightfoot, 2014), smart operations and maintenance (Huang et al., 2020) and value-based selling (Töytäri & Rajala, 2015). Thus, future research could examine the semiotics of the wider body of related research as well. Second, despite the evolution in academic discourse, the in situ practical names used for the given type of services vary by firm. For instance, Wärtsilä speaks about "lifecycle solutions" (Wärtsilä.com), and Rolls-Royce coins its business models based on flight hours TotalCare® or CorporateCare® (Rolls-Royce.com), while Hilti calls its power tools as-a-service offering as Fleet Management (Hilti.com). Understandably, the practical terminology used to describe the given type of services is even more scattered and nuanced than the theoretical terminology. Therefore, future research could map the various outcome-based offerings aggregately to spot differences, similarities and patterns and yield more granular typologies to accompany the extant availability/economic outcome-based contract typology (Böhm et al., 2016).

References

Baines, T., & Lightfoot, H. W. (2014). Servitization of the manufacturing firm: Exploring the operations practices and technologies that deliver advanced services. *International Journal of Operations & Production Management, 34*(1), 2–35.

Belsley, D. A., Kuh, E., & Welsh, R. E. (1980). *Regression diagnostics: Identifying influential data and sources of collinearity* (1st ed.). New York: John Wiley & Sons.

Blei, D., & Lafferty, J. (2006). Dynamic topic models. In *ICML 2006—Proceedings of the 23rd International Conference on Machine Learning*, (June, 25–29), 113–120.

Böhm, E., Backhaus, C., Eggert, A., & Cummins, T. (2016). Understanding outcome-based contracts. *Journal of Strategic Contracting and Negotiation, 2*(1–2), 128–149.

Breusch, T. S., & Pagan, A. R. (1979). A simple test for Heteroskedasticity and random coefficient variation. *Econometrica, 50*, 987–1007.

Brown, R. E., & Burke, J. J. (2000). Managing the risk of performance based rates. *IEEE Transactions on Power Systems, 15*(2), 893–898.

Carnie, A. (2006). *Syntax: A generative introduction* (2nd ed.). New York and Oxford: Wiley-Blackwell.

Cook, R. D. (1977). Detection of influential observation in linear regression. *Technometrics, 19*(1), 15–18.

Cook, R. D. (1979). Influential observations in linear regression. *Journal of the American Statistical Association, 74*(365), 169–174.

Cruse, D. A. (2000). *Meaning in language: An introduction to semantics and pragmatics* (1st ed.). New York: Oxford University Press.

Datta, P. P., & Roy, R. (2011). Operations strategy for the effective delivery of integrated industrial product-service offerings. *International Journal of Operations & Production Management, 31*(5), 579–603.

Essig, M., Glas, A. H., Selviaridis, K., & Roehrich, J. K. (2016). Performance-based contracting in business markets. *Industrial Marketing Management, 59,* 5–11.

Fehrenbacher, D. D., Kaplan, S. E., & Pedell, B. (2017). The relation between individual characteristics and compensation contract selection. *Management Accounting Research, 34,* 1–18.

Grubic, T., & Jennions, I. (2018). Do outcome-based contracts exist? The investigation of power-by-the-hour and similar result-oriented cases. *International Journal of Production Economics, 206,* 209–219.

Guajardo, J. A., Cohen, M. A., Kim, S. H., & Netessine, S. (2012). Impact of performance-based contracting on product reliability: An empirical analysis. *Management Science, 58*(5), 961–979.

Hou, J., & Neely, A. (2018). Investigating risks of outcome-based service contracts from a provider's perspective. *International Journal of Production Research, 56*(6), 2103–2115.

Huang, F., Chen, J., Sun, L., Zhang, Y., & Yao, S. (2020). Value-based contract for smart operation and maintenance service based on equitable entropy. *International Journal of Production Research, 58*(4), 1271–1284.

Hypko, P., Tilebein, M., & Gleich, R. (2010a). Benefits and uncertainties of performance-based contracting in manufacturing industries: An agency theory perspective. *Journal of Service Management, 21*(4), 460–489.

Hypko, P., Tilebein, M., & Gleich, R. (2010b). Clarifying the concept of performance-based contracting in manufacturing industries: A research synthesis. *Journal of Service Management, 21*(5), 625–655.

Jackendoff, R. (1990). *Semantic structures* (1st ed.). Cambridge, MA: MIT Press.

Jain, N., Hasija, S., & Popescu, D. (2013). Optimal contracts for outsourcing of repair and restoration services. *Operations Research, 61*(6), 1295–1311.

Kim, S. H., Cohen, M. A., Netessine, S., & Veeraraghavan, S. (2010). Contracting for infrequent restoration and recovery of mission-critical systems. *Management Science, 56*(9), 1551–1567.

Kleemann, F. C., & Essig, M. (2013). A providers' perspective on supplier relationships in performance-based contracting. *Journal of Purchasing and Supply Management, 19*(3), 185–198.

Klise, G. T., & Balfour, J. R. (2015). *A best practice for developing availability guarantee language in photovoltaic (PV) operation and maintenance agreements.* Retrieved from http://www.ntis.gov/help/ordermethods.aspx#online

Kohtamäki, M., Rabetino, R., & Möller, K. (2018). Alliance capabilities: A systematic review and future research directions. *Industrial Marketing Management, 68*(October 2017), 188–201.

Korkeamäki, L., & Kohtamäki, M. (2020). To Outcomes and Beyond: Discursively Managing Legitimacy Struggles in Outcome Business Models. *Industrial Marketing Management, 91*(February), 196–208.

Levinson, S. C. (1983). Pragmatics. In *Cambridge textbooks in linguistics* (1st ed.). Cambridge University Press.

Li, Y., Qiu, Y., & Wang, Y. D. (2014). Explaining the contract terms of energy performance contracting in China: The importance of effective financing. *Energy Economics, 45,* 401–411.

Ng, I. C. L., Ding, D. X., & Yip, N. (2013). Outcome-based contracts as new business model: The role of partnership and value-driven relational assets. *Industrial Marketing Management, 42*(5), 730–743.

Ng, I. C. L., & Nudurupati, S. S. (2010). Outcome based service contracts in the defence industry—Mitigating the challenges. *Journal of Service Management, 21*(5), 656–674.

Nowicki, D., Kumar, U. D., Steudel, H. J., & Verma, D. (2008). Spares provisioning under performance-based logistics contract: Profit-centric approach. *Journal of the Operational Research Society, 59*(3), 342–352.

Öner, K. B., Kiesmüller, G. P., & Van Houtum, G. J. (2015). On the upgrading policy after the redesign of a component for reliability improvement. *European Journal of Operational Research, 244*(3), 867–880.

Patra, P., Kumar, U. D., Nowicki, D. R., & Randall, W. S. (2019). Effective management of performance-based contracts for sustainment dominant systems. *International Journal of Production Economics, 208,* 369–382.

Rice, C. A., Beekhuizen, B., Dubrovsky, V., Stevenson, S., & Armstrong, B. C. (2019). A comparison of homonym meaning frequency estimates derived from movie and television subtitles, free association, and explicit ratings. *Behavior Research Methods, 51*(3), 1399–1425.

Rodd, J. M., Gaskell, M. G., & Marslen-Wilson, W. D. (2004). Modelling the effects of semantic ambiguity in word recognition. *Cognitive Science, 28*(1), 89–104.

Samra-Fredericks, D. (2005). Strategic practice, "discourse" and the everyday interactional constitution of "power effects". *Organization, 12*(6), 803–841.

Schaefers, T., Ruffer, S., & Böhm, E. (2021). Outcome-based contracting from the customers' perspective: A means-end chain analytical exploration. *Industrial Marketing Management, 93*(February), 466–481.

Selviaridis, K., & Van der Valk, W. (2019). Framing contractual performance incentives: effects on supplier behaviour. *International Journal of Operations and Production Management, 39*(2), 190–213.

Selviaridis, K., & Wynstra, F. (2015). Performance-based contracting: A literature review and future research directions. *International Journal of Production Research, 53*(12), 3505–3540.

Shapiro, S. S., & Wilk, M. B. (1965). An analysis of variance test for normality (complete samples). *Biometrika, 52*(3–4), 591–611.

Sjödin, D., Parida, V., Jovanovic, M., & Visnjic, I. (2020). Value creation and value capture alignment in business model innovation: A process view on outcome-based business models. *Journal of Product Innovation Management, 37*(2), 158–183.

Töytäri, P., & Rajala, R. (2015). Value-based selling: An organizational capability perspective. *Industrial Marketing Management, 45*(February), 101–122.

Tranfield, D., Denyer, D., & Smart, P. (2003). Towards a methodology for developing evidence-informed management knowledge by means of systematic review. *British Journal of Management, 14*(3), 207–222.

Van Ostaeyen, J., Van Horenbeek, A., Pintelon, L., & Duflou, J. R. (2013). A refined typology of product-service systems based on functional hierarchy modeling. *Journal of Cleaner Production, 51,* 261–276.

Visnjic, I., Jovanovic, M., Neely, A., & Engwall, M. (2017). What brings the value to outcome-based contract providers? Value drivers in outcome business models. *International Journal of Production Economics, 192*(October), 169–181.

Visnjic, I., Neely, A., & Jovanovic, M. (2018). The path to outcome delivery: Interplay of service market strategy and open business models. *Technovation, 72–73*(April), 46–59.

Online References

https://charteredabs.org/academic-journal-guide-2018-view/.

Merriam-Webster. (n.d.). Performance. In *Merriam-Webster.com dictionary*. Retrieved June 24, 2020, retrieved from https://www.merriam-webster.com/dictionary/performance.

Merriam-Webster. (n.d.). Outcome. In *Merriam-Webster.com dictionary*. Retrieved June 24, 2020, retrieved from https://www.merriam-webster.com/dictionary/outcome.

https://www.wartsila.com/energy/operate-and-maintain/lifecycle-solutions.

https://www.rolls-royce.com/investors/annual-report-2019.aspx#inner-downloads.

https://www.hilti.com/content/hilti/W1/US/en/services/tool-services/fleet-management.html.

The Features of Performance Measurement Systems in Value-Based Selling

Viktor Sundholm and Magnus Hellström

1 Introduction

Value-based selling has been identified as a key capability to sell industrial solutions. Because a solution comprises the value-in-use for a customer (Vargo & Lusch, 2004), quantifying and communicating the financial value-in-use is a key ingredient of the sales process (Töytäri & Rajala, 2015). When the sales force has the capabilities to understand the customer's business model, they can co-create the value-in-use *with* the customer, leading to improved business performance for the customer; through that, a deeper customer relationship and improved sales performance result (Terho et al., 2012).

In this chapter, we reflect on the value-based selling process from a performance measurement perspective. When reviewing the entire process of a performance measurement system, including designing performance measures, implementing the system, and updating it as needed (Bourne et al.,

V. Sundholm (✉) · M. Hellström
Laboratory of Industrial Management, Åbo Akademi University, Turku, Finland
e-mail: vsundhol@abo.fi

M. Hellström
e-mail: mhellstr@abo.fi

M. Hellström
School of Business and Law, University of Agder, Kristiansand, Norway

149

M. Kohtamäki et al. (eds.), *The Palgrave Handbook of Servitization*,
https://doi.org/10.1007/978-3-030-75771-7_10

2000), there are several aspects to account for in the value-based selling process. Successful performance measurement systems align the operations to the strategy (Kaplan & Norton, 1996) and provide the necessary information to challenge the strategy's content and validity (Ittner et al., 2003).

We synthesize solution strategy, value-based selling, and performance measurement in service operations theory to identify the features of performance measurement systems in value-based selling. There are several statements and indications in solution strategy and value-based selling research on the features of a performance measurement system, and the processes that are formed around it. Theory on performance measurement of industrial services also brings relevant insights (Jääskeläinen et al., 2014; Ukko et al., 2015). Through the theory synthesis, we cover a gap of performance measurement in value-based selling literature, as there has been no focused research within this area.

2   Theory Development

Solution Business Strategy

The term "solution business" is widely used. A common definition of *solutions* is a bundle of products and/or services that fully satisfies the needs and wishes of a customer (Tuli et al., 2007). Other researchers propose that a solution is a response to a customer problem (Stremersch et al., 2001) or solves a customer problem even before customers have considered their own products or service requirements (Davies et al., 2007). Some researchers also highlight the needs to co-identify and solve the problem with the customer (Terho et al., 2012; Luotola et al., 2017). While the customer need and problem certainly are fundamental facets of a solution, the problem is that the concept has become inflated to the extent that today "everyone is in the solutions business" (Adamson et al., 2012; for further critique on the concept, see also Nordin & Kowalkowski, 2010). Therefore, our view on a solution concept is that it goes beyond the explicit customer need (Adamson et al., 2012) toward changes in a market environment (cf., e.g., the term "market solution" in Storbacka & Nenonen, 2011). Solution providers strive to be leading developers of markets and industries in co-creation with their customers and their knowledge network, which is referred to as business-dominant logic (Wikström et al., 2009). In a sense, solution providers are forming business ecosystems with various customers that are based on the provider being a leading industry developer. The development is either based on increasing industry productivity or reducing the costs and environmental impact. This is done through either optimizing new build investments and industry operations or upgrading the installed base. The solution provider may even acquire a certain responsibility for maintaining or running the industry operations, depending on customer competence. Optimal operations and maintenance configuration should be the aim.

Researchers have also identified that solution providers have a hybrid strategy between product and solution business (Kujala et al., 2010). The level of relationship with the customers varies; some want to minimize their costs and focus on a rather transactional relationship with their supply chain, while others want co-creational relationships (Kowalkowski, 2011). Hence, customers can be classified into, for example (Baines & Lightfoot, 2014):

- customers who want to do it themselves;
- customers who want us to do it with them; and
- customers who want us to do it for them.

This brings in an important aspect of solution strategy implementation, especially for the sales force: identifying and providing input to segmenting customers according to product and solution business logics. Wikström et al. (2009) even outline four different business logics for industrial technology suppliers: product-, innovation and development-, service-, and business-dominant business logic. The scope of product and service supply depends greatly on the customer's own will and need to be a leading industry developer, to have the latest technology in their installed base, and also their own capabilities to execute the operations. This relates to the formation of industry architectures (Jacobides et al., 2006), where different firms develop competences to acquire a certain responsibility in the industry. In order to engage in the practice of solution business, the firm needs to have the capabilities to acquire the responsibility for a certain function within the system.

From a solution business strategy perspective, the value-based selling process serves as a direct channel to gather the information required to understand the solution providers' existing strategic position and the need to develop it. Researchers agree that the core of solution business strategy is the ability to improve the customer's business performance (Storbacka, 2011; Baines & Lightfoot, 2014; Rabetino et al., 2017). Solution providers develop their capabilities to provide combinations of products and services that meet the business, technical and operational needs of the customer (Gebauer, 2011). The sales force is key in implementing the solution business strategy, through designing and implementing business cases with the customers (Luotola et al., 2017). Implementing a solution strategy also involves finding the customers who are willing to engage in business relationships of value co-creation (Kowalkowski, 2011; Windahl & Lakemond, 2010). Identifying the level of relationship that the customers are willing to engage in has also been found to be a key to success in solution selling (Storbacka et al., 2011).

While the sales force engages in co-creating customized solutions with different customers, it typically builds on a more general modular solution development of products and services in the firm (Kohtamäki et al, 2019; Hellström, 2014). The information gathered by the sales force is an important input to solution development.

Value-Based Selling

Value-based selling involves incorporating the customer value into sales work, through quantifying and communicating the value of the offering (Terho et al., 2012; Töytäri & Rajala, 2015). The research area of value-based selling has received increasing attention among scholars as a natural development in solution selling. First, the relational aspect of selling was viewed as the primary means of selling solutions (Tuli et al, 2007), and subsequently, the importance of value-based selling has risen as an important process. Both relational and value-based selling are important aspects to view in sales. Relational selling stresses the importance of developing and maintaining deep relationships with solution customers and is a key to success in value-based selling. Value-based selling in turn accounts more for the processes and capabilities that are needed in order to sell value. Selling value is fundamental to solution sales, which is reflected in the definition of solution business—that it is the value-in-use for the customer that comprises a solution. Value-based selling literature outlines the main activities in the process of value-based selling:

1. Segmentation and identification of suitable customers (Terho et al., 2012; Töytäri and Rajala, 2015).
2. Value research of the customer business (Terho et al., 2012; Töytäri and Rajala, 2015).
3. Value proposition according to impact on the customer business (Corsaro, 2014; Terho et al., 2012; Töytäri and Rajala, 2015).
4. Communication of value, mutual target setting, and quantification of value (Anderson et al., 2006; Terho et al., 2012; Töytäri and Rajala, 2015).
5. Negotiate, offer, and deliver (Töytäri et al., 2012).

6. Verify and document impact (Anderson et al., 2006; Corsaro, 2014; Töytäri and Rajala, 2015).

Recent research on value-based selling outlines more detailed views of the customer-facing process, both from a contractual perspective (Liinamaa et al., 2016) and a design perspective (Luotola et al., 2017). This research outlines a three-stage process, including the customer perspective, divided into pre-sales, detail sales, and final sales.

Value-based selling requires a different process than transactional selling, emphasizing more activities that are based on involvement in the customer business (and investment) development. Transactional selling normally begins when the company receives a request for quotation (RFQ) from the customer, potentially preceded by some marketing activities (Cova et al., 1994), which can be viewed as detail sales as illustrated in Fig. 1. Value-based selling is different, as the seller is involved in creating the business case and investment specifications with the customer (pre-sales and detail sales). This requires a whole different skill set from a sales force; in fact, it has been found that only one-third of the sales force has the capabilities to change from product to solution selling (Ulaga & Loveland, 2014).

It is notable that the customer-facing value-based selling process outlined by Luotola et al. (2017) and Liinamaa et al. (2016) includes cooperation with several actors in the customer organization. As found in industrial sales

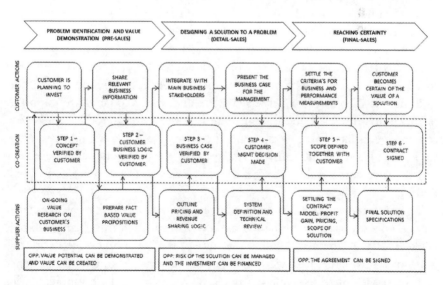

Fig. 1 Illustration of the value-based selling process (Adapted from Luotola et al. [2017])

literature (Webster & Wind, 1972), there are different actors in the customer organization that can influence a purchasing decision:

- Users—those members of the organization who use the purchased products and services
- Buyers—those with formal responsibility and authority for contracting with suppliers
- Influencers—those who influence the decision process directly or indirectly by providing information and criteria for evaluating alternative buying actions
- Deciders—those with authority to choose among alternative buying actions
- Gatekeepers—those who control the flow of information (and materials) into the buying center.

Performance Measurement in Service Operations

In service operations literature, the fundamental logic for performance measurement has been outlined to identify the features of performance measurement systems (Jääskeläinen et al., 2014), and has also been reviewed from the perspective of collaborative network performance measurement (Ukko et al., 2015; Ukko & Saunila, 2020).

Jääskeläinen et al. (2014) find three distinctive types of performance measurement for service performance: contingency-based measurement, customer-oriented measurement, and systemic measurement. Jääskeläinen et al. (2014) find that since service operations are unique, there is no universal means of measuring service operation performance. At the same time, they outline that the customer-perceived value and service quality are important factors to include in the performance measurement and that this goes beyond customer satisfaction. The systemic performance includes the customer's value, but also spans the entire service system. Measuring the systemic value is logical, as customer value creation should be tied to the system (Vargo et al., 2008).

The customer's role and involvement in the performance measurement of service operations are highlighted as key in implementing them (Ukko & Pekkola, 2016). Further, defining the state of the collaboration network that is formed through the service operations, the services and value elements, and the service providers' role in value creation are essential to implementing the performance measurement systems (Ukko et al., 2015; Ukko & Saunila,

2020). This points toward defining the systemic performance measurement identified by Jääskeläinen et al. (2014).

3   Theory Synthesis for a Performance Measurement Framework for Value-Based Selling

Our theoretical findings are summarized to three features of performance measurement in value-based selling. These three features are systemic, customer relationship, and sales process outcome. We also propose performance measurement processes throughout the value-based selling process. The sales outcome (top section in Fig. 2) is based on measuring the sales progress and resourcing of sales cases, and therefore operational performance measurement. The customer relationship performance measurement includes both operational and strategic measurement. This is due to that individual operational performance measures form the input to strategic analyses, such as input to the generic customer needs, and customer segmentation (as described in sect. "Customer Relationship Performance Measurement"). The systemic performance measurement moves to a strategic level, as an input to the value-based sales progress, while the value-based seller gathers important input required for the performance measurement (as described in sect. "Systemic Performance Measurement")

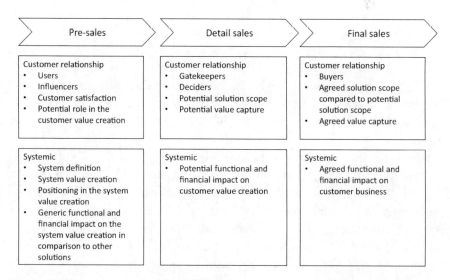

Fig. 2   Performance measurement throughout the value-based selling process

Systemic Performance Measurement

From a strategic perspective, the systemic performance measurement is based on an ongoing review of how different industrial systems are best operated and which the most beneficial system improvements would be, both through the new build perspective and potential upgrades. An important basis for this is defining the system (*i.e.,* the set of assets and through this the extent of impact), outlining the system value calculation formulae, and determining the role and responsibilities of different actors in the system according to set parameters in the formulae.

The basic formula that the solution provider needs to understand is the process-based calculation of the industrial system that their customers' assets function as part of. We classify the outlining of the systemic value process calculation as a performance measurement design process for solution providers; we argue that a key practice in this is for the firm to determine its position in the value stream according to a set parameter in the calculation. Different modules, or the combination of different modules in a solution offering impact the assets functionality through a set of several different parameters, which in turn impacts the system value creation. We further argue that without finding a parameter to position according to, the firm cannot be classed as a solution provider.

Our argument in positioning the solution provider according to a parameter is based on the logic that solution providers actually develop "market solutions" that bring a change to the industry environment (Storbacka & Nenonen, 2011). This also accounts for the customer perspective as identified in the service performance measurement literature through the impact on the customer assets, and serves as a basis to evaluating the overall systemic impact, also including the benefit to all different actors (Jääskeläinen et al., 2014). Researchers also highlight the need of determining each actor's role in a service network as the basis for performance measurement (Ukko & Saunila, 2020), which we find that is well suitable to do according to a parameter.

Another important performance measurement process that we identify in the solution business strategy and value-based selling literature (Anderson et al., 2006) is based on questioning the content and validity of the strategy. We find that a performance measurement process, based on benchmarking all potential investments in the industry, both on the new build and upgrades, and also the level of best-suited service requirements in the industry and for the customer, is required for strategy development. Viewing the strategy only from being the best at delivering specific functions through solutions is not enough. There may be, during this time, more beneficial system improvements through other types of functions. This type of information is also highly relevant for the value-based seller, as they need information comparing their offered business cases to the next best alternative (Anderson et al., 2006).

It is notable that the strategic performance measurement processes of the systemic value are all inputs required in the pre-sales phase of a value-based selling process (Luotola et al., 2017). As argued in the value-based selling literature, the sellers need to be able to quantify the value of business cases from different perspectives and discuss business cases through "value equations" (Anderson et al., 2006). Similarly, value-based sellers gather input on how customers and other actors view the formulas, and values applied to evaluating the functional and financial impact on the system- and customer value creation throughout the value-based selling process. These perspectives are crystalized throughout the value-based selling process, through the customer case during the detail phase and the final agreement in the final sales phase, forming a direct feedback loop to the strategic management. The seller may also receive input on the types of investments that the customers are considering and the values tied to these investments. Thus, the value-based seller becomes an important information source for both the performance measurement design process and benchmarking different potential improvements in the industry.

Customer Relationship Performance Measurement

The relational performance measurement moves to ensure the correct customer prioritization and focus from the firm. As the literature asserts, customers need to be segmented according to the type of relationship that they are willing to engage in and targeted accordingly (Baines & Lightfoot, 2014). Wrongful targeting results in wrong focusing of resource and knowledge sharing. Knowing how customers form their business relationships, however, requires input from the sellers. We find that there are three important performance measurement processes related to the customer relationship in value-based selling.

A first performance measurement feature that we identify is based on the amount of relevant actors found in the customer organization. In transactional (product and service-based) sales cases, the seller mainly corresponds with the buyers. In value-based (solution) sales cases, the seller gains the confidence of several actors in the customer organization. As a generic example for insight, we have structured the actors in the value-based sales process according to the framework of Webster and Wind (1972) in Fig. 1. Starting from the pre-sales phase, the seller must gain the confidence of users and influencers in order to get a first promotion in the customer organization. It is, however, notable that not all customer types have users in their organizations (Korkeamäki & Kohtamäki, 2020), as they may be pure owning customers. In this case, the influencers are the main actors required in the pre-sales phase. A notable factor is that measuring the amount of relevant actors in a customer organization moves from measuring customer activity to focused activity.

A second performance measurement feature is based on the customer need and value capture mechanisms. While the systemic performance measurement is based on the technical aspects of a business case, the customer relationship performance measurement moves toward identifying the potential role of the solution provider in the customer value creation, through services. This is also an important basis for the pricing mechanisms, if the customer service need is high enough then the outcome-based pricing is more likely possible (Sjödin et al., 2020). If the customers rather want to "do it themselves," then the sales case moves toward a product and service sales logic. This in turn is relevant for the sales planning, in where to focus the resourcing.

Another potential quantifiable input to the segmentation can be based on reviewing the sales progress of different cases with the customer according to the steps or phases defined in the value-based selling process. Customers with sales cases, progress past the pre-sales phase when they and the solution provider have similar views on how to view the value creation of industry systems. Passing the detail sales, in turn, involves there having been verifications from the customer operations and management of their confidence in the solution performance, while passing the final sales involves the customers being confident that the solution providers are the best ones to deliver.

We also find that monitoring customer satisfaction is an important input to the value-based seller. As customer satisfaction is actually a representation of the customer trust (Gustafsson et al., 2010) in the solution providers ability to provide value, the results from customer satisfaction may provide relevant insight on what the customer will most likely purchase.

4   Discussion

Theoretical Contributions

In our literature review, we have identified three key features of performance measurement systems for value-based selling: systemic, customer relationship, and sales process outcome. Further, we have identified their relevance during different phases of the value-based selling process and how activities in the value-based selling process provide input to the different strategic performance measurement processes.

The literature on performance measurement systems in service networks brings rich insight to implementation. It is notable that the implementation steps outlined by Ukko et al. (2015) relate strongly to activities outlined for the value-based selling process. This verifies our view on the link between the performance measurement systems in value-based selling and solution business strategy.

We recommend as further research to more closely review the type of performance measurement systems that can be formed for the value-based selling process and how to best implement them. The features we have outlined and potential performance measurement processes provide a basic direction for the type of systems that can be formed, but there are different options of how to form different performance measures based on the features we have outlined. A natural next step is to test different performance measures to refine the best practices in implementation. It is notable that implementation mainly seems to be an organizational issue rather than a technical one, and therefore studies in this area should be viewed from the organizational perspective.

We also find that especially the progress measurement of the value-based selling process brings potential links to the implementation of relational performance measurement as part of customer segmentation. The progress of different activities, such as input found to business case calculations and relationships gained in the customer organization, can be relevant to include in quantifiable customer segmentation.

Managerial Implications

We propose for managers in solution business to review their existing performance measurement systems and identify to what extent they can position their performance measurement processes in the features outlined in this article. In regards to shaping performance measurement processes around the outlined features, we propose that a natural start is to frame the industry system for the company, and different subsystems in it, to gain insight on the different perspectives from which the value needs to be quantified.

The next step is to outline the process calculations of different systems and position the firm's solutions according to set parameters in the formulae. Following up on implemented solution business cases for how they have impacted systemic value creation through the positioned parameter serves as a final verification.

An important factor in regards to the sales follow-up is to review the sales process, determining to what extent the value-based selling process can be applied in existing practices and if existing sales practices need reworking. Both successful and unsuccessful sales cases are essential input to find whether the value-based selling process is applicable to the firm's solution sales.

References

Adamson, B., Dixon, M., & Toman, N. (2012). The end of solution sales. *Harvard Business Review* (July–August) 61–68.

Anderson, J., Narus, J., & van Rossum, W. (2006). Customer value propositions in business markets. *Harvard Business Review* (March), 91–99.

Baines, T., & Lightfoot, H. W. (2014). Servitization of the manufacturing firm. *International Journal of Operations & Production Management, 34*(1), 2–35. https://doi.org/10.1108/IJOPM-02-2012-0086.

Bourne, M., Mills, J., Wilcox, M., Neely, A., & Platts, K. (2000). Designing, implementing and updating performance measurement systems. *International Journal of Operations & Production Management, 20*(7), 754–771. https://doi.org/10.1108/01443570010330739.

Corsaro, D. (2014). The emergent role of value representation in managing business relationships. *Industrial Marketing Management, 43*(6), 985–995. https://doi.org/10.1016/j.indmarman.2014.05.011.

Cova, B., Mazet, F., & Salle, R. (1994). From competitive tendering to strategic marketing: an inductive approach for theory-building. *Journal of Strategic Marketing, 2*(1), 29–48. https://doi.org/10.1080/09652549400000002.

Davies, A., Brady, T., & Hobday, M. (2007). Organizing for solutions: Systems seller vs. systems integrator. *Industrial Marketing Management, 36*(2), 183–193. https://doi.org/10.1016/j.indmarman.2006.04.009.

Gebauer, H. (2011). Exploring the contribution of management innovation to the evolution of dynamic capabilities. *Industrial Marketing Management, 40*(8), 1238–1250. https://doi.org/10.1016/j.indmarman.2011.10.003.

Gustafsson, M., Smyth, H., Ganskau, E., & Arhippainen, T. (2010). Bridging strategic and operational issues for project business through managing trust.

International Journal of Managing Projects in Business, 3(3), 422–442. https://doi.org/doi.org/10.1108/17538371011056066.

Hellström, M. (2014). Solution business models based on functional modularity—The case of complex capital goods. *Journal of Service Management, 25*(5), 654–676. https://doi.org/10.1108/JOSM-07-2013-0198.

Hellström M., Sifontes Herrera V.A., Wikström R., & Långstedt J. (2017). The service configurator—How to optimally split project scopes. In J. Vesalainen, K. Valkokari, & M. Hellström (Eds.), *Practices for network management*. Palgrave Macmillan. https://doi.org/10.1007/978-3-319-49649-8_16.

Ittner, C. D., Larcker, D. F., & Randall, T. (2003). Performance implications of strategic performance measurement in financial services firms. *Accounting, Organizations and Society, 28*(7–8), 715–741. https://doi.org/10.1016/s0361-3682(03)00033-3.

Jaaskelainen, A., Laihonen, H., & Lonnqvist, A. (2014). Distinctive features of service performance measurement. *International Journal of Operations & Production Management, 34*(12), 1466–1486. https://doi.org/10.1108/IJOPM-02-2013-0067.

Jacobides, M. G., Knudsen, T., & Augier, M. (2006). Benefiting from innovation: Value creation, value appropriation and the role of industry architectures. *Research Policy, 35*(8), 1200–1221. https://doi.org/10.1016/j.respol.2006.09.005.

Kaplan, R. S., & Norton, D. P. (1996). Linking the balanced scorecard to strategy. *California Management Review, 39*(1), 53–79. https://doi.org/10.2307/41165876.

Kohtamäki, M., Parida, V., Oghazi, P., Gebauer, H., & Baines, T. (2019). Digital servitization business models in ecosystems: A theory of the firm. *Journal of Business Research, 104*, 196–208. https://doi.org/10.1016/j.jbusres.2019.06.027.

Korkeamäki, L., & Kohtamäki, M. (2020). To outcomes and beyond: Discursively managing legitimacy struggles in outcome business models. *Industrial Marketing Management, 91*(2020), 196–208. https://doi.org/10.1016/j.indmarman.2020.08.023.

Kowalkowski, C. (2011). The service function as a holistic management concept. *Journal of Business & Industrial Marketing, 26*(7), 484–492. https://doi.org/10.1108/08858621111162280.

Kujala, S., Artto, K., Aaltonen, P., & Turkulainen, V. (2010). Business models in project-based firms—Towards a typology of solution-specific business models. *International Journal of Project Management, 28*(2), 96–106. https://doi.org/10.1016/j.ijproman.2009.08.008.

Liinamaa, J., Viljanen, M., Hurmerinta, A., Ivanova-Gongne, M., Luotola, H., & Gustafsson, M. (2016). Performance-based and functional contracting in value-based solution selling. *Industrial Marketing Management, 59*, 37–49. https://doi.org/10.1016/j.indmarman.2016.05.032.

Luotola, H., Hellström, M., Gustafsson, M., & Perminova-Harikoski, O. (2017). Embracing uncertainty in value-based selling by means of design thinking. *Industrial Marketing Management, 65,* 59–75. https://doi.org/10.1016/j.indmarman. 2017.05.004.

Nordin, F., & Kowalkowski, C. (2010). Solutions offerings: a critical review and reconceptualisation. *Journal of Service Management, 21*(4), 441–459. https://doi.org/10.1108/09564231011066105.

Rabetino, R., Kohtamäki, M., & Gebauer, H. (2017). Strategy map of servitization. *International Journal of Production Economics, 192,* 144–156. https://doi.org/10. 1016/j.ijpe.2016.11.004.

Sjödin, D., Parida, V., Jovanovic, M., & Visnjik, I. (2020). Value creation and value capture alignment in business model innovation: A process view on outcome-based business models. *The Journal of Product Innovation Management, 37*(2), 158–183. https://doi.org/10.1111/jpim.12516.

Storbacka, K. (2011). A solution business model: Capabilities and management practices for integrated solutions. *Industrial Marketing Management, 40*(5), 699–711. https://doi.org/10.1016/j.indmarman.2011.05.003.

Storbacka, K., & Nenonen, S. (2011). Scripting markets: From value propositions to market propositions. *Industrial Marketing Management, 40*(2), 255–266. https://doi.org/10.1016/j.indmarman.2010.06.038.

Storbacka, K., Polsa, P., & Sääksjärvi, M. (2011). Management practices in solution sales. *The Journal of Personal Selling & Sales Management, 31*(1), 35–54. Retrieved from https://www.econis.eu/PPNSET?PPN=647542595.

Stremersch, S., Wuyts, S., & Frambach, R. T. (2001). The purchasing of full-service contracts: An exploratory study within the industrial maintenance market. *Industrial Marketing Management, 30*(1), 1–12. https://doi.org/10.1016/S0019-850 1(99)00090-5.

Terho, H., Haas, A., Eggert, A., & Ulaga, W. (2012). 'It's almost like taking the sales out of selling'—Towards a conceptualization of value-based selling in business markets. *Industrial Marketing Management, 41*(1), 174–185. https://doi.org/10. 1016/j.indmarman.2011.11.011.

Töytäri, P., & Rajala, R. (2015). Value-based selling: An organizational capability perspective. *Industrial Marketing Management, 45,* 101–112. https://doi.org/10. 1016/j.indmarman.2015.02.009.

Tuli, K. R., Kohli, A. K., & Bharadwaj, S. G. (2007). Rethinking customer solutions: From product bundles to relational processes. *Journal of Marketing, 71*(3), 1–17. https://doi.org/10.1509/jmkg.71.3.1.

Ukko, J., & Pekkola, S. (2016). Customer-centered measurement of service operations: A B2B case study. *Operations Management Research, 9*(1), 11–21. https://doi.org/10.1007/s12063-016-0107-y.

Ukko, J., Pekkola, S., Saunila, M., & Rantala, T. (2015). Performance measurement approach to show the value for the customer in an industrial service network. *International Journal of Business Performance Management, 16*(2–3), 214–229. dx.doi.org/10.1504/IJBPM.2015.068726.

Ukko, J., & Saunila, M. (2020). Understanding the practice of performance measurement in industrial collaboration: From design to implementation. *Journal of Purchasing and Supply Management, 26*(1), https://doi.org/10.1016/j.pursup.2019.02.001.

Ulaga, W., & Loveland, J. M. (2014). Transitioning from product to service-led growth in manufacturing firms: Emergent challenges in selecting and managing the industrial sales force. *Industrial Marketing Management, 43*(1), 113–125. https://doi.org/10.1016/j.indmarman.2013.08.006.

Vargo, S. L., & Lusch, R. F. (2004). Evolving to a new dominant logic for marketing. *Journal of Marketing, 68*(1), 1–17. https://doi.org/10.1509/jmkg.68.1.1.24036.

Vargo, S. L., Maglio, P. P., & Akaka, M. A. (2008). On value and value co-creation: A service systems and service logic perspective. *European Management Journal, 26*(3), 145–152. https://doi.org/10.1016/j.emj.2008.04.003.

Webster, F. E., & Wind, Y. (1972). A general model for understanding organizational buying behavior. *Journal of Marketing, 36*, 12–19. https://doi.org/10.2307/1250972.

Wikström, K., Hellström, M., Artto, K., Kujala, J., & Kujala, S. (2009). Services in project-based firms—Four types of business logic. *International Journal of Project Management, 27*, 113–122. https://doi.org/10.1016/j.ijproman.2008.09.008.

Windahl, C., & Lakemond, N. (2010). Integrated solutions from a service-centered perspective: Applicability and limitations in the capital goods industry. *Industrial Marketing Management, 39*(8), 1278–1290. https://doi.org/10.1016/j.indmarman.2010.03.001.

Exploring Dynamic Capabilities to Facilitate a Smoother Transition from Servitization to Digital Servitization: A Theoretical Framework

Luna Leoni and Koteshwar Chirumalla

1   Introduction

In order to survive in the current competitive context—characterized by numerous and rapid changes—manufacturers are increasingly adopting servitization as a business strategy, offering a product-service combination in order to meet the renewed needs of consumers (Baines et al., 2009); thus, attaining sustainable competitive advantages (Raddats et al., 2019). Despite a growing body of literature on servitization, several researchers highlight the "non-maturity" of the concept and its strategy implementation as most companies are still limited to traditional product-related services compared to the advanced types of services, through which it is possible to achieve a higher competitive advantage (Rabetino et al., 2017; Raja et al., 2017).

The adoption of emerging digital technologies and Industry 4.0—e.g., smart sensors, internet of things (IoT), cloud computing, and augmented reality, together with real-time, intelligence, connectivity, and analytical

L. Leoni (✉)
Department of Management and Law, University of Rome Tor Vergata, Rome, Italy
e-mail: luna.leoni@uniroma2.it

K. Chirumalla
Mälardalen University, Eskilstuna, Sweden
e-mail: koteshwar.chirumalla@mdh.se

capabilities (e.g., Ardolino et al., 2018)—provides novel opportunities to industrial firms to enable advanced services in servitization, which is often referred to, in academia, as digital servitization (Kohtamäki et al., 2019; Sklyar et al., 2019). With the adoption of digital technologies, companies can develop smart and connected products with dedicated software-enabled systems, which enable capabilities such as monitoring, control, optimization, and autonomy as well as ecosystem collaboration, offering diagnostic, predictive, and remote services through new value propositions and business models (Kohtamäki et al., 2019; Porter & Heppelmann, 2015).

However, the successful transition toward digital servitization requires fundamental reconfiguration of resources, organizational structures and processes, work practices, infrastructure, culture, and value chains or ecosystems (Bustinza et al., 2015; Bustinza et al., 2018; Huikkola & Kohtamäki, 2017; Huikkola et al., 2016; Kohtamäki et al., 2019, 2020; Sklyar et al., 2019). In this vein, recent literature emphasizes how the theory of Dynamic Capability (Teece et al., 1997) is able to provide an interesting analytical framework for holistically studying such strategic organizational changes and transformation (Björkdahl, 2020; Coreynen et al., 2020; Kohtamäki et al., 2019; Pagoropoulos et al., 2017). In fact, during the shift to servitization, one of the major challenges for manufacturers is being able to acquire and properly manage additional capabilities afar those specifically centered on tangible products (Huikkola et al., 2016; Kindström et al., 2013; Raddats et al., 2017; Teece, 2007). Such capabilities are even more critical in the context of digital servitization, which requires manufacturers to acquire not only service-related capabilities but, increasingly, also those relating to digital technologies, the latter being a crucial tool to boost and ameliorate the service provision. Hence, it is fundamental for companies aspiring to properly understand, build, and adopt dynamic capabilities (here after referred as DCs) (Kohtamäki et al., 2019; Teece, 2007) in order to provide advanced services (Baines et al., 2017; Kindström et al., 2013) and to facilitate a smoother transition to digital servitization.

Most existing literature discusses different forms of general capabilities and DCs for servitization and digital servitization in a scattered way, lacking sufficient detail to support a smoother transition. Although the concept of DCs referred to in strategic management literature as building firms' long-term advantages and competitive flexibility in environmental dynamism, the uptake of this concept in digital servitization literature is still limited. Therefore, this chapter scans prior studies covering DCs for servitization and digital servitization to identify and compare the DCs needed to facilitate a smoother transition from "traditional forms" of servitization to digital servitization. The chapter addresses the following research questions:

RQ1:   What are the dynamic capabilities reported in the literature to successfully implement servitization and digital servitization?

RQ2:   According to literature, what are the main enablers that can facilitate the transition from "traditional" servitization to digital servitization?

In doing so, this chapter presents a theoretical framework of DCs to enable digital servitization, bringing to light 22 micro-foundations for servitization and digital servitization; thus, enhancing the understanding of how digital servitization can be built and nurtured from the currently ongoing servitization in industrial firms.

2   Theory Development

Defining Key Concepts

This chapter focuses on three main concepts: servitization, digital servitization, and DCs. Each of them is briefly described below and their main definitions are shown in Table 1.

Despite its widespread use, servitization is still subject to extensive debate because its implementation is far from simple and manufacturers tend to struggle with it (Rabetino et al., 2017; Raja et al., 2017). This is even truer if we consider digital servitization. Thus, in order to better understand how manufacturers can properly face the numerous challenges coming from servitization and digital servitization, recently published literature focuses on the importance of DCs, namely "the firm's ability to integrate, build, and reconfigure internal and external competences to address rapidly changing environments" (Teece et al., 1997: 516). The DCs approach has roots in the organization's resource-based view (RBV; Barney et al., 2001), explaining how firms can develop distinctive and difficult-to-replicate capabilities by adding, modifying, or reconfiguring resources/competences when the existing value-generating resources and capabilities become outdated due to environmental dynamism (Eisenhardt & Martin, 2000; Teece et al., 1997). Simply put, DCs describe firms' capacity to sense and shape opportunities and threats, seize opportunities, and reconfigure firms' intangible and tangible assets (Teece, 2007).

Table 1 Main concepts definitions

Concepts	Definitions	Main References
Servitization	It is a transformational process, which implies shifting from a product-centric to a service-centric business model and logic (i.e., shifting from selling product to selling product-service systems) It involves the innovation of a company's resource base, capabilities, structures, and processes, together with a redefinition of the firm mission, norms, and values	Neely (2008) Baines et al. (2009) Kindström and Kowalkowski (2014) Kowalkowski et al. (2017)
Digital servitization	It refers to the utilisation of digital technologies (e.g., IoT, big data, AI, and cloud computing) through which a company shifts from a product- to a service-centric business model by providing smart product-service-software systems that enable the company value creation It involves transforming industrial firms' (and related ecosystem) processes, capabilities, and offerings	Kohtamäki et al. (2019) Sjödin et al. (2020)
Dynamic capabilities	They refer to the firm's ability to purposefully integrate, build, and reconfigure both its internal and external competences in order to properly address rapid environmental changes They allow the firm to identify specific opportunity for change and—consequently—to formulate appropriate response and to implement ad hoc actions They can be classified into: • *Sensing capabilities*: the ability to detect and shape new technological and market opportunities as well as potential threats; • *Seizing capabilities*: the ability of addressing technological and market opportunities through new services, sheltering and exploiting new opportunities; and • *Reconfiguring capabilities*: the firm ability to match and manage the dependence between service strategy and organizational design in order to achieve strategic alignment and to create competitive advantage (i.e., to transform resources, processes, and operational skills)	Teece et al. (1997) Teece (2007)

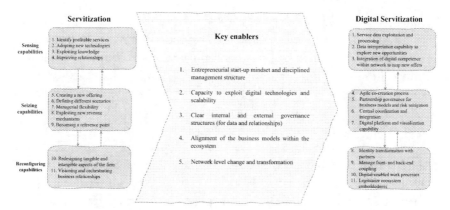

Fig. 1 Theoretical dynamic capabilities framework for digital servitization

A Theoretical Framework of Dynamic Capabilities to Enable Digital Servitization

The literature analysis of DCs for servitization and digital servitization shows 22 micro-foundations of sensing, seizing, and reconfiguring capabilities and five key enablers. Based on these results, the study derives a theoretical framework of dynamic capabilities to enable digital servitization, which could facilitate the transition from "traditional" servitization to "digital" servitization (see Fig. 1).

Dynamic Capabilities for Servitization

Findings reveal that a set of eleven specific activities is necessary to properly develop the DCs needed to successfully implement a servitization strategy. In particular, the sensing capabilities refer to the ability to carry out the following four different activities:

1. *Identify profitable services.* The literature emphasizes the importance for manufacturers to differentiate their offerings through valuable services. In other words, there is the need to identify services that—integrated with tangible products—consumers are willing to pay for (Fischer et al., 2010). In doing that, scholars stress the importance of recognizing services as financial opportunities that need to be visible in the firm's financial statement and performance measurement systems to make the organization aware of their potential (Gebauer et al., 2012, 2013; Kindström et al., 2013).

2. *Adopting new technologies.* If manufacturers want to accurately respond to customers' needs and competitors' actions, information needs to be systematically captured and relayed through ad hoc technologies that allow information-gathering, -filtering, and -processing mechanisms to become routines (Fischer et al., 2010; Kanninen et al., 2017; Kindström et al., 2013). In this way, firms can provide a satisfactory product-service combination to customers as well as to strategically respond to competitors. The adoption of new technologies may also involve other actors. In fact, as emphasized by Kindström et al. (2013) and Lütjen et al. (2019), establishing external cooperation (with ICT specialists, universities, research institutes, and the like) is a useful practice that may lead to a deeper understanding of new service opportunities.

3. *Exploiting knowledge.* Once information on customers is collected and made available throughout the firm through ad hoc technologies, manufacturers have to exploit this new knowledge by putting in place information evaluation mechanisms that allow only relevant knowledge to be retained within the company (Adam et al., 2018; Fischer et al., 2010; Kindström et al., 2013). However, knowledge exploitation also refers to the manufacturer's ability to investigate and understand external actors in order to undertake exchanges of knowledge with the latter capable of improving their sensing opportunities and capabilities (Lütjen et al., 2019; Raddats et al., 2017).

4. *Improving relationships.* A successful servitization strategy is conditioned by the existence of certain relational abilities (e.g., listening skills, open mindset) within the firms, which—on the one hand—allow the creation of a comfortable environment that allows building intimate and long-standing relationships with customers (Adam et al., 2018) and—on the other hand—increases the chance to evaluate opportunities together with external actors (Adam et al., 2018; Kindström et al., 2013; Kanninen et al., 2017; Lütjen et al., 2019).

The seizing capabilities refer to the ability to carry out the following five activities:

1. *Creating a new offering.* According to the previously identified profitable services, manufacturers are called to create a new offering that properly combines tangible products and intangible services. The creation of a new offering, thus conceived, requires interaction between the manufacturing company and other actors in order to create something innovative, not only in terms of products/services but also toward different value chains

and beyond industry and existing network borders (Fischer et al., 2010; Gebauer et al., 2012).

2. *Defining different scenarios.* As suggested by Fischer et al. (2010) and Gebauer et al. (2012), the seizing capability is strictly linked to the firm's capacity to define numerous potential scenarios and to formulate strategies for each of them. Even other actors may be invited to seize the different scenarios, leading them to propose new value constellations (Gebauer et al., 2012).

3. *Managerial flexibility.* The ability to seize one or more opportunities is also closely linked to the firm's ability to be flexible (Gebauer et al., 2017). This flexibility is mainly related to managers, who are called upon as being able to explore a broad range of different business opportunities through an open mindset (Fischer et al., 2010). The flexibility also refers to their ability to integrate different capabilities coming from different sources, i.e., integration between manufacturing firm capabilities and those belonging to other actors (included or not in the service ecosystem) (Adam et al., 2018; Fischer et al., 2010; Gebauer et al., 2013; Lütjen et al., 2019; Raddats et al., 2017).

4. *Exploiting new revenue mechanisms.* It basically consists of verifying the financial benefits (previously sensed) by assessing whether customers demand and pay for the provided services (Gebauer et al., 2012). Charging for services previously offered for free (Fischer et al., 2010) and basing revenue mechanisms on service availability and customer productivity (Kindström et al., 2013) are examples of this exploitation.

5. *Becoming a reference point.* As noted by Lütjen et al. (2019), firms offering (highly innovative) services need to be seen by other actors as pioneers to increase their chance of being involved in innovative collaboration projects, enhancing—in turn—their change to provide innovative services.

Finally, the reconfiguring capabilities are linked to the ability to carry out two specific activities:

1. *Redesigning tangible and intangible aspects of the firm.* Servitization requires the firm's structure and processes to be redesigned in a way through which the various activities related to products and services may "talk" without hindering each other (Fischer et al., 2010; Kindström et al., 2013). In particular, the firm needs to be able to restructure its resources according to the services' delivery process (Kindström et al., 2013). This usually involves the creation of a specific unit within the company dedicated

exclusively to services (Fischer et al., 2010). However, the firm's capacity to redesign tangible aspects of the firm (such as the structure and technical requirements) needs to be balanced by the capacity to also redesign intangible aspects. In this vein, Gebauer et al. (2012), Kanninen et al. (2017), and Kindström et al. (2013) report that one of the most difficult but crucial activities is the modification of the corporate culture to re-orient it toward services. In particular, the creation of this new culture requires time and strong managers' commitment to be successful (Kindström et al., 2013). These changes in the tangible and intangible aspects of the firm influence each other and one is the cause-effect of the other and vice versa. Moving to the inter-firm level, the redesign is expressed by a refining process of multiple actors' competencies and capabilities. In doing so, Gebauer et al. (2013) highlight the need to create a common language among all the involved actors to promote solid relationships between them and, thus, their capabilities' integration; meanwhile, Lütjen et al. (2019) advocate the relevance of integrating external knowledge. Adam et al. (2018) further stress the concept by emphasizing that the capacity to redesign the tangible and intangible aspects of the firm depends as much on the ability to learn (through a deep and active knowledge sharing among multiple actors) as on the ability to unlearn familiar practices.

2. *Visioning and orchestrating business relationships.* It mainly refers to the internal ability of the firm to face challenges. In fact, servitization usually creates internal resistance and conflicts that need to be overcome (Fischer et al., 2010) through the institution of a service-oriented mental model and flat hierarchies (Adam et al., 2018) and the removal of traditional roots and structures (Lütjen et al., 2019). At the inter-firm level, what emerges as critical is the ability to orchestrate the service system. In other words, there is the need to skillfully manage the reconfiguration of almost all the firm's aspects in a process of continuous alignment between internal and external resources and processes (Gebauer et al., 2012; Kindström et al., 2013). This reconfiguration mainly passes through a re-evaluation of the business relationships (Fischer et al., 2010) that allows rearranging the different roles played by the numerous actors, visioning and mobilizing them (Gebauer et al., 2013), as well as incorporating complementary resources (Kindström et al., 2013).

Dynamic Capabilities for Digital Servitization

Our literature analysis found that a set of eleven specific activities is necessary to properly develop the DCs needed to successfully implement a digital servitization strategy. In particular, the digitally enabling sensing capabilities refer to the ability to carry out the following three different activities:

1. *Service data exploitation and processing.* Data is critically important and an enabler for digital servitization. The initial efforts to install sensors and constantly generate service-related data from the field help firms to exploit data and process it further (Coreynen et al., 2017; Tronvoll et al., 2020) and to sense a need or a problem. Kohtamäki et al. (2019) stress the importance of having capabilities in detailed monitoring, control, and optimization for autonomous solutions.
2. *Data interpretation capability to explore new opportunities.* It refers to the capacity of firms to interpret the collected data for recognizing customers' needs or exploring new opportunities (Tronvoll et al., 2020; Ulaga & Reinartz, 2011). Coreynen et al. (2020) found that high-exploration firms are more likely to be oriented toward digital servitization when they have reached a medium level of exploitation.
3. *Integration of digital competence within the network to map new offerings.* Firms need to have the right resources or hire employees with data analytics skills to formulate hybrid offerings (Coreynen et al., 2017), and to drive new business models around data-related issues (Tronvoll et al., 2020). This requires the integration of business knowledge and expertise of multiple actors in the network to realize the full potential of digitalization (Kamalaldin et al., 2020).

The digitally enabling seizing capabilities refer to the ability to carry out the following four activities:

1. *Agile co-creation process.* Manufacturing firms need to rethink their value creation process in digital servitization. Rather than working with the traditional way of working, the firms need to adopt an agile micro-service innovation approach to manage the value co-creation process with customers (Sjödin et al., 2020). Moreover, strategic agility is considered a prerequisite for digital organizational transformation (Bustinza et al., 2018), helping firms to adopt different configurations. Additionally, firms need to have a strong service, entrepreneurial, and agile mindset and way of working to productize digital services (Tronvoll et al., 2020).
2. *Partnership governance for business models and risk mitigation.* Manufacturing firms need to establish a broader range of external partnerships with different actors in the value chain and in the ecosystem to access specialized competences and to build a network, e.g., with third-party software

vendors (Tronvoll et al., 2020). Moreover, firms need to redefine business model configurations involving ecosystem actors (Kohtamäki et al., 2019) since the transformation of a single firm is not enough to realize the digital servitization. This requires relational governance strategies to protect everyone's business interests, cost structure, revenue and incentives, and to overcome risks and uncertainties (Kamalaldin et al., 2020; Pagoropoulos et al., 2017; Ulaga & Reinartz, 2011).

3. *Central coordination and integration.* For the successful organization and transformation to digital servitization, manufacturing firms need within-firm centralization and integration (Sklyar et al., 2019). The central organization needs to create a common resource pool and a set of digital tools and training methods to support local organizations to strengthen their customer relationships (Sklyar et al., 2019).

4. *Digital platform and visualization capability.* Firms need to invest in building digital systems and platforms to provide customized digital services to customers and to manage the associated abundance of data (Kamalaldin et al., 2020; Tronvoll et al., 2020). Moreover, firms need to allocate dedicated resources and expertise to analyze and visualize massive data for optimizing the operational processes (Coreynen et al., 2017; Kamalaldin et al., 2020).

Finally, the reconfiguring capabilities are linked to the ability to carry out four specific activities:

1. *Identity transformation with partners.* Firms that are developing digital services need to transform their identity from a "product-service-centric" company to a "digital-centric" company. Since there is a higher dependency between actors in developing digital services, it is not just enough to transform an identity of a single company; rather, it requires an ecosystem actor's identity transformation (Tronvoll et al., 2020). Firms need to search for new skills and a competence base that would be more compatible with the combination of servitization and digitalization by using technologies such as IoT, AI, 5G, cloud computing, and data analytics (Kohtamäki et al., 2019).

2. *Manage front- and back-end coupling.* Digital servitization transforms the roles and responsibilities of both front- and back-end units, which need to be tightly integrated (Coreynen et al., 2017; Sklyar et al., 2019). The local organizations and digital service centers are more focused on identifying and deploying new digital opportunities and business models whereas

back-end units focus on their ability to effectively create solutions with the integration of front-end functions (Coreynen et al., 2017).

3. *Digital-enabled work processes.* Manufacturing firms need to develop digital work processes to enable the easy accumulation and access of data from many different sources within the ecosystem (Kamalaldin et al., 2020) to improve data transparency and information sharing.

4. *Legitimize ecosystem embeddedness.* Manufacturing firms need to set a vision of digital-centricity and use this as a frame of reference to be promoted across the ecosystem (Sklyar et al., 2019). It is important to establish trust building and relational and structural embeddedness within the ecosystem with the adoption of a proper legitimization mechanism (Sklyar et al., 2019; Tronvoll et al., 2020).

The theoretical analysis also identified five key enablers for digital servitization, as shown in the theoretical framework in Fig. 1. The key enablers that support the transition from "traditional" servitization to digital servitization are: (1) Entrepreneurial start-up mindset and disciplined management structure, (2) Capacity to exploit digital technologies and scalability, (3) Clear internal and external governance structures, (4) Alignment of the business models within the ecosystem, and (5) Network level change and transformation.

3   Discussion

Theoretical Contributions

This study offers new insights to enable digital servitization by presenting a theoretical framework, which compares the DCs and key enablers needed to facilitate a smoother transition from "traditional forms" of servitization to digital servitization. The findings extend previous research related to developing and organizing digital servitization (e.g., Bustinza et al., 2018; Coreynen et al., 2017; Sjödin et al., 2020; Sklyar et al., 2019), enhancing DCs for servitization (e.g., Fischer et al., 2010; Gebauer et al., 2012; Kanninen et al., 2017; Kindström et al., 2013) and for digital servitization (e.g., Coreynen et al., 2020; Kohtamäki et al., 2019; Pagoropoulos et al., 2017).

In fact, current literature on servitization and digital servitization does not provide exhaustive indications about the needed DCs and their even more detailed level of micro-foundations (Coreynen et al., 2017; Fischer et al.,

2010; Huikkola & Kohtamäki, 2017; Kindström et al., 2013; Kohtamäki et al., 2019; Parida & Wincent, 2019; Raddats et al., 2017; Salonen, 2011). Existing research on DCs focuses on either servitization or digital servitization, but not their combination—an essential topic for today's digitalization of firms—resulting in relatively abstract knowledge and lacking sufficient detail to support a smoother transition to digital servitization. Thus, this study fills this gap by identifying a set of 22 micro-foundations that companies need to carry out to properly develop sensing, seizing, and reconfiguring of DCs for servitization and digital servitization, relating them into a theoretical framework. In doing so, it extends the generic DCs' framework by offering a more fine-grained and complete view to properly succeed through servitization and digital servitization, as well as to holistically prepare the organization for a smoother transition from first to second by providing five enablers. This corresponds to the call for supporting companies in a smoother transition from traditional servitization to the digital one (Kohtamäki et al., 2019; Paiola & Gebauer, 2020; Paschou et al., 2020). Moreover, the framework contributes to the still-limited discussion on organizational and managerial activities through which firms actually introduce and organize digital servitization (e.g., Sjödin et al., 2020; Sklyar et al., 2019).

Thus, this chapter provides a broader view considering the firms' capability development and makes an important step in enhancing understanding of how digital servitization can be built and nurtured from the currently ongoing servitization in industrial firms. Firms require a clear understanding of their current position and capabilities in servitization work; without such knowledge, it is difficult to find a pathway for improving or defining a future position. Thus, this study examined the ongoing and emerging servitization work and identified the respective micro-foundations for each position, including the required key enablers for a successful transition. Such an approach considered the implementation of digitalization as a more continuous process and helped to efficiently build digital servitization in a step-by-step manner.

The comparison of DCs for servitization and digital servitization shows some interesting results. When it comes to sensing capabilities, it is evident that companies need to make a shift from exploiting knowledge to the exploitation of data/data management or in combination. For seizing capabilities, companies need to make a shift from basic managerial capabilities to managing agile platforms and partnership governance. For reconfiguring capabilities, companies need to make a shift from managing business partnerships to managing the transformation of networks and ecosystems with the support of digital work processes. Finally, the results confirm that transition to digital servitization does not only include digital technologies or data, but also firms' development of competences, work processes, organizational structures, and partnership management.

Managerial Implications

The theoretical framework presented in this chapter provides several practical implications that are particularly useful for practitioners and managers of manufacturing firms who want to undertake (or who have already undertaken) a transition process toward servitization and digital servitization.

Firstly, managers will benefit from a general and enriched understanding of which DCs are needed to be successful in servitization and digital servitization processes. Secondly, the theoretical framework can be interpreted as a map that contains all the specific DCs necessary to face the transition itself, facilitating practitioners in their understanding and management of the different steps through which the transition toward service-oriented business models takes place. Moreover, the "map" can also be useful in identifying the necessary changes—in terms of DCs—required for moving from servitization to digital servitization. Thirdly and lastly, the framework sheds light on the importance of the DCs developed through external actors. Accordingly, the ability of practitioners to adequately select partners within their service ecosystem as well as their ability to relate adequately with external actors (e.g., institutions, universities) assumes a crucial role.

References

Adam, M., Strähle, J., & Freise, M. (2018). Dynamic capabilities of early-stage firms: Exploring the business of renting fashion. *Journal of Small Business Strategy, 28*(2), 49–67.

Ardolino, M., Rapaccini, M., Saccani, N., Gaiardelli, P., Crespi, G., & Ruggeri, C. (2018). The role of digital technologies for the service transformation of industrial companies. *International Journal of Production Research, 56*(6), 2116–2132. https://doi.org/10.1080/00207543.2017.1324224.

Baines, T., Bigdeli, A. Z., Bustinza, O. F., Shi, V. G., Baldwin, J., & Ridgway, K. (2017). Servitization: Revisiting the state-of-the-art and research priorities. *International Journal of Operations & Production Management, 37*(2), 256–278. https://doi.org/10.1108/IJOPM-06-2015-0312.

Baines, T., Lightfoot, H., Benedettini, O., & Kay, J. (2009). The servitization of manufacturing: A review of literature and reflection of future challenges. *Journal of Manufacturing Technology Management, 20*(5), 547–567. https://doi.org/10.1108/17410380910960984.

Barney, J., Wright, M., & Ketchen, D.J. (2001). The resource-based view of the firm: Ten years after 1991. *Journal of Management*, 625–641. https://doi.org/10.1177%2F014920630102700601.

Björkdahl, J. (2020). Strategies for digitalization in manufacturing firms. *California Management Review, 62*(4), 17–36. https://doi.org/10.1177%2F0008125620920349.

Bustinza, O. F., Bigdeli, A. Z., Baines, T., & Elliot, C. (2015). Servitization and competitive advantage: The importance of organizational structure and value chain position. *Research-Technology Management, 58*(5), 53–60. https://doi.org/10.5437/08956308X5805354.

Bustinza, O. F., Gomes, E., Vendrell-Herrero, F., & Tarba, S. Y. (2018). An organizational change framework for digital servitization: Evidence from the Veneto region. *Strategic Change, 27*(2), 111–119. https://doi.org/10.1002/jsc.2186.

Coreynen, W., Matthyssens, P., & Van Bockhaven, W. (2017). Boosting servitization through digitization: Pathways and dynamic resource configurations for manufacturers. *Industrial Marketing Management, 60*, 42–53. https://doi.org/10.1016/j.indmarman.2016.04.012.

Coreynen, W., Matthyssens, P., Vanderstraeten, J., & van Witteloostuijn, A. (2020). Unravelling the internal and external drivers of digital servitization: A dynamic capabilities and contingency perspective on firm strategy. *Industrial Marketing Management, 89*, 265–277. https://doi.org/10.1016/j.indmarman.2020.02.014.

Eisenhardt, K. M., & Martin, J. A. (2000). Dynamic capabilities: What are they? *Strategic Management Journal, 21*(10–11), 1105–1121. https://doi.org/10.1002/1097-0266(200010/11)21:10/11%3C1105:AID-SMJ133%3E3.0.CO;2-E.

Fischer, T., Gebauer, H., Gregory, M., Ren, G., & Fleisch, E. (2010). Exploitation or exploration in service business development? Insights from a dynamic capabilities perspective. *Journal of Service Management, 21*(5), 591–624. https://doi.org/10.1108/09564231011079066.

Gebauer, H., Paiola, M., & Edvardsson, B. (2012). A capability perspective on service business development in small and medium-sized suppliers. *Scandinavian Journal of Management, 28*(4), 321–339. https://doi.org/10.1016/j.scaman.2012.07.001.

Gebauer, H., Paiola, M., & Saccani, N. (2013). Characterizing service networks for moving from products to solutions. *Industrial Marketing Management, 42*(1), 31–46. https://doi.org/10.1016/j.indmarman.2012.11.002.

Gebauer, H., Saul, C. J., Haldimann, M., & Gustafsson, A. (2017). Organizational capabilities for pay-per-use services in product-oriented companies. *International Journal of Production Economics, 192*, 157–168. https://doi.org/10.1016/j.ijpe.2016.12.007.

Huikkola, T., & Kohtamäki, M. (2017). Solution providers' strategic capabilities. *Journal of Business and Industrial Marketing, 32*(5), 752–770. https://doi.org/10.1108/JBIM-11-2015-0213.

Huikkola, T., Kohtamäki, M., & Rabetino, R. (2016). Resource realignment in servitization. *Research Technology Management, 59*(4), 30–39. https://doi.org/10. 1080/08956308.2016.1185341.

Kamalaldin, A., Linde, L., Sjödin, D., & Parida, V. (2020). Transforming provider-customer relationships in digital servitization: A relational view on digitalization. *Industrial Marketing Management, 89,* 306–325. https://doi.org/10.1016/j.ind marman.2020.02.004.

Kanninen, T., Penttinen, E., Tinnilä, M., & Kaario, K. (2017). Exploring the dynamic capabilities required for servitization. *Business Process Management Journal, 23*(2), 226–247. https://doi.org/10.1108/BPMJ-03-2015-0036.

Kindström, D., & Kowalkowski, C. (2014). Service innovation in product-centric firms: A multidimensional business model perspective. *Journal of Business & Industrial Marketing, 29*(2), 96–111.

Kindström, D., Kowalkowski, C., & Sandberg, E. (2013). Enabling service innovation: A dynamic capabilities approach. *Journal of Business Research, 66*(8), 1063–1073. https://doi.org/10.1016/j.jbusres.2012.03.003.

Kohtamäki, M., Parida, V., Oghazi, P., Gebauer, H., & Baines, T. (2019). Digital servitization business models in ecosystems: A theory of the firm. *Journal of Business Research, 104,* 380–392. https://doi.org/10.1016/j.jbusres.2019.06.027.

Kohtamäki, M., Parida, V., Patel, P. C., & Gebauer, H. (2020). The relationship between digitalization and servitization: The role of servitization in capturing the financial potential of digitalization. *Technological Forecasting and Social Change, 151,*. https://doi.org/10.1016/j.techfore.2019.119804.

Kowalkowski, C., Gebauer, H., Kamp, B., & Parry, G. (2017). Servitization and deservitization: Overview, concepts, and definitions. *Industrial Marketing Management, 60,* 4–10.

Lütjen, H., Schultz, C., Tietze, F., & Urmetzer, F. (2019). Managing ecosystems for service innovation: A dynamic capability view. *Journal of Business Research, 104,* 506–519.

Neely, A. (2008). Exploring the financial consequences of the servitization of manufacturing. *Operations management research, 1*(2), 103–118.

Pagoropoulos, A., Maier, A., & McAloone, T. C. (2017). Assessing transformational change from institutionalising digital capabilities on implementation and development of Product-Service Systems: Learnings from the maritime industry. *Journal of Cleaner Production, 166,* 369–380. https://doi.org/10.1016/j.jclepro. 2017.08.019.

Paiola, M., & Gebauer, H. (2020). Internet of things technologies, digital servitization and business model innovation in BtoB manufacturing firms. *Industrial Marketing Management, 89,* 245–264. https://doi.org/10.1016/j.indmarman. 2020.03.009.

Parida, V., & Wincent, J. (2019). Why and how to compete through sustainability: A review and outline of trends influencing firm and network-level transformation. *International Entrepreneurship and Management Journal, 15,* 1–19. https:// doi.org/10.1007/s11365-019-00558-9.

Paschou, T., Rapaccini, M., Adrodegari, F., & Saccani, N. (2020). Digital servitization in manufacturing: A systematic literature review and research agenda. *Industrial Marketing Management, 89,* 278–292. https://doi.org/10.1016/j.ind marman.2020.02.012.

Porter, M. E., & Heppelmann, J. E. (2015). How smart, connected products are transforming companies. *Harvard Business Review, 93*(10), 96–114.

Rabetino, R., Kohtamäki, M., & Gebauer, H. (2017). Strategy map of servitization. *International Journal of Production Economics, 192,* 144–156. https://doi.org/10.1016/j.ijpe.2016.11.004.

Raddats, C., Kowalkowski, C., Benedettini, O., Burton, J., & Gebauer, H. (2019). Servitization: A contemporary thematic review of four major research streams. *Industrial Marketing Management, 83,* 207–223. https://doi.org/10.1016/j.ind marman.2019.03.015.

Raddats, C., Zolkiewski, J., Story, V. M., Burton, J., Baines, T., & Bigdeli, A. Z. (2017). Interactively developed capabilities: Evidence from dyadic servitization relationships. *International Journal of Operations & Production Management, 37*(3), 382–400. https://doi.org/10.1108/IJOPM-08-2015-0512.

Raja, J. Z., Frandsen, T., & Mouritsen, J. (2017). Exploring the managerial dilemmas encountered by advanced analytical equipment providers in developing service-led growth strategies. *International Journal of Production Economics, 192,* 120–132. https://doi.org/10.1016/j.ijpe.2016.12.034.

Salonen, A. (2011). Service transition strategies of industrial manufacturers. *Industrial Marketing Management, 40*(5), 683–690. https://doi.org/10.1016/j.indmar man.2011.05.005.

Sjödin, D., Parida, V., Kohtamäki, M., & Wincent, J. (2020). An agile co-creation process for digital servitization: A micro-service innovation approach. *Journal of Business Research, 112,* 478–491. https://doi.org/10.1016/j.jbusres.2020.01.009.

Sklyar, A., Kowalkowski, C., Tronvoll, B., & Sörhammar, D. (2019). Organizing for digital servitization: A service ecosystem perspective. *Journal of Business Research, 104,* 450–460. https://doi.org/10.1016/j.jbusres.2019.02.012.

Teece, D. J. (2007). Explicating dynamic capabilities: The nature and microfoundations of (sustainable) enterprise performance. *Strategic Management Journal, 28*(13), 1319–1350. https://doi.org/10.1002/smj.640.

Teece, D. J., Pisano, G., & Shuen, A. (1997). Dynamic capabilities and strategic management. *Strategic Management Journal, 18*(7), 509–533. https://doi.org/10.1002/(SICI)1097-0266(199708)18:7%3C509:AID-SMJ882%3E3.0.CO;2-Z.

Tronvoll, B., Sklyar, A., Sörhammar, D., & Kowalkowski, C. (2020). Transformational shifts through digital servitization. *Industrial Marketing Management, 89,* 293–305. https://doi.org/10.1016/j.indmarman.2020.02.005.

Ulaga, W., & Reinartz, W. J. (2011). Hybrid offerings: How manufacturing firms combine goods and services successfully. *Journal of Marketing, 75*(6), 5–23. https://doi.org/10.1509%2Fjm.09.0395.

Dynamic Capabilities as Enablers of Digital Servitization in Innovation Ecosystems: An Evolutionary Perspective

María Alejandra Rodríguez, Leandro Lepratte,
and Rodrigo Rabetino

1   Introduction

The resource-based view (RBV), the dynamic capabilities view (DC), and the business model approach are the dominant perspectives in the servitization field (Rabetino et al., 2018). Recent literature reviews of the servitization-related research highlight the limited theoretical diversity and call for frameworks to study digital servitization at the ecosystem level rather than at the organizational level (Kohtamäki et al., 2019; Rabetino et al., 2018). A growing body of research, beyond the servitization literature, also considers the importance of dynamic capabilities in innovation ecosystems and focuses on dynamic capabilities in digital transformation processes (Lütjen et al., 2019; Parida et al., 2016). These processes require collaborative approaches, redefining the scope of firm-centered business models to others which

M. A. Rodríguez (✉) · L. Lepratte
Industrial Organization Department, National Technological University,
Concepción del Uruguay, Argentina
e-mail: rodrigueza@frcu.utn.edu.ar

L. Lepratte
e-mail: leprattel@frcu.utn.edu.ar

R. Rabetino
School of Management, University of Vaasa, Vaasa, Finland
e-mail: rodrigo.rabetino@uva.fi

© The Author(s), under exclusive license to Springer Nature
Switzerland AG 2021
M. Kohtamäki et al. (eds.), *The Palgrave Handbook of Servitization*,
https://doi.org/10.1007/978-3-030-75771-7_12

are ecosystem-driven and innovation-oriented (Rothaermel & Hess, 2007; Warner & Wäger, 2019).

The present chapter develops a multilevel framework on digital servitization that builds on the above research and integrates dynamic capabilities, business ecosystems, and innovation processes. In doing so, the chapter addresses the following research question: *what is the relationship between the development of dynamic capabilities at the level of business ecosystems and individual companies' business model innovation processes towards digital servitization?* The answer to this question includes two main discussions. First, the chapter discusses the specificities of digital capabilities. Second, the chapter argues how specific "digital capabilities" may serve as a value capture instrument to improve business performance.

The chapter is structured as follows. The second section introduces the relationship between dynamic capabilities and digital servitization. Section "Dynamic Capabilities and Digital Servitization" identifies the central concepts and their link to business model innovation processes. Next, the chapter reviews the advances in the conceptualization of digitalization capabilities. Section "Organizational Dynamic Capabilities and Ecosystems in Digital Servitization" includes contributions from studies on digital servitization, service-oriented ecosystems, configurations, digitalization capabilities, and organizational transformation. The chapter then presents a conceptual-explanatory framework in sect. "Dynamic Capabilities in Digital Servitization Innovation Ecosystems", shifting the analysis of digitalization capabilities from the firm- to the ecosystem-level. The framework also includes changes in structures and routines, technological and non-technological innovations, and their impact on business performance. Based on the previous discussions, section three summarizes the conceptual contribution and elaborates a heuristic proposal that includes tools and practices with managerial implications.

2   Theory Development

This section builds our conceptual discussion from the review of 37 publications on "digital servitization" systematically selected by using the SCOPUS database. From these articles, other studies related to "dynamic capabilities," "digital capabilities," and "digitalization capabilities" were selected and examined. Several studies link resources, capabilities, and servitization; studies specifically focused on dynamic capabilities, digital servitization. However, studies focusing on the relationship between dynamic capabilities, digital servitization, and ecosystems are still relatively recent (Paschou et al., 2020; Raddats et al., 2019). Next, we explore the most relevant concepts, processes, and results involved in this relationship.

Dynamic Capabilities and Digital Servitization

Digital servitization enables service innovation through digital technologies and innovative business models (Gebauer et al., 2020; Vendrell-Herrero et al., 2017), but it is not a straightforward endeavor (Rabetino et al., 2017). Firms face two major external contingencies: technological turbulence and competitive intensity (Coreynen et al., 2020). Additionally, the mere incorporation of digitizing assets does not imply an automatic process towards digital servitization. Developing appropriate business models that fit the firm's digital servitization strategies is critical. Strategic decisions configure different governance structures based on value creation and capture logics (Lerch & Gotsch, 2015; Sjödin et al., 2019). Thus, existing capabilities must be realigned, leading to a reconfiguration of resources and the development of new dynamic capabilities (Coreynen et al., 2017), not only technological but also organizational (Lerch & Gotsch, 2015). Business model-related capabilities drive and shape the innovation processes (Nylén & Holmström, 2015; Sjödin et al., 2020).

Digital servitization strategies also shape firm boundaries (Huikkola et al., 2020) as industry boundaries blur and companies reposition beyond the industry value chain and across an ecosystem. Firms often move from product-provider and industrializer-style business models to complex and digitalized models, such as integrated solutions provider, outcome provider, and platform provider (Kohtamäki et al., 2019). Therefore, "*digital*" and "*digitalization*" capabilities become increasingly more relevant too. As discussed below, both capabilities are implicit in digital servitization and can be analyzed from the perspective of dynamic capabilities at the firm and ecosystem level.

Previous studies used the dynamic capabilities approach to understand digital servitization (Lenka et al., 2017; Parida et al., 2016). Regarding the operationalization of dynamic capabilities, the distinction between "digitization" and "digitalization" must be considered (Ritter & Pedersen, 2020) (Table 1). "*Digitization*" is the process that has facilitated servitization for a long time. It is considered as the transformation of analog into digital. The

Table 1 Dynamic capabilities, digitalization, and digitization at the organizational level

Digital servitization at the organizational level	Digital servitization process	Dynamic capabilities related to Digital servitization	Dynamic capabilities orientations (outputs)
Digitization	Digitization resources and platforms	Digitization capabilities	Exploiting the technological possibilities, from analogic to digital
Digitalization	Complex socio-technical structures and processes	Digitalization capabilities	Exploration and exploitation are critical processes for business model innovation

digitization capabilities[1] are oriented to digitization resources and platforms. These capabilities focus on exploiting the technological possibilities of data transferability, expanding the communication frontiers. They also focus on increasing information, and facilitating the adoption of servitization strategies based on innovation ecosystems (Sklyar et al., 2019; Tronvoll et al., 2020). Digitization leads to commoditization unless it incorporates digitalization processes.

In contrast, "*digitalization*" emphasizes adopting the above technologies and how they can improve business performance. It represents the generation of more complex socio-technical structures and processes (Hinings et al., 2018). This incorporation requires developing new digital capabilities from the organizational viewpoint (Sklyar et al., 2019), which enable exploration and exploitation processes that are critical for business model innovation (Pisano, 2017; Teece, 2018).

As we will discuss in sect. "Organizational Dynamic Capabilities and Ecosystems in Digital Servitization", *digitalization capabilities* have shown to be critical to co-creating value with suppliers and customers (Kohtamäki et al., 2019). Therefore, these capabilities must be examined in the context of digital servitization ecosystems.

---

[1] There are also other related concepts (Paschou et al., 2020), such as IoT capabilities (Naik et al., 2020), ICT capabilities (Parida et al., 2016) and technology capabilities (Huikkola et al., 2020).

Organizational Dynamic Capabilities and Ecosystems in Digital Servitization

The reconfiguration of dynamic capabilities results from interactions with stakeholders, including suppliers, intermediates, and customers (Raddats et al., 2019). Therefore, because these capabilities have a *relational sense* (Kohtamäki et al., 2013), necessary to implement digital servitization strategies, co-generate capabilities, and co-create value in business networks and ecosystems (Henneberg et al., 2013). *Ecosystem* and business networks appear to be the right analytical levels for defining digital servitization strategies and business models (Kohtamäki et al., 2019; Lütjen et al., 2019). Regarding the organization of service ecosystems, evidence shows that centralized decision-making, together with a coherent implementation of digital platforms, improves firms' efficiency and responsiveness. Thus, understanding digital servitization-oriented business ecosystems' governance structures is crucial when evaluating digital technologies' effects on the structural flexibility between firms (Sklyar et al., 2019). The governance configurations that show the best performance are those that facilitate service innovation s. Those configurations based on relational governance offer a good fit with digital servitization processes. Suppliers and customers are key stakeholders to ensure successful cooperation and governance for value co-creation (Kohtamäki et al., 2019; Sjödin et al., 2020).

Likewise, Huikkola et al. (2020) consider that new specific capabilities are generated in closer interaction with customers, facilitating learning with them. Capabilities range from *generic* (e.g., digitization capabilities) to *relational* (e.g., system integration, project management, IT-systems, consulting, financial competencies, delivery, and aftersales services). The complex relationship between dynamic relational capabilities and digital servitization strategies redefines firm boundaries. They are determined by the interaction between business opportunities, the reconfiguration of digitization capabilities, and the resulting innovation processes. Thus, *complementary digitization capabilities* emerge (as digital assets) from feedbacks between *co-construction of knowledge, the cogeneration of capabilities, and relational governance configurations* (Coreynen et al., 2020; Huikkola & Kohtamäki, 2020; Kamalaldin et al., 2020; Sjödin et al., 2020).

Dynamic Capabilities in Digital Servitization Innovation Ecosystems

This section presents a conceptual framework for exploring and analyzing the relationship between dynamic capabilities development at the business ecosystem level and individual 'companies' business model innovation processes towards digital servitization. The framework assumes that digital servitization also depends on socio-technical interactions between global (outside-inside) and organizational (inside-outside) phenomena,[2] resulting from a systemic emergence[3] involving Digital Transformation—DT—(Warner & Wäger, 2019) and Servitization (Rabetino et al., 2018). From this assumption, dynamic capabilities are key factors to analyze how firms adapt to their environments (Teece, 2007, 2018). Simultaneously, the framework adds the notion of actor-rules system dynamics (Geels, 2020) and the multilevel analysis on transitions and socio-technical systems (Geels, 2004, 2020). Accordingly, *digital servitization is part of open-ended, non-linear, and uncertain, socio-technical transitions, which imply relationships between environmental and organizational dimensions.* DT develops from an ongoing techno-economic paradigm that involves an intensification of the service-oriented technological convergence (Adams et al., 2018; Kodama, 2014; Rabetino et al., 2018). The shift implies a new form of consumption, cultural changes, institutional redefinitions, new infrastructures, and business model reconfigurations.

Figure 1 gets inspiration from the contributions on evolutionary-systemic emergence and dynamic capabilities (Kay et al., 2018) and actor–rules system dynamics (Geels, 2020). It highlights the accumulated and strategic superior cognitive skills oriented to build and sustain competitive advantages (via technological, business, and innovation strategies) at the organizational level (Pisano, 2017; Teece, 2007). According to their type, strategies give rise to *organizational processes* (internal and external). In this context, the starting points are digital transformation (technological processes) and servitization (business processes). Both processes are evolutionary (Nelson & Winter, 1982) and generate systemic emergence phenomena, that is, properties that are more than the individual parts involved (Kay et al., 2018). Consequently,

---

[2] In the neo-Schumpeterian tradition of evolutionary studies, technological change and innovation processes are part of a complex dynamics on micro-meso-macro relations (Dopfer et al., 2004). As Rabetino et al. (2020) suggest, we assume that the above research stream shares ontological assumptions with the dynamic capabilities approach.

[3] The relationship between systemic emergence and dynamic capacities has been recently developed to explain the co-evolution in historical processes of capability generation and the complementarities between types of capabilities according to their level of complexity (Kay et al., 2018).

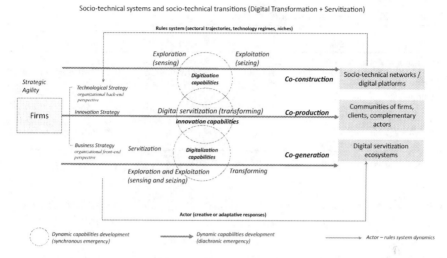

Fig. 1 Digital servitization and dynamic capabilities

the emerging transformation of both processes is digital servitization. The wider arrows indicate the emergence of dynamic capabilities in a diachronic sense (co-evolutionary), while the circles comprise a synchronic emergence (complementarities between capabilities).

Both types of systemic emergences in an organization are related. Synchronous ones consider the effects of complementarities between types of dynamic capabilities according to different levels of complexity. Diachronic ones cause changes in the firms' routines. Thus, digitization capabilities lead to changes in routines related to the co-construction of knowledge (sensing to seizing). Instead, digitalization capabilities introduce changes in the trajectory of the value cogeneration (seizing and sensing). The complementarity between both types of capabilities generates innovation capabilities, which cause changes in routines in the firms' co-production with other actors in their environment, mainly users or customers. Finally, organizational (socio-technical) transformations toward relational governance modes emerge from the relationship between strategies, processes, dynamic capabilities, and routines according to their typology (Table 2).

Following digital technological strategies, platforms generated and dynamize socio-technical networks. Servitization strategies allow the formation of business ecosystems. Simultaneously, innovation strategies facilitate communities of practice between firms, users, and complementary actors.

The above framework suggests that firms develop digital servitization strategies according to their path dependence (Dosi et al., 2016) within

Table 2 Digital Servitization and relational governance

Strategies	Processes	Dynamic capabilities[a]	Routines[b]	Organizational transformations
Technological	Digital transformation	Sensing to seizing	Knowledge co-construction	Digital platforms/socio-technical networks
Business	Servitization	Seizing and Sensing to transforming	Value cogeneration	Digital servitization ecosystems
Innovation	Digital servitization	Transforming	Co-production	Communities of practices

[a]Synchronous emergency, [b]Diachronic emergency

complex socio-technical transitions (Geels, 2010, 2020). Nevertheless, socio-technical shifts do not impact the firms in an entirely deterministic manner because they *operate in actor-rule system dynamics* (Geels, 2020). Here, two types of strategies are relevant: technological strategies and marketing strategies.

The *technological strategies* aim to execute *digital transformation* processes based on digitization capabilities at the organizational level. The specificity of *digitization capabilities* (Ritter & Pedersen, 2020) lies in the idea that they are oriented toward enhancing *sensing* resources, routines, and skills, internal to the organization and external. Concerning the latter, digital technologies allow opening firm boundaries and generating knowledge co-construction relationships with clients and other stakeholders through cross-platforms. Knowledge management from digital platforms creates a disruptive change in how sensing dynamic capabilities work (Teece, 2018). Thus, the *digitization capabilities generate organizational innovations of different scope*. Significantly, the external ones, for that firms develop relational capabilities generating different dynamics of socio-technical networks. These networks use unique relational governance modes that impact digital servitization-oriented technological strategies (Sjödin et al., 2019).

Accordingly, the digital transformation strategies imply incorporating digital technologies and the expansion of the dynamic sensing capabilities based on socio-technical networks and shared digital platforms. These conditions allow collecting large volumes of data as inputs to generate learning (seizing) about clients, suppliers, and even competitors. Knowledge co-construction, socio-technical network synergies, and the learning levels in a distributed knowledge environment show the degree of virtuosity that the firms' DT's technological strategies can have (Callon et al., 2002).

From the arguments above, firms define their *business strategies* based on digitization and relational capabilities.[4] Business strategies of digital servitization use the digitization and relational capabilities to innovate their business models (seizing), moving from goods-dominant to service-dominant exchange logic. Therefore, we assume that a minimum threshold of these capacities is required to promote dynamic capabilities oriented to seizing activities, with different modes and knowledge exploitation and exploration levels (seizing and sensing). In this context, the interaction between dynamic capabilities and business models has a central purpose, enhancing value co-creation (Lenka et al., 2017).

The business digitalization capabilities deal with co-creation processes that affect the value propositions according to different service-dominant logic (Lusch & Vargo, 2014; Taylor et al., 2020). By this, the platform ecosystems' organizational designs can be analyzed according to who owns the digital platform, the mechanisms of value co-creation, and the autonomy of the complementors (Hein et al., 2020). Therefore, innovations in marketing impact the firm-level and influence the firm level and the global configuration of the ecosystems where they participate (Taylor et al., 2020).

Along with technological strategies and digital-servitization-oriented business models, firms develop *innovation strategies* according to their ecosystem positioning. The digital servitization innovations processes are assumed to be systemic emergences, which relate socio-technical systems and socio-technical transitions (macro-level) and technology and business strategies and their corresponding dynamic capabilities (micro-level) (Geels, 2020; Nambisan et al., 2019). We focus on micro-level issues and assume that innovation activities in digital servitization contexts occur in *co-production* processes mediated by capabilities (Chen et al., 2015). Based on digital servitization-oriented platforms and ecosystems, co-production processes are dynamized in socio-technical networks that define services qualification and singularity (Callon et al., 2002).

New or improved product-services systems (PSS) or services can emerge among the digital servitization-oriented innovation strategies based on innovation models. They allow co-producing with clients and other complementary actors in spaces of distributed and situated cognition that generate *communities of actors* (Romero & Molina, 2011). Therefore, co-production starts changes in routines and capabilities at the networks/platforms level (incorporation of digital technologies and process innovations) and digital business ecosystems (marketing innovations). *Co-production* can also drive

---

[4] Several authors consider this process to be related to absorptive capacity (Cohen & Levinthal, 1990).

the emergence of new networks/platforms and digital business ecosystems guided by service-dominant logic.

As a complex process of organizational change, digital servitization executes three interconnected types of strategies. Each involves organizational transformations (Tronvoll et al., 2020) and specific value generation modes (Rabetino et al., 2017). *Technological strategies of digital servitization* involve routines and capabilities in organizational changes from planning to discovery, based on the generation and adaptation of networks/digital platforms, which aim at a specific form of *value appropriation and productivity*. From an *organizational back-end perspective*, digital technologies improve the firm's operational and R&D capabilities in terms of efficiency, resource allocation, and information on the business environment, key for decision-making and product and service development.

Based on digital servitization, business strategies drive organizational transformation from scarcity to abundance, understanding the dynamics of their digital servitization-oriented ecosystems. Central to this is how they carry out routines and capabilities to drive value co-creation and relationship management. Thus, from a *front-end organizational perspective*, business models based on digital servitization promote new types of integration and interaction with customers and complementary actors (Tronvoll et al., 2020). While those *innovation digital servitization-oriented strategies* transform the firms from a hierarchy to a partnership approach, they also consider open organizational modalities to generate value based on the co-production and configuration of communities with clients and complementary actors. Each of these organizational dimensions has its outcomes, modes of interaction, and logic of action and learning, which induce organizational transformations that drive organizational (socio-technical) innovations integrating people, technologies, infrastructures, cultures, and purposes[5] (Coreynen et al., 2017).

3   Discussion

Theoretical Contributions

At least three contributions of research emerge from the proposed framework. First, *from the dynamic capabilities approach*, the recognition of the complexity of the digital servitization process (Parida et al., 2016), together

---

[5] The literature related to *digital transformation* oriented to Industry 4.0 is already extensive and raises different models and analytical tools in socio-technical terms to analyze degrees of change in the firms and its networks (Bertolini et al., 2019).

with the operationalization and redefinition of capabilities in the context of digital servitization-oriented innovation ecosystems (Teece, 2018), gives way to exploring new operationalizations covering dynamic capabilities (Kohtamäki et al., 2020b). The second contribution follows the recurrent criticism observed in servitization concerning the lack of approaches that could deepen the understanding of the phenomenon using a multilevel approach (Rabetino et al., 2018). Our framework moves in that direction by reconciling such complementary approaches as dynamic capabilities, the economy of innovation (Arndt & Pierce, 2018; Nelson & Winter, 1982; Teece, 2018), socio-technical transitions, and actor-rules systemic dynamics (Geels, 2020; Lepratte, 2016). Finally, a meta-paradigmatic question is related to what Rabetino et al. (2020) observed when analyzing the strategic management field. Although different onto-epistemological positions may coexist, synergic approaches that answer the emerging canonical questions beyond positivism are needed (Luoto et al., 2017). Deepening a convergent perspective oriented to digital transformation processes and servitization poses challenges in this regard (Kohtamäki, Einola et al., 2020a; Kohtamäki, Parida et al., 2020; Kohtamäki et al., 2018). In any case, the socio-technical approach responds to the need for multilevel and multi-paradigmatic research (Geels, 2020) to study digital servitization (Rabetino et al., 2018).

Managerial Implications: Practices and Tools to Enhance Digitalization Capabilities

Enabling ambidexterity in the firms' strategic management is critical to face the paradoxes in servitization (Kohtamäki et al., 2020a). These circumstances also call for placing innovation at the top of the servitization management agenda (Sjödin et al., 2019), bearing in mind that the value capture process will be beyond the firm's boundaries and must focus on relational governance models (Vendrell-Herrero et al., 2017). Because old and new business models can coexist, strategic agility is a prerequisite (Bustinza et al., 2018; Tronvoll et al., 2020) to foster ambidextrous processes. Due to its importance, the agility to adapt resources and capabilities in collaboration with complementary actors in the ecosystem is another critical attribute that managers must develop. Managers must be prepared to identify changes and opportunities that generate socio-technical transitions and effect changes in their mindset (Bustinza et al., 2018; Huikkola & Kohtamäki, 2020; Sjödin et al., 2020). A successful digital servitization strategy calls for implementing coordinated efforts and redefining organizational culture, involving a closer link between business units (Sklyar et al., 2019). Another necessary condition is to develop relational capacities to interact and, above all, co-create value, with financial impact and in terms of quality, with customers and other stakeholders in a service ecosystem (Kohtamäki et al., 2020b).

References

Adams, T. L., Taricani, E., & Pitasi, A. (2018). The technological convergence innovation. *International Review of Sociology, 28*(3), 403–418.

Arndt, F., & Pierce, L. (2018). The behavioral and evolutionary roots of dynamic capabilities. *Industrial and Corporate Change, 27*(2), 413–424.

Bertolini, M., Esposito, G., Neroni, M., & Romagnoli, G. (2019). Maturity models in industrial Internet: A review. *Procedia Manufacturing, 39,* 1854–1863.

Bustinza, O. F., Gomes, E., Vendrell-Herrero, F., & Tarba, S. Y. (2018). An organizational change framework for digital servitization: Evidence from the Veneto region. *Strategic Change, 27*(2), 111–119.

Callon, M., Méadel, C., & Rabeharisoa, V. (2002). The economy of qualities. *Economy and Society, 31*(2), 194–217.

Chen, J.-S., Kerr, D., Tsang, S.-S., & Sung, Y. C. (2015). Co-production of service innovations through dynamic capability enhancement. *The Service Industries Journal, 35*(1–2), 96–114.

Cohen, W. M., & Levinthal, D. A. (1990). Absorptive capacity: A new perspective on learning and innovation. *Administrative Science Quarterly, 35*(1), 128–152.

Coreynen, W., Matthyssens, P., & Van Bockhaven, W. (2017). Boosting servitization through digitization: Pathways and dynamic resource configurations for manufacturers. *Industrial Marketing Management, 60,* 42–53.

Coreynen, W., Matthyssens, P., Vanderstraeten, J., & van Witteloostuijn, A. (2020). Unravelling the internal and external drivers of digital servitization: A dynamic capabilities and contingency perspective on firm strategy. *Industrial Marketing Management.*

Dopfer, K., Foster, J., & Potts, J. (2004). Micro-meso-macro. *Journal of Evolutionary Economics, 14*(3), 263–279.

Dosi, G., Grazzi, M., Marengo, L., & Settepanella, S. (2016). Production theory: Accounting for firm heterogeneity and technical change. *The Journal of Industrial Economics, 64*(4), 875–907.

Gebauer, H., Paiola, M., Saccani, N., & Rapaccini, M. (2020). Digital servitization: Crossing the perspectives of digitization and servitization. *Industrial Marketing Management.*

Geels, F. W. (2004). From sectoral systems of innovation to socio-technical systems: Insights about dynamics and change from sociology and institutional theory. *Research Policy, 33*(6), 897–920.

Geels, F. W. (2010). Ontologies, socio-technical transitions (to sustainability), and the multilevel perspective. *Research Policy, 39*(4), 495–510.

Geels, F. W. (2020). Micro-foundations of the multilevel perspective on socio-technical transitions: Developing a multi-dimensional model of agency through crossovers between social constructivism, evolutionary economics and neo-institutional theory. *Technological Forecasting and Social Change, 152,* 119894.

Hein, A., Schreieck, M., Riasanow, T., Setzke, D. S., Wiesche, M., Böhm, M., et al. (2020). Digital platform ecosystems. *Electronic Markets, 30*(1), 87–98.

Henneberg, S. C., Gruber, T., & Naudé, P. (2013). Services networks: Concept and research agenda. *Industrial Marketing Management, 42*(1), 3–8.

Hinings, B., Gegenhuber, T., & Greenwood, R. (2018). Digital innovation and transformation: An institutional perspective. *Information and Organization, 28*(1), 52–61.

Huikkola, T., & Kohtamäki, M. (2020). Agile new solution development in manufacturing companies. *Technology Innovation Management Review, 10*(3), 16–24.

Huikkola, T., Rabetino, R., Kohtamäki, M., & Gebauer, H. (2020). Firm boundaries in servitization: Interplay and repositioning practices. *Industrial Marketing Management, 90,* 90–105.

Kamalaldin, A., Linde, L., Sjödin, D., & Parida, V. (2020). Transforming provider-customer relationships in digital servitization: A relational view on digitalization. *Industrial Marketing Management.*

Kay, N. M., Leih, S., & Teece, D. J. (2018). The role of emergence in dynamic capabilities: A restatement of the framework and some possibilities for future research. *Industrial and Corporate Change, 27*(4), 623–638.

Kodama, F. (2014). MOT in transition: From technology fusion to technology-service convergence. *Technovation, 34*(9), 505–512.

Kohtamäki, M., Einola, S., & Rabetino, R. (2020). Exploring servitization through the paradox lens: Coping practices in servitization. *International Journal of Production Economics,* 107619.

Kohtamäki, M., Parida, V., Oghazi, P., Gebauer, H., & Baines, T. (2019). Digital servitization business models in ecosystems: A theory of the firm. *Journal of Business Research, 104,* 380–392.

Kohtamäki, M., Parida, V., Patel, P. C., & Gebauer, H. (2020). The relationship between digitalization and servitization: The role of servitization in capturing the financial potential of digitalization. *Technological Forecasting and Social Change, 151,.*

Kohtamäki, M., Partanen, J., Parida, V., & Wincent, J. (2013). Non-linear relationship between industrial service offering and sales growth: The moderating role of network capabilities. *Industrial Marketing Management, 42*(8), 1374–1385.

Kohtamäki, M., Rabetino, R., & Möller, K. (2018). Alliance capabilities: A systematic review and future research directions. *Industrial Marketing Management, 68,* 188–201.

Lenka, S., Parida, V., & Wincent, J. (2017). Digitalization capabilities as enablers of value co-creation in servitizing firms. *Psychology & Marketing, 34*(1), 92–100.

Lepratte, L. (2016). On the processes of technical change and development in Latin America: A proposed framework of analysis. In H. Horta, M. Heitor, & J. Salmi (Eds.), *Trends and challenges in science and higher education* (pp. 121–143). Springer.

Lerch, C., & Gotsch, M. (2015). Digitalized product-service systems in manufacturing firms: A case study analysis. *Research-Technology Management, 58*(5), 45–52.

Luoto, S., Brax, S. A., & Kohtamäki, M. (2017). Critical meta-analysis of servitization research: Constructing a model-narrative to reveal paradigmatic assumptions. *Industrial Marketing Management, 60,* 89–100.

Lusch, R. F., & Vargo, S. L. (2014). *Service-dominant logic: Premises, perspectives, possibilities.* Cambridge University Press.

Lütjen, H., Schultz, C., Tietze, F., & Urmetzer, F. (2019). Managing ecosystems for service innovation: A dynamic capability view. *Journal of Business Research, 104,* 506–519.

Naik, P., Schroeder, A., Kapoor, K. K., Ziaee Bigdeli, A., & Baines, T. (2020). Behind the scenes of digital servitization: Actualising IoT-enabled affordances. *Industrial Marketing Management.*

Nambisan, S., Wright, M., & Feldman, M. (2019). The digital transformation of innovation and entrepreneurship: Progress, challenges and key themes. *Research Policy, 48*(8), 103773.

Nelson, R. R., & Winter, S. G. (1982). *An evolutionary theory of economic change.* Harvard University Press.

Nylén, D., & Holmström, J. (2015). Digital innovation strategy: A framework for diagnosing and improving digital product and service innovation. *Business Horizons, 58*(1), 57–67.

Parida, V., Oghazi, P., & Cedergren, S. (2016). A study of how ICT capabilities can influence dynamic capabilities. *Journal of Enterprise Information Management, 29*(2), 179–201.

Paschou, T., Rapaccini, M., Adrodegari, F., & Saccani, N. (2020). Digital servitization in manufacturing: A systematic literature review and research agenda. *Industrial Marketing Management.* https://www.elgaronline.com/view/edcoll/978 1786433442/9781786433442.00012.xml.

Pisano, G. P. (2017). Toward a prescriptive theory of dynamic capabilities: Connecting strategic choice, learning, and competition. *Industrial and Corporate Change, 26*(5), 747–762.

Rabetino, R., Harmsen, W., Kohtamäki, M., & Sihvonen, J. (2018). Structuring servitization-related research. *International Journal of Operations & Production Management, 38*(2), 350–371.

Rabetino, R., Kohtamäki, M., & Federico, J. S. (2020). A (re)view of the philosophical foundations of strategic management. *International Journal of Management Reviews* (early view).

Rabetino, R., Kohtamäki, M., & Gebauer, H. (2017). Strategy map of servitization. *International Journal of Production Economics, 192,* 144–156.

Raddats, C., Kowalkowski, C., Benedettini, O., Burton, J., & Gebauer, H. (2019). Servitization: A contemporary thematic review of four major research streams. *Industrial Marketing Management, 83,* 207–223.

Ritter, T., & Pedersen, C. L. (2020). Digitization capability and the digitalization of business models in business-to-business firms: Past, present, and future. *Industrial Marketing Management, 86,* 180–190.

Romero, D., & Molina, A. (2011). Collaborative networked organisations and customer communities: Value co-creation and co-innovation in the networking era. *Production Planning & Control, 22*(5–6), 447–472.

Rothaermel, F., & Hess, A. (2007). Building dynamic capabilities: Innovation driven by individual-, firm-, and network-level effects. *Organization Science, 18*(6), 898–921.

Sjödin, D., Parida, V., & Kohtamäki, M. (2019). Relational governance strategies for advanced service provision: Multiple paths to superior financial performance in servitization. *Journal of Business Research, 101,* 906–915.

Sjödin, D., Parida, V., Kohtamäki, M., & Wincent, J. (2020). An agile co-creation process for digital servitization: A micro-service innovation approach. *Journal of Business Research.*

Sklyar, A., Kowalkowski, C., Tronvoll, B., & Sörhammar, D. (2019). Organizing for digital servitization: A service ecosystem perspective. *Journal of Business Research, 104,* 450–460.

Taylor, S. A., Hunter, G. L., Zadeh, A. H., Delpechitre, D., & Lim, J. H. (2020). Value propositions in a digitally transformed world. *Industrial Marketing Management, 87,* 256–263.

Teece, D. J. (2007). Explicating dynamic capabilities: The nature and microfoundations of (sustainable) enterprise performance. *Strategic Management Journal, 28*(13), 1319–1350.

Teece, D. J. (2018). Business models and dynamic capabilities. *Long Range Planning, 51*(1), 40–49.

Tronvoll, B., Sklyar, A., Sörhammar, D., & Kowalkowski, C. (2020). Transformational shifts through digital servitization. *Industrial Marketing Management.*

Vendrell-Herrero, F., Bustinza, O. F., Parry, G., & Georgantzis, N. (2017). Servitization, digitization and supply chain interdependency. *Industrial Marketing Management, 60,* 69–81.

Warner, K. S. R., & Wäger, M. (2019). Building dynamic capabilities for digital transformation: An ongoing process of strategic renewal. *Long Range Planning, 52*(3), 326–349.

Reviewing Service Types from a Transaction Cost Economics Perspective

Bart Kamp

1   Introduction

When looking at base, intermediate or advanced services (Baines & Lightfoot, 2013) that industrial users can source from outside suppliers, one observes how these services generate an increasing level of interdependence between customers and providers (Benedettini et al., 2015; Huikkola et al., 2016).

From a relational perspective (Dyer et al., 1998; Kamalaldin et al., 2020), this tends to be viewed as a positive and natural progression. However, this evolution can also entail risks (Oliva & Kallenberg, 2003) or raise questions about where to set the boundaries between the firms involved (Kohtamäki et al., 2019). Hence, not all users may be interested in strengthening their B2B relationships when moving from base to advanced services (Dyer et al., 2018). Moreover, the choice is not only between market-based and relational supply arrangements (Sjödin et al., 2019); a user of services may also opt for self-supply (Baines & Lightfoot, 2014; Valtakoski, 2017).

If increased interdependence through **servitization** may receive mixed reactions in practice (Wünderlich et al., 2015), while the **servitization**

3b. Theories of the firm in servitization

B. Kamp (✉)
Orkestra-Basque Institute of Competitiveness, San Sebastian, Spain
e-mail: bart.kamp@orkestra.deusto.es

© The Author(s), under exclusive license to Springer Nature Switzerland AG 2021
M. Kohtamäki et al. (eds.), *The Palgrave Handbook of Servitization*,
https://doi.org/10.1007/978-3-030-75771-7_13

community tends to display an optimistic attitude towards progressively closer B2B ties (Luoto et al., 2017), there is a risk that counterfactual evidence cannot be explained adequately. Hence, it seems logical to consider a theoretical framework that looks critically at governance choices for B2B arrangements. Following on from Geiger et al. (2012) and Böhm et al. (2016), this paper proposes transaction cost economics (TCE) as a framework for analyzing the logic behind the governance modes that industrial users can apply when adopting different service types.

2   Considering Service Provision from a Governance Mode Perspective

Transaction Cost Economics

TCE deals essentially with make-or-buy decisions (Powell, 1990; Williamson, 1985). To determine what is the best decision for a specific—in this context—service, it first considers the cost of providing the service through in-house means. Second, it considers the costs involved in contracting the service from a third party, including what it takes to find a suitable supplier, negotiate the terms, draw up a contract and monitor performance (Zou et al., 2019). As TCE applies an economistic logic to make-or-buy questions, it argues that companies seek to minimize costs (Williamson, 1975, 1985). As such, if external service provision generates savings compared to obtaining them in-house, firms can be expected to involve third parties (Kohtamäki et al., 2019).

Types of Governance Arrangements

When referring to governance arrangements for organizing service provision, TCE distinguishes between hierarchy, market and network solutions (Powell, 1990; Williamson, 1991).[1] Hierarchy represents the internalization of service activities and thus refers to in-house solutions. The hierarchy solution may involve assigning an available internal **structure** to do the job or acquiring an external entity. A market arrangement implies contracting an external party to deliver the service in question. I.e. purchasing the service on the 'spot market',

---

[1] In particular, as regards network solutions, it is possible to differentiate between contractual and relational governance (Wacker et al., 2016). Whereas a contract lays the foundation for the transaction to be carried out, relational adjustment may be needed to execute the transaction properly.

keeping the supplier at arm's length. Networks are hybrid governance arrangements through which the user engages in an ongoing relationship with an external supplier. These networks entail less of an arm's length relationship than market arrangements, but they are also less internalized than hierarchy solutions (Thorelli, 1986). The network option thus embodies a more interactive exchange relationship. Hence, Kohtamäki et al. (2019) refer to 'make-or-collaborate-or-buy decisions', as do Baines and Lightfoot (2014: 4).[2]

Determinants of Governance Arrangement Choices

To determine which governance arrangement is most adequate, TCE proposes the following criteria to be evaluated (Baker et al., 2002; Krickx, 1991):

Asset Specificity[3]

Williamson (1985: 55) defines asset specificity as '*durable investments that are undertaken in support of particular transactions*'. It refers to the resources needed to provide a specific service (Williamson, 1985). For instance: unique and novel expertise, investments in capital equipment, or R&D for an 'idiosyncratic' service (Williamson, 1975). In addition, asset specificity refers to dedicated technologies and investments that lose their value under alternative uses or which cannot easily be redeployed (Heide, 1994).

Similarly, operations that rely on substantial tacit knowledge are a form of asset specificity. This is typically the case for customized services, which cannot be transferred on a copy-paste basis to other situations.

Interaction Level

Interaction level refers to the degree of ongoing contact between exchange partners (Baker et al., 2002) for a specific service. Alternatively, Milgrom and Roberts (1992) talk of the frequency with which similar transactions occur and the period during which they are repeated (longevity of the interaction cycle). Boehlje's (1999) concept of 'task programmability' also relates

---

[2] Both market and network arrangements can consist of a 'single supplier to user' relationship or 'multiple suppliers to user' relationships. The latter can also be called ecosystems (Jacobides et al., 2018; Kohtamäki et al., 2019). This paper acknowledges this point, but it does not delve further into the number of actors involved in market or network arrangements.

[3] Note that while the term 'asset' has a tangible connotation, it can refer both to products and services.

to interaction level, as he links it to transactions that are often repeated. Additionally, there is 'depth of interaction', referring to how intense the interaction concerning services is between partners (White, 2005).

Uncertainties

Uncertainty may relate to behavioural insecurities. This encompasses the reliability of actors involved in a specific activity, including issues like loyalty, predictability of behaviour and whether the necessary competences are in place.

According to TCE, situations in which behavioural insecurities prevail may lead to opportunistic behaviour involving cheating, distortion of information and shirking of responsibility (Williamson, 1985). Likewise, they may lead to disappointing performance by the actors involved (Stouthuysen et al., 2012), even if transaction partners act in good faith.

This risk of behavioural uncertainty tends to be highest if the activity in question represents uncharted territory, a domain that the focal firm or possible partners does not master yet (Roehrich & Lewis, 2014), or if it is altogether new (Hypko et al., 2010). In addition, the complexity of a transaction magnifies uncertainties for its anticipated user (Milgrom & Roberts, 1992). This may also make it difficult for the party contracting the service to specify its expectations and to assess what is an appropriate outcome of the envisaged operation (Milgrom & Roberts, 1992). Accordingly, behavioural uncertainties may stem from a potential supplier's inability to give an exact explanation of what the client can expect, leading to situations of performance ambiguity (Wacker et al., 2016).

Alternatively, uncertainties can refer to proprietary insecurities. An activity requiring access to confidential information can entail legal and intellectual property risks (Williamson, 1985). To be protected against this type of risks, the focal firm may want to adopt strict contractual measures or adapt the governance mode.

Choosing Governance Arrangements Based on Determinant-Specific 'Scores'

With regard to the criteria to be evaluated when making governance arrangement choices (i.e. asset specificity, interaction level and uncertainties), TCE applies a high–low scale. This means that it either attributes a high or a low score to each of these respective criteria.

Asset Specificity

TCE argues that if the asset specificity of a product or service is high, the user must take additional precautions to prevent the underlying technology/know-how from falling into the hands of competitors (Klein, 1989) or to avoid exposure to other types of opportunistic hazard (Williamson, 1991).

In the case of idiosyncratic activities, the user will want to have tight control to mitigate transaction and agency costs. This can lead the user to either opt for a hierarchy governance mode, or choose a network arrangement if strict guarantees can be obtained.

The decision to adopt a hierarchy mode can involve internal development or acquisition of an external organization to gain control over critical supplies and avoid hold-ups (Krickx, 1991).

Alternatively, a user can decide to opt for a hybrid arrangement. As this entails (inter)dependence, selecting a competent and reliable partner is imperative (Ménard, 2004). The subsequent partnerships to be created are likely to be long-lasting (and perhaps exclusive) in nature, in order to prevent providers opting out or sharing insights with competitors. In fact, network modes are often selective rather than open systems, and developing steady partnerships and/or a stable ecosystem is a crucial element (Ménard, 2004).

Conversely, when dealing with a low-asset-specific service, a market arrangement can suffice. This is typically the case when the service in question relies on codified knowledge or a mature technology that is widely available on the market, and firms need not be concerned about protecting this knowledge from competitors (Hennart, 1989).

In a similar vein, Boehlje (1999) argues that if a transaction or service is well understood by several parties, it can be managed via a market arrangement. He calls this (high) 'task programmability', referring to tasks that can be accomplished by many providers and managed through impersonal coordination mechanisms.

Intervening Variables

Several scholars have pointed to the importance of looking at the proximity of a transaction to the user's core business to determine whether a hierarchy or network mode is preferable (Arnold, 2000; Prahalad & Hamel, 1990). To some extent, this idea can be related to what Williamson (1985) calls 'innovation potential'. If a transaction creates a differential source of value, or a way to sustain a firm's route to market, this means the transaction is important from the perspective of creating strategic advantage.

Consequently, the reasoning is that the closer a specific activity is to a firm's core competences and/or strategic intent, the greater the preference for internalization (Kroes & Ghosh, 2010). Conversely, if the activity in question is at some remove from the knowledge base of the focal firm, an argument can be made for relying on external expertise.

In addition, the speed with which the focal company wants the activity in question to be operational can be another important consideration for its choice of governance mode. For example, if a firm wishes to seize a first-mover advantage (Liebermann & Montgomery, 1988), it will need to quickly identify whether the necessary skills and knowledge are available in-house or elsewhere, in order to choose its make-or-buy solution.

Interaction Level

From a TCE perspective, the frequent repetition of interactions can constitute a reason to internalize the resources or service provided by an external party, or to create an internal unit to become self-sufficient (Williamson, 1985). Similarly, if the internalization option is discarded, a user may choose to diversify its sourcing channels to reduce dependence on a single external party.

Next, there is 'depth of interactions', referring to how intimate or cooperative the required interactions are and whether they lead to 'high encounter situations' (Zack, 2005). Deep interactions can be judged problematic in cases of high-asset-specificity (certainly when there are also strong uncertainty concerns, see below), and may make a contracting firm wary of allowing outsiders too much insight into its activities.

Intervening Variables

Firstly, it is worth noting that frequency is often subordinate to asset specificity. As Ménard (2004) postulates, asset specificity should take precedence over uncertainty and frequency when making governance mode choices. Consequently, internalization is deemed suitable in the case of high-asset-specificity activities, whereas diversification of sources is considered appropriate for low-asset-specificity operations.

Secondly, in addition to frequency, there is the issue of task programmability (Boehlje, 1999). If interactions are replicable in nature, they can be formalized and regulated through market transactions, particularly when the operations have low strategic value. Conversely, firms would likely favour hierarchy governance for strategic activities.

Lastly, interactions around a transaction should be viewed from the perspective of their (inter)dependence with other processes (Milgrom & Roberts, 1992) and their scope (White, 2005). It is paramount to assess to what extent they can be carried out without affecting other processes or, to the contrary, touch upon a system of linked activities. When dealing with stand-alone interactions, these can be left to the markets, but when dealing with transactions that are highly interconnected, users may want to place these under internal coordination mechanisms.

Uncertainties

TCE reasons that if on balance, uncertainties are high (Palmatier et al., 2007), users are inclined not to engage with suppliers and shy away from interdependence.

Certainly, risks due to high-asset-specificity lead companies to choose internalization (Jacobides et al., 2018) because it offers them protection against 'attendant behavioral risks' (Argyres & Zenger, 2012). If, conversely, these uncertainties are judged to be low, third parties may be permitted to take care of, or become involved in, operations, leading the firm to choose market or network arrangements.

Intervening Variables

Behavioural uncertainty can be reduced through control mechanisms available to a focal firm to monitor and check operators' activities in (new) business domains (Williamson, 1985). This can help to manage potential opportunistic behaviour by those in charge of the new operations, be they internal or external (Williamson, 1985).

Similarly, having existing experience or knowledge in the field of activity will also make expectations more concrete and enable performance and functionality indicators to be specified.

Applying TCE to Different Service Types

Servitization literature tends to distinguish between base, intermediate and advanced services when it comes to the service types chosen by industrial users (Baines & Lightfoot, 2013; Rabetino et al., 2017).

Base services typically refer to the provision of spare parts and replenishables (Baines & Lightfoot, 2013). Intermediate services, such as maintenance and repair, focus on supporting product condition (Oliva & Kallenberg, 2003). Advanced services include outcome-oriented services and the provision of capabilities (Baines & Lightfoot, 2013; Rabetino et al., 2015).

Clearly, these service types differ substantially in their level of distinctiveness, engagement with customers' business processes, level of competition, potential to create competitive advantage, and risks (Baines & Lightfoot, 2013; Oliva & Kallenberg, 2003).

Hence, in the following sections, we will assess base, intermediate and advanced services along the axes of asset specificity, frequency of interaction and uncertainties.

Aspects of Asset Specificity

When an external agent is allowed to deliver advanced services, a supplier can come to understand the nature of the customer's business, as well as the processes surrounding the service offering (Ruizalba et al., 2016). This constitutes a major difference between intermediate and advanced services: the former does not bring the service provider into the heart of a user's **value creation** operations to the same degree as the latter type of services (Baines et al., 2009). Obviously, in the case of base services, there is even less need for the user to give the service provider access to or insights into its business processes.

This also means that advanced services require (developing) much more tacit or insider knowledge than intermediate and base services. In fact, base services can often be performed building on standardized or taxonomic information, leading to fewer bespoke offerings.

As regards task programmability, or the degree to which alternative agents can deliver a given service type, advanced services are likely to be assigned to insiders or preferred vendors who are granted privileged insights. Contrarily, candidates for intermediate and base services will be more numerous and interchangeable and do not need (comprehensive) insights into a client's **value creation** activities.

Similarly, advanced services will typically require dedicated investments or the contracting of exclusive operators.

Assessment of Asset Specificity Per Service Type and Implications for Governance Mode

In the case of advanced services, and particularly if they involve access to confidential data, a trade-off arises between engaging external expertise or going for 'homebrewed' solutions. In sectors where data secrecy is common, like defence or aeronautics and automotive, there may be a tendency to opt for hierarchy solutions (Kamp, 2018). Conversely, when users of advanced services can afford to be less concerned about information spillover, they may favour network arrangements.

Intermediate services are less clear cut from an asset specificity perspective. When a user operates equipment according to standard specifications, inter-mediate services can be provided by external suppliers. However, when users upgrade their equipment's performance via internal tuning operations, they may be motivated to take care of intermediate services themselves (Kamp et al., 2017).

Base services tend to be characterized by low-asset-specificity. Hence, they can be disconnected from a user's core business, and there is little need to keep them in-house.

Ultimately, the governance choice will also depend on case-specific situations according to the intervening variables indicated earlier. Examples of these include (i) proximity of the service to the user's core business and internal knowledge base (Sjödin et al., 2018; Valtakoski, 2017); (ii) how much the service contributes to its competitive advantage or differential value; and (iii) the possibility of seizing first-mover advantages, as this will impact on the speed with which the user will want to have it available (Bigdeli et al., 2017).

Allowing an outsider to take part in an asset-specific operation will also depend on whether this may erode the service user's centrality or gatekeeping position in relation to the end market (Bigdeli et al., 2017; Bustinza et al., 2015).

Hypotheses:

H1A: When the asset specificity of the services to be provided is high, their user(s) will favour hierarchy modes. Conversely, when their asset specificity is low, the user(s) will favour market arrangements.

H1B: Advanced services tend to be characterized by higher asset specificity than intermediate services and base services.

Interaction Level

Clearly, delivering replenishables or spare parts in a regular manner is different from maintaining intensive contact with a user for the provision of advanced services that support a client's value-creating operations. Whereas the aforementioned base services may provide regular touchpoints without leading to extensive contact, the latter may indeed lead to or require stronger ties. Moreover, advanced services may come with an extended preparation period, helping to lengthen the relationship before the actual service is operational.

As regards task programmability, clearly the degree of predictability in terms of when and how to intervene through base and intermediate services is higher than in the case of advanced services. The latter will arguably entail much more crafting and fine-tuning of less linear programming. Also, since they are more interconnected with other processes or assets, multiple functional and performance parameters will need to be taken into account. At the same time, advanced services may need to consider more contingency variables.

Assessment of Interaction Level Per Service Type and Implications for Governance Mode

While regular contact between supplier and user for the provision of base services is indicative of frequency of interaction, such services may not need to be internalized, even less so if the inputs provided have a moderate to low degree of asset specificity.

Contrarily, advanced services that entail ongoing and intensive contact (in terms of either development and/or operational support), as well as interdependence between parties, may be a reason for their user to decide to take charge of these services in a hierarchy mode, or to utilize them via a closely connected network arrangement with third parties.

From the perspective of task programmability, or the need to craft and adjust services, base services tend to come with clear specifications, whereas this is increasingly less true for intermediate and particularly advanced services. Especially in the ramping-up phase, advanced services will require time for discovery, experimentation and mutual adjustment. Consequently, a closed environment or a sheltered context together with external parties in the form of a network arrangement would be beneficial.

Hypotheses:

H2A: When the services to be provided require in-depth and/or cooperative interaction, their user(s) will favour hierarchy modes. Conversely, when they require superficial and/or standardized interaction, their user(s) will favour market arrangements.

H2B: Advanced services tend to be characterized by more in-depth and/or cooperative interaction than intermediate services and base services.

Uncertainties

Utilizing services can generate several forms of uncertainty, particularly if the services are less mature and/or standardized. If a clear understanding exists of what is expected, the risk of non-compliance is limited. Conversely, in the case of novel services or when they are characterized by service complexity (Zou et al., 2019) and/or unclear specifications (Malleret, 2006), the uncertainties are considerable. Relying on outside contributors can then be risky, either for reasons of lack of competence or due to possible opportunistic behaviour. Also, in the case of (involuntary) lack of competence, an external supplier who is keen to provide a certain service may lack the experience and knowledge to envision and deliver the service (Valtakoski, 2017).

Accordingly, the risk of leaking proprietary information is clearly greater for advanced services than for the other types of services, particularly when using cloud technology, when exchanging large data sets and/or when there are concerns over cybersecurity (Kamp, 2018).

Assessment of Uncertainties Per Service Type and Implications for Governance Mode

The uncertainties surrounding advanced services are higher than those around base or intermediate services. Hence, from a risk perspective, it is more likely that users will want to internalize advanced services or establish network arrangements with rigorously selected outsiders, using detailed contracts and penalties to avoid breaches of said contracts.

Moreover, if the technologies or knowledge domains underpinning services to be provided lie outside the initial reach of the focal firm, it can either opt for internalization through acquisitions (Bustinza et al., 2019; Kamp, 2019) or reliance on a network arrangement, e.g. through ecosystems (Kamalaldin et al., 2020; Sjödin et al., 2019).

Hypotheses:

H3A: When the services to be provided involve considerable uncertain-ties, their user(s) will favour hierarchy modes. Conversely, when they involve limited uncertainties, their user(s) will favour market arrangements.

H3B: Advanced services tend to be characterized by more uncertainties than intermediate services and base services.

3   Discussion

Theoretical Contributions

From a theoretical perspective, it may be fair to state that **servitization** research has not yet put forward a taxonomy or framework to predict whether specific services are likely to be provided under a make, a collaborate or a buy arrangement. Therefore, by reviewing different service types based on the criteria that TCE applies to determine adequate governance choices for trans-actions, this paper contributes insights with regard to making such choices around service provision. Moreover, as there is a growing interest among the **servitization** community in advanced services, where issues like (service) specificity, interdependence (interaction) and uncertainty play an important role, looking to TCE seems particularly appropriate.

Overall, TCE's central axioms lead us to postulate that advanced services are less likely to be outsourced, which is in line with findings by Kowalkowski et al. (2011) and Bustinza et al., 2019).

Conversely, Kowalkowski et al. (2011) point to base services as being a good fit for market arrangements, whereas users of intermediate services can switch more freely across the governance arrangement spectrum (Fig. 1).

It is also worth noting that what may be considered an advanced service today could become mainstream tomorrow. This also means that what was initially an adequate governance arrangement for a service may change over time. In other words, if an advanced service matures and becomes a standard practice, its optimal governance could evolve from a hierarchy to a relational or market arrangement. It may thus be necessary to look at service types from a dynamic perspective and in terms of their lifecycle. In line with Cusumano

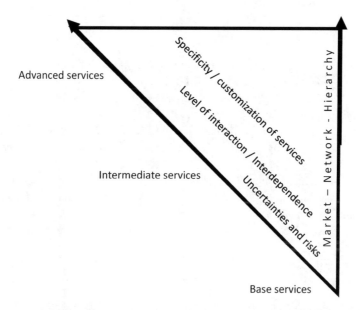

Advanced services

Specificity / customization of services

Level of interaction / Interdependence

Uncertainties and risks

Intermediate services

Market – Network – Hierarchy

Base services

Fig. 1 Type of services and their governance mode choices based on TCE criteria 'scores'

et al. (2015), one can argue that services that are in the early stages of their lifecycle have a considerable chance of being arranged in-house, while services in later stages become more suitable for network or market solutions. This may be explained by high (asset) specificity and uncertainty during their infancy and the fact that frequency of use may be low or uncertain. Such conditions may be a reason for users not to engage with external providers, but rather rely on internal resources. However, as a service matures, it will become more reliable and easier to understand, leading to the development of more standard uses. This would eventually clear the way for network or market options to govern them.

Managerial Implications

As regards implications for managers, this paper reviews the main determinants (and several underlying aspects per determinant) that TCE considers responsible for governance choices. As such, it can form the basis for a managerial checklist to determine which institutional arrangements service users (should) adopt when using base, intermediate or advanced services, and whether the preferences for such arrangements may (need to) change over time.

References

Argyres, N., & Zenger, T. (2012). Capabilities, transaction costs, and firm boundaries. *Organization Science, 23*(6), 1643–1657.

Arnold, U. (2000). New dimensions of outsourcing. *European Journal of Purchasing & Supply Management, 6*(1), 23–29.

Baines, T. S., Lightfoot, H. W., Benedettini, O., & Kay, J. M. (2009). The servitization of manufacturing. *Journal of Manufacturing Technology Management, 20*(5), 547–567.

Baines, T., & Lightfoot, H. (2013). *Made to serve*. Wiley.

Baines, T., & Lightfoot, H. (2014). Servitization of the manufacturing firm. *International Journal of Operations & Production Management, 34*(1), 2–35.

Baker, G., Gibbons, R., & Murphy, K. (2002). Relational contracts and the theory of the firm. *Quarterly Journal of Economics, 117,* 39–83.

Benedettini, O., Swink, M., Neely, A., Brown, S., & Brown, S. (2015). Why do servitized firms fail? *International Journal of Operations & Production Management, 35*.

Bigdeli, A., Bustinza, O., Vendrell-Herrero, F., & Baines, T. (2017). Network positioning and risk perception in servitization. *International Journal of Production Research*. https://doi.org/10.1080/00207543.2017.1341063.

Boehlje, M. (1999). Structural changes in the agricultural industries. *American Journal of Agricultural Economics, 81*(5), 1028–1041.

Böhm, E., Backhaus, Chr, Eggert, A., & Cummins, T. (2016). Understanding outcome-based contracts: Benefits and risks from the buyers' and sellers' perspective. *Journal of Strategic Contracting and Negotiation, 2*(1–2), 128–149.

Bustinza, O. F., Bigdeli, A. Z., Baines, T., & Elliot, C. (2015). Servitization and competitive advantage: The importance of organizational structure and value chain position. *Research-Technology Management, 58*(5), 53–60.

Bustinza, O. F., Lafuente, E., Rabetino, R., Vaillant, Y., & Vendrell-Herrero, F. (2019). Make-or-buy configurational approaches in product-service ecosystems and performance. *Journal of Business Research*. https://doi.org/10.1016/j.jbusres.2019.01.035.

Cusumano, M., Kahl, S., & Suarez, F. (2015). Services, industry evolution and the competitive strategies of product firms. *Strategic Management Journal, 36*(4), 559–575.

Dyer, J., & Singh, H. (1998). The relational view: Cooperative strategy and sources of interorganizational competitive advantage. *Academy of Management Review, 23*(4), 660–679.

Dyer, J., Singh, H., & Hesterly, W. (2018). The relational view revisited. *Strategic Management Journal, 39*(12), 3140–3162.

Geiger, I., Durand, A., Saab, S., & Kleinaltenkamp, M. (2012). The bonding effects of relationship value and switching costs in industrial buyer-seller relationships. *Industrial Marketing Management, 41*(1), 82–93.

Heide, J. B. (1994). Interorganizational governance in marketing channels. *Journal of Marketing, 58*(1), 71–85.

Hennart, J. F. (1989). Can the 'new forms of investment' substitute for the 'old forms?': A transaction costs perspective. *Journal of International Business Studies, 20*(Summer), 211–234.

Huikkola, T., Kohtamäki, M., & Rabetino, R. (2016). Resource Realignment in Servitization. *Research-Technology Management, 59,* 30–39.

Hypko, P., Tilebein, M., & Gleich, R. (2010). Benefits and uncertainties of performance-based contracting in manufacturing industries. *Journal of Service Management, 21*(4), 460–489.

Jacobides, M. G., Cennamo, C., & Gawer, A. (2018). Towards a theory of ecosystems. *Strategic Management Journal, 39,* 2255–2276.

Kamalaldin, A., Lindea, L., Sjödin, D., & V. Parida (2020). Transforming provider-customer relationships in digital servitization. *Industrial Marketing Management,* in press.

Kamp, B., Ochoa, A., & Diaz, J. (2017). Smart servitization within the context of industrial user–supplier relationships. *International Journal on Interactive Design and Manufacturing, 11,* 651–663.

Kamp, B. (2018). Expanding international business via smart services. In R. Van Tulder, A. Verbeke, & L. Piscitello (Eds.), *International business in the information and digital age*(pp. 273–293). Emerald.

Kamp, B. (2019). Restructuring for service business development. *International Journal of Business Environment, 10*(4), 281–305.

Klein, S. (1989). A transaction cost explanation of vertical control in international markets. *Academy of Marketing Science, 17*(3), 253–262.

Kohtamäki, M., Parida, V., Oghazi, P., Gebauer, H., & Baines, T. (2019). Digital servitization business models in ecosystems: A theory of the firm. *Journal of Business Research, 104*(11), 380–392.

Kowalkowski, Chr, Kindström, D., & Witell, L. (2011). Internalisation or externalisation? *Managing Service Quality, 21*(4), 373–391.

Krickx, G. (1991). Why transaction cost and resource dependence explanations can't be easily separated. In J. Thépot & R-A. Thiétart (Eds.), *Microeconomic contributions to strategic management* (pp. 143-167). Elsevier.

Kroes, J. R., & Ghosh, S. (2010). Outsourcing congruence with competitive priorities. *Journal of Operations Management, 28*(2), 124–143.

Liebermann, M., & Montgomery, D. (1988). First-mover advantages. *Strategic Management Journal, 9*(1), 41–58.

Luoto, S., Brax, S., & Kohtamäki, M. (2017). Critical meta-analysis of servitization research. *Industrial Marketing Management, 60,* 89–100.

Malleret, V. (2006). Value creation through service offers. *European Management Journal, 24*(1), 106–116.

Ménard, C. (2004). The economics of hybrid organizations. *Journal of Institutional and Theoretical Economics, 160*(3), 345–376.

Milgrom, P., & Roberts, J. (1992). *Economics, organization and management*. Englewood Cliffs, NJ: Prentice-Hall International.

Oliva, R., & Kallenberg, R. (2003). Managing the transition from products to services. *International Journal of Service Industry Management, 14*, 160–172.

Palmatier, R., Dant, R., & Grewal, D. (2007). A comparative longitudinal analysis of theoretical perspectives of interorganizational relationship performance. *Journal of Marketing, 71*(4), 172–194.

Powell, W. W. (1990). Neither market nor hierarchy: Network forms of organization. *Research in Organizational Behavior, 12*, 295–336.

Prahalad, C. K., & Hamel, G. (1990). The core competence of the corporation. *Harvard Business Review, 68*(3), 79–91.

Rabetino, R., Kohtamäki, M., Lehtonen, H., & Kostama, H. (2015). Developing the concept of life-cycle service offering. *Industrial Marketing Management, 49*, 53–66.

Rabetino, R., Kohtamäki, M., & Gebauer, H. (2017). Strategy map of servitization. *International Journal of Production Economics, 192*, 144–156.

Roehrich, J., & Lewis, M. (2014). Procuring complex performance: implications for exchange governance complexity. *International Journal of Operations & Production Management, 34*(2), 221–241.

Ruizalba, J., Soares, A., & Morales, J. (2016). Servitization and co-opetition in the pharmaceutical distribution. *Universia Business Review, 49*, 96–115.

Sjödin, D., Parida, V., Leksell, M., & Petrovic, A. (2018). Smart Factory Implementation and Process Innovation. *Research-Technology Management, 61*(5), 22–31.

Sjödin, D., Parida, V., & Kohtamäki, M. (2019). Relational governance strategies for advanced service provision. *Journal of Business Research, 101*, 906–915.

Stouthuysen, K., Slabbinck, H., & Roodhooft, F. (2012). Controls, service type and perceived supplier performance in interfirm service exchanges. *Journal of Operations Management, 30*(5), 423–435.

Thorelli, H. B. (1986). Networks: between markets and hierarchies. *Strategic Management Journal, 7*, 37–51.

Valtakoski, A. (2017). Explaining servitization failure and deservitization. *Industrial Marketing Management, 60*, 138–150.

Wacker, J. G., Yang, C., & Sheu, C. (2016). A transaction cost economics model for estimating performance effectiveness of relational and contractual governance. *International Journal of Operations and Production Management, 36*(11), 1551–1575.

White, S. (2005). Cooperation costs, governance choice and alliance evolution. *Journal of Management Studies, 42*(7), 1383–1412.

Williamson, O. E. (1975). *Markets and hierarchies*. New York: Free Press.

Williamson, O. E. (1985). *The economic institutions of capitalism*. New York: The Free Press.

Williamson, O. E. (1991). Comparative economic organization. *Administrative Science Quarterly, 36*, 269–296.

Wünderlich, N., Heinonen, K., Ostrom, A. L., Patricio, L., Sousa, R., Voss, C., et al. (2015). Futurizing smart service. *Journal of Services Marketing, 29*(6/7), 442–447.

Zack, M. (2005). The strategic advantage of knowledge and learning. *International Journal of Learning and Intellectual Capital, 2*(1), 1–20.

Zou, W., Brax, S., Vuori, M., & Rajala, R. (2019). The influences of contract structure, contracting process, and service complexity on supplier performance. *International Journal of Operations and Production Management, 39*(4), 525–549.

The Role of Financialization When Moving up the Service Ladder

Bart Kamp and Ibon Gil de San Vicente

1   Introduction

Servitization can be characterized as a change process (Lenka et al., 2018; Raddats et al., 2019). This is particularly true when defining it as '[t]he development of competences by manufacturing firms to deliver services and solutions to their clients' (Baines & Lightfoot, 2013).

When looking at the dimensions or layers of change upon which this transformation process can be built, one notes the following.

Kowalkowski et al. (2017) highlight that servitization entails a company shifting from a product-centric business logic to a service-centric approach. As such, cultural adaptation is one of the change layers involved in a servitization process. Moreover, in line with the argument put forward by Bigdeli et al. (2015, 2017) that servitization impacts the organizational structure of companies, it can be posited that servitization results in changes to a firm's

---

1c. New approaches in servitization research or as a contribution under Part 2.

B. Kamp (✉) · I. Gil de San Vicente
Orkestra-Basque Institute of Competitiveness, San Sebastián, Spain
e-mail: bart.kamp@orkestra.deusto.es

I. Gil de San Vicente
e-mail: igil@orkestra.deusto.es

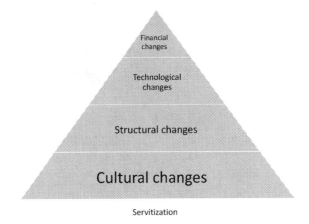

Fig. 1   Layers of change in servitization

organigramme. In addition, it has become commonly accepted that servitization leads to or requires 'technological' changes and digitalization (Kohtamäki et al., 2019; Sklyar et al., 2019; Vendrell-Herrero et al., 2017), particularly when moving into advanced services, as these often include the possibility of online monitoring and servicing.

Furthermore, there may be a financial dimension to servitization as a change process, in the sense that e.g. outcome-based contracts may emerge with new forms of service, and these may require financial innovations (Huikkola & Kohtamäki, 2018; Kamp, 2020). This is typically true of advanced services, as they feature usage-based revenue models (Bigdeli et al., 2020), tend to make use of risk–reward sharing agreements (Baines & Lightfoot, 2013), and typically incorporate features of a financial product (Huikkola & Kohtamäki, 2018).

Consequently, such advanced services can be likened to complex financial products, which require, for example, advanced financial management skills and (possibly) specific financial resources. As such, they can be seen as an example of the concept of 'financialization' as visualized in Fig. 1.

2   Theory Development: What Does Financialization Represent?

Financialization can be understood as the increasing preponderance of financial motives, markets, actors and institutions in the conduct of business (Epstein, 2005). It also refers to a shift from production-oriented management to a form of financial management (Erturk et al., 2008). Among other things, this change involves the (main) source of corporate return on investment among industrial companies shifting from the manufacture and sales of products to other activities and forms of trade that are monetized in the best possible manner through targeted financial strategies (Rosemary & Appelbaum, 2013). It also tends to lead to an increased focus on financial ratings (Froud et al., 2000), and cash flow and treasury management (Toxopeus et al., 2018).

Consequently, there are firms that used to make money by producing or trading goods and services which are increasingly basing their profits on financial activities (Epstein, 2005; Krippner, 2011; Palley, 2007). Think, for example, of initiatives by companies that have a dedicated financial arm or customer credit division in their organigram, such as GE Capital, Siemens Financial Services or ABB Finance (Kamp, 2020). Likewise, some companies may add a financial dimension to the products and services they offer (Brax & Visintin, 2017; Copani, 2014), in the form of leasing schemes or via product-as-a-service models. Similarly, outcome-based contracts have found their way into an increasing number of sectors (Ng & Nudurupati, 2010).

Despite the preceding, very few publications have focused on the role of the financial skills and resources behind companies' attempts to servitize. Gebauer et al. (2017) and de Oliveira et al. (2018) are among the few authors to address financial matters in relation to service development. Relevant issues in this regard are, among others, the complexity of financial management and risks around services, and the internal and external resources required for their implementation.

Different Service Types and the Need to Build in Financial Security

If we follow the standard subdivision of service types in servitization literature (i.e. base, intermediate and advanced services), it can be argued that the importance of dealing with financial uncertainties increases as we move up the service ladder from base to advanced services.

Why is this? A key aspect of servitization is that it fosters interdependence between buyers and suppliers. Accordingly, more advanced services involve more intimate and reciprocal forms of cooperation and exchange between business partners (Benedettini et al., 2015; Huikkola et al., 2016).

In other words, break-fix services or short-term operations in the form of repair and training (as examples of base and intermediate services) do not entail the level of intertwinement and mutual adjustment that availability- or outcome-based services to support customers' business processes (as a form of advanced services) generate.

Alongside the increasing interdependence that occurs when moving from base to advanced services, the degree of uncertainty that may surround the offering and roll-out of advanced services grows as well. See, for instance, Oliva and Kallenberg (2003), Eggert et al. (2014) and Josephson et al. (2016), who indicate that services exist in a variety of forms, and they differ in—among other things—their level of risk. In line with Ulaga and Reinartz (2011), they suggest that there are higher risks involved in advanced services compared to base or intermediate services.

One factor here is arguably the level of customization involved. Whereas base and intermediate services tend to be fairly standardized, advanced services are often more bespoke (Baines & Lightfoot, 2013).

Accordingly, for base and intermediate services, it is easier to predict how to carry them out and how to estimate their costs and performance, whereas with advanced services, it is not as easy to take past experiences as a point of reference for their fulfilment and the results and outcomes to be expected.

Another factor is the payment arrangements that may be involved in advanced services as well as their complexity. In particular, when pay-per-outcome and/or risk-reward sharing formulas come into play, they make the (financial) risks even more pronounced. Consequently, in order to cope with these, companies offering outcome-based service contracts are forced to look for financial solutions and support to deal adequately with the risks and uncertainties involved (Ehret & Wirtz, 2017). Similarly, Bigdeli et al. (2020) point out that successfully operating advanced services featuring usage-based revenue models requires competence in managing risk and the ability to discover new innovation pathways. This is required for the provider to ensure that the service can be sustainable from a profit-making perspective (Chesbrough et al., 2018).

All the above issues translate into financial insecurities and thus a need to deal with them, as Fig. 2 shows.

Dealing with Financial Insecurity in the Sphere of Advanced Services Through Financialization

When the concept of financialization is associated with advanced services—as the service type most exposed to financial insecurity—the implementation of

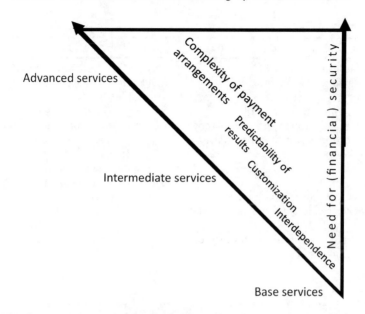

Fig. 2 Service types, increasing level of risks and uncertainty, and need for financial security

outcome-based contracts (OBS)[1]—as a specific form of advanced services—is deemed to have the implications as shown in Table 1.

Changes in accountancy and financial management practices
Outcome-based contracts drive service providers towards alternative methods of cost and income accounting, based on how the revenue streams from outcome-based services flow in. More precisely, they lead to a shift in interest from asset-based or capital expenditure-based accounting to activity-based accounting or accounting that is focusing on operational expenses. Whereas the former allocates costs to assets that are supposed to serve a specific purpose, the latter tracks and records cost based on actual operations performed. Similarly, there is a difference between cost accounting and charging based on a capital expenditure (CAPEX) and another based on an operational expenses (OPEX) approach. The first prompts suppliers to sell goods and collect payment for the value proposition upon delivery, whereas the second leads more easily to 'install now, pay later' (in instalments) practices. As Gebauer et al. (2010) assert, it can be argued that adopting

---

[1] Throughout this paper, different terms are used that we consider to be synonyms for outcome-based contracts, including: outcome-based services and usage-based services. The use of different terms reflects how they appear in publications by various scholars.

Table 1 Financial implications of providing outcome-based services

Aspect of outcome-based services (OBS)	Financial implication
1. OBS facilitate the use of pay-per-outcome/performance schemes	This increases the adoption of OPEX/activity-based bookkeeping principles
2. OBS augment the risks and uncertainties around the transparency and profitability of the operations to be performed	This incentivizes suppliers to look for support from financial specialists (asset finance companies and the like). Similarly, it encourages them to consider smart contracts to establish trustworthy payment practices
3. Overall, OBS make doing business and providing services more of a financial matter	This strengthens the role of the financial department/staff inside the company that provides the services
4. OBS foster the use of risk-reward sharing practices	This entails greater involvement of financial criteria and financial decision-makers on both the supplier and user sides in drawing up contracts

activity-based financial reporting and OPEX principles makes it more realistic for servitized earnings models to come into being.

At the same time, outcome-based contracts relate to financialization in the sense that they mirror the shift from the 'cult of ownership' to the 'cult of usership' (on the demand side). It also reflects the transition from production-oriented management to financial management (on the supply side). In the first case, asset ownership and the (on-balance) book value of assets (object-based accounting) is the way to grow a company's worth, whereas the second is more open to creating dedicated structures (including off-balance) to get new forms of doing business on track, such as modalities that rely on activity-based accounting. Obviously, the second 'position' is more favourable for experimenting with outcome-based service contracts.

H1:   OBS lead to changes in accountancy and financial management practices.

Changes of actor and technological approach to managing financial risks
Extant research highlights how outcome-based contracts transfer risks from the customer to the supplier (Benedettini et al., 2015; Josephson et al., 2016; Schaefers & Böhm, 2020). When providing e.g. production equipment on an OBS basis, the financial risks for the supplier stem, among other things, from downtime, overcapacity and underutilization and ineffective and inefficient execution of operations for which the equipment is used (Hypko et al., 2010; Guajardo et al., 2012). These risks can be aggravated if the supplier lacks

a good level of prior understanding concerning the processes in which the equipment will perform outcome-based services for a specific user. In this regard, customers may not always be willing or able to share the information required for the supplier and its equipment to successfully perform an OBS activity (Holmbom et al., 2014; Tuli et al., 2007).

Furthermore, there are risks and uncertainties relating to how the condition of the delivered equipment will evolve over the service lifetime, as well as its residual value at the end of the contract and the asset supplier's ability to subsequently reallocate or recoup value from the equipment that it provided.

Hence, suppliers need to prepare themselves well before putting such contracts in place. This has prompted different scholars to recommend the involvement of financial specialists to support OBS. In this vein, Raddats et al. (2017) speak of manufacturers' openness to collaborating with other companies to amplify their ability to offer and manage advanced services. Similarly, Bagozi et al. (2019) indicate that advanced services may require the participation of different organizations, including those that provide financial insurance. Gil de San Vicente and Kamp (2019) show that offering OBS may require firms to turn to independent financial service providers, like vendor finance companies or industrial asset management firms that provide customized financial services around industrial assets, i.e. financial specialists that are also more accustomed to managing such assets as a collateral. Once the contract is over or terminated early, this allows the service provider to recuperate the asset and—via an asset management partner— give it another use based on an appropriate valuation. As such, these external financial service providers facilitate the reconditioning, remarketing and repositioning of assets (cf. asset life cycle management—Belkadi et al., 2010; Rabetino et al., 2015).

In addition, as posited by Bagozi et al. (2019), it follows that while trust between business partners is critical, reliable systems and arrangements need to be put in place for outcome-based contracts as well, i.e. in the form of smart contracts[2] that rely on non-rejectable protocols to verify performance outcomes, which activate remuneration for the service provider.

Consequently, an OBS can be implemented between a supplier of goods, a user of the goods and, for example, a factoring company or an asset finance organization that incorporates a financial solution into the OBS that an industrial firm puts on the market (Davies, 2004). Under this contract, when the user reports a positive outcome from an operation involving the provided asset, this triggers a transaction towards the other actors. This underlines

---

[2] A smart contract is a set of computerized transaction protocols that execute the terms of a contract (Szabo, 1997).

the significance of fintech components, such as blockchains, for advanced services (Meroni & Plebani, 2018). Similarly, it highlights the importance of smart contracts to empower outcome-based services that are intended to align multi-party, long-term interests (Lopez Pintado et al., 2018).

In this model, events occurring on monitored equipment are stored as transactions in a blockchain, which provides shared and trusted data repositories for the OBS (Hull et al., 2016), while the smart contract guarantees transparency of operations and outcomes for all parties.

H2a: *OBS make it increasingly more important to engage with external financial actors.*

H2b: *OBS lead to an increasing interest in deploying financial technologies ('fintech') and their components (smart contracts, blockchain).*

Changes in the role of financial staff and skills for managing OBS

Position of the financial department in the service provider's organigram
Companies that are rooted in industrial management often may not give the financial department a very prominent position in their organizational structure. Hence, the financial department may be considered a staff unit. This means it has less authority within the firm and will chiefly fulfil a bookkeeping function (Doron et al., 2019).

When OBS become more important to the overall business of a firm and how it operates in its target market, it would be logical for the financial department to become a line unit with greater responsibility and initiative with regard to the company's business as a whole. Alternatively, a special department may be set up for financially complex service operations. This could be an autonomous unit to organize service project financing, revenue stream management, or even fundraising to pre-finance large operations (Gil de San Vicente & Kamp, 2020). If the latter option is chosen, this can even lead to a situation in which the newly created unit takes charge of special service project finances, whereas the traditional financial department is responsible for the conventional (service) business.

This option of creating an autonomous financial unit may also help in dealing in a focused manner with the structural complexities the financially innovative service business generates (Benedettini et al., 2017).

Importance of financial engineering skills and profiles within the company
Delivering OBS requires companies to possess appropriate financial skills and know-how. It may put a firm's ability to provide the right skill set for the new situation to the test, as well as its know-how in dealing with novel financing

arrangements (Kamp, 2020). Financial capabilities thus need to be brought up to speed, which requires adequately trained human resources.

The more radical the new financial modus operandi around advanced services deviates from conventional financial management, the more likely it will be that a firm will need to recruit financial specialists to lead it capably into the new situation.

Role of financial criteria in defining the company's strategy
Along with possible repositioning of the financial department within a firm, its influence on or contribution to company strategy may also have to be reviewed. That is if a firm is systematically operating in markets where competitiveness depends increasingly on financial engineering and innovative ways of generating revenue streams (or where OBS are coming more into vogue), the entire company strategy may also need to be imbued with financial 'values'.

Thus, in order to implement value propositions that entail important financial innovations, the financial department may have to expand its influence. Accordingly, the role of the financial department must become one of a 'strategic business partner' rather than an 'accounting controller' (Goretzki et al., 2013).

H3a:　*OBS up the importance of financial (management/engineering) skills.*
H3b:　*OBS increase the centrality of the financial department on the service provider side.*

Changes in the nature of B2B relationships
By aligning objectives, OBS create closer collaboration between the user and provider of these services (Guajardo et al., 2012). Consequently, they strengthen the interdependence of the parties involved.

This reciprocity is reinforced when risk-reward schemes are added (Baines & Lightfoot, 2013). When such schemes are developed, this also requires the involvement of the wider organization, beyond the service function (Bigdeli et al., 2018).

Arguably, the interorganizational relationship will then become more financial as well, and this is presumed to strengthen the involvement of the respective financial departments on the supplier and user sides. Or as Kamp and Parry (2017) voice: advanced services will have an impact on the financial governance of an impact on inter-firm relationships.

H4:　*OBS strengthens the financial dimension of B2B relationships.*

3   Discussion

In this paper, we have highlighted four spheres in which synergies between advanced services and outcome-based services, on one side, and financialization, on the other, may emerge. These are:

1. Accountancy and financial management practices;
2. Access to external financial actors and novel financial technologies ('fintech');
3. Development and leveraging of financial management and engineering skills within the firm;
4. Customer relationship management or B2B relationship management.

A general review of financialization concepts helps to shed light on the role of financial management, skills and innovation, and their ability to enable advanced services. Additionally, focusing on OBS also contributes to broadening our understanding of the transformation process (and the layers of change) that manufacturers go through when servitizing their business and as they move up the service ladder. Thus, offering advanced services increases the likelihood that implementers will undertake changes in their financial management and sourcing practices.

Theoretical Contributions

Therefore, as regards conceptual implications, we posit that adopting a financialization lens can broaden the development of theories around servitization. Notably, the hypotheses formulated here may form a basis for future research.

Managerial Implications

In terms of managerial implications, the possible impact on organizational structuring and the role of financial management within servitizing firms can serve as a point of reference for analysts and managers to assess (their) organizations to offer outcome-based services from the perspective of financialization.

References

Bagozi, A., Bianchini, D., De Antonellis, V., Garda, M., & Melchiori, M. (2019, December 2–4). Exploiting blockchain and smart contracts for data exploration as a service, iiWAS2019. Munich, Germany. http://doi.org/10.1145/3366030. 3366075

Baines, T., & Lightfoot, H. (2013). *Made to serve: Understanding what it takes for a manufacturer to compete through servitization and product-service systems.* Wiley.

Baines, T., & Lightfoot, H. (2014). Servitization of the manufacturing firm. *International Journal of Operations & Production Management, 34*(1), 2–35.

Belkadi, F., Troussier, N., Eynard, B., & Bonjour, E. (2010). Collaboration based on product lifecycles interoperability for extended enterprise. *International Journal on Interactive Design And Manufacturing, 4*, 169–179.

Benedettini, O., Swink, M., Neely, A., Brown, S., & Brown, S. (2015). Why do servitized firms fail? A risk-based explanation. *International Journal of Operations & Production Management, 35*.

Benedettini, O., Swink, M., & Neely, A. (2017). Examining the influence of service additions on manufacturing firms' bankruptcy likelihood. *Industrial Marketing Management, 60*, 112–125.

Bigdeli, A., Baines, T., Bustinza, O., & Guang Shi, V. (2015). *Holistic approach to evaluating servitization: A content, context, process framework.* Proceedings of the 22nd EurOMA Conference, Neuchatel, Switzerland.

Bigdeli, A., Bustinza, O., Vendrell-Herrero, F., & Baines, T. (2017). Network positioning and risk perception in servitization. *International Journal of Production Research.* https://doi.org/10.1080/00207543.2017.1341063.

Bigdeli, A., Baines, T., Schroeder, A., Brown, S., Musson, E., Guang Shi, V., et al. (2018). Measuring servitization progress and outcome: The case of 'advanced services'. *Production Planning and Control.* https://doi.org/10.1080/09537287. 2018.1429029.

Bigdeli, A., Baines, T., Kowalkowski, C., Kohtamäki, M., Parida, V., Raddats, C. ..., Rabetino, R. (2020). Advanced services as a basis for competitive advantage in manufacturing, Working Paper.

Böhm, E., Backhaus, Chr, Eggert, A., & Cummins, T. (2016). Understanding outcome-based contracts: benefits and risks from the buyers' and sellers' perspective. *Journal of Strategic Contracting and Negotiation, 2*(1–2), 128–149.

Brax, S., & Visintin, F. (2017). Meta-model of servitization: the integrative profiling approach. *Industrial Marketing Management, 60*(1), 17–32.

Chesbrough, H., Lettl, C., & Ritter, T. (2018). Value capture in open innovation systems: Value at the interface. *Journal of Product Innovation Management, 35*(6), 1–9.

Copani, G. (2014). Machine tool industry: Beyond tradition? In: G. Lay (Ed.), *Servitization in industry* (pp. 109–130). Springer Verlag.

Davies, A. (2004). Moving base into high-value integrated solutions: A value stream approach. *Industrial and Corporate Change, 13*(5), 727–756.

Doron, M., Baker, C. R., & Zucker, K. D. (2019). Bookkeeper-Controller-CFO: The rise of the Chief Financial and Chief Accounting Officer. *Accounting Historians Journal, 46*(2), 43–50.

Eggert, A., Hogreve, J., Ulaga, W., & Muenkhoff, E. (2014). Revenue and profit implications of industrial service strategies. *Journal of Service Research, 17,* 23–39.

Ehret, M., & Wirtz, J. (2017). Unlocking value from machines: business models and the industrial internet of things. *Journal of Marketing Management, 33*(1–2), 111–130.

Epstein, G. A. (Ed.) (2005). *Financialization and the world economy.* Edward Elgar.

Erturk, I., Froud, J., Johal, S., Leaver, A., & Williams, K. (Eds.) (2008). *Financialization at work.* London: Routledge.

Froud, J., Haslam, C., Johal, S., & Williams, K. (2000). Shareholder value and Financialization: Consultancy promises, management moves. *Economy and Society, 29*(1), 80–110.

Gebauer, H., Jennings, C., Haldimanna, M., & Gustafsson, A. (2017). Organizational capabilities for pay-per-use services in product-oriented companies. *International Journal of Production Economics, 192*(C), 157–168.

Gebauer, H., Paiola, M., & Edvardsson, B. (2010). Service business development in small and medium capital goods manufacturing companies. *Managing Service Quality, 20*(2), 123–139.

Gil de San Vicente, I., & Kamp, B. (2020). *So you want to servitize, but are you ready to financialize?* Proceedings of the Spring Servitization Conference 2020. Birmingham. ISBN 978 1 85449 429 0.

Goretzki, L., Strauss, E., & Weber, J. (2013). An institutional perspective on the changes in management accountants' professional role. *Management Accounting Research, 24*(1), 41–63.

Guajardo, J., Cohen, M., & Kim, S.-H. (2012). Impact of performance-based contracting on product reliability: An empirical analysis. *Management Science, 58*(5), 961–979.

Holmbom, M., Bergquist, B., & Vanhatalo, E. (2014). Performance-based logistics – an illusive [sic] panacea or a concept for the future? *Journal of Manufacturing Technology Management, 25*(7), 958–979.

Huikkola, T., Kohtamäki, M., & Rabetino, R. (2016). Resource realignment in servitization: A study of successful service providers explores how manufacturers modify their resource bases in transitioning to service-oriented offerings. *Research-Technology Management, 59,* 30–39.

Huikkola, T., & Kohtamäki, M. (2018). Business models in servitization. In: M. Kohtamäki, T. Baines, R. Rabetino, & A. Bigdeli (Eds.), *Practices and tools for servitization* (pp. 61–81). Palgrave Macmillan.

Hull, R., Batra, V. S., Chee,Y. M., Deutsch, A., Health, F. T., & Vianu, V. (2016). *Towards a shared ledger business collaboration language based on data-aware processes.* Proceedings of International Conference on Service Oriented Computing (ICSOC).

Hypko, P., Tilebein, M., & Gleich, R. (2010). Benefits and uncertainties of performance-based contracting in manufacturing industries: An agency theory perspective. *Journal of Service Management, 21*(4), 460–489.

Josephson, B. W., Johnson, J. L., Mariadoss, B. J., & Cullen, J. (2016). Service transition strategies in manufacturing implications for firm risk. *Journal of Service Research.* https://doi.org/1094670515600422

Kamp, B. (2020). Assessing the financial aptitude of industrial firms to implement servitised earnings models. *International Journal Of Business Environment, 11*(1), 1–10.

Kamp. B., & Gil de San Vicente, I. (2019). *Dealing with the financial implications of advanced services through alternative financial entities.* Proceedings of the Spring Servitization Conference 2019. Linköping. ISBN 978 1 85449 463 4.

Kamp, B., & Parry, G. (2017). Servitization and advanced business services as levers for competitiveness. *Industrial Marketing Management, 60,* 11–16.

Kohtamäki, M., Parida, V., Oghazi, P., Gebauer, H., & Baines, T. (2019). Digital servitization business models in ecosystems: A theory of the firm. *Journal of Business Research, 104*(C), 380–392.

Kowalkowski, C., Gebauer, H., Kamp, B., & Parry, G. (2017). Servitization and deservitization. *Industrial Marketing Management, 60,* 4–10.

Krippner, G. (2011). *Capitalizing on crisis: The political origins of the rise of finance.* Harvard University Press.

Lenka, S., Parida, V., Sjödin, D. R., & Wincent, J. (2018). Exploring the micro foundations of servitization: How individual actions overcome organizational resistance. *Journal of Business Research, 88*(C), 328–336.

López-Pintado, O., García-Bañuelos, L., Dumas,M., Weber, I., & Ponomarev, A. (2018). Caterpillar: A business process execution engine on the ethereum blockchain. CoRR abs/1808.03517 arXiv:1808.03517. http://arxiv.org/abs/1808.03517

Meroni, G., & Plebani, P. (2018). *Combining artifact-driven monitoring with blockchain: Analysis and solutions.* In Proceedings of 30th International Conference on Advanced Information Systems Engineering (CAiSE) (pp. 103–114).

Ng, I., & Nudurupati, S. (2010). Outcome-based service contracts in the defence industry – mitigating the challenges. *Journal of Service Management., 21*(5), 656–674.

Oliva, R., & Kallenberg, R. (2003). Managing the transition from products to services. *International Journal of Service Industry Management, 14*(2), 160–172.

Oliveira, M. G. d., Sousa Mendes, G. H. d., Albuquerque, A. A. d., & Rozenfeld, H. (2018). Lessons learned from a successful industrial product service system business model: Emphasis on financial aspects. *Journal of Business & Industrial Marketing, 33*(3), 365–376.

Palley, T. (2007). Financialization: What it is and why it matters (Working paper no. 525). Annandale-on-Hudson, NY: Levy Economics Institute of Badr College.

Rabetino, R., Kohtamäki, M., Lehtonen, H., & Kostama, H. (2015). Developing the concept of life-cycle service offering. *Industrial Marketing Management, 49,* 53–66.

Raddats, C., Zolkiewski, J., Story, V. M., Burton, J., Baines, T., & Ziaee Bigdeli, A. (2017). Interactively developed capabilities: Evidence from dyadic servitization relationships. *International Journal of Operations and Production Management, 37.*

Raddats, C., Kowalkowski, C., Benedettini, O., Burton, J., & Gebauer, H. (2019). Servitization: A contemporary thematic review of four major research streams. *Industrial Marketing Management, 83,* 207–223.

Rosemary, B., & Appelbaum, E. (2013). The impact of financialization on management and employment outcomes (Upjohn Working Paper 13-191). Kalamazoo, MI: W.E. Upjohn Institute for Employment Research.

Schaefers, S., & Böhm, E. (2020). Outcome-based contracting from the customers' perspective: A means-end chain analytical exploration. *Industrial Marketing Management.* https://doi.org/10.1016/j.indmarman.2020.06.002.

Sklyar, A., Kowalkowski, C., Tronvoll, B., & Sörhammar, D. (2019). Organizing for digital servitization: A service ecosystem perspective. *Journal of Business Research, 104,* 450–460.

Szabo, N. (1997). Formalizing and securing relationships on public networks. First Monday 2, 9.

Toxopeus, H., Achterberg, E., & Polzin, F. (2018). *Financing business model innovation: Bank lending for firms shifting towards a circular economy* (Sustainable Finance Lab working paper).

Tuli, K., Kohli, A., & Bharadwaj, S. (2007). Rethinking customer solutions: From product bundles to relational processes. *Journal of Marketing, 71*(3), 1–17.

Ulaga, W., & Reinartz, W. (2011). Hybrid offerings: How manufacturing firms combine goods and services successfully. *Journal of Marketing, 75,* 5–23.

Vendrell-Herrero, F., Bustinza, O., Parry, G., & Georgantzis, N. (2017). Servitization, digitization and supply chain interdependency. *Industrial Marketing Management, 60,* 69–81.

Servitization Process

Viewing Servitization Through a Practice-Theoretical Lens

Katja Maria Hydle and Marko Kohtamäki

1 Introduction

Servitization is the shift manufacturers undertake when turning from products to smart solutions (product-service-software systems) to gain a competitive edge, higher returns, and growth opportunities (Lightfoot et al., 2013; Matthyssens & Vandenbempt, 2008; Rabetino et al., 2015). Servitization and digital servitization (Coreynen et al., 2017; Kohtamäki et al., 2019) are far from easy or simple (Gebauer et al., 2005; Kallenberg & Oliva, 2003); they are complex, systemic, and lengthy processes and hence challenging to manage. Thus, servitization is complex and involve organizational change that calls for management tools that stretch beyond firm boundaries (Kohtamäki et al., 2018; Lightfoot et al., 2013). Servitization can be viewed through a variety of lenses and from a variety of theoretical perspectives; this chapter takes the practice-theoretical approach toward servitization.

Practice theories have gained popularity among academics (Brown & Duguid, 1991; Feldman & Orlikowski, 2011; Jarzabkowski, 2005; Johnson

K. M. Hydle (✉)
Department of Informatics, University of Oslo, Oslo, Norway
e-mail: katjahy@uio.no

M. Kohtamäki
University of Vaasa, Vaasa, Finland
e-mail: mtko@uwasa.fi

M. Kohtamäki et al. (eds.), *The Palgrave Handbook of Servitization*, https://doi.org/10.1007/978-3-030-75771-7_15

et al., 2003; Orlikowski, 2002; Schatzki et al., 2001), providing powerful frames to explain what people do and say (Schatzki, 2012; Schatzki et al., 2001). Understanding sayings and doings, so-called activities, is highly relevant for servitization since the transition from product logic to service logic involves activities that include bodily doings and sayings, as well as materials. Sayings and doings constitute social practices that are inherently social, and it is the social that carries the practices. "At the base of a practice, furthermore, lie those doings and sayings that are basic activities. Basic activities take place without the actor having to do something else: they are actions a person can perform without further ado" (Schatzki, 2012, p. 15). For instance, when typing on a keyboard, for the activity of viewing data logs and analysis for proactive support for a customer. We thus understand practices as composed of different activities, which themselves are formed by actions that, in turn, are constructed from basic doings and sayings (Schatzki, 2012).

Thus, we see practices being composed of activities, which are formed by sayings and doings involving material arrangements. This chapter contributes to the servitization literature by drawing from the practice-theoretical literature; while the primary emphasis is on Schatzki's practice theory, other theorists are considered, and the goal is to shed light on the practice-theoretical perspective toward servitization.

2   Servitization and Use of Practice Theory

There are several ways servitization can be understood by using practice theory. We propose three different angles: (1) servitization through practice emergence and dissolution; (2) transition through the action chains involved or the narratives used during servitization; and (3) performing a practice-based study of servitization. The first angle focuses mainly on the microlevel changes during servitization, while the second emphasizes macrolevel phenomena during servitization. The third angle is more all-encompassing, since a practice-based study may be in-depth and/or in breadth of the servitization transition. These three different ways of examining the servitization transition are not mutually exclusive.

Servitization Through Practice Emergence, Persistence and Dissolution

One way to focus on servitization is to uncover practice emergence and dissolution. From a practice-theoretical perspective, it is important to grasp and uncover the practices involved when manufacturing firms are changing from products to services. Uncovering particular practices in servitization entails focusing on the activities performed that hang together while developing intangible services in manufacturing firms. Uncovering the practices of service provision during servitization transition involves focusing on the new activities or the new ways these activities are organized, how existing activities are maintained, or even how certain activities and their organization dissolve. Following Schatzki (2012), the activities of a practice are "*organized by practical understandings, rules, teleoaffective structures and general understandings*" (2012, p. 15). "Practical understanding" refers to knowing how to carry out certain actions. Accordingly, the activities can be understood as organized by the practical understanding and the tacit knowledge that refers to the employees' know-how to perform the services. "Rules" refer to "explicitly formulated directive, remonstration, instruction or edict" (2012, p. 16). The activities are also organized by the rules to be interpreted, which involve explicit directives or procedures to follow, such as the internal instructions and templates and the applicable external standards or laws. "Teleoaffective structure" is the teleological hierarchies that are found in practice. The activities are organized by the teleoaffective structures (end-project-activity-combination) that are used when providing and delivering services to customers and obtaining customer satisfaction. "General understandings" are more abstract, representing the sense of worth, nature and value that form part of people's doings and sayings, and the "rightness" that particular actions are judged to have by performers of a practice. Practitioners' general understanding refers to the sense of the worth of the service provision that is expressed in employees' doings and sayings. A focus on the practices of service provision will uncover how the different activities form practices, how different practices are interrelated in bundles and how these bundles connect and form larger constellations (Schatzki, 2019). By identifying constellations of practices and arrangements for service provision, it will be possible to view how the transition from tangible products to intangible services takes form.

Further, the activities composing the practices are linked to material entities and arrangements. Material entities are understood as everything material, including human bodies. Focusing on servitization transition implies identifying the emergence of new practices related to services and the dissolution of other practices related to products, while also paying attention to those practices that persist (Schatzki, 2013). Practice persistence refers to the ongoing occurrence of the activities that compose a practice (Schatzki, 2013).

Emergence and dissolution of a practice will expose the locus of change and hence the servitization transition. Practice emergence takes place when a practice is sufficiently different from the existing practices to the practitioner (or the researcher). The evolution of a practice may involve new activities, or a new practice can collect together existing activities in a new way. Alternatively, part of the organization of the activities of a practice may be new, such as (1) the development of practical understanding, (2) new explicit formulations or rules, (3) different acceptable ends, tasks and actions, or (4) new common general understandings (Schatzki, 2013). The introduction of new material entities such as technology may also give emergence to a practice-arrangement bundle. In servitization, the introduction of simulation technology has enabled the emergence of new practices, for instance, technical user training for product support services, while dissolving existing practices.

Practice dissolution involves no longer performing the activities of a practice or dissolving or changing part of the organization of the practices (practical understanding, rules, teleoaffective structures and general understanding) through internal or external causes. Such causes may be small and internal, such as a new rule, or large societal changes, involving massive shifts in the organization of practices or responses from people resulting in the abandonment of existing practice-arrangement bundles (Schatzki, 2013). During servitization, several practice dissolutions take place, for instance, in relation to the transition from reactive support, in which customers are responded to based on products and installations involving a point-to-point sale whenever there is something wrong with the product, to proactive support involving data analysis of how the product is used and proactively following up on the usage of the product through a yearly subscription. The dissolution of practices and the organization of the practices involved in reactive support occur over time as the emergence of proactive support and related practices are gradually developed during servitization.

Servitization as a Transition Process

Servitization involves a change of focus from providing products to offering integrated solutions or services, and hence developing "From To," from the way the strategies, offerings and processes have been to how these are performed and the sayings and doings during the servitization journey (Kohtamäki et al., 2020). The change of focus involves a minimum of two different states of affairs, with a transition between them. There are two ways a focus on change can be studied: analyzing the action chains involved and/or the narratives used during the servitization transition.

According to practice theory (Schatzki, 2019), changes "emerge through, or result from, events and processes" (Schatzki, 2019, p. 7). An event is understood as something that happens, which may be either brief or extended in time. Processes are understood as continuous series of things happening (in line with Rescher [2000, p. 22]), as an "*integrated series of connected developments*," which can be identified by the results, or by the ongoing unfolding of advances (partly in line with Bergson understanding process as an advancing wave) (Schatzki, 2019, pp. 10–12). Material arrangements with which people's practices are entangled may include computers, mobile phones, tablets, software programs, machines, furniture, and even human bodies. Action chains are series of actions in which one action reacts to the prior action, such as answering an email. Chains of actions are composed of activities, where each of these activities is a linked component of one or several practices. Hence, action chains occur within and across practices (Schatzki, 2019). Furthermore, there are several types of action chains, such as interactions, exchanges, dialogues, governance, or randomness. Action chains form nexuses since they hang together, such as commercial arrangements between two companies.

Analyzing action chains necessitates an understanding of the practice-arrangement bundle and the constellations that these action chains are informed or shaped by. A practice-arrangement bundle is a set of linked practices and material arrangements, while constellations are linked bundles, meaning larger nexuses of practices and arrangements. Different service practices are linked and bundled, such as proactive maintenance, and several of these bundles form constellations or larger nexuses of practices and material arrangements, such as product-service bundling that could be coined socio-material practices in line with Orlikowski (2007, 2010). The action chains can be all the different series of actions in which an employee is involved in relation to other firms. Alternatively, such a different series of actions form larger nexuses, for instance, between a manufacturing firm and its customers. To focus on servitization as a change arising from nexuses of action chains, it is important to uncover the processes, events, and material arrangements that form part of the change.

Servitization as change can also be uncovered through the oral histories and narratives used by practitioners. Focusing on the sayings and the narratives used during servitization is another way to understand the transition. A practice in itself is composed of organized sayings (as well as doings of something) providing structure to work, often coined praxis by some theorists (Reckwitz, 2002; Whittington, 2006a). Practice entails what an employee says, while working with adding advanced services to a manufacturing firm may form part of a service practice. The sayings are often linked to the material entities s/he is using, such as the mobile phone or the PC, during customer meetings or while collaborating with other practitioners. A focus on sayings exposes the oral histories.

Oral histories, narratives, and storytelling are central practices in organizational transformation. Narratives are temporal, discursive constructions of the past, present, or future events (Czarniawska, 2004). Thus, narratives underline the temporal aspect in organizational discourse, separating these from other organizational discursive approaches (Vaara et al., 2016). For organizations, narratives form a central organizational practice. Antenarratives are seen as a specific form of organizational narrative, referring to microstories, which can represent sensemaking or sensegiving from past, current, or future events (Boje, 2001). Thus, narratives and antenarratives can be used in servitization research to understand the transition process over time. A narrative approach to a practice-based study enables a fluid and dynamic depiction of the transition process, exposing many voices and enhancing a rich interpretation (Cunliffe et al., 2004).

A Practice-Based Study of Servitization

A third way practice theories can be used in servitization is through performing a practice-based study of servitization. A practice-based study requires that the researcher understand what people do and say in their everyday work and how different people's activities are organized (Schatzki, 2012). A person participates in a number of practices every day. This means that the practices are not easily identified, and an observer and/or a researcher has to search to uncover them (Schatzki, 2012). Schatzki states that, "*Whereas material entities and activities can be directly perceived (this requires knowledge of the bundles to which they belong and of teleology as well as motivation), practices must be uncovered*" (2012, p. 24). For instance, when people collaborate, how people interact at a certain moment in time can be observed, but a pattern used for collaboration has to be uncovered over time. Service work is based on the activities of professionals, yet with a centrality of intellectual and symbolic skills in such (Alvesson, 2004), it is difficult to observe service work. On the other hand, activities can be perceived and observed, such as observing the activities of talking to a colleague while getting coffee in the morning, writing a project proposal, or being in a customer meeting. The practices of collaboration could involve all these activities of talking to a colleague, writing a project proposal or being in a meeting, yet not easily detected as part of the practices the first time they are observed. Rather, activities composing a practice are identified after having observed them over time or having been told about them recurrently. Hence, practices are more ethereal than activities (Schatzki, 2012).

Practices can be uncovered by following the central activities of service provision, such as writing a project offering and providing the service to the customer. Following different activities and perceiving them over time will provide an understanding of their worth or meaning in relation to other related activities and to service provision. The activities form action hierarchies that are provided to perform the service. In this sense, the end of the service provision is customer satisfaction, income, possibly customer retention and enhanced learning in the firm. Service provision, as such, can be understood as a practice that is shared across the different particulars of service deliveries to different customers. To uncover practices, a researcher needs to perform ethnography or use methods such as videotaping practices, meeting with the practitioners, performing participant observation, conducting interviews and obtaining the oral histories of the participants in a practice (Schatzki, 2012).

These three ways to uncover the servitization transition through practice theory expose different angles from which to identify the changes. The first, regarding practice emergence, persistence, or dissolution, focuses on the microlevel changes of the practices, the related actions, activities and the organization of the practices to uncover the servitization transition. The second, related to the action chains and the narratives used, mainly emphasizes the macrolevel changes of the servitization. Finally, a practice-based study of servitization aims at viewing the depth and breadth of servitization within one firm.

3   Servitization Research Using Practice Theory

There is a nascent body of servitization research using practice theory. In the following, we will emphasize existing research within three different lenses: microlevel changes, macrolevel changes, and servitization-as-practice.

Zooming in on Microlevel Servitization Practices

To view servitization and theorizing the practices, it is important to be able to adjust the focus. The understanding of "zooming in" set forth by Nicolini (2009; Palo et al., 2019) involves local accomplishments, such as real-time sets of doings and sayings, and the ability to perform a detailed study with the discursive and material elements involved. A zooming in would produce a detailed representation of practice, to get closer to the phenomena of interest and to better understand the related doings and sayings. With a granular analysis, often using ethnomethodological methods such as conversation analysis, zooming in could also entail foregrounding the tools and materials (Nicolini, 2009) used in servitization practices.

Some studies on servitization have zoomed in on doings and sayings when studying transformation processes. For instance, Kohtamäki et al. (2020) studied the paradoxical challenges in servitization and the practices used to cope with these paradoxes. Palo et al. (2019) studied servitization as a business model contestation, suggesting that contestations should be seen as a source of creative input for the organization. Nordin and Ravald (2016) found four practices to manage relational gaps: canceling, capitulating, combining, and convincing. In their study of narratives in servitization research, Luoto et al. (2017) identified four paradigmatic assumptions (constant development, realist ontology, positivist epistemology, and managerialism) shaping servitization research and calling for alternative narratives. Korkeamäki and Kohtamäki (2020) studied discursive legitimation strategies when implementing an outcome business model. Baines et al. (2020) identified a servitization model that depicts the transition through the four stages of exploration, engagement, expansion, and exploitation. Martinez et al. (2017) explored the manufacturer's servitization journey. They depicted servitization as a process of continuous change. Kohtamäki et al. (2018) published a book intending to collect practices and tools for servitization in the practice-theoretical spirit.

Zooming Out of Servitization Practices at the Macrolevel

"Zooming out" is switching the theoretical lenses to understand and view practices associated with the larger phenomena of organizational life (Nicolini, 2009). Zooming out provides an overview without going into extensive detail. Large social phenomena are, in practice, theory understood as large nexuses of practice-arrangement bundles or constellations as even larger bundles (Schatzki, 2016), such as corporations, ecosystems, industries, and economic systems. Zooming out may involve following connections in action, trailing the associations between practices through historical reconstruction or real-time shadowing (Nicolini, 2009). Another angle is to study the effects of different practice-arrangement bundles or constellations.

Research on servitization that has zoomed out would refer to studies that look beyond the nitty-gritty details of servitization processes and instead analyze servitization at the ecosystem level, moving beyond the boundaries of a single firm. Digital servitization has been seen as a phenomenon that extends beyond firm boundaries. While very few studies in servitization have actually used practice theory to analyze servitization, from micro- or macroperspectives, there are studies that look beyond firm boundaries into servitizing ecosystems. For instance, Sklyar et al. (2019) used an ecosystem perspective on digital servitization. Their study unfolds the digital servitization process, suggesting organizational integration and service centricity for improved coordination of activities. Huikkola et al. (2020) considered how servitization shapes boundaries by studying empirical cases of how servitization changes firm boundaries. Kohtamäki et al. (2019) described how digital servitization changes firm business models and boundaries, contextualizing and discussing the transition at the level of company ecosystems.

Servitization-as-Practice

Instead of either zooming in or zooming out on servitization practices, servitization-as-practice includes both micro and macro levels and has been proposed to describe tools and constructs that enable or disable servitization, that is, the change from standardized products and add-on services to complex integrated product-service solutions (Kohtamäki & Rajala, 2016; Kohtamäki et al., 2018). The understanding of servitization-as-practice has been inspired by the well-established strategy-as-practice (SAP) perspective in strategy research and the growing entrepreneurship-as-practice (EAP) community within entrepreneurship research. An understanding of servitization-as-practice will therefore look to SAP research to expose how the understanding of strategy has changed by using practice theory, which can illuminate how servitization research may evolve.

SAP reconceptualizes strategy as an inherently social activity; strategy is not something an organization *has* but rather something that its members *do*. SAP advocates the need to get closer to the phenomenon of interest and to better understand the "sayings" and "doings" in strategy work (Seidl & Whittington, 2014; Whittington, 2006a) by looking at that which is practically, explicitly, and implicitly associated with strategy. Practice theory is used as one theoretical foundation for the SAP perspective to shed light on the enacted nature of strategizing (Chia & MacKay, 2007; Feldman & Orlikowski, 2011; Jarzabkowski, 2004, 2005; Jarzabkowski et al., 2007; Jarzabkowski & Spee, 2009; Whittington, 2006a). In SAP, Jarzabkowski et al. define strategizing and strategy as "*a situated, socially accomplished activity, while strategizing comprises those actions, interactions and negotiations of multiple actors and the situated practices that they draw upon in accomplishing that activity*" (Jarzabkowski et al., 2007, pp. 7–8). SAP research uses practices to understand the relational and enacted nature of strategizing, the explicit strategizing practices and processes (Chia & MacKay, 2007; Jarzabkowski, 2008; Jarzabkowski et al., 2007; Jarzabkowski & Spee, 2009; Kornberger & Clegg, 2011; Rasche & Chia, 2009; Whittington, Whittington 2006a, 2006b, 2007) and the implicit strategizing, which is an immanent part of everyday practices and adaptive actions, whereas strategy-making is not necessarily an intentional goal orientation but instead is relative to past experiences and practical coping (Chia & Holt, 2006, 2009; Hydle, 2015; Vaara & Whittington, 2012).

Following the research on SAP, servitization-as-practice should emphasize the doings and sayings of servitization work, focusing on what is explicitly and implicitly linked to servitization, and practice theory can be one theoretical foundation to view the enacted servitization activities. Servitization-as-practice should therefore emphasize what practitioners do and say, their *servitizing*, not what the firms have; servitization-as-practice could therefore be an approach to view the enacted nature of *servitizing*. We understand *servitizing* as the activities and interactions involved by multiple actors and the use of materials when moving from products to services (Kohtamäki et al., 2020).

4   Discussion

Theoretical Contribution

This chapter uses a practice-theoretical lens on servitization, with a primary emphasis on Schatzki's practice theory. The chapter responded to calls for alternative narratives in servitization (Luoto et al., 2017), providing a specific and novel perspective on understanding servitization.

The use of practice theory on organizational phenomena is not novel; however, only a few studies use practice theory to understand servitizing. We propose three different angles to use practice theory on servitization: (1) servitization through practice emergence, persistence and dissolution; (2) servitization as a transition process; and (3) practice-based study of servitization. We also expose three different ways in which existing servitization research can be understood: zooming in on microlevel changes, zooming out on macrolevel changes, and servitization-as-practice. The contribution of this chapter is to reveal these different angles to view servitization and the understanding of servitizing.

Future Research Using Practice Theory in Servitization

Future research on servitization using practice theory may differently emphasize microlevel or macrolevel servitization phenomena or practice-based studies to uncover the transition. We suggest three different microlevel research directions, one at the macrolevel and one practice-based, to view organizational change.

Practice-theoretical research has much to give to servitization research. Being a socially constructed business transition, servitization as an implementation project requires managerial sayings and doings that enable simultaneous thriving or products, services and software development in an integrated manner. Certainly, few empirical studies exist on the sayings and doings in managerial work at different organizational levels during servitization (Kohtamäki et al., 2020; Palo et al., 2019). Hence, we propose:

Research direction 1. Managerial sayings and doings deserve practice-theoretical insight.

Servitization research should focus on managerial discourse and narratives to understand how managers construct servitization at their managerial work and how those constructions change. Managerial constructions and rhetoric can teach us much about the use of language when advancing servitization and how it shapes managerial practices:

Research direction 2. Servitization research should tap into the discursive constructions in servitization, e.g., how actors shape servitization through sayings and narrative constructions.

Moreover, despite the interplay between the product, services, software and humans, as a sociomaterial or sociotechnical phenomenon, very few studies exist of servitization as sociomaterial practice (Naik et al., 2020). For instance, the actual labor of a service worker is inherently sociomaterial. Without the tools and materials needed for the work, the service worker cannot do his/her job. Tools, tablets, virtual reality handsets, and artificial intelligence also shape the future of service work (Orlikowski, 2000). Interesting research opportunities exist under the concept of sociomateriality in servitization:

Research direction 3. Research is needed on the sociomaterial interplay between actors and their materials when planning and implementing servitization.

Based on the servitization literature, we know more about the practices used in advancing servitization. Little empirical research exists on how companies shape ecosystems during servitization and digital servitization. According to previous studies, companies need to reconstruct ecosystems (Kohtamäki et al., 2019; Sklyar et al., 2019), and these practices are often cocreated. How companies are actually crafting ecosystems, which tools they are using, and how and what practices are performed are still understudied, but important, phenomena:

Research direction 4. More research is needed about the practices used to shape the ecosystem when moving toward digital servitization and autonomous systems.

As suggested by many studies, servitization research has often been conducted by using multiple case settings (Rabetino et al., 2018). Multiple case studies can indeed provide important knowledge. However, the capacity of case studies to provide a detailed analysis of servitization practices is limited. In acknowledging that there are very few single case studies in servitization research, we call for studies using single case methods and conducting practice-based approaches. This would add to the existing body of servitization research:

Research direction 5. Servitization research should assess the depths of organizational change by using ethnographic methods and a practice-based study in single case studies.

References

Alvesson, M. (2004). *Knowledge work and knowledge intensive firms.* Oxford University Press.

Baines, T., Ziaee Bigdeli, A., Sousa, R., & Schroeder, A. (2020). Framing the servitization transformation process: A model to understand and facilitate the servitization journey. *International Journal of Production Economics, 221,*. https://doi.org/10.1016/j.ijpe.2019.07.036.

Boje, D. (2001). *Narrative methods for organizational and communication research.* Sage.

Brown, J. S., & Duguid, P. (1991). Organizational learning and communities-of -practice: Toward a unified view of working, learning and innovation. *Organization Science, 2*(1), 40–57.

Chia, R., & Holt, R. (2006). Strategy as practical coping: A Heideggerian perspective. *Organization Studies, 27*(5), 635–655. https://doi.org/10.1177/0170840606064102.

Chia, R., & Holt, R. (2009). *Strategy without design: The silent efficacy of indirect action.* Cambridge University Press.

Chia, R., & MacKay, B. (2007). Post-processual challenges for the emerging strategy-as-practice perspective: Discovering strategy in the logic of practice. *Human Relations, 60*(1), 217–242. http://search.ebscohost.com/login.aspx?dir ect=true&db=bth&AN=24240543&loginpage=Login.asp&site=ehost-live

Coreynen, W., Matthyssens, P., & Van Bockhaven, W. (2017). Boosting servitization through digitization: Pathways and dynamic resource configurations for manu-facturers. *Industrial Marketing Management, 60,* 42–53. https://doi.org/10.1016/j.indmarman.2016.04.012.

Cunliffe, A., Luhman, J., & Boje, D. (2004). Narrative temporality: Implications for organizational research. *Organization Studies, 25*(2), 261–286.

Czarniawska, B. (2004). *Narratives in Social Science Research.* Sage.

Feldman, M. S., & Orlikowski, W. J. (2011). Theorizing practice and practicing theory. *Organization Science,* 1–14.

Gebauer, H., Fleisch, E., & Friedli, T. (2005). Overcoming the service paradox in manufacturing companies. *European Management Journal, 23*(1), 14–26. https://doi.org/10.1016/j.emj.2004.12.006.

Huikkola, T., Rabetino, R., Kohtamäki, M., & Gebauer, H. (2020). Firm bound-aries in servitization: Interplay and repositioning practices. *Industrial Marketing Management, 90,* 90–105.

Hydle, K. M. (2015). Temporal and spatial dimensions of strategizing. *Organization Studies, 36*(5), 643–663. https://doi.org/10.1177/0170840615571957.

Jarzabkowski, P. (2004). Strategy as practice: Recursiveness, adaptation, and practices-in-use. *Organization Studies, 25*(4), 529–560. https://doi.org/10.1177/0170840604040675

Jarzabkowski, P. (2005). *Strategy as practice: An activity based approach.* Sage.

Jarzabkowski, P. (2008). Shaping strategy as a structuration process. *Academy of Management Journal, 51*(4), 621–650. http://search.ebscohost.com/login.aspx?dir ect=true&db=bth&AN=33664922&site=bsi-live

Jarzabkowski, P., Balogun, J., & Seidl, D. (2007). Strategizing: The challenges of a practice perspective. *Human Relations, 60*(1), 5–27. http://search.ebscohost. com/login.aspx?direct=true&db=bth&AN=24240521&loginpage=Login.asp& site=ehost-live

Jarzabkowski, P., & Spee, A. P. (2009). Strategy-as-practice: A review and future directions for the field. *International Journal of Management Reviews, 11*(1), 69–95.

Johnson, G., Melin, L., & Wittington, R. (2003). Micro strategy and strategizing: Towards an activity-based view. *Journal of Management Studies, 40*(1).

Kallenberg, R., & Oliva, R. (2003). Managing the transition from products to services. *International Journal of Service Industry Management, 14*(2), 160–172. https://doi.org/10.1108/09564230310474138.

Kohtamäki, M., Baines, T. S., Rabetino, R., & Bigdeli, A. Z. (Eds.). (2018). *Practices and tools for servitization: Managing Service Transition*: Palgrave Macmillan.

Kohtamäki, M., Einola, S., & Rabetino, R. (2020). Exploring servitization through the paradox lens: Coping practices in servitization. *International Journal of*

Production Economics, 226 (August), 1–15. https://doi.org/10.1016/j.ijpe.2020. 107619.

Kohtamäki, M., Parida, V., Oghazi, P., Gebauer, H., & Baines, T. (2019). Digital servitization business models in ecosystems: A theory of the firm. *Journal of Business Research, 104,* 380–392. https://doi.org/10.1016/j.jbusres.2019.06.027.

Kohtamäki, M., & Rajala, R. (2016). Theory and practice of value co-creation in B2B systems. *Industrial Marketing Management, 56,* 4–13. https://doi.org/10. 1016/j.indmarman.2016.05.027.

Korkeamäki, L., & Kohtamäki, M. (2020). To outcomes and beyond: Discursively managing legitimacy struggles in outcome business models. *Industrial Marketing Management, 91,* 196–208. https://doi.org/10.1016/j.indmarman.2020.08.023.

Kornberger, M., & Clegg, S. (2011). Strategy as performative practice: The case of Sydney 2030. *Strategic Organization, 9*(2), 136–162. https://doi.org/10.1177/ 1476127011407758.

Lightfoot, H. W., Baines, T., & Smart, P. (2013). The servitization of manufacturing: A systematic literature review of interdependent trends. *International Journal of Operations & Production Management, 33*(11/12), 1408–1434.

Luoto, S., Brax, S. A., & Kohtamäki, M. (2017). Critical meta-analysis of servitization research: Constructing a model-narrative to reveal paradigmatic assumptions. *Industrial Marketing Management, 60,* 89–100. https://doi.org/10.1016/j. indmarman.2016.04.008.

Martinez, V., Neely, A., Velu, C., Leinster-Evans, S., & Bisessar, D. (2017). Exploring the journey to services. *International Journal of Production Economics, 192*(October), 66–80.

Matthyssens, P., & Vandenbempt, K. (2008). Moving from basic offerings to value-added solutions: Strategies, barriers and alignment. *Industrial Marketing Management, 37*(3), 316–328. https://doi.org/10.1016/j.indmarman.2007.07.008.

Naik, P., Schroeder, A., Kapoor, K. K., Ziaee Bigdeli, A., & Baines, T. (2020). Behind the scenes of digital servitization: Actualising IoT-enabled affordances. *Industrial Marketing Management, 89,* 232–244. https://doi.org/10.1016/j.ind marman.2020.03.010.

Nicolini, D. (2009). Zooming in and out: Studying practices by switching theoretical lenses and trailing connections. *Organization Studies, 30*(12), 1391–1418. https://doi.org/10.1177/0170840609349875.

Nordin, F., & Ravald, A. (2016). Managing relationship gaps: A practitioner perspective. *Journal of Business Research, 69*(7), 2490–2497.

Orlikowski, W. J. (2000). Using technology and constituting structures: A practice lens for studying technology in organizations. *Organization Science, 11*(4), 404–428. http://search.ebscohost.com/login.aspx?direct=true&db=bth& AN=3629480&site=bsi-live

Orlikowski, W. J. (2002). Knowing in practice: Enacting a collective capability in distributed organizing. *Organization Science, 13*(3), 249–273.

Orlikowski, W. J. (2007). Sociomaterial practices: Exploring technology at work. *Organization Studies, 28*(9), 1435–1448. https://doi.org/10.1177/017084060 7081138.

Orlikowski, W. J. (2010). The sociomateriality of organisational life: Considering technology in management research. *Cambridge Journal of Economics, 34*(1), 125–141. https://doi.org/10.1093/cje/bep058.

Palo, T., Åkesson, M., & Löfberg, N. (2019). Servitization as business model contestation: A practice approach. *Journal of Business Research, 104,* 486–496. https://doi.org/10.1016/j.jbusres.2018.10.037.

Rabetino, R., Harmsen, W., Kohtamäki, M., & Sihvonen, J. (2018). Structuring servitization-related research. *International Journal of Operations & Production Management, 38*(2), 350–371. https://doi.org/10.1108/IJOPM-03-2017-0175.

Rabetino, R., Kohtamäki, M., Lehtonen, H., & Kostama, H. (2015). Developing the concept of life-cycle service offering. *Industrial Marketing Management, 49,* 53–66. https://doi.org/10.1016/j.indmarman.2015.05.033.

Rasche, A., & Chia, R. (2009). Researching strategy practices: A genealogical social theory perspective. *Organization Studies, 30*(7), 713–734. https://doi.org/10.1177/0170840609104809.

Reckwitz, A. (2002). Towards a theory of social practices: A development in culturalist theorizing. *European Journal of Social Theory, 5*(2), 243–263.

Rescher, N. (2000). *Process philosophy. A survey of basic issues.* University of Pittsburgh Press.

Schatzki, T. (2012). A primer on practices: Theory and research. In J. Higgs, R. Barnett, S. Billett, M. Hutchings, & F. Trede (Eds.), *Practice-based education: Perspectives and strategies* (pp. 13–26). Sense Publishers.

Schatzki, T. (2013). The edge of change: On the emergence, persistence, and dissolution of practices. In E. Shove & N. Spurling (Eds.), *Sustainable practice: Social theory and climate change* (pp. 31–46). Routledge.

Schatzki, T. (2016). Keeping track of large social phenomena. *Geographische Zeitschrift, 104*(1), 4–24.

Schatzki, T. (2019). *Social change in a material world.* Routledge.

Schatzki, T., Knorr Cetina, K. D., & von Savigny, E. (Eds.). (2001). *The practice turn in contemporary theory.* Routledge.

Seidl, D., & Whittington, R. (2014). Enlarging the strategy-as-practice research agenda: Towards taller and flatter ontologies. *Organization Studies, 35*(10), 1407–1421. https://doi.org/10.1177/0170840614541886.

Sklyar, A., Kowalkowski, C., Tronvoll, B., & Sörhammar, D. (2019). Organizing for digital servitization: A service ecosystem perspective. *Journal of Business Research, 104,* 450–460. https://doi.org/10.1016/j.jbusres.2019.02.012.

Vaara, E., Sonenshein, S., & Boje, D. (2016). Narratives as sources of stability and change in organizations: Approaches and directions for future research. *The Academy of Management Annals, 10*(1), 1–58.

Vaara, E., & Whittington, R. (2012). Strategy-as-practice: Taking social practices seriously. *The Academy of Management Annals, 6*(1), 285–336. https://doi.org/10.1080/19416520.2012.672039.

Whittington, R. (2006a). Completing the practice turn in strategy research. *Organization Studies, 27*(5), 613–634. https://doi.org/10.1177/0170840606064101.

Whittington, R. (2006b). Learning more from failure: Practice and process. *Organization Studies, 27*(12), 1903–1906. https://doi.org/10.1177/0170840606071945.

Whittington, R. (2007). Strategy practice and strategy process: Family differences and the sociological eye. *Organization Studies, 28,* 1575–1586.

Microfoundations of Servitization: An Individual-Level Perspective

Wim Coreynen

1   Introduction

Firms increasingly create value for customers by combining products and services into integrated solutions (Davies, 2004). They do so for a variety of reasons: to increase their competitive edge, to enhance customer loyalty, and to create new and stable revenue streams (Raddats et al., 2016). Yet moving from basic offerings to solutions is not easy, and firms often do not see immediate financial return, if at all (Gebauer et al., 2005). On top of explaining *why* product firms should rethink their business, the literature has started to stress *how* they can achieve growth through services (Kowalkowski et al., 2017). The last two decades, the majority of papers published has been concerned with finding how firms can alter their strategy, restructure their organization, and what type of capabilities they should develop to successfully create, sell, and deliver services (Raddats et al., 2019). Despite this variety of

W. Coreynen (✉)
School of Business and Economics, Vrije Universiteit Amsterdam, Amsterdam, The Netherlands
e-mail: w.coreynen@vu.nl

Utrecht University School of Economics, Utrecht University, Utrecht, The Netherlands

M. Kohtamäki et al. (eds.), *The Palgrave Handbook of Servitization*,
https://doi.org/10.1007/978-3-030-75771-7_16

highly relevant topics, most papers share one shortcoming: They view servitization entirely from the *firm* level while often neglecting the *individual* level (Rabetino et al., 2018; Rese & Maiwald, 2013).

In the increasing focus on strategy, structure and capabilities, the elementary truth about firms—that they are made up of individuals—seems to have been forgotten (Felin & Foss, 2005). Many strategy researchers choose the firm rather than the individual as the core level of analysis (Powell et al., 2011), yet people and their different characteristics are the building blocks of many collective phenomena and require careful consideration in both theory development and empirical research (Felin et al., 2012). Also, there have been several calls in recent servitization work to pay more attention to the role of individuals and their influence on organizational outcomes (e.g., Rabetino et al., 2017; Valtakoski, 2017).

This chapter discusses the current state of the microfoundations of servitization from an individual-level perspective. First, we briefly introduce the microfoundations movement and explain why it is a fruitful avenue for future research. Next, we consult and summarize prior research on individual-level components—namely cognitions, motivations, abilities, traits, and behavior—and their relationship with servitization. Based on these insights, we present a conceptual framework that can serve as inspiration for more microfoundational work to follow suit. We end this chapter by discussing its implications for theory and also management.

2   Theory Development

Microfoundations

A microfoundations approach explains collective phenomena, such as firms' innovation strategies, by considering lower-level entities, such as organizational processes and individuals, as well as their interactions (Felin et al., 2012). Conceptually, the microfoundations movement began in the early 2000s, as a reaction to the overemphasis on macro-level factors in strategy and organization theory, and empirical work started to take off in the 2010s (Felin et al., 2015). Researchers also started to focus on firms' microfoundations to build stronger conceptual foundations for servitization. For example, Kindström et al. (2013) identified several key microfoundations that allow product-centric firms to create dynamic capabilities for service innovation. So far, servitization scholars have applied a microfoundations approach only to a limited extent, and recent work calls for future studies to further explore the micro-level mechanisms of this service phenomenon (Valtakoski, 2017).

Exploring the microfoundations of servitization is a fruitful avenue for further research for two main reasons. First, as a multi-level approach, it aims to locate the cause(s) of a particular phenomenon at a level of analysis that is lower than the phenomenon itself (Felin et al., 2015). In other words: the microfoundations are concerned with at least two levels—the lowest level being the individual. Thus, in order to explain firm strategy and organizational behavior (as macro-level outcomes), the microfoundations approach considers individual-level factors as potential causes. For example, Gebauer et al. (2005) explain how different cognitive processes limit managers to extend into the service business (we will explain this study's results in further detail shortly). Second, it sheds light on firm-level heterogeneity by considering individual-level components, such as people's characteristics, abilities, and cognitions (Felin et al., 2012). In particular, behavioral strategy uses insights from cognitive and social psychology to enrich strategic management theory and practice (Powell et al., 2011). For example, Coreynen et al. (2020) recently found that decision-makers driven by different motives pursue servitization for different strategic purposes (we will also address this further later).

Cognitions

A person's cognitions are one of many building blocks to understand collective phenomena (Felin et al., 2012). Cognitive psychology focuses on the mental processes present within individuals (Powell et al., 2011). When people try to envision future scenarios and strategies, they rely on their cognitions, especially when there is little experience to draw on (Felin & Zenger, 2009).

Going back to the study by Gebauer et al. (2005), the authors found that several cognitive phenomena limit managers to extend into the service business: an overemphasis on tangible product characteristics, a failure to recognize the economic potential of services, and an aversion of the internal risks (e.g., the firm may not have the required capabilities) and external risks (e.g., customers may not be willing to share knowledge outside the firm) that come with servitization. These cognitions are often embedded in manufacturing firms, and changing them is often a process that should grow organically. When they are present, it has been found that managerial motivation to extend into service is limited and that the share of investments is small (Gebauer & Fleisch, 2007). Once managers overcome these cognitions—that is, when they put less emphasis on products' tangible features, see the value of services, and are less risk-averse—they are more likely to develop a service business strategy (Gebauer, 2009). On top, they will empower and coach employees to behave in a service-oriented way.

It is not only important that managers change their cognitions, but also employees should be convinced of the value of services. When employees see the financial potential of services, they will leverage them to augment the product offering and improve the customer relationship, which leads to better firm performance (Gebauer et al., 2010).

Motivations

Related to, yet different from, cognitions are a person's motivations, which refer to an individual's willingness to perform a task, and the level of effort they choose to exert (Johnstone et al., 2014). In short: motivation explains why people act a certain way. For instance, managers are motivated to extend into service when they place a high reward on it, perceive a high probability that they will be successful in their efforts and that their efforts will result in the reward (Gebauer et al., 2005).

McClelland (1987), one of the pioneering scholars to use a motivational perspective for studying entrepreneurial behavior (Frese & Gielnik, 2014), identified several key *intrinsic* motives, including the need to achieve (i.e., to excel by mastering difficult skills), to affiliate (i.e., to maintain good relations) and the need for power (i.e., to control and influence). In their empirical study, Coreynen et al. (2020) found that decision-makers driven by achievement or affiliation are likely to pursue servitization, whereas those driven by power are not. They also found that achievement-driven decision-makers prefer servitization to compete through highly innovative product-service offerings rather than low prices, for instance. Though this type of research is still in its infancy, it shows that people's underlying motivational structure influences how they behave in business.

Also from a service employee's point of view, it has been found that people are better at selling services when they are intrinsically motivated to do so (Ulaga & Loveland, 2014), and that people will deliver higher-quality services when they believe the nature of their work is interesting, fulfilling, and challenging, and when it allows them to use their abilities and personal skills (Kreye, 2016).

People can also be *extrinsically* motivated to sell and deliver high-quality services—for instance, some firms create different financial incentives and rewards systems to change employees' behavior (Antioco et al., 2008; Gebauer et al., 2010; Johnstone et al., 2014)—yet these extrinsic motivational drivers have been found less important than people's intrinsic motivation (Kreye, 2016).

Abilities

A person's ability refers to the knowledge and skills that are necessary to perform a job, and it is influenced by factors such as education, experience, and personality traits (Johnstone et al., 2014). The microfoundations movement considers individual abilities as the cornerstone for building firm capabilities (Helfat & Peteraf, 2015), and therefore they may be considered even more important (Felin & Hesterly, 2007). Some people have an aptitude for particular service skills and develop them more easily, while others may have an aversion to move into service-oriented roles (or they are limited in the role they can take in the organization) (Baines et al., 2013; Johnstone et al., 2014). It is estimated that only one-third of employees switch easily from selling products to services. The majority of salespeople needs massive train or need to be reassigned—sometimes firms even need to bring in new people with entirely different skills and mindsets (Ulaga & Reinartz, 2011). Therefore, recruitment and training are crucial success factors for servitization (Fliess & Lexutt, 2019; Kohtamäki et al., 2015).

Overall, employees in charge of delivering services need to possess both product and technical knowledge, combined with various excellent service delivery attitudes and behaviors (Johnstone et al., 2014). Also in digital servitization, which refers to the integration of service and technology, the right mindset and skills are considered at least as important as technical roles (Schymanietz & Jonas, 2020). So far, the literature discusses three main abilities that sales representatives of product firms should possess in order to successfully sell services.

First, sales reps should be more humanistic in their behavior, as opposed to people in production who think more technocratically (Baines et al., 2013). For example, they should be able to listen and appeal to the customer (Antioco et al., 2008), be empathetic with their problems (Baines et al., 2013), build close customer relationships (Rese & Maiwald, 2013), and remain knowledgeable about customers' goals and processes (Böhm et al., 2020). Second, they need to be able to go outside their comfort zone (Ulaga & Reinartz, 2011), modify their working routine to comply with customer requirements (Baines et al., 2013), and find creative solutions to solve customer problems (Matthyssens & Vandenbempt, 1998). Third, they need good networking skills, so they can access the right decision-makers in the customer organization—often higher-up in the hierarchy—and consult and coordinate with employees of their own organization (Baines et al., 2013; Böhm et al., 2020; Ulaga & Reinartz, 2011).

Traits

A person's ability to sell and deliver high-quality services is influenced by her/his personality traits (Johnstone et al., 2014). As one manager explained: *"Product salespeople are from Mars, while services sales people are from Venus"* (Ulaga & Reinartz, 2011: 13). So far, there has been limited research into the personality traits associated with successful servitization. Two relevant studies are by Ulaga and Loveland (2014) and Baines et al. (2013), who identified several traits related to high service sales and positive customer experience, respectively.

First, employees should be intelligent and eager to learn. They should be able to think abstractly (i.e., focus on the big picture rather than on the practical details), be open to experiment with new ideas, techniques and procedures to find answers to their own questions, and work to continuously improve themselves. Second, they should be authentic and have a desire to help others. They should genuinely commit to helping customers and also be prepared to tell them the truth. Third, they should be dependable and strive hard to honor all commitments until the assignment is completed. Finally, they should be resilient and emotionally stable, so they can better deal with the pressures and stress associated with working with customers.

Behavior

Depending on an individual's cognition, motivation, and ability to extend into service, (s)he will either support or resist servitization (Rese & Maiwald, 2013). When managers see the value of servitization, they are more likely to behave in a service-oriented way by empowering employees to respond to a broader range of customer problems, setting rewards, coaching, and supporting them in solving customer problems. This in turn increases employees' valuation of services, leading them to start serving customers as trusted advisors, problem solvers and performance enablers (Gebauer et al., 2010). They may even change their working hours and tasks to match customer demand (Baines et al., 2013).

When faced with organizational resistance to servitization, employees can adopt several tactics (Lenka et al., 2018). In case of cultural resistance, which often occurs when manufacturers do not see the value of servitization, employees can build awareness and convince others (i.e., evangelizing) to adopt service initiatives. For instance, they can demonstrate how services relate to the overall goals of the firm (Antioco et al., 2008). When there is structural resistance—meaning the firm's structure simply does not allow employees to pursue new service ideas—they can work covertly and without authorization (i.e., bootlegging). For example, a business unit of a stainless-steel pump manufacturer developed its own sales approach focused on offering customers "peace-of-mind" (Shankar et al., 2009) rather than just selling equipment (Coreynen, 2019). In case of strategic resistance—that is, the firm emphasizes the pursuit of other business opportunities—employees can leverage internal (or external) resources and try to define the agenda, including success criteria, to keep servitization implementation moving (Antioco et al., 2008). Finally, in case of procedural resistance, they can collaborate with colleagues to overcome internal obstacles to servitization initiatives. For instance, personnel can convince top management by presenting the gains that they will obtain from supporting services (Antioco et al., 2008).

Conceptual Framework

Recently, Coreynen et al., (2020: 190) defined the microfoundations of servitization as "*the influence of individual-level factors on firm-level service decisions, actions and outcomes.*" Based on this definition and the consulted literature, we present the following preliminary conceptual framework (see Fig. 1). Its purpose is to further advance research in the microfoundations of servitization by further unraveling the influence of individual-level factors—cognitions, motivations, abilities, traits, behavior, and more—on firm-level components, such service strategies, capabilities, organization, culture, and performance.

Because the microfoundations are a multi-level approach that aims to locate the causes of particular phenomena at a lower level of analysis than the phenomenon itself (Felin & Foss, 2005), we draw a dividing line between *firm*-level and *individual*-level components. Also, we separate firms' performance and people's behavior, which are *extrinsic* and directly noticeable, from their *inherent* components such as firms' culture and people's motivations, which are often less observable. For example, a firm's growth can be easily measured by calculating its revenues or profits, but it is more difficult to put

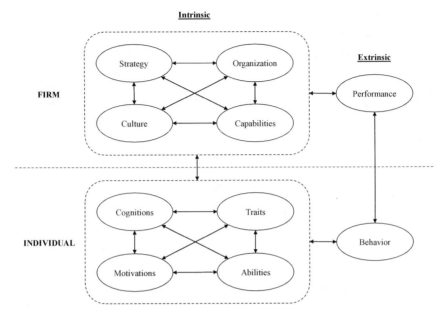

Fig. 1 Conceptual framework

a number on a firm's service strategy and culture. Similarly, it is easier to observe a person's behavior than her/his cognitions and motivations.

Based on the consulted literature, we are able to see several connections (for sake of clarity, we do not plot all relationships in Fig. 1). For example, depending on managers' *motivations* and *cognitions vis-à-vis* services, firms are more (or less) less likely to develop a service business *strategy* (Coreynen et al., 2020; Gebauer, 2009); managers with problem-solving *abilities* are likely to make sound *strategic* investments related to business model design (Helfat & Peteraf, 2015); when managers and employees *behave* in a service-oriented way, the satisfaction and loyalty of customers will be enhanced and the *performance* of their firm increases (Gebauer et al., 2010); firms also *perform* better at selling and delivering high-quality services when employees are *motivated* to do so (Kreye, 2016; Ulaga & Loveland, 2014), and so on. Plotting these connections reveal many potential direct, moderating, and mediating relationships (Venkatraman, 1989), which have either already been confirmed by prior research or require further investigation. Also, the components presented in Fig. 1 cover a variety of more specific research topics, such as a person's *intrinsic* versus *extrinsic* motives (Coreynen et al., 2020; Kreye, 2016), her/his ability to *listen* and *appeal* to the customer (Antioco et al., 2008), and personality traits, such as *introversion, openness,* and *conscientiousness,* which have been associated with successfully selling services (Ulaga &

Loveland, 2014), and for which scales can be drawn from literature, such as McClelland's (1987) Big Three motives and the HEXACO Personality Inventory (Lee & Ashton, 2004).

We purposefully use no single but double arrows for Fig. 1. Though the purpose of microfoundations research is to find individual-level causes for firm-level phenomena (suggesting arrows that point upwards and right-wards), the relationships are more complex. For example, when firms alter their *strategy*, the *motivation* of employees to sell services will change (Ulaga & Loveland, 2014), suggesting a downwards pointing arrow. Also, when firms initially *perform* bad at providing services, the *motivation* of managers may disappear (Gebauer et al., 2005), suggesting a downwards and left-wards pointing arrow. In sum, rather than proposing direct, causal effects between individual-level and firm-level service components, we consider the relationships to be more complex and very much interrelated.

Of course, Fig. 1 does not take into account *all* individual-level factors that may influence servitization. For instance, people's education, job tenure and social network (Felin et al., 2012) are left out for the simple reason that—to the best of our knowledge—there currently is no literature available on the matter. It could be argued, for example, that job tenure negatively relates to managers' motivation to develop service opportunities. Managers that have been around the firm for a long time may prefer the status quo—that is, they focus on improving and selling highly innovative products—whereas later generations, who are more familiar with service platforms such as Uber and Spotify, may be more likely to explore new business models. Furthermore, on the firm-level side, additional elements such as firms' HRM practices may also be considered. Though HRM is found to significantly influence firms' performance (Homburg et al., 2003; Kohtamäki et al., 2015), its foun-dations probably also lie at the level of the individual. For example, HR managers' cognitions, motivations, and abilities probably strongly influence a firm's personnel recruitment and training practices.

3   Conclusion

Theoretical Implications

This chapter calls for further research into the microfoundations of servitiza-tion. For too long, the strategy and management domain and the servitization research field in particular have looked at firms emphasizing heterogeneous strategies and leveraging different capabilities with varying degrees of success, implicitly sidelining the people that build the organization as homogeneous, malleable beings. Yet in the context of industrial services, the people component is an important driver for creating competitive advantage (Matthyssens & Vandenbempt, 1998). In sum: heterogeneity not only exists on the firm-level, but it is present on all levels—the individual being the most basic, foundational level that should be considered (Felin et al., 2015).

Based on a diverse set of articles, this chapter shows that people are made of different components—cognitions, motivations, abilities, traits, behavior and more—that either support or hinder firms in their service transition (Rese & Maiwald, 2013). Furthermore, by plotting these individual and firm-level components as well as their relationships onto a conceptual framework, we provide inspiration for more microfoundational work to follow suit. This chapter thus joins the call for more theoretical foundations and substantial theoretical extensions in servitization research from a micro-level, individual perspective (Rabetino et al., 2017; Valtakoski, 2017).

Managerial Implications

Moving from basic offerings to integrated solutions is not only a matter of changing the organization to better sell services on top of products, it also requires a transformation of the people involved. Managers should be aware of the complex interactions between different individual-level components (Gebauer et al., 2010), such as cognitions, motivations, abilities, and traits, and be closely involved in shaping and managing people's beliefs, skills and behavior. A service-oriented mindset should be shared by the *entire* organization, not just the people that deal with customers (Kohtamäki et al., 2015).

In order to win over people's hearts and minds about servitization, there should be more internal discussions about the benefits and risks of maintaining the current product business versus developing new services. Individuals with a strong service conviction should take the lead in convincing others to adopt new service initiatives, thus generating more organization-wide support (Lenka et al., 2018). Also, employees should receive proper training in order to create, sell, and deliver services. This requires entirely different skillsets, such as the ability to listen and be empathic to customer problems (Ulaga & Loveland, 2014). Managers should also actively reconsider the way employees are assessed and compensated (Homburg et al., 2003), for example, by emphasizing customer satisfaction and retention numbers rather than pure sales figures. Finally, when recruiting personnel, the firm should use different criteria that focus not only on experience and skills but also on motivations and personality.

References

Antioco, M., Moenaert, R. K., Lindgreen, A., & Wetzels, M. G. M. (2008). Organizational antecedents to and consequences of service business orientations in manufacturing companies. *Journal of the Academy of Marketing Science, 36*(3), 337–358. https://doi.org/10.1007/s11747-008-0085-1

Baines, T., Lightfoot, H., Smart, P., & Fletcher, S. (2013). Servitization of manufacture: Exploring the deployment and skills of people critical to the delivery of advanced services. *Journal of Manufacturing Technology Management, 24*(4), 637–646. https://doi.org/10.1108/17410381311327431

Böhm, E., Eggert, A., Terho, H., Ulaga, W., & Haas, A. (2020). Drivers and outcomes of salespersons' value opportunity recognition competence in solution selling. *Journal of Personal Selling & Sales Management, 0*(0), 1–18. https://doi.org/10.1080/08853134.2020.1778484

Coreynen, W. (2019). *Essays on servitization* (PhD Thesis). University of Antwerp.

Coreynen, W., Vanderstraeten, J., van Witteloostuijn, A., Cannaerts, N., Loots, E., & Slabbinck, H. (2020). What drives product-service integration? An abductive study of decision-makers' motives and value strategies. *Journal of Business Research, 117*, 189–200. https://doi.org/10.1016/j.jbusres.2020.05.058

Davies, A. (2004). Moving base into high-value integrated solutions: A value stream approach. *Industrial and Corporate Change, 13*(5), 727–756. https://doi.org/10.1093/icc/dth029

Felin, T., & Foss, N. J. (2005). Strategic organization: A field in search of microfoundations. *Strategic Organization, 3*(4), 441–455. https://doi.org/10.1177/1476127005055796

Felin, T., Foss, N. J., Heimeriks, K. H., & Madsen, T. L. (2012). Microfoundations of routines and capabilities: Individuals, processes, and structure. *Journal of Management Studies, 49*(8), 1351–1374. https://doi.org/10.1111/j.1467-6486.2012.01052.x

Felin, T., Foss, N. J., & Ployhart, R. E. (2015). The microfoundations movement in strategy and organization theory. *Academy of Management Annals, 9*(1), 575–632. https://doi.org/10.5465/19416520.2015.1007651

Felin, T., & Hesterly, W. S. (2007). The knowledge-based view, nested heterogeneity, and new value creation: Philosophical considerations on the locus of knowledge. *The Academy of Management Review, 32*(1), 195–218. JSTOR. https://doi.org/10.2307/20159288

Felin, T., & Zenger, T. R. (2009). Entrepreneurs as theorists: On the origins of collective beliefs and novel strategies. *Strategic Entrepreneurship Journal, 3*(2), 127–146. https://doi.org/10.1002/sej.67

Fliess, S., & Lexutt, E. (2019). How to be successful with servitization – Guidelines for research and management. *Industrial Marketing Management, 78*, 58–75. https://doi.org/10.1016/j.indmarman.2017.11.012

Frese, M., & Gielnik, M. M. (2014). The psychology of entrepreneurship. *Annual Review of Organizational Psychology and Organizational Behavior, 1*(1), 413–438. https://doi.org/10.1146/annurev-orgpsych-031413-091326

Gebauer, H. (2009). An attention-based view on service orientation in the business strategy of manufacturing companies. *Journal of Managerial Psychology, 24*(1), 79–98. https://doi.org/10.1108/02683940910922555

Gebauer, H., Edvardsson, B., & Bjurko, M. (2010). The impact of service orientation in corporate culture on business performance in manufacturing companies. *Journal of Service Management, 21*(2), 237–259. https://doi.org/10.1108/09564231011039303

Gebauer, H., & Fleisch, E. (2007). An investigation of the relationship between behavioral processes, motivation, investments in the service business and service revenue. *Industrial Marketing Management, 36*(3), 337–348. https://doi.org/10.1016/j.indmarman.2005.09.005

Gebauer, H., Fleisch, E., & Friedli, T. (2005). Overcoming the service paradox in manufacturing companies. *European Management Journal, 23*(1), 14–26. https://doi.org/10.1016/j.emj.2004.12.006

Helfat, C. E., & Peteraf, M. A. (2015). Managerial cognitive capabilities and the microfoundations of dynamic capabilities. *Strategic Management Journal, 36*(6), 831–850. https://doi.org/10.1002/smj.2247

Homburg, D. C., Fassnacht, M., & Guenther, C. (2003). The role of soft factors in implementing a service-oriented strategy in industrial marketing companies. *Journal of Business-to-Business Marketing, 10*(2), 23–51. https://doi.org/10.1300/J033v10n02_03

Johnstone, S., Wilkinson, A., & Dainty, A. (2014). Reconceptualizing the service paradox in engineering companies: Is HR a missing link? *IEEE Transactions on Engineering Management, 61*(2), 275–284. https://doi.org/10.1109/TEM.2013.2289738

Kindström, D., Kowalkowski, C., & Sandberg, E. (2013). Enabling service innovation: A dynamic capabilities approach. *Journal of Business Research, 66*(8), 1063–1073. https://doi.org/10.1016/j.jbusres.2012.03.003

Kohtamäki, M., Hakala, H., Partanen, J., Parida, V., & Wincent, J. (2015). The performance impact of industrial services and service orientation on manufacturing companies. *Journal of Service Theory and Practice, 25*(4), 463–485. https://doi.org/10.1108/JSTP-12-2013-0288

Kowalkowski, C., Gebauer, H., & Oliva, R. (2017). Service growth in product firms: Past, present, and future. *Industrial Marketing Management, 60*, 82–88. https://doi.org/10.1016/j.indmarman.2016.10.015

Kreye, M. E. (2016). Employee motivation in product-service system providers. *Production Planning & Control, 27*(15), 1249–1259. https://doi.org/10.1080/09537287.2016.1206219

Lee, K., & Ashton, M. C. (2004). Psychometric properties of the HEXACO personality inventory. *Multivariate Behavioral Research, 39*(2), 329–358. https://doi.org/10.1207/s15327906mbr3902_8

Lenka, S., Parida, V., Sjödin, D. R., & Wincent, J. (2018). Exploring the microfoundations of servitization: How individual actions overcome organizational resistance. *Journal of Business Research, 88,* 328–336. https://doi.org/10.1016/j.jbusres.2017.11.021

Matthyssens, P., & Vandenbempt, K. (1998). Creating competitive advantage in industrial services. *Journal of Business & Industrial Marketing, 13*(4/5), 339–355. https://doi.org/10.1108/08858629810226654

McClelland, D. C. (1987). *Human motivation.* CUP Archive.

Powell, T. C., Lovallo, D., & Fox, C. R. (2011). Behavioral strategy. *Strategic Management Journal, 32*(13), 1369–1386. https://doi.org/10.1002/smj.968

Rabetino, R., Harmsen, W., Kohtamäki, M., & Sihvonen, J. (2018). Structuring servitization-related research. *International Journal of Operations & Production Management, 38*(2), 350–371. https://doi.org/10.1108/IJOPM-03-2017-0175

Rabetino, R., Kohtamäki, M., & Gebauer, H. (2017). Strategy map of servitization. *International Journal of Production Economics, 192,* 144–156. https://doi.org/10.1016/j.ijpe.2016.11.004

Raddats, C., Baines, T., Burton, J., Story, V. M., & Zolkiewski, J. (2016). Motivations for servitization: The impact of product complexity. *International Journal of Operations & Production Management, 36*(5). https://doi.org/10.1108/IJOPM-09-2014-0447

Raddats, C., Kowalkowski, C., Benedettini, O., Burton, J., & Gebauer, H. (2019). Servitization: A contemporary thematic review of four major research streams. *Industrial Marketing Management.* https://doi.org/10.1016/j.indmarman.2019.03.015

Rese, M., & Maiwald, K. (2013). The individual level of servitization: Creating employees' service orientation. *IFAC Proceedings Volumes, 46*(9), 2057–2062. https://doi.org/10.3182/20130619-3-RU-3018.00429

Schymanietz, M., & Jonas, J. M. (2020, January 7). *The roles of individual actors in data-driven service innovation – A dynamic capabilities perspective to explore its microfoundations.* 53rd Hawaii International Conference on System Sciences. https://doi.org/10.24251/HICSS.2020.142

Shankar, V., Berry, L. L., & Dotzel, T. (2009). A practical guide to combining products + services. *Harvard Business Review, 87*(11), 94–99.

Ulaga, W., & Loveland, J. M. (2014). Transitioning from product to service-led growth in manufacturing firms: Emergent challenges in selecting and managing the industrial sales force. *Industrial Marketing Management, 43*(1), 113–125. https://doi.org/10.1016/j.indmarman.2013.08.006

Ulaga, W., & Reinartz, W. J. (2011). Hybrid offerings: How manufacturing firms combine goods and services successfully. *Journal of Marketing, 75*(6), 5–23. https://doi.org/10.1509/jmkg.75.6.5

Valtakoski, A. (2017). Explaining servitization failure and deservitization: A knowledge-based perspective. *Industrial Marketing Management, 60*, 138–150. https://doi.org/10.1016/j.indmarman.2016.04.009

Venkatraman, N. (1989). The concept of fit in strategy research: Toward verbal and statistical correspondence. *The Academy of Management Review, 14*(3), 423–444. https://doi.org/10.2307/258177

Revitalizing Alignment Theory for Digital Servitization Transition

Bieke Struyf, Paul Matthyssens, and Wouter Van Bockhaven

1 Introduction

With the rise of Industry 4.0 technology, manufacturing companies increasingly look toward services as a way of extending their revenue stream and/or reinforcing their competitive position (Bustinza et al., 2018; Coreynen et al., 2017; Kohtamäki, Parida et al., 2020). Provided that product and price are becoming decreasingly less powerful means of differentiation, human interaction and service support are growing in importance as distinguishing factors in B2B relationships (Matthyssens & Vandenbempt, 2008). Servitization, or

B. Struyf (✉) · P. Matthyssens · W. Van Bockhaven
Antwep Management School, Antwerp, Belgium
e-mail: Bieke.Struyf@ams.ac.be

P. Matthyssens
e-mail: paul.matthyssens@uantwerp.be

W. Van Bockhaven
e-mail: wouter.vanbockhaven@ams.ac.be

B. Struyf · P. Matthyssens
Faculty of Business and Economics, University of Antwerp, Antwerp, Belgium

P. Matthyssens
Department of Economics, Quantitative Methods and Business Strategy,
University of Milano-Bicocca, Milano, Italy

M. Kohtamäki et al. (eds.), *The Palgrave Handbook of Servitization*,
https://doi.org/10.1007/978-3-030-75771-7_17

261

the addition of services to manufacturers' core product offerings to create addi-tional customer value (Raddats et al., 2019: 207; Vandermerwe & Rada, 1988) builds on these factors and has been shown to lead to increased and steadier profits, improved customer relationships and market differentiation (Oliva & Kallenberg, 2003; Rabetino et al., 2017).

Digitalization enables and encourages the development of (advanced) services (Coreynen et al., 2017; Kohtamäki et al., 2019) and has given rise to digital servitization, a strategy in which firms provide customers with technology-enabled knowledge-based services (Bustinza et al., 2018; Coreynen et al., 2017). Even though a high level of servitization might be required to financially benefit from digitalization (Kohtamäki, Parida et al., 2020), digital servitization has been identified as a potential answer to the *service paradox*, the phenomenon in which increased revenues following servitization are accompanied by decreasing profits (Gebauer et al., 2005: 14).

Despite clear benefits, the transition toward digital servitization has proven to be challenging. Lack of market readiness (Coreynen et al., 2017), slow adaptation of the organizational identity and the accompanying business model (Tronvoll et al., 2020), and complex ecosystem relationships (Sklyar et al., 2019) are only a few elements holding companies back from effec-tively implementing digital servitization. Since Rapaccini et al. (2020) stated that the COVID-19 crisis will likely accelerate the transition toward digital, and stress the importance of advanced services for manufacturing compa-nies' future crises resilience, understanding what facilitates an effective move toward digital servitization becomes important.

Matthyssens and Vandenbempt (2008) previously proposed alignment as a solution to overcome barriers to the transition from basic products to services-based solutions. Alignment, or the *appropriateness* or agreement between *competitive situation, strategy, organization culture and leadership* (Chorn, 1991: 20) is said to be an iterative process shaped through endless interactions between internal and external stakeholders, organizational resources, and the company's strategic path in order to effectively respond to environmental changes and internal tensions (Yeow et al., 2018). Reaching peak effectiveness requires full alignment (Chorn, 1991). Tsoukas and Chia (2002), however, indicated that—although organizations organize for change—they are them-selves simultaneously shaped by the same change processes. Organizational practices and routines which are instigated to support strategic transitions are subject to continuous change due to interactions between organizational actors. Hence, unexpected implications are likely to occur throughout the implementation of strategic change, making continuous alignment essential to keep navigating toward the desired end goal and eventually reap the benefits from digitalization (Günther et al., 2017).

The importance of continuous alignment is strengthened by the radical and integrative nature of Industry 4.0 (Kagermann, 2015; Yeow et al., 2018). In this paradigm, systems are built upon systems and weaved across business units, value chain partners, and novel actors, which are added to a firm's ecosystem the more it evolves toward the development of complex, total value solutions (Frank et al., 2019; Gebauer et al., 2013). Being able to realize a digital strategy embedded in a growing web of interdependent actors necessary for value creation and delivery, requires a different approach, including high levels of external alignment (Adner & Kapoor, 2010; Berghman et al., 2006). Simultaneously, the disruptive nature of Industry 4.0 technology is expected to evoke strong emotional responses at individual and organizational levels which are likely to interfere with learning and mobilization processes essential to the establishment of the required organizational change (Huy, 1999; Vuori & Huy, 2016).

Digital servitization (DS) thus poses considerable challenges to organizational (internal) and market (external) alignment, both which are required in order to financially benefit from DS implementation (Kohtamäki et al., 2020; Sklyar et al., 2019). So far, however, alignment theory has not been applied as an additional lens to DS. Building on the work from Matthyssens and Vandenbempt (2008) we therefore ask ourselves: **How can alignment theory contribute to opening the black box of digital servitization transition success or failure?**

By answering this question, we contribute to literature and managerial practice in several ways. First, we answer the call by Tronvoll et al. (2020) for an examination of inter- and intrafirm tensions associated with digital servitization transition (DST). The application of an alignment theory lens allows us to boost understanding of the incurring conflicts as well as gain insight into factors contributing to effective DST. Additionally, the work of Alghisi and Saccani (2015), which focuses on internal and external alignment challenges in servitization companies, is extended by the introduction of digitalization as an additional complication. Finally, the developed alignment framework for DST can inspire future theory development and help practitioners to reduce risks by facilitating internal and external accord as they transition toward DS.

In what follows, we first assess the main literature on alignment theory after which servitization alignment challenges are reviewed. Next, the DST framework is introduced and discussed. We conclude with an overview of contributions, limitations and potential future research avenues which follow from the account.

2   Theory Development

Alignment Theory

The idea that alignment might contribute to supernatural profits (Powell, 1992) through increased organizational efficiency (Chorn, 1991) has generated continuous interest for the subject in the fields of among others, management literature (Kathuria et al., 2007; Matthyssens & Vandenbempt, 2008), information systems research (Venkatraman et al., 1993; Yeow et al., 2018), and human resource development (Alagaraja & Shuck, 2015; Saks & Gruman, 2014).

Traditionally, alignment theory has mostly focused on the internal fit between strategy, structure, and culture (Quiros, 2009; Sender, 1997). Given increasing interfirm interdependencies resulting from digitalization and the accompanying high integration of systems (Horváth & Szabó, 2019; Vendrell-Herrero et al., 2017), both internal processes and the organization's environment are to be considered upon the evaluation of digital servitization transitions (Matthyssens & Vandenbempt, 2008; Sklyar et al., 2019). Following Chorn (1991) and Sender (1997) we define alignment as an organization's pursuit of systematic agreement between competitive strategy, organizational structure and culture, leadership style, and the external environment.

Alignment theory finds its origin in congruence theory (Quiros, 2009) in which correspondence between context (inputs), organization (transformation process), and results (output) is investigated (Nadler & Tushman, 1988). According to the congruence model by Nadler and Tushman (1988), changes in the external environment are translated into strategy upon which the organization and its underlying mechanisms are transformed in order to realize the strategy and render proper results. Berghman et al. (2006), however, proposed a more proactive, market driving approach. Rather than simply reacting to market trends, companies would be able to align their offer with the market and meet customer expectations by anticipating changes in them. Such an approach would increase an organization's ability to create new customer value, break the industry recipe, and contribute to manufacturers' sustainable competitive advantage.

Whatever the direction of adaptation, both alignment and congruence theory consider strategy as a bridging tool between the internal and external environment. Day (1994) presented strategy development as one of the spanning processes which allows alignment between the *internal appraisal of the firms and the external assessment of environmental opportunities and threats* (Kathuria et al., 2007: 504). This indicates that strategy development largely depends on management's subjective perception and interpretation of organizational tensions and market changes. Literature supports the idea that mental models or cognitive maps of decision-makers strongly influence managerial actions and the way information is interpreted (Day, 1994; Matthyssens & Vandenbempt, 2003). Leadership thus (unconsciously) plays a distinct steering role in alignment processes (Hodgkinson & Healey, 2014).

Alignment not only matters in strategy development. It also plays an important part during the implementation process in which "higher level" congruencies between strategy, structure, culture and the larger system find their translation into "lower level" revisions of organizational resources, capabilities, and processes which eventually enable strategy realization (Kathuria et al., 2007). In the context of technology adoption, past research shows implementation often fails precisely due to the lack of alignment between the implemented technology and the organizational goals (Venkatraman et al., 1993).

Companies effective at harmonizing the internal organization with the market environment might enjoy superior performance (Yeow et al., 2018). Indeed, alignment has been shown to facilitate the accomplishment of organizational objectives (Quiros, 2009) and holds the potential for boosting financial performance (Böhm et al., 2017). Powell (1992) pointed toward alignment as a possible strategic resource to the extent that alignment followed from integrative capacity or organizational skill. Porter (1996: 13) even coined strategic fit *fundamental* to the sustainability of competitive advantage.

Not all is gold that glitters though. Literature demonstrates that while aiming for accord, alignment practices can make organizations more susceptible to inertia, limiting their potential for change. This is called the *alignment paradox* (Tallon & Kraemer, 2003: 1). By enabling success for one strategy, alignment simultaneously reduces an organization's agility, hindering the successful implementation of the next strategy (Yeow et al., 2018).

Nonetheless, achieving "perfect harmony" remains challenging (Alghisi & Saccani, 2015; Yeow et al., 2018). Chorn (1991: 23) referred to alignment as an unachievable yet worth pursuing *moving target*. The challenge would lie in the interdependency of the different elements which mutually influence each other through constant interaction (Quiros, 2009). Digitalization only increases those interdependencies (Sklyar et al., 2019; Yeow et al., 2018). Implementation of highly integrated systems and technology enable co-creation activities which cross company boundaries, making organizations gradually more vulnerable to the larger network in which they become embedded (Adner & Kapoor, 2010; Horváth & Szabó, 2019). Aligning the competitive strategy and internal organization with the external environment thus becomes more important and difficult as companies transition toward digital servitization (Sklyar et al., 2019; Yeow et al., 2018). Organizational alignment too is expected to be hampered by digitalization. The disruptive nature of digital technology (Kagermann, 2015) would among others require a new digital mindset (Ringberg et al., 2019) and ditto skills (Saunila et al., 2019). Emotions are expected to run high in response to the (digital) strategic change (Huy, 1999), especially in cases where the implementation of technology puts the organizational identity into question (Hodgkinson & Healey, 2014; Tronvoll et al., 2020). Indeed, Horváth and Szabó (2019) found organizational resistance to be a significant hindrance to the implementation of Industry 4.0 technology.

Digitalization thus boosts the internal and external alignment challenge (Yeow et al., 2018). Yet, transitioning toward servitization alone can already be a daring feat (Zhang & Banerji, 2017). In the following section, servitization alignment challenges are presented.

Aligning for Servitization

Several authors have identified organizational and market alignment as enablers of successful servitization transitions (Matthyssens & Vandenbempt, 2008; Palo et al., 2019). Exploratory research by Alghisi and Saccani (2015) discerned strategy, organizational culture and structure, and service portfolio as internal aspects requiring alignment. Customers and the service network were found to be central to market alignment. We structure our discussion around these five elements after which challenges to alignment and the importance of leadership for effective change management are reviewed.

Regarding strategy, the implementation of servitization has been described as an intrinsically complex, incremental, discontinuous, emergent process that often takes place *without a clearly directed effort* (Matthyssens & Vandenbempt, 2008; Raddats et al., 2019: 214; Tronvoll et al., 2020). According to Palo et al. (2019), servitization follows from repeated business model contestations in which the prevalent goods-dominant logic conflicts with a developing service-based logic. Organizational practices and capabilities, the business model and the service offer, as well as co-creating value partners are adapted gradually in response to these collisions as the company moves toward the new dominant paradigm.

After all, the shift in dominant logic from product vendor to service provider significantly affects every aspect of organizational life requiring realignment at different levels of the company (Gebauer et al., 2005; Rabetino et al., 2017). Kowalkowski et al. (2017) distinguished among other issues with the adaptation of organizational structure and the adoption of a service culture in organizations looking to benefit from service business opportunities. Yet, accordance between strategy and organizational structure, and an organizational culture which supports a service mindset are essential to service growth and securing profits from servitization (Neu & Brown, 2005; Palo et al., 2019; Zhang & Banerji, 2017).

Another element which considerably contributes to ensuring financial benefits, is the alignment of the offer with the market. Manufacturers could do well to create a balanced service portfolio of standardized and customized solutions (Matthyssens & Vandenbempt, 2010). Balancing both might enable scalability of the service portfolio (Alghisi & Saccani, 2015) and help counter the service paradox (Gebauer et al., 2005). Furthermore, customers must be effectively charged for the additional benefits they receive (Gebauer et al., 2005; Matthyssens & Vandenbempt, 2008). This might entail some (initial) convincing and proper framing of the solution toward clients (Alghisi & Saccani, 2015; Coreynen et al., 2017). New capabilities among which service capabilities, customer and supplier interface capabilities, and knowledge management capabilities will need to be developed to enable a successful servitization transition (Alghisi & Saccani, 2015; Saunila et al., 2019; Sousa & da Silveira, 2017). For indeed, understanding the customer's perspective is vital to continuously develop novel value propositions which fit customers' interests and their processes (Liinamaa et al., 2016; Zhang & Banerji, 2017). Developing an organizational culture and structure which enables customers' knowledge absorption in a proactive manner can considerably contribute to external alignment and strategic advantage (Berghman et al., 2006; Kamalaldin et al., 2020). Changes in organizational culture and structure can also enable organizations in becoming market driving. According to Berghman et al. (2006), marketing could even play a central role in the servitization change process.

In addition, the need for cultural alignment extends beyond the internal organization to include customers and the wider service network (Alghisi & Saccani, 2015). According to Palo et al. (2019: 494), servitization involves a collective change in which *the entire service and sales departments, the organization and its customers must engage in collective practices, and/or align their practices accordingly.* For servitization to be successful, customers need to understand the value of services and agree with the shift from ownership to access and/or fruition of product benefits (Alghisi & Saccani, 2015). The service network, in its turn, needs to buy into the premise of actively providing advanced services. Careful selection of partners can contribute to establishing common ground (Alghisi & Saccani, 2015). In addition to a shared service mindset, trust and commitment between co-creating service network partners is crucial for the creation and delivery of complex services (Palo et al., 2019). This can be difficult in an industry which traditionally has been plagued by mistrust. Strong relationship management skills will need to be developed to replace rivalry with deliberate, constructive partnerships.

More alignment challenges can be encountered at the lower organizational level. Processes, resources, financial targets, and value propositions all need to be readjusted to fit the new strategy (Kowalkowski et al., 2017; Oliva & Kallenberg, 2003; Rabetino et al., 2017). Proper harmonization requires successful organizational change (Sender, 1997). Unfortunately, effectively transforming a manufacturing company to profit from servitization is still one of the most significant challenges for servitization practitioners (Baines et al., 2017; Bigdeli et al., 2017). The necessary learning processes and mobilization of actors could be hindered by strong emotions evoked by the radical nature of changes in organizational identity (Huy, 1999; Vuori & Huy, 2016).

Literature has illustrated the impact of management and the importance of leadership (style) for effective change management (Seah et al., 2014; Vuori & Huy, 2016). Kim and Toya (2019) found that in Japanese manufacturing firms charismatic leadership enabled the transformation process whereas autocratic and autonomous leadership hindered the transition toward provision of service. Leadership and commitment were presented as essential to the translation of strategy into befitting organizational routines, processes and behavior (Alghisi & Saccani, 2015) and the service orientation of management's values and behavior was found to have a direct effect on servitization performance (Fliess & Lexutt, 2019). Alghisi and Saccani (2015: 1230) even named *top management vision, motivation, leadership and everyday commitment [...] extraordinary levers* for successful servitization transition.

On a more general level, adaptive leadership strategies and organizational culture have been identified as considerably influencing firms' adaptive capacity (Seah et al., 2014). According to Chorn (1991), managing the interdependencies between situation, strategy, culture, and leadership in order to achieve alignment, is the main responsibility of management. By shaping the organizational context to fit the servitization strategy, leadership may well (indirectly) influence employee behavior and thus facilitate the transition toward servitization (Chorn, 1991; Seah et al., 2014). Despite the promised benefits, however, little research has been undertaken in this area. Further exploration of the role of leadership in servitization transition processes is warranted (Kowalkowski et al., 2017).

To sum up, transitioning toward servitization causes tensions to rise both internally and externally to the organization. By focusing on aligning the service strategy, the internal organization, the service portfolio, customers, and the service network, manufactures can enhance their chances at successfully realizing servitization. In the next section, we develop a framework for digital servitization transition by applying this alignment lens. Propositions for future studies are developed.

An Alignment Lens for Digital Servitization Transition

The digitalization of the manufacturing industry offers new opportunities for servitization (Coreynen et al., 2017; Kohtamäki et al., 2019). Alignment challenges, however, are expected to intensify with the implementation of digital technologies. The disruptive nature of digitalization (Vendrell-Herrero et al., 2017), the increase in interdependencies between organization, customers, and the service network which follows from it (Adner & Kapoor, 2010; Horváth & Szabó, 2019), and the potential for the design and delivery of increasingly complex data-enabled solutions (Gebauer et al., 2013; Sklyar et al., 2019) are likely to enhance internal and external incongruencies, boosting the need for alignment in order to effectively profit from the digital servitization strategy (Kohtamäki et al., 2019; Tronvoll et al., 2020).

Digitalization or *the use of digital technology to provide new value-creating and revenue-generating opportunities* (Sklyar et al., 2019: 450) is said to add complexity to servitization (Kohtamäki et al., 2019). Matthyssens and Vandenbempt (2008) already recognized a growing degree of intricacy between co-creating value chain partners of advanced services. Digitalization now supports this trend through high integration of systems across firm boundaries (Kohtamäki et al., 2019). Hence, challenges to organizational and market alignment become intertwined.

In this paragraph, we focus on *digital* servitization. We investigate how the intertwinement between organizational and market alignment challenges affects the servitization alignment challenges formerly distinguished by Alghisi and Saccani (2015). Based on literature and building on the authors' model, we examine the intensifying effect of digitalization and identify five essential thrusts for DST alignment. Figure 1 shows the resulting framework.

Our discussion starts at the spine of the framework where digital service strategy and the digital service portfolio, elements central to solving the paradoxical tension between internal and external demands, are located. Next, we examine changes to relationships with customers and the wider service network following the introduction of digitalization. We round up at the organizational level where we take a closer look at changes to organizational culture and structure, and the facilitating power of leadership. Throughout the discussion levers for DST alignment are highlighted.

Digitalization firstly intensifies the challenge of effectively translating opportunities, in this case technological opportunities, into a coherent service strategy. Aside from converting technology into customer-oriented value propositions (Gebauer et al., 2005), congruency between digitalization and servitization levels should be guarded (Kohtamäki, Parida et al., 2020). Misalignment could lead to the occurrence of a *digitalization paradox,* a situation in which manufacturers struggle to realize returns on their digital investments *despite the demonstrated ability of digitalization to enhance revenue* (Gebauer et al., 2020: 314). We recognize the formulation of a clear digital service strategy as the first thrust to DST.

Digitalization also intensifies the challenge of configuring *business models to include service offerings* to fit the new service strategy (Palo et al., 2019: 486). Since digitalization embeds a firm even further into its ecosystem, business models and the digital service portfolio need to be increasingly aligned with the business models of ecosystem partners (Kohtamäki et al., 2019). The reason is twofold. First, a manufacturer's potential digital service offering often relies on capabilities and technologies of fellow ecosystem actors (Kohtamäki et al., 2019). Second, existing service revenues and partnerships with customers and suppliers might become endangered when digitalization supports the extension of services both upstream and downstream the value chain (Gebauer et al., 2020; Vendrell-Herrero et al., 2017) leading to an intensification of competition (Alghisi & Saccani, 2015). The wish to safeguard relationships which are essential to value creation and capture might hinder the extension of the digital service portfolio (Paiola et al., 2013). Effective harmonization of a company's digital service portfolio with the interests and capabilities of its ecosystem partners is therefore identified as a second thrust to DST.

This also includes proper alignment with customers' wants and expectations. Customer-centricity and a service-centric mindset are *essential for the successful development and adoption of novel digital service offerings* (Sklyar

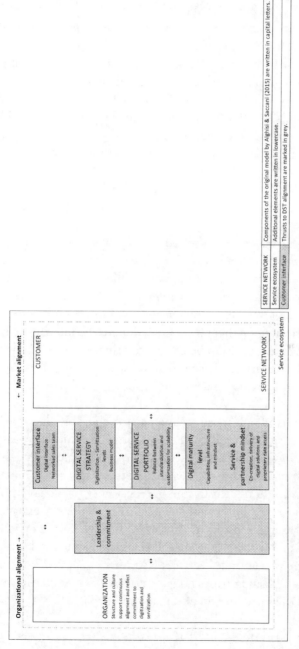

Fig. 1 Alignment framework for DST (*Source* Adapted from Alghisi and Saccani [2015])

et al., 2019; Tronvoll et al., 2020: 8). Digitalization both challenges and offers opportunities for customer alignment.

On the one hand, it makes it increasingly difficult to charge customers effectively for the services rendered (Alghisi & Saccani, 2015; Coreynen et al., 2017). Customers, who already suffered from *service for free* attitude (Fliess & Lexutt, 2019; Matthyssens, 2019: 2), now need to be convinced to pay for *digital* services (Gebauer et al., 2020). Yet the addition of digital technologies increases the complexity of the solutions offered (Gebauer et al., 2020). Lack of digital capabilities and immature digital infrastructures (Kamalaldin et al., 2020; Saunila et al., 2019) coupled with absence of trust and a missing service mindset on the customer's side (Alghisi & Saccani, 2015; Bagheri et al., 2019), can hinder customers in their comprehension, lowering their willingness to pay. Even more so, when digital services require customers to change their ways of working. In such instances, digital solutions might even be met with resistance (Coreynen et al., 2017; Huy, 1999; Saunila et al., 2019).

Additionally, Gebauer et al. (2020: 322) warned manufacturers about falling into the *freemium* trap or setting prices too low themselves. The latter might occur when firms expect customers' willingness to pay to be lowered due to a reduction in personal service interventions. The former refers to situations in which basic versions of digital applications are offered free of charge to customers discouraging them from upgrading to the full paid version. Such practices increase the risk of not being able to achieve the critical mass of sales necessary to render a service offer profitable, especially since high investments are required to turn DS into a commercial success (Kohtamäki, Parida et al., 2020).

On the other hand, advanced technologies such as big data might enable access to and the spreading of customer information and knowledge (Fliess & Lexutt, 2019; Tronvoll et al., 2020). Proactive knowledge absorption from customers and other market participants can enable manufactures to continuously create and deliver superior customer value and novel solutions (Berghman et al., 2006; Saunila et al., 2019.), thereby enhancing their competitive advantage. Customers, however, still need to be open to implementing highly innovative solutions and sharing proprietary information in order to optimize the advanced services (Günther et al., 2017; Saunila et al., 2019). Hence, establishing trust and generating customer buy-in gains a new dimension with the introduction of digitalization (Bagheri et al., 2019; Fliess & Lexutt, 2019).

According to Bustinza et al. (2018), manufacturers aiming at DS should arrange their organizational structure to facilitate continuous alignment between the digital service strategy and the customers' needs. The strategic resource value of the customer interface is therefore expected to grow. Sklyar et al. (2019) suggested enhancing the customer interface through heightened intrafirm integration. Developing a "networked sales team" (NST) might support this goal while adding a human component to the customer interface. An NST would assemble employees from among other sales, technical support, customer service, and management. The integrated team would collaborate to increase customer knowledge absorption, and present digital solutions as a united, multilingual front toward clients. Arguments for the idea can be found in Saunila et al. (2019) who discovered that, for clients to make use of digital channels, a certain level of trust needs to be present. The power of human factors in digital business environments was stressed. They also mentioned the importance of extending sales activities to proactively asking feedback from clients. This could help tie-in customers who might otherwise easily switch digital providers. By systematically combining insights from sales and customer services, an NST could contribute to a deeper understanding of customers' requirements. Big data can deliver powerful insights. Without context, however, data might be insufficient to truly understand customer preferences and motivations (Günther et al., 2017). Indeed, Saunila et al. (2019) found that comprehension of changes in the external environment was best understood through conversations with customers and exchanges with their production process.

The importance of customers for effective DST alignment is undeniable (Fliess & Lexutt, 2019; Kamalaldin et al., 2020). Given that a customer interface can considerably add to customer knowledge absorption and alignment (Saunila et al., 2019; Sklyar et al., 2019), the structural establishment of a customer interface, consisting of digital and non-digital components, is identified as a third thrust for DST alignment.

Digitalization further enhances the market alignment challenge by boosting the need for harmonization of practices and capabilities, and the establishment of common ground among value-creating partners, which are gathered in the service ecosystem and comprise among others customers and the wider service network. After all, cross-company integration both increases with and is required for digitalization (Sklyar et al., 2019). This makes having a shared digital service mindset and congruent digital maturity levels important levers to the DST alignment process. Kamalaldin et al. (2020) pointed toward the need for alignment of digital assets and competences, possession of complementary digitalization capabilities, digitally enabled knowledge-sharing routines, and a partnership mindset between customer and manufacturer. Co-evolution of capabilities and mutual adjustment of processes between ecosystem actors was said to be an essential element to successfully delivering advanced services (Fliess & Lexutt, 2019; Matthyssens et al., 2009). Moreover, since digital solutions are built on top of each other, selecting the right co-creating partner becomes even more crucial. According to Kamalaldin et al. (2020), DS converts relationships from transactional to relational, leading to long-term interdependencies which can enable and/or hinder the future success of the company. Achieving congruency between the "hard" (digital infrastructure) and "soft" (capabilities and mindset) ecosystem is required for all actors to benefit from DS (Sklyar et al., 2019) and is therefore identified as the fourth thrust to DST alignment.

Finally, digitalization also defies alignment at the organizational level (Yeow et al., 2018). Like for servitization transitions, processes and structures need to be adapted to support the digital strategy (Horváth & Szabó, 2019; Kamalaldin et al., 2020). For DS, however, radically new capabilities must be acquired (Saunila et al., 2019) by employees willing to accept and work with technology which might eventually threaten their own job (Horváth & Szabó, 2019). While dealing with an intensified organizational identity challenge (Tronvoll et al., 2020) and the rearrangement of power following business unit integration and decision-making decentralization (Matthyssens, 2019; Tronvoll et al., 2020), employees need to be kept motivated and engaged in order for organizational learning and change to occur. Solid change management, materialized in continuous and iterative change cycles (Tronvoll et al., 2020; Yeow et al., 2018) combined with adapted organizational routines to support the absorption of and effective response to "emotional" information (Hodgkinson & Healey, 2014), could facilitate the radical organizational change process required for DST (Huy, 1999; Vendrell-Herrero et al., 2017). We acknowledge leadership and commitment as the fifth and final thrust to DST alignment.

Alghisi and Saccani (2015: 1227) already marked leadership and top management commitment as *crucial for successful service business development*. According to Kohtamäki et al. (2019), digitalization reinforces the want for full organizational and top management's commitment to service provision in order to turn the service strategy profitable. Bustinza et al. (2018) also recognized commitment to digital solutions as central to organizational alignment. The authors pinpointed strategic agility which enables swift, flexible decision-making as a prerequisite for DST as well. Lewis et al. (2014) stated that strategic agility can be enhanced by paradoxical leadership, a leadership style in which paradoxes are treasured as essential ingredients to high performance. Given the high presence of paradoxes in servitization (Kohtamäki, Einola et al., 2020) and the increasing ambiguity following digitalization, exploring paradoxical leadership as a lever for DST alignment could be valuable.

In short, digitalization and its high integration of systems are leading to the intertwinement of organizational and market alignment challenges. Externally, service strategy, business models, and digital service offerings require increasing alignment with service ecosystem partners. Successful harmonization of digital capabilities and infrastructures facilitates integration and enhances opportunities for the joint creation and delivery of digitally enabled solutions. Shared service and partnership mindset complements knowledge-sharing routines by establishing trust between (un)familiar actors, enabling access to proprietary data and supporting the mobilization of ecosystem partners among others. Enlarging the customer interface and adding a networked sales team might speed up market alignment by strengthening ties across businesses (externally) and business units (internally) contributing to enhanced understanding of customers' needs, on the one hand, and the generation of novel digital solutions, on the other.

Internally, several factors raise the need for change management. Organizational structure and culture should support continuous alignment. Top management's commitment to digitalization and servitization as well as leadership style are key ingredients to the organizational alignment exercise.

3 Conclusion

With this paper, we have investigated alignment theory as a potential additional lens to digital servitization transition. Several theoretical and managerial contributions were made.

To scholars we suggest an integrative framework indicating key factors which make up a coherent DST journey. Two central learnings emerge. First, the framework extends the work of among others Alghisi and Saccani (2015) by including digitalization as an additional challenge to servitization transition alignment. Applying alignment theory to DST has allowed us to open the black box to understand what contributes to DST success or failure. Secondly, the framework suggests levels which might improve imminent DSTs. As this is a conceptual paper, future research could investigate the optimal composition, characteristics, and capabilities of an effective networked sales team, explore alternative ways to establishing a strong customer interface, and test the power of paradoxical leadership for successful DST.

To practitioners the paper offers a framework which can be applied to their own organization when embarking on a DST. Three lessons can be distilled. First, the framework implies that leadership will need to integrate two paradoxical forces. Organizational and market challenges are competing for attention yet require an integrative approach due to their increasing intertwinement. Second, the model highlights five thrusts which are central to DST alignment and can support practitioners in the definition and roll-out of their strategic plan toward DS. Lastly, this study suggests leadership can smoothen DST by taking up a central, active role in aligning internal and external interests, and building bridges across business units and cross-company.

This study is not without limitations. First, its conceptual nature omits empirical corroboration. Future research should test the framework in different settings to verify our findings and add granularity to the model. Applying the framework to SMEs and MNEs, for example, might lead to different results. Literature shows that both groups are often faced with distinct challenges given their specific characteristics. The current framework does not yet allow for this distinction. Furthermore, this paper solely focuses on optimizing alignment. Given that misalignment is unavoidable for companies aiming to thrive in a high-velocity business environment, investigating how firms can most effectively organize for misalignment could further increase our understanding.

Acknowledgements This paper was written in the context of the Paradigms 4.0 project. The authors gratefully acknowledge the financial support received by the Flanders Research Foundation (FWO) which made this research possible.

References

Adner, R., & Kapoor, R. (2010). Value creation in innovation ecosystems: How the structure of technological interdependence affects firm performance in new technology generations. *Strategic Management Journal, 31*(3), 306–333.

Alagaraja, M., & Shuck, B. (2015). Exploring organizational alignment-employee engagement linkages and impact on individual performance: A conceptual model. *Human Resource Development Review, 14*(1), 17–37.

Alghisi, A., & Saccani, N. (2015). Internal and external alignment in the servitization journey–Overcoming the challenges. *Production Planning & Control, 26*(14–15), 1219–1232.

Bagheri, S., Kusters, R. J., & Trienekens, J. J. M. (2019). Customer knowledge transfer challenges in a co-creation value network: Toward a reference model.

International Journal of Information Management, 47(December 2018), 198–214. https://doi.org/10.1016/j.ijinfomgt.2018.12.019

Baines, T., Bigdeli, A. Z., Bustinza, O. F., Shi, V. G., Baldwin, J., & Ridgway, K. (2017). Servitization: Revisiting the state-of-the-art and research priorities. *International Journal of Operations & Production Management, 37*.

Berghman, L., Matthyssens, P., & Vandenbempt, K. (2006). Building competences for new customer value creation: An exploratory study. *Industrial Marketing Management, 35*(8), 961–973.

Bigdeli, A. Z., Baines, T., Bustinza, O. F., & Shi, V. G. (2017). Organisational change towards servitization: A theoretical framework. *Competitiveness Review: An International Business Journal, 27*.

Böhm, E., Eggert, A., & Thiesbrummel, C. (2017). Service transition: A viable option for manufacturing companies with deteriorating financial performance? *Industrial Marketing Management, 60*, 101–111.

Bustinza, O. F., Gomes, E., Vendrell-Herrero, F., & Tarba, S. Y. (2018). An organizational change framework for digital servitization: Evidence from the Veneto region. *Strategic Change, 27*(2), 111–119.

Chorn, N. H. (1991). The "alignment" theory: Creating strategic fit. Management decision.

Coreynen, W., Matthyssens, P., & Van Bockhaven, W. (2017). Boosting servitization through digitization: Pathways and dynamic resource configurations for manufacturers. *Industrial Marketing Management, 60*, 42–53. https://doi.org/10.1016/j.indmarman.2016.04.012.

Day, G. S. (1994). The capabilities of market-driven organizations. *Journal of Marketing, 58*(4), 37–52.

Fliess, S., & Lexutt, E. (2019). How to be successful with servitization–Guidelines for research and management. *Industrial Marketing Management, 78*, 58–75.

Frank, A. G., Dalenogare, L. S., & Ayala, N. (2019). Industry 4.0 technologies: Implementation patterns in manufacturing companies. *International Journal of Production Economics, 210*, 15–26.

Gebauer, H., Fleisch, E., & Friedli, T. (2005). Overcoming the service paradox in manufacturing companies. *European Management Journal, 23*(1), 14–26.

Gebauer, H., Fleisch, E., Lamprecht, C., & Wortmann, F. (2020). *Growth paths for overcoming the digitalization paradox*. Business Horizons.

Gebauer, H., Paiola, M., & Saccani, N. (2013). Characterizing service networks for moving from products to solutions. *Industrial Marketing Management, 42*(1), 31–46.

Günther, W. A., Mehrizi, M. H. R., Huysman, M., & Feldberg, F. (2017). Debating big data: A literature review on realizing value from big data. *The Journal of Strategic Information Systems, 26*(3), 191–209.

Hodgkinson, G. P., & Healey, M. P. (2014). Coming in from the cold: The psychological foundations of radical innovation revisited. *Industrial Marketing Management, 43*(8), 1306–1313. https://doi.org/10.1016/j.indmarman.2014.08.012.

Horváth, D., & Szabó, R. Z. (2019). Driving forces and barriers of Industry 4.0: Do multinational and small and medium-sized companies have equal opportunities? *Technological Forecasting and Social Change, 146,* 119–132.

Huy, Q. N. (1999). Emotional capability, emotional intelligence, and radical change. *Academy of Management Review, 24*(2), 325–345. https://doi.org/10. 5465/AMR.1999.1893939.

Kagermann, H. (2015). Change through digitization—Value creation in the age of industry 4.0. In *Management of permanent change* (p. 23).

Kamalaldin, A., Linde, L., Sjödin, D., & Parida, V. (2020). Transforming provider-customer relationships in digital servitization: A relational view on digitalization. *Industrial Marketing Management, 89,* 306–325.

Kathuria, R., Joshi, M. P., & Porth, S. J. (2007). Organizational alignment and performance: past, present and future. *Management Decision, 45.*

Kim, S., & Toya, K. (2019). Leadership style required for the transition to servitization in Japan. *Journal of Manufacturing Technology Management, 30.*

Kohtamäki, M., Einola, S., & Rabetino, R. (2020). Exploring servitization through the paradox lens: Coping practices in servitization. *International Journal of Production Economics, 226,* 107619.

Kohtamäki, M., Parida, V., Oghazi, P., Gebauer, H., & Baines, T. (2019). Digital servitization business models in ecosystems: A theory of the firm. *Journal of Business Research, 104,* 380–392.

Kohtamäki, M., Parida, V., Patel, P. C., & Gebauer, H. (2020). The relationship between digitalization and servitization: The role of servitization in capturing the financial potential of digitalization. *Technological Forecasting and Social Change, 151,.*

Kowalkowski, C., Gebauer, H., Kamp, B., & Parry, G. (2017). Servitization and deservitization: Overview, concepts, and definitions. *Industrial Marketing Management, 60,* 4–10. https://doi.org/10.1016/j.indmarman.2016.12.007.

Lewis, M. W., Andriopoulos, C., & Smith, W. K. (2014). Paradoxical leadership to enable strategic agility. *California Management Review, 56*(3), 58–77.

Liinamaa, J., Viljanen, M., Hurmerinta, A., Ivanova-Gongne, M., Luotola, H., & Gustafsson, M. (2016). Performance-based and functional contracting in value-based solution selling. *Industrial Marketing Management, 59,* 37–49.

Matthyssens, P. (2019). Reconceptualizing value innovation for Industry 4.0 and the Industrial Internet of Things. *Journal of Business & Industrial Marketing, 34.*

Matthyssens, P., & Vandenbempt, K. (2003). Cognition-in-context: reorienting research in business market strategy. *Journal of Business & Industrial Marketing, 18,* 595–606.

Matthyssens, P., & Vandenbempt, K. (2008). Moving from basic offerings to value-added solutions: Strategies, barriers and alignment. *Industrial Marketing Management, 37*(3), 316–328. https://doi.org/10.1016/j.indmarman.2007.07.008.

Matthyssens, P., & Vandenbempt, K. (2010). Service addition as business market strategy: Identification of transition trajectories. *Journal of Service Management, 21,* 693–714.

Matthyssens, P., Vandenbempt, K., & Weyns, S. (2009). Transitioning and co-evolving to upgrade value offerings: A competence-based marketing view. *Industrial Marketing Management, 38*(5), 504–512. https://doi.org/10.1016/j.indmarman.2008.08.008.

Nadler, D., & Tushman, M. (1988). *Strategic organization design.*

Neu, W. A., & Brown, S. W. (2005). Forming successful business-to-business services in goods-dominant firms. *Journal of Service Research, 8*(1), 3–17.

Oliva, R., & Kallenberg, R. (2003). Managing the transition from products to services. *International Journal of Service Industry Management, 14.*

Paiola, M., Saccani, N., Perona, M., & Gebauer, H. (2013). Moving from products to solutions: Strategic approaches for developing capabilities. *European Management Journal, 31*(4), 390–409.

Palo, T., Åkesson, M., & Löfberg, N. (2019). Servitization as business model contestation: A practice approach. *Journal of Business Research, 104,* 486–496.

Porter, M. E. (1996). What is strategy? *Harvard Business Review, 74*(6), 61–78.

Powell, T. C. (1992). Organizational alignment as competitive advantage. *Strategic Management Journal, 13*(2), 119–134.

Quiros, I. (2009). Organizational alignment. *International Journal of Organizational Analysis, 17,* 285–305.

Rabetino, R., Kohtamäki, M., & Gebauer, H. (2017). Strategy map of servitization. *International Journal of Production Economics, 192,* 144–156.

Raddats, C., Kowalkowski, C., Benedettini, O., Burton, J., & Gebauer, H. (2019). Servitization: A contemporary thematic review of four major research streams. *Industrial Marketing Management, 83,* 207–223.

Rapaccini, M., Saccani, N., Kowalkowski, C., Paiola, M., & Adrodegari, F. (2020). Navigating disruptive crises through service-led growth: The impact of COVID-19 on Italian manufacturing firms. *Industrial Marketing Management, 88,* 225–237.

Ringberg, T., Reihlen, M., & Rydén, P. (2019). The technology-mindset interactions: Leading to incremental, radical or revolutionary innovations. *Industrial Marketing Management, 79,* 102–113.

Saks, A. M., & Gruman, J. A. (2014). What do we really know about employee engagement? *Human Resource Development Quarterly, 25*(2), 155–182.

Saunila, M., Ukko, J., & Rantala, T. (2019). Value co-creation through digital service capabilities: The role of human factors. *Information Technology & People.*

Seah, M., Hsieh, M.-H., & Huang, H.-Y. (2014). Leader driven organizational adaptation. *Management Decision, 52.*

Sender, S. W. (1997). Systematic agreement: A theory of organizational alignment. *Human Resource Development Quarterly, 8*(1), 23–40.

Sklyar, A., Kowalkowski, C., Tronvoll, B., & Sörhammar, D. (2019). Organizing for digital servitization: A service ecosystem perspective. *Journal of Business Research, 104,* 450–460.

Sousa, R., & da Silveira, G. J. (2017). Capability antecedents and performance outcomes of servitization. *International Journal of Operations & Production Management, 37*.

Tallon, P. P., & Kraemer, K. L. (2003). Investigating the relationship between strategic alignment and information technology business value: The discovery of a paradox Creating business value with information technology: Challenges and solutions (pp. 1–22). IGI Global.

Tronvoll, B., Sklyar, A., Sörhammar, D., & Kowalkowski, C. (2020). Transformational shifts through digital servitization. *Industrial Marketing Management, 89*, 293–305.

Tsoukas, H., & Chia, R. (2002). On organizational becoming: Rethinking organizational change. *Organization Science, 13*(5), 567–582.

Vandermerwe, S., & Rada, J. (1988). Servitization of business: Adding value by adding services. *European Management Journal, 6*(4), 314–324.

Vendrell-Herrero, F., Bustinza, O. F., Parry, G., & Georgantzis, N. (2017). Servitization, digitization and supply chain interdependency. *Industrial Marketing Management, 60*, 69–81.

Venkatraman, N., Henderson, J. C., & Oldach, S. (1993). Continuous strategic alignment: Exploiting information technology capabilities for competitive success. *European Management Journal, 11*(2), 139–149.

Vuori, T. O., & Huy, Q. N. (2016). Distributed attention and shared emotions in the innovation process: How Nokia lost the smartphone battle. *Administrative Science Quarterly, 61*(1), 9–51. https://doi.org/10.1177/0001839215606951.

Yeow, A., Soh, C., & Hansen, R. (2018). Aligning with new digital strategy: A dynamic capabilities approach. *The Journal of Strategic Information Systems, 27*(1), 43–58.

Zhang, W., & Banerji, S. (2017). Challenges of servitization: A systematic literature review. *Industrial Marketing Management, 65*, 217–227.

Managerial Heuristics in Servitization Journey

Tuomas Huikkola and Marko Kohtamäki

1   Introduction

Manufacturers have started to sell different types of services to their clients, ranging from product-related after-sales services (e.g., spare parts, maintenance services) to more comprehensive solutions (e.g., operations & maintenance services, turnkey projects), enabled by digital technologies such as the Internet of Things (IoT) (Kohtamäki et al., 2019; Kowalkowski et al., 2017; Töytäri et al., 2018; Visnjic et al., 2017) to generate advantages in B2B markets (Ulaga & Reinartz, 2011). This strategic transition is profound, as it has forced manufacturers to alter their strategies (Gebauer et al., 2010), business models (Huikkola & Kohtamäki, 2018; Storbacka et al., 2013), routines and capabilities (Ulaga & Reinartz, 2011), offerings (Kohtamäki & Partanen, 2016), and organization structures (Neu & Brown, 2005). The existing servitization literature has comprehensively studied the antecedents, processes, and outcomes of this strategic change (Rabetino et al., 2018; Raddats et al., 2019) but remains relatively silent about what types of managerial heuristics,

T. Huikkola (✉) · M. Kohtamäki
University of Vaasa, Vaasa, Finland
e-mail: thui@uwasa.fi

M. Kohtamäki
e-mail: mtko@uwasa.fi; mtko@uva.fi

© The Author(s), under exclusive license to Springer Nature
Switzerland AG 2021
M. Kohtamäki et al. (eds.), *The Palgrave Handbook of Servitization*,
https://doi.org/10.1007/978-3-030-75771-7_18

so-called simple rules, companies use when managing servitization strategy implementation.

This conceptual article aims to generate an evidence-based perspective on managerial heuristics in servitization to understand how to implement a servitization strategy. Based on the four propositions presented in this article, we encourage servitization scholars to study in-depth what types of "simple rules" manufacturers have crafted to facilitate service business development and reflect on what they have learned along the way. Companies may use simple rules to guide them toward the decided direction in a controllable yet flexible manner.

2   Theory Development

Defining Managerial Heuristics

Heuristics are described as mental shortcuts (Newell & Simon, 1972; Tversky & Kahneman, 1974) that provide fast, effective, and frugal decision-making approaches for managers (Artinger et al., 2015), especially in high-velocity markets and foggy environments (Brown & Eisenhardt, 1997; Eisenhardt, 1989; Maitland & Sammartino, 2015; Sull & Eisenhardt, 2012). Managerial heuristics are approaches to solving ill-structured problems that logic and probability theory are not capable of addressing (Artinger et al., 2015; Groner et al., 1983; Vuori & Vuori, 2014). Often, too little or too much information is available or too little time and resources are available to conduct a proper analysis (Bingham & Eisenhardt, 2014; Bingham et al., 2007; Eisenhardt & Sull, 2001). Relying on heuristics during decision-making can lead to negative (Kahneman, 2011; Kahneman & Klein, 2009), positive (Bingham & Eisenhardt, 2011, 2014; Eisenhardt & Sull, 2001; Maitland & Sammartino, 2015), or mixed outcomes (Wübben & Wangenheim, 2008). Adverse outcomes typically arise from humans' universal framing and anchoring errors, cognitive biases, shortcuts, and the dominance of intuitive systems and fast thinking (Davenport, 2020; Kahneman, 2011), whereas positive outcomes emerge from expert heuristics (Bingham & Eisenhardt, 2011), i.e., the process of learning through repetition and accumulated experience (Bingham & Eisenhardt, 2011, 2014). Although relying upon past experiences may be harmful for firms' continued existence, heuristics have been identified as particularly useful in ill-structured problems when the level of uncertainty remarkably increases (Artinger et al., 2015; Bingham & Eisenhardt, 2014; Gigerenzer & Gaissmaier, 2011) and firms lack the time or resources to conduct proper analysis (Maitland & Sammartino, 2015). Because heuristics are the opposite of rational decision-making, namely, slow thinking, some have argued that they lead to second-best decisions (Kahneman, 2011), whereas others have found that heuristics can lead to effective results (Artinger et al., 2015; Wübben & Wangenheim, 2008) or even better decisions overall (Bingham & Eisenhardt, 2014; Sull & Eisenhardt, 2012).

Kahneman and Klein (2009) argue that heuristic thinking and decision-making are more likely to work under predictable conditions—after the decision-maker has an opportunity to learn the regularities of that environment. Gigerenzer and Gaissmaier (2011) criticize this view and suggest that rational approaches do not work in "large worlds" where information is incomplete and all alternatives cannot be properly identified. Bingham and Eisenhardt (2014) respond that simple rules work best in managing processes that can be easily understood and adopted by personnel. Among practitioners, heuristics typically take the form of thumb rules/simple rules (Eisenhardt & Sull, 2001). Existing studies on the use of (expert) heuristics have shown positive effects in the context of sports and games (e.g., poker) (Sull & Eisenhardt, 2015), investment decisions (Antretter et al., 2020), and business strategies (Bingham & Eisenhardt, 2011; Maitland & Sammartino, 2015). Next, we introduce key types of heuristics regarding servitization, namely, selection, procedural, priority, and temporal heuristics (Sull & Eisenhardt, 2015), that guide managers and organization members to execute strategy in practice.

Selection Heuristics in Servitization

Selection heuristics refer to rules of thumb that guide firms in which sets of opportunities (e.g., market or product/service opportunities) firms decide to pursue (Bingham & Eisenhardt, 2011). In practice, selection heuristics specify, for example, what particular countries and geographical areas firms decide to enter, technologies to invest in, products/services to sell, or what customers/customers' needs to serve. In the servitization literature, little is known about *why* manufacturers have decided to enter certain markets (e.g., China) and *how* they have reasoned that entering this market is a better idea than other alternatives. For example, the Finnish elevator manufacturer KONE decided to sell its new machine, roomless elevators, and associated services first to the Netherlands because it enabled the firm to enter other EU markets after that, and the Netherlands was considered one of the leading and most adaptable countries for new, radical solutions (Michelsen,

2013). Another important and strategic decision for a firm is to select which customers it tries to target and what underlying needs the firm attempts to address by providing certain solutions. For example, in China, KONE decided first to serve the most demanding customers to polish the brand, gain reputation among them, and gain a foothold in that market. It reasoned that this approach would enable it to sell more easily to other customers, because customers have framed KONE as the leading manufacturer in that sector. Hence, KONE was anchored as the "premium seller" that customers compared to other alternatives, not the other way round. Firms also vary between products, services, and technologies they sell to different markets. For example, manufacturers may decide to sell O&M services only to certain customers, whether to those leading customers who want to free up their resources to reallocate resources to other, more profitable business areas or to those new customers who do not possess competencies or resources in-house to run such operations themselves (e.g., financial institutions), not for those customers located in the middle. In practice, these lessons learned can lead to certain stipulated rules (simple heuristics), such as "sell services only to developed countries", "when launching new services, enter US markets first", or "target only tier one customers when selling O&M solutions".

Proposition 1 *Manufacturers learn selection heuristics when they gain more experience with opportunities to capture downstream.*

Procedural Heuristics in Servitization

Procedural heuristics accord with guidelines and rules of thumb on how to execute a selected opportunity (Bingham & Eisenhardt, 2011). In practice, procedural heuristics are linked to entry modes (e.g., acquisition, greenfield investment), dedicated approaches to managing different functions (e.g., sales, recruiting, R&D, marketing or pricing), or different mechanisms used for defining a firm's business scope and boundaries (e.g., investments, divestments, stake-ins). For example, this form of simple heuristics could take forms such as "expand services organically", "never make service-related acquisitions", "sell solutions only to C-level executives", or "take service aspect into account already in the product-design phase". Typically, these rules of thumb are crafted based on accumulated experience and "trial-and-error". For example, if a firm has failed to make acquisitions, the management team can forbid the organization from making them or create a rule of thumb based on the lessons learned (e.g., "never acquire a firm bigger than you").

In services, managers may have noticed that selling solutions to lower level contacts is futile because they lack authority to make decisions and they do not see the services' value (Reinartz & Ulaga, 2008). Based on this observation, management can stipulate a rule of thumb that services must be sold to only decision-makers who are located higher in the customer's hierarchy (e.g., top management team) and have the authority to make larger scale decisions.

Proposition 2 *Manufacturers learn procedural heuristics when they gain more experience learning how to capture more service-related opportunities.*

Priority and Temporal Heuristics in Servitization

Temporal heuristics revolve around time, such as sequence, pace, and rhythm (Bingham & Eisenhardt, 2011). In practice, sequence heuristics can relate to the order of provided services, such as "always start with product-related services such as maintenance services, then move to customer-process focused services such as data analytics". Pace heuristics deal with stages such as "complete one region before beginning the next", whereas rhythm heuristics refer, for example, to the number of service-related acquisitions per year (e.g., "acquire at least 5 small service companies annually"). Temporal heuristics can, for example, lead to certain rules of thumb such as "always serve tier one customers first, then tier-two customers, and after that, sell services to tier three customers". *Priority heuristics*, on the other hand, are defined as deliberate rules of thumb that help firms rank and prioritize certain opportunities over others. For example, this can take rules of thumb such as "prioritize US customers over others" or "prefer selling analytics services first to German customers because Germany is a benchmark for other European countries' customers".

Proposition 3 *Manufacturers learn temporal and priority heuristics in servitization after they have learned selection and procedural heuristics.*

Table 1 below describes potential heuristics that managers can apply to manage servitization and facilitate organizational learning and renewal through examples in different business areas, such as geographic expansion, offerings, technologies, and customers served.

Table 1 Illustrations of managerial heuristics in servitization.

	Strategic focus of services			
	Geographic area	Offerings	Technologies	Customers
Selection heuristics and examples of rules of thumb in the servitization context	Sell services to US markets; do not sell services to developing markets	Sell only product-related services, not customer-process related services	Invest in service-related technologies in which our competitors will invest or have already invested	Sell O&M solutions only to tier-one customers
Procedural heuristics and examples of rules of thumb in the servitization context	Use service acquisitions as key mechanisms when entering US markets	Take services into account already in product-design phase	Never develop service-related technologies alone; always ally with your competitors	Sell services to customer's top management team level
Temporal heuristics and examples of rules of thumb in the servitization context	When selling IoT related solutions, sell first to Germany, then to Scandinavia, then to others	Always start with simple services, then move to more complex solutions, never progress other way around	Adopt service-related technologies that US or Swedish customers have accepted first, then leverage to other customers	Sell new services first to tier-one customers, then to tier-two customers, then to tier-three customers
Priority heuristics and examples of rules of thumb in the servitization context	Prioritize selling services to countries that have greater density of our flagship products	Rank services sold to customers based on their profitability	Prioritize service technologies with open standards	Rank customers based on their profitability

Learning Through Servitization

The organizational learning literature is extensive, and extant studies have shown that firms learn from experiences and through repetition, namely, through routines (Antretter et al., 2020; Bingham & Eisenhardt, 2011; Feldman & Pentland, 2003). However, the existing learning literature is relatively silent about *what* firms have actually learned along the way (Bingham & Eisenhardt, 2011). Moreover, little is known about how firms learn, in which order when they servitize, and what they learn along the way. Bingham and Eisenhardt (2011) found that companies learn heuristics in common structures and that they have specific development orders, starting from opportunity recognition (selection heuristics). After selection heuristics, they learn procedural heuristics, i.e., how to proceed in each process. Next, companies learn temporal and priority heuristics. Future servitization studies should delve deeper into two questions: (1) What manufacturers learn when they servitize? and (2) In which developmental order they learn when they servitize? Servitization is a purposeful context to study learning and organizational renewal processes, as it is a strategic yet specific renewal process. It is possible to study what companies learn when they servitize (e.g., in different geographic areas, technologies, offerings, and customers), and it can be measured (e.g., service sales development, level of internationalization, and number of different services).

Proposition 4 *Manufacturers learn heuristics in the following order when they servitize: (a) selection, (b) procedural, (c) temporal, and (d) priority heuristics.*

3   Discussion

Servitization has become an increasingly interesting business opportunity for manufacturers to ensure more stable income, better profit margins, and increased understanding of customers' business processes (Tuli et al., 2007; Ulaga & Reinartz, 2011). Many manufacturers have successfully servitized their businesses, and extant studies have widely investigated antecedents, processes, and outcomes of servitization (Rabetino et al., 2018). However, little is known about *what* manufacturers have actually learned along the way, why they have learned what they have learned, and how managerial heuristics have evolved during that transition, i.e., how firms have revamped and altered their simple rules to drive this strategic change when they have progressed in servitization.

Theoretical Contributions

This conceptual paper shows that the use of simple rules can be reflections of organizational learning and that they can reveal what manufacturers have learned when they have servitized their businesses. Hence, this article contributes to both the (1) servitization and (2) organizational learning literature by developing a framework of different heuristics in the servitization context. First, this article contributes to the servitization literature by suggesting that the use of different simple heuristics can reveal *what* firms learn, *why* they learn what they learn, and *how* they learn when they servitize, hence contributing to the discussion of learning in customer relationships (Töytäri et al., 2018; Tuli et al., 2007), technologies (Hasselblatt et al., 2017), geographic expansion (Aquilante & Vendrell-Herrero, 2019), and offerings (Kohtamäki & Partanen, 2016; Ulaga & Reinartz, 2011) in the servitization context. The propositions and framework presented in this article advance the servitization literature by illustrating different types of simple rules when companies enter new geographic areas, develop new offerings and technologies, and decide to serve different customers and customer needs. Second, this article sheds light on organizational learning theory by identifying development orders and cycles of learning heuristics. Challenging the traditional organizational learning literature that typically studies learning through an antecedent-behavior-outcome framework (Bingham & Eisenhardt, 2011), servitization provides an interesting context to study the *content* of learning, i.e., what issues manufacturers actually learn on their servitization journeys (simple rules reflect this learning in practice). These microfoundations of organizational learning shed light on learning behind the established simple rules, i.e., what issues have taught them to craft certain rules to drive the change. For example, in the traditional learning literature, studies have investigated how they can learn from acquisitions by using the number of acquisitions as a proxy to evaluate their success.

Managerial Implications

This book chapter helps managers craft their simple rules to navigate under an ever-changing business environment. Even though this study does not directly tell how these simple rules are created, this suggests that managers can systematically create a few thumb rules to redirect the company in each process and strategic domain. These simple rules can potentially help firms leverage their organizational assets by giving guidelines on where to reallocate resources (selection heuristics), how to reallocate resources (procedural heuristics), and in which order (temporal and priority heuristics). Following the work by Eisenhardt and Sull (2001), we suggest that firms should establish three–five simple rules for each process to redirect the company. These rules should be based on accumulated management experience, and these rules must be altered occasionally when times change and service knowledge increases within the company.

Future Research Avenues

Because this article is conceptual, it paves the way for future empirical studies about the evolution of heuristics in the servitization context. First, this article encourages future servitization studies to investigate what manufacturers learn when they servitize, i.e., what contents they learn (e.g., what have service acquisitions taught them?). Second, future servitization studies could explore why they learn what they learn, i.e., what incidents have affected those learning outcomes (e.g., what special event happened during the acquisition process that facilitated organizational learning?). Third, future servitization studies could shed light on how manufacturers learn when they servitize, i.e., what are the specific developmental orders of heuristics when firms create value through services (e.g., do firms apply the following order of learning heuristics: selection, procedural, temporal, priority when they servitize their businesses?). Do they follow the same, exact patterns or do these learning patterns vary between the companies? Moreover, servitization scholars could delve deeper into the evolution of simple rules in servitization, i.e., how firms revamp their simple rules to manage the servitization process more effectively.

References

Antretter, T., Blohm, I., Siren, C., Grichnik, D., Malmstrom, M., & Wincent, J. (2020). Do algorithms make better—and Fairer—Investments Than Angel Investors? *Harvard Business Review.* https://hbr.org/2020/11/do-algorithms-make-better-and-fairer-investments-than-angel-investors.

Artinger, F., Petersen, M., Gigerenzer, G., & Weibler, J. (2015). Heuristics as adaptive decision strategies in management. *Journal of Organizational Behavior, 36*(S1), 33–52.

Aquilante, T., & Vendrell-Herrero, F. (2019). Bundling and exporting: Evidence from German SMEs. Bank of England working papers 781, Bank of England.

Bingham, C. B., Eisenhardt, K. M., & Furr, N. R. (2007). What makes a process a capability? Heuristics, strategy, and effective capture of opportunities. *Strategic Entrepreneurship Journal, 1*(1–2), 27–47.

Bingham, J. B., & Eisenhardt, K. M. (2011). Rational heuristics: The 'simple rules' that strategists learn from process experience. *Strategic Management Journal, 32,* 1437–1464.

Bingham, C. B., & Eisenhardt, K. M. (2014). Response to Vuori and Vuori's commentary on "Heuristics in the strategy context". *Strategic Management Journal, 35*(11), 1698–1702.

Brown, S. L., & Eisenhardt, K. M. (1997). The art of continuous change: Linking complexity theory and time-pace devolution in relentlessly shifting organizations. *Administrative Science Quarterly, 42*(1), 1–34.

Davenport, T. H. (2020). How to make better decisions about Coronavirus. *MIT Sloan Management Review.* https://sloanreview.mit.edu/article/how-to-make-better-decisions-about-coronavirus/.

Eisenhardt, K. M. (1989). Making fast strategic decisions in high-velocity environments. *Academy of Management Journal, 32*(3), 543–576.

Eisenhardt, K. M., & Sull, D. N. (2001). Strategy as simple rules. *Harvard Business Review, 79*(1), 106–116.

Feldman, M. S., & Pentland, B. T. (2003). Reconceptualizing organizational routines as a source of flexibility and change. *Administrative Science Quarterly, 48*(1), 94–118.

Gebauer, H., Edvardsson, B., Gustafsson, A., & Witell, L. (2010). Match or mismatch: Strategy-structure configurations in the service business of manufacturing companies. *Journal of Service Research, 13*(2), 198–215.

Gigerenzer, G., & Gaissmaier, W. (2011). Heuristic decision making. *Annual Review of Psychology, 62,* 451–482.

Groner, M., Groner, R., & Bischof, W. F. (1983). Approaches to heuristics: A historical review. In R. Groner, M. Groner, & W. F. Bischof (Eds.), *Methods of heuristics* (pp. 1–18). Erlbaum.

Hasselblatt, M., Huikkola, T., Kohtamäki, M., & Nickell, D. (2017). Modeling manufacturer's capabilities for the Internet of Things. *Journal of Business & Industrial Marketing, 33*(6), 822–836.

Huikkola, T., & Kohtamäki, M. (2018). Business models in servitization. In M. Kohtamäki, T. Baines, R. Rabetino, & A. Bigdeli (Eds.), *Practices and tools for servitization: Managing service transition.* Palgrave-Macmillan.

Kahneman, D., & Klein, G. (2009). Conditions for intuitive expertise: A failure to disagree. *American Psychologist, 64*(6), 515–526.

Kahneman, D. (2011). *Thinking, fast and slow.* Farrar, Straus and Giroux.

Kohtamäki, M., & Partanen, J. (2016). Co-creating value from knowledge-intensive business services in manufacturing firms: The moderating role of relationship learning in supplier-customer interactions. *Journal of Business Research, 69*(7), 2498–2506.

Kohtamäki, M., Parida, V., Oghazi, P., Gebauer, H., & Baines, T. (2019). Digital servitization business models in ecosystems: A theory of the firm. *Journal of Business Research, 104,* 380–392.

Kowalkowski, C., Gebauer, H., & Oliva, R. (2017). Service growth in product firms: Past, present, and future. *Industrial Marketing Management, 60,* 82–88.

Maitland, E., & Sammartino, A. (2015). Decision making and uncertainty: The role of heuristics and experience in assessing a politically hazardous environment. *Strategic Management Journal, 36*(10), 1554–1578.

Michelsen, K.-E. (2013). *Perhe, yrittäjyys ja yritys teollisuuden vuosisadalla.* Otava.

Neu, W., & Brown, S. (2005). Forming successful business-to-business services in goods-dominant firms. *Journal of Service Research, 8*(3), 3–17.

Newell, A., & Simon, H. A. (1972). *Human problem solving.* Prentice Hall.

Rabetino, R., Harmsen, W., Kohtamäki, M., & Sihvonen, J. (2018). Structuring servitization related research. *International Journal of Operations and Production Management, 38*(2), 350–371.

Raddats, C., Kowalkowski, C., Benedettini, O., Burton, J., & Gebauer, H. (2019). Servitization: A contemporary thematic review of four major research streams. *Industrial Marketing Management.* https://doi.org/10.1016/j.indmarman.2019.03.015.

Reinartz, W. J., & Ulaga, W. (2008). How to sell services more profitably? *Harvard Business Review, 86*(5), 90–96.

Storbacka, K., Windahl, C., Nenonen, S., & Salonen, A. (2013). Solution business models: Transformation along four continua. *Industrial Marketing Management, 42*(5), 705–716.

Sull, D., & Eisenhardt, K. M. (2012). Simple rules for a complex world. *Harvard Business Review, 90*(9), 68–74.

Sull, D., & Eisenhardt, K. M. (2015). *Simple rules: How to thrive in a complex world.* Hodder Stoughton.

Tuli, K. R., Kohli, A. K., & Bharadwaj, S. G. (2007). Rethinking customer solutions: From product bundles to relational processes. *Journal of Marketing, 71*(3), 1–17.

Tversky, A., & Kahneman, D. (1974). Judgment under uncertainty: Heuristics and biases. *Science, 185*(4157), 1124–1131.

Töytäri, P., Turunen, T., Klein, M., Eloranta, V., Biehl, S., & Rajala, R. (2018). Aligning the mindset and capabilities within a business network for successful adoption of smart services. *Journal of Product Innovation Management, 35*(5), 763–779.

Ulaga, W., & Reinartz, W. J. (2011, November). Hybrid offerings: How manufacturing firms combine goods and services successfully. *Journal of Marketing, 75,* 5–23.

Visnjic, I., Jovanovic, M., Neely, A., & Engwall, M. (2017). What brings the value to outcome-based contract providers? Value drivers in outcome business models. *International Journal of Production Economics, 192,* 169–181.

Vuori, N., & Vuori, T. (2014). Comment on "Heuristics in the strategy context" by Bingham and Eisenhardt (2011). *Strategic Management Journal, 35*(11), 1689–1697.

Wübben, M., & Wangenheim, F. V. (2008). Instant customer base analysis: Managerial heuristics often "get it right". *Journal of Marketing, 72*(3), 82–93.

Narrative Network as a Method to Understand the Evolution of Smart Solutions

Suvi Einola, Marko Kohtamäki, and Rodrigo Rabetino

1   Introduction

In this era of the Internet of Things, the social and material are more inter-connected than ever before. We combine various digital tools and functions in our everyday lives without paying attention; when running, we check our GPS-linked watch to see how much we still need to run. The same watch tells us when to go to sleep, answers our phone, sends and receives emails, and tells us how our night was, and what the weather will be like today. These opportunities that the Internet of Things has to offer are changing our personal lives, the lives of organizations, and the processes of organizing (Andal-Ancion et al., 2003), as well as the lives of traditional manufac-turing companies. Previously, manufacturing companies succeeded with quite simplistic, "produce a lot, and sell a lot" of business models, but the trans-formation toward digitalization has driven the firms to change their business

S. Einola (✉) · M. Kohtamäki · R. Rabetino
University of Vaasa, Vaasa, Finland
e-mail: suvi.einola@uwasa.fi; suvi.einola@univaasa.fi

M. Kohtamäki
e-mail: mtko@uwasa.fi

R. Rabetino
e-mail: rodrigo.rabetino@uwasa.fi; rodrigo.rabetino@univaasa.fi

M. Kohtamäki et al. (eds.), *The Palgrave Handbook of Servitization*,
https://doi.org/10.1007/978-3-030-75771-7_19

model from pure product manufacturing towards smart solutions (product-service-software system), a transition often coined as servitization (Rabetino et al., 2017), or later on, with an emphasis on digital, digital servitization (Coreynen et al., 2017; Kohtamäki et al., 2019b). Both servitization and digital servitization, as change processes, are far from simple (Kohtamäki et al., 2020). Tangible products that meet intangible services—products, services, and software—are bundled together into smart solutions to create value for the customer and the manufacturer. Thus, servitization meets the digital, and the manufacturer goes through a transition, where the digital and servitization are developed at least partially in parallel. Multiple studies have suggested this. However, the previous digital servitization literature is relatively silent on this interplay and how it could be framed. The present study intends to use a narrative network as a method to understand the interplay between digitalization and servitization.

The narrative approach has been argued to have a key role in the social sciences for decades (Bakhtin, 1981; Boje, 1995, 2008; Vaara & Tienari, 2011). In this chapter, we use the narrative network as a methodological tool to understand the evolution of smart solutions. As Berger and Luckman already concluded in 1966, when reality is socially constructed, and social can be illustrated as a network of different stories (Abbott, 1992), it seems interesting to study the interconnection of the social and material, for instance, the interplay between human activities (sayings and doings) (Schatzki, 2012), and the digital tools. Indeed, Pentland and Feldman (2007: 781) suggest that this interconnection *"can be conceptualized and empirically summarized as patterns of narrative fragments connected into networks."* We draw from their idea of narrative network, in which the term narrative is used *"to emphasize a set of actions or events that embodies coherence or unity of purpose"* and the term network *"to emphasize that these actions can be interconnected in many different ways"* (Pentland & Feldman, 2007, p. 781). To summarize, the narrative network includes two ingredients, network nodes representing *"things that happen"* and network edges representing their consecutive relationship (Pentland et al., 2017). That is to say, that in organizational life, or social life more generally, there is not only one "correct" narrative to describe what is going on in our lives or how to define organizational happenings (Weick et al., 2005), but also many optional narratives, or pieces of stories. Those pieces of stories, narratives, build the narrative fragments we aim to study in this article. Although narratives can be considered more broadly than in this article, for this article, we narrow the meaning of narrative as series of events or discursive actions *"to make up the core story"* (Pentland & Feldman, 2007,

p. 782), which facilitates organizational sensemaking (Einola et al., 2017) and sensegiving.

This conceptual book chapter intends to extend the discussion about the interplay between digitalization and servitization by introducing a narrative network as a method to understand the interplay and therefore the evolution of smart solutions. As such, the narrative network provides a microlevel lens to study the co-evolution of digital servitization.

2   Theory Development

The narrative network approach draws from various theories, such as organizational routines (Feldman, 2000; Feldman & Pentland, 2003; Goh & Pentland, 2019), structuration theory (Giddens, 1984), and actor–network theory (Latour, 2005). A narrative network comprises two core elements as narratives in general: happenings and their sequential relationship (Pentland & Feldman, 2007). Those happenings, pieces of stories, are seen as network nodes, which can have several features, such as who, when, why, etc. (Pentland et al., 2017). At the center of building a narrative network is the question "*what happens next*" (Pentland & Feldman, 2007: 788) to emphasize the sequential essence of the narrative network. Furthermore, the narrative network outlines the set of pathways at each point, so the question of "what happens next" becomes a question about network structure, or as Goh and Pentland (2019: 1920) sophistically express it, "*The narrative network framework provides a starting point for operationalizing the conditions for morphogenesis.*" Finally, in all pieces of stories, the sequence labels the development of actions (Pentland et al., 2020).

Using the concept of narrative network theory, we aim to understand the evolution of smart services by modeling the paths manufacturing companies have taken on their way toward outcome-based services and smart solutions.

Narratives of Servitization

As a transition from products to product-service systems, servitization involves strategic and structural components, e.g., strategy-structure fit (Forkmann et al., 2017; Kohtamäki et al., 2019a). Hence, servitization requires strategic decisions and actions and the development of structures and capabilities to support this major transition. We consider this transition through ten sequential narratives or core stories.

Since the beginning of the Second Industrial Revolution in 1870, manufacturing companies have used more or less the same business logic: cost reduction and profit maximization through mass production, large-scale manufacturing with standardized products (Ramírez, 1999). These traditional *(A) manufacturing products* with add-on services are also the starting point of our analysis (Oliva & Kallenberg, 2003). After a centuries-old manufacturing tradition, companies started to see new business opportunities in adding some simple services and systems to their manufactured products (Matthyssens & Vandenbempt, 2008). In the value systems of industrial manufacturing companies, we have also witnessed movement regarding make-or-buy decisions, integration, and disintegration (Hobday et al., 2005). One way to see the structure of the architecture of an industrial value system has been from raw material supplies, to components suppliers, systems supplies, solution integrators, operators, and customers (Davies, 2004; Rabetino & Kohtamäki, 2018). While value systems are not all the same or equal, and value system architectures involve much variety, the transition from a system supplier position toward the downstream has been seen as a means to increase competitive advantage (Brady et al., 2005). *(B) Supplying simple systems* has been a strategic position for many manufacturers looking to move toward the downstream (Rabetino & Kohtamäki, 2018). Thus, when traditional manufacturers' perception about customers was that they "*destroy the value*"(Ramírez, 1999: 61), we later observed the emerging customer emphasis in the literature concerning manufacturing firms (Wise & Baumgartner, 1999). To some extent, manufacturing firms woke up to **emphasize customer needs** (Kindström, 2010; Rabetino et al., 2017) to co-produce value together with customers (Vargo & Lusch, 2004).

Although starting to understand the role of customer needs and add-on services, many companies maintained their *(D) cost-based pricing* practices when selling products, add-on services, and simple systems. Cost-based pricing supports effective but sub-optimizing exchange behaviors with an emphasis on low costs and short-term profits, resulting in low seller differentiation and power (Ulaga & Eggert, 2006). To differentiate, servitizing companies started *(E) integrating products* and *services into* **solutions** to become customized integrated solution providers (Kohtamäki et al., 2019a, 2019b). The provision of integrated solutions intended to decrease the buyer's transaction costs by integrating more complex offerings into systems, bringing customers closer to the servitizing manufacturers (Bigdeli et al., 2018; Huikkola et al., 2020), the manufacturers moving downstream (Wise & Baumgartner, 1999). Furthermore, delivering complex integrated solutions required a more in-depth *(F)* **understanding of the role of value** co-creation

(Rabetino et al., 2017). Value co-creation is often divided into two separate although intertwined, interaction processes, co-creation, and co-production, in which value co-creation is an outcome of the consumption process, and co-production is the interaction in developing the value proposition and creating the core offering (Kohtamäki & Rajala, 2016; Lusch & Vargo, 2006).

To be able to co-create value, companies *(G) started to manage customer relationships* more in-depth. Despite the evident need for good customer relationship management, many companies struggled significantly with execution (Grönroos & Helle, 2010; Richards & Jones, 2008; Vargo & Lusch, 2004). Furthermore, while getting to know customers and building trust through value co-creation, servitizing companies found business potential from *(H) building life-cycle solutions* (Rabetino et al., 2015). Life-cycle solutions include "*the services that support the pre-sales phase (services that contribute to design and construction), the sales phase (services that augment the product offering and basic services for the installed base), and the after-sales phase (advanced services for the installed base)*" (Rabetino et al., 2015: 56). This shift toward life-cycle solutions dramatically changed the logic behind the business. As services and solutions started to bring revenues to the servitizing companies, the logic behind offering and prizing changed. Where earlier companies used cost-based pricing (and some of them competition-based pricing), the most advanced companies *(I) started to change towards value-based offering and pricing* (also coined customer value-based pricing) to answer the main question behind this logic: "*How can we create additional customer value and increase customer willingness to pay, despite the competition?*" (Hinterhuber & Liozu, 2018).

In this study, the final phase of the evolution of servitization is coined *(J) offering outcome-based services*, which also prior literature has recognized and acknowledged to be the most progressed model of the servitization process (Baines et al., 2017; Korkeamäki & Kohtamäki, 2020; Visnjic et al., 2017). The basic idea of outcome-based services is that the business logic is flipped from selling products and services to selling and guaranteeing outcomes (Sjödin et al., 2020a). Figure 1 illustrates the narrative fragments and interconnection between the ten phases of servitization.

Narratives of Digitalization

Digitalization has been defined as the "use of digital technologies *to change a business model and provide new revenue and value-producing opportunities; it is the process of moving to a digital business*" (Gartner Glossary, 2020). This chapter defines digitalization as the transition process from sensor

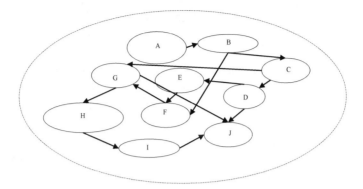

Fig. 1 Narrative fragments of servitization with their interconnectedness

development through remote monitoring and optimization all the way to autonomous systems (Porter & Heppelmann, 2015).

The digital transformation started to change manufacturers' business logic irrevocably in the early 2000s. The first steps toward digitalization were taken, when companies started *(1) sensor development* to add simple sensors to their products to collect data about the usage of the products (Rymaszewska et al., 2017). As sensors started to provide data on the products, companies developed monitoring and *(2) remote diagnostics* and found new business opportunities by diagnosing problems remotely and moving from " *'just in case' to 'just in time'*" maintenance (Brax & Jonsson, 2009: 545). With the help of sensors collecting real-time data and developed remote diagnostics, companies started to put effort into anticipating the possible failures of the equipment and initiate maintenance in response to equipment conditions found by various sensors before breakdowns or problems (Grubic & Peppard, 2016; Swanson, 2001), coined here as *(3) predictive maintenance*.

Furthermore, remote real-time monitoring enabled companies to launch *(4) remote control* for the installed base in which some of the problems or errors in the usage of the equipment could actually be noticed and even repaired from a distance. For this purpose, companies built separate control rooms using remote diagnostics to enable, e.g., reliability programs (Grubic & Peppard, 2016). Since the amount of data companies gather and analyze has exploded in the last two decades, the most important task is handling those data to prevent information overload and enable new business opportunities (Opresnik & Taisch, 2015). For these purposes, *(5) big data analytics* offers speed and efficiency for the utilization of the gathered data. Big data analytics aims to improve the performance of the equipment. Overall, the interconnection between various equipment and systems enables *(6) optimization through data analytics* to expand and deepen their offerings towards optimization and outcome-based services (Kohtamäki et al.,).

(7) Artificial intelligence is one of the major next steps in the evolution of digitalization. It will transform the services (Rymaszewska et al., 2017) and the business model of servitizing companies and reshape competition (Porter & Heppelmann, 2015). The solutions artificial intelligence can offer for servitizing companies are still in their infancy. However, we have already seen such features as machine learning supporting preventive decisions (Paschou et al., 2020) and digital customer services such as fleet management by AI-enabled optimizations (Sjödin et al., 2020b). As the digitalization process of manufacturing companies proceeds, some of the manufacturers become more like software companies (Immelt, 2017; Töytäri et al., 2018) in processes where software becomes a more relevant part of the manufacturing firm's offerings, sometimes progressing to a stage where the company may begin offering also *(8) software as service*. Furthermore, companies may also progress toward a platform provider business model connecting multiple providers and customers through software (Kohtamäki et al.,). Again the question regarding firm boundaries and make-or-buy decision, is highly relevant in these settings (Kohtamäki et al., 2019a, 2019b).

Finally, fully autonomous systems narrate the final phase of the evolution of digitalization. Although we have witnessed rapid transition towards autonomous ships, cars, etc., it seems that the transition towards this level is still at the very beginning, for "*equipment operating in this category is capable of completing pre-assigned missions, handling deviations, and learning from its operational environment*" (Thomson et al., 2021). However, in different industries, this development toward (9) *autonomous systems* is still in its infancy. Figure 2 synthesizes the narrative fragments and interconnection between the nine phases of digitalization.

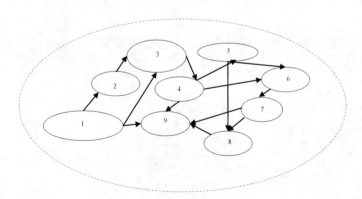

Fig. 2 Narrative fragments of digitalization with their interconnectedness

Narrative Network of Digital Servitization

Scholars started using digital servitization as a concept to merge digitalization and servitization. Digital servitization is often defined *"…as the transition toward smart product-service-software systems that enable value creation and capture through monitoring, control, optimization, and autonomous function. To gain value from digital servitization, firms must capitalize on three dimensions of digital offerings (i.e., products, services, and software), which should work together"* (Kohtamäki et al., 2019a, 2019b: 383). Studies have revealed the interplay between digitalization and servitization, and have already provided some preliminary evidence on the financial feasibility of the digital servitization business model (Kohtamäki et al., 2020). Hence, we draw on previous literature to describe manufacturers' evolution towards digital servitization and smart solutions by constructing a narrative network between servitization and digitalization.

Narrative fragments on the right and left sides of Fig. 3 are structured sequentially to form narratives (Czarniawska, 1997). The left side narrates the evolution of servitization and the right side narrates the evolution of digitalization. The middle column illustrates the chronological and coherent interconnectedness between servitization and digitalization. By doing so, the figure builds a narrative network of digital servitization. Round arrows elucidate the connection among various narrative fragments over a consecutive chronological order inside both phenomena, where straight arrows show the interconnectedness between studied phenomena.

The narrative network of digital servitization builds a story of the co-evolution of digitalization and servitization, with an emphasis on their interplay. Thus, it demonstrates how digital technologies enable the creation

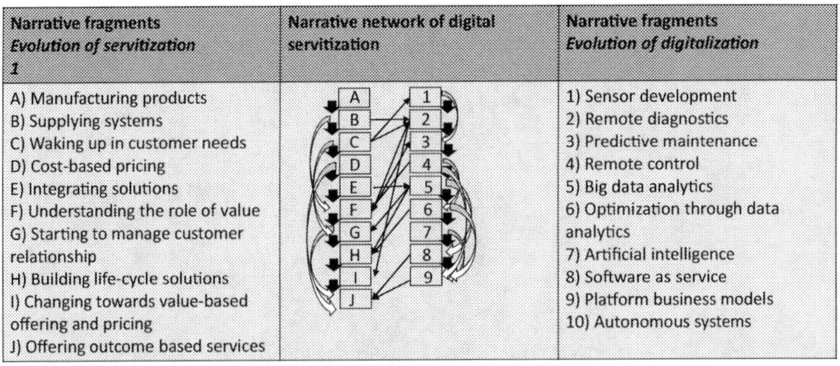

Narrative fragments Evolution of servitization 1	Narrative network of digital servitization	Narrative fragments Evolution of digitalization
A) Manufacturing products B) Supplying systems C) Waking up in customer needs D) Cost-based pricing E) Integrating solutions F) Understanding the role of value G) Starting to manage customer relationship H) Building life-cycle solutions I) Changing towards value-based offering and pricing J) Offering outcome based services	A 1 B 2 C 3 D 4 E 5 F 6 G 7 H 8 I 9 J	1) Sensor development 2) Remote diagnostics 3) Predictive maintenance 4) Remote control 5) Big data analytics 6) Optimization through data analytics 7) Artificial intelligence 8) Software as service 9) Platform business models 10) Autonomous systems

Fig. 3 The narrative network of digital servitization

and development of new types of smart solutions. In the early stage of servitization, products (A) provided the opportunity to develop sensors and remote diagnostics. When companies started to supply systems (B), remote diagnostics (2) facilitated the emergence of a new business model, and already back then, enabled companies to take first steps toward value-based offering and pricing (I) through predictive maintenance services (3). In addition, remote diagnostics (2) fostered both the understanding of the role of value (Töytäri et al., 2018) (4) and customer relationship management (G). When companies started to integrate more complex solutions (E), big data analytics (5) provided possibilities to not only reduce costs (Opresnik & Taisch, 2015) but also to provide value by controlling and optimizing these systems. Remote diagnostics, together with smart algorithms and big data analytics, enable a manufacturer to offer life-cycle solutions (H). However, this requires data and a proper understanding of the customer's processes and needs. Remote diagnostics increase customer data, enabling improved (4) control and (6) optimization (Porter & Heppelmann, 2015), and providing value-based pricing opportunities for outcome-based services (J). In this instance, the software may also be provided as a service (8). Furthermore, with the help of data analytics (5) and artificial intelligence (7), companies can broaden their scope further to expand their offerings to platforms and autonomous systems (9) (Kohtamäki et al., 2019a, 2019b) in the near future.

Narrative Network as a Methodological Tool

Finding out how to crystallize specific representations or happenings into generalized patterns is essential to understanding organizations (Tsoukas & Chia, 2002; Weick, 1995). Perhaps the narrative network as a method can provide a specific lens to build shared understanding around organizational developmental steps, as the narrative network further organizations "*to visualize patterns of action without losing touch with the specific performances that make up these patterns*" (Feldman & Pentland, 2003: 791). The narrative network includes two key components as any narrative: (1) happenings (network nodes) and (2) their consecutive relationship in the continuous process of actions (network edges) (Pentland et al., 2017). The narrative network can act as a tool to describe and visualize patterns of actions in and around organizations (Yeow & Faraj, 2011). When building the narrative network, the most critical thing is to answer the question "what happens next" and bear in mind that the relation between narrative fragments should follow chronology and coherence (Pentland et al., 2017). To summarize, the narrative network, as a methodological lens, provides a conceptual tool for *"everything that follows"* (Pentland et al., 2017: 26).

3   Discussion of the Narrative Network of the Evolution of Smart Solutions

Theoretical Contribution

Products, technologies, and software artifacts have value only when used by actors (Grubic, 2014). Thus, in the interconnection between the social and material, the actor and the artifact, play a key role when discussing the evolution of smart solutions. In the end, the evolution of smart solutions, from manufacturing products to offering outcome-based services, is far from easy, which is why companies struggle with these solutions (Kohtamäki et al., 2020). To fully understand the complexity of this evolution process, one needs to understand the interconnectedness of all the phases of the process and all the actors inside these processes, the tight intertwining between the material and social, which continues to rewrite the future of smart solutions.

The contribution of this article is twofold. As the first theoretical contribution, we extend the discussion about the complex interplay between digitalization and servitization during their co-evolution. We used the narrative network to uncover the evolution of digital servitization and smart solutions. In doing so, this chapter describes ten narrative fragments of servitization, nine narrative fragments of digitalization, and the dynamic interplay of the fragments, narrative network. First, we frame both servitization and digitalization separately and then build an interconnection between both of these phenomena. This discussion contributes to the digital servitization literature (Kohtamäki et al., 2019a, 2019b; Paschou et al., 2020; Sklyar et al., 2019), considering its evolution since the turn of the millennium until recently. As the second contribution, this article introduces a narrative network as a method to understand the interplay between servitization and digitalization and, therefore, the evolution of smart solutions. As such, the narrative network provides a microlevel lens to study the co-evolution of digital servitization. The narrative network unravels the interplay between these dimensions coherently and consecutively, where the reader can follow the temporal and spatial narrative uniquely.

Managerial Implications

For managers in digital servitization companies, this book chapter provides some insight into the complexity and interconnectedness of the elements included in the lengthy change process of digital servitization. Perhaps this chapter gives managers ideas for more in-depth processing of different phases of the change and the possibility to recognize different narratives inside the process. Moreover, perhaps the method can also act as a vehicle when planning the digital servitization process, and communication around it.

Future Research Directions

Future studies could collect in-depth ethnographic-type field data about the interconnected processes of digital servitization and build an empirical narrative network to understand the evolution of smart solutions through narrative fragments inside servitizing companies. Furthermore, one could compare digital servitization processes in different organizations or at different organizational levels by using a narrative network as a method. In general, servitization scholars could more often use a cognitive lens (Einola, 2017) and narrative methods to increase understanding about the complex change process that companies face when moving from traditional manufacturing towards digital servitization and smart solutions. As such, we concur with the previous call (Luoto et al., 2016) for alternative narratives in servitization research.

References

Abbott, A. (1992). Notes on narrative positivism. *Sociological Methods & Research, 20*(4), 428–455.

Andal-Ancion, A., Cartwright, P. A., & Yip, G. S. (2003, Summer). *MIT Sloan Management Review, 44*(4), 34–41.

Baines, T., Ziaee Bigdeli, A., Bustinza, O. F., Shi, V. G., Baldwin, J., & Ridgway, K. (2017). Servitization: Revisiting the state-of-the-art and research priorities. *International Journal of Operations and Production Management, 37*(2), 256–278.

Bakhtin, M. (1981). *The dialogic imagination: Four essays by MM Bakhtin*. University of Texas Press.

Berger, P. L., & Luckman, T. (1966). *The social construction of reality: A tratise in the sociology of knowledge*. Doubleday.

Bigdeli, A. Z., Bustinza, O., Vendrell-Herrero, F., & Baines, T. (2018). Network positioning and risk perception in servitization: Evidence from the UK road transport industry. *International Journal of Production Research, 56*(6), 2169–2183.

Boje, D. M. (1995). Stories of the storytelling organization: A postmodern analysis of Disney as "Tamara-Land." *Academy of Management Journal, 38*(4), 997–1035.

Boje, D. M. (2008). *Storytelling organizations.* Sage.

Brady, T., Davies, A., & Gann, D. M. (2005). Creating value by delivering integrated solutions. *International Journal of Project Management, 23*(5), 360–365.

Brax, S. A., & Jonsson, K. (2009). Developing integrated solution offerings for remote diagnostics: A comparative case study of two manufacturers. *International Journal of Operations and Production Management, 29*(5), 539–560.

Coreynen, W., Matthyssens, P., & Van Bockhaven, W. (2017). Boosting servitization through digitalization: Pathways and dynamic resource configurations for manufacturers. *Industrial Marketing Management, 60,* 42–53.

Czarniawska, B. (1997). *Narrating the organization: Dramas of institutional identity.* University of Chicago Press.

Davies, A. (2004). Moving base into high-value integrated solutions: A value stream approach. *Industrial and Corporate Change, 13*(5), 727–756.

Einola, S. (2017). Making sense of strategic decision making. In M. Kohtamäki (Ed.), *Real-time strategy and business intelligence: Digitizing practices and systems* (pp. 149–166). Palgrave Macmillan.

Einola, S., Kohtamäki, M., Parida, V., & Wincent, J. (2017). Retrospective relational sensemaking in R&D offshoring. *Industrial Marketing Management, 63,* 205–216.

Feldman, M. S. (2000). Organizational routines as a source of continuous change. *Organization Science, 11*(6), 611–629.

Feldman, M. S., & Pentland, B. T. (2003). Reconceptualizing organizational routines as a source of flexibility and change. *Administrative Science Quarterly, 48*(1), 94–118.

Forkmann, S., Henneberg, S. C., Witell, L., & Kindström, D. (2017). Driver configurations for successful service infusion. *Journal of Service Research, 20*(3), 275–291.

Gartner Glossary. (2020). *Digitalization.* https://www.gartner.com/en/information-technology/glossary/digitalization.

Giddens, A. (1984). *The constitution of society.* University of Califonia Press.

Goh, K. T., & Pentland, B. T. (2019). From actions to paths to patterning: Toward a dynamic theory of patterning in routines. *Academy of Management Journal, 62*(6), 1901–1929.

Grönroos, C., & Helle, P. (2010). Adopting a service logic in manufacturing: Conceptual foundation and metrics for mutual value creation. *Journal of Service Management, 21*(5), 564–590.

Grubic, T. (2014). Servitization and remote monitoring technology: A literature review and research agenda. *Journal of Manufacturing Technology Management, 25*(1), 100–124.

Grubic, T., & Peppard, J. (2016). Servitized manufacturing firms competing through remote monitoring technology: An exploratory study. *Journal of Manufacturing Technology Management, 27*(2), 154–184.

Hinterhuber, A., & Liozu, S. (2018). Is it time to rethink your hiring strategy? *MIT Sloan Management Review, 109*(5), 16–17.

Hobday, T., Davies, A., & Prencipe, A. (2005). Systems integration: A core capability of the modern corporation. *Industrial and Corporate Change, 14*(6), 1109–1143.

Huikkola, T., Rabetino, R., Kohtamäki, M., & Gebauer, H. (2020). Firm boundaries in servitization: Interplay and repositioning practices. *Industrail Marketing Management, 90*(June), 90–105.

Immelt, J. (2017). How I remade GR: And what I learned along the way. *Harvard Business Review, 95*(5), 42–51.

Kindström, D. (2010). Towards a service-based business model: Key aspects for future competitive advantage. *European Management Journal, 28*(6), 479–490.

Kohtamäki, M., Einola, S., & Rabetino, R. (2020). Exploring servitization through the paradox lens: Coping practices in servitization. *International Journal of Production Economics, 226*, 107619.

Kohtamäki, M., Henneberg, S. C., Martinez, V., Kimita, K., & Gebauer, H. (2019a). A configurational approach to servitization. *Service Science, 11*(3), 213–240.

Kohtamäki, M., Parida, V., Oghazi, P., Gebauer, H., & Baines, T. (2019b). Digital servitization business models in ecosystems: A theory of the firm. *Journal of Business Research, 104*(November), 380–392.

Kohtamäki, M., & Rajala, R. (2016). Theory and practice of value co-creation in B2B systems. *Industrial Marketing Management, 56*, 4–13.

Korkeamäki, L., & Kohtamäki, M. (2020). To outcomes and beyond: Discursively managing legitimacy struggles in outcome business models. *Industrial Marketing Management, 91*(February), 196–208.

Latour, B. (2005). *Reassembling the social: An introduction to actor-network theory.* Oxford University Press.

Luoto, S., Brax, S. A., & Kohtamäki, M. (2016). Critical meta-analysis of servitization research: Constructing a model-narrative to reveal paradigmatic assumptions. *Industrial Marketing Management, 60*, 89–100.

Lusch, R. F., & Vargo, S. L. (2006). Service-dominant logic: Reactions, reflections and refinements. *Marketing Theory, 6*(3), 281–288.

Matthyssens, P., & Vandenbempt, K. (2008). Moving from basic offerings to value-added solutions: Strategies, barriers and alignment. *Industrial Marketing Management, 37*(3), 316–328.

Oliva, R., & Kallenberg, R. (2003). Managing the transition from products to services. *International Journal of Service Industry Management, 14*(2), 160–172.

Opresnik, D., & Taisch, M. (2015). The value of big data in servitization. *International Journal of Production Economics, 165*, 174–184.

Paschou, T., Rapaccini, M., Adrodegari, F., & Saccani, N. (2020). Digital servitization in manufacturing: A systematic literature review and research agenda. *Industrial Marketing Management, 89*(January 2019), 278–292.

Pentland, B. T., & Feldman, M. S. (2007). Narrative networks: Patterns of technology and organization. *Organization Science, 18*(5), 781–795.

Pentland, B. T., Mahringer, C. A., Dittrich, K., Feldman, M. S., & Wolf, J. R. (2020). Process multiplicity and process dynamics: Weaving the space of possible paths. *Organization Theory, 1*(3), 1–21.

Pentland, B. T., Recker, J., & Wyner, G. (2017). Rediscovering handoffs. *Academy of Management Discoveries, 3*, 284–301.

Porter, M. E., & Heppelmann, J. E. (2015). How smart, connected products are transforming companies. *Harvard Business Review*, 2015(October).

Rabetino, R., & Kohtamäki, M. (2018). To servitize is to reposition: Utilizing a Porterian view to understand servitization and value systems. In *Practices and tools for servitization: Managing service transition* (pp. 325–341).

Rabetino, R., Kohtamäki, M., & Gebauer, H. (2017). Strategy map of servitization. *International Journal of Production Economics, 192*(October 2015), 144–156.

Rabetino, R., Kohtamäki, M., Lehtonen, H., & Kostama, H. (2015). Developing the concept of life-cycle service offering. *Industrial Marketing Management, 49*(August), 53–66.

Ramírez, R. (1999). Value co-production: Intellectual origins and implications for practice and research. *Strategic Management Journal, 20*(1), 49–65.

Richards, K. A., & Jones, E. (2008). Customer relationship management: Finding value drivers. *Industrial Marketing Management, 37*(2), 120–130.

Rymaszewska, A., Helo, P., & Gunasekaran, A. (2017). IoT powered servitization of manufacturing: An exploratory case study. *International Journal of Production Economics, 192*(February), 92–105.

Schatzki, T. R. (2012). A primer on practices: Theory and research. In J. Higgs, R. Barnett, S. Billett, M. Huthings, & F. Trede (Eds.), *Practice-besed education: Perspectives and strategies* (pp. 13–26). Sense Publishers.

Sjödin, D., Parida, V., Jovanovic, M., & Visnjic, I. (2020a). Value creation and value capture alignment in business model innovation: A process view on outcome-based business models. *Journal of Product Innovation Management, 37*(2), 158–183.

Sjödin, D., Parida, V., Kohtamäki, M., & Wincent, J. (2020b). An agile co-creation process for digital servitization: A micro-service innovation approach. *Journal of Business Research, 112*(March), 478–491.

Sklyar, A., Kowalkowski, C., Tronvoll, B., & Sörhammar, D. (2019). Organizing for digital servitization: A service ecosystem perspective. *Journal of Business Research, 104*(February), 450–460.

Swanson, L. (2001). Linking maintenance strategies to performance. *International Journal of Production Economics, 70*(3), 237–244.

Thomson, L., Kamalaldin, A., Sjödin, D., & Parida, V. (2021). A maturity framework for autonomous solutions in manufacturing firms: The interplay of technology, ecosystem, and business model. *International Entrepreneurship and Management Journal* (In press).

Töytäri, P., Turunen, T., Klein, M., Eloranta, V., Biehl, S., & Rajalaet, R. (2018). Aligning the mindset and capabilities within a business network for successful adoption of smart services. *Journal of Product Innovation Management, 35*(5), 763–779.

Tsoukas, H., & Chia, R. (2002). On organizational becoming: Rethinking organizational change. *Organization Science, 13*(5), 567–582.

Ulaga, W., & Eggert, A. (2006). Value-based differentiation in business relationships: Gaining and sustaining key supplier status. *Journal of Marketing, 70*(1), 119–136.

Vaara, E., & Tienari, J. (2011). On the narrative construction of multinational corporations: An antenarrative analysis of legitimation and resistance in a cross-border merger. *Organization Science, 22*(2), 370–390.

Vargo, S. L., & Lusch, R. F. (2004). Evolving to a new dominant logic for marketing. *Journal of Marketing, 68*(1), 1–17.

Visnjic, I., Jovanovic, M., Neely, A., & Engwall, M. (2017). What brings the value to outcome-based contract providers? Value drivers in outcome business models. *International Journal of Production Economics, 192*(December 2015), 169–181.

Weick, K. E. (1995). *Sensemaking in organizations*. Sage.

Weick, K., Sutcliffe, K., & Obstfeld, D. (2005). Organizing and the process of sensemaking. *Organization Science, 16*(4), 409–421.

Wise, R., & Baumgartner, P. (1999). Go downstream: The new profit imperative in manufacturing. *Harvard Business Review*, (September–October), 133–141.

Yeow, A., & Faraj, S. (2011). Using narrative networks to study enterprise systems and organizational change. *International Journal of Accounting Information Systems, 12*(2), 116–125.

A Conceptual Guideline to Support Servitization Strategy Through Individual Actions

Shaun West, Paolo Gaiardelli, Anet Mathews, and Nicola Saccani

1 Introduction

It is generally agreed that the servitization of manufacturing calls for organizations to radically innovate all components of their strategy or business model (Gebauer et al., 2005). In particular, changes required by servitization entail different strategic (Baines et al., 2009), organizational, and network challenges (Oliva et al., 2012), that can be categorized around many different perspectives (Alghisi & Saccani, 2015). By definition, such change creates a major impact on the culture of a firm in terms of organizational intensity and

S. West (✉) · A. Mathews
Institute of Innovation and Technology Management, Lucerne University of
Applied Sciences and Arts, Lucerne, Switzerland
e-mail: shaun.west@hslu.ch

P. Gaiardelli
Department of Management, Information, and Production Engineering,
University of Bergamo, Bergamo, Italy
e-mail: paolo.gaiardelli@unibg.it

N. Saccani
Department of Industrial and Mechanical Engineering, University of Brescia,
Brescia, Italy
e-mail: nicola.saccani@unibs.it

© The Author(s), under exclusive license to Springer Nature
Switzerland AG 2021
M. Kohtamäki et al. (eds.), *The Palgrave Handbook of Servitization*,
https://doi.org/10.1007/978-3-030-75771-7_20

service specificity (Mathieu, 2001a), and involves a gradual and consistent adaptation of the whole business model (Zott et al., 2011).

Although many scholars have analyzed service transformation factors, benefits, and paradoxes from different perspectives (Brax, 2005; Kohtamäki et al., 2020), including strategy, marketing, operations, organization, and behavioral angles (Gebauer, 2009), relatively few works have focused on the everyday actions that have to be addressed by the management team to accomplish a successful service process transformation (Baines & Shi, 2015; Lütjen et al., 2017). In other words, there are limited models for servitization as a change process, while literature provides very few indications on how organizations undergoing servitization face daily challenges to achieve successful operations (Baines et al., 2017).

On these premises, in this chapter we will discuss how the management of a servitized company implements its day-by-day actions for efficient and effective product-service solutions. Through a model, developed around seven categories of servitization barriers identified by Hou and Neely (2013) and three categories of dynamic capabilities suggested by Kindström et al. (2013), we will detail servitization barriers and the actions necessary to address them effectively. Moreover, exploiting the results of West and Gaiardelli (2016) from interviews conducted with service managers and associated sources in industry, we will provide examples of barriers firms faced.

Since our aim is to understand how organizations overcome servitization barriers through managerial actions, this is done by focusing on the analysis of adopted measures undertaken at individual level, consistently with Lenka et al. (2018). Specifically, we will refer to middle management actions, due to this group's role as the primary management in day-by-day service operations.

Finally, the interpretation of the empirical evidence through the adopted model allows us to provide a guideline for developing a roadmap to overcome internal and external forces that influence the transition to services.

The chapter is based on the research findings of West et al. (2014), West and Gaiardelli (2016), West and Gaiardelli (2017), and West et al. (2018, 2019), supported by additional analysis of prior studies and expert interviews.

2   Theory Development

The aim of this section is to provide a theoretical foundation before introducing a guideline to develop solutions to servitization challenges. First, there is a discussion about the concept of servitization barriers and how they can be addressed, followed by an analysis of existing studies that adopt categorization of servitization barriers. The study is the foundation for the construction of a model we have used to classify servitization barriers and to identify and describe individual actions implemented by service managers to overcome them.

Theoretical Concepts of Barriers to Servitization

Implementation of a servitization strategy requires a highly sophisticated process (Brax, 2005) that leads companies to consider different aspects. Such complexity can bring firms to encounter different types of paradoxes (Kohtamäki et al., 2020) thus calling for suitable and coherent strategies to avoid servitization failure (Valtakoski, 2017). In particular, the adoption of day-to-day actions emerges as essential to reconcile the strategic view with distinctive operations characteristics. These actions are usually taken by people in middle management who are also confronted by other types of barriers, whether structural, procedural, or cultural (Lenka et al., 2018).

The barriers are not static but change over time, and actions employed by management are only successful when they are able to evolve, involving different capabilities dynamically. As suggested by Kindström et al. (2013), the three aspects of sensing, seizing, and reconfiguring constitute the dynamic capabilities a servitized firm needs to deliver service innovation effectively.

Studies About Categorization of Servitization Barriers

From the first appearance of the concept of servitization of manufacturing in literature (Vandermerwe & Rada, 1988), scholars have been committed to better understand the main barriers to its implementation. Over the years these barriers have been explored from different perspectives, which may concern their types and nature (Rabetino et al., 2017), and companies' distinctive characteristics (Confente et al., 2015) rather than stages of the service transformation process (Baines et al., 2017).

Among others, the work of Hou and Neely (2013) that summarized the results of a literature review conducted on 166 papers, identified seven main categories of barriers to create service excellence, namely: customers; organizational structure and culture; knowledge and information; products and activities; competitors, suppliers and partners; economic and finance; and society and environment. The work of Lütjen et al. (2017) is complementary as it classifies servitization barriers into three main groups: (i) strategy-related barriers, (ii) market-related barriers, and (iii) implementation-related barriers.

Strategic barriers are often associated with the cannibalization of existing businesses within the firm's portfolio (Benedettini et al., 2017). In other words, they describe the difficulties that top management encounters when it has to decide how to allocate its resources to develop a service business, trying to capture new portions of the market without eroding the existing business. Market-related barriers concern the difficulty for customers (Wang et al., 2016) and partners to accept the process of service transformation, due to their existing behaviors and usage habits (Steinberger et al., 2009; White et al., 1999). Finally, implementation-related barriers concern the way organizations develop their strategy to deal with a servitization journey effectively and efficiently. This group of barriers, according to Hou and Neely (2013) includes adaptations to customer value propositions, organization of delivery systems, skills and capabilities required, and organizational structures, as well as customers' and partners' relationships (Christopher, 2004; Martinez et al., 2010; Visnjic Kastalli & Van Looy, 2013) as they are becoming integrated into the customer's processes with their knowledge, skills and resources (Vargo & Lusch, 2008). In particular, changing the mindset to service is fundamental where customization, flexibility, and innovation are becoming more and more important (Turunen & Toivonen, 2011).

Theoretical Model

The main results of existing studies available in literature on the identification and categorization servitization barriers, were refined through the results of interviews conducted with the service managers and associates from industry. These were used to build a general model to group together servitization barriers and help develop appropriate guidelines for managerial actions to address those servitization barriers (Fig. 1). The approach is based on the assumption of a strategy with a clearly defined vision for servitization within the firm.

As we intended to assess how firms organize their operations to effectively address servitization barriers, we adopted a dynamic capabilities perspective (Teece et al., 1997). Accordingly, our model was built on the three categories suggested by Kindström et al. (2013), and further expanded by taking into account the origin of the impetus for managerial action, i.e., whether it is: (i) internal, when the perception of the problem emerges from within the company or (ii) external, when the issue is detected externally by the company, i.e., in the network or in the ecosystem where it operates (Table 1).

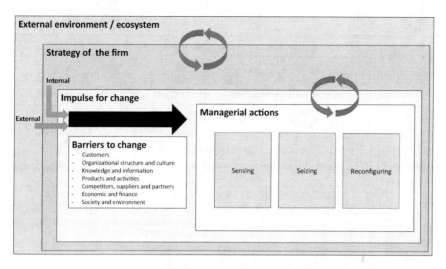

Fig. 1 Interrelationships between the external environment and wider ecosystem, strategy of the firm and the actions necessary to support changes and overcome barriers (Based on, Teece et al. [1997], Kindström et al. [2013], and on Hou and Neely [2013])

Table 1 Examples of individual actions to overcome organizational barriers (based on Hou and Neely [2013], and West and Gaiardelli [2016])

Categories	Examples of barriers faced by management
Competitors, suppliers, and partners	Expanding your capabilities
	Coordinating cooperation in the supply chain
	Transforming agents and distributors into service partners
	Developing a common (business) language
	Transforming our partners into a service force
	Managing measurement performance with your partners
	Working with installers
Society and environment	Converting free to fee (change internal and external mentalities)
	Dealing with conflicting demands to standardize and localize
	Managing long-term contractual commitments at corporate level with local laws
	Identifying the main legal implications for our organization
	Understanding tax and transfer pricing issues
Customers	Having effective sales for services
	Coordinating (process) cooperation with our customers/end users
	Reaching the end user when the equipment is sold via an installer/external partner
	Promoting our solution to the end user when the equipment/service is delivered via an external partner
	Our customers explicitly ask us for new services
	Managing our delivery when our customers want to perform some of the service tasks themselves

(continued)

Table 1 (continued)

Categories	Examples of barriers faced by management
Economic and finance	Moving away from cost plus, or time and materials-based pricing
	Considering margins and price effectively
	Managing the margin reduction that occurs due to more service (spares have high margins)
	Developing our service business when we have no cash to invest
	Managing dealer discounts better
Knowledge and information	Shareing know-how more effectively
	Share service feedback with the equipment designers in a better way
	Identify new project management skills needed for services
	Learn more about the equipment operation
	Mix know-how from installers and customers
Products and activities	Professionalizing service delivery
	Understanding the installed base
	Designing and delivering advanced services
	Developing services that support new equipment sales
	Developing digital services at customer's request
Organizational structure and culture	Educating managers who do not think of service as a real business
	Geting R&D to consider the whole equipment lifecycle
	Obtaining top management involvement
	Educating HR and employees
	Helping the firm to see service as a real business unit (BU) with a profit and loss sheet
	Reducing internal resistance to developing a service business

Analysis of Results

This section outlines how the management of a servitized company implements its day-to-day actions for efficient and effective product-service solutions. This is within the context of the constraints imposed upon the firms that restrict individual action in responding (Rungtusanatham & Salvador, 2008). The examples are given in Table 2 for organizational barriers and Table 3 for external barriers. The examples are based on 40+ interviews, and survey data from over 150 individuals (West et al. 2019) are categorized according to Hou and Neely (2013) and explored according to Lütjen et al. (2017).

Table 2 Examples of individual actions to overcome organizational barriers

Category	Sensing: new approaches to opportunity discovery	Seizing: capitalizing on service innovation opportunities	Reconfiguring: shifting the competitive arena
Organizational structure and culture	Initiative came from the CEO and the top management to double their service business	A manager seized the opportunity to convert a loss-making manufacturing facility into a service center with the aim to grow volume and margins in service	Introduced an organizational structure supported the service business, demonstrating that was no longer a second priority
Products and services	The firm invested in R&D to develop service solutions that are independent of the product, but essential to the product lifecycle	A group within the commercial team took the lead to sell the new services for the whole of the product lifecycle	Sales for lifecycle services were separated from the traditional transactional service business. The team was supported with technical input to help create modular solutions
Knowledge and information	Tracking the products allowed the company to see where they are located and what they are used for, to provide the end users with customized services throughout the entire lifecycle of the product	Using the data generated, the firm gained new insights into how customers were using the equipment, this helped to create triggers for sales and pro-active support services	Focus on operational insights to establish a new level of transparency in performance, resulting in a restructuring of operations to allow employees to engage in the service business

(continued)

Table 2 (continued)

Category	Sensing: new approaches to opportunity discovery	Seizing: capitalizing on service innovation opportunities	Reconfiguring: shifting the competitive arena
Customers	The firm invested in developing service solutions that would maintain the performance of their product throughout the lifecycle based on customer and field service feedback	Developed an innovative service offer, that was independent of their traditional product portfolio, and in doing so reduced the downtime for their customers during maintenance	By co-creating service offers the firm was able to win customers' trust and develop a long-term relationship with them. This was hard to achieve initially, as service customers were the owners and operators of the equipment, whereas the new equipment business' customers were the installers of the equipment
Competitors, suppliers, and partners	The company had a headcount cap but staff were told to grow sales	Growing sales without headcount results in more spares sales. The innovation was based around this, and a leader asked if the business could work more effectively with supply chain partners to achieve the "unachievable"	A manager fostered a closer relationship with a selection of installers to support them better when bidding for equipment to go into new projects, to install them correctly, and to provide ongoing support. The firm gained product and ongoing service sales while improving customer satisfaction

Category	Sensing: new approaches to opportunity discovery	Seizing: capitalizing on service innovation opportunities	Reconfiguring: shifting the competitive arena
Economic and finance	The company brought all the service business under one department with a separate P&L statement, to show that the service business is profitable and worth the investment. This helped them acquire a higher budget for their transformation, which is a necessary investment in the initial stages of servitization	The service business moved to focus on cash generation from services rather than focusing mainly on the margin. This was necessary because as the firm grew service sales, the spares margins were diluted	By having wider delegation with pricing, the firm moved away from a cost-plus pricing strategy. This resulted in improved finance performance and less effort in the quoting process
Society and environment	The firm worked to develop an environment where sharing was normal and valued it rather than considered it as a distraction. Doing so supported the development of better solutions and reduced risks in the firm	Long-term contractual agreements were developed and became an important part of the business. They needed to be executed locally but held centrally to allow the firm to gain the maximum value from them and improve the customer experience	A service center manager created a new opportunity by collaborating with other locations. As well as creating business value it created social value within the firm

Table 3 Examples of individual actions to overcome external barriers

Barrier	Sensing: new approaches to opportunity discovery	Seizing: capitalizing on service innovation opportunities	Reconfiguring: shifting the competitive arena
Organizational structure and culture	Benchmarking showed that some firms with effective servitization strategies had separate service (business) development functions	A manager set up a service-focused development program. The development was funded on a bootstrap basis	Service managers searched for possible new services that they could develop based on current customer problems. This was counter to the traditional culture in the firm where development was centrally directed
Products and services	Customers complained that services were not "professional" in the way they were delivered	A manager linked up the service development with the front link staff, to create a direct channel to speed up innovation	A service manager used journey mapping to identify both the actors and their touchpoints, starting an improvement of customer experience
Knowledge and information	Customers were correct with their statements that the firm did not know-how the equipment was actually operated and maintained. Sales were supposed to lead with capturing operational information	A database of the installed base was set up and segmented, using customer outcomes and mindsets. This was based on a modified CRM platform	In one service shop sales taught the other staff in the workshop how to share information and how to then use the CRM system so that lessons could be more widely shared

Barrier	Sensing: new approaches to opportunity discovery	Seizing: capitalizing on service innovation opportunities	Reconfiguring: shifting the competitive arena
Customers	A competitor analysis showed that digital servicing was gaining momentum within the market. While there are only small players offering digital services in the market, major players had started to actively invest in digitalization and were looking to implement servitization	To move into the new areas the firm acquired a service business, whose reputation for excellence among the customers makes it possible to introduce and expand the service portfolio into a purely manufacturing firm	Following the acquisition, a local manager started to collaborate with the new colleagues to provide a new offer for our combined customers
Competitors, suppliers, and partners	A competitor asked the firm to service the customer's equipment as they could not do it due to not having a local service center for the customer	New models based on do-it-yourself, do-it-with-me, and do-it-together were developed to allow customer or third-party integration into the service delivery	By having more degrees of freedom, one service center trained their agents to deliver routine maintenance and troubleshooting, thereby improving customer experience
Economic and finance	Understanding tax and transfer pricing issues to allow the company to "think global = act local," without this change, sharing resources would have been all but impossible	Tax and cash flow were added as additional dimensions for innovation within advanced service contracts. They needed to be executed locally but held centrally to gain the maximum value from them and to improve the customer experience	In a service shop, the manager changed cash flow for a repair project to match the customer's income. In doing so, risk was reduced and margins increased

(continued)

Table 3 (continued)

Barrier	Sensing: new approaches to opportunity discovery	Seizing: capitalizing on service innovation opportunities	Reconfiguring: shifting the competitive arena
Society and environment	Customers complained about service not being delivered in a professional way, yet they received the services for free. Deeper feedback confirmed that customers would be willing to pay for some services if delivered professionally	The firm moved from fee to free and would charge the "customer" for the services provided. Innovation was based around what customers valued and what they would pay for	By telling sales that they could provide services for free, but their cost would be taken from the sales budget changed mindsets. Many new "hidden" services were identified

3   Supporting Servitization Change Management

Empirical evidence suggests that barriers to servitization may differ in type and nature and that there is no common pattern. Indeed, firms will have different starting points, although in general the process begins with a strategic decision made by senior management. This is in line with much of the change literature (Pettigrew, 1988; Pye & Pettigrew, 2005; Whipp et al., 1989) that states there is no one "right way" to deliver a change program. The motivation can come from a strategic choice to move into services (Baines et al., 2009; Gebauer, 2007, Mathieu, 2001b), from a change in the market, or from an acquisition process. Indeed, managerial actions may differ in time and methods, depending not only on the nature of the barrier, but also on where the impetus for change comes from (internally or externally) and on the awareness of each individual manager in understanding the situation and adapting its choices to the context in which the firm is operating operates. Nevertheless, the study suggests that individual actions can be adapted on a systematic basis by management to tackle and overcome them, supporting the execution of the strategy and its ongoing evolution.

On these premises and on the basis of what has been learned from successful experiences, a guideline has been developed to support the initiation of individual actions to deal with servitization barriers in a structured way. The guideline (Fig. 2) consists of five main steps and assumes that a strategy for service has already been defined. The five steps are:

i. **Identify the barriers**—service managers should identify the barriers to developing service excellence. It is anticipated that many barriers are likely to be found. These are within the strategic environment of the firm and can be internal or external to the firm.

ii. **Categorize the service barriers**—the barriers should then be categorized and segmented into internal and external barriers.

iii. **Assess the barriers**—for each barrier confirm its importance (e.g., 1: not important, 3: important, 5: critical) and its maturity (e.g., 1: employees have no awareness, no processes in place, 3: employees have some awareness, some processes, 5: employees are fully aware, and processes are used and improved). This will help to show the key barriers to focus upon.

iv. **Prioritize the barriers**—following the identification of the key barriers to focus upon, take them, and place them on a 2 × 2 matrix with the axes of effort and importance necessary to overcome the barrier. This will help you identify how best to schedule the actions.

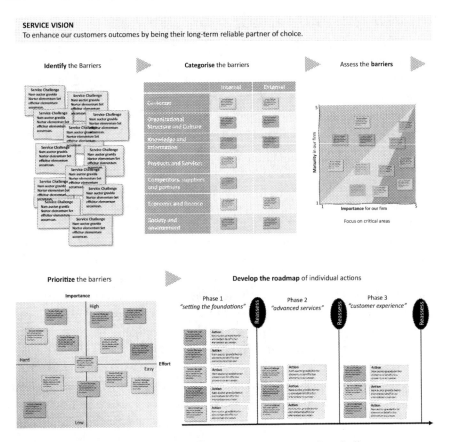

Fig. 2 A framework to create a roadmap to overcome service challenges

v. **Develop the roadmap of individual actions**—once you have priori-
tized the barriers all the individual actions necessary to overcome each
barrier need to be scheduled on a roadmap. The roadmap should be
divided into phases where you have around three–five barriers and their
actions assigned to each phase. Name each phase based on what its focus
and define the duration for each phase. At the end of each phase, it is
important to reassess the barriers and their actions, so the road map can
be revised, providing an opportunity to re-adjust and redefine the next
actions.

Theoretical Contribution

This chapter builds upon the theoretical framework of West et al. (2019) based on over 150 surveys and 40 interview insights (with over 40 h of recordings) and provides a guideline to building a road map to support a firm's servitization strategy. The study confirms Hou and Neely's (2013) point of view about servitization barriers and provides practical support for the assessment of the operational challenges. Integrating the work of Kindström et al. (2013), it also shows how it is possible to link individual managerial actions to support the strategic vision and in doing so uses the change management theory of Teece et al. (1997). The approach is also in agreement with both the prior works of Alghisi and Saccani (2015) and Gebauer (2009) and confirms that leaders have practical challenges in implementing servitization strategies in their organizations. Finally, integrating the approach with a framework that supports service leaders to build an actionable roadmap focused on change management is new, and allows the research to be implemented in a way to support rather than observe servitization change management.

Managerial Implications

The development of a guideline to support the development of a roadmap that supports a firm's servitization strategy has been described. The guideline allows mangers and leaders to overcome barriers that are important in their firm though individual actions. The guideline offers a structured approach to building an individual roadmap for the firm. This is important, as the literature confirms that there is not a single standardized approach to the process of servitization for a firm, due to the multitude of contextual issues. The choice to embark on the process of servitization is strategic, and we believe that the roadmap that is produced as a result of the framework will support firms to successfully deliver that strategy through a well-designed change management roadmap.

References

Alghisi, A., & Saccani, N. (2015). Internal and external alignment in the servitization journey-overcoming the challenges. *Production Planning and Control*. https://doi.org/10.1080/09537287.2015.1033496.

Baines, T., Ziaee Bigdeli, A., Bustinza, O. F., Shi, V. G., Baldwin, J., & Ridgway, K. (2017). Servitization: Revisiting the state-of-the-art and research priorities.

International Journal of Operations and Production Management. https://doi.org/10.1108/IJOPM-06-2015-0312.

Baines, T., & Shi, V. G. (2015). A Delphi study to explore the adoption of servitization in UK companies. *Production Planning and Control.* https://doi.org/10.1080/09537287.2015.1033490.

Baines, T., Lightfoot, H., Peppard, J., Johnson, M., Tiwari, A., Shehab, E., & Swink, M. (2009). Towards an operations strategy for product-centric servitization. *International Journal of Operations and Production Management.* https://doi.org/10.1108/01443570910953603.

Benedettini, O., Swink, M., & Neely, A. (2017). Examining the influence of service additions on manufacturing firms' bankruptcy likelihood. *Industrial Marketing Management.* https://doi.org/10.1016/j.indmarman.2016.04.011.

Brax, S. (2005). A manufacturer becoming service provider: Challenges and a paradox. *Managing Service Quality.* https://doi.org/10.1108/09604520510585334.

Christopher, M. (2004). *Logistics and supply chain management: Creating value added networks.* Financial Times/Prentice Hall.

Confente, I., Buratti, A., & Russo, I. (2015). The role of servitization for small firms: Drivers versus barriers. *International Journal of Entrepreneurship and Small Business, 26*(3), 312–331. https://doi.org/10.1504/IJESB.2015.072394.

Gebauer, H. (2007). The logic for increasing service revenue in product manufacturing companies. *International Journal of Services and Operations Management.* https://doi.org/10.1504/IJSOM.2007.013462.

Gebauer, H. (2009). An attention-based view on service orientation in the business strategy of manufacturing companies. *Journal of Managerial Psychology.* https://doi.org/10.1108/02683940910922555.

Gebauer, H., T. Friedli., E., & Fleisch, E. (2005). Overcoming the service paradox in manufacturing companies. *European Management Journal 23*(1): 14–26.

Hou, J., & Neely, A. (2013). Barriers of servitization: Results of a systematic literature review. In T. Baines, B. Clegg, & D. Harrison (Eds.), *Spring servitization conference.* Proceedings of the 2013 Spring Servitization conference "Servitization in the multi-organisation enterprise" (pp. 189–195).

Kindström, D., Kowalkowski, C., & Sandberg, E. (2013). Enabling service innovation: A dynamic capabilities approach. *Journal of Business Research.* https://doi.org/10.1016/j.jbusres.2012.03.003.

Kohtamäki, M., Einola, S., & Rabetino, R. (2020). Exploring servitization through the paradox lens: Coping practices in servitization. *International Journal of Production Economics.* https://doi.org/10.1016/j.ijpe.2020.107619.

Lenka, S., Parida, V., Sjödin, D. R., & Wincent, J. (2018). Exploring the microfoundations of servitization: How individual actions overcome organizational resistance. *Journal of Business Research.* https://doi.org/10.1016/j.jbusres.2017.11.021.

Lütjen, H., Tietze, F., & Schultz, C. (2017). Service transitions of product-centric firms: An explorative study of service transition stages and barriers in Germany's energy market. *International Journal of Production Economics*. https://doi.org/10. 1016/j.ijpe.2017.03.021.

Martinez, V., Bastl, M., Kingston, J., & Evans, S. (2010). Challenges in transforming manufacturing organisations into product-service providers. *Journal of Manufacturing Technology Management*. https://doi.org/10.1108/174103810110 46571.

Mathieu, V. (2001a). Service strategies within the manufacturing sector: Benefits, costs and partnership. *International Journal of Service Industry Management*. https://doi.org/10.1108/EUM0000000006093.

Mathieu, V. (2001b). Product services: From a service supporting the product to a service supporting the client. *Journal of Business and Industrial Marketing*. https:// doi.org/10.1108/08858620110364873.

Oliva, R., Gebauer, H., & Brann, J. M. (2012). Separate or integrate? Assessing the impact of separation between product and service business on service performance in product manufacturing firms. *Journal of Business-to-Business Marketing*. https://doi.org/10.1080/1051712X.2012.647797.

Pettigrew, A. M. (1988). *The management of strategic change*. John Wiley and Sons Ltd.

Pye, A., & Pettigrew, A. (2005). Studying board context, process and dynamics: Some challenges for the future. *British Journal of Management*. https://doi.org/ 10.1111/j.1467-8551.2005.00445.x.

Rabetino, R., Kohtamäki, M., & Gebauer, H. (2017). Strategy map of servitization. *International Journal of Production Economics*. https://doi.org/10.1016/j.ijpe. 2016.11.004.

Rungtusanatham, M. J., & Salvador, F. (2008). From mass production to mass customization: Hindrance factors, structural inertia, and transition hazard. *Production and Operations Management*. https://doi.org/10.3401/poms.1080. 0025.

Steinberger, J. K., van Niel, J., & Bourg, D. (2009). Profiting from megawatts: Reducing absolute consumption and emissions through a performance-based energy economy. *Energy Policy*. https://doi.org/10.1016/j.enpol.2008.08.030.

Teece, D. J., Pisano, G., & Shuen, A. (1997). Dynamic capabilities and strategic management. *Strategic Management Journal*, *18*(7), 509–533.

Turunen, T. T., & Toivonen, M. (2011). Organizing customer-oriented service business in manufacturing. *Operations Management Research*. https://doi.org/10. 1007/s12063-011-0047-5.

Valtakoski, A. (2017). Explaining servitization failure and deservitization: A knowledge-based perspective. *Industrial Marketing Management*. https://doi.org/ 10.1016/j.indmarman.2016.04.009.

Vandermerwe, S., & Rada, J. (1988). Servitization of business: Adding value by adding services. *European Management Journal*. https://doi.org/10.1016/0263-2373(88)90033-3.

Vargo, S. L., & Lusch, R. F. (2008). Service-dominant logic: Continuing the evolution. *Journal of the Academy of marketing Science, 36,* 1–10. https://doi.org/10.1007/s11747-007-0069-6.

Visnjic Kastalli, I., & Van Looy, B. (2013). Servitization: Disentangling the impact of service business model innovation on manufacturing firm performance. *Journal of Operations Management.* https://doi.org/10.1016/j.jom.2013.02.001.

Wang, Q., Zhao, X., & Voss, C. (2016). Customer orientation and innovation: A comparative study of manufacturing and service firms. *International Journal of Production Economics.* https://doi.org/10.1016/j.ijpe.2015.08.029.

West, S., & Gaiardelli, P. (2016). Driving the servitization transformation through change management: Lessons learnt from industrial cases. In T. Baines, J. Burton, D. Harrison, & J. Zolkiewski (Eds.), *Proceedings of the 2016 Spring Servitization Conference 2016 "Servitization: Shift, Transform, Grow"* (pp. 209–216). Manchester Business School.

West, S.S. & Gaiardelli, P. (2017). Driving The Servitization Transformation Through Change Management: Lessons Learnt From Ten Industrial Cases. *Frontiers in Service 2017*, Fordham University. New York.

West, S., Gaiardelli, P., Bigdeli, A., & Baines, T. (2018). Exploring operational challenges for servitization: An European Survey. In A. Bigdeli, T. Frandsen, J. Raja, & T. Baines (Eds.), *Proceedings of 2018 Spring Servitization Conference "Driving Competitiveness through Servitization"* (pp. 9–17).

West, S., Gaiardelli, P., & Mathews, A. (2019). Overcoming the challenges of change management associated with servitization: Lessons from 20 practical cases. In A. Z. Bigdeli, C. Kowalkowski, D. Kindström, & T. Baines (Eds.), *Proceedings of 2018 Spring Servitization Conference "The Spring Servitization Conference 2019: Delivering Services Growth in the Digital Era"* (pp. 9–17).

West, S., Schmitt, P., & Siepen, S. A. (2014). A comparative assessment of the service cultures of industrial businesses in the DACH region of Europe and their impact on business performance. In *Proceedings of the 2014 EUROMA Conference "Operations Management in an Innovation Economy"* Palermo June 2014.

Whipp, R., Rosenfeld, R., & Pettigrew, A. (1989). Managing strategic change in a mature business. *Long Range Planning.* https://doi.org/10.1016/0024-6301(89)90106-4.

White, A., Stoughton, M., & Feng, L. (1999). *Servicizing: The quiet transition to extended product responsibility.* Tellus Institute.

Zott, C., Amit, R., & Massa, L. (2011). The business model: Recent developments and future research. *Journal of Management.* https://doi.org/10.1177/0149206311406265.

Employee Reactions to Servitization as an Organizational Transformation

Mădălina Pană and Melanie E. Kreye

1   Introduction

When managing the organizational transition from offering products to services, employee engagement and buy-into the servitization strategy is a core determinant of the success of the transformation. However, upon commencing such a transition, a lack of service employees (Burton et al., 2017; Lütjen et al., 2017) as well as difficulties retaining skilled and trained service specialists (Huikkola et al., 2016) present major impediments for traditional manufacturers to overcome to integrate services into their businesses. Although the specific needs of each industry and organization may vary, focusing on employees is justified due to the necessity of aligning their operational roles and competencies with the future service practices (Baines et al., 2013; Lütjen et al., 2017). More specifically, organizational transformation involves changes that require employees to respond to a new set of job requirements and perform in the context of a different business approach.

M. Pană (✉) · M. E. Kreye
Department of Technology, Management and Economics,
Technical University of Denmark (DTU Management), Kongens Lyngby,
Denmark
e-mail: mpana@dtu.dk

M. E. Kreye
e-mail: mkreye@dtu.dk

M. Kohtamäki et al. (eds.), *The Palgrave Handbook of Servitization*,
https://doi.org/10.1007/978-3-030-75771-7_21

327

In this context, the reactions of employees, visible in the level and direction of their efforts during the transformation (Herscovitch & Meyer, 2002), are divided between two extremes, support and rejection, with resistance in the middle (Rese & Maiwald, 2013).

The role of managers in identifying and handling employees' reactions is critical for engaging employees in the organizational transformation process (Bareil & Gagnon, 2005; Oreg et al., 2011). Identifying the type of employee reaction (support, resistance, or rejection) enables managers to recognize the relevant stakeholders that could be called "change agents" in the process (Oreg et al., 2011; Rese & Maiwald, 2013), and then, enabling these key stakeholders to engage in the organizational transformation drives the success of the process (Bel et al., 2018).

This chapter seeks to answer the following research question: *How can employee reactions to the organizational transformation of servitization be managed to encourage employee engagement?* We present a review of the literature on servitization, organizational behavior, and organizational psychology to connect employee reactions to servitization to management responses directed toward gaining employees engagement. We integrate these insights into a framework of employee reactions in servitization.

2   Theory Development

Employee reactions can range from support for the servitization strategy to rejection of it, which becomes evident in voluntary turnover (Ulaga & Loveland, 2014). Between the two extreme points is resistance, which can be used in a positive manner if management responds to it appropriately (Ford et al., 2008). Bareil and Gagnon (2005) describe a continuous approach for helping employees contribute to an organizational transformation, consisting of clarifying employees' reasons of concerns during the organizational transformation and responding with suitable management practices for helping employees involved in the transformation. For clarifying employees' reasons of concerns, management attention is directed toward observing and categorizing employees' reactions during the organizational transformation. In this section, we review the relevant literature on employee reactions and management responses to determine how to encourage employee engagement in the servitization journey. Figure 1 depicts the link between employee reactions, suitable management responses, and resultant employee engagement based on the continuous approach by Bareil and Gagnon (2005).

Fig. 1 Framework of employee reactions, suitable management responses, and employee engagement

Support for Servitization

Support as reaction. Employee support for servitization can vary substantially (Herscovitch & Meyer, 2002). Support may consist of following rules and procedures related to the transformation even without fully agreeing with the implemented changes (compliance with change). For example, administrative staff members responsible for back-office service processes may be willing to provide necessary information for service operations without actively supporting in the new business strategy (Kreye, 2016). By contrast, at the highest level of effort, employee support may entail a desire to assist the process of change and promote it within the organization (championing the change process) (Herscovitch & Meyer, 2002). This often describes the attitude of service engineers who go out to customer sites and engage in service-based collaboration (Kreye et al., 2015). In addition, employees high level of support toward the organizational transformation of servitization is also visible in their efforts in exploring and identifying service business growth opportunities (Baines et al., 2020). Between the extreme points, a moderate degree of employee support requires making some sacrifices to advance the organizational transformation in terms of engaging in cooperative behavior (Herscovitch & Meyer, 2002); for example, marketing employees may need to collaborate with customers because of the often broader value proposition provided by services instead of products (Vargo & Lusch, 2008).

Suitable management responses. Supportive employees can be a vital resource in the organizational transition because they can champion the change process. Here, the focus is on involving supportive employees to reduce the cultural and process barriers of servitization (Lenka et al., 2018). In addition, supportive employees may be further engaged as leaders in the servitized business (Rabetino et al., 2017). Nonetheless, despite the range of employee support for servitization, organizational transformation generally requires active support to effectively allocate the resources necessary to achieve the expected service quality (Baik et al., 2019) and reduce internal barriers such as a product-focused culture, doubts, and values that decrease servitization efforts (Lenka et al., 2018). Active support must be based on employees having a shared identity with the organization and their corresponding subunit (Rese & Maiwald, 2013), and it may be easier to create employee support in organizational units that are close to service-based activities, such as marketing. For marketing employees, the transition from products to services presents the opportunity to focus on how service offerings create customer value and then advertising such services accordingly—this is the key role of marketing (Vargo & Lusch, 2004). Hence, the service orientation of an organization aligns its advertising requirements with the principles of marketing, which in turn establishes the necessary motivation that helps employees to actively support the service business.

Rejection of Servitization and Voluntary Turnover

Rejection and voluntary turnover. At the complete opposite pole of employee support is the rejection of the servitization strategy, where employees choose to leave the organization because of disagreement with the organizational transformation. Voluntary turnover can hence be seen as rejection of the adoption of the service business approach (Ulaga & Loveland, 2014). Specific observable behaviors that predict voluntary turnover, such as initial lateness and subsequent absence from work (Harrison et al., 2006), can be used as indicators for future rejection of organizational transformation.

The reasons for rejecting organizational transformation toward servitization tend to be related to a lack of service-related competencies. For example, Ulaga and Loveland (2014) acknowledged the challenge faced by sales employees, skilled in selling products, in replying to the demands of service sales. Similarly, changes in the operational requirements of their work may cause employees to reject the transformation. For example, although technical specialists may have the required competencies to provide services, having to travel more frequently for work due to their position as frontline employees may lead to voluntary turnover (Zarpelon Neto et al., 2015). Thus, rejection may be a sign of various employee concerns regarding the organizational transformation.

Suitable management responses. In contending with rejection behaviors, such as voluntary turnover, suitable managerial responses can be divided into two categories. First, employee intentions can be measured before the actual behavior is observed to identify the general predisposition of employees (Morrell et al., 2004). For example, Bothma and Roodt (2013) demonstrated that turnover intention is a realistic predictor of actual turnover behavior.

In addition, they validated a specific scale that measures turnover intention through, for instance, frequency of thoughts related to leaving one's employment as well as the level of enthusiasm for the upcoming working days. This first approach offers a meaningful management tool for predicting and preparing for employee turnover. Second, managers can attempt to learn the reasons for employee turnover once it has occurred (Morrell et al., 2004). This consists of understanding individual reasons for leaving. Both management responses enable the organization to learn from the initial rejection of the organizational transformation and improve internal functioning and processes (Morrell et al., 2004).

Resistance to Servitization

Resistance as reaction. Between the two poles of employee reaction depicted above is resistance, which describes the effort involved in opposing the organizational transformation. Herscovitch and Meyer (2002) described two levels of resistance in terms of active and passive resistance. In active resistance, employees make strong efforts to ensure that the organizational transformation will not be implemented. This can be observed in disruptive behaviors, such as sales employees' actively arguing for the value of product sales by citing their higher profit margins and continued opportunities for business growth (Reinartz & Ulaga, 2008). By contrast, passive resistance is visible in employee efforts that are directed toward diminishing the potential of succeeding with the transformation (Herscovitch & Meyer, 2002). For example, sales employees may continue engaging in product sales because they are more familiar with this process (Ulaga & Loveland, 2014). This behavior demonstrates passive resistance because it indicates that employees may prefer the product (traditional) business and attribute less value and importance to the new service business (Matthyssens & Vandenbempt, 2010).

A possible reason for resistance may be employees' fear of leaving their comfort zone. For example, sales employees may be uncomfortable with service sales approaches that require networking, joint decision-making between various stakeholders, and discussions with points of contact that are in leadership positions (Ulaga & Loveland, 2014). In addition, the resistance of sales employees may arise from concerns about losing their traditional commission (Reinartz & Ulaga, 2008). In some cases, the transition from products to services requires a transition from free services to paid services, which increases the discomfort and resistance of sales employees who used free services to foster positive customer interactions (Ulaga & Loveland, 2014).

Suitable management responses. To handle employee resistance, managers of the organizational transformation may adopt two primary approaches. First, managers can use the resistance positively to create awareness and keep organizational transformation as a recurring topic of discussion (Ford et al., 2008). Assessing resistance can be a helpful means of analyzing the feasibility of the organizational transformation (Kets De Vries & Balazs, 1999) and for revising and reconsidering managerial decisions regarding implementation decisions (Ford et al., 2008). Second, managers can use specific responses to mitigate the resistance and support the service business. Reinartz and Ulaga (2008) stressed the importance of supporting sales employees through training to assist them in overcoming their comfort with their product-related roles to become able to support the service buyer's decision-making. In addition, they emphasized the necessity of hiring specialized employees that support the service sales, such as service engineers with knowledge about customer operations. Reinforcing the focus on services can be supported by projects and internal communication developed around the service culture (Rabetino et al., 2017).

Table 1 provides an overview of the three described employee reactions and possible management responses based on the literature on servitization, organizational behavior, and organizational psychology. It summarizes the key points for understanding employee reactions in the context of servitization.

Employee Engagement

Employee engagement is visible in employees' presence in their individual roles at the cognitive, emotional, and physical levels (Kahn, 1990). Specifically, presence in one's working role refers to authentically sharing personal thoughts, feelings, ideas, and so forth (Kahn, 1992), which requires both cognitive and emotional effort. However, due to the difficulties of evaluating the intensity and availability of personal effort in a working role, Macey and Schneider (2008) propose looking for observable engagement behaviors such as *"innovative behaviors, demonstrations of initiative, proactively seeking opportunities to contribute, and going beyond what is, within specific frames of reference, typically expected or required"* (p. 15). Taking the initiative to identify and create opportunities to contribute within the organization is critical in servitization due to the necessity of having employees prepared to learn and grow within a changing business environment (Martinez et al., 2017). In addition, service quality depends on the performers of the service-related task (Levitt, 1972; Kreye, 2016; Baik et al., 2019), and thus, it is crucial for employees to be engaged in their working roles and in the organization.

Table 1 Employee reactions and suitable responses of managers in servitization transformation

Reaction	Support for servitization	Resistance to servitization	Rejection of servitization and voluntary turnover
Definition and description	• Effort oriented toward accepting servitization or even helping the service business to succeed	• Efforts directed toward opposing the new service and diminishing the potential to succeed in the organizational transformation	• Withdrawal from an organization that does not follow the traditional business model
Observable behavior	• Complying with the new business requirement (Herscovitch & Meyer, 2002) • Active support for the new process and operations at customer sites (Kreye et al., 2015)	• Insisting on product-sales procedures and the potential to grow the products market to avoid engagement with service sales approach (Reinartz & Ulaga, 2008) • Using typical, well-known sales approaches that focus on characteristics of the products. (Ulaga & Reinartz, 2011)	• Manifesting a lack of interest and effort through counterproductive behaviors such as delays and absenteeism (Harrison et al., 2006)
Possible reasons for reaction	• Shared identity with the organization and the subunit to which one belongs (Rese & Maiwald, 2013)	• Fear of not being in control in the new service-sales approach (Ulaga & Loveland, 2014) • Fear of losing commissions from product sales (Reinartz & Ulaga, 2008) • Discomfort due to charging for formerly free added services (Ulaga & Loveland, 2014)	• Lack of necessary competencies for service-related demands (Ulaga & Loveland, 2014) • Increase in necessary frequency of travel as a demand of the service business (Zarpelon Neto et al., 2015)

(continued)

Table 1 (continued)

Reaction	Support for servitization	Resistance to servitization	Rejection of servitization and voluntary turnover
Suitable responses from management	• Involvement of supportive employees in reducing the internal resistance (Lenka et al., 2018) • Delegation of leadership roles to supportive employees who actively engage in helping the servitization journey (Rabetino et al., 2017)	• Acknowledgment of reasons for resistance with the aim of improving the decision-making process (Ford et al., 2008) • Specific responses, such as training and hiring specialized personnel to support the sales employees (Reinartz & Ulaga, 2008) • Promoting a service culture through projects and internal communication (Rabetino et al., 2017)	• Measurement of employee turnover intentions and clarification of the reasons for their turnover behavior (Morrell et al., 2004)

3   Discussion

This section explains the main value of the insights regarding employee reactions both from a theoretical perspective (section "Theoretical Contribution") and practical perspective (section "Managerial Implications"). We further discuss the main challenges for future work in this context.

Theoretical Contribution

This chapter contributes to the theory on servitization by providing insights into employee reactions and suitable management responses to encourage or create employee engagement during the organizational transformation. This is based on an integration of the literature on organizational behavior and organizational psychology with descriptions and observations in servitization. This chapter hence illuminates and specifies employee reactions, which have thus far been described and observed in the servitization literature (Buschmeyer et al., 2016; Huikkola et al., 2016; Kreye, 2016) but have not explained in the underlying causes and reasons of employees. Showing the potential reasons for employee rejection of a servitization strategy, as well as support or resistance, this chapter offers unique insights into the organizational challenges when implementing servitization.

This chapter further offers valuable management approaches as a response to the different employee reactions. This is based on the explanations regarding underlying causes and reasons and hence identifies management responses based on robust reasoning utilizing insights from the organizational behavior and organizational psychology literature. This integration of related literature streams is a novel contribution to the servitization literature, which has thus far not been able to identify active management responses to employee reactions (Kreye, 2016). This chapter hence offers unique value and insights for management scholars and as well as servitization practitioners (elaborated in section "Managerial Implications").

Managerial Implications

The overview of management responses and related discussion yields concrete implications for management. To foster employee engagement, managers must first identify and understand the specific employee reaction they face, and then they can determine a suitable response. The detailed overview of the various employee reactions (Table 1) enables researchers to define observable patterns of employee behavior during the servitization journey. This is useful, especially for further operationalization of support, rejection, and resistance as reactions to the servitization. This enables managers to develop measurement tools as follows. When faced with employee support for the servitization journey, managers can acknowledge employees' contributions by involving them in removing the obstacles of the servitization and, in some cases, creating the opportunity for them to assume a leadership position within the service business to create employee engagement. When faced with employee rejection of the servitization journey, managers can approach this situation as a learning opportunity and evaluate the process of implementing servitization within the organization. In so doing, the effect of the organisational transformation as well as the extent to which employees are affected by the transformation can be clarified and considered in the process of managing the employees' transition to service operations. When dealing with resistance to servitization, managers can consider two suitable responses. Either they can learn about the concerns motivating the resistance and use them to improve the management of the organizational transformation, or they can emphasize the relevance of servitization through focusing specific attention on service culture and operational capabilities development. The first response allows employees to express their concerns and managers to see a different viewpoint, whereas the second response helps employees to develop their skills and to assimilate new working approaches.

If managers choose a suitable response for each employee reaction, they can benefit by gaining information and engagement for the proposed organizational transformation. This is critical in servitization due to the necessity of creating new operational capabilities while maintaining the focus on developing the new service business.

4   Conclusions

This chapter provides an overview of the range of employee reactions to the servitization transformation. On the basis of the presentation of an overview of the literature on organizational behavior and organizational psychology, we contribute core insights on employee reactions and management responses that can drive employee engagement into the discussion on servitization. For each long-term reaction, such as support, resistance, and rejection, we propose observable behaviors, reasons for these behaviors as well as management responses that could help the overall process of engaging the employees and gaining the internal support for developing the service capabilities. This chapter thus provides a distilled overview of the key points drawn from the existing literature. The presented key point further the theoretical insights into servitization as an organizational transformation and contribute to managerial perspectives by highlighting approaches that help employee engagement and servitization transformation.

References

Baik, K., Kim, K. Y., & Patel, P. C. (2019). The internal ecosystem of high performance work system and employee service-providing capability: A contingency approach for servitizing firms. *Journal of Business Research, 104,* 402–410. https://doi.org/10.1016/j.jbusres.2019.02.028.

Baines, T., Lightfoot, H., Smart, P., & Fletcher, S. (2013). Servitization of manufacture: Exploring the deployment and skills of people critical to the delivery of advanced services. *Journal of Manufacturing Technology Management, 24*(4), 637–646. https://doi.org/10.1108/17410381311327431.

Baines, T., Ziaee Bigdeli, A., Sousa, R., & Schroeder, A. (2020). Framing the servitization transformation process: A model to understand and facilitate the servitization journey. *International Journal of Production Economics, 221,* 107463. https://doi.org/10.1016/j.ijpe.2019.07.036.

Bareil, C., & Gagnon, J. (2005). Facilitating the individual capacity to change. *Gestion 2000, 22*(5), 177–194.

Bel, B. R., Smirnov, V., & Wait, A. (2018). Managing change: Communication, managerial style and change in organizations. *Economic Modelling, 69,* 1–12. https://doi.org/10.1016/J.ECONMOD.2017.09.001.

Bothma, C. F. C., & Roodt, G. (2013). The validation of the turnover intention scale. *SA Journal of Human Resource Management, 11*(1). https://doi.org/10.4102/sajhrm.v11i1.507.

Burton, J., Story, V. M., Raddats, C., & Zolkiewski, J. (2017). Overcoming the challenges that hinder new service development by manufacturers with diverse services strategies. *International Journal of Production Economics, 192,* 29–39. https://doi.org/10.1016/j.ijpe.2017.01.013.

Buschmeyer, A., Schuh, G., & Wentzel, D. (2016). Organizational transformation towards product-service systems – empirical evidence in Managing the Behavioral Transformation Process. *Procedia CIRP, 47,* 264–269. https://doi.org/10.1016/j.procir.2016.03.224.

Ford, J. D., Ford, L. W., & D'Amelio, A. (2008). Resistance to change: The rest of the story. *Academy of Management Review, 33*(2), 362–377. https://doi.org/10.5465/amr.2008.31193235.

Harrison, D. A., Newman, D. A., & Roth, P. L. (2006). How important are job attitudes? Meta-analytic comparisons of integrative behavioral outcomes and time sequences. *Academy of Management Journal, 49*(2), 305–325. https://doi.org/10. 5465/AMJ.2006.20786077.

Herscovitch, L., & Meyer, J. P. (2002). Commitment to organizational change: Extension of a three-component model. *Journal of Applied Psychology, 87*(3), 474–487. https://doi.org/10.1037/0021-9010.87.3.474.

Huikkola, T., Kohtamäki, M., & Rabetino, R. (2016). Resource realignment in servitization. *Research-Technology Management, 59*(4), 30–39. https://doi.org/10. 1080/08956308.2016.1185341.

Kahn, W. A. (1990). Psychological conditions of personal engagement and disengagement at work. *Academy of Management Journal, 33*(4), 692–724. https://doi. org/10.5465/256287.

Kahn, W. A. (1992). To be fully there: Psychological presence at work. *Human Relations, 45*(4), 321–349. https://doi.org/10.1177/001872679204500402.

Kets De Vries, M. F. R., & Balazs, K. (1999). Transforming the mind-set of the organization: A clinical perspective. *Administration and Society, 30*(6), 640–675. https://doi.org/10.1177/00953999922019030.

Kreye, M. E. (2016). Employee motivation in product-service system providers. *Production Planning and Control, 27*(15), 1249–1259. https://doi.org/10.1080/ 09537287.2016.1206219.

Kreye, M. E., Roehrich, J. K., & Lewis, M. A. (2015). Servitising manufacturers: the impact of service complexity and contractual and relational capabilities. *Production Planning and Control, 26*(14–15), 1233–1246. https://doi.org/10.1080/095 37287.2015.1033489.

Lenka, S., Parida, V., Sjödin, D. R., & Wincent, J. (2018). Exploring the microfoundations of servitization: How individual actions overcome organizational resistance. *Journal of Business Research, 88,* 328–336. https://doi.org/10.1016/j. jbusres.2017.11.021.

Levitt, T. (1972). Production-line approach to service. *Harvard Business Review, 50*(5), 41–52.

Lütjen, H., Tietze, F., & Schultz, C. (2017). Service transitions of product-centric firms: An explorative study of service transition stages and barriers in Germany's energy market. *International Journal of Production Economics, 192,* 106–119. https://doi.org/10.1016/j.ijpe.2017.03.021.

Macey, W. H., & Schneider, B. (2008). The meaning of employee engagement. *Industrial and Organizational Psychology, 1*(1), 3–30. https://doi.org/10.1111/j. 1754-9434.2007.0002.x.

Martinez, V., Neely, A., Velu, C., Leinster-Evans, S., & Bisessar, D. (2017). Exploring the journey to services. *International Journal of Production Economics, 192,* 66–80. https://doi.org/10.1016/j.ijpe.2016.12.030.

Matthyssens, P., & Vandenbempt, K. (2010). Service addition as business market strategy: Identification of transition trajectories. *Journal of Service Management, 21*(5), 693–714. https://doi.org/10.1108/09564231011079101.

Morrell, K. M., Loan-Clarke, J., & Wilkinson, A. J. (2004). Organisational change and employee turnover. *Personnel Review, 33*(2), 161–173. https://doi.org/10.1108/00483480410518022.

Oreg, S., Vakola, M., & Armenakis, A. (2011). Change recipients' reactions to organizational change: A 60-year review of quantitative studies. *The Journal of Applied Behavioral Science, 47*(4), 461–524. https://doi.org/10.1177/0021886310396550.

Rabetino, R., Kohtamäki, M., & Gebauer, H. (2017). Strategy map of servitization. *International Journal of Production Economics, 192*, 144–156. https://doi.org/10.1016/j.ijpe.2016.11.004.

Reinartz, W., & Ulaga, W. (2008). How to sell services more profitably. *Harvard Business Review, 86*(5), 90–96.

Rese, M., & Maiwald, K. (2013). The Individual Level of Servitization: Creating Employees' Service Orientation. *IFAC Proceedings Volumes, 46*(9), 2057–2062. https://doi.org/10.3182/20130619-3-RU-3018.00429.

Ulaga, W., & Loveland, J. M. (2014). Transitioning from product to service-led growth in manufacturing firms: Emergent challenges in selecting and managing the industrial sales force. *Industrial Marketing Management, 43*(1), 113–125. https://doi.org/10.1016/j.indmarman.2013.08.006.

Ulaga, W., & Reinartz, W. J. (2011). Hybrid offerings: How manufacturing firms combine goods and services successfully. *Journal of Marketing, 75*(6), 5–23. https://doi.org/10.1509/jm.09.0395.

Vargo, S. L., & Lusch, R. F. (2004). The four service marketing myths: Remnants of a goods-based, manufacturing model. *Journal of Service Research, 6*(4), 324–335. https://doi.org/10.1177/1094670503262946.

Vargo, S. L., & Lusch, R. F. (2008). From goods to service(s): Divergences and convergences of logics. *Industrial Marketing Management, 37*(3), 254–259. https://doi.org/10.1016/j.indmarman.2007.07.004.

Zarpelon Neto, G., Pereira, G. M., & Borchardt, M. (2015). What problems manufacturing companies can face when providing services around the world? *Journal of Business & Industrial Marketing, 30*(5), 461–471. https://doi.org/10.1108/JBIM-05-2012-0090.

Co-creating Value in Servitization

Salesforce Transformation to Solution Selling

Anna Salonen and Harri Terho

1 Introduction

Few manufacturers have eluded the imperative to go "downstream" in the value chain (Wise & Baumgartner, 1999), and for many, this has meant the adoption of a solutions-based business approach. The organizationally complex transformation from product selling to solution selling places new requirements on the sales function at both the organization and individual salesperson levels (Panagopoulos et al., 2017; Reinartz & Ulaga, 2008; Ulaga & Loveland, 2014; Worm et al., 2017).

In particular, recent research has recognized the critical role salespeople play in developing solution offerings and communicating their value-in-use potential to customers (Panagopoulos et al., 2017). This salesperson solution selling enactment plays a critical role in subsequent solution selling performance (Panagopoulos et al., 2017). However, many product-oriented salespeople are reluctant and/or unable to engage in solution selling (Ulaga & Loveland, 2014; Ulaga & Reinartz, 2011), which presents a major constraint on the manufacturer's servitization efforts.

A. Salonen (✉) · H. Terho
University of Turku, Turku, Finland
e-mail: anna.k.salonen@utu.fi

H. Terho
e-mail: harri.terho@utu.fi

© The Author(s), under exclusive license to Springer Nature
Switzerland AG 2021
M. Kohtamäki et al. (eds.), *The Palgrave Handbook of Servitization*,
https://doi.org/10.1007/978-3-030-75771-7_22

To advance the theory and practice of servitization, the purpose of this book chapter is to describe the requirements of solution selling at the salesforce level, which then forms the basis for building appropriate organizational structures and forms of support to facilitate a salesforce-wide transformation to solution selling.

This review is organized as follows: First, we provide an overview of the conceptual foundations of solution selling and position it in the wider servitization stream of research. Second, we explain how the understanding of the requirements posed by solution selling has progressed from an analysis of organizational-level conditions to the individual salesperson level. Third, we discuss how an organization can facilitate a salesforce-level transformation to solution selling.

2   Theory Development

Conceptual Foundations of Solution Selling

The roots of academic discussion on the concept of solution selling trace back to engineering practices, when suppliers of military weapons systems in the 1940s and 1950s began to develop better ways of managing the development and delivery of complex weapons systems (Hobday et al., 2005). Industrial marketing scholars picked up the idea of selling complex product systems through the concept of systems selling (see e.g., Mattsson, 1973). Systems selling required a change in the sales approach of industrial products (Page & Siemplenski, 1983) through the incorporation of a consultative orientation (Hanan, 1986). Later, "system" was specified to refer to a physical product system, whereas a solution was said to incorporate, in addition to the physical product system, strategic and consultative business activities (Davies et al., 2006).

From these conceptual origins, research on solution selling later evolved further as part of the interdisciplinary servitization stream of research (Vandermerwe & Rada, 1988). Viewed through the servitization lens, solution selling represents an enactment of the service-dominant logic on behalf of manufacturers (Vargo & Lusch, 2004, 2008) as they gradually transition to providing more advanced services (Salonen, 2011). This typically means extending the manufacturer's scope of supply through the integration of previously disintegrated product-based components into functional systems (Matthyssens & Vandenbempt, 2008) and the deployment of output-based services that target the customer's process (Ulaga & Reinartz, 2011). In doing so, the manufacturer's focus shifts to a collaborative process of value co-creation (Vargo & Lusch, 2008), as it engages customers in relational processes during the various phases of the solution life cycle that precede and follow the integration of product- and/or service-based components into customized responses to complex customer needs (Evanschitzky et al., 2011; Tuli et al., 2007).

Organizational Requirements of Solution Selling

A principle challenge for a manufacturer undergoing a solution transformation is building an organization that is able to interact with the customer in fundamentally different ways. Managers reared up in product-based organizations excel at designing and manufacturing superior products, as well as managing the processes involved in making and selling them. Thus, the transformation to solution selling requires the development of new organizational capabilities and structures.

To mitigate these challenges, Davies et al. (2006) suggest setting up an organizational structure composed of a customer-facing front-end organization, a supportive back-end organization, and a flexible core that provides oversight, coordination, and leadership for effectively delivering standardized, repeatable solutions. The customer-facing front-end is responsible for capturing customer insights and transferring the learnings to the back-end organization. The customer-facing front-end organization also manages strategic engagements with the customer and develops value propositions, integrates solutions, and provides operational services (Storbacka, 2011). Due to the high degree of trust and collaboration needed in the co-creation of customer solutions, the seller typically initially develops solutions with a limited number of key customers (Cova & Salle, 2007). Experimentation with lead customers then allows the vendor to develop effective value propositions as well as value quantification and verification tools, as it builds organizational capabilities for value-based selling in the solution business context (Terho et al., 2012, 2017; Töytäri & Rajala, 2015).

While the customer-facing units described above are in charge of developing commercialization capabilities that ensure value creation through the solution business model, the back end takes charge of ensuring the manufacturer's value capture ability (Storbacka, 2011). At the core of these efforts lies the implementation of the principle of modularity (Davies et al., 2006). This means limiting variety through the definition of a clear solution architecture that specifies the modules that make up the solution, which allows salespeople to sell mass-customized solutions (Kowalkowski et al., 2015; Salonen,

2011; Salonen et al., 2018; Storbacka, 2011). In cases of highly complex, fully tailored turnkey solutions, opportunities to modularize the offering are limited (Salonen & Jaakkola, 2015). In these cases, a separate project organization unit staffed with suitable individuals typically handles the solution selling and delivery.

If the firm is able to modularize the solution offering, this builds the organizational readiness to implement a broader solution transformation through repeatable, mass-customized solutions that enable better value capture (Salonen et al., 2018). However, the transformation is constrained by the fact that the salesperson-level requirements for solution selling are vastly different from those of product selling (Reinartz & Ulaga, 2008; Ulaga & Loveland, 2014). Since replacing large portions of the salesforce is costly and disruptive to existing business and sales routines, manufacturers undergoing a solution transformation need to find ways to deal with this constraint. The first step in addressing this challenge is to develop an in-depth understanding of how these requirements differ, as this will form the basis for building the appropriate organizational structures and forms of support to facilitate a salesforce transformation to solution selling.

Salesperson-Level Requirements in Solution Selling (Selling Process and Proficiencies)

The seminal study by Tuli et al. (2007) introduced a customer-centric view of solution business. According to this perspective, customers ultimately judge solutions as relational processes instead of customized and integrated bundles of goods and services. Consequently, an effective solution selling process should go beyond the mere task of customizing an offering to meet customer needs. The requirements' definition, deployment, and post-deployment support arise as additional critical components of solution provision for customers, and thus call for a relational sales process.

Salespeople play a key role in implementing these four stages into practice through solution selling involvement, which captures the degree to which a salesperson engages in activities that help his/her firm provide end-to-end solutions for the salesperson's customers (Panagopoulos et al., 2017). The initial phases of this process focus on gaining a deep understanding of the customer's business and designing effective solutions for the customer's needs. In later stages, salespeople need to ensure the correct delivery of the solution and to maintain a continuous and supportive dialogue with the customer after deployment of the solution into the customer's process. Such an involvement is systematically linked to increased sales performance and is stronger under higher levels of a firm's product portfolio scope, sales unit cross-functional cooperation, and customer–supplier relationship tie strength (Panagopoulos et al., 2017).

Along similar lines, Worm et al. (2017) demonstrated that a firm's solution sales capabilities, defined as the degree to which the salesforce is able to identify the appropriate decision-makers and provide proficient justification for the solutions offering, are critical for their solution selling performance. Ulaga and Kohli (2018) further note that salespeople play a key role in reducing the customer's need uncertainty, process uncertainty, and outcome uncertainty during the different stages of the solution selling process. To do so, salespeople need to provide pertinent information to key stakeholders within the customer and supplier organizations, and to encourage adaptive behavior of the parties involved. Thus, salespeople need to be able to demonstrate the value-in-use potential of the abstract offerings often by engaging new types of customer stakeholders, such as business decision-makers, instead of buyers (Terho et al., 2012, 2017).

Previous solution selling research has thus provided strong evidence for the critical role salespeople play in the context of solution selling. At the same time, it appears difficult to build the required salesperson-level competences. Bonney and Williams (2009), in their conceptual study, were among the first to argue that the salesperson-level requirements of solution selling are fundamentally different from those of product selling. Subsequently, several authors have explored the specific nature of these requirements. For instance, Ulaga and Loveland's (2014) qualitative study among top managers provided a structured exploration of key salesperson proficiencies and required personality traits in solution selling. They identified 13 traits that help salespeople develop the required proficiencies to succeed in solution selling. These include high learning, customer service, and teamwork orientation, as well as intrinsic motivation and general intelligence.

Other studies have elaborated on these traits. For instance, Friend and Malshe (2016) found that salespeople need to possess network and relationship management-specific skills to craft customer solutions in an ecosystem context. Key skills include diversity sensitivity, multipoint probing, orchestration, and stability preservation. Koponen et al. (2019), in turn, elaborate on the broader communication competences required for international solution selling, relating them to four components: behavioral, affective, cognitive, and general sales acumen. Behavioral competence helps salespeople to act effectively in interactions through relational communication skills, personal selling skills, and language skills. Affective competence refers to the motivation to engage in interpersonal interaction, manifested in motivations, positive and open attitudes, and cultural sensitivity. Cognitive competence refers to the knowledge and understanding of effective and appropriate interpersonal communication behaviors. Finally, sales acumen is related to sales-specific knowledge and skills, including the strategic understanding of business-to-business sales and leadership skills.

Böhm et al. (2020) empirically studied the antecedents and outcomes of salespeople's value opportunity recognition (VOR) competence. VOR refers to the cognitive process that individual salespeople use to detect misallocations of resources, define associated customer problems, and develop solutions that generate value for the customer and profit for the supplier (Bonney & Williams, 2009). Böhm et al. (2020) found that customer knowledge is the key driver of VOR, and salespeople can compensate for a lack of technical knowledge by forging strong relationships with the back-end organization, thus implying the need for a team selling structure for solution sales. The formalization of sales hinders the salesperson's ability to leverage their customer relationships for VOR but helps them to work more effectively with the back-end organization to recognize value opportunities (Böhm et al., 2020).

Key Ways to Implement a Salesforce Transformation to Solution Selling

At the organizational level, firms have two options for initiating solution sales. One is to build up a dedicated solution unit staffed with individuals with the appropriate capabilities, experience, and personality traits. The second is to implement a broader, salesforce-wide transformation to solution selling.

Regarding a salesforce-wide transformation to solution selling, some argue that the requirements of product selling and solution selling differ so substantially that firms that want to develop an organizational capability to sell solutions need to recruit new salespeople for the solution selling tasks (Reinartz & Ulaga, 2008; Ulaga & Loveland, 2014). This challenge is caused by a total re-orientation in the required selling approach. Different personality traits are even potentially required, which are difficult to change with mere training and compensation schemes. However, recent research suggests that product-centric salespeople can be engaged in solution selling if the organization provides appropriate support tailored to individual salespeople's needs (Salonen et al., 2020).

In the initial stages of a manufacturer's solution transformation, a dedicated solution selling salesforce typically makes the most sense. Levihn and Levihn (2016) found in the case organization they studied that those sales branches that separated the solution business from the product business were more successful. Best practice units hired new salespeople for the solution selling task from their customers as a way to gain the required in-depth understanding of the customer's industry, business model, and underlying needs (Levihn & Levihn, 2016). Organizational separation also finds strength from the findings of Paiola et al. (2012), who found, in the context of service sales, that organizational separation of a newly recruited salesforce improved the commitment and financial performance of the new salesforce.

At the same time, a key challenge related to the creation of a dedicated solution salesforce is that it is costly to implement and places limits on the manufacturer's ability to follow the industrialization path to service-based growth (Kowalkowski et al., 2015). In these cases, solutions sales typically represent a relatively small proportion of the firm's overall operations and consist of project-based, fully tailored solutions with customer-specific, premium pricing. Yet, in many cases, firms will want to strive for a broader shift to solution business by investing in the development of modular solution architecture and the associated organizational processes (Rajala et al., 2019; Salonen et al., 2018). In these cases, the manufacturer needs to consider whether and how it can implement a broader salesforce-wide transformation to solution selling that involves its existing product-centric salesforce.

While the development of sufficient industrialization capabilities removes many of the organizational constraints of a salesforce-wide transformation to solution selling, managing the transformation process is still far from easy given the vastly different salesperson-level requirements. However, as demonstrated by Salonen et al. (2020), it is possible, albeit with some restrictions. More specifically, the study reveals that not all salespeople can engage in a solution transformation, as there are necessary threshold requirements in the form of salesperson value-based selling capability (Terho et al., 2012, 2017). However, beyond this threshold condition, a heterogeneous salesforce can engage if the organization offers the right type of transformation support.

The required type of organizational support depends on the salesperson's characteristics. While some exceptional and highly motivated salespersons with prior experience in selling complex offerings transition virtually without any organizational support, others need exhaustive support. Salespeople who are typically the most difficult to transform perceive a transition to solution selling as risky and have no prior experience in solution sales. Firms can provide the needed support through either top-down organizational actions or, more informally, operational-level support. Organizational support can take place though training or communication of expectations by sales management, whereas dedicated solution champions who engage in market shaping (Nenonen et al., 2019) offer operational-level support to salespeople (Salonen et al., 2020).

The finding regarding the role of solution champion market shaping suggests that organizational support required in a transformational context extends beyond the boundaries of the focal organization. This is because a large-scale transformation from product selling to solution selling often requires negotiation of institutional resistance from customers (Hartmann et al., 2018), which is beyond the capacity of any individual salesperson. Solution champions can help the salesperson redesign the exchange, reconfigure the networks of the actors, or reform institutions (Baker et al., 2019; Nenonen et al., 2019). In doing so, they create opportunities for salespeople to engage in solution selling.

Lastly, solution selling and value-based selling studies indicate that sales organizations should always provide their salespeople with a basic toolset to succeed in solution selling during all phases of the sales cycle (Töytäri & Rajala, 2015). In the initial phases of sales, clear sales strategy elements facilitate solution selling effectiveness. Segmentation and prioritization schemes help salespeople to better understand customer requirements and to target resource-intensive solution selling investments for those customers who are best served through solution selling initiatives (see Panagopoulos & Avlonitis, 2010; Terho et al., 2015; Töytäri & Rajala, 2015). Similarly, the development of clear relationship objectives, selling models, and different sales channels to reach and serve different types of customers helps salespeople to effectively adapt the selling process to different customers (Töytäri & Rajala, 2015). This is particularly important in cases when industrial companies continue to maintain their traditional offerings while expanding into solution business through servitization. In such a situation, some customers may wish to merely place orders for fairly standardized offerings, while others may need a complex solution that is integrated as a fully tailor-made project. Customers who do not require the salesperson's expertise can largely manage their own purchase journeys through automated, often web-based channels, while others will need extensive support through a dedicated salesforce.

3   Discussion

The purpose of this chapter was to develop an understanding of the requirements of solution selling at the salesforce level, which forms the basis for building appropriate organizational structures and forms of support to facilitate a salesforce-wide transformation to solution selling. Based on this review, we conclude that solution selling involvement by salespeople plays a key role in ensuring subsequent solution selling performance (Panagopoulos et al., 2017; Worm et al., 2017). However, given that the requirements for solution selling differ drastically from those of product selling, facilitating salesperson solution selling involvement is difficult to realize in practice.

Rather than attempt an immediate firm-wide transformation to solution selling, we suggest that the manufacturer proceed in stages. In the first stage, setting up a dedicated solution salesforce and staffing it with suitable salespeople is a good way to initiate the complex transformation. Such a unit can recruit salespeople with appropriate capabilities, experience, and personality traits (Ulaga & Loveland, 2014). Alternatively, the manufacturer could scan the existing salesforce for suitable individuals. Here, the presence of value-based selling capability is a necessary threshold competence (Salonen et al., 2020; Terho et al., 2012, 2017). Additionally, skills such as communication competence (Koponen et al., 2019) and attitudes such as learning orientation, intrinsic motivation, and teamwork orientation (Ulaga & Loveland, 2014) are likely to support salespeople's success in solution selling.

At the same time, to realize a large-scale solution transformation, manufacturers need to find ways of engaging salespeople who may not possess the optimal set of skills, attitudes, or personality traits. Doing so is possible as long as the manufacturer (1) understands that a salesforce transformation to solution selling is both an individual- and organizational-level phenomenon, and (2) is able to manage the complex interplay of these conditions (Salonen et al., 2020). This includes the provision of appropriate organizational support tailored to individual salespeople's needs. Additionally, organizations should provide supportive sales tools for the salesforce, including documented reference cases, solution configurators, and value quantification and pricing tools (Terho et al., 2017; Töytäri & Rajala, 2015).

References

Baker, J. J., Storbacka, K., & Brodie, R. J. (2019). Markets changing, changing markets: Institutional work as market shaping. *Marketing Theory, 19*(3), 301–328.

Böhm, E., Eggert, A., Terho, H., Ulaga, W., & Haas, A. (2020). Drivers and outcomes of salespersons' value opportunity recognition competence in solution selling. *Journal of Personal Selling & Sales Management, 40*(3), 180–197.

Bonney, L. F., & Williams, B. C. (2009). From products to solutions: The role of salesperson opportunity recognition. *European Journal of Marketing, 43*(7/8), 1032–1052.

Cova, B., & Salle, R. (2007). Introduction to the IMM special issue on 'Project marketing and the marketing of solutions' A comprehensive approach to project marketing and the marketing of solutions. *Industrial Marketing Management, 36*(2), 138–146.

Davies, A., Brady, T., & Hobday, M. (2006). Charting a path towards integrated solutions. *MIT Sloan Management Review, 47*(3), 39–48.

Evanschitzky, H., Wangenheim, F. V., & Woisetschläger, D. M. (2011). Service & solution innovation: Overview and research agenda. *Industrial Marketing Management, 40*(5), 657–660.

Friend, S., & Malshe, A. (2016). Key skills for crafting customer solutions within an ecosystem: A theories-in-use perspective. *Journal of Service Research, 19*(2), 174–191.

Hanan, M. (1986). Consultative selling, get to know your customers' problems. *Management Review, 75*(4), 25–31.

Hartmann, N. N., Wieland, H., & Vargo, S. L. (2018). Converging on a new theoretical foundation for selling. *Journal of Marketing, 82*(2), 1–18.

Hobday, M., Davies, A., & Prencipe, A. (2005). Systems integration: A core capability of the modern corporation. *Industrial and Corporate Change, 14*(6), 1109–1143.

Koponen, J., Julkunen, S., & Asai, A. (2019). Sales communication competence in international B2B solution selling. *Industrial Marketing Management, 82*, 238–252.

Kowalkowski, C., Windahl, C., Kindström, D., & Gebauer, H. (2015). What service transition? Rethinking established assumptions about manufacturers' service-led growth strategies. *Industrial Marketing Management, 45*(February), 59–69.

Levihn, U., & Levihn, F. (2016). The transition from product to solution selling: The role and organization of employees engaged in current business. *Journal of Business-to-Business Marketing, 23*(3), 207–219.

Matthyssens, P., & Vandenbempt, K. (2008). Moving from basic offerings to value-added solutions: Strategies, barriers, and alignment. *Industrial Marketing Management, 37*, 316–328.

Mattsson, L. G. (1973). Systems selling as a strategy on industrial markets. *Industrial Marketing Management, 3*, 107–120.

Nenonen, S., Storbacka, K., & Windahl, C. (2019). Capabilities for market-shaping: Triggering and facilitating increased value creation. *Journal of the Academy of Marketing Science, 47*(4), 617–639.

Page, A. L., & Siemplenski, M. (1983). Product systems marketing. *Industrial Marketing Management, 12*, 89–99.

Paiola, M., Gebauer, H., & Edvardsson, B. (2012). Service business development in small- to medium-sized equipment manufacturers. *Journal of Business-to-Business Marketing, 19*, 33–66.

Panagopoulos, N. G., & Avlonitis, G. J. (2010). Performance implications of sales strategy: The moderating effects of leadership and environment. *International Journal of Research in Marketing, 27*(1), 46–57.

Panagopoulos, N. G., Rapp, A. A., & Ogilvie, J. L. (2017). Salesperson solution involvement and sales performance: The contingent role of supplier firm and customer-supplier relationship characteristics. *Journal of Marketing, 81*(4), 144–164.

Rajala, R., Brax, S., Virtanen, A., & Salonen, A. (2019). The next phase in servitization: Transforming integrated solutions into modular solutions business. *International Journal of Operations and Production Management, 39*(5), 630–657.

Reinartz, W., & Ulaga, W. (2008). How to sell services more profitably. *Harvard Business Review, 86*(5), 90–96.

Salonen, A. (2011). Service transition strategies of industrial manufacturers. *Industrial Marketing Management, 40*(5), 683–690.

Salonen, A., & Jaakkola, E. (2015). Firm boundary decisions in solution business: Examining internal vs. external resource integration. *Industrial Marketing Management, 51,* 171–183.

Salonen, A., Rajala, R., & Virtanen, A. (2018). Leveraging the benefits of modularity in the provision of integrated solutions: A strategic learning perspective. *Industrial Marketing Management, 68,* 13–24.

Salonen, A., Terho, H., Böhm, E., Rajala, R., & Virtanen, A. (2020). Engaging a product focused sales force in solution selling: Interplay of individual and organizational conditions. *Journal of the Academy of Marketing Science.* https://link.springer.com/article/10.1007/s11747-020-00729-z.

Storbacka, K. (2011). A solution business model: Capabilities and management practices for integrated solutions. *Industrial Marketing Management, 40*(5), 699–711.

Terho, H., Eggert, A., Haas, A., & Ulaga, W. (2015). How sales strategy translates into performance: The role of salesperson customer orientation and valuebased selling. *Industrial Marketing Management, 45,* 12–21.

Terho, H., Eggert, A., Ulaga, W., Haas, A., & Böhm, E. (2017). Selling value in business markets: Individual and organizational factors for turning the idea into action. *Industrial Marketing Management, 66,* 42–55.

Terho, H., Haas, A., Eggert, A., & Ulaga, W. (2012). 'It's almost like taking the sales out of selling'—Towards a conceptualization of value-based selling in business markets. *Industrial Marketing Management, 41*(1), 174–185.

Töytäri, P., & Rajala, R. (2015). Value-based selling: The organizational capability perspective. *Industrial Marketing Management, 45*(February), 101–112.

Tuli, K. R., Kohli, A. K., & Bharadwaj, S. G. (2007). Rethinking customer solutions: From product bundles to relational processes. *Journal of Marketing, 71*(3), 1–17.

Ulaga, W., & Loveland, J. M. (2014). Transitioning from product to service-led growth in manufacturing firms: Emergent challenges in selecting and managing the industrial sales force. *Industrial Marketing Management, 43*(1), 113–125.

Ulaga, W., & Reinartz, W. J. (2011). Hybrid offerings: How manufacturing firms combine goods and services successfully. *Journal of Marketing, 75*(6), 5–23.

Ulaga, W., & Kohli, A. (2018). The role of a solutions salesperson: Reducing uncertainty and fostering adaptiveness. *Industrial Marketing Management, 69,* 161–168.

Vandermerwe, S., & Rada, J. (1988). Servitization of business: Adding value by adding services. *European Management Journal, 6*(4), 314–324.

Vargo, S., & Lusch, R. (2004). Evolving to a new dominant logic for marketing. *Journal of Marketing, 68,* 1–17.

Vargo, S., & Lusch, R. (2008). From goods to service(s): Divergences and convergences of logics. *Industrial Marketing Management, 37,* 254–259.

Wise, R., & Baumgartner, P. (1999). Go downstream. *Harvard Business Review, 77*(5), 133.

Worm, S., Bharadwaj, S. G., Ulaga, W., & Reinartz, W. J. (2017). When and why do customer solutions pay off in business markets? *Journal of the Academy of Marketing Science, 45*(4), 490–512.

Digital Servitization: Strategies for Handling Customization and Customer Interaction

Katja Maria Hydle, Magnus Hellström, Tor Helge Aas,
and Karl Joachim Breunig

1   Introduction

Balancing customization and standardization is likely enabled through modularity for production as well as service companies (Aas & Pedersen, 2013; Bask et al., 2011; Hellström et al., 2016). Achieving such a balance is a key challenge for manufacturing firms when servitizing. Research on manufacturing firms' interactions with their customers as they pursue servitization strategies has focused on different forms of customer engagement (Carlborg et al., 2018) and customizing solutions (Jagstedt et al., 2018). Customer centricity is suggested to be a core property for services, which

K. M. Hydle (✉)
Department of Informatics, University of Oslo, Oslo, Norway
e-mail: katjahy@uio.no

K. M. Hydle · M. Hellström · T. H. Aas
School of Business and Law, University of Agder, Kristiansand, Norway
e-mail: magnus.hellstrom@uia.no

T. H. Aas
NORCE, Norwegian Research Centre AS, Oslo & Kristiansand, Norway
e-mail: tor.h.aas@uia.no

K. J. Breunig
Oslo Business School, Oslo Metropolitan University, Oslo, Norway
e-mail: karjoa@oslomet.no

© The Author(s), under exclusive license to Springer Nature
Switzerland AG 2021
M. Kohtamäki et al. (eds.), *The Palgrave Handbook of Servitization*,
https://doi.org/10.1007/978-3-030-75771-7_23

are essentially co-created (e.g., Vargo & Lusch, 2008). Moreover, research has emphasized the role of managing information when pursuing a balance between customization and standardization (Cenamor et al., 2017; Hellström, 2014). At the same time, recent service theory has departed from emphasizing heterogeneity as a key services criterion, as new digital technologies provide opportunities for increased mass adaptation and standardization (e.g., Sawhney, 2016).

Overall, the digital servitization trend, understood as the use of digital tools to move from a product-centric business model to a service-centric one, is strengthening, which has significant implications for business model innovation (Kohtamäki et al., 2019; Paiola & Gebauer, 2020). Digital servitization particularly enables effective value creation (Kohtamäki et al., 2019); although customers expect customization, manufacturing firms work toward standardization, increasing efficiency and capturing value. In the servitization literature, services are often treated as a homogenous group of offerings; in contrast, we believe that different digitalization processes and outcomes can be expected, depending on the type of service. Therefore, it is time to take stock of recent developments in digital servitization and discuss and conceptualize the implications of digitalization for different types of services, with a focus on the tension between customization and standardization on the one hand and the degree of customer interaction on the other. Hence, we ask the following research question: How does digitalization enable firms to balance standardization and customization when they co-create value with customers?

This conceptual chapter was motivated by an empirical study of five manufacturing firms in the oil and gas industry at different stages of servitization. We use insights from this study to illustrate our main arguments (Siggelkow, 2007).

We continue by defining key concepts in service customization by categorizing industrial services and digitalization. Then, we present various types of industrial service offerings and typologies for their classification. Thereafter, we describe associations among customer interaction, customization, digitalization and different types of industrial service, with an overview of the digital technologies used in servitization. Finally, we discuss the strategic implications of this work for servitized firms.

2   Theory Development

Standardization, Customization and Customer Interaction

Standardization relates to the pursuit of economies of scale; it is based on the logic that the more you make of something, the more you save in standardizing both the process and the output. However, competitive advantage derives not only from operational excellence and low-cost production (Porter, 1996) but also from differentiation and more careful customer orientation, which results in a huge interest in mass customization (Davis, 1987). A recent literature review found that one key value creation process of servitizing manufacturers is to customize the offering (Garcia Martin et al., 2019). The central idea underlying mass customization is the pursuit of meeting specific customer needs at near-mass-production efficiency. Hence, mass customization remains relevant for servitizing manufacturers. A few studies have addressed this from the perspective of achieving balance, seeing modularity as the enabler (Bask et al., 2011; Hellström et al., 2016). It is, however, clear that digitalization also constitutes an enabler in achieving such balance in service provision, for example, through platforms (Cenamor et al., 2017).

Therefore, this study seeks to understand how customers participate in digital service provision using two dimensions: the degrees of standardization/customization and customer interaction (e.g., Consoli & Elche-Hortelano, 2010; Hansen et al., 1999; Larsson & Bowen, 1989; Løwendahl, 2005; Maister, 1993; Ramírez, 1999; Schmenner, 1986). Standardization refers to the reduction or elimination of customized, one-time, seldom-used solutions that involve variability, added costs and quality problems. Customization refers to tailoring offerings to meet customers' specific needs; its varying degrees run along a continuum ranging from customized to standardized services, depending on the extent to which a service can be codified and delivered (Hansen et al., 1999; Løwendahl, 2005; Maister, 1993).

The degree of customer interaction refers to the extent of customer involvement in the provision of an offering. A common understanding is that services are co-produced through interaction between customers and service providers (Amara et al., 2009; Bettencourt et al., 2002) and that their quality is evaluated when the service is used (Normann, 1984). However, this conceptualization needs to be nuanced (Breunig et al., 2014; Grönroos, 2011). Services are sometimes created in collaboration with customers, with simultaneous provision and consumption; customers are not always involved, however, such as when service providers receive orders from customers and then deliver the requested services. In this vein, Kvålshaugen et al. (2015) identified four generic types of services: standardized-provided, standardized–co-produced, customized-provided and customized–co-produced. Indeed, servitization is changing the buyer–supplier relationships toward the use of more relational business practices, and digitalization provides means (e.g., through efficient knowledge-sharing routines) to master this change (Kamalaldin et al., 2020). Moreover, digital service innovation may develop incrementally through agile co-creation processes that are typical in software engineering (Sjödin et al., 2020).

The relationship between standardization/customization and customer interaction is a powerful construct for understanding servitization as it aids in identifying how companies can manage their industrial services and interact differently with their customers. However, different types of industrial services may require different degrees of customer interaction.

Industrial Service Types

There are various service classifications. Baines and Lightfoot (2014) suggest a classification that catches the role of the customer: based on customer profiles, industrial services (i.e., those provided by manufacturers) are classified as basic (for "do-it-yourself" customers), intermediate (for customers who want manufacturers to do it with them) and advanced (for customers who want manufacturers to do it for them). In this classification, it is mainly the advanced services that are delivered by deploying information and communication technologies (Baines & Lightfoot, 2014). Another framework based on this classification is the servitization pyramid, with a horizontal dimension regarding service focus that distinguishes between product focus versus customer process and a vertical dimension exposing value proposition that distinguishes between input, performance and results (Coreynen et al., 2017).

However, for this analysis, the more fine-grained classification of Partanen et al. (2017) is used. It consists of five categories (pre-sales, R&D, operational, product support and product lifecycle services), each with sub-categories, resulting in a total of 15 distinct types of industrial services (see Table 1). This classification is useful for the operationalization of servitization efforts when services are changing due to digitalization. For example, the existing industrial service "technical user training" (a product support service) may become location-independent when assisted by virtual reality (VR) technology. However, to fully grasp what digital servitization is about, we need to look at the characteristics of the digitalization.

Table 1 Degrees of standardization/customization and customer interaction for traditional and digital industrial services

Industrial services	Type of service	Standardization/ Customization	Customer interaction	Digital services	Digital tools	Digital processes	Standardization/ Customization	Customer interaction
Pre-sales services	Product demonstration	Standardized	High	Simulations	VR	Representing	Standardized	Low
	Customer seminar	Standardized	High	Learning lab/simulations	VR	Representing	Standardized	Low
R&D services	Research service	Customized	Low	Data analysis	IoT	Informating	Customized	Low
	Prototype design	Customized	Low	Additive manufacturing	3D	Informating, representing	Customized	Low
	Feasibility studies	Customized	High	Data analysis	IoT	Informating	Customized	Low
Operational services	Project management	Customized	High	CAD/CAM	Robotics, Digital twin	Automating, mediating	Standardized	Low/High
	Service for operating the product sold for the customer	Customized	High	Automation	Robotics	Automating	Standardized	Low
	Service for operating customer's process	Customized	High	Proactive support, Service for monitoring customer's process	VR	Representing	Standardized	Low
Product support services	Warranty	Standardized	Low	Data analysis	IoT	Informating	Customized	Low

(continued)

Table 1 (continued)

Industrial services	Type of service	Standardization/ Customization	Customer interaction	Digital services	Digital tools	Digital processes	Standardization/ Customization	Customer interaction
	Technical user training	Customized	High	Simulations	VR	Representing	Standardized	Low
	Customer consulting and support by phone	Standardized	High	Proactive support, Data analysis	IoT	Informating	Customized	Low
Product life-cycle services	Installation services	Customized	High	Simulations, Real-time instructions	VR, AR	Representing, mediating	Standardized	Low/High
	Repair services	Customized	High	Data analysis, Real-time instructions/smart flying engineers	IoT, AR	Informating, mediating	Standardized	Low/High
	Spare parts Maintenance	Standardized Customized	Low High	Data analysis Smart maintenance	IoT IoT, AR	Informating Informating, mediating	Standardized Standardized	Low Low/High

Characteristics of Digitalization

There are basic characteristics of digital technology that can be used as a foundation for understanding how digitalization enables servitization. Zuboffs (1985) seminal work exposes how information technology facilitates moving from industrialism to knowledge-based societies through "automating" and "informating." Automating is about using information technology to automate tasks and reproduce human skills, providing precision and uniformity in production. When automating activities, data are registered by the equipment or machine. The term "automating" is highly relevant in servitization since many service provisions are time-consuming and repetitive, such as (condition) monitoring and fault detection. In contrast, informating refers to the process that translates descriptions and measurements of activities, events and objects into information that becomes visible to the employees and that may be relevant for decision-makers. Informating can be an unintended result of computer-based automation, but it can also be a conscious decision designed to obtain and exploit information that can be used in business, such as improvement and innovation of products and services (Zuboff, 1985, p. 8). Informating in relation to servitization reflects the possibility of using data generated through automated or digitalized service processes to improve and further capitalize on the service.

Automating and informating represent two facets of digital work, while interactive (collaborative) aspects of it may be conceptualized through notions of digital representing and mediating (Jonsson et al., 2018). Digital representing emphasizes content and "how IT is used to monitor and produce digital content" (Jonsson et al., 2018, p. 218), while digital mediating emphasizes the medium and "how IT can be used for digitally mediated cooperative work" (Jonsson et al., 2018, p. 218). Digital representing and mediating highlight two ways that digital technology may be used by servitized firms. Jonsson et al. (2018) use the example of a condition-based maintenance service, where representing may refer to information that can be obtained from the monitored machine and where mediating may refer to how technology is used when maintenance workers and/or data analysts collaborate.

In the following, we will use the concepts of automating and informating to highlight the basic characteristics of digital technology, while representing and mediating are key characteristics of how digital technologies are implicated in work practices when exposing digital processes undertaken by the services. According to the service-dominant logic, customers are co-creators or producers of value (Vargo & Lusch, 2008). How this co-production happens (in terms of customization/standardization and customer interaction) as services become increasingly digital and involve automating, informating, representing and mediating has not been conceptualized to our knowledge.

Degrees of Customization and Customer Interaction in Industrial Services

By mapping different industrial service types (Partanen et al., 2017) onto Kvålshaugen et al. (2015) juxtaposition of the degrees of standardization/customization and customer interaction, a clear pattern emerges (Fig. 1). Overall, most industrial services involve high degrees of customer interaction and customization. Operational, product support and product lifecycle services are customized and co-produced; interaction with customers during service performance is important, and solutions and outcomes are tailored to specific customer needs. Repair services for equipment on an oil rig may serve as an example: The customer, who may be the rig operator, calls the supplier's 24-hour call center, describes the issue and asks for help. Representatives of the customer and the supplier engage in a point-to-point sale for the repair work, which may take a few hours or up to 4 weeks. When the customer

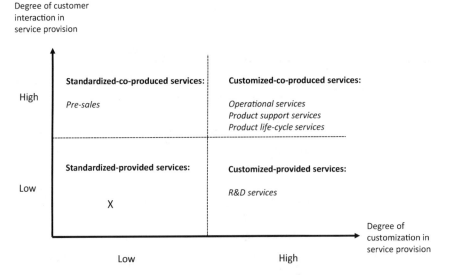

Fig. 1 Degree of customer interaction and customization of different industrial services

agrees to the repair service, a service engineer is flown to the rig to repair the product; they explain the problem to the rig staff and demonstrate how to deal with it in the future. The rig employees thus learn from the service engineer during this visit.

Pre-sales services are more standardized (i.e., not individually customized) but involve a high degree of customer interaction, for example via product demonstrations and seminars attended by potential and existing customers. Most R&D services are customized-provided (involving a high degree of customization with less customer interaction), except for feasibility studies, which are typically tailored to customers' strategic needs and performed in close collaboration with customers or their representatives. Only sub-categories related to warranties and spare parts are standardized-provided.

Impacts of Digitalization on Customization and Customer Interaction in Industrial Services

Industrial services are changing drastically through digital servitization. The use of digital technology in relation to products such as the internet of things (IoT) (including sensors), virtual reality (VR), artificial reality (AR), robotics and automation completely alters services, their outreach and provision (Parida et al., 2019). Returning to the example of repair services on an offshore oil rig, digital technologies enable the manufacturing firm to run a proactive rather than reactive support center, with engineers using digital monitoring (which covers all on-rig operations) to remotely detect errors and digital tools such as digital twins to find potential solutions. When a repair job must be performed by someone physically present on the rig, AR can be used to guide the rig crew, eliminating the need to dispatch an engineer from the manufacturer. In our empirical study, we identified cases in which the application of digital technology reduced the time spent performing repair jobs on offshore rigs from 4 weeks to 1 hour. This example involves customer consultation through the product support center and product lifecycle and repair services. Digital technology transforms product lifecycle services to standardized–co-produced or even standardized-provided services, with a low degree of customization and a low to high degree of customer interaction, depending on the type of technology used.

Digitalization also changes other service types, perhaps with the exception of R&D services. Product support services use mainly data analysis and the IoT and are customized with little customer interaction. Pre-sales and operational services involve simulations, automation and proactive support;

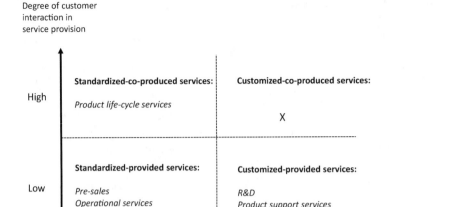

Fig. 2   Degree of customer interaction and customization for digital services

these are standardized-provided services with low degrees of customer inter-action and customization. Thus, digitalized industrial services tend to be standardized-provided, and fewer are customized–co-produced (Fig. 2). Tech-nology is the driver of digital industrial services, as addressed in the next section.

Digital Technologies Used in Industrial Service Customization and Customer Interaction

Different digital technologies give rise to different customization and interac-tion patterns (Fig. 3). IoT technologies (i.e., sensors) provide companies with huge amounts of data that can reduce customer interaction while enabling more service customization. Using the basic characteristics of information technology, data through IoT that reduces customer interaction and enables customization relates to the process of informating. However, robotics, VR and AR are associated with low degrees of customization. Robotics relates to the process of automating, where information technology is used to auto-mate tasks and mechanically reproduce human skills. In contrast, VR is a way to implicate digital technology in work practices, where the content is important, as in digital representing. Finally, AR, in addition to representing content, is also about the medium used for cooperative work, as in digital mediating. AR, but not VR or robotics, appears to enable a high degree of

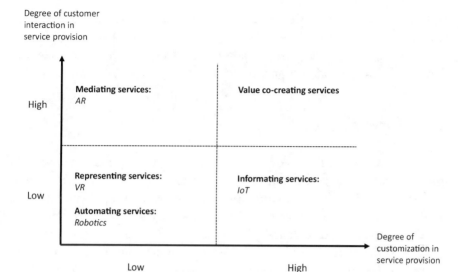

Fig. 3 Degree of customer interaction and customization for different digital technologies

customer interaction. For example, a rig crew can perform maintenance on a product such as a ventilator with direction from a servitized firm's service center staff via AR. Thus, the use of IoT technologies leads to the provision of customized-provided services through informating processes, whereas AR is associated with standardized–co-produced services through mediating processes; VR enables representing services; and robotics use automating processes associated with standardized-provided services (Fig. 3). No technology seems to lead to high degrees of customization and customer interaction, which may indicate that these services require value co-creation with customers, in which digital technologies enable the communication, while the real value lies in the interaction (Grönroos, 2011; Løwendahl, 2005). The servitization literature exposes that interaction for value co-creation may be increased in breadth and depth through digitalization capabilities such as intelligence, connectivity and analytics (Lenka et al., 2017). Following these complementary insights, digitalization capabilities are necessary for value co-creating with customers.

This conceptual analysis suggests that industrial digitalized service provisions enable firms to shift from: (i) customized–co-produced to standardized-provided services and representing and automating services; (ii) customer interaction to increased customer knowledge; and (iii) servitization to the professionalization of services and further development of customized–co-produced services. Table 1 shows the shift and the whole range of traditional and digitalized industrial services according to the degree of standardization/customization and customer interaction.

3   Discussion

We set out to answer the following question: How does digitalization enable firms to balance standardization and customization when they co-create value with customers? Drawing on the framework of Kvålshaugen et al. (2015) combined with theories on servitization and digitalization, we have conceptualized the implications of digital servitization on the degree of customization and standardization of services and customer interaction. Our conceptualization suggests that different digital technologies have different impacts on customization and customer interaction according to service type (Figs. 1 and 3, Table 1). With digitalization, many of Davis's (1987) ideas on mass customization are becoming a reality. The idea of mass customization builds on what could be termed "economies of customer interaction" (Piller & Möslein, 2002). Therefore, we further classified different technologies' relationships to service types in terms of customer interaction (Figs. 2 and 3, Table 1).

Theoretical Contributions

Servitization can strengthen companies' performance (Aas & Pedersen, 2011) and competitiveness, especially in the long term (Visnjic et al., 2016); however, the transition from products to services is very challenging (Alghisi & Saccani, 2015), as it entails a shift in logic (Wikström et al., 2009). Product-oriented businesses are often characterized by standardized, homogeneous solutions and volume production, whereas more service-oriented companies are characterized by heterogeneous, specialized knowledge-intensive delivery (Fisk et al., 1993), often customized to individual customers' needs.

Industrial services have traditionally been delivered for specific needs and have involved intense customer interaction (i.e., customized and co-produced). However, our conceptualization indicates that the digitalization of these industrial services involves a shift in logic. We argue that digital technology paradoxically enables service standardization (and higher-volume production) with less customer interaction as these technologies increasingly replace human interaction through the processes of automating and representing (Jonsson et al., 2018; Zuboff, 1985). The figuration of mediating, however, enables new forms of collaboration that involve standardization with high customer interaction. Moreover, the process of informating increasingly comes into play and simultaneously creates more data and knowledge about customers. We contend that servitized companies utilize a kind of economy of interaction (Piller & Möslein, 2002), not in the sense of interaction frequency or volume but in terms of appropriate data collection and smart data analysis.

To harness customer data from sensors and the IoT, servitizing companies build analytical capabilities and new knowledge bases that can be used strategically to (further) enhance (new) services. This process implies that digitalized services are characterized by standardized solutions, as are products, but also by detailed, customized, mass-adapted delivery to customers. For example, data analytics can yield detailed information about a drilling crew's performance relative to that of other crews on the same oil platform (or other platforms) in a translational process in which measures of activities, events and objects have become information. Such informating processes (Zuboff, 1988) involve how microdata can be used to scale the analytics down to the product level or aggregate them up to the crew, organization, rig or even geographic region level.

Thus, digital services are characterized by the provision of standardized solutions that are not only informating but also representing and mediating. Our main contribution to the servitization literature is that we demonstrate how industrial services shift from customized and co-created to mainly standardized-provided and informating when digitalized. Classically, customized–co-produced services are related to professional services, in which experienced and knowledgeable professionals employed by service providers work closely with customers to co-create solutions (Løwendahl, 2005; von Nordenflycht, 2010). The development and enhancement of such professional services may be the next step for servitized manufacturing firms to address future customer-related challenges. Although these firms will then compete with other service firms, they may have a competitive advantage, given their product-related knowledge. Future studies of digital industrial services should closely examine the evolving professionalization of servitized firms.

Managerial Implications

This chapter can aid managers of servitized manufacturing firms who wish to utilize digital technologies in their service provision. These complex changes go far beyond the technological dimension and should be managed wisely. The conceptualization advocated in this chapter may help firms know how to develop insight and knowledge about their customers based on collected data rather than on interaction, while retaining interaction between customers and the manufacturers' installed base of products and systems. Just as manufacturers shift to new knowledge bases when initiating servitization (Davis, 2004), further enhancement of knowledge about customers via data collection manifests their positions and potentially enables further value stream migration. The conceptual models presented in this chapter may serve as guiding frameworks for managers responsible for transformations that move their firms toward digital servitization.

4   Concluding Remarks

Our analysis suggests that digital technologies influence industrial services and opportunities for customization and customer interaction, thereby extending extant knowledge (e.g., Sawhney, 2016) on opportunities for increased mass adaptation and standardization of services in the context of servitization. The dimensions of standardization and customization for industrial services are almost the opposite when these services are digitalized. The use of digital characteristics exposes the digital processes underlying these services: Informating, automating and representing expose low customer interaction, while mediating represents high customer interaction; however, informating exposes customized services, while automating, representing and mediating expose standardized services.

Future studies could examine the transformation of customer interaction into customer knowledge through informating services. How service firms increasingly practice high customer interaction through mediating is another important future research area. An issue that should be addressed carefully is the question of who owns customer data and the resulting customer knowledge, which are becoming the new trading goods.

References

Aas, T. H., & Pedersen, P. E. (2011). The impact of service innovation on firm-level financial performance. *Service Industries Journal, 31*(13), 2071–2090. https://doi.org/10.1080/02642069.2010.503883.

Aas, T. H., & Pedersen, P. E. (2013). The usefulness of componentization for specialized public service providers. *Managing Service Quality, 23*(6), 513–532. https://doi.org/10.1108/MSQ-10-2012-0138.

Alghisi, A., & Saccani, N. (2015). Internal and external alignment in the servitization journey—Overcoming the challenges. *Production Planning & Control, 26*(14–15), 1219–1232. https://doi.org/10.1080/09537287.2015.1033496.

Amara, N., Landry, R., & Doloreux, D. (2009). Patterns of innovation in knowledge-intensive business services. *Service Industries Journal, 29*(4), 407–430. https://doi.org/10.1080/02642060802307847.

Baines, T., & Lightfoot, H. W. (2013). *Made to serve: How manufacturers can compete through servitization and product service systems.* Wiley.

Baines, T., & Lightfoot, H. W. (2014). Servitization of the manufacturing firm: Exploring the operations practices and technologies that deliver advanced services. *International Journal of Operations & Production Management, 34*(1), 2–35. https://doi.org/10.1108/IJOPM-02-2012-0086.

Bask, A., Lipponen, M., Rajahonka, M., & Tinnilä, M. (2011). Framework for modularity and customization: Service perspective. *Journal of Business & Industrial Marketing, 26*(5), 306–319. https://doi.org/10.1108/0885862111111 44370.

Bettencourt, L. A., Ostrom, A. L., Brown, S. W., & Roundtree, R. I. (2002). Client co-production in knowledge-intensive business services. *California Management Review, 44*(4), 100–128.

Breunig, K. J., Kvålshaugen, R., & Hydle, K. M. (2014). Knowing your boundaries: Integration opportunities in international professional service firms. *Journal of World Business, 49*(4), 502–511. https://doi.org/10.1016/j.jwb.2013.12.004.

Carlborg, P., Kindström, D., & Kowalkowski, C. (2018). Servitization practices: A co-creation taxonomy. In M. Kohtamäki, T. Baines, R. Rabetino, & A. Z. Bigdeli (Eds.), *Practices and tools for servitization: Managing service transition* (pp. 309–321). Springer International Publishing.

Cenamor, J., Rönnberg Sjödin, D., & Parida, V. (2017). Adopting a platform approach in servitization: Leveraging the value of digitalization. *International Journal of Production Economics, 192*, 54–65. https://doi.org/10.1016/j.ijpe.2016.12.033.

Consoli, D., & Elche-Hortelano, D. (2010). Variety in the knowledge base of Knowledge Intensive Business Services. *Research Policy, 39*(10), 1303–1310. https://doi.org/10.1016/j.respol.2010.08.005.

Coreynen, W., Matthyssens, P., & Van Bockhaven, W. (2017). Boosting servitization through digitization: Pathways and dynamic resource configurations for manufacturers. *Industrial Marketing Management, 60*, 42–53. https://doi.org/10.1016/j.indmarman.2016.04.012.

Davis, S. (1987). *Future perfect.* Addison-Wesley.

Davis, T. R. V. (2004). Different service firms, different international strategies. *Business. Horizons, 47*(6), 51–59. http://search.ebscohost.com/login.aspx?direct=true&db=bth&AN=15032461&site=ehost-live.

Fisk, R. P., Brown, S. W., & Bitner, M. J. (1993). Tracking the evolution of the services marketing literature. *Journal of Retailing, 69*(1), 61–103. https://doi.org/10.1016/S0022-4359(05)80004-1.

Garcia Martin, P. C., Schroeder, A., & Ziaee Bigdeli, A. (2019). The value architecture of servitization: Expanding the research scope. *Journal of Business Research, 104*, 438–449. https://doi.org/10.1016/j.jbusres.2019.04.010.

Grönroos, C. (2011). Value co-creation in service logic: A critical analysis. *Marketing Theory, 11*(1), 279–301. https://doi.org/10.1177/1470593111408177.

Hansen, M. T., Nohria, N., & Tierney, T. (1999). What's your strategy for managing knowledge?. *Harvard Business Review, 77*(2), 106–116. http://eho stvgw2.epnet.com/start_direct2.asp?key=204.179.122.140_8000_-176300783& site=direct&return=n&db=buh&jn=HBR&scope=site.

Hellström, M. (2014). Solution business models based on functional modularity— The case of complex capital goods. *Journal of Service Management, 25*(5), 654–676. https://doi.org/10.1108/JOSM-07-2013-0198.

Hellström, M., Wikström, R., Gustafsson, M., & Luotola, H. (2016). The value of project execution services: A problem and uncertainty perspective. *Construction Management and Economics, 34*(4–5), 272–285. https://doi.org/10.1080/01446193.2016.1151062.

Jagstedt, S., Hedvall, K., & Persson, M. (2018). The virtue of customising solutions: A managerial framework. In M. Kohtamäki, T. Baines, R. Rabetino, & A. Z. Bigdeli (Eds.), *Practices and tools for servitization: Managing service transition* (pp. 291–308). Springer International Publishing.

Jonsson, K., Mathiassen, L., & Holmström, J. (2018). Representation and mediation in digitalized work: Evidence from maintenance of mining machinery. *Journal of Information Technology, 33*(3), 216–232. https://doi.org/10.1057/s41 265-017-0050-x.

Kamalaldin, A., Linde, L., Sjödin, D., & Parida, V. (2020). Transforming provider-customer relationships in digital servitization: A relational view on digitalization. *Industrial Marketing Management, 89*, 306–325. https://doi.org/10.1016/j.ind marman.2020.02.004.

Kohtamäki, M., Parida, V., Oghazi, P., Gebauer, H., & Baines, T. (2019). Digital servitization business models in ecosystems: A theory of the firm. *Journal of Business Research, 104*, 380–392. https://doi.org/10.1016/j.jbusres.2019.06.027.

Kvålshaugen, R., Hydle, K. M., & Brehmer, P.-O. (2015). Innovative capabilities in international professional service firms: Enabling trade-offs between past, present, and future service provision. *Journal of Professions and Organization, 2*(2), 148–167. https://doi.org/10.1093/jpo/jov005.

Larsson, R., & Bowen, D. E. (1989). Organization and customer: Managing design and coordination of services. *Academy of Management Review, 14*(2), 213–233.

Lenka, S., Parida, V., & Wincent, J. (2017). Digitalization capabilities as enablers of value co-creation in servitizing firms. *Psychology & Marketing, 34*(1), 92–100.

Løwendahl, B. R. (2005). *Strategic management of professional service firms* (3rd ed.). Copenhagen Business School Press.

Maister, D. H. (1993). *Managing the professional service firm*. The Free Press.

Normann, R. (1984). *Service management*. Wiley.

Paiola, M., & Gebauer, H. (2020). Internet of things technologies, digital servitization and business model innovation in BtoB manufacturing firms. *Industrial Marketing Management*. https://doi.org/10.1016/j.indmarman.2020.03.009.

Parida, V., Sjödin, D., & Reim, W. (2019). Reviewing literature on digitalization, business model innovation, and sustainable industry: Past achievements and future promises. *Sustainability, 11*(2), 391. https://www.mdpi.com/2071-1050/11/2/391.

Partanen, J., Kohtamäki, M., Parida, V., & Wincent, J. (2017). Developing and validating a multi-dimensional scale for operationalizing industrial service offering. *Journal of Business & Industrial Marketing, 32*(2), 295–309. https://doi.org/10.1108/JBIM-08-2016-0178.

Piller, F., & Möslein, K. (2002). *Economies of interaction and economies of relationship: Value drivers in a customer centric economy.* Paper presented at the ANZAM-IFSAM 2002 Conference, Brisbane, Australia.

Porter, M. E. (1996, November–December). What is strategy? *Harvard Business Review,* 61–78.

Ramírez, R. (1999). Value co-production: Intellectual origins and implications for practice and research. *Strategic Management Journal, 20*(1), 49–65. http://www.jstor.org/cgi-bin/jstor/printpage/01432095/sp030025/03x0201s/0.pdf?backcontext=table-of-contents&dowhat=Acrobat&config=jstor&userID=90a4153b@bi.no/01cc99331600501b1832b&0.pdf.

Sawhney, M. (2016, September). Putting products into services. *Harvard Business Review, 94,* 82–89.

Schmenner, R. W. (1986). How can service businesses survive and prosper?. *Sloan Management Review, 27*(3), 21–32. http://search.ebscohost.com/login.aspx?direct=true&db=bth&AN=4021720&site=bsi-live.

Siggelkow, N. (2007). Persuasion with case studies. *Academy of Management Journal, 50*(1), 20–24. https://doi.org/10.5465/amj.2007.24160882.

Sjödin, D., Parida, V., Kohtamäki, M., & Wincent, J. (2020). An agile co-creation process for digital servitization: A micro-service innovation approach. *Journal of Business Research, 112,* 478–491. https://doi.org/10.1016/j.jbusres.2020.01.009.

Vargo, S. L., & Lusch, R. F. (2008). Service-dominant logic: Continuing the evolution. *Journal of the Academy of Marketing Science, 36*(1), 1–10. https://doi.org/10.1007/s11747-007-0069-6.

Visnjic, I., Wiengarten, F., & Neely, A. (2016). Only the brave: Product innovation, service business model innovation, and their impact on performance. *Journal of Product Innovation Management, 33*(1), 36–52. https://doi.org/10.1111/jpim.12254.

von Nordenflycht, A. (2010). What is a professional service firm? Toward a theory and taxonomy of knowledge intensive firms. *Academy of Management Review, 35*(1), 155–174. http://search.ebscohost.com/login.aspx?direct=true&db=bth&AN=45577926&site=ehost-live.

Wikström, K., Hellström, M., Artto, K., Kujala, J., & Kujala, S. (2009). Services in project-based firms—Four types of business logic. *International Journal of Project Management, 27*(2), 113–122. https://doi.org/10.1016/j.ijproman.2008.09.008.

Zuboff, S. (1985). Automate/informate: The two faces of intelligent technology. *Organizational Dynamics, 14*(2), 5–18. https://doi.org/10.1016/0090-2616(85)90033-6.

Zuboff, S. (1988). *In The age of the smart machine: The future of work and power.* Basic Books.

Relational Transformation for Digital Servitization

Anmar Kamalaldin, Lina Linde, David Sjödin, and Vinit Parida

1 Introduction

Digital Servitization

Digitalization is considered by both practitioners and academics as a source of competitive advantage, as it is opening up new opportunities for value creation and value capture. In light of that, manufacturers are increasingly undergoing a servitization transition from providing products to providing

A. Kamalaldin (✉) · L. Linde · D. Sjödin · V. Parida
Entrepreneurship and Innovation, Luleå University of Technology, Luleå, Sweden
e-mail: anmar.kamalaldin@ltu.se

L. Linde
e-mail: lina.linde@ltu.se

D. Sjödin
e-mail: david.sjodin@ltu.se

V. Parida
e-mail: vinit.parida@ltu.se

D. Sjödin
USN Business School, University of South Eastern Norway, Notodden, Norway

V. Parida
Department of Management, University of Vaasa, Vaasa, Finland

M. Kohtamäki et al. (eds.), *The Palgrave Handbook of Servitization*,
https://doi.org/10.1007/978-3-030-75771-7_24

services and solutions enabled by digital technologies (Hasselblatt et al., 2018; Kohtamäki et al., 2019). This trend is referred to as *digital servitization* (Vendrell-Herrero & Wilson, 2017), and can be defined as *"the transformation in processes, capabilities, and offerings within industrial firms and their associated ecosystems to progressively create, deliver, and capture increased service value arising from a broad range of enabling digital technologies such as the Internet of Things (IoT), big data, Artificial Intelligence (AI), and cloud computing"* (Sjödin et al., 2020: 478). An example of digital services is ABB's remote optimization service which is offered through its collaborative operations centers for gearless mill drives, employing its technological expertise and digital technologies. Remote services can enable the provider to offer availability guarantees (Lerch & Gotsch, 2015), as remote monitoring and diagnostics allow for proactive maintenance, for example (Allmendinger & Lombreglia, 2005). Typically, providers adopt a digital servitization strategy to generate new revenue streams and differentiate themselves from their competitors (Opresnik & Taisch, 2015; Scherer et al., 2016). Though, this necessitates a transformation in provider–customer relationships to move from transactional product-centric models to relational service-oriented engagement (Kamalaldin et al., 2020; Pagoropoulos et al., 2017; Reim et al., 2018; Sjödin et al., 2020).

Provider–Customer Relationships in Digital Servitization

Digital servitization requires the provider to undertake bigger responsibility for the customer's core processes (Lerch & Gotsch, 2015), and thus, provider–customer relationship must transform to one that is based on a logic of co-creation, long-term commitment, and high investment in the relationship. However, many companies struggle with various relational challenges, such as how to balance between control and trust, and between risk and reward (Reim et al., 2018), how to determine the appropriate level of customization, how to ensure transparency and data sharing, and integrate digital systems (Coreynen et al., 2017).

To address these challenges, this chapter integrates insights from literature on digitalization and servitization with the theoretical perspective of the relational view, which argues that competitive advantage is a result of inter-firm relations and joint input of partners (Dyer & Singh, 1998; Dyer et al., 2018). The relational view suggests four determinants of inter-organizational competitive advantage: complementary resources and capabilities, relation-specific assets, knowledge-sharing routines, and effective governance. Dyer and Singh suggest that these determinants can generate relational rents, defined as the *"supernormal profit jointly generated in exchange relationship that cannot be generated by either company in isolation and can only be created through the joint idiosyncratic contributions of the specific alliance partners"* (Dyer & Singh, 1998: 662).

This chapter conceptualizes the determinants of relational rent in the context of digital servitization, and presents a *relational transformation framework for digital servitization*. The framework is based on four relational components that evolve as the provider–customer relationship progresses: complementary digitalization capabilities, relation-specific digital assets, digitally enabled knowledge-sharing routines, and partnership governance (Kamalaldin et al., 2020).

2   A Relational Transformation Framework for Digital Servitization

The framework highlights that *complementary digitalization capabilities* represent the key trigger for initiating and preserving a digital servitization relationship, hence, complementarity is the foundation for partnership. To progress with this partnership, the provider and customer must continue to invest in *relation-specific digital assets*, and enhance *digitally enabled knowledge-sharing routines*, in order to maximize the potential of their relationship. Furthermore, *partnership governance* must be gradually transformed to a relational trust-based approach in order to fully leverage the potential of digitalization.

The following sections provide further details and elaborations on each of the relational components and explain how they evolve across three phases (*foundational, intermediate, and advanced*). These phases are empirically derived from the study of Kamalaldin et al. (2020), supplemented by insights from research describing the typical transformation process phases in the context of servitization and digitalization (e.g. Baines et al., 2020; Iansiti & Lakhani, 2014; Lerch & Gotsch, 2015). The framework is presented in Table 1, providing an overview on the different phases of digital servitization relationships.

Complementary Digitalization Capabilities

Having specialized competences and expertise is necessary for implementing digital technologies (Ardolino et al., 2018). Digitalization capabilities such as intelligence, connectivity, and analytics (Lenka et al., 2017) are essential

Table 1 A relational transformation framework for digital servitization

	Foundational phase *Exploratory phase for building the partnership's foundation with the new partner*	Intermediate phase *Developmental phase for collaborating to increase the value of the partnership*	Advanced phase *Strategic phase for driving long-term investments in continuous innovation*
Complementary digitalization capabilities The synergy-sensitive specialized digital competences and expertise (such as connectivity) that each partner possess, which when combined, their value increases	• Evaluate the benefits of combining provider's expertise and customer's business knowledge	• Monitor partner's capability evolution and reassess complementarity	
Relational-specific digital assets The specialized digital assets that are of strategic importance for the relationship, including both physical assets (such as machinery) and human assets (such as dedicated digital experts)	• Invest in building digital systems • Assign dedicated staff for managing digital systems	• Develop digital platform tailored to customer's systems • Allocate time and resources to gain know-how of business processes	• Enable offer customization and efficiency based on digital platform • Build joint digital and analytics team to keep track of key operational processes

	Foundational phase *Exploratory phase for building the partnership's foundation with the new partner*	Intermediate phase *Developmental phase for collaborating to increase the value of the partnership*	Advanced phase *Strategic phase for driving long-term investments in continuous innovation*
Digitally enabled knowledge-sharing routine The purposefully designed processes and interactions between partners that allow specialized knowledge to be transferred, recombined, or created, enabled by digital means (such as data analytics)	• Collect operational data from physical assets to monitor performance • Undertake ad-hoc discussions to utilize insights from operational data	• Accumulate and connect data from multiple sources to enable transparency and optimization • Set up regular interactions between partners to integrate data into joint operations	• Align incentives to enable increased data transparency and analysis • Establish a multi-level joint team to use data for continuous improvement and innovation
Partnership governance The safeguard used by partners to enforce what they have agreed, including both formal safeguards (such as financial penalties) and informal safeguards (such as reputation)	• *Contractual governance* to safeguard partners' interests	• *Transitional governance* to revise the contract and realign incentives	• *Relational governance* to focus on mutually beneficial improvements

for this endeavor. When a company does not have all the required digitalization capabilities, it fills the gap by partnering with other companies, and customers usually involve providers in operations that fall outside their core competences (Sjödin et al., 2018). Thus, complementary digitalization capabilities are the trigger for initiating and preserving the provider–customer relationship in digital servitization.

Foundational phase: if a digital servitization relationship is to be initiated, partners should evaluate the benefits of combining the digital expertise of the provider and the operational business knowledge of the customer. Sought after benefits include improved efficiency and optimized resource utilization through digital services, for example.

Intermediate and advanced phases: given the rapid development of digital technologies, it is vital to continue monitoring the evolution of partner's capabilities and reassess complementarity throughout the phases of the relationship. In order to maintain the rationale for continuing a partnership, partners should keep up with the speed of development that enables value creation.

Empirical example: in order to improve efficiency through digital services, a mining company complemented its knowledge in mining operations and minerals processing with its provider's expertise in digital mining equipment and control systems. The provider possessed the digitalization capabilities that the mining company lacked, enabling them to integrate the machines fleet and control systems to pinpoint further optimization opportunities. This complementarity was continuously evaluated and reassessed for subsequent projects (Kamalaldin et al., 2020).

Relation-Specific Digital Assets

When complementary digitalization capabilities are present, partners are motivated to invest in relation-specific digital assets. These are specialized assets of strategic importance for the relationship. For example, in order for a provider to offer availability guarantees for machines and plants, it has to link customer's plants with its digital architecture via a compatible connectivity and network (Lerch & Gotsch, 2015). However, relation-specific digital assets do not only include physical assets such as machinery, but also human assets such as know-how and staff dedicated to drive digitalization within the relationship. In particular, partners gradually invest in aligning their digital technologies, and in developing digital competence, and both evolve throughout the phases of the relationship.

Foundational phase: at this early phase of the relationship, the investments in relation-specific digital assets are largely focused on building the digital systems needed for providing the digital services. This includes, for example, installing sensors and digitally connecting the machine fleet. To facilitate this, dedicated staff are assigned to manage digital systems and services, as it is important to commit human resources to the digitalization efforts.

Intermediate phase: when the provider–customer relationship enters an intermediate phase, their focus turns to developing a tailored digital platform which facilitates the implementation of various digital services across different functions. For example, through this platform, the customer's operations team can check the performance of equipment and order optimization services, and the provider's account managers can assess how they can better help the customer. Moreover, at this phase, both sides tend to dedicate more resources to improve staff's know-how of business processes and digital operations, potentially opening the door to further opportunities.

Advanced phase: at this phase, the digital platform can become an enabler for identifying new solutions for efficiency improvement and offer customization, and in turn, increasing the potential for further value creation. What is more, the provider and customer are likely to establish a joint analytics team, including members from both sides, in order to keep track of key operations and further develop digital competence.

Empirical example: an energy and utilities company established a relationship with a provider of automation technologies. At the *foundational phase*, the provider's applications were built on the digital systems of the energy company, and dedicated engineers were assigned for joint operations. At an *intermediate phase*, a joint digitalization center was formed, and a digital platform was developed. This platform was improved at the relationship's *advanced phase* to enable resolution to operational problems such as the positioning of water leakages. Moreover, a joint team was established for developing additional solutions (Kamalaldin et al., 2020).

Digitally Enabled Knowledge-Sharing Routines

In addition to investing in relation-specific digital assets, partners should also set up digitally enabled knowledge-sharing routines. These are purposefully designed processes and interactions between partners that facilitate knowledge exchange. The purpose of these routines is to enable specialized knowledge to be transferred, recombined, or created (Grant, 1996). In digital servitization relationships, these knowledge-sharing routines are, unsurprisingly, digitally enabled and data-driven. Whilst digital technologies allow partners to easily communicate and share data and information (Gago & Rubalcaba, 2007; Martín-Peña et al., 2018), this does not necessarily translate into improved knowledge-sharing or performance. Thus, it is key to translate data into knowledge, and transform it into valuable insights and actions (Lenka et al., 2017). This can be enabled through digital services that are reliant on machine intelligence, where real-time data is automatically collected, validated, stored, and transformed into actionable knowledge (Allmendinger & Lombreglia, 2005). Consequently, partners should not only seek to enhance the transparency of knowledge-sharing, but also develop the associated processes to utilize the data and knowledge; processes which should gradually evolve across the phases of the relationship.

Foundational phase: at the relationship's foundational phase, the focus is on collecting data from physical assets to monitor performance in support of the digital services. Therefore, it is important to set up the required technologies, such as sensors, as well as digital systems for storing data, from the beginning of the relationship. Naturally, data has little value if not utilized, so, partners need to collaborate to maximize value from the collected data. At this phase, insights from operational data tend to be utilized in an ad-hoc and unstructured way. For example, this can simply take the form of conversations and feedback among operators.

Intermediate phase: at this phase of the relationship, partners shift focus from monitoring to optimizing operations. The provider and customer collaborate to accumulate and connect data from multiple sources to enable further transparency and optimization. For example, accumulating data from the whole fleet of machines and from the entire process can enable partners to identify operational problems and to use analytics to optimize operations. At this phase, partners also seek better ways to utilize knowledge, and regular interactions become more structured with the aim to integrate data into joint operations. These interactions are conducted at different levels, including operational meetings as well as managerial meetings.

Advanced phase: at this phase, the focus of knowledge-sharing routines shift from coordination to integration. Consequently, partners align incentives to enable comprehensive data exchange and analysis, with the aim of enhancing transparency and to achieve mutual benefits. This helps to maintain trust in the relationship, allowing both parties to recognize the business opportunities that may emerge from open data exchange. Thus, a key aspect of the relational transformation in this endeavor is about overcoming possible reluctance to sharing data, and this reluctance tends to be minimized when trust is built and benefits of open data exchange are recognized. In order to effectively utilize data and knowledge, partners may establish a joint R&D team at this phase to foster continuous improvement and innovation and agree on priorities.

Empirical example: a forestry company, together with an equipment provider, installed digital hardware and software for monitoring machines' performance. This laid the foundation for knowledge-sharing and ad-hoc discussions of production efficiency at the *foundational phase* of the relationship. At the *intermediate phase*, data was accumulated from various machines, enabling better site management. Additionally, semi-annual meetings were held between the forestry company's operators and the equipment provider's mechanics for discussing performance improvements. At the *advanced phase*, the partners integrated their data in order to facilitate a digital service package, and a joint team was established for exploring new opportunities and the latest digital innovations in the industry (Kamalaldin et al., 2020).

Partnership Governance

Governance may be considered as the key differentiator that allows for the development of the other relational components, as it is the safeguard for enforcing what partners have agreed upon (Dyer et al., 2018). Governance mechanisms include formal means such as legal contracts and financial penalties (Reim et al., 2018; Williamson, 1983), as well as informal safeguards like goodwill, trust, and reputation (Gulati, 1995; Larson, 1992; Powell, 1990; Uzzi, 1997; Weigelt & Camerer, 1988). In the context of digital servitization, a key paradox in governing a relationship is related to balancing between control and flexibility (Svahn et al., 2017), as the latter is necessary for innovation and exploiting new digital opportunities. Therefore, the provider and customer should agree on governance mechanisms for their partnerships, where they adjust the balance between control and flexibility over time to improve governance efficiency. Indeed, as the relationship develops, more emphasis tends to be put on informal mechanisms, given that mutual trust evolves over time. *"Digital servitization partnerships often begin with a highly contractual governance approach, then develop into the phase of transitional governance, and eventually on to a highly relational governance approach as the relationship matures"* (Kamalaldin et al., 2020: 317).

Foundational phase: at the start of the relationship, partners are inclined to initiate a highly *contractual governance* approach with high levels of control to safeguard their interests. The initial contract tends to be very detailed, as trust is yet to be built. Partners are likely to define key performance indicators to drive value creation. Partners may also account for certain scenarios that they want to safeguard themselves from.

Intermediate phase: it is obviously not feasible to anticipate every possible scenario that can occur, since unexpected events may happen throughout the relationship. Therefore, as the relationship develops, partners may consider adding contractual incentives to facilitate a transition to a partnership built on trust. Thus, they establish a *transitional governance* approach to revise the contract and realign incentives. Mechanisms such as "reward-penalty" and "gain-pain sharing" may be incorporated. As the term suggests, the aim of transitional governance is to set the stage for the transition from a highly contractual governance approach to a more relational one.

Advanced phase: when the relationship progresses well, and partners feel more confident about each other's capabilities, they work to establish a *relational governance* approach that is based on trust with no tight control. This enables them to concentrate on mutually beneficial improvements rather than on monitoring partner's behavior. Trust also enables more efficient collective review of performance, as well as efficient negotiation processes.

Empirical example: at the *foundational phase* of a relationship between a telecom equipment provider and a network provider, their contract was laid out in meticulous details, including tight boundary conditions and back-stops. However, at the *intermediate phase*, they revised the contract to incorporate "reward-penalty" mechanisms to align incentives, and data-driven KPIs formed a foundation for contract re-negotiation. At the *advanced phase*, the governance approach was transformed toward an emphasis on relational benefits and upholding a "win–win" situation in contract implementation (Kamalaldin et al., 2020).

3   Discussion

Digital servitization requires a transformation in provider–customer relationships. Failing to adapt to the new relational requirements may limit the possibility to benefit from digitalization. This chapter advances knowledge on the transformation of industrial provider–customer relationships in digital servitization by combining insights from the literature on digitalization and servitization with the relational view (Dyer & Singh, 1998; Dyer et al., 2018). The relational transformation framework for digital servitization presented in this chapter highlights four relational components that are important to consider (complementary digitalization capabilities, relation-specific digital assets, digitally enabled knowledge-sharing routines, and partnership governance), and shows how they evolve across the different phases of the provider–customer relationship. The framework carries theoretical implications for the emerging digital servitization literature, as well as managerial implications for managers who are active in digital servitization initiatives.

Theoretical Contributions

By integrating the theoretical perspective of the relational view (Dyer & Singh, 1998; Dyer et al., 2018) in the context of digital servitization, we contribute to the servitization literature which has been criticized for being phenomena driven and lacking theoretical application (Rabetino et al., 2018). We show that the relational view is a useful theoretical lens for understanding provider–customer relationships, which must be transformed in order to benefit from digital servitization (Pagoropoulos et al., 2017). The relational view provides a more dynamic perspective compared to the resource-based view. Whilst the resource-based view highlights how a firm derives competitive advantage by having valuable, rare, inimitable, and non-substitutable resources (Barney et al., 2001), it does not consider the fact that these resources may extend beyond the boundaries of a single firm and may be complemented by a partner's resources and capabilities. Due to the rapid development of digital technologies, it is evident that no firm can keep pace on its own (Bogers et al., 2018), and thus, the provider–customer relationship is an important unit of analysis in investigating digital servitization.

Furthermore, we contribute to digital servitization literature by shedding light on both sides of the provider–customer relationship. Existing literature has mainly focused on the provider perspective, and it is necessary to include the less-studied customer perspective to understand digital servitization relationships (Coreynen et al., 2017; Holmlund et al., 2016; Raddats et al., 2019; Tuli et al., 2007; Valtakoski, 2017). The framework this chapter presents takes into consideration both provider and customer perspectives, viewing them as partners who cooperatively co-create value. Thus, it provides a more holistic transformation model for the relationship at its different phases, as opposed to models that mainly focus on the provider's transformation (e.g. Lerch & Gotsh, 2015).

Whilst literature on servitization and digitalization emphasizes the necessity for relational and trust-based governance approaches (e.g. Reim et al., 2018; Sarker et al., 2012; Sjödin et al., 2019), the focus is mainly on comparing relational governance and contractual governance. The framework presented in this chapter takes a step further by illuminating how the governance approach can be progressively adapted over the different phases of the digital servitization relationship. The framework shows how partnership governance transforms from contractual governance at the foundational phase, to transitional governance at the intermediate phase, to relational governance at the advanced phase.

Managerial Implications

The framework offers guidance for providers and customers pursuing transformation of their relationships to maximize benefits from digital servitization, as it underlines what to focus on at each phase of the relationship. This can help managers at both sides to make informed decisions and prioritize resources.

Moreover, the framework can serve as a template for facilitating negotiations and discussions between the provider and customer based on the activities highlighted for different phases. For example, they may discuss how relation-specific digital assets (such as a digital platform) should co-evolve with digitally enabled knowledge-sharing routines (such as accumulating data from multiple sources). This emphasizes the interconnection between the different relational components that partners should pay attention to, as focusing on one to the neglect of the other may not generate the anticipated value.

Additionally, the framework supports managers in developing governance mechanisms in the different phases of the provider–customer relationship. The framework emphasizes that the partnership governance approach should progressively develop over time to improve efficiency, and hence, managers from both sides should continuously revise it based on experience.

References

Allmendinger, G., & Lombreglia, R. (2005). Four strategies for the age of smart services. *Harvard Business Review, 83*(10), 131.

Ardolino, M., Rapaccini, M., Saccani, N., Gaiardelli, P., Crespi, G., & Ruggeri, C. (2018). The role of digital technologies for the service transformation of industrial companies. *International Journal of Production Research, 56*(6), 2116–2132.

Baines, T., Bigdeli, A. Z., Sousa, R., & Schroeder, A. (2020). Framing the servitization transformation process: A model to understand and facilitate the servitization journey. *International Journal of Production Economics, 221*, 107463.

Barney, J., Wright, M., & Ketchen, D. J., Jr. (2001). The resource-based view of the firm: Ten years after 1991. *Journal of Management, 27*(6), 625–641.

Bogers, M., Chesbrough, H., & Moedas, C. (2018). Open innovation: Research, practices, and policies. *California Management Review, 60*(2), 5–16.

Coreynen, W., Matthyssens, P., & Van Bockhaven, W. (2017). Boosting servitization through digitization: Pathways and dynamic resource configurations for manufacturers. *Industrial Marketing Management, 60*, 42–53.

Dyer, J. H., & Singh, H. (1998). The relational view: Cooperative strategy and sources of interorganizational competitive advantage. *Academy of Management Review, 23*(4), 660–679.

Dyer, J. H., Singh, H., & Hesterly, W. S. (2018). The relational view revisited: A dynamic perspective on value creation and value capture. *Strategic Management Journal, 39*(12), 3140–3162.

Gago, D., & Rubalcaba, L. (2007). Innovation and ICT in service firms: Towards a multidimensional approach for impact assessment. *Journal of Evolutionary Economics, 17*(1), 25–44.

Grant, R. M. (1996). Prospering in dynamically-competitive environments: Organizational capability as knowledge integration. *Organization Science, 7*(4), 375–387.

Gulati, R. (1995). Does familiarity breed trust? The implications of repeated ties for contractual choice in alliances. *Academy of Management Journal, 38*(1), 85–112.

Hasselblatt, M., Huikkola, T., Kohtamäki, M., & Nickell, D. (2018). Modeling manufacturer's capabilities for the internet of things. *Journal of Business & Industrial Marketing, 33*(6), 822–836.

Holmlund, M., Kowalkowski, C., & Biggemann, S. (2016). Organizational behavior in innovation, marketing, and purchasing in business service contexts—An agenda for academic inquiry. *Journal of Business Research, 69*(7), 2457–2462.

Iansiti, M., & Lakhani, K. R. (2014). Digital ubiquity: How connections, sensors, and data are revolutionizing business. *Harvard Business Review, 92*(11), 19.

Kamalaldin, A., Linde, L., Sjödin, D., & Parida, V. (2020). Transforming provider-customer relationships in digital servitization: A relational view on digitalization. *Industrial Marketing Management, 89*, 306–325.

Kohtamäki, M., Parida, V., Oghazi, P., Gebauer, H., & Baines, T. (2019). Digital servitization business models in ecosystems: A theory of the firm. *Journal of Business Research, 104*(11), 380–392.

Larson, A. (1992). Network dyads in entrepreneurial settings: A study of the governance of exchange relationships. *Administrative Science Quarterly*, 76–104.

Lenka, S., Parida, V., & Wincent, J. (2017). Digitalization capabilities as enablers of value co-creation in servitizing firms. *Psychology & Marketing, 34*(1), 92–100.

Lerch, C., & Gotsch, M. (2015). Digitalized product-service systems in manufacturing firms: A case study analysis. *Research-Technology Management, 58*(5), 45–52.

Martín-Peña, M. L., Díaz-Garrido, E., & Sánchez-López, J. M. (2018). The digitalization and servitization of manufacturing: A review on digital business models. *Strategic Change, 27*(2), 91–99.

Opresnik, D., & Taisch, M. (2015). The value of big data in servitization. *International Journal of Production Economics, 165*, 174–184.

Pagoropoulos, A., Maier, A., & McAloone, T. C. (2017). Assessing transformational change from institutionalising digital capabilities on implementation and development of product-service systems: Learnings from the maritime industry. *Journal of Cleaner Production, 166*, 369–380.

Powell, W. W. (1990). Neither market nor hierarchy: Network forms of organization. In B. M. Staw & L. L. Cummings (Eds.), *Research in organizational behaviour.* (Vol. 12, pp. 295–336). JAI Press.

Rabetino, R., Harmsen, W., Kohtamäki, M., & Sihvonen, J. (2018). Structuring servitization-related research. *International Journal of Operations & Production Management, 38*(2), 350–371.

Raddats, C., Kowalkowski, C., Benedettini, O., Burton, J., & Gebauer, H. (2019). Servitization: A contemporary thematic review of four major research streams. *Industrial Marketing Management, 83*, 207–223.

Reim, W., Sjödin, D., & Parida, V. (2018). Mitigating adverse customer behaviour for product-service system provision: An agency theory perspective. *Industrial Marketing Management, 74*, 150–161.

Sarker, S., Sarker, S., Sahaym, A., & Bjørn-Andersen, N. (2012). Exploring value cocreation in relationships between an ERP vendor and its partners: A revelatory case study. *MIS Quarterly, 36*(1), 317–338.

Scherer, J. O., Kloeckner, A. P., Ribeiro, J. L. D., Pezzotta, G., & Pirola, F. (2016). Product-service system (PSS) design: Using design thinking and business analytics to improve PSS design. *Procedia CIRP, 47*, 341–346.

Sjödin, D., Parida, V., Jovanovic, M., & Visnjic, I. (2020). Value creation and value capture alignment in business model innovation: A process view on outcome-based business models. *Journal of Product Innovation Management, 37*(2), 158–183.

Sjödin, D., Parida, V., & Kohtamäki, M. (2019). Relational governance strategies for advanced service provision: Multiple paths to superior financial performance in servitization. *Journal of Business Research, 101*, 906–915.

Sjödin, D., Parida, V., Kohtamäki, M., & Wincent, J. (2020). An agile co-creation process for digital servitization: A micro-service innovation approach. *Journal of Business Research, 112*, 478–491.

Sjödin, D. R., Parida, V., Leksell, M., & Petrovic, A. (2018). Smart factory implementation and process innovation. *Research-Technology Management, 61*(5), 22–31.

Svahn, F., Mathiassen, L., & Lindgren, R. (2017). Embracing digital innovation in incumbent firms: How Volvo cars managed competing concerns. *MIS Quarterly, 41*(1), 239–253.

Tuli, K. R., Kohli, A. K., & Bharadwaj, S. G. (2007). Rethinking customer solutions: From product bundles to relational processes. *Journal of Marketing, 71*(3), 1–17.

Uzzi, B. (1997). Social structure and competition in interfirm networks: The paradox of embeddedness. *Administrative Science Quarterly, 42*, 35–67.

Valtakoski, A. (2017). Explaining servitization failure and deservitization: A knowledge-based perspective. *Industrial Marketing Management, 60*, 138–150.

Vendrell-Herrero, F., & Wilson James, R. (2017). Servitization for territorial competitiveness: Taxonomy and research agenda. *Competitiveness Review: An International Business Journal, 27*(1), 2–11.

Weigelt, K., & Camerer, C. (1988). Reputation and corporate strategy: A review of recent theory and applications. *Strategic Management Journal, 9*(5), 443–454.

Williamson, O. E. (1983). Credible commitments: Using hostages to support exchange. *The American Economic Review, 73*(4), 519–540.

Service-Dominant Logic: A Missing Link in Servitization Research?

Maria Åkesson and Nina Löfberg

1   Introduction

Parallel to the evolving literature on servitization, the notion of service-dominant (S-D) logic has evolved as a perspective on marketing (e.g. Vargo & Lusch, 2004). The research fields of servitization and S-D logic have mainly developed separately, even though they are highly relevant to each other. We argue that S-D logic can be seen as a missing link in servitization research; a foundational service business logic, comprising a firm's mission and its employees' mental models, which has been omitted from previous research, to explain and understand how firms can manage servitization.

S-D logic as a business logic means that service is a perspective of value creation, rather than an output (Edvardsson et al., 2005). Moreover, service is the fundamental unit of exchange and value is considered to be co-created through resource integration in service ecosystems, and decided as value-in-use (Vargo & Lusch, 2004, 2016). This can be compared to a business logic based on the traditional goods-dominant (G-D) logic, where value is considered to be created by the producer and embedded in an offering (Vargo &

M. Åkesson · N. Löfberg (✉)
Service Research Center, Karlstad University, Karlstad, Sweden
e-mail: nina.lofberg@kau.se

M. Åkesson
e-mail: maria.akesson@kau.se

© The Author(s), under exclusive license to Springer Nature
Switzerland AG 2021
M. Kohtamäki et al. (eds.), *The Palgrave Handbook of Servitization*,
https://doi.org/10.1007/978-3-030-75771-7_25

389

Lusch, 2004). In this mindset, services are considered to be a different type of output to goods (Edvardsson et al., 2005), and managed accordingly.

Combining S-D logic and servitization is not completely new. Many aspects of S-D logic, e.g. offering solutions to customer needs (e.g. Davies, 2004; Ng et al., 2013), the importance of emphasizing the knowledge and skills of employees (e.g. Auguste et al., 2006; Smith et al., 2014), the importance of value creation and value-in-use (e.g. Smith et al., 2014), and the emphasis on relationships in business networks (Ford, 2011), have been discussed both in a servitization context and in B2B marketing research. Demonstrably, S-D logic is also applicable to manufacturing firms (Baines et al., 2017; Kowalkowski, 2010; Ng et al., 2012; Vargo & Lusch 2008, 2011).

In this chapter, we combine S-D logic and servitization research to create a framework that contributes to an improved theoretical basis for servitization. First, we describe what constitutes S-D logic and how it has been discussed in previous servitization research. Then, we present a model that combines the research fields and shows what S-D logic means for servitization. Finally, we discuss three implications for theory and practice; (1) a definition of servitization, (2) a foundational service business logic to guide servitization, and (3) a holistic view of servitization.

2   S-D Logic and Servitization Research

S-D logic is based on 11 foundational premises that have recently been rationalized into five axioms (Vargo & Lusch, 2016). In what follows, we present the axioms and discuss what they entail for servitization.

Service Is the Fundamental Basis of Exchange

The first axiom: *Service is the fundamental basis of exchange*, originates from the idea that service (knowledge and skills) is prominent to goods and that it is the activities arising from the knowledge and skills of people that are transmitted during the service-for-service exchange (Vargo & Lusch, 2004). It is, hence, knowledge and skills that comprise the source of value. In other words, just having a good without the relevant knowledge and skills regarding how to use it will not create value. An important outcome of this reasoning is that S-D logic uses the term "services" (plural) to refer to units of output. The value-creating process that reflects the process of doing something beneficial is referred to as *service* (Edvardsson et al., 2005; Vargo & Lusch, 2008).

Combining S-D logic and servitization, this first axiom would mean a change in the view of what is being sold: an output (goods, services, or both) or knowledge and skills as solutions to a problem or need. This seemingly small distinction has major implications for servitization since the latter alternative per se includes a more holistic approach than the limited view of offering an output entails. For instance, when a manufacturing firm collects data from an installed base, the data per se is not what creates value. Rather, the value lies in the process of doing something beneficial to the data, such as when an employee with specialized knowledge interprets that data. This interpretation can then lead to a customized solution for the customer. Offering solutions to customer needs is nothing new in servitization research; rather, researchers in the field of integrated solutions have been discussing this for quite a while (e.g. Davies, 2004; Ng et al., 2013). Moreover, the importance of emphasizing the knowledge and skills of employees during the servitization process has also been discussed before (e.g. Auguste et al., 2006; Smith et al., 2014).

Value Is Co-created by Multiple Actors

The second axiom: *Value is co-created by multiple actors, always including the beneficiary* (Vargo & Lusch, 2016), implies that firms cannot offer value but propositions of value. These value propositions are made up of combinations of resources, such as knowledge and skills or raw materials, which can be combined into, e.g. goods, services, or solutions with the aim of co-creating value with other actors. In a G-D logic perspective, the service provider is considered the sole value creator since value is seen as embedded in the output (often during a production process). In S-D logic, the offering can be seen as having no value until acted upon by actors (Vargo & Lusch, 2004). A normative misunderstanding of this axiom is that it implies that firms should always involve their customers in, e.g. the design, creation, or completion of a firm's output, and, hence, in the co-production of value. Vargo and Lusch (2016), however, state that co-production is relatively optional, while co-creation, on the other hand, is not. This axiom is about the co-creation of value as the purpose of exchange, which is not something an individual actor does alone. As such, the axiom highlights the multi-actor nature of the process of value creation.

Adopting this view would mean a manufacturing firm creating value with other actors, e.g. customers or partners. In understanding what value should be co-created, understanding customer processes is unavoidable. This implies the need to spend time at customer sites and to keep business processes as transparent as possible. It implies that collaborations are necessary, and that value is created for multiple actors, not just the manufacturing firm itself. To illustrate this, imagine a manufacturing firm, during a planned customer visit, noticing that an important bolt is about to fall off a machine they have sold. By solving the problem before the bolt falls off, a major breakdown can be prevented. Meanwhile, the manufacturing firm's R&D unit gets feedback that enables learning and knowledge creation for the future. Hence, value is created through the integration of resources provided by many actors. The importance of value creation in relation to servitization is also something that has been discussed in previous research (e.g. Smith et al., 2014).

All Actors Are Resource Integrators

The third axiom highlights the fact that all *social and economic actors are resource integrators* (Vargo & Lusch, 2016). The actors are the ones carrying the most important resource: knowledge and skills. These operant resources are superior to other resources since they are the ones acting upon other resources (e.g. raw material) (Vargo & Lusch, 2004). As such, the actors, e.g. customers, partners, and employees, are seen as enacting active roles and can thus also enact the roles of, for instance, innovators or designers. Emphasizing this kind of relationship between partners is not new in B2B research and practice: The Industrial Marketing and Purchasing (IMP) group has a tradition of studying industrial networks with a particular focus on the relationships between suppliers and customers (see, e.g. Andersson et al., 1994; Ford, 2011).

However, the S-D logic perspective is more focused on creating an understanding of the co-created experience, which involves an ecosystem of actors and resource-integrating activities. The actors act upon the value proposition of the manufacturing firm by means of resource integration and integrating the value proposition into their own value creation process (Vargo & Lusch, 2008). This implies that value differs between referents and must be assessed separately (Vargo & Lusch, 2016). Therefore, deep knowledge of customers and their situations is needed in order to offer the most suitable value proposition to each customer (Löfberg & Åkesson, 2018).

Therefore, the third axiom means that value does not occur in isolation, but through the integration of resources from many sources (Vargo & Lusch, 2016). A key implication of this axiom is that other actors' resources constitute an important aspect to consider when understanding the value to be co-created: Therefore, it is necessary to create interaction opportunities together with, e.g. customers, but also between employees and various information and communication systems and between the different goods and services that constitute the resources enabling value co-creation. Thus, the redeployment and reconfiguration of a company's resource base, as well as its organizational capabilities and structures, is necessary (Baines et al., 2009).

Value Is Always Determined by the Beneficiary

The implication of the fourth axiom: *Value is always uniquely and phenomenologically determined by the beneficiary* (Vargo & Lusch, 2016), is that value occurs when the service is useful to the beneficiary, e.g. a customer. This is often referred to as value-in-use. The notion of value-in-use has a long tradition in B2B marketing research (e.g. LaPierre, 1997), but for reasons of convenience, many companies have focused on value-in-exchange (Vargo & Lusch, 2004), which views the customer as passive and left out of value-creating activities.

Servitization entails the need for a service business model whereby the manufacturing firm commits itself to improving its customers' value-in-use, e.g. guaranteeing up-time (Kowalkowski et al., 2017). If value is created in use, this means that a manufacturing firm needs to understand what its customers value. This cannot be decided by a technician developing a new offering, since the risk exists that such a process will be driven by management without taking the customer perspective into consideration. As Vargo and Akaka (2009) put it, this risk might entail an internal focus on design specifications, operational processes, and other actions aimed at enhancing the efficiency of the manufactured good per se. The value created during one customer process might differ from other customer processes and might also vary over time. This is linked to viewing value as experiential (Vargo & Lusch, 2008). Therefore, we argue that servitization processes take place within a dynamic environment since experiences may differ. Thus, staying close to the customer (and other actors) in order to be prepared for any changes that arise is a prerequisite. It is not enough to merely monitor the customer, something that has been much easier using technologies that enable remote services, for instance. Rather, it is more a question of *connecting with* the customer and the environment, the entire experience, and not just "good use", as explained by Bettencourt et al. (2014).

Value Co-creation Is Coordinated Through Institutions

According to axiom 5, *value co-creation is coordinated through actor-generated institutions and institutional arrangements* (Vargo & Lusch, 2016). This axiom refers to the acknowledgement that S-D logic's view of the role of institutions is that they exist within coherent ecosystems. Institutions provide the building blocks for resource integration and service-exchange activities in overlapping ecosystems, as such making up the social context (Chandler & Vargo, 2011). According to S-D logic, understanding such service ecosystems is fundamental to understanding value co-creation (Vargo & Lusch, 2016). A service ecosystem can be seen as an arena where multiple resource integrations occur; these enable and facilitate the successful realization of value propositions. The ecosystem view of S-D logic clearly contrasts with G-D logic's dominant dyadic view of relationships (Banoun et al., 2016).

This axiom stresses the need for resources from the ecosystem in order to co-create value because firm output is only one input into value co-creation. We do not co-create alone; co-creation is closely linked to context, depending on the resources available to the actors. This can differ and depends on access to resources from market, public and private sources, as well as on personal and unique knowledge and skills (Vargo & Lusch, 2011). Previous research emphasizing the complexity of good-service transitions has stressed the breadth of the knowledge and skills required to make the transition (e.g. Auguste et al., 2006; Smith et al., 2014).

A manufacturing firm that wants to adopt S-D logic must acknowledge the structures and coordinating mechanisms that the service ecosystem provides. The institutions prevailing within the ecosystem, e.g. norms, routines, rules, and the use of a certain language, must be understood. These institutions can be inhibitory when it comes to thinking in new ways, which servitization implies. Basically, this means that issues can be related to routinized ways of thinking and acting which constrain human behaviour. To succeed with servitization, these prevailing institutions need to be changed (Kindström & Kowalkowski, 2014).

Servitization Model Based on S-D Logic

In combining the research fields of servitization and S-D logic, Fig. 1 illustrates a model of how the axioms could constitute a service business logic. The inner circle comprises the key concepts of the five axioms; service, value co-creation, resource integration, value-in-use, and ecosystems. The outer circle illustrates the servitization activities, which are: offer solutions, offer value

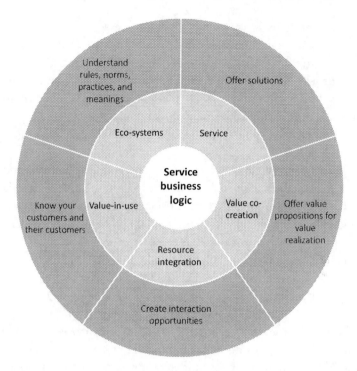

Fig. 1 The make-up of a service business logic

propositions for value realization, create interaction opportunities, know your customers and their customers, and understand rules, norms, practices, and meanings.

3   Discussion

Combining the research fields of S-D logic and servitization results in three implications for theory and practice; (1) a definition of servitization, (2) a foundational service business logic to guide servitization, and (3) a holistic view of servitization.

A Definition of Servitization

Since the early literature, servitization has been based on the idea that it is some kind of transition process (e.g. Oliva & Kallenberg, 2003; Vendrell-Herrero et al., 2014). Researchers describe how manufacturing firms expand their goods offerings with services, and how the service part of their businesses increases and simultaneously becomes more advanced (see, e.g. Davies, 2004; Galbraith, 2002; Wise & Baumgartner, 1999). Often, this view implies that firms develop their service businesses as they leave one transition step for another. However, the transition process idea has been criticized, with researchers arguing that manufacturing firms often need to be undergoing different steps at the same time (Kowalkowski et al., 2015; Raddats & Kowalkowski, 2014).

The view of servitization as a transition process implies that the service offering is key to deciding the level of servitization. Since services are seen as another type of output, the transition process view is consistent with G-D logic. Using an S-D logic approach, the type of offering will not be key to deciding the level of servitization. Rather, disparate types of offerings can be managed simultaneously (cf. Kowalkowski, 2011) in order to solve a customer problem or fulfil a need, i.e. service is exchanged for service (Vargo & Lusch, 2004). It has been argued that G-D and S-D logics are two different ways of enabling a firm to servitize (Kowalkowski, 2010).

Thus, the question then remains: Is a firm servitizing if it adds more advanced services to its offerings (the G-D logic way), or is it necessary to change the mindset of the employees and apply a foundational service business logic (the S-D logic way)? Previous research is not consistent as regards what constitutes servitization. However, in line with Kowalkowski et al. (2017), we argue that servitization needs to include a change of business logic, e.g. if a firm offers another type of service as a new output of its production, continuing with its G-D logic way of doing business, then there will be no servitization. On the other hand, if the firm wants to offer solutions and change its business logic to a value creation perspective, where interactions take place with others within the ecosystem, value is co-created, etc., then servitization will be a fact.

Our reasoning is in line with, e.g. Kowalkowski et al. (2017) as we define servitization as a change process from a goods logic to a service business logic. During this process, activities and outcomes are guided by a value creation perspective on service; consequently, a mindset change within the organization becomes necessary.

A Foundational Service Business Logic to Guide Servitization

A foundational service business logic would offer clear direction and guidance during servitization efforts, even though activities may vary within or between firms. In research focusing on the different steps of a transition process, this lack of a solid foundation becomes clear. Researchers have not agreed on a transition process and different steps are identified in different studies, with these often being only vaguely described. This could be because transition processes vary between firms, e.g. the study by Martinez et al. (2017: 78) shows that: *"service journeys do not follow a single path or even share the same point of departure"*.

Discussing servitization on the business logic level will provide a clear direction and a common ground, even though the practical ways of achieving it might differ. From this fundamental perspective, servitization is seen as a change of value creation perspectives that would apply to firms with different kinds of offerings, in different industries and so on. It could also apply to manufacturing firms that develop their products or service businesses, or to service firms with a goods business logic. Due to this change of mindset, all servitization activities will start out from customer needs, how these can be met using solutions, and in doing so how value can be created with other actors within the ecosystem. A prerequisite for the foundational service business logic, thus, is close relationships between actors, e.g. customers and service providers, and the transparency of business processes. A clear understanding of each other's needs will probably enhance the odds of achieving a win–win situation, resulting in value being realized for all the involved actors.

However, adopting this mindset within an organization would change various aspects of how doing business is viewed, e.g. service innovation will include closer collaboration with customers than before, and knowing customer processes will be even more important since the focus will be on customer needs. Creating business models with the mindset that value is co-created and experienced differently (depending on the context) paves the way for new possibilities, e.g. value-based pricing. Even the firm's mission would be different when focusing on the value created rather than on the products and services per se.

These are just a few examples showing how a foundational service business logic can guide activities, with each firm needing to decide whether servitization is suitable for its business or not. Previous research has shown that it is hard to offer solutions without knowing one's customers very well (e.g. Davies, 2004). However, for those intending to offer basic services (as another type of output), or to operate in a traditional industry where others within the ecosystem are reluctant as regards close collaboration, resource integration, etc., the adoption of a service business logic could be complicated or even unnecessary.

A Holistic View of Servitization

Even though the discussion about a foundational business logic has been missing, the axioms of S-D logic can all be found, implicitly or explicitly, in the servitization literature (e.g. Baines et al., 2017; Bjurklo et al., 2009; Kowalkowski et al., 2017; Ng et al., 2012). This means that the various aspects, and their importance, have not been overlooked. Rather, it has been stressed that servitization needs a system-wide change to be successful (Gebauer et al., 2010; Rabetino et al., 2017). The need for a mindset change which pervades the entire firm, its network, and the ecosystem within which it operates has been called for (Kastalli et al., 2013; Ng et al., 2013). We argue that a response to this call would be the adoption of a holistic view of servitization, based on the axioms constituting the S-D logic, since this would foster servitization more than the different parts being managed separately would.

Viewing servitization as holistic allows a service ecosystem, consisting of resource integration leading to realized value-in-use through the co-creation of value as performed by multiple actors, to emerge. Imagine a scenario where one of these aspects was left out, resource integration with customers for instance: Trying to solve a customer problem by offering a new service developed by an R&D department detached from close resource integration with other actors, e.g. the customer, would most likely result in an output responding to managerial thoughts about what the customer is in need of and will value. This is something that will not necessarily result in realized value-in-use for the customer.

However, viewing servitization as holistic entails that all parts of the service business logic are important and need to coexist. The effect of this reasoning, when applied to the above example, is the addition of resource integration with the customer. This opportunity for other actors than the professional developers at the R&D department to significantly contribute to novel and useful service innovations could lead to co-created solutions which are not just easier to sell, due to being directed at solving the customer's problem, but which are also, as a consequence, better suited to realizing the sought after value-in-use. Previous research has to some extent acknowledged this kind of customer-initiated value proposition (Ballantyne & Varey, 2006), but not against the backdrop of a holistic view of servitization.

This is just one example illustrating the importance of viewing servitization as holistic. It is key to understand the importance of each part and to figure out how these parts all harmoniously coexist, a state of affairs that will never be achieved when removing one of the parts from the whole. In other words, servitization needs all aspects making up the foundational service business logic to be realized.

Theoretical Contributions

Using S-D logic as a complementary theory for understanding servitization, important theoretical contributions can be made. We present a model that combines the research fields and shows what S-D logic means for servitization. Based on that, implications for servitization theory and practice are discussed. First, we define servitization as a change process from a goods to a service business logic. This definition emphasizes the importance of a change of mindset within the firm, towards a value creation perspective on service. Second, we add another dimension to the academic debate in terms of a foundational service business logic that guides servitization. The level of abstraction that this foundational service business logic offers can guide both servitization researchers and practitioners. Finally, the importance of adopting a holistic view of servitization is highlighted. The different axioms and related topics have been discussed in servitization research before; however, we argue that they are closely interrelated and dependent on each other and thus need to be discussed accordingly. To summarize, S-D logic has been a missing link in servitization research and, in this chapter, we have shown how it can contribute towards an improved theoretical basis for servitization.

Managerial Implications

S-D logic is suitable for guiding managers in expanding their service businesses towards solutions. Guided by the axioms, new perspectives on service, value co-creation, resource integration, value-in-use, and ecosystems emerge. Our model shows how these different parts are both interrelated and important. Initiating the servitization process with a change of business logics creates a solid foundation for the following activities and outcomes. It opens up new business opportunities regarding, e.g. business models, service innovation, capabilities, and sales, all focused on value creation.

Future Research

Although the different axioms have previously been discussed in servitization research, more knowledge is needed to understand how firms can apply them in order to guide servitization activities in practice, e.g. regarding service innovation, business model development, or capabilities. Moreover, the holistic view of servitization needs further investigation. Servitizing firms need to work on different activities at the same time, with research being sparse on how the efforts of, e.g. different departments can be coordinated, or in what order they are to be performed. There are several research fields that can be integrated into servitization research to drive conceptualization and theory, e.g. organizational change theory or institutional theory. Finally, we argue that more action research is needed to truly understand the servitization efforts being made by manufacturing firms.

References

Auguste, B. G., Harmon, E. P., & Pandit, V. (2006). The right service strategies for product companies. *McKinsey Quarterly, 1*(40), 41–51.

Andersson, J. C., Håkansson, H., & Johansson, J. (1994). Dyadic business relationships within a business network context. *Journal of Marketing, 58*(4), 1–15.

Baines, T. S., Lightfoot, H. W., Benedettini, O., & Kay, J. M. (2009). The servitization of manufacturing: A review of literature and reflection on future challenges. *Journal of Manufacturing Technology Management, 20,* 547–567.

Baines, T., Bigdeli, A. Z., Bustinza, O. F., Shi, V. G., Baldwin, J., & Ridgway, K. (2017). Servitization: Revisiting the state-of-the-art and research priorities.

Ballantyne, D., & Varey, R. J. (2006). Creating value-in-use through marketing interaction: The exchange logic of relating, communicating and knowing. *Marketing Theory, 6*(3), 335–348.

Banoun, A., Dufour, L., & Andiappan, M. (2016). Evolution of a service ecosystem: Longitudinal evidence from multiple shared services centers based on the economies of worth framework. *Journal of Business Research, 69*(8), 2990–2998.

Bettencourt, L. A., Lusch, R. F., & Vargo, S. L. (2014). A service lens on value creation: Marketing's role in achieving strategic advantage. *California Management Review, 57*(1), 44–66.

Bjurklo, M., Edvardsson, B., & Gebauer, H. (2009). The role of competence in initiating the transition from products to service. *Managing Service Quality: an International Journal, 19*(5), 493–510.

Chandler, J. D., & Vargo, S. L. (2011). Contextualization and value-in-context: How context frames exchange. *Marketing Theory, 11*(1), 35–49.

Davies, A. (2004). Moving base into high-value integrated solutions: A value stream approach. *Industrial and Corporate Change, 13*(5), 727–756.

Edvardsson, B., Gustafsson, A., & Roos, I. (2005). Service portraits in service research: A critical review. *International Journal of Service Industry Management, 16*(1), 107–121.

Ford, D. (2011). IMP and service-dominant logic: Divergence, convergence and development. *Industrial Marketing Management, 40*(2), 231–239.

Galbraith, J. R. (2002). Organizing to deliver solutions. *Organizational Dynamics, 31,* 194–207.

Gebauer, H., Edvardsson, B., & Bjurklo, M. (2010). The impact of service orientation in corporate culture on business performance in manufacturing companies. *Journal of Service Management, 21*(2), 237–259.

Kastalli, I. V., Van Looy, B., & Neely, A. (2013). Steering manufacturing firms towards service business model innovation. *California Management Review, 56*(1), 100–123.

Kindström, D., & Kowalkowski, C. (2014). Service innovation in product-centric firms: A multidimensional business model perspective. *Journal of Business & Industrial Marketing, 29*(2), 96–111.

Kowalkowski, C. (2010). What does a service-dominant logic really mean for manufacturing firms? *CIRP Journal of Manufacturing Science and Technology, 3*(4), 285–292.

Kowalkowski, C. (2011). Dynamics of value propositions: Insights from service-dominant logic. *European Journal of Marketing, 45*(1–2), 277–294.

Kowalkowski, C., Gebauer, H., Kamp, B., & Parry, G. (2017). Servitization and deservitization: Overview, concepts, and definitions. *Industrial Marketing Management, 60,* 4–10.

Kowalkowski, C., Windahl, C., Kindström, D., & Gebauer, H. (2015). What service transition? Rethinking established assumptions about manufacturers' service-led growth strategies. *Industrial Marketing Management, 45,* 59–69.

Lapierre, J. (1997). What does value mean in business-to-business professional services? *International Journal of Service Industry Management, 8*(5), 377–397.

Löfberg, N., & Åkesson, M. (2018). Creating a service platform–how to co-create value in a remote service context. *Journal of Business & Industrial Marketing, 33*(6), 768–780.

Martinez, V., Neely, A., Velu, C., Leinster-Evans, S., & Bisessar, D. (2017). Exploring the journey to services. *International Journal of Production Economics, 192,* 66–80.

Ng, I. C., Ding, D. X., & Yip, N. (2013). Outcome-based contracts as new business model: The role of partnership and value-driven relational assets. *Industrial Marketing Management, 42*(5), 730–743.

Ng, I., Parry, G., Smith, L., Maull, R., & Briscoe, G. (2012). Transitioning from a goods-dominant to a service-dominant logic: Visualising the value proposition of Rolls-Royce. *Journal of Service Management, 23*(3), 416–439.

Oliva, R., & Kallenberg, R. (2003). Managing the transition from products to services. *International Journal of Service Industry Management, 14*(2), 160–172.

Rabetino, R., Kohtamäki, M., & Gebauer, H. (2017). Strategy map of servitization. *International Journal of Production Economics, 192,* 144–156.

Raddats, C., & Kowalkowski, C. (2014). A reconceptualization of manufacturers' service strategies. *Journal of Business-to-Business Marketing, 21*(1), 19–34.

Smith, L., Maull, R., & Ng, I. C. L. (2014). Servitization and operations management: A service dominant-logic approach. *International Journal of Operations and Production Management, 34*(2), 242–269.

Vargo, S. L., & Akaka, M. A. (2009). Service-dominant logic as a foundation for service science: Clarifications. *Service Science, 1*(1), 32–41.

Vargo, S. L., & Lusch, R. F. (2004). Evolving to a new dominant logic for marketing. *Journal of Marketing, 68*(1), 1–17.

Vargo, S. L., & Lusch, R. F. (2008). From goods to service(s): Divergences and convergences of logics. *Industrial Marketing Management, 37*(3), 254–259.

Vargo, S. L., & Lusch, R. F. (2011). It's all B2B... and beyond: Toward a systems perspective of the market. *Industrial Marketing Management, 40*(2), 181–187.

Vargo, S. L., & Lusch, R. F. (2016). Institutions and axioms: An extension and update of service-dominant logic. *Journal of the Academy of Marketing Science, 44*(1), 5–23.

Vendrell-Herrero, F., Parry, G., Bustinza, O. F., & O'Regan, N. (2014). Servitization as a driver for organizational change. *Strategic Change, 23*(5–6), 279–285.

Wise, R., & Baumgartner, P. (1999, September–October). Go downstream: The new profit imperative in manufacturing. *Harvard Business Review*, 133–141.

Value Co-creation in Digitally-Enabled Product-Service Systems

Shaun West, Wenting Zou, Eugen Rodel, and Oliver Stoll

1   Introduction

Increasingly today value creation within digitally-enabled PSS is based on co-creation, both for the development of the initial concept and for the delivery of the service (Kohtamäki et al., 2019). Valtakoski (2017), describes how two actors combine explicit and tacit knowledge that results in value co-creation. Digitally-enabled PSS uses data to drive value creation, data alone

S. West (✉)
Institute of Innovation and Technology Management, Lucerne University of Applied Science and Art, Lucerne, Switzerland
e-mail: shaun.west@hslu.ch

W. Zou
Industrial Engineering and Management, Aalto University, Espoo, Finland
e-mail: wenting.zou@aalto.fi

E. Rodel
Thingminds, Lachen, Switzerland
e-mail: er@thingminds.ch

O. Stoll
School of Computing, Engineering and Built Environment, Institute of Innovation and Technology Management, Lucerne University of Applied Science and Art, Glasgow Caledonian University, Glasgow, UK
e-mail: oliver.stoll@hslu.ch

M. Kohtamäki et al. (eds.), *The Palgrave Handbook of Servitization*,
https://doi.org/10.1007/978-3-030-75771-7_26

403

cannot create value (Lee et al., 2014). The processing of data and its presentation should be coupled with its context, as processed data, seen in context, can help create usable, significant or meaningful answers and create knowledge and understanding (Choo, 2007; Frické, 2009; Rowley, 2007). Shedroff (1999) defined three elements where interaction design can support value co-creation between a dispersed ecosystem of actors: control and feedback between the parties; productivity; and adaptability.

These three elements are in line with the concepts reported in the managerial literature about Service-Dominant (S-D) logic in PSS. Vargo and Lusch (2004, 2008), state that value is continuously created through simultaneous interactions of different actors, who act as the resource integrators, forming ecosystems of service offerings and exchanges (Sklyar et al., 2019). Value is determined by the beneficiary in the context of co-creation. Actors generate value together through the reciprocal application of resources (Baraldi et al., 2012). The system integrator orchestrates the ecosystem to ensure that each member remains in good health and is able to actively contribute (Kindström & Kowalkowski, 2014). By encouraging the involvement of knowledgeable actors from the supply and system network, the co-creation process will actively involve actors from both the supply network and the customer network (Cova & Salle, 2008). The value co-creation in PSS was described by West et al. (2018), in a paper that proposed a process to support ecosystem engagement in PSS value creation.

Servitization (Vandermerwe & Rada, 1988) describes the innovation of an organization's capabilities and processes to shift from goods to services or "*moving towards supplying integrated solutions*" (Windahl et al., 2004: 221). Digitization is considered an enabler and driver for value co-creation and novel business models in servitization studies (Kohtamäki et al., 2019). Due to this digital transformation, firms are rapidly moving toward operation optimization and process automation based on digital technologies; for instance, Rolls-Royce, Wärtsilä, and Caterpillar have all used a variety of sensor-based technologies to support digitally-enabled product-service system (PSS) solutions (Grubic & Jennions, 2018; Rymaszewska et al., 2017).

Despite the obvious benefits, the transition toward digital servitization inevitably increases complexity for companies. Digitally-enabled PSS entails transformation in terms of business model configuration rather than simply changes to value propositions (Kohtamäki et al., 2019). Developing new business models often requires value co-creation through in-depth interactions and extensive integration of capability between servitizing companies and their customers. The interactions are often based on a variety of service components that include the exchange of information between different actors. All these changes inevitably increase risks and complexities for manufacturing companies during a collaborative process with their customers, which complicates the design of service offerings. However, transforming traditional PSS into digitally-enabled PSSs with clearly defined value propositions is a process that is poorly researched, and there remains a need for a conceptual framework to address the deficit (Kohtamäki et al., 2019). Based on the literature described above, such a framework should focus on value co-creation and relationships, couple this with the traditional PSS design methodologies, and also support the longer-term transformation of data into information, and knowledge building. This chapter focuses on the value co-creation and resource integration necessary for an orchestrator to successfully overcome the challenges that they face.

2   Theory Development

Servitization provides an extension to a firm's offering, based on developing a broad range of services to support customer functions, which provides a market strategy for a firm that is aiming to gain a competitive advantage (Vandermerwe & Rada, 1988). Companies believe servitization will enable them to create value-adding capabilities that should be more sustainable and help to defend them against the competition (Baines et al., 2009). The shift to value-added services and value-in-use business models (Kohtamäki et al., 2019) has driven servitization to a more customer-centric approach based on value co-creation, furthermore digital servitization business models can support value co-creation and value capture (Kohtamäki et al., 2019).

PSS can be considered a way to deliver a servitization strategy, as PSS integrates product and service offerings that deliver value-in-use (Baines et al., 2009). The subjects of PSS research (Baines et al., 2009) included the detailed practices and models needed to deliver integrated products and services to address the challenges faced by manufacturers in a servitization transformation.

Paiola and Gebauer (2020) described the service-oriented impact of Internet of Things (IoT) technologies on B2B manufacturing firms' business models and proposed a map of digital servitization that helps to focus attention on the impact of a firms' business model. Porter and Heppelmann (2014) provided two different classifications in order to understand "smart products"; the first deals with the ecosystem: product, smart product, smart connected product, product system, and system of systems. The second

describes four possible levels of automation: monitoring, control, optimization, and autonomy. Kowalkowski and Ulaga (2017) proposed a classification
of industrial services that is useful for understanding the nature of the services
based on the nature of the value proposition offered to the recipient (i.e.,
product lifecycle, asset efficiency, process support, or process delegation).
Kohtamäki et al. (2019) combined the approach of Porter and Heppelmann
(2014) with the traditional PSS models to create a 3D cube that identified
different solution spaces (Fig. 1).

In order to capture value, at least two actors need to be actively involved
in the service ecosystem (Raja et al., 2020). Valtakoski (2017) based the
value co-creation process on the integration of explicit and tacit knowledge
components from actor A and B (ie., the supplier and customer) to develop
a solution (Fig. 2), and in a digital world this requires the additional integration of data from both actors. Value co-creation processes can take different
forms characterized by different types of participant engagement, depending
on the roles, responsibilities, and involvement of the various actors. There is a
strong ecosystem aspect, because many actors and machines can be involved
in value creation. It is known that the customer has an important role as a
value co-creator (Payne et al., 2008), but if companies are collaborating with
partners, they sometimes do not get the necessary trust to succeed. Shedroff
(1999) links value co-creation to three elements from interaction design:

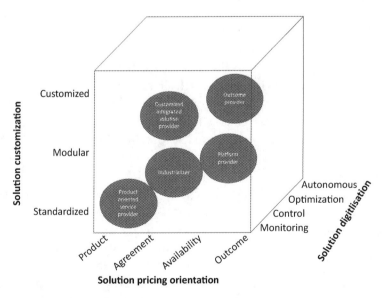

Fig. 1 Understanding the characteristics of solution offerings in digital servitization
business models (based on Kohtamäki et al., 2019)

i. control and feedback between the parties—the ability of the person who receives the information to manage and provide feedback to those who have generated it.

ii. productivity—the ability to (co)create experience.

iii. adaptability—the ability to advance management processes by modifying the data and information based on who receives the information.

Grönroos (2011) expands value co-creation along the product lifecycle, focusing on the beginning of life (BOL) and the middle of life (MOL) from the model (Terzi et al., 2010) that is shown in an adapted form in Fig. 3. The objective of the design phase is to develop a solution in the BOL that supports value creation based on the value-in-use during the MOL phase. There are likely to be both traditional goods-dominant and Service Design (S-D) logic approaches creating conflicts within the firm. The optimization of value and linking of key spheres in both BOL and MOL phases can be seen in the model created by Valtakoski (2017). Furthermore, Bertoni et al. (2013) use visualization of the value in a PSS in the design phase (BOL) as part of an attempt to link BOL and MOL value creation. Journey mapping can be used as a tool to identify value co-creation opportunities as it describes the journey

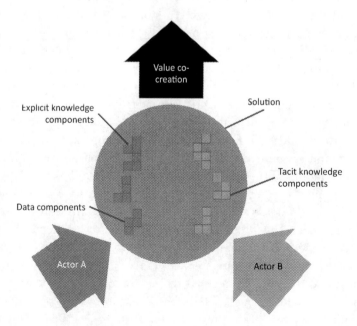

Fig. 2 Value co-creation based on a bundle of knowledge and integrated with data (based on Valtakoski, 2017)

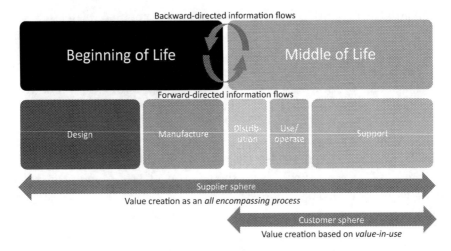

Fig. 3 Value creation along the lifecycle (based on Grönroos, 2011; Terzi et al., 2010; Wuest et al., 2016)

of customers visually, clearly showing their touchpoints and actor interrelationships (Lemon & Verhoef, 2016). Journey mapping in combination with personas can provide a deeper understanding of value co-creation opportunities by identifying the actors involved along the lifecycle, along with the resource and knowledge that they may possess (West et al., 2020). This can then be used to support the value co-creation process by integrating contextual information to help build understanding and knowledge (Pirola et al., 2014). PPS consists of actors, stakeholders, and beneficiaries in the context of servitization (Kuijken et al., 2017), in addition to the machines within the system. Many tools, such as the customer value proposition canvas developed by Osterwalder (2014), fail to capture the contextual aspect of value co-creation and are limited to a single actor or segment of actors, leading to a misrepresentation of the value that is co-created.

The more products become distribution mechanisms for services, and the more the focus shifts toward intangible resources, co-creation and relationships, the more a company moves into the domain of S-D logic (Vargo and Lusch, 2004, 2008) and value-in-use, and away from goods-based logic. This implies a reframing of the company and its role in value creation (Table 1). It is shown that the value from smart services unfolds when looking at them through S-D logic (West et al., 2018). Based on Grönroos (2011), the design and manufacture phase of the product should aim to develop a platform that can maximize the value-in-use throughout the MOL phase. This requires value co-creation processes similar to those defined by Valtakoski, A. (2017)

Table 1 S-D logic directions for marketing practitioners (Vargo and Lusch, 2008)

Goods logic (from...)	Service logic (to...)
... thinking about the purpose of the firm's activity as making something (goods or services)	... a process of assisting customers in their own value-creation processes
... thinking about value as something produced and sold	... thinking about value as something co-created with the customer and other value-creation partners
... thinking of customers as isolated entities	... understanding them in the context of their own networks
... thinking of firm resources primarily as operand—tangible resources such as natural resources	... thinking of firm resources as operant—usually intangible resources such as knowledge and skills.
... thinking of customers as targets	... thinking of customers as resources
... making efficiency primary	... increasing efficiency through effectiveness

to be active in both the BOL and MOL phases, reinforcing the S-D logic (Vargo and Lusch, 2008).

The transformation of data into information is known as information design, that of information into knowledge as interaction design (Shedroff, 1999). Liew (2007) provided a detailed overview for understanding data, information, knowledge, and their interrelationships, and the interrelationships between data, information, knowledge, and wisdom were further explored by Aven (2013). Bagheri et al. (2015) explore the development of knowledge within the context of PSS. To drive value creation, digitally-enabled PSS requires data, but that data must be transformed into valuable, meaningful information (or insights). Context and personal judgment can then be combined to help create knowledge, by interpolating the information available to each actor through interactions with others (Choo, 2007). By adding the judgment of actors to knowledge, wisdom can be created, this can include ethical values, which makes the wisdom personal and unique to an actor (Rowley, 2007). The difference between a passive and an interactive experience is defined by the amount of feedback, control of the audience, co-creativity, productivity, communication, and adaptivity that is generated (Shedroff, 1999).

The value co-generation process is supported by the application of resources by integrators assisting customers in their own value-creation processes (Vargo and Lusch, 2004, 2008), as confirmed by Valtakoski (2017). To support the value co-creation process, and by default the transformation of information into knowledge along the lifecycle and therefore the twin spheres of the supplier and the customer, requires ongoing efforts by integrators. The actors who act as resource integrators need to understand the perspectives of value creation within the different spheres, along with having an understanding of data and purpose of the information. To integrate the actors and the resources they need to know when different actors are active along the lifecycle, particularly as some actors move into beneficiary roles. Finally, the integrator needs to understand the knowledge building process and therefore where knowledge exists and where and when it can actively be applied. The role of the integrators set out here was described by Hertog (2000) in relation to innovation, and by Kohtamäki and Partanen (2016) who considered how to moderate learnings from supplier–customer interactions within industrial environments.

3   Discussion

This section details a generic framework to support the development of value co-creation in digitally-enabled PSS and is based on the literature described in previous sections. Because of the evolving nature of the literature, this is an initial framework that will need further testing and adaptation. The chapter concludes by describing the managerial implications associated with the move to digitally-enabled PSS, and the academic implications. The academic implications present some gaps in the current literature that represent areas for future research.

Framework

The framework starts from the assumption that many of the building blocks are in place in a firm, rather than starting from a clean canvas; in effect building upon an existing PSS, the associated value propositions and the firms' business models. It is also built upon the premise that the new value proposition is based on providing additional value and delivering it in a new form. To that end, a framework is proposed, that is built upon the dyadic relationship (although these are in effect an oversimplification of the situation) between two actors (i.e., the consumer and the provider) that allows explicit knowledge and tacit knowledge to be integrated into a "solution" and, in doing so, provide value co-creation for the beneficiaries (Valtakoski, 2017). This confirms the importance of using technical and domain expertise when developing new or extending existing PSS value propositions. The framework also integrates the three key aspects from interactive design, namely: control and feedback between the parties; productivity; and adaptability.

The integration of the customer and supplier at each stage supports the development of a PSS platform that will provide opportunities for value co-creation during the MOL phase (Fig. 4). Information flows between the different phases of the lifecycle were described by Wuest et al. (2016), but there is a need to orchestrate these flows (in effect, create feedback) between the actors and between the phases, allowing both tacit and explicit information to be integrated by the actors into a solution and then lead to value co-creation. The framework must also support productivity from the co-creation through joint experiences or working, and it must have the ability to provide information that is suitable for the actor receiving it, in a form that enables the recipient to use it to make decisions and to build their knowledge base. Every transaction or touchpoint provides opportunity for value co-creation. The MOL therefore provides many opportunities for co-creation, as the operational and technology environment changes. The framework helps to challenge the status quo by focusing on the equipment and on delivering the key outcomes to the PSS beneficiaries. It does this by integrating the four aspects that support value co-creation, namely the perspectives of value co-creation, data and information, relationships, and knowledge building, along the lifecycle and between activities (e.g., design, manufacture, etc.) within each phase. In doing so, the framework builds upon the findings of West et al. (2018) where the focus was on value co-creation and knowledge creation

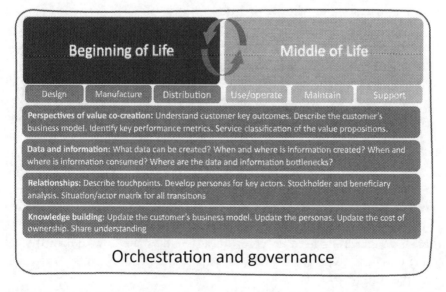

Fig. 4 Framework for supporting value co-creation within the context of digitally-enabled PSS (based on Grönroos, 2011; Terzi et al., 2010; Wuest et al., 2016)

mainly from the middle of life phase within the perspective of PSS. The Framework in Fig. 4 identifies the important role of a so-called "moderator" or "resource integrator" to orchestrate the value co-creation and to govern the overall process.

Implications for the Beginning of Life Phase

The development of digitally-enabled PSS involves many disciplines, and people with different expertise each need to give their input at the right stage to support value co-creation. In early stages, such as the design phase, the expertise of business, engineering, and computer science are required on a high level. Having these three relevant domains involved leads to a sustainable design, e.g., by preventing managers from developing digitally-enabled PSS which are technically not feasible, or IT specialists developing services that are not cost-effective. Grönroos (2011) stated that the value co-creation in the BOL phase is driven by the supplier, nevertheless the BOL in a PSS provides the platform for value-in-use in the MOL phase. Therefore, the integration of information that different actors have is important and in line with the backward and forward information flows identified by Wuest et al. (2016).

Implications for the Middle of Life

Digital technologies (within PSS) have been analyzed in relation to the development of new forms of agreements or revenue models related to asset operation and asset life management. They enable new value propositions to be developed for PSS, and in some cases new business models. However, there is a paradox, which suggests that although companies may invest in digitization, they often fail to achieve the expected revenue enhancement. This is because many firms struggle to successfully modify their business models and then fail to deliver their value propositions due to limits within these firms based on resources, capabilities, and processes. Therefore, understanding how new value propositions are developed in response to investing in digital technologies is crucial for manufacturing companies. Furthermore, there is an increasing need for companies to understand how to identify and assess potential commercial offers under the umbrella of value co-creation with the customer.

Orchestration and Governance Along the Lifecycle

Orchestration and governance (Fig. 4) are in place to support long-term value co-creation for both the supplier and the customer over the whole PSS lifecycle, here the use of a "resource integrator" to orchestrate the resecure integration is critical to successful value co-creation over the lifecycle.

The current and future portfolio of services needs careful management and integration with the other steps in the framework. The range of customer key outcomes must be shared, the various business models analyzed, contract performance measures compared, and various digital PSS modules overseen, all through the assessment of the service classification. Similarly, relationships need to be overseen, with the ability to feedback and suggest changes to existing contracts. The customer experience can be gauged using the touchpoints and the actor definitions and this is different to the contract performance metrics, which are generally factual. The relationship analysis here deals with the emotional aspects of digital PSS and it provides valuable early warnings about problems and challenges that may later have an impact on existing contracts, even where outcomes are currently being delivered. Data and information, as well as knowledge building are relevant again, and here much of the emphasis needs to be placed on ensuring effective sharing of knowledge.

In order to achieve this level of value co-creation, relationships between the company and the customer can be described as "*valuable bridges, as they give one actor access to the resources of another*" (Harland, 1996: 68). Business relationships that perform will play a crucial role in digitally-enabled PSS, as smart solutions require integration across company boundaries, and manufacturers need to enable and maintain long-term smooth collaboration with their customers to facilitate successful technological and service innovation. In digitally-enabled PSS the complexity of PSS and the long-term horizon for delivery need an equally long-term orientation between manufacturing firms and their customers, which in turn requires a healthy relationship. The orchestration and governance should be institutionalized within the supplier's business, part of this would be through the application of appropriate tools (Pezzotta et al., 2016, 2018; Lemon & Verhoef, 2016; Pirola et al., 2014).

Theoretical Contributions

The theory development section introduced many theoretical concepts developed by researchers from various fields. This contribution shows that linking existing concepts and theories can lead to the development of new holistic frameworks that builds on existing knowledge. The framework that is presented faces the challenge of complexity coming from systems and multi-actor perspectives. Used in combination with existing theory, these challenges could be faced. The combination of multidisciplinary and multi-level theory can add new value, depth, and breadth to the knowledge base.

Managerial Implications

This is a framework that focuses on the BOL and MOL phases of a lifecycle model to support value co-creation in digitally-enabled PSS value propositions. Given the evolution of traditional PSS to digitally-enabled PSS, the framework integrates continual feedback. It links important aspects that already exist and assumes that there is already a PSS in existence at the company. The framework challenges the integrator's team at both phases to understand the customer's outcomes, their value creation process, the avatars and the actors who are involved with the development, delivery and use of the value proposition. It assumes that the firm has existing processes in place that support both product and service development, and uses these as the foundation to reflect upon when considering the additional digital aspects that allow the building of digitally-enabled value propositions.

References

Aven, T. (2013, March). A conceptual framework for linking risk and the elements of the data–information–knowledge–wisdom (DIKW) hierarchy. *Reliability Engineering & System Safety, 111*, 30–36.

Bagheri, S., Kusters, R., & Trienekens, J. (2015). The customer knowledge management lifecycle in PSS value networks: Towards process characterization. In M. Massaro & A. Garlatti (Eds.), *Proceedings of the 16th European Conference on Knowledge Management* (pp. 66–77).

Baines, T. S., Lightfoot, H. W., Benedettini, O., & Kay, J. M. (2009). The servitization of manufacturing: A review of literature and reflection on future challenges. *Journal of Manufacturing Technology Management, 20*(5), 547–567. https://doi.org/10.1108/17410380910960984.

Baraldi, E., Gressetvold, E., & Harrison, D. (2012). Resource interaction in inter-organizational networks: Foundations, comparison, and a research agenda, *Journal of Business Research, 65*(2), 266–276.

Bertoni, A., Bertoni, M., & Isaksson, O. (2013). Value visualization in Product Service Systems preliminary design. *Journal of Cleaner Production, 53*, 103–117. https://doi.org/10.1016/j.jclepro.2013.04.012.

Choo, C. W. (2007). The knowing organization: How organizations use information to construct meaning, create knowledge, and make decisions. 1-384. https://doi.org/10.1093/acprof:oso/9780195176780.001.0001.

Cova, B., & Salle, R. (2008). Marketing solutions in accordance with the SD logic: Co-creating value with customer network actors. *Industrial Marketing Management, 37*, 270–277.

Frické, M. (2009). The knowledge pyramid: A critique of the DIKW hierarchy. *Journal of Information Science.* https://doi.org/10.1177/0165551508094050.

Grönroos, C. (2011). Value co-creation in service logic: A critical analysis. *Marketing Theory.* https://doi.org/10.1177/1470593111408177.

Grubic, T., & Jennions, I. (2018). Do outcome-based contracts exist? The investigation of power-by-the-hour and similar result-oriented cases. *International Journal of Production Economics, 206,* 209–219. https://doi.org/10.1016/j.ijpe.2018.10.004.

Harland, C. M. (1996). Supply chain management: Relationships, chains and networks. *British Journal of Management, 7*(S1), S63–S80.

Hertog, P. Den. (2000). Knowledge-intensive business services as co-producers of innovation. *International Journal of Innovation Management.* https://doi.org/10.1142/s136391960000024x.

Kindström, D., & Kowalkowski, C. (2014). Service innovation in product-centric firms: A multidimensional business model perspective, *Journal of Business & Industrial Marketing, 29*(2), 151–163. https://doi.org/10.1108/JBIM-08-2013-0165.

Kohtamäki, M., & Partanen, J. (2016). Co-creating value from knowledge-intensive business services in manufacturing firms: The moderating role of relationship learning in supplier-customer interactions. *Journal of Business Research.* https://doi.org/10.1016/j.jbusres.2016.02.019.

Kohtamaki, M., Parida, V., Oghazi, P., Gebauer, H., & Baines, T. (2019). Digital servitization business models in ecosystems: A theory of the firm. *Journal of Business Research, 104,* 380–392.

Kowalkowski, C., & Ulaga, W. (2017). *Service strategy in action: A practical guide for growing your B2B service and solution business.* Service Strategy Press.

Kuijken, B., Gemser, G., & Wijnberg, N. M. (2017). Effective product-service systems: A value-based framework. *Industrial Marketing Management, 60,* 33–41. https://doi.org/10.1016/j.indmarman.2016.04.013.

Lee, J., Kao, H. A., & Yang, S. (2014). Service innovation and smart analytics for Industry 4.0 and big data environment. In *Procedia CIRP.* https://doi.org/10.1016/j.procir.2014.02.001.

Lemon, K. N., & Verhoef, P. C. (2016). Understanding customer experience throughout the customer journey. *Journal of Marketing, 80*(6), 69–96.

Liew, A. (2007). Understanding data, information, knowledge and their inter-relationships. *Journal of Knowledge Management Practice, 8*(2), 1–16.

Osterwalder, A. (2014). *Value proposition design: How to create products and services customers want.* Wiley.

Paiola, M., & Gebauer, H. (2020). Internet of things technologies, digital servitization and business model innovation in BtoB manufacturing firms. *Industrial Marketing Management, 89,* 245–264. https://doi.org/10.1016/j.indmarman. 2020.03.009.

Payne, A. F., Storbacka, K., & Frow, P. (2008). Managing the co-creation of value. *Journal of the Academy of Marketing Science, 36*(1), 83–96. https://doi.org/10. 1007/s11747-007-0070-0.

Pezzotta, G., Pirola, F., Rondini, A., Pinto, R., & Ouertani, M. Z. (2016). Towards a methodology to engineer industrial product-service system—Evidence from power and automation industry. *CIRP Journal of Manufacturing Science and Technology.* https://doi.org/10.1016/j.cirpj.2016.04.006.

Pezzotta, G., Sassanelli, C., Pirola, F., Sala, R., Rossi, M., Fotia, S., Koutoupes, A., Terzi, S., & Mourtzis, D. (2018). The Product Service System Lean Design Methodology (PSSLDM). *Journal of Manufacturing Technology Management.* https://doi.org/10.1108/jmtm-06-2017-0132.

Pirola, F., Pezzotta, G., Andreini, D., Galmozzi, C., Savoia, A., & Pinto, R. (2014). *Understanding customer needs to engineer Product-Service Systems.* Paper presented at the IFIP International Conference on Advances in Production Management Systems.

Porter, M. E., & Heppelmann, J. E. (2014). How smart, connected products are transforming competition. *Harvard Business Review, 92*(11), 64–88.

Raja, J. Z., Frandsen, T., Kowalkowski, C., & Jarmatz, M. (2020). Learning to discover value: Value-based pricing and selling capabilities for services and solutions. *Journal of Business Research, 114,* 142–159. https://doi.org/10.1016/j.jbusres.2020.03.026.

Rowley, J. (2007). The wisdom hierarchy: Representations of the DIKW hierarchy. *Journal of Information Science.* https://doi.org/10.1177/0165551506070706.

Rymaszewska, A., Helo, P., & Gunasekaran, A. (2017). IoT powered servitization of manufacturing—An exploratory case study. *International Journal of Production Economics.* https://doi.org/10.1016/j.ijpe.2017.02.016.

Shedroff, N. (1999). Information interaction design: A unified field theory of design. *Information Design,* 267–292.

Sklyar, A., Kowalkowski, C., Tronvoll, B., & Sörhammar, D. (2019). Organizing for digital servitization: A service ecosystem perspective. *Journal of Business Research.* https://doi.org/10.1016/j.jbusres.2019.02.012.

Terzi, S., Bouras, A., Dutta, D., Garetti, M., & Kiritsis, D. (2010). Product lifecycle management—From its history to its new role. *International Journal of Product Lifecycle Management.* https://doi.org/10.1504/IJPLM.2010.036489.

Valtakoski, A. (2017). Explaining servitization failure and deservitization: A knowledge-based perspective. *Industrial Marketing Management.* https://doi.org/10.1016/j.indmarman.2016.04.009.

Vandermerwe, S., & Rada, J. (1988). Servitization of business: Adding value by adding services. *European Management Journal, 6*(4), 314–324. https://doi.org/10.1016/0263-2373(88)90033-3.

Vargo, S. L., & Lusch, R. F. (2004). Evolving to a new dominant logic for marketing. *Journal of Marketing, 68*(1), 1–17. https://doi.org/10.1509/jmkg.68.1.1.24036.

Vargo, S. L., & Lusch, R. F. (2008). From goods to service(s): Divergences and convergences of logics. *Industrial Marketing Management, 37*(3), 254–259. https://doi.org/10.1016/j.indmarman.2007.07.004.

West, S., Gaiardelli, P., & Rapaccini, M. (2018a). Exploring technology-driven service innovation in manufacturing firms through the lens of Service Dominant logic. *IFAC Papersonline, 51*(11), 1317–1322. https://doi.org/10.1016/j.ifacol.2018.08.350.

West, S., Gaiardelli, P., Resta, B., & Kujawski, D. (2018b). Co-creation of value in Product-Service Systems through transforming data into knowledge. *IFAC-PapersOnLine.* https://doi.org/10.1016/j.ifacol.2018.08.349.

West, S., Stoll, O., Østerlund, M., Müller-Csernetzky, P., Keiderling, F., & Kowalkowski, C. (2020). Adjusting customer journey mapping for application in industrial product-service systems. In *International Journal of Business Environment, 11.* https://doi.org/10.1504/IJBE.2020.110911.

Windahl, C., Andersson, P., Berggren, C., & Nehler, C. (2004). Manufacturing firms and integrated solutions: Characteristics and implications. *European Journal of Innovation Management, 7*(3), 218–228. https://doi.org/10.1108/14601060410549900.

Wuest, T., Wellsandt, S., & Thoben, K. D. (2016). Information quality in PLM: A production process perspective. *IFIP Advances in Information and Communication Technology.* https://doi.org/10.1007/978-3-319-33111-9_75.

Manufacturers' Service Innovation Efforts: From Customer Projects to Business Models and Beyond

Vicky M. Story, Judy Zolkiewski, Jamie Burton, and Chris Raddats

1 Introduction

The role of services in manufacturing firms is growing in importance for businesses and national economies (Raddats et al., 2019). Servitization, the process of adding services to an existing portfolio of offerings, is argued to be crucial for manufacturing firms seeking differentiation and competitive advantage (Burton et al., 2017; Rabetino et al., 2015). This has driven increased attention to service innovation research and new service development (NSD) processes (Witell et al., 2016). However, this literature remains fragmented; is mainly project-level research (Biemans & Griffin, 2018), service success rates are not encouraging (Storey et al., 2016), and

V. M. Story (✉)
Loughborough University, Loughborough, UK
e-mail: V.M.Story@lboro.ac.uk

J. Zolkiewski · J. Burton
University of Manchester, Manchester, UK
e-mail: judy.zolkiewski@manchester.ac.uk

J. Burton
e-mail: Jamie.Burton@Manchester.ac.uk

C. Raddats
University of Liverpool, Liverpool, UK
e-mail: chrisr@liverpool.ac.uk

© The Author(s), under exclusive license to Springer Nature Switzerland AG 2021
M. Kohtamäki et al. (eds.), *The Palgrave Handbook of Servitization*,
https://doi.org/10.1007/978-3-030-75771-7_27

the reported firm-level performance outcomes of service innovation activity are often equivocal. This appears exacerbated for servitizing firms, grappling with transitioning from being product-centric to service-centric (Baines et al., 2009; Burton et al., 2017). Service innovation research highlights that service context matters (Biemans et al., 2016), as does the type of innovation (Jaakkola & Hallin, 2018; Storey et al., 2016). Studies also suggest that the level at which we study innovation matters because the competencies and success factors for individual service innovations can clash with competencies and approaches at the firm or ecosystem levels.

Servitization is typically described as an organizational transformation process, where a manufacturer moves away from a product-oriented focus to having a service-oriented focus (Rabetino et al., 2018; Raddats et al., 2019). The literature is developing in terms of the 'big picture', such as understanding barriers and enablers (Burton et al., 2017) and the project-level picture in terms of single innovation projects (Bustinza et al., 2019), and how they can offer value to groups of customers (Johansson et al., 2019), literature on service innovation in servitizing firms remains sparse (Johansson et al., 2019) and performance outcomes equivocal. Despite the recognition that some firms build successful portfolios of innovative service offerings that deliver competitive advantage and profit (Baines et al., 2020), there is less work on how firms can develop strong offering portfolios or how they can achieve the desired performance outcomes.

NSD literature has extensively explored success factors (e.g. Storey et al., 2016), what Pettigrew (1987) term the 'content' aspects (i.e. what has changed). While servitization work has studied the 'what', 'why', and 'how' at different points (Baines et al., 2020), research is fragmented and does not typically take a more holistic view of the interplay between content, context, and process aspects. Furthermore, the process of developing a portfolio of new service value propositions within servitizing firms (Skålén et al., 2015), which would come under the 'content' and 'process' aspects (i.e. what have manufacturers have changed and how did, or should, change occur) (Baines et al., 2020), and the macro-level interactions occurring within servitizing firms (the 'context' aspect) receive limited attention.

Negative performance outcomes are typically attributed to the challenges of implementing service-oriented business models (Visnjic Kastalli & Van Looy, 2013), but might also be due to variation in the type of service innovation introduced, the nature and size of the service portfolio, and difficulties related to implementing servitization at the firm and ecosystem level. Therefore, servitization researchers need to better understand how service innovation efforts can deliver positive performance outcomes beyond the project level, adopting the view that change is multi-level, made up of an interplay between content, context, and process (Pettigrew, 1987).

The wealth of literature that already exists on service innovation (e.g. Biemans et al., 2016; Snyder et al., 2016), alongside the developing service innovation-focused servitization literature, provides useful insights for theorizing about service innovation practices in servitizing firms, and forms the basis of our theoretical development. Theory building is critical to the development of a research field because it provides the foundation upon which knowledge can be built, resulting in a deeper, richer understanding of organizational behavior (Klein et al., 1999; Witell et al., 2016). In adopting a multilevel theory building approach, we respond to calls for greater variety and depth when theorizing about the servitization-innovation performance relationship (Martinez et al., 2017), by offering a research framework that will enable a clearer picture to be built with regard to different types of servitization efforts and their outcomes.

Service innovation is considered on a continuum from incremental to radical (Witell et al., 2016) and manufacturers often seek radical service innovations to achieve improved performance, yet many service innovations are incremental improvements on existing offerings (Johansson et al., 2019). This is further complicated by the fact that service innovations are considered at different levels in terms of the innovation system: individual service innovation projects, offering portfolio (the mix of base, intermediate, and advanced services offered (Baines & Lightfoot, 2013), business model, ecosystem, industry and beyond. However, few papers discuss how service innovations diffuse across innovation levels. The chapter proposes a research framework that brings together innovation 'newness' (incremental to radical), the firm's service strategy (product-focused, hybrid and service-focused), and the 'innovation level' (project, offering portfolio, business model, etc.), as a means of classifying and understanding the linkages between three key service innovation dimensions. In doing so, we more holistically represent the potential interactions between service innovation efforts and choices made by servitizing firms, which, if studied systematically, should allow for a better understanding of how performance outcomes can be achieved.

2   Theory Development

The Service Innovation Concept

Several articles offer detailed explanations of what service innovation is (e.g. Lusch & Nambisan, 2015), arguing that in order to move theory forward, clear conceptual definitions are required (Witell et al., 2016). For example, Skålén et al. (2015: 137) define service innovation as "*the creation of new value propositions by means of developing existing or creating new practices and resources in new ways*". Such a definition highlights several key characteristics of service innovations, three of which link back to the work of Schumpeter (1934), that: (1) to be classified as an innovation, an invention must be launched or 'put into practice'; (2) there has to be an element of 'newness' (but services can be incremental revisions, line extensions, or radically new, including both re-combinative innovations [new combinations of existing characteristics into a new offering], or new to the world); and (3) there is a distinction between process (New Service Development—NSD) and output (service innovation). In terms of (3), however, there is less consistency. Many studies use them interchangeably, but, in line with Snyder et al. (2016), we argue that it is important to distinguish between the process (also recognizing the importance of 'context' and 'content' in this) and the 'output' (new services), which then drive performance outcomes.

Some definitions also explore service innovations from a value perspective and articulate value creation from the perspective of one or more actors (Ostrom et al., 2010). Thus, the perspective of 'value for whom' is also important when examining service innovation. Furthermore, Witell et al. (2016: 2871) note a key difficulty for firms in balancing innovation efforts across different types, "*making trade-offs between exploitation and exploration or incremental and radical innovation if they are to survive, let alone prosper*". Thus, our framework needs to consider different types of innovations and recognize the unique elements of these different types.

Service Innovation Categorizations

In reviewing categories of service innovation, Snyder et al. (2016) highlight four distinct aspects for categorizing service innovations: (1) degree of change (incremental—radical)—conceptualized as 'newness' in some studies; (2) type of change (product vs process); (3) newness, conceptualized as who the service is new for (the firm or the market), and thus, distinct from aspect (1); and (4) means of provision (technology vs people). Work often focuses on differences and similarities between service types to build a clearer understanding of what drives success in service innovation efforts (Biemans et al., 2016). However, Snyder et al. (2016) note that categories are frequently neither exhaustive nor mutually exclusive, with some seen as continuums, with blurred boundaries between types. The categorization process is also complicated by service innovations being explored at different levels (the individual project, the firm-level, or the ecosystem level).

That said, of the four Snyder et al., (2016) identified, a widely accepted distinction is the radical and incremental categorization (Witell et al., 2016). Innovation is often portrayed as a continuum from incremental to radical, with the term, newness, applied at a product/service level (Chester Goduscheit & Faullant, 2018), portfolio-level (Heimonen & Kohtamäki, 2019), firm-level (Story et al., 2015), industry-level (Dolfsma & Van der Velde, 2014), and country-level (Tellis et al., 2009). Services with minor changes to characteristics are typically categorized as incremental, whereas services that have a totally new set of characteristics are categorized as radical (Witell et al., 2016).[1] However, even when we know the degree of change, where an innovation sits on the continuum is not always clear, making it difficult to offer meaningful analysis of service innovation outcomes (Storey et al., 2016).

Within servitization literature, researchers also highlight different innovation levels. Figure 1 outlines the product-level categorizations articulated in extant research, which all view services from the perspective of whether they are more product-focused or more service-focused. Some offer reasonably comparable categories, while others cover a broader range of services. Thus, Fig. 1 shows these categories across a continuum.

What is clear from Fig. 1 is that consensus for categorizing service innovations has not been reached, despite the importance of this for understanding how service innovation occurs in servitizing firms. Only once research can be positioned within a clear, consistent categorization framework, will performance outcomes of different approaches become clear. In looking to draw from the long-standing service innovation literature and the servitization literature, our work returns to the notion of 'newness', in terms of how new these service innovations are. Some servitization researchers directly articulate this notion. For instance, at one end of the continuum, Kowalkowski et al. (2012) focus on 'agile incrementalism' as firms seek to continually adapt services to changing market opportunities. On the other, Johansson et al. (2019) call for manufacturers to develop radical service innovations.

---

[1] Biemans et al. (2016) provide a comprehensive review of service innovation typologies.

Author(s)	Product-focused------------------	Continuum --------------Service-focused	
Mathieu (2001)	SSPs (e.g. after-sales services/ repairs and maintenance)	SSCs (e.g. R&D Services - reward sharing contracts)	
Tukker (2004)	Product-oriented	Use-oriented	Results-oriented
Baines and Lightfoot (2013)	Base (e.g. installation)	Intermediate (e.g. maintenance, technical support)	Advanced (e.g. risk and reward sharing contracts)
Cusumano, Kahl and Suarez, (2015)	Smoothing services: facilitate product sale/usage	Adapting services: enhance product use	Substitution services: replace product purchase
Ulaga and Reinartz (2011)	Hybrid offerings: made up of innovative product and service combinations		
Jaakkola & Hallin, 2018 & Kohtamäki et al., 2019	Productized or smart solutions: bundles of products, services, expertise, and software		

Fig. 1 Servitization classifications on a continuum from product-focused to service-focused

Firm Service Strategy Categorizations

Innovation research more generally (e.g. Storey et al., 2016), and servitization research (e.g. Burton et al., 2017; Coreynen et al., 2020) recognizes the need for a firm-level understanding of service innovation activities. At the firm-level, servitization strategies are discussed in terms of firms being more product- or service-focused (Baines et al., 2009). Product-centric firms have portfolios of services directly coupled to their products, where products are foregrounded in decision-making. Service-centric firms focus more on aligning services to customers' processes. In many studies, product-level categorizations are used as proxies for service strategies (Raddats et al., 2019); however, these do not easily capture the 'strategic intent of the firm', where firms may have a range of offerings, but the overall balance of these will be driven by the firm's strategy. In this work we are not attempting to explore the specifics of *how* products and services are combined, we are instead interested in combining several of the firm-level strategies concepts to suggest a continuum from product-centric strategic intent through a hybrid strategic intent where neither dominates, through to a service-centric strategic intent, with the premise being that different firm-level strategies are likely to have different performance outcomes and boundary conditions.

Innovation Levels

Innovation is studied at different levels: project, portfolio, organization, ecosystem, sector, and economy. Previous research largely focused on examining service innovations at one level; for example, the project level (de Brentani, 1989), the team level (Lievens & Moenaert, 2000), or the organizational level (Jaakkola & Hallin, 2018). However, most services are not developed and delivered in isolation, but include portfolio- and organization-level considerations. The organizational arrangements for service innovation are more complex, ranging from temporary ad hoc structures for individual projects to more enduring complex business models and/or industry structures. Organizational structures can create stability and a focus on long-term visions (Jaakkola & Hallin, 2018), but they are also known to constrain (Heracleous et al., 2017). Nor are services developed in isolation, often relying on interactions with other ecosystem actors (Sjödin et al., 2019).

Furthermore, only limited work exists on the differences between the commercial success of individual service innovations and how these innovations contribute to longer-term firm-level performance outcomes. For example, Storey et al. (2016) examined the difference between the short-term commercial success of a single innovation and achieving firm-level Strategic Competitive Advantage (SCA), identifying unique critical success factors for each. Exploring service innovation efforts across the different levels should help to elucidate how the activities that occur at each level combine to contribute to or reduce performance outcomes.

The use of multilevel theory has been highlighted as a means of bridging gaps in theory development through a recognition of the multilevel systems involved in complex organizational research contexts (Turner, 2005), such as servitization, by focusing on three different levels of influencers, which are nested within one another, and evolve and change over time (Vargo et al., 2015), namely: macro-level (industry-wide and beyond) factors, meso-level (firm business model and portfolio) factors, and micro-level (individual projects) factors. Thus, adopting an ecosystem-level, multilayered perspective is needed to understand how resources are integrated at the various system levels (i.e. micro, meso, and macro) (Edvardsson et al., 2011). The literature on the key issues at the three levels will now be summarized.

There are several reviews of micro-level service innovation providing a detailed examination of current project-level thinking (e.g. Biemans et al., 2016), exploring such aspects as: the topics studied; research design focus; and data sources. Within this literature, a key debate is still around whether products and services are different when it comes to innovation efforts.

However, the applicability of traditional distinctions in contemporary service contexts is questioned and some recommend a single framework for studying product and service innovation activities, rather than seeing them as distinct (Storey et al., 2016). While there is limited work in the servitization literature examining service innovation at a project level, Rabetino et al. (2017) demonstrate how manufacturers can work with customers to co-develop new project-based solutions. Meanwhile, Lightfoot and Gebauer's (2011) study of service innovation highlighted heterogeneity in the innovation success determinants (e.g. importance of different NSD phases) across 24 projects. Here, again, there is debate around the interplay between product and service innovation, primarily because services typically compete with more established product development activities for limited resources and often remain inextricably linked to products (Burton et al., 2017).

At the meso-level, authors highlight the importance of considering service innovation efforts at the portfolio-level, recommending that firms adopt a more strategic approach to servitization portfolios (Burton et al. 2017; Heimonen & Kohtamäki, 2019). This is also supported by work highlighting the importance of economies of scope and scale in relation to achieving an advantage (Teece, 2007; Visnjic Kastalli & Van Looy, 2013). Nordin et al. (2011) discuss strategies for service provision based on customization, bundling, and widening ranges of offerings. Other work highlights modularity as a viable approach for managing complexity and building productivity gains (Gremyr et al., 2019). Kowalkowski et al. (2015) highlight the importance of balancing service expansion and standardization activities, and that services perform different roles, creating a complementary co-existence between offerings that need to be managed. Thus, in the same way that product research highlights that different products offer different advantages to a firm, we know that service innovations can bring different advantages (Heimonen & Kohtamäki, 2019). Work also highlights that different types of services are more prominent under particular industry conditions or under different stages of an industry's lifecycle (Cusumano et al., 2015), and can be driven by diverse customer needs (Johnstone et al., 2008). Other work highlights that servitization can result in short-term performance sacrifices for longer-term benefits, noting that service revenues should not be judged at the individual level, because this may not capture such things as portfolio-level cannibalization effects (Visnjic Kastalli & Van Looy, 2013), or at only one point in time, because of the temporal nature of innovation performance outcomes. Thus, for many firms, service innovation activities are a complex process of taking a portfolio-level approach to balancing customization and standardization (Matthyssens & Vandenbempt, 2010).

At the meso-level again, research has begun to foreground the role of business models in servitization, and how the design and management of new service-oriented business models are key to firms' servitization efforts (Kowalkowski et al., 2017). The business model level offers the opportunity to analyze bundles of practices related to revenue models, structures, and transactions (Baines et al., 2020). Business model transformation is seen as key to the servitization process (Kowalkowski et al., 2017), but research also suggests that firms must often manage multiple parallel business models (Kowalkowski et al., 2015), which often compete for dominance, creating tensions (Burton et al., 2016; Palo et al., 2019).

At a macro-level, business ecosystems are "*a relatively self-contained, self-adjusting system of mostly loosely coupled social and economic (resource integrating) actors*" (Lusch & Nambisan, 2015: 161) existing at industry or wider levels. Ecosystems have gained currency in describing collaborative efforts in developing and delivering service innovation (Koskela-Huotari et al., 2016) and for servitization (Bustinza et al., 2019), because they offer a holistic, multi-actor lens and enable examination of systemic, dynamic, and contextual aspects surrounding actor activities (Sklyar et al., 2019). When they operate effectively, ecosystems allow firms to deliver value that no one organization could create in isolation (e.g. Adner, 2006). However, ecosystem structures may vary for different service offerings and delivery modes, and for different firm service strategies, with actors in a service ecosystem depending on one another in different ways (Story et al., 2020).

An Integrative Framework of Service Innovation Activities

Organizations, and the ecosystems in which they operate, are inherently multilevel systems, and how companies integrate complex product and service innovation strategies requires a broader, multilevel perspective (Chester Goduscheit & Faullant, 2018), that enables a more integrated understanding of explored phenomena (Klein et al., 1999). Given that many firms struggle to transition to service strategies that deliver positive performance outcomes (Burton et al., 2017), a central question then relates to how service innovation knowledge, skills, and capabilities diffuse from individual customer projects to business models and beyond; how firms can achieve the right balance between incremental and radical innovations; and how a firm's service strategy affects these choices.

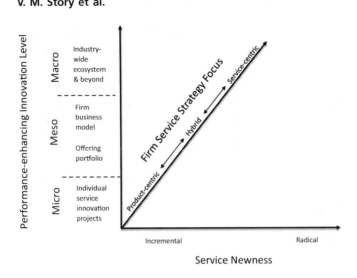

Fig. 2 Integrative research framework of service innovation activities

The research framework presented (Fig. 2) is designed as a mechanism to consider similarities, differences, and relationships between three key characteristics of service innovation in servitizing firms, so that future work can better position their study and contribution. Building on service innovation literature and the unique context of servitization, it recognizes the importance of the type of innovation, focusing on service newness of the new services, and whether the firm is more product-centric or service-centric. In doing so, the framework helps to categorize three key dimensions that need to be explored in understanding how service innovations begin at the micro-level as one-off service innovation projects, and portfolio offerings through firm business models (meso-level) to the ecosystem, industry-wide, and beyond (macro-level) and thus increase their potential to enhance performance. Key issues for each of the dimensions and their interactions are outlined below.

3   Discussion

Framework Implications

Servitization is often described as a transformational process whereby firms move from being product-centric to service-centric through developing base services, through intermediate to advanced services, with performance outcomes linked to advanced service provision (Baines et al., 2020). However, work has critiqued the presentation of servitization as a unidirectional approach based on a manufacturer's service strategies (Burton et al., 2017). The mixed evidence in terms of the performance implications of adding services suggests that the servitization—performance relationship is likely to be complex and non-linear, moderated by a variety of factors (boundary conditions) (Sjödin et al., 2019). However, until we understand the interplay between the different aspects involved, understanding performance outcomes will be difficult. Research framework 1.2 helps to articulate these different factors in such a way as to enable the performance implications of these key characteristics to be more systematically examined and compared.

In terms of newness, radical innovation is often hailed as a key driver of firm performance, but research suggests that incremental service innovation is at least as prevalent as radical service innovation (Raddats et al., 2019). Indeed, we might expect incremental projects to diffuse up the innovation levels quicker and more easily than more radical service innovations because there is a better fit with current operations, culture, and business models, but equally, we know that radical innovations can drive business model innovations that create game-changing effects higher up the innovation levels. For many firms, understanding how to move from 'low-hanging fruit', where margins are worthwhile without significant investment or culture change, to wide-scale servitization efforts that bring positive performance through appropriate portfolio decision-making efforts, and economies of scale and scope, is hard.

We argue that part of understanding how to improve performance will be to understand how project innovation leads to portfolio-level changes that deliver cost efficiencies through standardization or offer growth potentials that will make them profitable in the longer term. Alternatively, insights may also be gained by looking at mismatches across different elements (Gebauer et al., 2010). Furthermore, it is important that we begin to understand how firms can balance incremental and radical projects. Innovation literature highlights several tensions that arise from simultaneous exploration and exploitation efforts (Heracleous et al., 2017), with some researchers advocating the structural separation of activities related to incremental and radical innovations (Witell et al., 2016) and others advocating an integrated approach. However, many manufacturing firms attempting servitization face issues in embedding radical service innovations into their portfolios (Burton et al., 2017), often due to more product-focused processes and structures (Gremyr et al., 2019), highlighting a key interaction between innovation newness and the firm's service strategy focus.

When trying to understand the performance outcomes of service innovation efforts, the level at which a service innovation is studied is likely to matter. For instance, we need to understand what makes for a successful service innovation project, while also understanding the implications of service innovation activities at the firm-level, to support decision-making about where R&D resources are spent and how groups of offerings perform. This is important because, as the number of offerings increases, the explanatory power of a single project decreases (Story et al., 2015). Therefore, as service portfolios grow, firm, and ecosystem level decisions become more important.

Equally important then is whether macro-level factors in the ecosystem or industry stifle or support innovation efforts. Contestations at the firm and ecosystem level are likely to both drive change and create stability with regard to service innovation efforts, which, some argue, is where the main challenges and opportunities lie (Palo et al., 2019). This is likely to translate into firms needing to find a way to balance service innovation efforts across several dimensions: product versus service innovation efforts; incremental and radical service offerings; and ensuring that the right balance of base, intermediate, and advanced services are offered that match customer requirements. This is even more important for digital technologies, which support servitization efforts but also blur boundaries between actors, sectors, and markets (Coreynen et al., 2020). However, we know that these interactions are likely to bring tensions (Burton et al., 2016), not just in terms of the new and the old, or between products and services, but also between incremental and radical innovation efforts.

A change of organizational focus to become service-centric brings with it a requirement to redesign structures, business models, and organizational processes. However, literature is still unclear as to whether the transition occurs as part of a planned strategic organizational effort or as an emergent process, focusing on the project level and then looking to scale (Luoto et al., 2017). In reality, it is likely to be a bit of both, because while individual projects often drive transformation efforts, these projects sit within an organization and their ecosystem. Furthermore, it is harder to measure the economic impact and performance of service innovations, due to intangible benefits (Gallouj & Savona, 2009).

Determining the right portfolio is not a straightforward decision, and often goes hand-in-hand with the need to transform business models (Palo et al., 2019). Not doing so can lead to a firm ending up with a mismatch between their strategic market offerings and their organizational arrangements (Gebauer et al., 2010). Research also suggests that the different levels feed up and down (Koskela-Huotari et al., 2016). For example, Mukherjee et al. (2020) articulate how macro-level planning can help to overcome micro-level managerial myopia and help managers with decision-making at the project level, through reframing the rules in which their sense-making processes occur (e.g. Weick, 1995). By working both up and down the innovation levels, a common cognitive understanding can be built, that should support better performance outcomes for those involved. Thus, meso-level activities are important because business models can be powerful tools for framing and organizing servitization practices, but more work needs to be done to understand the activities that occur at each level and how they interact, to help firms to achieve better performance outcomes.

Theoretical Contributions

This chapter makes three important theoretical contributions. First, developing a framework of service innovation in servitizing firms should support the development of theory through enabling organization of related concepts that enable the relationships between these concepts to be articulated, allowing for classification and theory building efforts (Snow & Ketchen, 2014). In building on earlier work in both the service innovation and the servitization literature, this framework offers a mechanism for both classifying innovation efforts and developing an understanding of the interlinkages between the dimensions explored. By looking across the levels and understanding the impact of different types of innovations and the different types of firm-level strategic intent, this might help us to identify key threats related to value 'destruction' (Visnjic Kastalli & Van Looy, 2013), thereby achieving value creation for firms, customers, and the economy; from individual offerings to industry-wide impacts. In offering this framework, we seek to provide better direction to servitization researchers by moving beyond descriptive categorizations of service offerings or organizational approaches to highlight that research needs to explore issues within each level. For example, understanding key similarities and differences between incremental and radical service innovation within servitizing firms, and the implications of firm culture on these activities, as well as exploring the interactions between activities at the three different levels, to understand how innovation knowledge, skills, and capabilities diffuse between the micro, meso, and macro levels.

Second, the multilevel approach captures the embedded nature of the activities that occur at each level, and is, therefore, likely to bring greater understanding than studying them in isolation. Most work focuses on the project level, the overall firm-level (e.g. barriers and enablers), or, more recently, the ecosystem level. However, the insights outlined here, suggest that the meso-level portfolios and business models are particularly important, and while research is developing in this area, more work is needed to understand these aspects and their interactions across the micro and macro levels in support of improved servitization outcomes.

Third, our framework looks to foreground the processes involved in servitization activities, both within and across the dimensions articulated. Exploring how servitizing firms develop in relation to their service innovation efforts responds to calls regarding building knowledge of the change processes, answering questions related to 'how does, or should, change occur' (Baines et al., 2020), so that the activities are undertaken to support a firm's transition from manufacturer to successfully achieving growth and revenue benefits.

In articulating potential interactions between three key service innovation dimensions, the framework offers a research agenda for servitization researchers that will enable knowledge to be built about the service innovation–performance relationship. Performance outcomes cannot be explained by only looking at one area, but by seeing service innovation in the context of a firm's service strategies, and how these service innovation efforts diffuse across the ecosystem. Only through a systematic development of knowledge will a fuller picture be built of how performance outcomes are affected by these intertwined decisions.

Managerial Implications

From a practitioner's perspective, it is important to highlight that servitization efforts are a balance of developing the right incremental and radical services, which match with the firm-level service strategy, and that decisions should be seen in the context of micro, meso, and macro influences. Furthermore, it is important that organizations consider the interactive nature of decisions at the individual service, portfolio, business model, and beyond, if they are to succeed in making the transformation from a manufacturer to a profitable provider of services that create value for customers, themselves, and ecosystem partners.

References

Adner, R. (2006). Match your innovation strategy to your innovation ecosystem. *Harvard Business Review, 84*(4), 98.

Baines, T., Bigdeli, A. Z., Sousa, R., & Schroeder, A. (2020). Framing the servitization transformation process: A model to understand and facilitate the servitization journey. *International Journal of Production Economics, 221,* 107463.

Baines, T. S., & Lightfoot, H. (2013). Servitization of the manufacturing firm: Exploring the operations practices and technologies that deliver advanced services. *International Journal of Operations and Production Management, 34*(1), 2–35.

Baines, T., Lightfoot, H., Peppard, J., Johnson, M., Tiwari, A., Shehab, E., et al. (2009). Towards an operations strategy for product-centric servitization. *International Journal of Operations & Production Management, 29*(5), 494–519.

Biemans, W., & Griffin, A. (2018). Innovation practices of B2B manufacturers and service providers: Are they really different? *Industrial Marketing Management, 75*, 112–124.

Biemans, W. G., Griffin, A., & Moenaert, R. K. (2016). Perspective: New service development: How the field developed, its current status and recommendations for moving the field forward. *Journal of Product Innovation Management, 33*(4), 382–397.

Burton, J., Story, V. M., Raddats, C., & Zolkiewski, J. (2017). Overcoming the challenges that hinder new service development by manufacturers with diverse services strategies. *International Journal of Production Economics, 192*, 29–39.

Burton, J., Story, V., Zolkiewski, J., Raddats, C., Baines, T. S., & Medway, D. (2016). Identifying tensions in the servitized value chain: If servitization is to be successful, servitizing firms must address the tensions the process creates in their value network. *Research-Technology Management, 59*(5), 38–47.

Bustinza, O. F., Gomes, E., Vendrell-Herrero, F., & Baines, T. (2019). Product–service innovation and performance: The role of collaborative partnerships and R&D intensity. *R&D Management, 49*(1), 33–45.

Chester Goduscheit, R., & Faullant, R. (2018). Paths toward radical service innovation in manufacturing companies—A service-dominant logic perspective. *Journal of Product Innovation Management, 35*(5), 701–719.

Coreynen, W., Matthyssens, P., Vanderstraeten, J., & van Witteloostuijn, A. (2020). Unravelling the internal and external drivers of digital servitization: A dynamic capabilities and contingency perspective on firm strategy. *Industrial Marketing Management* (in press).

Cusumano, M. A., Kahl, S. J., & Suarez, F. F. (2015). Services, industry evolution, and the competitive strategies of product firms. *Strategic Management Journal, 36*(4), 559–575.

de Brentani, U. (1989). Success and failure in new industrial services. *Journal of Product Innovation Management, 6*(4), 239–258.

Dolfsma, W., & Van der Velde, G. (2014). Industry innovativeness, firm size, and entrepreneurship: Schumpeter Mark III? *Journal of Evolutionary Economics, 24*(4), 713–736.

Edvardsson, B., Tronvoll, B., & Gruber, T. (2011). Expanding understanding of service exchange and value co-creation: A social construction approach. *Journal of the Academy of Marketing Science, 39*(2), 327–339.

Gallouj, F., & Savona, M. (2009). Innovation in services: A review of the debate and a research agenda. *Journal of Evolutionary Economics, 19*(2), 149.

Gebauer, H., Edvardsson, B., Gustafsson, A., & Witell, L. (2010). Match or mismatch: Strategy-structure configurations in the service business of manufacturing companies. *Journal of Service Research, 13*(2), 198–215.

Gremyr, I., Valtakoski, A., & Witell, L. (2019). Two routes of service modularization: Advancing standardization and customization. *Journal of Services Marketing, 33*(1), 73–87.

Heimonen, J., & Kohtamäki, M. (2019). Measuring new product and service portfolio advantage. *International Entrepreneurship and Management Journal, 15*(1), 163–174.

Heracleous, L., Papachroni, A., Andriopoulos, C., & Gotsi, M. (2017). Structural ambidexterity and competency traps: Insights from Xerox PARC. *Technological Forecasting and Social Change, 117,* 327–338.

Jaakkola, E., & Hallin, A. (2018). Organizational structures for new service development. *Journal of Product Innovation Management, 35*(2), 280–297.

Johansson, A. E., Raddats, C., & Witell, L. (2019). The role of customer knowledge development for incremental and radical service innovation in servitized manufacturers. *Journal of Business Research, 98,* 328–338.

Johnstone, S., Dainty, A., & Wilkinson, A. (2008). In search of 'product-service': Evidence from aerospace, construction, and engineering. *The Service Industries Journal, 28,* 861–875.

Klein, K. J., Tosi, H., & Cannella, A. A., Jr. (1999). Multilevel theory building: Benefits, barriers, and new developments. *Academy of Management Review, 24*(2), 248–253.

Kohtamäki, M., Parida, V., Oghazi, P., Gebauer, H., & Baines, T. (2019). Digital servitization business models in ecosystems: A theory of the firm. *Journal of Business Research, 104,* 380–392.

Koskela-Huotari, K., Edvardsson, B., Jonas, J. M., Sörhammar, D., & Witell, L. (2016). Innovation in service ecosystems—Breaking, making, and maintaining institutionalized rules of resource integration. *Journal of Business Research, 69*(8), 2964–2971.

Kowalkowski, C., Gebauer, H., & Oliva, R. (2017). Service growth in product firms: Past, present, and future. *Industrial Marketing Management, 60,* 82–88.

Kowalkowski, C., Kindström, D., Alejandro, T. B., Brege, S., & Biggemann, S. (2012). Service infusion as agile incrementalism in action. *Journal of Business Research, 65*(6), 765–772.

Kowalkowski, C., Windahl, C., Kindström, D., & Gebauer, H. (2015). What service transition? Rethinking established assumptions about manufacturers' service-led growth strategies. *Industrial Marketing Management, 45,* 59–69.

Lievens, A., & Moenaert, R. K. (2000). New service teams as information-processing systems: Reducing innovative uncertainty. *Journal of Service Research, 3*(1), 46–65.

Lightfoot, H. W., & Gebauer, H. (2011). Exploring the alignment between service strategy and service innovation. *Journal of Service Management, 22*(5), 664–683.

Lusch, R. F., & Nambisan, S. (2015). Service innovation: A service-dominant logic perspective. *MIS Quarterly, 39*(1), 155–175.

Luoto, S., Brax, S. A., & Kohtamäki, M. (2017). Critical meta-analysis of servitization research: Constructing a model-narrative to reveal paradigmatic assumptions. *Industrial Marketing Management, 60,* 89–100.

Martinez, V., Neely, A., Velu, C., Leinster-Evans, S., & Bisessar, D. (2017). Exploring the journey to services. *International Journal of Production Economics, 192,* 66–80.

Mathieu, V. (2001). Product services: From a service supporting the product to a service supporting the client. *Journal of Business and Industrial Marketing, 16,* 39–61.

Matthyssens, P., & Vandenbempt, K. (2010). Service addition as business market strategy: Identification of transition trajectories. *Journal of Service Management, 21*(5), 693–714.

Mukherjee, M., Ramirez, R., & Cuthbertson, R. (2020). Strategic reframing as a process enabled with scenario research. *Long Range Planning, 53*(5), 101933.

Nordin, F., Kindström, D., Kowalkowski, C., & Rehme, J. (2011). The risks of providing services. *Journal of Service Management, 22*(3), 390–408.

Ostrom, A. L., Bitner, M. J., Brown, S. W., Burkhard, K. A., Goul, M., Smith-Daniels, V., et al. (2010). Moving forward and making a difference: Research priorities for the science of service. *Journal of Service Research, 13*(1), 4–36.

Palo, T., Åkesson, M., & Löfberg, N. (2019). Servitization as business model contestation: A practice approach. *Journal of Business Research, 104,* 486–496.

Pettigrew, A. (1987). Context and action in the transformation of the firm. *Journal of Management Studies, 24*(6), 649–670.

Rabetino, R., Harmsen, W., Kohtamäki, M., & Sihvonen, J. (2018). Structuring servitization-related research. *International Journal of Operations and Production Management, 38*(2), 350–371.

Rabetino, R., Kohtamäki, M., & Gebauer, H. (2017). Strategy map of servitization. *International Journal of Production Economics, 192,* 144–156.

Rabetino, R., Kohtamäki, M., Lehtonen, H., & Kostama, H. (2015). Developing the concept of life-cycle service offering. *Industrial Marketing Management, 49,* 53–66.

Raddats, C., Kowalkowski, C., Benedettini, O., Burton, J., & Gebauer, H. (2019). Servitization: A contemporary thematic review of four major research streams. *Industrial Marketing Management, 83,* 207–223.

Schumpeter, J. A. (1934). The theory of economic development: An inquiry into profits, capital. Credit, interest, and the business cycle.

Sjödin, D., Parida, V., & Kohtamäki, M. (2019). Relational governance strategies for advanced service provision: Multiple paths to superior financial performance in servitization. *Journal of Business Research, 101,* 906–915.

Skålén, P., Gummerus, J., Von Koskull, C., & Magnusson, P. R. (2015). Exploring value propositions and service innovation: A service-dominant logic study. *Journal of the Academy of Marketing Science, 43*(2), 137–158.

Sklyar, A., Kowalkowski, C., Tronvoll, B., & Sörhammar, D. (2019). Organizing for digital servitization: A service ecosystem perspective. *Journal of Business Research, 104,* 450–460.

Snow, C. C., & Ketchen, D. J., Jr. (2014). Typology-driven theorizing: A response to Delbridge and Fiss. *Academy of Management Review, 39*(2), 231–233.

Snyder, H., Witell, L., Gustafsson, A., Fombelle, P., & Kristensson, P. (2016). Identifying categories of service innovation: A review and synthesis of the literature. *Journal of Business Research, 69*(7), 2401–2408.

Storey, C., Cankurtaran, P., Papastathopoulou, P., & Hultink, E. J. (2016). Success factors for service innovation: A meta-analysis. *Journal of Product Innovation Management, 33*(5), 527–548.

Story, V. M., Boso, N., & Cadogan, J. W. (2015). The form of relationship between firm-level product innovativeness and new product performance in developed and emerging markets. *Journal of Product Innovation Management, 32*(1), 45–64.

Story, V., Zolkiewski, J., Verleye, K., Nazifi, A., Hannibal, C., Grimes, A., & Abboud, L. (2020). Stepping out of the shadows: Supporting actors' strategies for managing end-user experiences in service ecosystems. *Journal of Business Research* (in press).

Teece, D. J. (2007). Explicating dynamic capabilities: The nature and microfoundations of (sustainable) enterprise performance. *Strategic Management Journal, 28*(13), 1319–1350.

Tellis, G. J., Prabhu, J. C., & Chandy, R. K. (2009). Radical innovation across nations: The preeminence of corporate culture. *Journal of Marketing, 73*(1), 3–23.

Tukker, A. (2004). Eight types of product-service system: Eight ways to sustainability? Experiences from Suspronet. *Business Strategy and the Environment, 13,* 246–260.

Turner, J. H. (2005). A new approach for theoretically integrating micro and macro analysis. In *The Sage handbook of sociology* (pp. 405–422).

Ulaga, W., & Reinartz, W. J. (2011). Hybrid offerings: How manufacturing firms combine goods and services successfully. *Journal of Marketing, 75*(6), 5–23.

Vargo, S. L., Wieland, H., & Akaka, M. A. (2015). Innovation through institutionalization: A service ecosystems perspective. *Industrial Marketing Management, 44*(1), 63–72.

Visnjic Kastalli, I., & Van Looy, B. (2013). Servitization: Disentangling the impact of service business model innovation on manufacturing firm performance. *Journal of Operations Management, 31*(4), 169–180.

Weick, K. E. (1995). *Sensemaking in organizations* (Vol. 3). Sage.

Witell, L., Snyder, H., Gustafsson, A., Fombelle, P., & Kristensson, P. (2016). Defining service innovation: A review and synthesis. *Journal of Business Research, 69*(8), 2863–2872.

Configurational Servitization Approach: A Necessary Alignment of Service Strategies, Digital Capabilities and Customer Resources

Tinhinane Tazaïrt and Isabelle Prim-Allaz

1 Introduction: The Complexity of Servitization

In order to face down competition and enhance their market share, manufacturing companies need to address their businesses differently, developing either complementary offers or a core transformation of their offer into one that integrates services. These changes can lead to a better response to customer needs, quite often in innovative ways.

Servitization (Vandermerwe & Rada, 1988) is an evolution of the value proposition of manufacturing firms. It consists of a shift from a product-centric offer to an offer combining products and services, or to a use-centric or a result-centric offer (Baines et al., 2009; Mathieu, 2001).

Servitization is perceived by firms as a way of both improving their competitiveness (Vandermerwe & Rada, 1988) and reaching a higher level of profitability (Gebauer et al., 2011). The service offerings are more likely to provide higher margins and profitability due to their low comparability (Frambach et al., 1998; Neu & Brown, 2005; Oliva & Kallenberg, 2003) and

T. Tazaïrt (✉) · I. Prim-Allaz
Lumière Lyon 2 University, Lyon, France
e-mail: tinhinane.tazairt@univ-lyon2.fr

I. Prim-Allaz
e-mail: isabelle.prim-allaz@univ-lyon2.fr

© The Author(s), under exclusive license to Springer Nature
Switzerland AG 2021
M. Kohtamäki et al. (eds.), *The Palgrave Handbook of Servitization*,
https://doi.org/10.1007/978-3-030-75771-7_28

437

to allow manufacturers to be less concerned with price competition (Malleret, 2006).

The research to date highlights that the servitization of manufacturing companies has not always fulfilled its promised performance. Many tensions are observed in the literature, including the so-called service paradox (Gebauer et al., 2005; Neely, 2007). Empirical studies demonstrate that the financial benefits resulting from servitization are not always positive or perceptible (Gebauer et al., 2005; Neely, 2007). The service development in manufacturing firms should improve their performance, but this is not always the case in practice (Gebauer et al., 2005). This paradox is possibly reinforced by a digitalization paradox, digitalization being considered as a driver as well as an enabler of servitization (Vendrell-Herrero et al., 2017). The digitalization paradox reflects the fact that the revenues attributable to digitalization are much lower than the costs engaged (Sjödin et al., 2020). This lack of performance may appear in particular when firms simultaneously develop both their servitization and their digitalization (Vendrell-Herrero et al., 2017).

One way of overcoming these paradoxes is to better understand servitization and its conditions of success. As there is no consensus in the literature on defining servitization, we reexamine the current understanding of servitization and we propose to highlight the heterogeneity of this concept, which is multifaceted and faces different approaches (Table 1): either offer-oriented, processes-oriented, uses or results-oriented or innovation-oriented. These approaches reflect different servitized value propositions (SVP).

The value proposition addresses the relationship between customer needs and supplier offers (Osterwalder and Pigneur, 2010), and some scholars put the customer and its resources as a focal point of servitization (Baines et al., 2009, 2013; Vandermerwe & Rada, 1988), showing the importance of the customer in the servitized value proposition. In Sect. 2, we present and discuss key components of servitization (strategy, value proposition, customer resources and digital capabilities) that companies have to combine. Service strategies and their related servitized value proposition have to be considered through the interplay with the roles given to customers and digitalization in order to perform as expected.

In Sect. 3, we argue that there are different paths to a successful servitization. Based on configuration theory, we propose an integrative framework to help manufacturing firms to implement servitization according to their chosen strategy. We defend the idea that firms may perform as expected while implementing different configurations of service strategies, digital capabilities and customer resources (Ambroise et al., 2018).

Table 1 The necessary reexamination of the current understanding of servitization: different servitization approaches

Servitization approaches	Authors	Definition
Offer	Vandermerwe and Rada (1988), Vestrepen and Van Den Berg (1999), Mathieu (2001), Robinson et al. (2002), Oliva and Kallenberg (2003), Ward and Graves (2007) and Baines et al. (2007, 2013)	The *offer-oriented* approach to servitization is considered as an extension or transformation of the offer via a combination of simple services added to products. Companies tend to offer a set of products, services, support, self-service and knowledge through the integration of a "products and services" duality in its global offer, the aim being to take advantage of the benefits associated with services without disrupting the business model
Processes	Mathieu (2001), Neely (2007), Baines et al. (2007, 2013) and Kowalkowski et al. (2017)	The *process-oriented* approach to servitization is considered as a set of transformational processes through which a company moves from a product-oriented to a service-oriented model, transforming the product offering into a use or a result offer. Scholars propose that service-oriented businesses tend to transform their processes in order to respond differently to the market, leading to new forms of services. This approach foresees a shift from an industrial process to a service-based process
		(continued)

Table 1 (continued)

Servitization approaches	Authors	Definition
Uses and results	Oliva and Kallenberg (2003), Lewis et al. (2004) and Baines et al. (2007, 2013)	The **use and result-oriented** approach to servitization is considered as a strategy that changes the way in which functionalities are delivered to their markets. This refers to the service typology (basic, intermediate and advanced services) of Baines et al. (2009). The use and results-oriented servitization approach recommends the creation of services with new functionalities that are measurable and might provide greater added value, resulting in a performance contract proposal, through selling use or result. This may lead to business model disruption
Innovation	Tellus Institute (1999), Desmet et al. (2013), Neely (2007), Baines et al. (2007, 2013), Parida et al. (2015), Huikkola and Kohtamäki (2017) and Sjödina et al. (2020)	The **innovation-oriented** approach to servitization is a way to innovate through services and improve the core activity of manufacturing firms: manufacturing firms are increasingly integrating services into their offerings in order to pursue innovation objectives. The innovation-oriented approach looks at servitization through two approaches: innovating through the process and innovating for, and with, the customer

2   Theory Development

Understanding the different servitization approaches can help manufacturing companies to better address their servitized value proposition. In the meantime, adopting a value proposition perspective can facilitate a better implementation of servitization. These approaches—offer-oriented, processes-oriented, uses or results-oriented and innovation-oriented—are not mutually exclusive and refer to different value propositions (Table 1).

Value Propositions and Service Strategies

Baines et al. (2019) recommend rethinking servitized value propositions in terms of customers' roles and resources. They define the value proposition (VP) offered to customers as the capacity of firms to combine their offerings (as providers) with the outcomes (the customer benefits inherent to the use of these offerings). In other words, the VP "is presented as a statement that clearly identifies for customers what they will receive and what it will do for them" (p. 4). This definition is completed by "how customers will contribute throw their own proposals (roles and resources)." Indeed, it is important to consider the servitized value proposition (SVP) of the resources brought by customers in specific transactions and in the whole relationship (Moeller, 2010). Customers may play different roles, with different levels of integration in the value chain.

Baines et al. (2013) suggest a configurative definition of servitization, which integrates the customers in the definition of services, giving specific roles to them and necessitating a different organization according to the types of services. Indeed, the authors propose three types of customized servitization: (1) basic added services for the "*do it themselves*" category of customers; (2) intermediate services to the "*do it with them*" customers; and (3) advanced service for the "*do it for them*" customers. In doing so, the authors fully integrate the customer in their definition of servitization and put the focus on the heterogeneity of customer roles. Many companies emphasize customer roles in their servitized value proposition, showing how to favor a customer-service configuration with shared value creation between customers and suppliers (Neely, 2007). As they move to servitization, manufacturing companies may offer different value propositions to their customers.

We propose three different levels of value propositions for services, inspired by Baines et al. (2019). The first level corresponds to proposing merely added services such as simple product spares, training materials, documentation, breakdown services, consumables and maintenance tools (Baines et al.,

2019; Teyssier et al., 2018). We name this VP the basic VP. The second level integrates product break/fix, assured maintenance and performance advisory services (Baines et al., 2019) as well as predictive maintenance, monitoring to improve customers' use of equipment, outsourcing, co-design or co-production activities (Gebauer et al., 2010; Teyssier et al., 2018). We name this second type of VP an output-oriented VP. The third level of VP proposes to integrate customers more in the service production in terms of asset, process and platform (Baines et al., 2019) where suppliers (non-transfer of property rights and of associated risks) provide an integrated product-service solution that guarantees different customers' outcomes. We name this VP a customer outcomes-oriented VP.

These VPs are the declination of a variety of strategies. Ambroise et al. (2018) identify three of them: proposing added services to the core offer; activities reconfiguration; and business model reconfiguration (Table 2).

In a certain way, these strategies are closed to the typology of customer roles proposed by Baines et al. (2013)—"do it themselves"; "do it with them";

Table 2 Service strategies and servitized value propositions (Ambroise et al., 2018; Baines et al., 2019)

The AS strategy (-*do it themselves*-) does not fundamentally change the customer's value chain but allows the supplier to extend its offer and expand opportunities. Ownership is transferred from the supplier to the customer, along with the associated risks. This corresponds to the first level of VP, the basic one, where manufacturing companies propose products and product spares to the customer (Baines et al., 2019), training materials, documentation, breakdown services, consumables and maintenance tools (Teyssier et al., 2018)
The AR strategy (-*do it with them*-) helps manufacturing companies to become providers of products and services by integrating customers into their business model and value chain: this allows them to co-develop offers and/or processes with the customer and to outsource services. We name this second level of VP "output-oriented": it integrates product break/fix, assured maintenance and performance advice, predictive maintenance and monitoring to improve customers' use of equipment, outsourcing, co-design or co-production activities (Baines et al., 2019; Gebauer et al., 2010; Teyssier et al., 2018)
The BMR strategy (-*do it for them*-) involves a change in the business model of the supplier and the customer as well as in their relationship model. It refers to the industrial supplier accepting a use or result-oriented arrangement with its customer, which will change not only their offerings but also their mutual organisational processes and their revenue and profit equations. Therefore, this strategy has significant strategic, organisational and financial implications for both the provider and the customer (Ambroise et al., 2018). Suppliers have to integrate customers more in terms of asset, process and platform (Baines et al., 2019), and they provide an integrated product-service solution that guarantees different customers' outcomes. We name this VP "the customer outcomes oriented" VP

"do it for them"—that takes explicitly into account the resources brought by the customers. Vargo and Lusch (2008) point out the necessity of bringing customers to deliver "applied resources for value creation and collaboratively (interactively) create value" (p. 7). In line with Vargo and Lusch (2004), Baines and Lightfoot (2013) show the key role of customers assuming that the customer is always a co-producer, implying value creation in an interactive manner.

Manufacturing firms increasingly aim to offer a comprehensive commercial proposal by integrating the customers in the offer (Vandermerwe & Rada, 1988). They put the customer in a central position. The contribution of the customers to the servitized value creation must be considered during the servitized process itself, the customer having more or less active roles in the value proposition design and implementation. Indeed, the customer can contribute to the offer with different levels of resources: a passive customer is considered as a mere consumer; an active one is considered as a producer; and a proactive one is considered as an initiator.

Services Strategies, Digital Capabilities and Customer Resources

Mobilizing customer resources and considering the customer as a co-producer induces greater information exchange. Servitization globally involves a better knowledge of customer needs and more interactions that are nowadays greatly facilitated by digitalization. Customers and digitalization are both keys in elaborating an appropriate value proposition: technologies contribute to improving the value of the offer delivered to customers and the value brought by customers (Ambroise et al., 2018; Coreynen et al., 2017; Tukker, 2004).

Digitalization can help to move to a product-service system (Frank et al., 2019) in which digital capabilities are needed to interact and create value with customers (Lenka et al., 2017). Gobble (2018) considers digitalization as a form of process and business model innovation that enables the exploitation of new opportunities to create and capture value (Gobble, 2018) by enhancing customers' analytics and insights, operational efficiency and marketing learning (Ramaswamy & Ozcan, 2018). We note here the necessary link between digital processes and customers.

Developing a service offering also requires us to reconsider interactions and interfaces with customers (Ambroise et al., 2018) and promotes the development of digital capabilities in companies (Parida et al., 2015) to improve customer relations. Nevertheless, the customer interface required differs depending on the service strategy implemented (Ambroise et al.,

2018). This interface defines the potential of firms to collect data and automatize part of the relationship.

As mentioned above, these strategies, **AS, AR and BMR**, need to address different digital capabilities relating to the customer interface required: **informative, collaborative and productive** (Teyssier et al., 2018). The first category of capabilities (informative) makes it possible to capture and store information about customers and the environment that the front office receives and generates. The second type of capabilities (collaborative) enables both information exchanges between customers and the back office and co-creating activities; and the third (productive) improves internal operational processes, including design and manufacturing processes, flow and supply chain management (Teyssier et al., 2018).

Companies must take into account their digital capabilities and cutomer resources in their servitized value proposition. This is especially true in B2B activities in which suppliers are looking for a better understanding of the value creation process (Coreynen, 2017) in order to improve their value proposition and thus move their business to more customer-integrated models (Grandval & Ronteau, 2011). Informative capabilities are particularly important when developing added services; while collaborative capabilities are important when proposing activities reconfigurations. Productive capabilities are key to business model reconfiguration strategy (Teyssier et al., 2018).

To conclude, we define the servitized value proposition as an iterative process that allows: (i) the identification of customer needs; and (ii) the formulation of an optimal response by suppliers through service development and integrated digital capabilities to enable an innovative and configurative model of servitization. The servitized value proposition has to be considered through interaction with the roles given to customers and digitalization in order to perform as expected (Martín-Peña et al., 2019).

Companies that integrate new services by simultaneously developing digitalization processes may face a digital service paradox (DSP) due to the difficulty in finding the right articulation and structure between servitization and digitalization. We define the DSP as a risk of failure in the financial performance of manufacturing companies that are trying to enhance their offerings toward more services while enhancing their digital capabilities to meet customers' needs at the same time. In order to overcome this DSP, we argue for the necessity of articulating between: (i) customer resources by showing the importance of the customer (and the need to consider it as a resource with varying degrees of integration in the chosen servitized value proposition); and (ii) digitalization capabilities to develop new services, and for their integration in the servitized value proposition design. As there is a multiplicity of possible combinations of servitization strategies, customer resources and digitization capabilities, one must consider that different configurations may lead to better performance.

In the next section, we present an integrative framework combining service strategies, digital capabilities and customer resources to design and implement efficient servitized value propositions (Table 3).

3 Toward a Configurational Orientation of Servitization

Ambroise et al. (2018) demonstrate that there is no one best way to implement a service strategy and that customer roles and interfaces have to be adapted to the chosen strategy. As a consequence, we advocate the need for a configurational approach that recognizes the alignment of service strategies, digital capabilities and customer resources to be a necessity.

As service strategies are multiple and potentially very heterogeneous, there is a risk of mismatch between the servitization strategy that is implemented, digital capabilities and customer resources. This can result in a financial failure and a potential deservitization (Kowalkowski et al., 2017). Therefore, firms have to be aware of the need to choose relevant configurations (Bowen et al., 1989).

We previously pointed out the complexity and heterogeneity of servitization, both of which often lead manufacturing firms to misunderstand the concept. To design their servitized value proposition, manufacturing firms must have a comprehensive framework of servitization that takes into account service strategies, customer roles and resources and firms' digital capabilities. Previous work has shown that a plethora of different service strategies on offer means that there is no one best way to servitize. A configurational approach is proposed in order to take into account this heterogeneity. Implementing a servitization strategy is not a "straight road to success" (Gebauer et al., 2010: 198).

Dimensions of the Configurational Approach and Need for an Alignment of Service Strategy, Customer Roles and Resources and Digital Capabilities

In developing the research area of servitization, scholars would be well advised to identify the conditions for successful implementation of servitization in manufacturing companies. Our essay offers a valuable contribution to the field by providing a perspective that understands the configurations of servitized value propositions and considers their strategies and underlying structures as well as their resource contingencies.

Instead of looking for a single condition to determine outcomes, the configuration theory allows for different conditions of a successful outcome, considering there is no one best way to achieve performance but a set of combinations (Böhm et al., 2017; Meyer et al., 1993).

The configuration logic is that different interactions between the three domains (strategy, structure, resources) may bring about successful servitization (Kohtamäki, Henneberg et al., 2019). Scholars assume that superior performance can be reached with different pathways: companies should not have a single and common reading of their performance. They have to deal with their own organizational and strategic characteristics (Böhm et al., 2017).

Moreover, the configurational approach advocates nonlinearity and equifinality (Meyer et al., 1993; Ragin, 2008) which means that the key attributes are multidimensional, possibly interrelated and have potentially a mutual amplificatory effect. Indeed, researchers have shown that firms with more coherent characteristics outperform firms with less coherent characteristics (Meyer et al., 1993; Vorhies & Morgan, 2003). Multiple configurations lead to superior performance as long as their individual conditions are aligned (Böhm et al., 2017; Doty et al., 1993).

Drawing on the research literature to date, we propose that companies adopt a relevant alignment of service strategy, digital capabilities and customer resources. The service strategies typology proposed by Ambroise et al. (2018), added services (AS), activities reconfiguration (AR) and business model reconfiguration strategies (BMR), is complementary to the one proposed by Baines and Lightfoot (2013) (*"do it themselves-do it with them-do it for them"*). Crossing the two typologies makes it possible to better understand the role customers are expected to perform according to the specific strategy implemented.

Table 3 presents the different attributes for designing and realizing the chosen service strategy based on a configurational approach. When implementing an AS strategy, manufacturing companies are positioned in an offer-oriented and/or a processes-oriented approach to servitization, which implies greater digital informative capabilities.

To address an AR strategy, companies can design either/both a result, processes or uses-oriented servitization approach where digital collaborative capabilities are needed. Besides, to implement a BMR strategy, companies can adopt either/both processes, uses or innovation-oriented servitization approaches, with digital productive capabilities.

As represented in Table 3, when implementing their strategy manufacturing firms can adopt "either/both" of the different servitization approaches (Kohtamäki et al., 2020), but they must coherently reconsider their offering according to their resources and capabilities (digital capabilities, organizational model, etc.), and also according to roles that customers play. Customers have to be considered as a resource, but the level of their contribution will vary according to the implemented service strategy and to the type of resources they deliver toward the design and realization of the servitized value proposition.

As shown in Table 3, the customers' integration into the servitized value proposition varies according to the chosen servitization strategy determining the role customers play and the resources they provide to the supplier. Indeed, a passive customer will only participate with basic resources, such as mere information. This low level of integration may be sufficient if the manufacturing firm decides to implement an AS strategy. If proposing an AR strategy, however, customers are expected to endorse the producer. There is a higher level of expectation for them to participate and collaborate in designing the servitized value proposition. Finally, when implementing a BMR service strategy, customers have a high degree of integration in the servitized value proposition of the company: they become proactive.

Adopting a configurational approach to servitization leads to blurring the boundaries of each servitization approach (Fig. 1) to fix the heterogeneity behind this concept. We propose that manufacturing firms manage their offer according to the necessary alignment of service strategies, digital capabilities and customer resources as a necessary and sufficient condition to succeed in implementing servitization.

Table 3 A configurational approach to servitization

Service strategy	Added services	Activities reconfiguration	Business model reconfiguration
Servitized value propositions (Inspired by Baines et al., 2019)	Basic VP	Output-oriented VP	Customer outcomes-oriented VP
Customer roles (status)	Do it themselves	Do it with them	Do it for them
Digital capabilities	Informative capabilities	Collaborative capabilities	Productive capabilities
Customer as a resource: Customer integration in the servitized value proposition design	Passive customer : "consumer"	Active customer : "producer"	Proactive customer
Servitization approaches	Offer	Result	Innovation

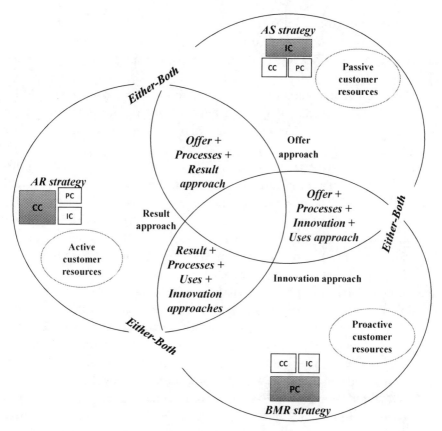

Fig. 1 Blurring boundaries through a configurational approach to servitization

Multiple Pathways to Succeed in Implementing Servitization

Manufacturing firms need to better understand the concept of servitization and its conditions of success. To help managers of manufacturing firms to come to terms with the challenges of servitization, we first proposed an innovative reading to address its heterogeneity and, through this, help them to better understand servitization and position their offers in line with their value proposition and thus with one of these different approaches.

To better support this shift from a product-centric to a service-user or service-centric model, we suggest adopting a customer-centric logic, which is common to all the approaches presented above. Moreover, to facilitate servitized value proposition design, we present a comprehensive framework that helps manufacturing firms to position their offers according to a necessary alignment of service strategies, digital capabilities and customer resources.

In line with their value propositions and the chosen servitization approaches, which correspond to their definition of servitization, companies can implement servitization in different ways and all perform as expected (Table 3).

Indeed, when implementing an AS service strategy, companies address a basic value proposition in which a lower degree of customer integration (passive customer) is needed, and only digital informative capabilities are needed.

In the AR service strategy, in order to address an efficient and output-oriented VP, companies need more customer integration (active customer) and essentially digital collaborative capabilities are needed.

Companies that want to implement a BMR service strategy address a customer outcomes-oriented VP, in which a high level of customer integration (proactive customer), and essentially productive capabilities are needed.

These approaches suggest different levels of maturity in the servitization map of manufacturing companies (Rabetino et al., 2017). As a consequence, multiple pathways can lead to success in servitization. Identifying the right alignment between service strategies, customer resources and digital capabilities may be challenging. However, this alignment between those concepts is required to deliver a better value proposition to their customers (Table 3) and to perform according to qualified value proposition proposals.

To conclude, we assume that there is no one best way to implement servitization, and in designing the chosen servitized value proposition companies need to consider a relevant alignment between service strategies, digital capabilities and customer resources. Our contribution provides them with a framework for determining this alignment, depending on their chosen strategy.

Acknowledgements The authors acknowledge the Coactis research center and the Auvergne-Rhône-Alpes Region for their financial support through the AURA-PMI project.

References

Ambroise, L., Prim-Allaz, I., & Teyssier, C. (2018). Financial performance of servitized manufacturing firms: A configuration issue between servitization strategies and customer-oriented organizational design. *Industrial Marketing Management, 71,* 54–68. https://doi.org/10.1016/j.indmarman.2017.11.007.

Baines, T. S., Lightfoot, H. W., Benedettini, O., & Kay, J. M. (2009). The servitization of manufacturing: A review of literature and reflection on future challenges.

Journal of Manufacturing Technology Management, 20(5), 547–567. https://doi.org/10.1108/17410380910960984.

Baines, T. S., Ziaee Bigdeli, A., Anders, K. M., Andrews, D., Benbow, S. A., Kapoor, K., Machan, I. H., & Tumber, N. (2019). *Customer value propositions for servitization: A mini-guide for manufacturers seeking to compete through advanced services.* The Advanced Services Group, Aston Business School.

Böhm, E., Eggert, A., & Thiesbrummel, C. (2017). Service transition: A viable option for manufacturing companies with deteriorating financial performance? *Industrial Marketing Management, 60,* 101–111. https://doi.org/10.1016/j.indmarman.2016.04.007.

Bowen, B. E., Siehl, C., & Schneider, B. (1989). A framework for analyzing customer service orientations in manufacturing. *The Academy of Management Review, 14,* 75–95.

Baines, T., & Lightfoot, H. (2013). *Made to serve: A model of the operations practices and technologies that deliver servitization.* Cranfield University Press. Retrieved from http://dspace.lib.cranfield.ac.uk/handle/1826/9504.

Baines, T. S., Lightfoot, H. W., Evans, S., Neely, A., Greenough, R., Peppard, J., ... Wilson, H. (2007). State-of-the-art in product-service systems. *Proceedings of the Institution of Mechanical Engineers, Part B: Journal of Engineering Manufacture, 221*(10), 1543–1552. https://doi.org/10.1243/09544054JEM858.

Baines, T., Lightfoot, H., Smart, P., & Fletcher, S. (2013). Servitization of manufacture: Exploring the deployment and skills of people critical to the delivery of advanced services. *Journal of Manufacturing Technology Management, 24*(4), 637–646. https://doi.org/10.1108/17410381311327431.

Coreynen, W., Matthyssens, P., & Van Bockhaven, W. (2017). Boosting servitization through digitization: Pathways and dynamic resource configurations for manufacturers. *Industrial Marketing Management, 60,* 42–53. https://doi.org/10.1016/j.indmarman.2016.04.012.

Desmet, S., Van Dierdonck, R., Van Looy, B., & Gemmel, P. (2013). *Servitization: Or why services management is relevant for manufacturing environments* (pp. 430–442). Pearson Education Limited: Essex (UK).

Doty, D. H., Glick, W. H., & Huber, G. P. (1993). Fit, equifinality, and organizational effectiveness: A test of two configurational theories. *The Academy of Management Journal, 36*(6), 1196–1250. https://doi.org/10.2307/256810.

Frambach, R. T., Barkema, H. G., Nooteboom, B., & Wedel, M. (1998). Adoption of a service innovation in the business market: An empirical test of supply-side variables. *Journal of Business Research, 41*(2), 161–174. https://doi.org/10.1016/S0148-2963(97)00005-2.

Frank, A. G., Mendes, G. H. S., Ayala, N. F., & Ghezzi, A. (2019). Servitization and Industry 4.0 convergence in the digital transformation of product firms: A business model innovation perspective. *Technological Forecasting and Social Change, 141,* 341–351. https://doi.org/10.1016/j.techfore.2019.01.014.

Gebauer, H., Fleisch, E., & Friedli, T. (2005). Overcoming the service paradox in manufacturing companies. *European Management Journal, 23*(1), 14–26. https://doi.org/10.1016/j.emj.2004.12.006.

Gebauer, H., Gustafsson, A., & Witell, L. (2011). Competitive advantage through service differentiation by manufacturing companies. *Journal of Business Research, 64*(12), 1270–1280. https://doi.org/10.1016/j.jbusres.2011.01.015.

Gebauer, H., Paiola, M., & Edvardsson, B. (2010). Service business development in small and medium capital goods manufacturing companies. *Managing Service Quality: An International Journal, 20*(2), 123–139. https://doi.org/10.1108/09604521011027561.

Gobble, M. M. (2018). Digitalization, digitization, and innovation. *Research-Technology Management, 61*(4), 56–59. https://doi.org/10.1080/08956308.2018.1471280.

Grandval, S., & Ronteau, S. (2011). *Business model: Configuration et renouvellement.* Paris: Hachette.

Huikkola, T., & Kohtamäki, M. (2017). Solution providers' strategic capabilities. *Journal of Business & Industrial Marketing, 32*(5), 752–770. https://doi.org/10.1108/JBIM-11-2015-0213.

Kohtamäki, M., Einola, S., & Rabetino, R. (2020). Exploring servitization through the paradox lens: Coping practices in servitization. *International Journal of Production Economics*, 107619. https://doi.org/10.1016/j.ijpe.2020.107619.

Kowalkowski, C., Gebauer, H., Kamp, B., & Parry, G. (2017). Servitization and deservitization: Overview, concepts, and definitions. *Industrial Marketing Management, 60*, 4–10. https://doi.org/10.1016/j.indmarman.2016.12.007.

Kohtamäki, M., Henneberg, S. C., Martinez, V., Kimita, K., & Gebauer, H. (2019). A configurational approach to servitization: Review and research directions. *Service Science, 11*(3), 29.

Lenka, S., Parida, V., & Wincent, J. (2017). Digitalization capabilities as enablers of value co-creation in servitizing firms: Digitalization capabilities. *Psychology & Marketing, 34*(1), 92–100. https://doi.org/10.1002/mar.20975.

Lewis M., Portioli Staudacher A., Slack N. (2004). *Beyond products and services: Opportunities and threats in servitization.* (n.d.). https://re.public.polimi.it/handle/11311/535488#.YL_f8fkzaM8.

Malleret, V. (2006). La rentabilité des services dans les entreprises industrielles, enquête sur un postulat, communication au 26ème Congrès de l'AFC.

Martín-Peña, M.-L., Sánchez-López, J.-M., & Díaz-Garrido, E. (2019). Servitization and digitalization in manufacturing: The influence on firm performance. *Journal of Business & Industrial Marketing, ahead-of-print* (ahead-of-print). https://doi.org/10.1108/JBIM-12-2018-0400.

Mathieu, V. (2001). Product services: From a service supporting the product to a service supporting the client. *Journal of Business & Industrial Marketing, 16*(1), 39–61. https://doi.org/10.1108/08858620110364873.

Meyer, A. D., Tsui, A. S., & Hinings, C. R. (1993). Configurational approaches to organizational analysis. *Academy of Management Journal, 36*(6), 1175–1195. https://doi.org/10.5465/256809.

Moeller, S. (2010). Characteristics of services—A new approach uncovers their value. *Journal of Services Marketing, 24*(5), 359–368. https://doi.org/10.1108/08876041011060468.

Neely, A. (2007). Exploring the financial consequences of the servitization of manufacturing. *Operations Management Research, 1,* 103–118. https://doi.org/10.1007/s12063-009-0015-5.

Neu, W. A., & Brown, S. W. (2005). Forming successful business-to-business services in goods-dominant firms. *Journal of Service Research, 8*(1), 3–17. https://doi.org/10.1177/1094670505276619.

Oliva, R., & Kallenberg, R. (2003). Managing the transition from products to services. *International Journal of Service Industry Management, 14*(2), 160–172. https://doi.org/10.1108/09564230310474138.

Osterwalder, A., Pigneur, Y., (2010). *A handbook for visonaries, game changers, and challengers*. New Jersey: John Wiley and Sons.

Parida, V., Sjödin, D. R., Lenka, S., & Wincent, J. (2015). Developing global service innovation capabilities: How global manufacturers address the challenges of market heterogeneity. *Research-Technology Management, 58*(5), 35–44. https://doi.org/10.5437/08956308X5805360.

Rabetino, R., Kohtamäki, M., & Gebauer, H. (2017). Strategy map of servitization. *International Journal of Production Economics, 192,* 144–156. https://doi.org/10.1016/j.ijpe.2016.11.004.

Ragin, C. C. (2008). *Redesigning social inquiry: Fuzzy sets and beyond*. University of Chicago Press.

Ramaswamy, V., & Ozcan, K. (2018). Offerings as digitalized interactive platforms: A conceptual framework and implications. *Journal of Marketing, 82*(4), 19–31. https://doi.org/10.1509/jm.15.0365.

Robinson, T., Clarke-Hill, C. M., & Clarkson, R. (2002). Differentiation through service: A perspective from the commodity chemicals sector. *The Service Industries Journal, 22*(3), 149–166. https://doi.org/10.1080/714005092.

Sjödin, D., Parida, V., Kohtamäki, M., & Wincent, J. (2020). An agile co-creation process for digital servitization: A micro-service innovation approach. *Journal of Business Research*. https://doi.org/10.1016/j.jbusres.2020.01.009.

Tellus Institute. (1999). Servicizing: *The quiet transition to extended product responsibility*. Boston, MA: Tellus Institute.

Teyssier C., Ambroise L., Prim-Allaz I., & Perez M. (2018). Digitalisation et stratégies de servicisation des PMI, CIFEPME, Toulouse, Octobre.

Tukker, A. (2004). Eight types of product–service system: Eight ways to sustainability? Experiences from SusProNet. *Business Strategy and the Environment, 13*(4), 246–260. https://doi.org/10.1002/bse.414.

Vandermerwe, S., & Rada, J. (1988). Servitization of business: Adding value by adding services. *European Management Journal, 6*(4), 314–324. https://doi.org/10.1016/0263-2373(88)90033-3.

Vargo, S. L., & Lusch, R. F. (2004). The four service marketing myths: Remnants of a goods-based, manufacturing model. *Journal of Service Research, 6*(4), 324–335. https://doi.org/10.1177/1094670503262946.

Vargo, S. L., & Lusch, R. F. (2008). Service-dominant logic: Continuing the evolution. *Journal of the Academy of Marketing Science, 36*(1), 1–10. https://doi.org/10.1007/s11747-007-0069-6.

Vendrell-Herrero, F., Bustinza, O. F., Parry, G., & Georgantzis, N. (2017). Servitization, digitization and supply chain interdependency. *Industrial Marketing Management, 60,* 69–81. https://doi.org/10.1016/j.indmarman.2016.06.013.

Verstrepen, S., Deschoolmeester, D., & van den Berg, R. J. (1999). Servitization in the automotive sector: Creating value and competitive advantage through service after sales. In K. Mertins, O. Krause, & B. Schallock (Eds.), *Global production management: IFIP WG5.7 International conference on advances in production management systems september 6–10, Berlin, Germany* (pp. 538–545). Boston, MA: Springer US. https://doi.org/10.1007/978-0-387-35569-6_66.

Vorhies, D. W., & Morgan, N. A. (2003). A configuration theory assessment of marketing organization fit with business strategy and its relationship with marketing performance. *Journal of Marketing, 67*(1), 100–115. https://doi.org/10.1509/jmkg.67.1.100.18588.

Ward, Y., & Graves, A. (2007). Through-life management: The provision of total customer solutions in the aerospace industry. *International Journal of Services Technology and Management, 8*(6), 455. https://doi.org/10.1504/IJSTM.2007.013942.

Managing Product-Service Operations

Digital Servitization and Modularity: Responding to Requirements in Use

Ellen Hughes, Glenn Parry, and Philip Davies

1   Introduction

A major challenge faced by manufacturers when moving into advanced services is providing bespoke service offerings at scale. Traditionally manufacturers have operated in a closed system in which products are designed for a fixed use. The traditional firm perspective on value is 'exchange': value is created at the point of exchange, e.g. goods exchanged for money (Ng, Parry, Smith, et al., 2012). Advanced services operate in an open system where value is phenomenological (Ng & Smith, 2012), which is to say that value is emergent and co-created with customers who use service offerings in a variety of contexts (Smith et al., 2014). To meet the different customer's requirements that arise from use in multiple contexts, service providers have relied on human resources to meet customer requirements, absorbing the variety of

E. Hughes
Bristol Business School, University of the West of England, England, UK
e-mail: Ellen.Hughes@uwe.ac.uk

G. Parry (✉)
Surrey Business School, University of Surrey, Guildford, UK
e-mail: g.parry@surrey.ac.uk

P. Davies
Henley Business School, University of Reading, Reading, UK
e-mail: Philip.davies@henley.ac.uk

© The Author(s), under exclusive license to Springer Nature
Switzerland AG 2021
M. Kohtamäki et al. (eds.), *The Palgrave Handbook of Servitization*,
https://doi.org/10.1007/978-3-030-75771-7_29

their emergent demands (Green et al., 2017). This chapter demonstrates how modularity and digitisation of a product can allow the product to be flexible, helping to absorb variety in use.

The chapter begins by discussing in greater detail the challenge to manufacturers in serving customer's varied requirements in use. It then synthesises the literature on digitisation and modular systems theory, specifically focusing on the perception of modularity as a closed system, and the change to an open systems approach, underpinned by digital technologies (Davies et al., 2020). An example is then used to explore how modularity and digitisation can create a product that can be flexible to heterogeneous requirements in use.

2   Theoretical Background

Servitization as an Open System

Servitization describes an observed strategy where firms seek additional value by adding services to their core offerings (Vandermerwe & Rada, 1988). When servitization occurs in professional service firms, such as lawyers or consultants, the business model and approach to value creation remains the same. However, product-centric firms such as manufacturers must develop new capabilities in order to create service-centric business models (Kowalkowski et al., 2016). In advanced services (Ziaee Bigdeli et al., 2018) firms move beyond the delivery of traditional services to offer customised, dynamic, and complex services that adapt to customer's changing needs. The provider firms responsibilities are extended (Baines & Lightfoot, 2014) as an intimate understanding of the customers' operations is required if the provider is to support a customer's core activities. Service providers must build a relationship with the customer that extends across the life cycle of the service offering (Story et al., 2017).

Traditionally, manufacturers have designed goods in a closed system whereby a boundary is drawn between the producer and customer at the point of exchange (Kimbell, 2011). Whilst this is in part reflective of the payment mechanism used to transfer ownership between the two parties, the boundary also allows organisations to separate design and context (i.e. where the product is used) such that product purpose and hence the design is fixed (Garud et al., 2008; Simon 1996) and customer requirements frozen in the form of stable specification of required functionality and performance attributes (Henfridsson et al., 2014). As a result of the separation of design and context, many of the theoretical and practical insights developed within manufacturing new product development (NPD) adopt a stable process that requires structural and functional requirements to be specified during the design cycle and frozen prior to their transfer to the production department (Baldwin & Clark, 2000). When manufacturers draw their boundary they create a closed system where the customer and their context are treated as exogenous to the manufacturing organisation. Products are designed for fixed and predictable use, with value realised 'in exchange' across the boundary (Smith et al., 2014), e.g. a TV for the money.

In services, the provider operates in an open system in which the boundary between the provider and customer, and between design and context, is blurred (Ng, 2014; Ng & Smith, 2012). The provider is involved at the point of use, so the focus of value is when the customer utilises the service providers resources to gain a benefit, co-creating value in use (Prahalad & Ramaswamy, 2004). In advanced services providers shift their focus to enabling customers to realise desired outcomes of value within their specific use context (Smith et al., 2014); use-value is measured as the benefits customers gain in context (Akaka & Parry, 2019). Value in use requires providers to understand contextual variety, which may stem from differences between individual customer preference, industries, and/or the physical environment in which a service is accessed (Palmatier, 2008). Servicing heterogeneous customer requirements introduces complexity into the system; product manufacturers are no longer able to separate customer-induced variety from their design and manufacturing processes (Ng et al., 2009).

To address the service challenge, advanced services often utilise new technology (Cenamor et al., 2017; Green et al., 2017). Digital sensors embedded in products (the internet of things [IoT]), can provide data to support digitally enabled advanced services [DEAS] (Kowalkowski & Brehmer, 2008; Vendrell-Herrero & Wilson, 2016). Provider firms can also benefit from advances in 3D printing, which when combined with a modular systems approach allows firms to tailor products to customers' requirements (Davies et al., 2020).

Modularity and Digitisation

Digital components embedded in a product offer opportunities for value creation and capture through monitoring, control, optimisation, and autonomy (Porter & Heppleman, 2014). Digital components operate to sense and capture information on the use and condition of products; to connect digitalised products through a wireless network; and to generate data to be analysed and transformed into useful insights and actionable directives (Lenka et al., 2017). Digitisation also offers manufacturers the potential to engage in complex and dynamic interactions with customers, e.g. using embedded sensors to analyse real time and historical user data to tailor maintenance and deliver increased operational efficiency (Parida et al., 2015). With such data, manufactures can identify and react to customers changing and emergent needs and customise offerings to meet heterogeneous demands (Lenka et al., 2017). Cenamor et al. (2017) discussion on modular platform architecture highlighted the importance of the information module to understanding context and enabling the reconfiguration of product and service modules.

Modularity is a general systems concept that allows organisations to offer both flexibility and efficiency in their offerings (Baldwin & Clark, 2000). Modularity can be described as '*the degree to which a system's components can be separated and re-combined, and it refers both to the tightness of coupling between components and the degree to which the "rules" of the system architecture enable (or prohibit) the mixing and matching of components*' (Schilling, 2000: 312). A modular system decomposes products and processes into separate components or process stages, named 'modules' (Langlois & Robertson, 1992). Modules are connected together by standardised interfaces, enabling modular systems to be readily adapted as components can be interchanged (Sanchez, 1995). Baldwin and Clark (Baldwin & Clark, 1997) highlight the importance of modular design rules for modular offerings, as these rules define the architecture that specifies which modules are created and their function within the system; the interfaces that loosely connect modules to one another; and the standards that ensure compatibility and conformity of modules across the system.

Modularity literature tends to favour a closed systems perspective, creating a boundary between design and use context (Ng, 2014). This follows Simon's (1962) scientific approach to design, where design and context are separated allowing firms to benefit from the ability to change aspects of the design during the development process (MacCormack et al., 2001; Ulrich, 1995), economies of scale in production (Salvador, 2007), and the ability to leverage supply chain capabilities to incorporate modules designed and manufactured externally (Fixson, 2005). The early specification supports module decoupling (i.e. one module can be changed without requiring changes in another module) and allows modules to be upgraded through life (Pil & Cohen, 2006). The careful planning of the structural and functional elements, the decoupling of modules, and definition of how they interface with one another allows organisations to augment modules (add or change them) through a product life cycle (Wouters et al., 2011). Gil (2007) refers to this as *planned flexibility*, which is useful when there is uncertainty in future demand. However, the freezing of the structural and functional elements pre-production effectively minimises the opportunity for redesign once the offering has been produced (Henfridsson et al., 2014).

One of the key managerial decisions for modularity is the degree of flexibility planned into the architecture during design (Engel et al., 2017). Organisations embedding flexibility that permits future module augmentation (Baldwin & Clark, 2000) only provide limited flexibility in the form of differences in degree (Yoo et al., 2010). In closed systems, design decisions are made on the assumption that no rework of the architecture will be needed at a later date (Verganti, 1997). Implicit in this approach is that all requirements can be captured in advance of use and that the scope of requirements remains stable once the offering has been designed, produced, and exchanged with the customer for use. Following the closed system approach means accommodating change beyond the architectural specification defined during design is difficult and costly, particularly when change is made to the physical product (Davies et al., 2020).

Products with known long life cycles have flexibility designed at the beginning. Unexpected advances in technology, development of new modules and emergence of new customer requirements, will likely render the architecture obsolete. This ultimately requires the product to be re-modularised (Lundqvist et al., 1996), which can be done at a high cost (Gil, 2007; Wouters et al., 2011). In advanced services, where requirements emerge in use and the organisation are required to match that variety in order to maintain a contracted level of performance (Ng, Parry, Smith, et al., 2012; Smith et al., 2014), closed systems are problematic when emergent changes are required that are not part of the designed 'planned flexibility'. Davies et al. (2020) find that organisations who incorporate emerging requirements post-production do so by diminishing the degree of modularity present in their architecture, losing efficiency gains, and potentially increasing coordination costs through life; effectively impacting upon their long-term viability.

Traditional approaches to product design limit flexibility post-production, and so people are employed within systems to absorb variety in service. Ng and Briscoe (2012) encouraged the servitization community to consider how products can be made more flexible, stimulating innovation in design of delivery systems so products could absorb variety in use.

Optimising Me Manufacturing Systems: An Illustrative Case Study

Advances in manufacturing technology extend the scope of modularity to an open systems environment. This case study, drawn from an innovation in healthcare, illustrates how modularity and digital technology can be used to create a flexible responsive product and enable organisations to accommodate a degree of variety in use.

The Optimising Me Manufacturing System [OMMS] is an innovation in the manufacture and delivery of immunotherapy treatment for certain forms of cancer. Traditional healthcare systems involve centralised, laboratory-based manufacture of therapeutics (medicine), which are treated as products. Drug delivery occurs in a separate hospital setting, perceived as the service. OMMS breaks from this, servitizing treatment by creating a micro-factory device that is worn on the body. The device monitors the patient, manufactures a bespoke therapeutic treatment, and delivers it to them, all via an on-body system. Developments in material technology enable an automated modular system contained within the device, to responsively manufacture bespoke therapeutic treatments, and deliver them to changing patient needs. The personalised medicines that OMMS will deliver are manufactured from an individual's own blood cells (Iyer et al., 2018; Piscopo et al., 2018). One such example, CAR T cell therapy, removes, modifies, and re-infuses a patient's own immune cells to attack cancer in their body.

The current process of manufacture and delivery of CAR T cell therapy is expensive, lengthy, and contains potential risks. Blood cells are taken from a patient in hospital and transported to a centralised laboratory, where the cells are used as starting material for the manufacture of the therapeutic treatment. Manufacturing processes are labour intensive and undertaken by skilled operators, involve open handling and the use of many pieces of specialised equipment. Once manufactured, the therapy treatment is transported back to the hospital and administered to the patient. Transportation and other lab-based processes have potential risks in terms of contamination, operator error, and side effects to the patient (Iyer et al., 2018; Vormittag et al., 2018; Wang & Rivière, 2016). The manufacturing process is expensive, as is the patients' long stay in hospital under specialist care. Manufacturing and logistics processes may extend to 30 days, a long wait for patients with rapidly developing cancer (Olweus, 2017).

Demand for the therapy is growing, but the potential benefits of the treatment can only be achieved if it is reliably delivered to patients at scale, with affordable costs, whilst meeting customers' heterogeneous requirements.

To address these issues a fully automated machine for closed end-to-end processing was proposed by Kaiser et al. (2015), removing the need for transportation and preservation processes (Wang & Rivière, 2016), and allowing decentralised manufacture close to patient (Harrison et al., 2018; Kaiser et al., 2015). Automated manufacturing machines, an example of which is the CliniMACS Prodigy, are adaptable and can rapidly change between protocols using a different programme to manufacture specific therapies (Kaiser et al., 2015). However, the machines themselves are expensive, currently ~$155,000, must be used in clean rooms by specialised operators, use disposable items at ~$26,000 per patient, and can only manufacture for one patient at a time, which can take up to 24 days. Committing to this route locks the healthcare provider into a single source provider, their qualified related sundries, reagents, and suppliers, and reduces flexibility of manufacture. The approach makes little difference to the patient experience, maintaining the product/service value in exchange ethos of centralised manufacture of the therapeutic product, with the service as the administering hospital.

The OMMS modular micro-factory device offers an alternative solution that moves towards value in use. It is a wearable 'sealed device', located on the body, so risks associated with open handling and transportation are removed. Process stages are miniaturised and modularised to give portability, allowing mobility and potentially treatment in the patient's home, lowering costs associated with long hospital stays, transport, and laboratory processing. The device will be 3D printed to fit the individual patient's body, enabling a secure fit, facilitating different use contexts. Internally, the device is formed of a set of distinct modules (Ulrich & Seering, 1988). Each module contains a processing unit, which performs a discrete function in the manufacturing stage. Modules are connected through standardised interfaces (Sanchez, 1995), which bind the modules together to form the process stages (Yoo, 2013). Blood is taken straight from the patient into the device where it is used as the starting material in the manufacturing process. The process is optimised for immediate delivery, which simplifies manufacturing (Ohno, 1988; Womack & Jones, 1996). Once manufactured, the therapeutic is infused directly to the patient, reducing time to treatment. The device is digitalised (Vendrell-Herrero & Wilson, 2016), with biosensors embedded within each module connected to a data controller. Biosensors respond to an individual patient's starting material and make adjustments to physical elements within a processing unit (for example, modifying channel widths) to change manufacturing pathways, creating a bespoke therapeutic product. Biosensors also test the product, constantly checking for cell viability and quality. Adjustments are dynamic, continually responding to patient's requirements in real time.

Through its modular design, use of digital technology, and the dynamic functionality of physical elements contained within the modules, the OMMS micro-factory enables the hyper-local manufacture and delivery of a bespoke therapeutic product at scale (Salvador, 2007). The flexibility of a modular system combined with 3D printing offers three further benefits: First, modules can be rapidly combined in response to patient needs: decisions about the form and function of the device can be postponed until requirements emerge in use (Davies et al., 2020); Second, in the development stages of the OMMS system, the device can be augmented for additional functionality (Wouters et al., 2011). Due to high standards of manufacture and the need for clinical trials, innovations in healthcare can take many years to come to market. Through the use of modular design, a proto micro-factory can be manufactured in the early stages of development, to perform one or two processes in treatment manufacture, with additional modules incorporated as they are approved for clinical use. This has the additional benefit of allowing time for more gradual socio-technical adjustments to the new healthcare device, increasing the chances of success of the innovation (Walrave et al., 2018); Third, modularity will allow for the replacement or upgrade of individual modules (Pil & Cohen, 2006).

Combined these benefits enable the OMMS system to provide a bespoke treatment, delivered to the patient within their own context, maintaining contractual agreements with healthcare providers, whilst incorporating technological and medical advances into the service delivery system (Ng, Parry, McFarlane, et al., 2012).

3   Discussion

Theoretical Contribution

Using an example from health care innovation, modularity is shown to enable service providers to meet heterogeneous requirements in use, supporting the argument for an open systems approach in modularity theory, enabled by digital technology (Davies et al., 2020). In a closed system, designing for contextual variety entails segmenting customer groups and designing a targeted service provision based on generalised characteristics of the group (Palmatier, 2008). Using the OMMS example, this would involve sizing one device to fit a child and another to fit an adult, and having a set number of treatment pathways. In an open system, device size and shape are not predetermined, but are responsive to an individual patients' body shape. Equally, the OMMS system treatment pathways are dynamically responsive to requirements in use.

Servitization literature is commonly concerned with the ways in which firms create value through services that are additions to their products. The current CAR T treatment is a product (the therapeutic) delivered within hospitals as part of a health service system. The move to small-scale product manufacturing via automation using the CliniMACS Prodigy manufacturing platform shifts therapeutic production from centralised to decentralised locations. This impacts the logistics process, but it does not alter the service experience provided to the patient. The patient remains in the hospital and is the recipient of the therapeutic product delivered within the hospital setting. The OMMS device seeks to create an advanced service, delivering therapeutics within contexts beyond the hospital bed, responding in real time to patients' changing treatment need whilst contributing to the quality of their life.

The OMMS example highlights the potential of a product to adapt and absorb variety and thus improve a service offering. In the existing literature, products are perceived as fixed parts of the service. The product is an operand resource (Vargo & Lusch, 2004) as it is perceived as static. The people who form the surrounding support are the operant resources and are dynamic, helping to absorb variety through application of their skills to ensure the therapeutic is correctly manufactured and delivered safely to the patient. Through the application of modularity in combination with digital technologies, the physical product can become flexible and contributes towards the ability of the system to adapt to requirements in use, in a scalable manner.

Modularity and digitalisation pose a new challenge to established service systems. Doctors will need to develop new knowledge competencies as services move from skilled operators monitoring therapeutic manufacture, towards medical devices that undertake manufacture and analysis and output digital information (Harrison et al., 2018). The OMMS device enables treatment to be delivered in new service contexts; therapy delivery is potentially moved from a hospital setting to the patient's home. Further research is required to understand what changes in human resources may be needed in response to flexible, digitised products.

4   Conclusions and Managerial Implications

This chapter has challenged a number of assumptions surrounding the physical product within servitization. Building on existing research discussing modular solutions, this chapter has proposed an alternative pathway that integrates an open systems perspective that acknowledges complexity manifests from variety in use and that the product is able to help absorb some of this variety. Accepting an open systems perspective allows us to move beyond normative assumptions that the product is fixed and stable in use and start to understand how to design for open systems characterised by emergence and customer endogeneity.

This has a number of implications for practising managers. We highlight how variability introduced by the customer in their context has implications for the viability of the service system. By acknowledging the customer is endogenous, a challenge for practice is how to optimise the whole system, which includes the context of use and customer resources, as opposed to just the organisations delivery system that traditionally treated the customer as passive or exogenous to the system. This requires a shift away from a one-sided, product-centric view of servitization towards a more holistic view of the service system as mandated by more advanced service contracts. Whilst a number of challenges still exist and the illustrative case we have used is novel, the core findings presented are useful at a general level for organisations to begin thinking about how an open systems perspective could create new sources of competitive advantage.

References

Akaka, M. A., & Parry, G. (2019). Value-in-context: An exploration of the context of value and the value of context. In P. P. Maglio, C. A. Kieliszewski, J. C. Spohrer, K. Lyons, L. Patricio, & Y. Sawatani (Eds.), *Handbook of service science, Volume II* (pp. 457–77). Springer.

Baines, T., & Lightfoot, H. W. (2014). Servitization of the Manufacturing firm exploring the operations practices and technologies that deliver advanced services. *International Journal of Operations & Production Management, 34*(1), 2–35.

Baldwin, C., & Clark, K. (1997). Managing in the age of modularity. *Harvard Business Review, 75*(5), 84–93.

Baldwin, C., & Clark, K. (2000). *Design rules: The power of modularity*. MIT Press.

Cenamor, J., Sjödin, D. R., & Parida, V. (2017). Adopting a platform approach in servitization: Leveraging the value of digitalization. *International Journal of Production Economics, 192*, 54–65.

Davies, P., Parry, G., Alves, K., & Ng, I. (2020). How additive manufacturing allows products to absorb variety in use: Empirical evidence from the defence industry. *Production Planning & Control*, 1–18.

Engel, A., Browning, T. R., & Reich, Y. (2017). Designing products for adaptability: Insights from four industrial cases. *Decision Sciences, 48*(5), 875–917.

Fixson, S. K. (2005). Product architecture assessment: A tool to link product, process, and supply chain design decisions. *Journal of Operations Management, 23*(3–4), 345–369.

Garud, R., Jain, S., & Tuertscher, P. (2008). Incomplete by design and designing for incompleteness. *Organizational Studies, 29*(3), 351–371.

Gil, N. (2007). On the value of project safeguards: Embedding real options in complex products and systems. *Research Policy, 36*(7), 980–999.

Green, M. H., Davies, P., & Ng, I. C. L. (2017). Two strands of servitization: A thematic analysis of traditional and customer co-created servitization and future research directions. *International Journal of Production Economics, 192*, 40–53. https://doi.org/10.1016/j.ijpe.2017.01.009.

Harrison, R. P., Ruck, S., Rafiq, Q. A., & Medcalf, N. (2018). Decentralised Manufacturing of cell and gene therapy products: Learning from other healthcare sectors. *Biotechnology Advances, 36*(2), 345–357.

Henfridsson, O., Mathiassen, L., & Svahn, F. (2014). Managing technological change in the digital age: The role of architectural frames. *Journal of Information Technology, 29*(1), 27–43. https://doi.org/10.1057/jit.2013.30.

Iyer, R. K., Bowles, P. A., Kim, H., & Dulgar-Tulloch, A. (2018). Industrializing autologous adoptive immunotherapies: Manufacturing advances and challenges. *Frontiers in Medicine, 5*, 150.

Kaiser, A., Assenmacher, M., Schröder, B., Meyer, M., Orentas, R., Bethke, U., & Dropulić, B. (2015). Towards a commercial process for the manufacture of genetically modified T cells for therapy. *Cancer Gene Therapy, 22*(2), 72–78.

Kimbell, L. (2011). Designing for service as one way of designing services. *International Journal of Design, 5*(2), 41–52.

Kowalkowski, C., & Brehmer, P. O. (2008). Technology as a driver for changing customer-provider interfaces: Evidence from industrial service production. *Management Research News, 31*, 746–757.

Kowalkowski, C., Gebauer, H. Kamp, B., & Parry, G. (2016). Servitization and deservitization: Overview, concepts, and definitions. *Industrial Marketing Management*.

Langlois, R. N., & Robertson, P. L. (1992). Networks and innovation in a modular system: Lessons from the microcomputer and stereo component industries. *Research Policy, 21*(4), 297–313.

Lenka, S., Parida, V., & Wincent, J. (2017). Digitalization capabilities as enablers of value co-creation in servitizing firms. *Psychology & Marketing, 34*(1), 92–100.

Lundqvist, M., Sundgren, N., & Trygg, L. (1996). Remodularization of a product line: Adding complexity to project management. *Journal Of Product Innovation Management, 13*(4), 311–324.

MacCormack, A., Verganti, R., & Iansiti, M. (2001). Developing products on 'internet time': The anatomy of a flexible development process. *Management Science, 47*(1), 133–150.

Ng, I., & Briscoe, G. (2012). Value, variety and viability: New business models for co-creation in outcome-based contracts. 06/12. Coventry.

Ng, I., Parry, G., McFarlane, D., & Tasker, P. (2012). Transitioning from a goods-dominant to a service-dominant logic. *Journal of Service Management, 23*(3), 416–439.

Ng, I., Parry, G., Smith, L., Maull, R., & Briscoe, G. (2012). Transitioning from a goods-dominant to a service-dominant logic, ed. R. Verma. *Journal of Service Management, 23*(3), 416–439.

Ng, I. C. L. (2014). *Creating new markets in the digital economy: Value and worth.* Cambridge University Press.

Ng, I. C. L., Maull, R., & Yip, N. (2009). Outcome-based contracts as a driver for systems thinking and service-dominant logic in service science: Evidence from the defence industry. *European Managment Journal, 6,* 377–387.

Ng, I. C. L., & Smith, L. A. (2012). An integrative framework of value. *Review of Marketing Research.*

Ohno, T. (1988). *Toyota production system—Beyond large scale production.* Productivity Press.

Olweus, J. (2017). Manufacture of CAR T cells in the body. *Nature Biotechnology, 35*(6), 520–521.

Palmatier, R. (2008). Interfirm relational drivers of customer value. *Journal of Marketing, 72,* 76–89.

Parida, V., Rönnberg Sjödin, D., Lenka, S., & Wincent, J. (2015). developing global service innovation capabilities: How global manufacturers address the challenges of market heterogeneity. *Research-Technology Management, 58*(5), 35–44.

Pil, F. K., & Cohen, S. K. (2006). Modularity: Implications for imitation, innovation, and sustained advantage. *Academy of management Review, 31*(4), 995–1011.

Piscopo, N. J., Mueller, K. P., Das, A., Hematti, P., Murphy, W. L., Palecek, S. P., Capitini, C. M. & Saha, K. (2018). Cells, bioengineering solutions for manufacturing challenges in CAR T cells. *Biotechnology Journal, 13*(2), 1–10.

Porter, M. E., & Heppleman, J. E. (2014, November 1). How smart, connected products are transforming competition. *Harvard Business Review,* 64–88.

Prahalad, C. K., & Ramaswamy, V. (2004). Co-creation experiences: The next practice in value creation. *Journal of Interactive Marketing, 18*(3), 5–14.

Salvador, F. (2007). Toward a product system modularity construct: Literature review and reconceptualization. *IEEE Transactions on Engineering Management, 54*(2), 219–240.

Sanchez, R. (1995). Strategic flexibility in product competition. *Strategic Management Journal, 16*(S1), 135–159.

Schilling, M. A. (2000). Toward a general modular systems theory and its application to interfirm product modularity. *Academy of Management Review, 25*(2), 312–334.

Simon, H. A. (1962). The architecture of complexity. *Proceedings of the American Philosophical Society, 106*(6), 467–482.

Simon, H. A. (1996). *The sciences of the artificial*. MIT Press.

Smith, L., Maull, R., & Ng, I. (2014). Servitization and operations management: A service dominant-logic approach. *International Journal of Operations & Production Management, 34*(2), 242–269.

Story, V. M., Raddats, C., Burton, J., Zolkiewski, J., & Baines, T. (2017). Capabilities for advanced services: A multi-actor perspective. *Industrial Marketing Management, 60,* 54–68.

Ulrich, K. (1995). The role of product architecture in the manufacturing firm. *Research Policy, 24*(3), 419–440.

Ulrich, K., & Seering, W. (1988). Function sharing in mechanical design. *Artificial Intelligence*, 342–346.

Vandermerwe, S., & Rada, J. (1988). Servitization of business: Adding value by adding services. *European Management Journal, 6*(4), 314–324.

Vargo, S. L., & Lusch, R. F. (2004). Evolving to a new dominant logic for marketing. *Journal of Marketing, 68*(1), 1–17.

Vendrell-Herrero, F., & Wilson, J. R. (2016). Servitization for territorial competitiveness: Taxonomy and research agenda. *Competitiveness Review, 26*(5).

Verganti, R. (1997). *R&D management*. Blackwell.

Vormittag, P., Gunn, R., Ghorashian, S., & Veraitch, F. (2018). A guide to manufacturing CAR T cell therapies. *Current Opinion in Biotechnology, 53,* 164–181.

Walrave, B., Talmar, M., Podoynitsyna, K., Romme, A. G., & Verbong, G. (2018). A multi-level perspective on innovation ecosystems for path-breaking innovation. *Technological Forecasting and Social Change, 136,* 103–113.

Wang, X., & Rivière, I. (2016). Clinical manufacturing of CAR T cells: Foundation of a promising therapy. *Molecular Therapy Oncolytics, 3,* 16015.

Womack, J., & Jones, T. (1996). *Lean thinking*. Simon & Schuster Ltd.

Wouters, M., Workum, M., & Hissel, P. (2011). Assessing the product architecture decision about product features—A real options approach. *R&D Management, 41*(4), 393–409.

Yoo, Y. (2013). The tables have turned: How can the Information systems field contribute to technology and innovation management research? *Journal of the Association for Information Systems, 14*(5), 227–236.

Yoo, Y., Henfridsson, O., & Lyytinen, K. (2010). The new organizing logic of digital innovation: An agenda for information systems research. *Information Systems Research, 21*(4), 724–735.

Ziaee Bigdeli, A., Baines, T., Schroeder, A., Brown, S., Musson, E., Guang Shi, V., & Calabrese, A. (2018). Measuring servitization progress and outcome: The case of 'advanced services'. *Production Planning & Control, 29*(4), 315–332.

Service Integration: Supply Chain Integration in Servitization

Khadijeh Momeni

1 Introduction

Many manufacturing firms in various industries, such as aerospace, ship-yards and engineering, have shifted their focus from selling products and basic services to providing integrated products and services (called integrated solutions, product-service systems or servitized offerings) to fulfil customers' business or operational needs (Rabetino et al., 2018). This strategic transition, which is called servitization, has been a growing interest in manufacturing firms to enhance their competitive position and business performance (Baines et al., 2009). Adding services to the product offering not only affects the manufacturing firms involved but also changes the traditional manufacturing supply chain and affects intra- and inter-organizational structures (Baines et al., 2009).

Over the past decade, servitization has been identified as not a solo journey but a joint strategic effort by several organizations in the supply chain (Ayala et al., 2017; Burton et al., 2016; Martinez et al., 2017). Firms engaged in servitization must integrate with a network of actors that include component suppliers, intermediaries and customers (Burton et al., 2016). Because

K. Momeni (✉)
Department of Industrial and Engineering Management, Tampere University, Tampere, Finland
e-mail: Khadijeh.momeni@tuni.fi

© The Author(s), under exclusive license to Springer Nature
Switzerland AG 2021
M. Kohtamäki et al. (eds.), *The Palgrave Handbook of Servitization*,
https://doi.org/10.1007/978-3-030-75771-7_30

manufacturing firms do not possess all the required resources and capabilities to achieve their servitization goal, they need to collaborate with several partners that can support the design and delivery of the offering (Shah et al., 2020; Windahl & Lakemond, 2006).

As the service business is an important source of revenue for some manufacturing firms, the service supply chain (SSC) becomes a key enabler of this transformation (Iakovaki et al., 2009). Baltacioglu et al. (2007: 112) defined SSC as "*the network of suppliers, service providers, consumers and other supporting units that performs the functions of transaction of resources required to produce services; transformation of these resources into supporting and core services; and the delivery of these services to customers*". SSC can be categorized into either a service-only supply chain or a product-service supply chain (Wang et al., 2015). The service provision in manufacturing firms belongs to the product-service supply chain where physical products develop and deliver through the supply chain, but services have a significant role for most of the supply chain partners (Nagariya et al., 2020). To develop a comprehensive picture of supply chain integration in servitization, this chapter proposes a service integration framework that explains the integration of supply chain partners to enable the integration of service business in the firm's existing value chain. The scope of this chapter is limited to manufacturing firms, and thus other SSC clusters (e.g. a logistics SSC is out of the scope of this study).

2   Theory Development

Service Integration in Terms of Dimensions, Levels, Modes and Service Types

As explained, the business relationships for the servitization of manufacturing firms are not limited to service units, and they require the integration and management of complex interfaces between multiple organizational units and firms (Burton et al., 2016). This section uses supply chain integration as the theoretical lens and focuses on the extant servitization literature on intra- and inter-organizational relationships. Supply chain integration is defined as the collaborative management of intra- and inter-organizational interfaces (Flynn et al., 2010; Schoenherr & Swink, 2012). The literature on supply chain integration recognizes the importance of considering both internal and external perspectives to maximize supply chain value for all the actors involved (Flynn et al., 2010). Internal integration enables external integration (Flynn et al., 2010) by facilitating the flow of products, services, information, money and

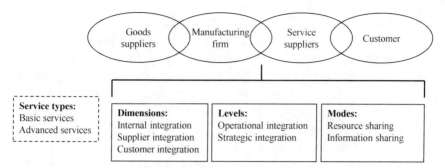

Fig. 1 Service integration framework elements

decisions to increase customer value at low cost and high speed (Zhao et al., 2011).

The service integration framework aims to conceptualize the supply chain integration to enable integrating service business into the firm's existing value chain. As Fig. 1 illustrates, this framework explores supply chain integration by distinguishing the supply chain dimensions (i.e. internal, supplier and customer integration), levels (i.e. operational and strategic integration), modes (i.e. resource and information sharing) and type of services (i.e. basic and advanced services). It should be noted that Fig. 1 is a simplified version of a supply chain and its partners; in practice, the manufacturing firm might have different types of supply chain structures and partners.

Research conceptualizes supply chain integration as consisting of three dimensions: internal, supplier and customer integration (Flynn et al., 2010; Schoenherr & Swink, 2012; Zhao et al., 2011).

Internal integration involves cross-functional collaborative and information activities through synchronized processes and systems (Schoenherr & Swink, 2012). These synchronized processes aim to meet customers' needs as well as facilitate external integration (Flynn et al., 2010). Internal integration mainly features information system integration and cross-functional cooperation (Zhao et al., 2011).

Supplier integration refers to structuring inter-organizational strategies, practices and procedures into collaborative, synchronized and manageable processes to fulfil customers' needs (Zhao et al., 2015). Supply chain integration mainly involves coordination and information-sharing activities that enable the firm to understand suppliers' processes, capabilities and constraints (Schoenherr & Swink, 2012). In the context of servitization, suppliers can be divided into goods suppliers and service suppliers. Whereas goods suppliers are more active in the upstream value chain through equipping the required components of the system, service suppliers in the downstream act as intermediaries between the firm and customers to deliver some or all services.

Customer integration involves collaborative and information-sharing activities between the firm and its customers; this enables the firm to identify expectations and business opportunities and, consequently, respond to customers' needs (Schoenherr & Swink, 2012). Customer integration decreases the threat of competitors, improves customer willingness to pay a premium price and increases customer loyalty (Droge et al., 2004).

Supply chain integration can be considered at two levels: operational integration and strategic integration (He & Lai, 2012). *Operational integration* focuses on the integration of processes and information flows, and it usually occurs during a specific service activity, such as service development, sales and delivery (He & Lai, 2012). *Strategic integration* focuses on collaboration with external partners to create common interests, agree on a shared vision and carry out collective actions (He & Lai, 2012). Strategic integration concerns the integration of supply chain partners independently of a specific service operation and enhances the long-term relationship (Momeni & Martinsuo, 2019a).

Regarding the modes of integration, supply chain integration can be carried out through two major modes: *resource sharing* (i.e. people, physical possessions, technologies and properties) and *information sharing* (Nagariya et al., 2020). While information can be considered part of organizational resources, it is defined as a separate mode to emphasize the importance of information (and knowledge) flow in the supply chain.

Finally, previous literature has identified that supply chain integration needs can differ based on the type of services offered by manufacturing firms (Saccani et al., 2014; Shah et al., 2020). Most of the services can be categorized into *basic* and *advanced* services (Sousa & da Silveira, 2017). Basic services, such as installation, provision of spare parts, maintenance and repair, focus on installing and maintaining basic product functionality (Sousa & da Silveira, 2017). Advanced services, such as training, consulting, risk/revenue sharing contracts or rental agreements, focus on outcome assurance and create value for the customer beyond the basic functionality of the product (Baines et al., 2013). Advanced services are characterized by high interaction with the customer to co-create value in a way that addresses the specific customer's needs (Sousa & da Silveira, 2017).

The following sections explore each dimension of service integration in terms of integration levels, modes and types of services.

Internal Integration

The manufacturing firm may use different organizational structures to integrate service functions: (1) a dedicated service organization to provide all services (Oliva et al., 2012; Sousa & da Silveira, 2017), (2) a specific service unit to handle advanced services and (3) a functional structure managing both products and services, outsourcing some services and overseeing other services through business functions (Alghisi & Saccani, 2015; Bustinza et al., 2015). However, organizational functions involved in servitized offerings usually specialize in their own activities (Oliva et al., 2012). This distinction creates conflicts over expectations, preferences and priorities that need to be overcome through integration efforts between functions (Oliva & Watson, 2011).

Servitization literature has emphasized the criticality of strategic integration through linking the servitization strategy with critical processes and key practices (Rabetino et al., 2017). The literature has also explored internal integration at the operational level. The service development process strongly depends on the cross-functional collaboration between product and service development teams (Lenka et al., 2018). Moreover, integrations between after-sales services and engineering functions, as well as with production, marketing (Paslauski et al., 2016) and sales (Kindström et al., 2015; Momeni & Martinsuo, 2019b), have been identified as enablers for the success of servitization. Cross-functional collaboration, which occurs through both information and resource sharing, increases information flow within the organization and in its relationship with customers, thus enhancing strategic integration with customers and revealing opportunities for fulfilling customer requirements (Kindström et al., 2015).

While the scope of basic services is often limited to the service unit, advanced services usually require integration with other organizational functions (Baines et al., 2013). For example, advanced services, such as technical consulting, often require information and knowledge sharing among product development, sales units and service units; the product-service system delivery needs information sharing between project teams, service units and sales units and modernization and upgrades require integration between product development, sales units and service units (Momeni & Martinsuo, 2018).

Internal integration is considered an important enabler of servitization, but it is insufficient for achieving the servitization goal. However, internal integration helps manufacturing firms develop external integration with other partners in the supply chain to access more resources and capabilities (Shah et al., 2020).

Supplier Integration

As explained previously, servitized manufacturing firms collaborate with two types of suppliers in the value chain: goods suppliers in the upstream and service suppliers in the downstream.

While the firm–supplier relationship has usually been treated as a dyadic relationship, it can also become triadic (Bastl et al., 2012; Finne & Holmström, 2013). Especially in the case of complex systems, the supplier may provide some specific services (e.g. training, repair) directly to the customer (Bastl et al., 2012). This change makes supply chain relationships more complex and requires closer collaboration between manufacturing firms and suppliers (Finne & Holmström, 2013). Moreover, depending on the position of the manufacturing firm in the value chain, either the firm can be a system integrator that couples systems together and provides services to the customers, or another supplier can have the integrator role or deliver some specific services to the customers (Finne & Holmström, 2013).

Thus, to manage this increased uncertainty and complexity in the supply chain, manufacturing firms attempt to enhance integration with key suppliers (Shah et al., 2020).

Studies on servitization in the downstream of the value chain are moving away from a dyadic interaction between a manufacturing firm and supplier by acknowledging the role of intermediaries (Karatzas et al., 2017). The manufacturing firms use service suppliers with the necessary knowledge and capabilities as external support to overcome servitization challenges (Ayala et al., 2019). In general, the relationship between the manufacturing firm and the service suppliers can be divided into three main categories: (1) the service offering is developed by the firm and delivered by the service supplier, (2) the service offering is developed and delivered by the service supplier or (3) both the firm and the service supplier collaborate in developing and delivering the offering (Ayala et al., 2019). The choice of arrangement mainly depends on the financial objectives, the chosen level of customer relationship, the characteristics of service components and the current or targeted level of servitization (Ayala et al., 2017).

Manufacturing firms make use of extensive operational collaboration with goods suppliers during the development, production and delivery of integrated products and services (Finne & Holmström, 2013). They do the same with service suppliers during new service development (Aminoff & Hakanen, 2018; Ayala et al., 2019) and service delivery (Karatzas et al., 2017). While successful collaboration between manufacturing firms and suppliers requires operational integration through frequent and open information exchange and the right operational linkages, it also needs strategic integration through developing trust-based governance, more formalized cooperative norms and reciprocal adaptation in the processes (Bastl et al., 2012; Saccani et al., 2014).

Supplier integration depends more on a greater exchange of information and know-how between the firms (Martinez et al., 2017). The firms need to create strong links of information and knowledge exchange between different systems, procedures and routines (Bastl et al., 2012). Previous studies have also reported some resource sharing efforts between manufacturing firms and suppliers, such as joint engineering meetings with goods suppliers to design the offering or offer some services (e.g. training) to the end customer by the service supplier (Bastl et al., 2012).

Integration with goods suppliers becomes more important for developing and delivering basic services (Shah et al., 2020). For basic services, such as maintenance that requires technical expertise (Sousa & da Silveira, 2017), integration with key suppliers can help manufacturing firms enhance manufacturing-based capabilities (e.g. production technologies for certain spare parts), thus enabling the development and delivery of basic services (Shah et al., 2020). However, recent studies in the context of digital servitization show that specific types of suppliers (e.g. software providers, platform providers) are becoming more important in developing and delivering advanced services (Kohtamäki et al., 2019). However, regarding integration with the service supplier, the partners collaborate more in the provision of advanced services. For basic services, the information exchange between the manufacturing firm and service suppliers is low and limited to technical and operational aspects (Saccani et al., 2014). Delivering advanced services requires stronger integration through the exchange of technical- and customer-related information (Saccani et al., 2014). It can be argued that the position of service suppliers, i.e. having a direct connection with the customers and their service-specific capabilities, makes them the important partner in delivering advanced services (Ayala et al., 2017; Saccani et al., 2014).

Customer Integration

Services have a relational nature (Windahl & Lakemond, 2006), thus the role of the customer in servitization is paramount (Kindström & Kowalkowski, 2009). On one hand, in order to integrate services into the product offerings of manufacturing firms, firms need to acknowledge customers' needs and integrate different components to deliver higher value to customers (Oliva &

Kallenberg, 2003). On the other hand, customers are considerably engaged in the service production flow (Chen et al., 2015).

Customer integration occurs at both the operational level and strategic level. Previous studies have explored operational integration through customer engagement and co-creation of value, especially during service design and development (Chen et al., 2015; Windahl & Lakemond, 2006). Servitization also encourages strategic integration with customers to help manufacturing firms increase customer readiness, understand the current and future needs of customers, utilize the customer's inputs and resources in developing the offering, create demand and maintain long-term strategic agreements with customers (Shah et al., 2020). Customer integration has a broad scope and includes different modes of integration, such as information sharing and customer resource sharing, including customers themselves, physical possessions, data, technologies and properties (Alghisi & Saccani, 2015; Chen et al., 2015; Moeller, 2008).

Basic services, such as installation and maintenance, are characterized by a transaction-based nature and a low-intensity relationship between the firm and customer (Saccani et al., 2014; Sousa & da Silveira, 2017). Customers are not usually involved in the service process and expect that the manufacturing firm possesses the manufacturing-based capabilities (i.e. technical expertise) required for these services (Saccani et al., 2014). Customer integration becomes more important in offering advanced services (Shah et al., 2020). Advanced services have a relationship-based nature that demands service-specific capabilities, such as expertise in designing and delivering service processes and the ability to design services and products jointly (Sousa & da Silveira, 2017). For delivering advanced services, such as outcome-based contracts, the manufacturing firm becomes more dependent on the customer and its resources (Ng et al., 2011). Because the manufacturing firm does not have much control over customers, the provision of advanced services strongly depends on the flow of information between the firm and the customer (Ng et al., 2011).

3   Discussion

Theoretical Contributions

The supply chain of manufacturing firms relies on information, resources and collaboration among different partners (Nagariya et al., 2020). Supply chain integration, i.e. strategic collaboration with supply chain partners (Zhao

et al., 2015), has been underscored in the operations and product manufacturing literature (Flynn et al., 2010). Offering services to customers also
requires close collaboration with different internal and external organizations
(Nagariya et al., 2020). The close relationship with customers has been especially emphasized in several studies (e.g. Chen et al., 2015; Moeller, 2008).
However, a servitized offering is different from a pure product or pure service
offering in terms of the variety of involved resources (Shah et al., 2020).
The increased number of partners expands interdependency, creating more
complexity, uncertainty and tensions in the supply chain (Burton et al., 2016;
Shah et al., 2020).

This study contributes to the discussion on supply chain integration in
servitization literature by providing a big picture of the supply chain integration dimensions, the levels and modes of integration and the integration
needs in relation to the type of services. The service integration framework integrates different aspects of supply chain integration that need to be
considered in the servitization context. The service integration framework
depicted in Fig. 2 highlights that providing integrated products and services
to customers is about understanding not only the nature of the offering and
its responsibility for certain functions but also the nature of the interaction
and collaboration between functions (Ng et al., 2011).

To create value for the customer and other firms in the supply chain,
manufacturing firms attempt to integrate several supply chain process activities within the firm and with other firms in the supply chain (Katunzi, 2011).
When managing collaboration with internal and external organizations, the
manufacturing firms focus on the following three dimensions: internal integration, supplier integration and customer integration. First, manufacturing

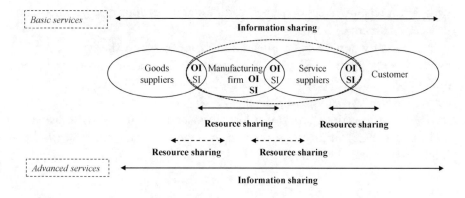

OI: Operational integration   SI: Strategic integration

Fig. 2 Service integration framework

firms need continuous collaboration and information flow within the firm (Oliva & Watson, 2011) because the provision of integrated products and services is not limited to individual functions but requires the collaboration of all functional departments, such as sales, production, procurement and services (Shah et al., 2020). Second, manufacturing firms need strong relationships with suppliers to utilize their information, resources and capabilities to ensure the successful development and delivery of new products and services (Ayala et al., 2019). Third, close collaboration with customers helps manufacturing firms develop a deep understanding of customer demands and utilize customers' resources in the process of developing and delivering services (Kindström & Kowalkowski, 2009).

Service integration occurs at two main levels: operational and strategic. As presented in Fig. 2, manufacturing firms need both operational and strategic integration between different functions in the firm to ensure that the servitization goal is reached. The strategic alliance between functions enables smooth operational collaboration (Rabetino et al., 2017), and operational integration facilitates external integration to access more resources and capabilities needed for the servitization strategy (Shah et al., 2020). While the need for strategic collaboration with suppliers has been acknowledged, manufacturing firms utilize more operational than strategic collaboration with suppliers (Bastl et al., 2012). Manufacturing firms are less willing to share strategic information with suppliers (Bastl et al., 2012) and also have less control over the adaptation of goals and processes (Momeni & Martinsuo, 2019a). The provision of services also requires both operational and strategic integration with customers. While operational collaboration helps manufacturing firms fulfil the specific needs of customers (Kindström & Kowalkowski, 2009), strategic integration enables long-term relationships with customers, increases customer readiness and develops new products and services (Shah et al., 2020).

The need for supply chain integration varies based on the type of service (Saccani et al., 2014). Basic services require less integration efforts, and their provision is usually limited to supplier integration to provide spare parts and deliver services to customers (Shah et al., 2020). On the other hand, advanced services require various types of information and resource sharing between multiple partners within the supply chain, especially with customers (Chen et al., 2015; He & Lai, 2012).

Managerial Implications

The concept of service integration explained in this chapter is appropriate for managers to identify the intra- and inter-organizational interfaces that are involved in the integration of products and services. Bundling product and service components cannot always guarantee that the servitization goal will be achieved, but manufacturing firms must pay attention to the supply chain and consider all partners as crucial actors for integrating service business in the value chain of the firm. Different elements of service integration presented in the framework would be helpful when executing the servitization strategy to identify neglected or improvement-needed areas. Managers need to identify the key partners in the supply chain for each type of offering that enable or facilitate the successful development, sales and delivery of the services. Identifying these key partners, their roles and their impact will help managers focus their resources on enhancing the key relationships in the supply chain. Depending on the supply chain structure of the firm (e.g. presence of a service supplier), all dimensions are equally important as they complement each other and facilitate successful servitization.

References

Alghisi, A., & Saccani, N. (2015). Internal and external alignment in the servitization journey—Overcoming the challenges. *Production Planning & Control, 26*(14–15), 1219–1232. https://doi.org/10.1080/09537287.2015.1033496.

Aminoff, A., & Hakanen, T. (2018). Implications of product centric servitization for global distribution channels of manufacturing companies. *International Journal of Physical Distribution and Logistics Management, 48*(10), 1020–1038. https://doi.org/10.1108/IJPDLM-06-2018-0231.

Ayala, N. F., Gerstlberger, W., & Frank, A. G. (2019). Managing servitization in product companies: The moderating role of service suppliers. *International Journal of Operations and Production Management, 39*(1), 43–74. https://doi.org/10.1108/IJOPM-08-2017-0484.

Ayala, N. F., Paslauski, C. A., Ghezzi, A., & Frank, A. G. (2017). Knowledge sharing dynamics in service suppliers' involvement for servitization of manufacturing companies. *International Journal of Production Economics, 193,* 538–553. https://doi.org/10.1016/j.ijpe.2017.08.019.

Baines, T. S., Lightfoot, H. W., Benedettini, O., & Kay, J. M. (2009). The servitization of manufacturing: A review of literature and reflection on future challenges. *Journal of Manufacturing Technology Management, 20,* 547–567. https://doi.org/10.1108/17410380910960984.

Baines, T., Lightfoot, H., Smart, P., & Fletcher, S. (2013). Servitization of manufacture: Exploring the deployment and skills of people critical to the delivery of advanced services. *Journal of Manufacturing Technology Management, 24*(4), 637–646. https://doi.org/10.1108/17410381311327431.

Baltacioglu, T., Ada, E., Kaplan, M. D., Yurt, O., & Kaplan, Y. C. (2007). A new framework for service supply chains. *Service Industries Journal, 27*(2), 105–124. https://doi.org/10.1080/02642060601122629.

Bastl, M., Johnson, M., Lightfoot, H., & Evans, S. (2012). Buyer-supplier relationships in a servitized environment: An examination with Cannon and Perreault's framework. *International Journal of Operations and Production Management, 32*(6), 650–675. https://doi.org/10.1108/01443571211230916.

Burton, J., Story, V., Zolkiewski, J., Raddats, C., Baines, T. S., & Medway, D. (2016). Identifying tensions in the servitized value chain. *Research Technology Management, 59*(5), 38–47. https://doi.org/10.1080/08956308.2016.1208042.

Bustinza, O. F., Bigdeli, A. Z., Baines, T., & Elliot, C. (2015). Servitization and competitive advantage: The importance of organizational structure and value chain position. *Research Technology Management, 58*(5), 53–60. https://doi.org/10.5437/08956308X5805354.

Chen, J.-S., Kerr, D., Tsang, S.-S., & Sung, Y. C. (2015). Co-production of service innovations through dynamic capability enhancement. *The Service Industries Journal, 35*(1–2), 96–114. https://doi.org/10.1080/02642069.2014.979405.

Droge, C., Jayaram, J., & Vickery, S. K. (2004). The effects of internal versus external integration practices on time-based performance and overall firm performance. *Journal of Operations Management, 22*(6), 557–573. https://doi.org/10.1016/j.jom.2004.08.001.

Finne, M., & Holmström, J. (2013). A manufacturer moving upstream: Triadic collaboration for service delivery. *Supply Chain Management, 18*(1), 21–33. https://doi.org/10.1108/13598541311293159.

Flynn, B. B., Huo, B., & Zhao, X. (2010). The impact of supply chain integration on performance: A contingency and configuration approach. *Journal of Operations Management, 28*(1), 58–71. https://doi.org/10.1016/j.jom.2009.06.001.

He, Y., & Lai, K. K. (2012). Supply chain integration and service oriented transformation: Evidence from Chinese equipment manufacturers. *International Journal of Production Economics, 135*(2), 791–799. https://doi.org/10.1016/j.ijpe.2011.10.013.

Iakovaki, A., Srai, J. S., & Harrington, T. (2009, January). Service supply chain integration in multi-organisation networks—Applying integration enablers and aligning process capabilities. *14th Annual Cambridge Manufacturing Symposium,* 1–16. http://www2.ifm.eng.cam.ac.uk/cim/symposium2009/proceedings/16_iakovaki.pdf.

Karatzas, A., Johnson, M., & Bastl, M. (2017). Manufacturer-supplier relationships and service performance in service triads. *International Journal of Operations and Production Management, 37*(7), 950–969. https://doi.org/10.1108/IJOPM-11-2015-0719.

Katunzi, T. M. (2011). Obstacles to process integration along the supply chain: Manufacturing firms perspective. *International Journal of Business and Management, 6*(5), 105–113. https://doi.org/10.5539/ijbm.v6n5p105.

Kindström, D., & Kowalkowski, C. (2009). Development of industrial service offerings: A process framework. *Journal of Service Management, 20*(2), 156–172. https://doi.org/10.1108/09564230910952753.

Kindström, D., Kowalkowski, C., & Alejandro, T. B. (2015). Adding services to product-based portfolios an exploration of the implications for the sales function. *Journal of Service Management, 26*(3), 372–393. https://doi.org/10.1108/JOSM-02-2014-0042.

Kohtamäki, M., Parida, V., Oghazi, P., Gebauer, H., & Baines, T. (2019). Digital servitization business models in ecosystems: A theory of the firm. *Journal of Business Research, 104,* 380–392. https://doi.org/10.1016/j.jbusres.2019.06.027.

Lenka, S., Parida, V., Sjödin, D. R., & Wincent, J. (2018). Towards a multi-level servitization framework: Conceptualizing ambivalence in manufacturing firms. *International Journal of Operations and Production Management, 38*(3), 810–827. https://doi.org/10.1108/IJOPM-09-2016-0542.

Martinez, V., Neely, A., Velu, C., Leinster-Evans, S., & Bisessar, D. (2017). Exploring the journey to services. *International Journal of Production Economics, 192,* 66–80. https://doi.org/10.1016/j.ijpe.2016.12.030.

Moeller, S. (2008). Customer Integration—A Key to an Implementation Perspective of Service Provision. *Journal of Service Research, 11*(2), 197–210. https://doi.org/10.1177/1094670508324677.

Momeni, K., & Martinsuo, M. M. (2018). Allocating human resources to projects and services in dynamic project environments. *International Journal of Managing Projects in Business, 11*(2), 486–506. https://doi.org/10.1108/IJMPB-07-2017-0074.

Momeni, K., & Martinsuo, M. (2019a). Going downstream in a project-based firm: Integration of distributors in the delivery of complex systems. *International Journal of Project Management, 37*(1), 27–42. https://doi.org/10.1016/j.ijproman.2018.09.007.

Momeni, K., & Martinsuo, M. (2019b). Integrating services into solution offerings in the sales work of project-based firms. *International Journal of Project Management, 37*(8), 956–967. https://doi.org/10.1016/j.ijproman.2019.09.004.

Nagariya, R., Kumar, D., & Kumar, I. (2020). Service supply chain: From bibliometric analysis to content analysis, current research trends and future research directions. *Benchmarking, 28*(1), 333–369. https://doi.org/10.1108/BIJ-04-2020-0137.

Ng, I., Parry, G., Maull, R., & McFarlane, D. (2011). Complex engineering service systems: A grand challenge. In *Complex engineering service systems* (pp. 439–454). Springer. https://doi.org/10.1007/978-0-85729-189-9_23.

Oliva, R., Gebauer, H., & Brann, J. M. (2012). Separate or integrate? Assessing the impact of separation between product and service business on service performance in product manufacturing firms. *Journal of Business-to-Business Marketing, 19*(4), 309–334. https://doi.org/10.1080/1051712X.2012.647797.

Oliva, R., & Kallenberg, R. (2003). Managing the transition from products to services. *International Journal of Service Industry Management, 14*(2), 160–172. https://doi.org/10.1108/09564230310474138.

Oliva, R., & Watson, N. (2011). Cross-functional alignment in supply chain planning: A case study of sales and operations planning. *Journal of Operations Management, 29*(5), 434–448. https://doi.org/10.1016/j.jom.2010.11.012.

Paslauski, C. A., Ayala, N. F., Tortorella, G. L., & Frank, A. G. (2016). The last border for servitization. *Procedia CIRP, 47*, 394–399. Elsevier B.V. https://doi.org/10.1016/j.procir.2016.03.056.

Rabetino, R., Harmsen, W., Kohtamäki, M., & Sihvonen, J. (2018). Structuring servitization-related research. *International Journal of Operations and Production Management, 38*(2), 350–371. https://doi.org/10.1108/IJOPM-03-2017-0175.

Rabetino, R., Kohtamäki, M., & Gebauer, H. (2017). Strategy map of servitization. *International Journal of Production Economics, 192*, 144–156. https://doi.org/10.1016/j.ijpe.2016.11.004.

Saccani, N., Visintin, F., & Rapaccini, M. (2014). Investigating the linkages between service types and supplier relationships in servitized environments. *International Journal of Production Economics, 149*, 226–238. https://doi.org/10.1016/j.ijpe.2013.10.001.

Schoenherr, T., & Swink, M. (2012). Revisiting the arcs of integration: Cross-validations and extensions. *Journal of Operations Management, 30*(1–2), 99–115. https://doi.org/10.1016/j.jom.2011.09.001.

Shah, S. A. A., Jajja, M. S. S., Chatha, K. A., & Farooq, S. (2020). Servitization and supply chain integration: An empirical analysis. *International Journal of Production Economics, 229*(January), https://doi.org/10.1016/j.ijpe.2020.107765.

Sousa, R., & da Silveira, G. J. C. (2017). Capability antecedents and performance outcomes of servitization: Differences between basic and advanced services. *International Journal of Operations and Production Management, 37*(4), 444–467. https://doi.org/10.1108/IJOPM-11-2015-0696.

Wang, Y., Wallace, S. W., Shen, B., & Choi, T. M. (2015). Service supply chain management: A review of operational models. *European Journal of Operational Research, 247*, 685–698. https://doi.org/10.1016/j.ejor.2015.05.053.

Windahl, C., & Lakemond, N. (2006). Developing integrated solutions: The importance of relationships within the network. *Industrial Marketing Management, 35*(7), 806–818. https://doi.org/10.1016/j.indmarman.2006.05.010.

Zhao, G., Feng, T., & Wang, D. (2015). Is more supply chain integration always beneficial to financial performance? *Industrial Marketing Management, 45*(1), 162–172. https://doi.org/10.1016/j.indmarman.2015.02.015.

Zhao, X., Huo, B., Selen, W., & Yeung, J. H. Y. (2011). The impact of internal integration and relationship commitment on external integration. *Journal of Operations Management, 29*(1–2), 17–32. https://doi.org/10.1016/j.jom.2010.04.004.

Network Structures in Service Provision

Melanie E. Kreye

1   Introduction

As the academic understanding of servitization has matured over time, an interesting trend in terms of the development of described network structures can be observed. Initially, research studies have focused on service dyads, concentrating on the requirements of manufacturers wishing to engage in services to develop novel capabilities for developing and delivering services and conversely adapting their internal structures and capability base (Baines et al., 2007). Here, the main insights typically focus on the lack of internal complementarity between service operations and manufacturing (Oliva et al., 2012), creating difficulties in engaging with customers and provide the desired value. For example, Fang et al. (2008) highlight that the transition towards services can create internal confusion, tension and even conflict between the service and product-focused operations because of the need to focus around customer needs and processes (Sampson & Froehle, 2006).

Recently, research studies have focused around more complex network structures for service provision, including the contribution of intermediaries or multiple suppliers (Raddats et al., 2019). Here, different sets of capabilities between partners can be combined with the aim to achieve collective

M. E. Kreye (✉)
Department of Technology, Management and Economics, Danish Technical University, Lyngby, Denmark
e-mail: mkreye@dtu.dk

© The Author(s), under exclusive license to Springer Nature
Switzerland AG 2021
M. Kohtamäki et al. (eds.), *The Palgrave Handbook of Servitization*,
https://doi.org/10.1007/978-3-030-75771-7_31

487

benefits faster, at less cost, with greater flexibility and with less risk (Kreye & Perunovic, 2020b). Yet, operational challenges and the ability to achieve service performance in these set-ups differ substantially from earlier works focusing on the service dyad.

The aim of this chapter is to critically discuss the network structures currently described in the servitization literature and offer insights on the specific benefits, challenges, and performance factors. More specifically, we describe service dyads, service triads and service networks as the network structures typically highlighted in the literature and found in managerial practice (Raddats et al., 2019). We seek to provide a concise overview of the state-of-the-art on this topic.

2   Theory Development

This section is structured with the increasing organizational and operational complexity of the network structures for service provision in mind. First, we describe service dyads, then service triads and finally service networks before summarising the insights in an overview table.

Service Dyads

Most servitization research has focused on service dyads, which are long-term relationships between provider and customer firms (Vargo & Lusch, 2008). As servitization changes the nature of the relationship between manufacturer and their customers (Kreye et al., 2015; Wise & Baumgartner, 1999), the service encounter is embedded in a series of exchanges with planned and administered individual transactions (Tax et al., 2013). Inputs from provider and customer are intrinsically entwined to jointly produce service performance (Sampson & Froehle, 2006). Both partners are operationally dependent on each other, including commitment and level of contribution to achieve the desired value.

Relationships in service dyads are complex as the customer has multiple contact channels with the provider (Sampson, 2012). Reversely, a service provider uses multiple channels to deliver the service. These channels include personal interaction through service engineers repairing or maintaining the product (Kreye et al., 2015) and impersonal interaction through, e.g. digital monitoring technology or remote operations (Larivière et al., 2017). As a result, a service provider needs the capability of integrating the different channels to deliver the outcome of the service. This can pose a challenge in the service dyad due to the high level of complexity in services with regard to information exchange and communication (Breidbach et al., 2013).

In service dyads, performance is highly dependent on customer responsiveness (Sampson & Spring, 2012). This in turn requires the service provider to be customer oriented in their operational set-up through flexible processes and close inter-personal relationships between provider and customer employees (Kreye, 2016). Performance is related to the customer's evaluation of the service quality, which includes a combination of different factors. For example, technical quality focuses around factors, such as performance output or equipment up-time often defined in the service contract (Caldwell & Howard, 2014). In contrast, functional quality focuses around factors, such as reliability (of employees and materials), responsiveness and appearance and quality of physical facilities and equipment (Kreye, 2017b). Furthermore, relationship quality, describing the customer's perceived trade-off between benefits of the delivered service and sacrifices in terms of relationship-specific investments (Ulaga, 2003), will strongly affect the customer's evaluation of the value they receive (Grönroos, 2011).

In sum, the research on service dyads is manifold and has described the different benefits, challenges and performance factors through various research studies across industry sectors. Many of these studies contrast service-based needs to the manufacturing traditions of the provider company, offering thus specific insights for managers to engage in the transition towards becoming a service provider. The research results can thus be seen as an important basis for following research studies on more complex network structures, including service triads and service networks.

Service Triads

In service triads, the service is delivered directly by a supplier to a buyer's customer (Wynstra et al., 2015). The three partners can combine their capabilities to create competitive advantage in the triad. While the buyer (often the servitized manufacturer) provides the necessary technological capabilities and know-how, the supplier provides direct customer access, often through a dispersed network of front line service engineers. Service triads can often be found in cross-national set-ups (Ndubisi et al., 2015) and span legal, regulatory and often cultural borders (Kreye, 2017a). Here, the supplier enables spanning of geographical and often cultural distances.

Service triads create unique organizational and operational challenges because of increased complexity in terms of interactions, operations and relationships (Li & Choi, 2009). Managing and governing the triadic relationship is required to achieve the above mentioned benefits as delicate trade-offs between autonomy to the supplier and tight control of delivered quality level can shape long-term relationships in the triad (Ndubisi et al., 2015). However, additional challenges and risks arise. For example, the buyer may risk to lose the value of direct customer contact and information exchange in the long-term as this role is fulfilled by the supplier (Wynstra et al., 2015). Similarly, the typical cross-national set-up can involve operational challenges due to missing infrastructure or legal frameworks in the receiving country (Kreye, 2017a).

As a result, performance in service triads is determined by the interaction between the partners in addition to the technical and functional quality (Caldwell & Howard, 2014). In a recent study by Karatzas et al. (2016), the authors found that it was the *combination* between different relationship characteristics and contextual factors, such as contract value, that determined service performance in triads. Specific relationship characteristics span all three triad partners and include operational interdependence, cooperative and contractual norms and mutual relationship-specific investments.

In sum, the body of literature on service triads has emerged more recently and much of the insights are strongly based on the service-dyad literature. Despite existing contributions of the unique benefits and challenges of service triads, further work is required to advance academic understanding in this area. Specifically, studies regarding the performance factors in service triads needs further expanding as this will not only be affected by service characteristics, provider and supplier capabilities and relationships (Karatzas et al., 2016), but also factors related to the often cross-national set-up (Elango & Wieland, 2015).

Service Networks

A service network is a constellation of multiple business actors, who collaborate to provide an integrated service based on complex and diverse customer needs (Löfberg et al., 2015; Windahl & Lakemond, 2006). Service networks form because a single company does not have the necessary capabilities to develop or deliver the specific service and the in-house development of these capabilities is not economically feasible (Gebauer et al., 2013). Service networks can be vertical or horizontal in nature (Gebauer et al., 2013), which means that the service package can address one or multiple equipment lifecycle stages through combining different capabilities of various partners. As a result, the nature of relationships and dynamics in service networks can vary substantially based on the chosen network structure and contextual factors.

Benefits of service networks are customer centric, as the customer receives a one-stop solution for their specific needs. In turn, the manufacturer gains access to capabilities not possessed within their organization, enabling them to achieve service growth (Jaakkola & Hakanen, 2013). However, networks also pose significant challenges based on the organizational and often operational complexity. One critical task is to integrate the different product and service offerings provided by the different suppliers into a single customer offering (Gebauer et al., 2013). This requires long-term collaboration between individual partners and ideally the network (Kreye & Perunovic, 2020b). However, dynamic changes in the network based on new business opportunities and hence new network configurations of capabilities pose additional challenges in this context (Spring & Araujo, 2013).

As targeted performance studies in service networks are still missing, important insights can be taken from the service dyad and service triad descriptions provided above and combine these with the wider organizational network literature (Kreye & Perunovic, 2020a; Windahl & Lakemond, 2006). Examples here are the relationship strength between individual actors and the network as a whole (Windahl & Lakemond, 2006), the integrator firm's position in the network (Windahl & Lakemond, 2006) and hence their ability to affect partner behaviour and deliverables (Kreye & Perunovic, 2020b) and an individual firm's network horizon and additional contextual factors.

In sum, the academic understanding on service networks is still nascent and currently relatively diverse due to the strong variations in network structures. As important insights on the benefits and challenges emerge, academic understanding matures and behaviour and determinants in service networks can be better and more accurately explained. Important gaps remain on performance factors of service networks. Existing insights from the service dyad and service triad literatures can be expected to provide only sparse insights into the more complex and diverse empirical settings of service networks. Hence, much more targeted and detailed studies need to be done in this area.

Table 1 summarises the discussions in this section and provides an overview of the definitions, benefits, challenges and performance factors of service dyads, service triads and service networks.

Table 1 Summary of organizational set-ups in servitization

	Service dyads	Service triads	Service network
Description	= Long-term and close relationships between provider and customer (Vargo & Lusch, 2008) Typical constellation:	= a buyer contracts a supplier to deliver a service directly to the buyer's customer (Wynstra et al., 2015) Typical constellation:	= constellation of multiple business actors, who collaborate to provide an integrated service based on complex and diverse customer needs (Löfberg et al., 2015; Windahl & Lakemond, 2006) Exemplar constellation:
Opportunities	Customer lock-in (Kreye et al., 2015) through long-term and committed relationships with multiple contact channels and customised processes (Sampson & Froehle, 2006) Higher profit margins and more stable cash flow (Wise & Baumgartner, 1999) create new competitive advantage (Vandermerwe & Rada, 1988) Improve customer operational efficiency and reduce costs of equipment operation and maintenance	Unique combination of capabilities to provide combined competitive advantage (Wynstra et al., 2015) Buyer often provides technological capabilities and know-how Supplier often provides direct customer access (Finne & Holmström, 2013), especially in cross-national set-ups (Kreye, 2017a) Added benefits from service dyad set-up, such as customer lock-in and stable cash flow.	One-stop customer solution for complex needs and customer requirements (Löfberg et al., 2015; Windahl & Lakemond, 2006) Access to external capabilities required for successful service growth at the manufacturer (Windahl & Lakemond, 2006)

	Service dyads	Service triads	Service network
Challenges	Need to manage service-based processes, which require operational flexibility based on varying customer inputs (Sampson & Froehle, 2006)	Relational and governance concerns Trade-off between granting autonomy to supplier and tight control of service activities and delivered service quality determine dynamics in the triad (Ndubisi et al., 2015)	Organizational and operational challenges arising from network complexity, including relationship characteristics and governance (Jaakkola & Hakanen, 2013; Kreye & Perunovic, 2020b)
	Need to integrate information from multiple customer contact channels with customer (Breidbach et al., 2013)	Buyer risk of losing benefits from direct customer access (Wynstra et al., 2015)	Additional challenges arise from integral dynamism in network configuration and capability integration (Spring & Araujo, 2013)
	High levels of operational uncertainty due to variability and unpredictability of service operations and strong operational dependence on customer inputs (Kreye et al., 2014)	Additional challenges when operations are set in countries with missing infrastructure or legal frameworks (Kreye, 2017a)	
Performance	Determined by customer evaluation of, e.g. technical quality (= what is delivered in comparison to service contract), functional quality (= how it is delivered) and relationship quality (= sacrifices made through relationship specific investments) (Kreye, 2017b)	Combination of relationship characteristics, including operational interdependencies, cooperative and contractual norms, and contextual factors, such as contract value (Karatzas et al., 2016)	Targeted investigations still missing Likely performance determinants based on service and network literature streams include Relationship characteristics between individual partners (Windahl & Lakemond, 2006) Network configuration and positioning of individual firms (Kreye & Perunovic, 2020a) Firm's network horizon (Windahl & Lakemond, 2006) Contextual factors, such as industry dynamics and regulatory frameworks

3   Discussion

This section discusses the provided insights on the different network structures both from an academic perspective (section "Theoretical Contributions") and practical perspective (section "Managerial Implications"). We will highlight the main challenges for future work in this context.

Theoretical Contributions

The theoretical contribution of this research results from the critical discussion of the state-of-the-art of network structures in service provision. Based on a detailed review, important insights from core works within the diverse field of servitization are provided and summarised in a concise and yet detailed overview (see Table 1). This overview provides insights into the specific nature of the reviewed network structures (service dyads, service triads and service networks) while the accommodating descriptions give an idea of the logical development within the servitization literature. This enables the academic community to take stock of existing understanding in the field and develop strategies for future research where gaps remain.

The contribution from this research further relates to the identified gaps briefly outlined in sections "Service Dyads", "Service Triads", and "Service Networks". Specifically, the more recently explored network structures of service triads and service networks provide important areas for further investigations to improve academic understanding and close existing gaps in knowledge. For example, insights into the unique dynamics of relationships in service triads and resulting performance effects are still nascent and only emerging insights have been provided (Karatzas et al., 2016). Initial suggestions regarding the importance of *combinations* of performance factors (rather than individual performance factors prevalent in the service dyad literature) are promising and require much more detailed and elaborate studies. Similarly, academic knowledge on performance in service networks requires much further work. Here, further understanding needs to be created as the specific dynamics resulting from the structural set-up will critically affect performance. More specifically, studies into the performance of service networks could show that diverse combinations of different factors can create unique performance effects in this context.

Managerial Implications

The insights provided in this chapter offer some meaningful implications for managers involved in servitization and the provision of engineering services. The provided overview enables informed decision making regarding the network structures of service provision. In other words, managers can make more informed choices regarding the specific organizational structure focusing on the specific nature of the service offering and industry context by basing these choices on the expected benefits and expected performance effects created by the organization structure. This then enables managers to direct their attention to the specific challenges identified in Table 1. This chapter shows that these challenges are relatively unique based on the specific organizational structure and require targeted management attention.

Next Steps

To research network structures in servitization, further work is needed to elaborate understanding on service triads and service networks in more detail. The identified gaps described above already give some indication into specific research objectives and directions.

On a more fundamental note, many research studies tend to focus on single party perspective or dyad perspective, even when attempting to study triads or networks (Kreye & Van Donk, 2021). Existing works typically study a focal organization within a network (Rabetino et al., 2017; Ramirez Hernandez & Kreye, 2021; Zhang & Banerji, 2017), ignoring input from other network actors. Insights on the dynamics within the complex network structures are rare and require more elaborate investigations into the inputs, motives and contributions of all actors. This will enable more elaborate and detailed insights into the governance of these networks for successful servitization, including coordination and control mechanisms (Karatzas et al., 2016; Selviaridis, 2016). This will further offer valuable insights into network management to achieve successful performance outcomes for all actors, including long and short term performance measures.

4   Conclusions

This chapter provides an overview of the different network structures for service provisions, illuminating specifically the benefits, challenges and performance factors of service dyads, service triads and service networks. This complements existing studies focusing on the specific organizational structure currently found in the servitization literature. This chapter provides a distilled overview of the diverse understanding on this topic.

References

Baines, T. S., Lightfoot, H. W., Evans, S., Neely, A., Greenough, R., Peppard, J., Roy, R., Shehab, E., Braganza, A., Tiwari, A. and Alcock, J.R., Angus, J. P., Bastl, M., Cousens, A., Irving, P., Johnson, M., Kingston, J., Lockett, H., Martinez, V., Michele, P., Tranfield, D., Walton, I. M., & Wilson, H. (2007). State-of-the-art in Product-Service Systems. *Proceedings of the Institution of Mechanical Engineers—Part B—Journal for Engineering Manufacture, 221,* 1543–1552. https://doi.org/10.1243/09544054jem858.

Breidbach, C. F., Kolb, D. G., & Srinivasan, A. (2013). Connectivity in service systems: Does technology-enablement impact the ability of a service system to co-create value? *Journal of Service Research, 16*(3), 428–441. https://doi.org/10.1177/1094670512470869.

Caldwell, N., & Howard, M. (2014). Contracting for complex performance in markets of few buyers and sellers. *International Journal of Operations & Production Management, 34*(2), 270–294. https://doi.org/10.1108/IJOPM-10-2013-0444.

Elango, B., & Wieland, J. R. (2015). Impact of country effects on the performance of service firms. *Journal of Service Management, 26*(4), 588–607. https://doi.org/10.1108/JOSM-02-2015-0056.

Fang, E. (Er), Palmatier, R. W., & Steenkamp, J.-B. E. M. (2008). Effect of service transition strategies on firm value. *Journal of Marketing, 72*(5), 1–14. https://doi.org/10.1509/jmkg.72.5.1.

Finne, M., & Holmström, J. (2013). A manufacturer moving upstream: Triadic collaboration for service delivery. *Supply Chain Management: An International Journal, 18*(1), 21–33.

Gebauer, H., Paiola, M., & Saccani, N. (2013). Characterizing service networks for moving from products to solutions. *Industrial Marketing Management, 42*(1), 31–46. https://doi.org/10.1016/j.indmarman.2012.11.002.

Grönroos, C. (2011). A service perspective on business relationships: The value creation, interaction and marketing interface. *Industrial Marketing Management, 40*(2), 240–247. https://doi.org/10.1016/j.indmarman.2010.06.036.

Jaakkola, E., & Hakanen, T. (2013). Value co-creation in solution networks. *Industrial Marketing Management, 42*(1), 47–58. https://doi.org/10.1016/j.indmarman.2012.11.005.

Karatzas, A., Johnson, M., & Bastl, M. (2016). Relationship determinants of performance in service triads: A configurational approach. *Journal of Supply Chain Management, 52*(3), 28–47. https://doi.org/10.1111/jscm.12109.

Kreye, M. E. (2016). Employee motivation in Product-Service-System providers. *Production Planning & Control, 27*(15), 1249–1259. https://doi.org/10.1080/09537287.2016.1206219.

Kreye, M. E. (2017a). Can you put too much on your plate? Uncertainty exposure in servitized triads. *International Journal of Operations & Production Management, 37*(12), 1722–1740. https://doi.org/10.1108/IJOPM-06-2016-0357.

Kreye, M. E. (2017b). Relational uncertainty in service dyads. *International Journal of Operations & Production Management, 37*(3), 363–381.

Kreye, M. E., Newnes, L. B., & Goh, Y. M. (2014). Uncertainty in competitive bidding—A framework for product—Service systems. *Production Planning & Control, 25*(6), 462–477. https://doi.org/10.1080/09537287.2012.705354.

Kreye, M. E., & Perunovic, Z. (2020a, April). Performance in publicly funded innovation networks (PFINs): The role of inter-organisational relationships. *Industrial Marketing Management, 86,* 201–211. https://doi.org/10.1016/j.indmarman.2019.11.018.

Kreye, M. E., & Perunovic, Z. (2020b). You don't forget where you come from: Linking formation and operations in publicly funded innovation networks. *Production Planning & Control, 31*(10), 816–828. https://doi.org/10.1080/09537287.2019.1693066.

Kreye, M. E., Roehrich, J. K., & Lewis, M. A. (2015). Servitising manufacturers: The impact of service complexity and contractual and relational capabilities. *Production Planning & Control, 26*(14), 1233–1246. https://doi.org/10.1080/09537287.2015.1033489.

Kreye, M. E., & Van Donk, D. P. (2021). Exploring servitization in the Business-to-Consumer context. *International Journal of Operations & Production Management.*

Larivière, B., Bowen, D., Andreassen, T. W., Kunz, W., Sirianni, N. J., Voss, C., Wünderlich, N. V., & De Keyser, A. (2017). "Service Encounter 2.0": An investigation into the roles of technology, employees and customers. *Journal of Business Research, 79,* 238–246. https://doi.org/10.1016/j.jbusres.2017.03.008.

Li, M. E. I., & Choi, T. Y. (2009). Triads in services outsourcing: Bridge, bridge decay and bridge transfer. *Journal of Supply Chain Management, 45*(3), 27–39. https://doi.org/10.1111/j.1745-493X.2009.03169.x.

Löfberg, N., Witell, L., & Gustafsson, A. (2015). Service manoeuvres to overcome challenges of servitisation in a value network. *Production Planning & Control, 26*(14), 1188–1197. https://doi.org/10.1080/09537287.2015.1033491.

Ndubisi, N. O., Capel, C. M., & Ndubisi, G. C. (2015). Innovation strategy and performance of international technology services ventures: The moderating effect of structural autonomy. *Journal of Service Management, 26*(4), 548–564. https://doi.org/10.1108/JOSM-04-2015-0118.

Oliva, R., Gebauer, H., & Brann, J. M. (2012). Separate or integrate? Assessing the impact of separation between product and service business on service performance in product manufacturing firms. *Journal of Business-to-Business Marketing, 19*(4), 309–334. https://doi.org/10.1080/1051712X.2012.647797.

Rabetino, R., Kohtamäki, M., & Gebauer, H. (2017). Strategy map of servitization. *International Journal of Production Economics, 192,* 144–156. https://doi.org/10.1016/j.ijpe.2016.11.004.

Raddats, C., Kowalkowski, C., Benedettini, O., Burton, J., & Gebauer, H. (2019, April). Servitization: A contemporary thematic review of four major research streams. *Industrial Marketing Management, 83,* 207–223. https://doi.org/10.1016/j.indmarman.2019.03.015.

Ramirez Hernandez, T., & Kreye, M. E. (2021). Uncertainty profiles in engineering-service development: Exploring supplier co-creation. *Journal of Service Management,* forthcoming.

Sampson, S. E. (2012). Visualizing service operations. *Journal of Service Research, 15*(2), 182–198. https://doi.org/10.1177/1094670511435541.

Sampson, S. E., & Froehle, C. M. (2006). Foundations and implications of a proposed unified services theory. *Production & Operations Management, 15*(2), 329–343. http://search.ebscohost.com/login.aspx?direct=true&db=buh&AN=22404199&site=ehost-live.

Sampson, S. E., & Spring, M. (2012). Customer roles in service supply chains and opportunities for innovation. *Journal of Supply Chain Management, 48*(4), 30–50. https://doi.org/10.1111/j.1745-493X.2012.03282.x.

Selviaridis, K. (2016). Contract functions in service exchange governance: Evidence from logistics outsourcing. *Production Planning and Control, 27*(16), 1373–1388. https://doi.org/10.1080/09537287.2016.1224397.

Spring, M., & Araujo, L. (2013). Beyond the service factory: Service innovation in manufacturing supply networks. *Industrial Marketing Management, 42*(1), 59–70. https://doi.org/10.1016/j.indmarman.2012.11.006.

Tax, S. S., McCutcheon, D., & Wilkinson, I. F. (2013). The Service Delivery Network (SDN): A customer-centric perspective of the customer journey. *Journal of Service Research, 16*(4), 454–470. https://doi.org/10.1177/1094670513481108.

Ulaga, W. (2003). Capturing value creation in business relationships: A customer perspective. *Industrial Marketing Management, 32*(8), 677–693. https://doi.org/10.1016/j.indmarman.2003.06.008.

Vandermerwe, S., & Rada, J. (1988). Servitization of business: Adding value by adding services. *European Management Journal, 6*(4), 314–324.

Vargo, S. L., & Lusch, R. F. (2008). Service-dominant logic: Continuing the evolution. *Journal of the Academy of Marketing Science, 36*(1), 1–10.

Windahl, C., & Lakemond, N. (2006). Developing integrated solutions: The importance of relationships within the network. *Industrial Marketing Management, 35*(7), 806–818. https://doi.org/10.1016/j.indmarman.2006.05.010.

Wise, R., & Baumgartner, P. (1999). Go downstream: The new profit imperative in manufacturing. *Harvard Business Review, 77*(5), 133–141.

Wynstra, F., Spring, M., & Schoenherr, T. (2015). Service triads: A research agenda for buyer–supplier–customer triads in business services. *Journal of Operations Management, 35,* 1–20. https://doi.org/10.1016/j.jom.2014.10.002.

Zhang, W., & Banerji, S. (2017, June). Challenges of servitization: A systematic literature review. *Industrial Marketing Management, 65*, 217–227. https://doi.org/10.1016/j.indmarman.2017.06.003.

Organizational Structures in Servitization: Should Product and Service Businesses Be Separated or Integrated?

Sophie Peillon

1 Introduction

In a contingency perspective, "*structure follows strategy*" (Chandler, 1962), and changes in strategy are associated with changes in organizational architecture (Mintzberg, 1990). The scientific literature on servitization has explored the alignment between strategy, structure, and environment, and considers alignment between service strategy and organizational design as essential to the success of the transition to service (Ambroise et al., 2018; Auguste et al., 2006; Gebauer, Edvardsson, Gustafsson, et al. 2010; Gebauer & Kowalkowski, 2012; Neu & Brown, 2005, 2008; Raddats & Burton, 2011).

The provision of services requires the manufacturer not only to develop new market offerings but also to support these offerings with new and unfamiliar organizational structures, capabilities, and processes (Davies et al., 2006; Oliva & Kallenberg, 2003). These structures, capabilities, and processes differ to those of production operations, and the challenge is to define what form they should take to support the effective delivery of integrated product/service offerings. Specifically, service success depends on a supportive organizational design (Baines et al., 2017), and the change of internal structures is needed to support business transformation (Zhang &

S. Peillon (✉)
Mines Saint-Etienne, Institut Henri Fayol, Saint-Étienne, France
e-mail: sophie.peillon@mines-stetienne.fr

Banerji, 2017). It follows that "*one of the most significant challenges for prac-titioners of servitization is how to transform a manufacturing organization to exploit the opportunity*" (Baines et al., 2017: 256).

Shepherd and Ahmed (2000) were the first to point out the interrelation between the offering of integrated solutions and the organizational structure (Biege et al., 2012), going as far as to say that "*the biggest area to be impacted by adopting a 'solutions' model is that of the organisational structure*" (Shepherd & Ahmed, 2000: 105). Organizational structure "*refers to the formal allo-cation of work roles and the adoption of a management mechanism to control internal activities and support the implementation of business strategy within an organization*" (Zhang & Banerji, 2017: 220).

Within the servitization process, the tasks and activities related to the provision of services should be integrated into the hierarchy of the manu-facturing company. Thus, manufacturers need to make decisions regarding the way they can properly integrate additional service-providing activities and/or units (Biege et al., 2012; Bustinza et al., 2015). More specifically, manufacturers need to determine whether to integrate a service organization in the strategic business units (SBUs) for products, or to set up a separate service organization or SBU for services in addition to the product SBUs (Gebauer, Edvardsson, et al., 2010). The appropriate organizational structure for services in manufacturing is a central question discussed in the litera-ture (Fliess & Lexutt, 2019), and, from a managerial perspective, there is still little guidance available for manufacturers regarding the way organizational structures and processes should be developed (Biege et al., 2012).

Despite nearly two decades of study and lively debate, conceptual and empirical work on organizational structures in servitization still remains divergent. In order to help alleviate the current stalemate, this chapter calls for a new direction in research on organizational structures in servitization, especially regarding its epistemological foundations. We begin by reviewing the terms of the "to separate or integrate" debate, then suggest avenues for studying organizational structures in servitization within alternative episte-mological paradigms.

2   Organizational Structures in Servitization

Table 1 provides an overview regarding the main statements provided by the literature on organizational structures in servitization, which are further detailed in sections "Separating Product and Services Activities" and "Inte-grating Product and Services Activities".

Table 1 Main statements in literature on organizational structures in servitization

Organizational structures in servitization	– The alignment between service strategy and organizational design is essential to the success of the transition to service	Ambroise et al. (2018), Auguste et al. (2006), Gebauer, Edvardsson, Gustafsson, et al. (2010), Gebauer and Kowalkowski (2012), Neu and Brown (2005, 2008), and Raddats and Burton (2011)
	– The provision of services requires new and unfamiliar organizational structures, capabilities and processes (different from those of production operations)	Baines et al. (2017), Davies et al. (2006), Oliva and Kallenberg (2003), and Zhang and Banerji (2017)
	– Practically, little guidance is available for manufacturers regarding organizational structures	Biege et al. (2012)
Separation	– Is the first step in the transition toward servitization	Oliva and Kallenberg (2003)
	– Is the prevalent organizational structure among "servitized" companies	Oliva et al. (2012) and Raddats et al. (2019)
	– Is the most appropriate organizational structure for advanced services, when differentiation is the key mechanism underlying competitive advantage, or when services are designed as an independent growth business	Bustinza et al. (2015), Fliess and Lexutt (2019), and Raddats et al. (2019)
	– Has a positive impact on company performance	Fliess and Lexutt (2019), Gebauer, Edvardsson, et al. (2010), Gebauer, Edvardsson, Gustafsson, et al. (2010), and Oliva et al. (2012)
	Since it enables:	
	– Full control of the targeting of customers and the development, pricing, selling, and delivery of services	Gebauer, Edvardsson, et al. (2010)
	– Support and protection of the service culture	Gebauer, Edvardsson, et al. (2010), Oliva et al. (2012), Oliva and Kallenberg (2003), and Raddats et al. (2019)

(continued)

Table 1 (continued)

	– The deployment of dedicated staff (sales force and service technicians)	Gebauer, Edvardsson, et al. (2010), Oliva et al. (2012), and Oliva and Kallenberg (2003)
	– A stronger strategic commitment toward service business	Fliess and Lexutt (2019)
	– The implementation of a specific IS, leading to transparency and awareness of how important services are	Oliva and Kallenberg (2003) and Gebauer et al. (2005)
Integration	Is the most appropriate:	
	– When services are intended to protect or enhance the value of the product business	Auguste et al. (2006)
	– When competitive advantage is based on customer satisfaction	Bustinza et al. (2015)
	– In order to offer repeatable customer solutions	Gebauer and Kowalkowski (2012)
	– In complex markets (e.g., IT) to ensure proper alignment with customers' needs	Neu and Brown (2005, 2008)
	Since it enables/favors:	
	– Internal collaboration and synergies between product and service activities, thanks to cross-functional communication, information-sharing, decentralized decision-making, and teamwork	Fliess and Lexutt (2019), Neu and Brown (2005, 2008), and Windahl and Lakemond (2006)
	– External collaboration and communication with customers	Neu and Brown (2005, 2008)
	– A more effective integration of product and service offerings, higher levels of accountability, transparency and delivery speed	Rabetino et al. (2017)
Other possible "moderators"	Internal:	
	– Service maturity	Raddats et al. (2019)
	– Organizational size	Baines et al. (2017)
	– Existing structure of the firm	Windahl and Lakemond (2006)
	External:	
	– Relationships within the network	Windahl and Lakemond (2006)
	– Position in the value chain	Bustinza et al. (2015)
	– Nature of competitive advantage	Galbraith (2002); Bustinza et al. (2015)
	– Industry and market conditions	Raddats and burton (2011)

Separating Product and Services Activities

Separation of product and service activities has been shown to be the prevalent organizational structure among companies (Oliva et al., 2012); Raddats et al., 2019). Separating services from the product business means that firms create a distinct SBU for services that fully control the targeting of customers and the development, pricing, selling, and delivery of service offerings. As a distinctive SBU, the service organization takes over the financial responsibilities for profit-and-loss in the service business (Gebauer, Edvardsson, et al., 2010).

There are several arguments in favor of adopting this view. First of all, manufacturers seeking service growth often have dedicated service SBUs (Raddats et al., 2019), and studies have shown that an independent service organization has a positive impact on company performance (Fliess & Lexutt, 2019; Gebauer, Edvardsson, et al., 2010; Gebauer, Edvardsson, Gustafsson, et al. 2010; Oliva et al., 2012). Moreover, a separate service organization with profit-and-loss responsibility enables support and protection of the service culture, operating as a service company with dedicated staff, processes, and systems (Gebauer, Edvardsson, et al., 2010; Oliva et al., 2012; Oliva & Kallenberg, 2003), and emphasizes strategic commitment toward service business (Fliess & Lexutt, 2019).

In their study of 11 capital equipment manufacturers, Oliva & Kallenberg (2003) reported that consolidating existing service offerings under a single organizational unit was the first step in their transition toward servitization. It facilitates the deployment of dedicated staff, especially a sales force and service technicians, and the implementation of a specific information system that monitors business operations. This in turns allows accounting transparency for the service business and raises awareness on the importance of services for the overall performance of the firm. Finally, it supports the creation and protection of the emerging service culture. The authors conclude that the creation of a separate organization is a crucial success factor in the effective handling of a service offering. These results are in line with those from Gebauer et al. (2005) who showed, based on a study of 30 equipment manufacturing companies, that firms which were successful in increasing service revenue ran decentralized service organizations with profit-and-loss responsibility. They conclude that in manufacturing companies, the service organization must operate like a professional service organization using similar performance measures such as customer satisfaction, employee satisfaction and business success.

Moreover, separation is generally considered as vital for building or reinforcing a service culture. A dedicated sales force and specialized service technicians make it easier to break with the traditional "product-centric" culture (Windahl & Lakemond, 2006). The creation of an organizational structure dedicated to services protects the emerging service culture from the predominant values in the manufacturing organization (Oliva & Kallenberg, 2003), can help "kick start" a service culture in the organization (Raddats et al., 2019), and strengthens the creation of a service orientation in the corporate culture (Gebauer, Edvardsson, et al., 2010).

On the whole, the establishment of a stand-alone service business unit is considered the most appropriate organizational structure, especially for manufacturers whose strategy is to offer advanced services, such as usage- or performance-based contracts (Fliess & Lexutt, 2019; Raddats et al., 2019).

However, separation is also seen as suffering from certain limitations, such as higher costs and risks (Mathieu, 2001). In addition, a dedicated service SBU is not necessarily the optimal organizational design for manufacturers whose services are either immature or designed to "defend" existing products businesses (Auguste et al., 2006) or when services are highly developed (Raddats et al., 2019). This has led some researchers to either contest or moderate the superiority of separation over integration.

Integrating Product and Services Activities

Integrating services into product SBUs means that the services are attached to the product functions and the product SBU takes over service responsibilities. Product sales are also responsible for the service sales; service delivery is organized within the product manufacturing; the profit-and-loss calculation is made for the total offering of products and services based on total sales, as well as product and service costs (Gebauer, Edvardsson, et al., 2010).

The arguments in favor of integration are twofold. Firstly, integration enables the synergies that are needed between product and service activities in order to provide solutions. Secondly, it allows a better alignment with markets and customers' needs.

Integrating the service organization into the product organization enables synergies and knowledge spillovers (Fliess & Lexutt, 2019; Neu & Brown, 2005, 2008). Integration facilitates cross-functional communication, information sharing, decentralized decision making, teamwork and cooperation, which are all considered critical for solution sales (Fliess & Lexutt, 2019). Systems integration, for instance, constitutes a core capability for solution providers, and rests on organizational structures that support interaction between different disciplines and departments (Windahl & Lakemond, 2006). Through integrating the service business with the product business, companies can deploy and combine their product-related and service-related skills and competencies in unique ways (Fliess & Lexutt, 2019). Rabetino et al. (2017) confirm that implementing end-to-end structures enables companies to integrate offerings more effectively and to achieve higher levels of accountability, transparency, and delivery speed.

In addition, in order to achieve success in the business of integrated solutions, companies must build their organizations around their customers' current and future needs (Davies et al., 2006). Yet, an integration of production and service responsibilities combined with strong internal and external collaboration makes it possible to better align the strategy with market needs, and consequently contributes to the success of service development (Neu & Brown, 2005, 2008). In particular, there must be continuous communication between the customer and the service organization (Gebauer et al., 2005). Collaboration with customers allows a better understanding of the complexity of their needs and validates the proper alignment of the service strategy with market needs (Neu & Brown, 2005, 2008). In highly complex markets, such as the I.T. sector, success requires the firm to adapt its strategy and organization to fit the market environment, and this is often best achieved by keeping services in combined units with products and services (Neu & Brown, 2005).

More broadly, a number of researchers emphasize the need for a customer orientation in organizational structures. Customer-facing units bringing together products and services are the most appropriate structures to offer repeatable customer solutions. Gebauer and Kowalkowski (2012) advocate for customer-focused SBUs, which bring together products and services into sector- or customer-specific solutions. According to Galbraith (2002), manufacturers that intend to bundle their products together with services into effective solutions require strong customer-centric profit centers. He argues for a separation between, on the one hand, back-end technology- and product-oriented units and, on the other hand, front-end customer-facing units, which aim to gain a thorough understanding of the customers and deliver tailored solutions.

Other authors suggest a more nuanced approach, in which the choice of the right organizational structure depends on the chosen service strategy and/or on the type of services offered. For instance, Auguste et al. (2006) suggest that integrated product and services SBUs are appropriate for when services are intended to protect or enhance the value of the product business through differentiation; whereas independent service SBUs are suitable for when services are designed as an independent growth business. Bustinza et al.

(2015) consider the organizational structure issue in relation to the company's position in the value chain. They conclude that a specialist service unit or outsourcing are suited to specific advanced services when differentiation is the key mechanism underlying competitive advantage; whereas services should be developed directly by business functions when competitive advantage is based on customer satisfaction.

Finally, neither theoretical contributions nor empirical evidence allow for a definitive answer to the question of integrating or separating product and service activities (Oliva et al., 2012). Some partial conclusions can nevertheless be drawn. First, there is a consensus that reconfiguring organizational structure is both challenging and a key decision to make. Second, most studies converge to conclude that organizational structure follows strategy, and that the question of integrating or separating service activities depends on the strategy being followed and on the type of services being developed. But other factors are also mentioned as being influential, such as the service maturity (Raddats et al., 2019), organizational size (Baines et al., 2017), existing structure of the firm, relationships with external actors (Windahl & Lakemond, 2006), nature of competitive advantage (Bustinza et al., 2015; Galbraith, 2002), position in the value chain (Bustinza et al., 2015), industry and market conditions (Raddats & Burton, 2011). Thus, while the organizational structure depends on the service strategy, there are many factors at various levels that may moderate the strength of this relationship. Thus, the decision to integrate/separate product and service activities appears far more complex, and the handling of this complexity may call for a reconsideration of the paradigmatic assumptions that underlie the research on organizational structures in servitization.

3   Discussion

The Need for a Paradigmatic Evolution

Several paradigmatic assumptions have become institutionalized in research on servitization, among which realist ontology, positivist epistemology, and managerialism (Luoto et al. 2017). These assumptions also underlie the specific area on organizational structures in servitization.

In a realist ontology perspective, the real world is seen as consisting of intangible structures that exist independently of the knower and process of knowing. Consequently, the *"secrets of servitization"* are considered as separate entities or truths that researchers should reveal to the world (Luoto et al.,

2017: 96). In this regard, servitization is envisioned as showing intrinsic properties that should be uncovered and considered as a scientific truth which in turn should be validated, especially through quantification, in order to provide generalizable knowledge. This realist ontology also underpins the research on organizational structures in servitization, with a large proportion of studies seeking to uncover the most effective strategy-structure configuration and establish it as a scientific truth. Conversely, it could be argued that servitization knowledge is contextually and historically grounded, and that researchers might search for phenomenological insights into organizational structures in servitization rather than a scientific truth, in order to provide *"theoretically driven contributions and situational new knowledge focused on meaning"* (Tronvoll et al., 2011).

Similarly, a positivist epistemology means that *"servitization is seen to consist of universal laws,"* and as *"a forward-unidirectional process across the continuum from goods- to service-focused"* (Luoto et al., 2017: 96). Nevertheless, this vision is starting to be questioned, and some researchers point out other possible paths, such as reversed servitization (Finne et al., 2013), service defusion (Kowalkowski et al., 2012), servitization failure and deservitization (Valtakoski, 2017). In this perspective, there may not be an optimal organizational design and the organizational structure may change over time to adapt to internal and external contingencies. Rather than seeking to uncover the most effective strategy-structure configuration, researchers may then identify and better understand the various factors influencing decisions regarding organizational structures.

Finally, servitization research is based on a managerialist assumption as managers are generally considered *"the focal actors contributing to the regeneration of the manufacturing firm"* (Luoto et al., 2017: 97), and failures related to servitization can only be attributed to irrational management and poor process design. Managerialism for instance underlies the conception of culture in servitization research, managers being often considered as having to *"inculcate service-related climate and culture"* (Bowen et al., 1989), whereas Schein (2004: 11) considers culture as *"the result of a complex group learning process that is only partially influenced by leader behavior."* The nature of service culture and the relationship between organizational culture and organizational structures in servitization should thus be studied further.

Luoto et al. (2017) encourage future research to take a critical stance and challenge these paradigmatic dominances, calling for paradigmatic alternatives or multiple paradigms. In order to move beyond the *status quo* on separation vs. integration of product and service activities, we suggest studying organizational structures in servitization by moving from a positivist paradigm to alternative paradigms. We claim that organizational structures in servitization are a complex phenomenon which calls for paradigms and methods able to capture this complexity. While recognizing that, to a great extent, servitization research builds on case studies (Rabetino et al., 2018), these are performed in a tradition of "qualitative positivism," applying positivist assumptions to case study research, which tend to decontextualize the case studies in order to search for regularities (Welch et al., 2011). We suggest that interpretivism, constructionism, and critical realism could provide fruitful paradigmatic frameworks to enrich and deepen the research on organizational structures in servitization. In particular, these paradigms affirm the value of contextualization in relation to theorizing, and allow for interpretive sensemaking and contextualized explanation which seeks to explain "without laws" (Welch et al., 2011).

Table 2 presents the main characteristics of each paradigm, the "philosophy" of case study research within each paradigm and suggests the way research questions on organizational structures in servitization could be formulated. These are then specified and exemplified in the interpretive/constructionist and critical realist paradigms.

Studying Organizational Structures in Servitization Within Alternative Epistemological Paradigms

First, both interpretive/constructionist and critical realism paradigms enable a more dynamic and emergent approach to servitization, as called for by more and more authors. Research on organizational structures would therefore focus on understanding the way they are shaped and how they evolve during the servitization journey. For instance, Kowalkowski et al. (2012) insist on the explorative nature of the servitization process, and suggest an incremental approach based on organizational flexibility and responsiveness. Thus, the way organizational structures support or hinder this incremental process and the implementation of flexibility and responsiveness should be studied further.

Second, some authors underline the continuous tensions that punctate the servitization process, such as the management of intertwining goals and the co-existence of different roles (Kowalkowski et al., 2012, 2015). In this perspective, the integration/separation of product and service activities should not be considered as a choice to be made, but as an irreducible paradox which companies must cope with, calling for a "both-and" rather than an "either-or" thinking (Kohtamäki et al., 2020). Therefore, a dialogic approach where varying constructions are compared and contrasted could be employed in

Table 2 Possible approaches to research on organizational structures in servitization (based on Avenier & Thomas, 2015; Tronvoll et al., 2011; Welch et al., 2011)

	Positivist	Interpretive/constructionist	Critical realist
Approach	Static & a priori	Dynamic & emergent	
Basic ontological & epistemological position	Ontological and epistemological realism (reality exists and is knowable)	Ontological and epistemological relativism (multiple interrelated/constructed realities)	Ontological realism and epistemological relativism (reality exists but is not directly observable)
Actors' role	Actors viewed as passive receivers	Actors viewed as active partners	
Goal	To obtain a fixed language system and identify regularities and patterns	To obtain phenomenological insight, revelation, and open language system	To identify causal mechanisms and the conditions under which they are activated
Form of knowledge	Falsifiable statements	Actionable propositions and narratives	Testable statements and actionable propositions
Main research methods	Snapshot methods, lab experiments, surveys Positivist case studies	Dynamic and time capture methods	
Case study research Goal	Inductive theory building	Interpretive sensemaking	Contextualized explanation
Nature of Research process	Objective search for generalities	Subjective search for meaning	Subjective search for causes
Outcome	Explanation (testable propositions, cause-effect linkages)	Understanding (actor's subjective experiences)	Explanation (causal mechanisms)
Strength	Induction, internal validity	Thick description	Causes-of-effects explanations

(continued)

Table 2 (continued)

	Positivist	Interpretive/constructionist	Critical realist
Attitude to generalization	Generalization to population/to theory	"Particularization" (not generalization)	Contingent and limited generalizations
Nature of causality	Regularity model (associations between events, cause-effect relationships)	Too simplistic and deterministic a concept	Causal mechanisms and contextual conditions under which they work
Role of context	Explanations isolated from the context	Contextual description necessary for understanding	Context integrated into explanations
Main research question regarding OS in servitization	What is the most effective strategy-structure configuration in servitization?	How do servitization process and organizational structure interact with each other over time in different contexts?	How and why does a given strategy-structure configuration occur in servitization?

order to further study the tensions between product and service organizations (including structures, cultures, HRM policies, etc.) and the way companies face them.

Third, research on servitization should leave behind its managerialist approach and turn its attention to the social dimensions underlying the servitization process. Instead of focusing on how managers can improve the servitization process by changing corporate cultures and frames, research should rather consider servitization as an organizational change process, where political, social and cultural dimensions are of major importance (Kowalkowski et al., 2012). In particular, research should consider the role of cognition and learning, and of individual skills and behaviors in shaping and adapting organizational structures. For instance, how is organizational design affected by cognitive models, tacit knowledge, or organizational learning? How do interpersonal cooperation, knowledge-sharing practices, mutual goal-setting, and trust influence organizational structures?

Finally, the organizational structure issue would also benefit from being studied in a critical realist paradigm, especially through contextualized explanations. These aim to account for why and how events are produced, providing contingent generalizations and explaining "without laws," thus avoiding possible "overgeneralizations" (Welch et al., 2011). Certain conclusions drawn by research on organizational structures in servitization may indeed suffer from this limitation, for example, the studies from Neu & Brown (2005, 2008) which are highly specific to the IT sector. Authors should therefore integrate the context into their explanations in order to understand the causal dynamics of the particular organizational design. Studies should better identify, in different settings, the factors that led to or influenced the choice between separation and integration, their interdependencies, and their causal role in leading to a specific organizational design. For instance, Lexutt (2020) adopts this perspective and underlines the causal complexity between strategy, structure, leadership, and culture dimensions.

Table 3 provides a synthesis of the approaches that need to be developed in order to move beyond the current "separate/integrate" stalemate.

To conclude, we suggest that, in the same way as for service research, the preoccupation with the positivistic paradigm has limited the development of research on organizational structures in servitization. Research should be expanded beyond the positivistic paradigm to better understand its organizational antecedents and consequences. In particular, research on organizational structures in servitization would benefit from taking various paradigmatic points of departure that could lead to the development of new approaches.

Table 3 What could be questioned on organizational structures in servitization in a pluralist stance?

Within a dynamic and emergent approach to servitization	Studying organizational structures' evolution during the servitization journey: How do organizational structures support/hinder the servitization process? How are organizational structures modified and adapted throughout the servitization journey? How are organizational flexibility and responsiveness implemented?
Within a dialogic approach to servitization	Studying the tensions between product and service organizations: How do irreducible tensions between product and service activities (cultures, HRM practices, etc.) influence organizational design? How do organizational structures pacify or accentuate the tensions between product and service activities?
Within a social approach to servitization	Studying the role of actors in relation to organizational design: How do people (not only managers) contribute to the co-creation of the servitization process and to organizational design? How do cognitive models, tacit knowledge, and organizational learning interplay with organizational structures? How do interpersonal cooperation, knowledge-sharing practices, mutual goal-setting, and trust influence organizational structures?
Within a critical realist approach to servitization	Studying the causal mechanisms leading to a specific (separate/integrate) organizational structure and the conditions under which they do—and do not—operate: What is the role of corporate culture, decentralization, collaboration, and management commitment in designing the organizational structure? What is the role of internal and external factors such as organizational size, existing structure of the firm, relationships within the network, position in the value chain, industry and market conditions, nature of competitive advantage, etc.?

These approaches could provide new and deeper insights on organizational structures in servitization, that could in turn serve as more reliable bases for the quantitative studies that are also called for (Rabetino et al., 2018).

References

Ambroise, L., Prim-Allaz, I., Teyssier, C., & Peillon, S. (2018). The environment-strategy-structure fit and performance of industrial servitized SMEs. *Journal of Service Management, 29*(2), 301–328.

Auguste, B. G., Harmon, E. P., & Pandit, V. (2006). The right service strategies for product companies. *The McKinsey Quarterly, 1,* 40–51.

Avenier, M., & Thomas, C. (2015). Finding one's way around various methodological guidelines for doing rigorous case studies: A comparison of four epistemological frameworks. *Systèmes D'information & Management, 20*(1), 61–98.

Baines, T., Bigdeli, A. Z., Bustinza, O. F., Shi, V. G., Baldwin, J., & Ridgway, K. (2017). Servitization: Revisiting the state-of-the-art and research priorities. *International Journal of Operations and Production Management, 37*(2), 256–278.

Biege, S., Lay, G., & Buschak, D. (2012). Mapping service processes in manufacturing companies: Industrial service blueprinting. *International Journal of Operations and Production Management, 32*(8), 932–957.

Bowen, D. E., Siehl, C., & Schneider, B. (1989). A framework for analyzing customer service orientations in manufacturing. *Academy of Management Review, 14*(1), 75–95.

Bustinza, O. F., Bigdeli, A. Z., Baines, T., & Elliot, C. (2015). Servitization and competitive advantage: The importance of organizational structure and value chain position. *Research Technology Management, 58*(5), 53–60.

Chandler, A. (1962). *Strategy and structure: Chapters in the history of the industrial enterprise.* MIT Press.

Davies, A., Brady, T., & Hobday, M. (2006). Charting a path toward integrated solutions. *MIT Sloan Management Review, 47*(3), 39–48.

Finne, M., Brax, S., & Holmström, J. (2013). Reversed servitization paths: A case analysis of two manufacturers. *Service Business: an International Journal, 7*(4), 513–537.

Fliess, S., & Lexutt, E. (2019). How to be successful with servitization—Guidelines for research and management. *Industrial Marketing Management, 78,* 58–75.

Galbraith, J. R. (2002). Organizing to deliver solutions. *Organizational Dynamics, 31*(2), 194–207.

Gebauer, H., Edvardsson, B., & Bjurko, M. (2010). The impact of service orientation in corporate culture on business performance in manufacturing companies. *Journal of Service Management, 21*(2), 237–259.

Gebauer, H., Edvardsson, B., Gustafsson, A., & Witell, L. (2010). Match or mismatch: Strategy-structure configurations in the service business of manufacturing companies. *Journal of Service Research, 13*(2), 198–215.

Gebauer, H., Fleisch, E., & Friedli, T. (2005). Overcoming the service paradox in manufacturing companies. *European Management Journal, 23*(1), 14–26.

Gebauer, H., & Kowalkowski, C. (2012). Customer-focused and service-focused orientation in organizational structures. *Journal of Business and Industrial Marketing, 27*(7), 527–537.

Kohtamäki, M., Einola, S., & Rabetino, R. (2020). Exploring servitization through the paradox lens: Coping practices in servitization. *International Journal of Production Economics, 226,* 107619.

Kowalkowski, C., Kindström, D., Alejandro, T. B., Brege, S., & Biggemann, S. (2012). Service infusion as agile incrementalism in action. *Journal of Business Research, 65*(6), 765–772.

Kowalkowski, C., Windahl, C., Kindström, D., & Gebauer, H. (2015). What service transition? Rethinking established assumptions about manufacturers' service-led growth strategies. *Industrial Marketing Management, 45*(1), 59–69.

Lexutt, E. (2020). Different roads to servitization success—A configurational analysis of financial and non-financial service performance. *Industrial Marketing Management, 84,* 105–125.

Luoto, S., Brax, S. A., & Kohtamäki, M. (2017). Critical meta-analysis of servitization research: Constructing a model-narrative to reveal paradigmatic assumptions. *Industrial Marketing Management, 60,* 89–100.

Mathieu, V. (2001). Service strategies within the manufacturing sector: Benefits, costs and partnership. *International Journal of Service Industry Management, 12*(5), 451–475.

Mintzberg, H. (1990). The design school: reconsidering the basic premises of strategic management. *Strategic Management Journal, 11,* 171–195.

Neu, W. A., & Brown, S. W. (2005). Forming successful business-to-business services in goods-dominant firms. *Journal of Service Research, 8*(1), 3–17.

Neu, W. A., & Brown, S. W. (2008). Manufacturers forming successful complex business services: Designing an organization to fit the market. *International Journal of Service Industry Management, 19*(2), 232–251.

Oliva, R., Gebauer, H., & Brann, J. M. (2012). Separate or Integrate? Assessing the Impact of Separation Between Product and Service Business on Service Performance in Product Manufacturing Firms. *Journal of Business-to-Business Marketing, 19*(4), 309–334.

Oliva, R., & Kallenberg, R. (2003). Managing the transition from products to services. *International Journal of Service Industry Management, 14*(2), 160–172.

Rabetino, R., Harmsen, W., Kohtamäki, M., & Sihvonen, J. (2018). Structuring servitization-related research. *International Journal of Operations & Production Management, 38*(2), 350–371.

Rabetino, R., Kohtamäki, M., & Gebauer, H. (2017). Strategy map of servitization. *International Journal of Production Economics, 192,* 144–156.

Raddats, C., & Burton, J. (2011). Strategy and structure configurations for services within product-centric businesses. *Journal of Service Management, 22*(4), 522–539.

Raddats, C., Kowalkowski, C., Benedettini, O., Burton, J., & Gebauer, H. (2019). Servitization: A contemporary thematic review of four major research streams. *Industrial Marketing Management,* 1–17.

Schein, E. H. (2004). *Organizational culture and leadership* (3rd ed.). Jossey-Bass.

Shepherd, C., & Ahmed, P. K. (2000). From product innovation to solutions innovation: A new paradigm for competitive advantage. *European Journal of Innovation Management, 3*(2), 100–106.

Tronvoll, B., Brown, S. W., Gremler, D. D., & Edvardsson, B. (2011). Paradigms in service research. *Journal of Service Management, 22*(5), 560–585.

Valtakoski, A. (2017). Explaining servitization failure and deservitization: A knowledge-based perspective. *Industrial Marketing Management, 60,* 138–150.

Welch, C., Piekkari, R., Plakoyiannaki, E., & Paavilainen-Mäntymäki, E. (2011). Theorising from case studies: Towards a pluralist future for international business research. *Journal of International Business Studies, 42*(5), 740–762.

Windahl, C., & Lakemond, N. (2006). Developing integrated solutions: The importance of relationships within the network. *Industrial Marketing Management, 35*(7), 806–818.

Zhang, W., & Banerji, S. (2017). Challenges of servitization: A systematic literature review. *Industrial Marketing Management, 65,* 217–227.

Coordinating and Aligning a Service Partner Network for Servitization: A Motivation-Opportunity-Ability (MOA) Perspective

Jawwad Z. Raja and Thomas Frandsen

1   Introduction

Since the publication of the now seminal paper by Vandermerwe and Rada (1988) over 30 years ago, the domain of servitization has gained much traction. A recent extensive bibliometric review of the servitization domain—and the related communities (product-service systems, solution business, and service science)—consisting of over 1,000 papers is evidence of this increased attention (Rabetino et al., 2018). A vast body of literature now addresses the issues manufacturers encounter when attempting to shift toward greater service provision to deliver advanced service and solution offerings (Baines et al., 2009; Bigdeli et al., 2017; Parida et al., 2015; Raja et al., 2013; Reim et al., 2019).

Although the servitization literature has grown considerably over the last three decades, the understanding of the challenges of managing a service partner network is not as well developed (Parida et al., 2015; Raja & Frandsen, 2017). Servitizing firms are often dependent on external partner

J. Z. Raja (✉) · T. Frandsen
Department of Operations Management, Copenhagen Business School, Frederiksberg, Denmark
e-mail: jr.om@cbs.dk

T. Frandsen
e-mail: tfr.om@cbs.dk

© The Author(s), under exclusive license to Springer Nature
Switzerland AG 2021
M. Kohtamäki et al. (eds.), *The Palgrave Handbook of Servitization*,
https://doi.org/10.1007/978-3-030-75771-7_33

organizations to realize opportunities for delivering services (Reim et al., 2019; Spring & Araujo, 2013), especially in cases where abilities do not exist internally to do so. To understand the service partner network, we adopt the motivation-opportunity-ability (MOA) framework (Blumberg & Pringle, 1982; Boudreau et al., 2003; MacInnis et al., 1991; Rothschild, 1999) to how partner organizations need to be *motivated* to behave in a way which is congruent with the goals of the focal firm, which—in turn—requires the focal firm to provide the *opportunity* and *ability* for service partners to deliver. To align the MOA elements, there is a need for coordination of efforts across the different actors so that any change to one aspect of the MOA of one actor is likely to influence the MOA elements of other actors in a network. We contribute to the servitization domain by arguing that it is a perennial management challenge of continuously trying to align and coordinate MOA elements within a service network, which may account for the challenges that firms encounter in servitizing.

This chapter is structured as follows: next, we provide the theoretical background, followed by an illustrative case of a global Danish manufacturer, highlighting their efforts and challenges in coordinating a service partner network. We discuss how the need for coordination and alignment among the different actors in a supply network is a key concern and how changes to one actor's MOA is likely to impinge on others in the network.

2   Theoreticl Background

In this section we discuss the service supply network consideration perspective, followed by an elaboration of the MOA framework.

Service Supply Network Considerations

Although a number of notable studies within a servitization context on buyer–supplier relationships (e.g., Bastl et al., 2012; Finne & Holmström, 2013; Johnson & Mena, 2008; Saccani et al., 2014) and network perspectives (e.g., Bigdeli et al., 2018; Hedvall et al., 2019) exist, there is a need for further research that addresses the challenges of coordinating an internal and external service partner network for servitizing firms. Previous research has demonstrated that more complex service supply network configurations might be necessary to create value for customers (Chakkol et al., 2014; Windahl & Lakemond, 2006), with some arguing that the "service network represents the missing link between the manufacturer and customers" (Reim et al., 2019, p. 469).

Servitizing firms are confronted with choices as to whether they invest and develop in the requisite market knowledge and capabilities for service provision internally (Jovanovic et al., 2019) or opt for developing an external service partner network (Chakkol et al., 2014; Kowalkowski et al., 2011; Raja & Frandsen, 2017). Partnering with external actors affords opportunities to extend the reach of the firm without the need for investing in the development of an internal service capability (Kowalkowski et al., 2011). It is not unprecedented that many firms need to look beyond their own firm boundaries to expand the service business. Moreover, the delivery of complex services is likely to necessitate the need for cooperation and management of inter-firm dependencies across the business network (Kowalkowski et al., 2011, 2016). Lately, the discussion of service supply network considerations has also extended to factor in the local industrial ecosystem perspective (Kohtamäki et al., 2019).

A firm's network is a necessary consideration as it is likely to play an important role in the realization of opportunities (Spring & Araujo, 2013). Thus, dependency on a supply network necessitates that the servitizing focal firm understands its customer base and, most importantly, how its service partners may contribute to value creation. Reim et al. (2019) posit that "prior studies have assumed that the service strategies of service network actors and manufacturers are inheritably aligned [and that there are] challenges related to the ability of the service network to provide advanced services" (p. 469). We contend that the MOA framework is a useful basis for exploring the managerial challenges that servitizing manufacturers may encounter when relying on *both* an internal and external service partner network.

MOA Framework

Within the extant literature, it is argued that human behavior can be considered as a function of a person's motivation, opportunity, and ability (MOA) and that these three elements, when considered holistically, are the antecedents to action (Blumberg & Pringle, 1982; Boxall & Purcell, 2016; Siemsen et al., 2008). The following elaborates further on these elements:

- *Motivation* is considered an important factor in guiding human behavior toward outcomes which are perceived as desirable (Boudreau et al., 2003) and has a strong self-interest component (Rothschild, 1999). Motivation includes factors such as willingness, readiness, interest, or desire (MacInnis et al., 1991), which set a person or organization up for action in terms of the effort they are willing to exercise if they can see the benefits.

- *Opportunity* pertains to "situations in which the benefits of acting towards a certain goal are clearly discernible. The willingness on the part of the individual or firm may be present but the means by which to achieve that goal may not. Thus, it is necessary to understand how conducive a given context or situation is to realizing the identified opportunity" (Raja & Frandsen, 2017, p. 1659).

- *Ability* pertains to the skills, knowledge, attitudes, and behavior necessary in the pursuit of desired goals. Ability thus is a requirement in order for an individual to complete a given task competently. Organizations may strive to address issues related to ability with staff by recruiting those that meet the desired criteria in terms of skills, knowledge, and attitudes. They may also invest in the training and development of staff to provide the necessary ability to achieve goals.

Blumberg and Pringle (1982) suggest that these three MOA elements are mutually reinforcing and important in directing the behavior of individuals and/or organizations,[1] and thus, any analysis needs to account for all three elements.

Within a servitization context, motivation has been explored and delineated into three notable categories: competitive, demand-based and economic motivations (for detailed overview see Oliva & Kallenberg, 2003; Raddats et al., 2016; Wise & Baumgartner, 1999). According to Raddats et al. (2016), "motivations for manufacturers to servitise are often assumed to be a truism and homogenous for all companies and sectors. In practice this is unlikely; circumstances will differ and this will have a profound effect on the servitisation process" (p. 573). Hence, there is a need to not only understand the differing motivations that may exist but also how they may vary across actors within a service network. In terms of the opportunity within a servitization context, there is a considerable challenge for firms in transforming from their traditional manufacturing base to being able to exploit the services and solutions opportunity presented in new markets (Raja et al., 2017). Lastly, ability within servitization pertains to the skills, knowledge, and attitudes of workers required to perform within a service mode of operation. It may be incumbent upon firms not only to consider the ability of their own employees, but also that of partner organizations.

---

[1] The MOA framework has typically been used at an individual level to examine human behavior, which can also be applied at an organizational level of analysis (see Karatzas et al., 2020; Raja & Frandsen, 2017).

Within the servitization domain, there have been a few notable studies that have drawn on the MOA framework. Johnstone, Wilkinson, and Dainty (2014) undertook two in-depth case studies of firms adopting servitization strategies arguing for the need to move beyond the focus on the financial returns and consider other challenges. Drawing on the MOA elements, they examined the human resource considerations in explaining the service paradox (Gebauer et al., 2005). More recently, Karatzas et al. (2020) deployed the MOA framework to examine a service network for a commercial vehicle manufacturer. With a specific focus on training, they found that "manufacturer-led formal training improves the performance of both company-owned and independent service units, but the effect is stronger for the latter" (Karatzas et al., 2020, p. 1103). This raises important implications for servitizing firms that turn to external service partners and the need to provide them with training so that they have the requisite skills, knowledge, and ability to perform.

Building on the above, we consider that there is utility in the MOA framework for extending the understanding of servitization, especially within a service supply network context, which we consider in this chapter by discussing a case study undertaken involving a manufacturer and its internal and external service network. The MOA framework adopted complements existing studies within the domain of servitization that have addressed the difficulties manufacturers encounter in transitioning toward services. Each of the MOA elements provides a means of understanding the main drivers within a service network and the challenges encountered in addressing them. Importantly, the need to consider how the different elements reinforce one another is addressed within the servitization context. Moreover, we contribute to the servitization domain by further advancing our understanding of the service network perspective.

3   Case Illustration

To explore the supply network perspective using the MOA framework, we draw upon a case study undertaken with a large Danish manufacturer, PumpCo (a pseudonym), operating globally. PumpCo provides capital equipment and solutions across an array of industries, with a large installed base of products. Recently, the company has expanded its market share in Asia, specifically targeting China as its second home market, after Europe. PumpCo has developed a full range of services (e.g., spare parts, repair and

maintenance, transportation, and the preventative and predicative maintenance) to fully fledged customer solutions for Western markets. The Chinese
market offered opportunities to provide these services.

This case draws on data collected in two distinct rounds: (1) from the
headquarters (HQ) in Denmark and (2) from the Chinese subsidiary and
the authorized service partner network (ASPN). In total, we conducted 25
interviews over an extended period with key informants related to the service
business. During these interviews, we asked about the different elements
of the MOA framework from the perspective of each actor (the HQ, the
Chinese subsidiary, and the ASPN). We followed the process laid out for
template analysis (King, 2004) using the MOA framework. A more detailed
overview is provided in Raja and Frandsen (2017).

4   Findings

Drawing on the MOA framework, in this section, we provide insights into
the key issues and obstacles each actor encountered.

Motivation

PumpCo: At the HQ, senior management was cognizant of the changing
competitive environment in which the number of new entrants was
increasing, leading to price competition. To address this issue, PumpCo's
motivation was to ensure they were perceived differently to their competitors.
This meant not mimicking the competition but focusing on the combination of products and services into solutions that addressed specific customer
needs. As such, advanced service offerings were considered an effective way to
address these customer needs and compete in the different markets. PumpCo
was motivated as part of its global strategy to ensure that services were
delivered in a standardized way, using procedures for sales and training for
subsidiaries to maintain and ensure consistent products and service quality
across the globe.

Subsidiary: As the company's new second home market, the importance
of the Chinese subsidiary to PumpCo was elevated, and the personnel in
the Chinese subsidiary needed to grow the customer base by targeting and
securing high value contracts. This meant targeting larger customers such
as municipalities or government bodies in specific regions of the country.
The subsidiary was motivated to a large extent by being part of an established and highly recognized global organization renowned for its innovations

and product quality. The need to grow the service business was not lost on personnel in the subsidiary, and targeting the installed base was deemed a starting point. Within the subsidiary in China, the service department was considered a cost center, resulting in the provision of services being largely outsourced to the ASPN. It was considered cheaper to deliver services for the large part through the external service partner network than through the hiring, training, and use of PumpCo engineers.

ASPN: The motivation of the authorized service providers (ASPs) within the service network was to satisfy customers and establish long-term relationships, while increasing revenue. To do so successfully depended on being an authorized partner of PumpCo, which in turn provided legitimacy in the eyes of customers when delivering services. The ASPN was positioned in such a way that it possessed knowledge of the customer base, making external service providers valuable to PumpCo for growing and delivering services in China. The Chinese subsidiary was responsible for the accreditation of the ASPs, requiring them to meet a stringent criterion to maintain their operating license as an authorized partner. The ASPs generally sought recognition for their work from PumpCo and the Chinese subsidiary but some ASPs felt this was lacking in recent times.

Opportunity

PumpCo: For the HQ, services afforded an opportunity to make inroads into the Chinese market, making service an important part of the business strategy. Customers purchasing more complex products also valued services, which presented an opportunity. Thus, services were viewed as a way of increasing revenues and a means of greater profitability. Digitalization was an important part of realizing this opportunity by capturing usage data on the installed base and utilizing their analytical capabilities to provide customized solutions that meet customer needs, such as more efficient energy utilization.

However, PumpCo was confronted with a number of difficulties in delivering more advanced services, notably the need for specific capabilities for which the ASPN was not trained or experienced in. The challenge that PumpCo HQ experienced was appreciating complexities of the Chinese market, which are typically based on close and personal relationships with customers (*Guanxi*) (cf. Xin & Pearce, 1996). Thus, this called for a different approach than those utilized in other markets.

Subsidiary: With the Chinese market being assigned as the "second home market" by the HQ, the subsidiary was presented with an opportunity to play a greater role in growing the business, especially by expanding the business to yet unexploited areas. The challenge, however, was that, although PumpCo HQ considered services an important part, the Chinese subsidiary did not place the same level of emphasis on services as essential to its strategy to secure growth for the future. Deemed more important by the subsidiary was PumpCo's reputation for product quality in the Chinese marketplace. Given the pivotal position of the external service providers in the network and their close personal relations with customers, they were considered vital in progressing the service strategy in China.

Internally, within the Chinese subsidiary, the difficulties largely pertained to negotiating a local strategy for managing the ASPN with PumpCo HQ. This primarily resulted from hierarchical differences between management personnel in the HQ and in the subsidiary, where the senior service manager at PumpCo's HQ was positioned far higher in their organizational hierarchy than their counterpart in the Chinese subsidiary. In addition, the Chinese subsidiary lacked the necessary investment and infrastructure to provide services internally on a large scale, which in turn meant the ability to exploit opportunities for service was highly contingent on the ASPN.

Externally two main challenges were experienced with regard to competitors: (1) other international competitors entering the Chinese market and (2) newly emerging, local competitors that were reverse-engineering PumpCo's products and selling them at far lower prices.

ASPN: For service delivery, the ASPN found itself more optimally placed to deliver services as it was more costly for PumpCo engineers to provide the type of service support the majority of customers required, i.e., predominately standard services. PumpCo also did not have the desire to invest and coordinate a large dispersed service workforce considering the market was still in an early phase of development. As for advanced services, this was something that would take time to actualize, with necessary investment from PumpCo to develop the external service partner network. As a consequence, the ASPN was presented with the opportunity to leverage its position between the Chinese subsidiary and the customers because detailed knowledge of the installed base was not readily available to the subsidiary but was instead rather dependent on the ASPN. Not surprisingly, the ASPN was able to prioritize its self-interest, i.e., maintain their positions as key brokers and maximize revenues for themselves. Understandably, they did not wish to give up their position and relationships with the customers as these provided an important means of selling more products and parts, while pushing more basic services that they provided.

Ability

PumpCo: In terms of ability, PumpCo's main capabilities reside in the product business due to its technical knowledge and expertise in developing innovative products. This expertise manifests itself in the vast portfolio of specialized products that PumpCo has accumulated for a range of customers. Although the core capabilities reside in the products, PumpCo has also been investing in the development of the service business to expand further. The challenge is that local conditions do not allow for the service business to be scaled in the same way the product business has, requiring the need for sensitivity to local conditions. As described previously, in non-Western markets, PumpCo is very reliant on the ASPN for the distribution of products and delivery of basic services to customers. The service delivery model is very much reliant on its ASPN and the need to work in cooperation with one another. As such, PumpCo HQ stipulates the standards that the ASPN must be compliant with. Likewise, the ASPN requires accreditations from PumpCo to be considered a legitimate service partner for their products.

Subsidiary: The Chinese subsidiary, until recently, had predominately focused on selling products. In recent years, the strategy shifted toward the greater incorporation of services to grow. In this respect, it was deemed that the subsidiary did not possess the requisite ability to provide basic services on a large scale. The ASPN was however able to support and deliver the services. This then led to the challenge of managing the ASPs, as the HQ had concerns about allowing too much discretion over customer contact, fearing the resulting relationships between the ASPN and the customers might be detrimental for PumpCo. As a consequence, dependency on the ASPN was considered a "necessary evil" by PumpCo's HQ to penetrate the Chinese market. Paradoxically, the successes of the ASPN were deemed "potential" lost opportunities, or even losses, for PumpCo. At the same time, management recognized the need for programs to further develop the competency level of the ASPN, which was not considered fully capable of delivering advanced services (cf. Reim et al., 2019). The challenge for the Chinese subsidiary then was one of reconciling the need to grow the service business via the service partner network knowing they were not fully capable of delivering the full spectrum of services.

ASPN: The ASPN found itself in a fairly strong position in terms of access to and knowledge of customers, and coupled with personal relationships that had been developed, it played a vital role in delivering services. As mentioned, although the opportunities for basic services existed on a larger scale, the necessary skills for more advanced services were found to be lacking within the ASPN. So, while the ASPN had access to customers across a fairly vast geographical area, PumpCo considered them to be no more than suppliers of basic services and cheaper labor for the Chinese market. To large extent, this is attributable to technicians within the ASPN not having received the necessary formal training, something which PumpCo HQ attempted to address through training manuals. Unfortunately, this was neither considered adequate, nor was it customized to address the needs of high-end customers. The general feeling was that the training from HQ could have been more extensive. Moreover, a constant gripe of the ASPN was that they did not receive sufficient guidance or appropriate product briefings from the Chinese subsidiary, which consequently severely limited their ability to deliver the quality of work that was required. Whereas, PumpCo considered the cost of training external partners to high levels of risk to their business and instead preferred to develop such capabilities in internal engineers and technicians.

Table 1 summarizes the key factors driving the MOA elements described above and the challenges encountered for each actor.

5   Coordinating and Aligning MOA Elements Across the Supply Network

Our research findings suggest that organizations are confronted with the perennial task of trying to align the MOA elements to further their servitization strategy not only at the individual actor level but also across actors. We argue that changes in one of the MOA elements is likely to impinge on other elements within and across actors. As a result, there is the perennial need to seek alignment in respect of the actions taken to advance a service strategy. Dependency on an external service partner network presents additional complexities for management in terms of coordinating the actions of multiple actors to achieve alignment. This implies that servitization is as much a managerial challenge of coordination and alignment as it is a structural challenge of developing the appropriate strategy and structure for the business.

Therefore, there is a need to understand the dynamic—that is, the constant change, activity, and unfolding—relationship among the MOA elements, relating to the ways in which PumpCo HQ seeks to develop a service strategy that internally aligns the MOA. PumpCo has a clear motivation with respect to their service strategy, yet the ability to actualize service opportunities has not been fully grasped. To address this, PumpCo HQ has sought to support its Chinese subsidiary. However, decisions undertaken at the subsidiary level

Table 1 Key drivers and challenges summary of MOA elements

	Motivation		Opportunity		Ability	
	Key drivers	Challenges	Key drivers	Challenges	Key drivers	Challenges
HQ	• Address customer needs with integration of products and services • Expand service and solutions business • Increase competitiveness • Strengthen company competitiveness with services • Mitigate against price competition from low cost entrants into market	• Transferring know-how of solutions developed in Western markets to emerging markets	• Targeting very large public and private customers to provide solutions for complex infrastructures • Utilizing advanced technology to remotely monitor an installed base • Offering integrated product and service offerings with a possibility to operate a network • Increasing revenues with service • Preventing reverse engineering of equipment by providing aftermarket services	• Knowledge of installed base resides predominately with external network partners • Developing personal relationships in Chinese market	• Ability to set global strategy • Wide range of specialized capital equipment for diverse customer needs • Experience delivering high-end solutions in other markets	• Product focus hinders service capability development • Ability to onboard subsidiary to sell advanced services

(continued)

Table 1 (continued)

	Motivation		Opportunity		Ability	
	Key drivers	Challenges	Key drivers	Challenges	Key drivers	Challenges
Subsidiary	• Grow customer base • Strongly identify with PumpCo • Provide service for the installed base via ASPN • Support customers with knowledge and solutions that are customized • Target high value contracts with bigger customers	• Outsourcing of service delivery to external partners (ASPN) as the service business is considered a cost center	• Placing greater emphasis on growing business in the second home market • Leveraging product brand to tap into service opportunities • Coordinating ASPN for delivering services • Developing longer-term relationships with customers	• Competition from low-cost, local service providers • Reverse engineering of products by local manufacturers • Dependency on ASPN • Attaining external service partner loyalty • ASPN retains knowledge of customers and installed bases • Translating global strategy to local market needs • Level of internal investment and infrastructure to support service capability development	• Local knowledge • Ability to deliver advanced services and solutions in some areas • Highly skilled PumpCo service engineers for large projects • Ability to deliver basic services to customers across the Chinese market via ASPN	• Scalability issue with services • Resource allocation determined by HQ • Ability to learn from other markets globally • Knowledge of installed base with ASPN

	Motivation		Opportunity		Ability	
	Key drivers	Challenges	Key drivers	Challenges	Key drivers	Challenges
ASPN	• Increase revenue • Maintain and improve position in network • Obtain recognition from PumpCo China and partner with them • Maintain authorized service partner status	• Rewards and recognition not available	• Possessing knowledge of installed base • Building up close relationships with customers for selling further services • Providing cheaper service for the low-end of the market in comparison to PumpCo engineers and technicians	• Retaining accreditation • Delivering service level requirements	• Local knowledge of customers • Well-positioned in the social network (*guanxi*) with customers to deliver service and highly trusted • Readily available labor to deliver basic services	• Knowledge of the high-end segment of market for advanced services • Limited training from PumpCo for offerings • Limited pool of qualified service engineers

tilt toward increasing dependency on external service providers, which, in turn, creates opportunities and motivation among the ASPN, which has the ability to provide—albeit mostly *basic*—service on a large scale. This point is not lost on PumpCo HQ as it recognizes the lack of capabilities of the subsidiary and ASPN to realize opportunities in the Chinese market in terms of ensuring consistency of service delivery and the skills for more advanced services and solutions as part of the global service strategy. To support and develop the ASPN's ability to deliver, the HQ sought to leverage its abilities and provide training to, and certification of, the ASPN.

The complexities of coordinating and aligning the MOA elements across the different actors are discussed below.

- *Dynamic 1a and 1b—Developing a service strategy within PumpCo HQ*: The motivation for the HQ was to expand the business in China by emphasizing the provision of services and allotting it as the "second home market." PumpCo wished to be perceived differently from competitors. To do so, the focus was placed on customers by utilizing internal abilities through combining products and services into integrated solutions for customers.
- *Dynamic 2a, 2b, and 2c—Realizing motivation and opportunity in the Chinese subsidiary*: PumpCo China was largely motivated by the prospect of growing its market share. The Chinese subsidiary's main ambition is to expand its customer base and secure larger, more lucrative contracts. Moreover, PumpCo personnel in China were motivated to create opportunities for service sales, although they lacked the internal service technicians and engineers necessary to expand the business. This, in turn, impacted PumpCo's ability to provide services reliably across a country the size of China.
- *Dynamic 3a—Leverage abilities in the subsidiary*: Although opportunities for growth were clearly evident, the question of whether the country subsidiary possessed the ability to *realize* the opportunity was contested internally in PumpCo. To further the service strategy, PumpCo deployed expatriate managers from the HQ to the Chinese subsidiary to relay the priority to local management. Given the service business was locally considered to be a cost center, this consequently led to the outsourcing of service provision being a more appealing option than servicing using in-house capabilities, which were predominately maintained for customers requiring advanced services.
- *Dynamic 4a and 4b—Opportunities for the external service partner network*: The Chinese subsidiary has little difficulty in recruiting external service

partners given the reputational capital PumpCo possess for its products. Hence, services present an enticing opportunity for those that become ASPs. For external partners, selling services is an opportunity to increase their revenues which drives their motivations. Moreover, given the limited control from PumpCo China, external service partners are in a fairly strong position to benefit and even act opportunistically. The external network is positioned as an intermediary between PumpCo and the end customers, highly trusted by the latter and very knowledgeable about the installed base. Although the ASPN was able to provide support services to the low-end market (cf. Gebauer, 2006), such as repair and maintenance, the move toward realizing opportunities for more complex and advanced offerings is found to be somewhat beyond the current capabilities of external partners.

- *Dynamic 5a—Ability to deliver service contingent on ASPN*: PumpCo's Chinese subsidiary resolved its ability issue by turning to its external ASPN, which allowed it to service the extensive installed base across the country. For PumpCo HQ and the Chinese subsidiary, there was a realization that they were not currently in a position to assume full control over the end customer's operations, hence the ASPN proved an important part of the service strategy in the immediate and long term.
- *Dynamic 6a—PumpCo leveraging its global capabilities*: For PumpCo the main challenges were to, first, develop the necessary abilities locally and, second, support the transfer and sharing of knowledge from other markets to support the development of advanced offerings on a larger scale (cf. Reim et al., 2019). To do this required the monitoring and development of the skill levels of the ASPN. In this regard, PumpCo HQ devised a new policy of annually re-accrediting external service partners based on a stringent ability criterion.

Figure 1 illustrates the MOA elements of each actor, with the lines and corresponding numbers indicating how the dynamics described above unfold within the network. Clearly evident is the motivation and opportunity for growing services within PumpCo and its Chinese subsidiary, though the ability to do so is—to a large extent—dependent on the external ASPN, which presents numerous managerial challenges for PumpCo.

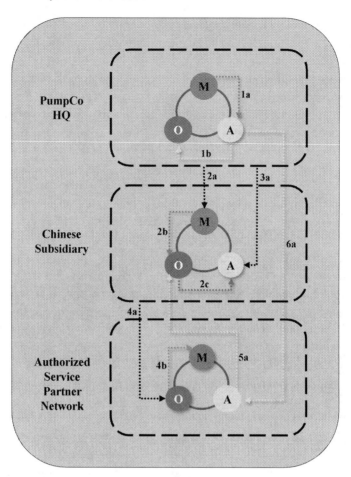

Fig. 1 Coordinating MOA elements in the service supply network

6 Concluding Remarks and Managerial Considerations

To date, research examining servitization phenomenon by drawing on the MOA elements tends to focus on the focal firm (Johnstone et al., 2014). We concur with these studies that the MOA elements within an organization need to be mutually reinforcing (Blumberg & Pringle, 1982; Johnstone et al., 2014). However, we also suggest that this needs to occur across a supply network, which includes additional managerial complexities and challenges of coordinating and aligning the different elements across the supply network actors. As such, each of the MOA elements need to be recognized as important for enabling strategic change in support of services and to instigate motivation, create opportunities, and develop abilities not only for the focal firm but also across the network.

We argue that there is a need to shift away from solely structural considerations and toward the managerial challenges of coordinating and aligning the different MOA elements for the actors in the network. For example, as illustrated above, the motivation of PumpCo HQ to actualize the service strategy will impact the opportunity and ability of other actors within the supply network. Although aligning the MOA elements may involve adjustments to structural and infrastructural decision categories (Rudberg & Olhager, 2003), we suggest this to be a more dynamic managerial process in which the different actors in the network impact, and are impacted by, the decisions and actions of others. Although notable previous research on servitization addresses the role of external partner networks (Kowalkowski et al. , 2011, 2016) and buyer–supplier relationships (Bastl et al., 2012; Saccani et al., 2014), the managerial challenges of coordination and alignment are not as well explored. We contribute to this body of research by focusing on external service partner networks and the challenges of coordinating and aligning activities in a supply network by drawing on the MOA framework. Of particular note is the need for ongoing managerial attention to coordination and alignment in order to mutually reinforce the MOA elements. Changing MOA in one part of the network is likely to have implications for the MOA elements in other parts of the network and underscores the dynamic nature and managerial efforts required on an ongoing basis.

References

Baines, T., Lightfoot, H., Peppard, J., Johnson, M., Tiwari, A., Shehab, E., & Swink, M. (2009). Towards and operations strategy for product-centric servitization. *International Journal of Operations & Production Management, 29*(5), 494–519.

Bastl, M., Johnson, M., Lightfoot, H., & Evans, S. (2012). Buyer-supplier relationships in a servitized environment: An examination with Cannon and Perreault's framework. *International Journal of Operations & Production Management, 32*(6), 650–675.

Bigdeli, A. Z., Baines, T., Bustinza, O. F., & Shi, V. G. (2017). Organisational change towards servitization: A theoretical framework. *Competitiveness Review: An International Business Journal.*

Bigdeli, A. Z., Bustinza, O. F., Vendrell-Herrero, F., & Baines, T. (2018). Network positioning and risk perception in servitization: Evidence from the UK road transport industry. *International Journal of Production Research, 56*(6), 2169–2183.

Blumberg, M., & Pringle, C. D. (1982). The missing opportunity in organizational research: Some implications for a theory of work performance. *Academy of Management Review, 7*(4), 560–569.

Boudreau, J., Hopp, W., McClain, J. O., & Thomas, L. J. (2003). On the interface between operations and human resources management. *Manufacturing & Service Operations Management, 5*(3), 179–202.

Boxall, P., & Purcell, J. (2016). *Strategy and human resources management* (4th ed.). Palgrave Macmillan.

Chakkol, M., Johnson, M., Raja, J., & Raffoni, A. (2014). From goods to solutions: How does the content of an offering affect network configuration? *International Journal of Physical Distribution & Logistics Management, 44*(1/2), 132–154.

Finne, M., & Holmström, J. (2013). A manufacturer moving upstream: Triadic collaboration for service delivery. *Supply Chain Management: An International Journal, 18*(1), 21–33.

Gebauer, H. (2006). Entering low-end markets: A new strategy for Swiss companies. *Journal of Business Strategy, 27*(5), 23–31.

Gebauer, H., Fleisch, E., & Friedli, T. (2005). Overcoming the service paradox in manufacturing companies. *European Management Journal, 23*(1), 14–26.

Hedvall, K., Jagstedt, S., & Dubois, A. (2019). Solutions in business networks: Implications of an interorganizational perspective. *Journal of Business Research, 104,* 411–421.

Johnson, M., & Mena, C. (2008). Supply chain management for servitised products: A multi-industry case study. *International Journal of Production Economics, 114*(1), 27–39.

Johnstone, S., Wilkinson, A., & Dainty, A. (2014). Reconceptualizing the service paradox in engineering companies: Is HR a missing link? *IEEE Transactions on Engineering Management, 66*(2), 275–284.

Jovanovic, M., Raja, J. Z., Visnjic, I., & Wiengarten, F. (2019). Paths to service capability development for servitization: Examining an internal service ecosystem. *Journal of Business Research, 104,* 472–485.

Karatzas, A., Papadopoulos, G., & Godsell, J. (2020). Servitization and the effect of training on service delivery system performance. *Production and Operations Management, 29*(5), 1101–1121.

King, N. (2004). Using templates in the thematic analysis of texts. In C. Cassell & G. Symon (Ed.), *Essential guide to qualitative methods in organizational research* (pp. 256–270). Sage.

Kohtamäki, M., Parida, V., Oghazi, P., Gebauer, H., & Baines, T. (2019). Digital servitization business models in ecosystems: A theory of the firm. *Journal of Business Research, 104,* 380–392.

Kowalkowski, C., Kindström, D., & Carlborg, P. (2016). Triadic value propositions: When it takes more than two to tango. *Service Science, 8*(3), 282–299.

Kowalkowski, C., Kindström, D., & Witell, L. (2011). Internalisation or externalisation? Examining organisational arrangements for industrial services. *Managing Service Quality: An International Journal, 21*(4), 373–391.

MacInnis, D. J., Moorman, C., & Jaworski, B. J. (1991). Enhancing and measuring consumers' motivation, opportunity, and ability to process brand information from ads. *The Journal of Marketing, 55,* 32–53.

Oliva, R., & Kallenberg, R. (2003). Managing the transition from products to services. *International Journal of Service Industry Management, 14*(2), 160–172.

Parida, V., Sjödin, D. R., Lenka, S., & Wincent, J. (2015). Developing global service innovation capabilities: How global manufacturers address the challenges of market heterogeneity. *Research-Technology Management, 58*(5), 35–44.

Rabetino, R., Hermsen, W., Kohtamäki, M., & Sihvonen, J. (2018). Structuring servitization-related research. *International Journal of Operations & Production Management, 38*(2), 350–371.

Raddats, C., Baines, T., Burton, J., Story, V. M., & Zolkiewski, J. (2016). Motivations for servitization: The impact of product complexity. *International Journal of Operations & Production Management, 36*(5), 572–591.

Raja, J. Z., Bourne, D., Goffin, K., Çakkol, M., & Martinez, V. (2013). Achieving customer satisfaction through integrated products and services: An exploratory study. *Journal of Product Innovation Management, 30*(6), 1128–1144.

Raja, J. Z., & Frandsen, T. (2017). Exploring servitization in China: Challenges of aligning motivation, opportunity, and ability in coordinating an external service partner network. *International Journal of Operations & Production Management, 37*(11), 1654–1682.

Raja, J. Z., Frandsen, T., & Mouritsen, J. (2017). Exploring the managerial dilemmas encountered by advanced analytical equipment providers in developing service-led growth strategies. *International Journal of Production Economics, 192,* 120–132.

Reim, W., Sjödin, D. R., & Parida, V. (2019). Servitization of global service network actors—A contingency framework for matching challenges and strategies in service transition. *Journal of Business Research, 104,* 461–471.

Rothschild, M. L. (1999). Carrots, sticks, and promises: A conceptual framework for the management of public health and social issue behaviours. *The Journal of Marketing, 63*(4), 24–37.

Rudberg, M., & Olhager, J. (2003). Manufacturing networks and supply chains: An operations strategy perspective. *Omega, 31*(1), 29–39.

Saccani, N., Visintin, F., & Rapaccini, M. (2014). Investigating the linkages between service types and supplier relationships in servitized environments. *International Journal of Production Economics, 149,* 226–238.

Siemsen, E., Roth, A. V., & Balasubramanian, S. (2008). How motivation, opportunity, and ability drive knowledge sharing: The constraining-factor model. *Journal of Operations Management, 26*(3), 426–445.

Spring, M., & Araujo, L. (2013). Beyond the service factory: Service innovation in manufacturing supply networks. *Industrial Marketing Management, 42*(1), 59–70.

Vandermerwe, S., & Rada, J. (1988). Servitization of business: Adding value by adding services. *European Management Journal, 6*(4), 314–324.

Windahl, C., & Lakemond, N. (2006). Developing integrated solutions: The importance of relationships within the network. *Industrial Marketing Management, 35*(7), 806–816.

Wise, R., & Baumgartner, P. (1999). Go downstream: The new profit imperative in manufacturing. *Harvard Business Review, 77*(5), 133–141.

Xin, K. K., & Pearce, J. L. (1996). Guanxi: Connections as substitutes for formal institutional support. *Academy of Management Journal, 39*(6), 1641–1658.

Index

© The Editor(s) (if applicable) and The Author(s), under exclusive
license to Springer Nature Switzerland AG 2021
M. Kohtamäki et al. (eds.), *The Palgrave Handbook of Servitization*,
https://doi.org/10.1007/978-3-030-75771-7

Printed in the United States
Baker & Taylor Publisher Services